1976

Psychological Deprivation in Childhood

Psychological Deprivation in Childhood

J. Langmeier and Z. Matějček

EDITED BY G. L. MANGAN

A HALSTED PRESS BOOK

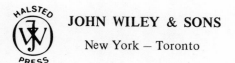

JOHN WILEY & SONS
New York — Toronto

First edition (Czechoslovakian) *Psychická deprivace v dětství (Psychological Deprivation in Childhood)* published by Státní Zdravotnické Nakladatelství, Prague, 1963

Second edition (Czechoslovakian), 1968

Third edition (English published and © University of Queensland Press, St. Lucia, Queensland, 1975

Printed and bound by Dai Nippon Printing Co. (HK) Ltd., Hong Kong

Published in the U.S.A., Canada, and Latin America by Halsted Press, a Division of John Wiley & Sons, Inc., New York

ISBN 0-470-51718-2
Library of Congress Catalog Card No. 75-16185

Library of Congress Cataloging in Publication Data

Langmeier, Josef.
    Psychological deprivation in childhood.
    "A Halsted Press book."
    Translation of Psychická deprivace v dětství.
    Bibliography: pp. 417-81
    Includes indexes.
    1. Parental deprivation. 2. Social isolation.
    I. Matějček, Zdeněk, joint author. II. Title.
    [DNLM: 1. Child psychology. 2. Maternal deprivation. WS350 L284p]
    BF723.D4L313 1975   155.9'2   75-16185
    ISBN 0-470-51718-2

Contents

Illustrations

Preface

Following World War II, there was a period of radical social, political, and economic re-organization in Czechoslovakia. Rapid industrialization and agricultural collectivization demanded an increased work force, and employment of women in some areas approached 100 per cent. There was increasing provision of kindergartens and nurseries, and these, with the traditional institutions offering permanent or part-time care, formed a highly integrated network of child-care facilities.

This system had both social and ideological goals. It was not only a helping agency, it also claimed to provide the most suitable environment for the rearing of all children. Not only was the uniform system of progressive and efficiently organized professional care considered superior to average family care from a medical-developmental point of view, it was also a much more appropriate vehicle of authority and cultural norms in educating the new citizen with a sense of collective responsibility. With increasing state involvement in child rearing, the woman's status as a mother inevitably declined particularly where her changed status was accompanied by newly created economic demands in a developing consumer society.

Not unexpectedly, these developments had important implications for child care. As familial values retreated in the face of extra-familial demands, and as the percentage of the child population under permanent or part-time institutional care increased, the traditional problem of the orphan child was replaced by the new problem of the social orphan, the child of uninterested or divorced parents, or from broken families. The model of child deprivation became the "collectivized" child, the child who was denied full and direct emotional relationships with the mother in the family, who was inundated with some stimuli and refused others during a long stay in an institution, for which he was often developmentally unprepared. Increasing incidence of illness in nurseries, problems about daily separation, difficulties in emotional adaptation and establishment of the first emotional attachments, and at times serious personality disorders were direct outcomes of this type of care.

*   *   *

This was the context in which the authors of the present volume were working. The first edition of the book, published in 1963, was an attempt to evaluate the available research and clinical material on the effects of institutional care in Czechoslovakia, so as to provide a practical basis for improvements in such care. With the mushrooming of studies in psychological deprivation in the sixties, a second, updated edition was published in 1968 to incorporate the relevant new material.

In this English edition, Langmeier and Matějček have attacked the problem of psychological deprivation on a much broader front. They have adopted a more comparative-social approach than is usual in deprivation studies, and have derived models of child deprivation from content analysis of books on child rearing in the nineteenth and twentieth centuries, which they have contrasted with deprivation models in contemporary societies. In this way, they have attempted to identify the general factors underlying deprivation, and what is contributed specifically by cultural, economic, and geographical events and circumstances.

From their own extensive clinical experience, and from a careful appraisal of the Western and Eastern European and U.S. literature, the authors conclude that even under relatively uniform institutional conditions, there is no unique picture or syndrome of the deprived child, but different "types" of deprived personality. Psychological deprivation, therefore, should not be viewed as a single factor inhibiting the child's development in a specific way, but as a broad context in which developmental retardation occurs. The nature and degree of retardation vary according to the individual child's resources and deficiencies, to which needs are inadequately satisfied, and to his developmental level.

*   *   *

Consideration of these factors is the main content of the book. The treatment is encyclopaedic and eclectic, the perspective historical and contemporary. The authors give a balanced and detailed account of deprivation in the family and in institutions, the effects of long-

and short-term deprivation, the role of internal organismic and external environmental factors, the importance of social and cultural milieus and forces. They have drawn extensively on source material from experimental and developmental psychology and sociology, and have shown a proper concern for definitional and methodological issues. Perhaps most importantly, they have offered a multi-level theory of psychological deprivation as a framework in which diagnostic, therapeutic, and preventive problems can be attacked. Throughout the book, there is a wealth of case studies and drawings, particularly by deprived children of their families, which serve as a sort of leitmotif for the illustrative section of the book. Overall, the authors have woven an intricate and highly interesting fabric.

The material presented has considerable relevance and applicability to a wide spectrum of problems in our society. These range from "global" concerns such as the threat of "alienation" or "relevance deprivation" in a modern society advancing under the aegis of a rapidly accelerating technology, to highly specific problems such as the most appropriate care for handicapped (i.e. sensorily deprived) children and children of working mothers. The latter problem particularly has been the subject of much well-intentioned but psychologically unsophisticated comment in recent years.

Psychological deprivation is obviously an extremely complex problem. Since it is concerned with the relationship between the demands of the developing organism and of society, it has implications for many areas of social practice. The book, therefore, should be of interest to teachers and psychologists, to students of social work and medicine — to all those who are directly or indirectly involved in the care of children.

*   *   *

It seems fitting, as a final comment, to record that this volume originated in a country placed in the middle of Europe, a crucible of different ideologies and influences, a country which nurtured Hus, Comenius, and Masaryk, as well as Freud, Husserl, and Kafka, a country which is strongly dedicated to ideals of freedom, respect for the individual and his right to full development. The clash between conflicting ideologies was probably felt here more strongly than in many other countries, and from this conflict there emerged a strong reform movement directed towards a new understanding of child care, the function of the mother and the family, of the individual and the collective. Since the studies in psychological deprivation described here were a source of inspiration in this movement, this book is offered as a record of these reforming efforts and as a contribution to the universal goal of world humanism.

Translation from the original Czech text was by Peter Anger, Dip. Psych. Thanks are due to the University of Queensland Press for initial financial support.

Gordon L. Mangan
Department of Experimental Psychology
University of Oxford
August, 1972

1 Concepts of psychological deprivation

At times scientific discovery is prompted by internal and external pressures which redirect attention to important questions which have been neglected for prolonged periods, either because other problems have been given priority or because we lacked adequate methodology for their solution. When such problems are "rediscovered", therefore, it is not surprising that data are interpreted rather extravagantly, and that interest in the area becomes fashionable. Under these conditions, systematic investigation and critical appraisal of the issues develop slowly.

The problem of psychological deprivation is almost a classic example of such a process. It is referred to in very early chronicles. For example, the thirteenth century chronicler Salimbeni of Parma (A. Peiper, 1955) recorded an anecdote about the Emperor Frederick the Second. He committed children to the care of nurses who were given strict instructions to feed and bathe their charges, but to refrain from cuddling, petting, or speaking. The Emperor hypothesized that if the children lacked language models, their speech would be the oldest, most original language of mankind. His scientific curiosity remained unsatisfied, however, as all the children died. They could not survive, as Salimbeni notes, without "loving words" and happy facial expressions from their nurses. There is also on record (reported by R. A. Spitz, 1945) an extract from the diary of a Spanish bishop around the year 1760: "in an orphanage children become sad, and many of them die because of this sadness".

Usually the fairy tales, myths, legends, and folk-lore delve even further into the past than the chroniclers' accounts to provide information about child-rearing practices. We observe here the glorification of motherly love, which can never be compensated for, and the figure of the stepmother representing all that is evil and destructive. Compared with this, we find the idealized picture of the neglected child living amongst animals or wicked people, homeless, without love or emotional support, and, against such odds, growing into a handsome young man or beautiful woman, with a fully developed personality and strong moral character. However, if Romulus and Remus had been fostered by a she-wolf, as described in the Roman legend, they would probably have resembled the "wolf children" we shall describe later on. It is unlikely that they would have been the founders of Rome. The movie image of Tarzan, the handsome and fearless child of nature, is sheer fantasy when considered against the deprivational studies.

Descriptions of childhood portrayed by Turgenev, Dickens, Zola, and other realistic novelists present a contrasting picture. From the middle of the last century to the present day, literature is rich in descriptions of human character and destiny, in which circumstances which today we would describe as deprivational have played a significant role. This applies equally to actual persons — notorious conquerors, rulers, dictators, assassins, and criminals — whose bizarre and seemingly unpredictable behaviour has profoundly influenced the course of history.

Two such examples are the Italian anarchist Luigi Lucheni, who assassinated the Austrian Empress Elizabeth in 1898, and Lee Oswald, who was accused of the assassination of President Kennedy in 1963. Lucheni did not know his mother, who, pregnant, left her native village in Italy at the age of eighteen and went to Paris. The boy was left in a maternity ward a few days after birth, was then placed in St. Anthony's foundling home in Paris, and later in a foundling home in Parma. At twelve months of age he was committed to foster care. At the age of nine years (according to the biographer of Empress Elizabeth, E.C. Corti, 1937), he was working on the railway. As a young man he showed a desire to travel. He wandered from country to country, and finally, after journeying from Rijeka to Trieste, penniless and unemployed, he was deported to Italy.

With regard to Oswald, for whose crime the Warren Commission could find no logical motive, we quote this extract from an article by I. Klíma (*Literární Noviny*, Prague, 1965, no. 4):

> We cannot avoid, when reading his life history, at least pity, if not sympathy, for this man who was constantly hounded in childhood, led an isolated existence, and who from childhood developed the strange combination of restlessness and anarchism. A posthumous child, born a few weeks after the outbreak of World War II, Lee Oswald spent part of his early life in an orphanage. His childhood was characterized by constant changes. His mother, always in search of something,

alternated husbands, jobs and environments. Usually she did not stay more than six months in one place. The succession of schools young Lee attended were just impersonal buildings. When he rebelled and played truant from school, he was sent to a psychiatric clinic for assessment. The report noted — "the boy is very isolated, avoids contact, prefers to spend his time alone, reading or watching TV ... he is emotionally very disturbed".

If we consider historically the growth of scientific interest in the problem of psychological deprivation, and the development of an adequate methodology for its study, we can distinguish four periods.
1. The first "empirical" period covers approximately the second half of the last century, and up to the thirties of this century. During this period, observations and experimental data were recorded but no serious attempt was made to systematically treat and analyze the data. In some cases the emphasis was medical-social, in others philanthropical. This body of data includes observations by paediatricians in orphanages, in children's hospitals, and in other children's institutes, and reports about the tragic death rate and lowered vitality of institutionalized children.

A great upsurge of interest in psychological deprivation followed World War I and the great economic depression of the early thirties. The establishment and development of post-war social services, the far-reaching improvements in hygienic conditions in institutions, and progress in all fields of medicine led to the important observation that with institutionalized children the death rate could be drastically reduced and dangerous epidemics prevented. Even under these improved conditions, however, it was obvious that institutionalized children, compared with children living in families, were less resistant to all unfavourable influences, and that their development was retarded and unbalanced. A decisive role in this unfavourable development was assigned to psychological factors.

2. The second period can be described as the "alarm" period. It spans the thirties and forties of this century, and was heralded by the studies of the Vienna school of C. Bühler. She and her co-workers systematically investigated the mental development of children exposed to environmental conditions which varied in degree of impoverishment. Studies by this group were often methodologically sounder than some later studies which gained wider acceptance and provoked greater interest. A number of factors contributed to this predicament — in the interim the public at large had been prepared to accept such findings; World War II had brought to light new, shocking accounts of deserted and suffering children;

and while later findings were incorporated into the broad, generally accepted framework of psychoanalytic thought, the Vienna school failed to provide a sufficiently broad psychological theory to account for their findings.

Even at this early stage, H. Hetzer (1929–1932) studied children with bad social and economic backgrounds, children "without families" and from "foster families". In addition, Bühler's group conducted the first systematic investigation into psychological hospitalism. Interest in this field was created both by an increase in the number of social and medical institutions involved in child care, and by a recognition of the medical problems resulting from institutional care (high mortality in baby institutes).

These two factors probably provided the impetus for the initial studies of R. A. Spitz, which pre-date World War II. These studies are important because of their comprehensiveness, the precise observational methods employed, and the theoretical importance of the conclusions advanced.

Beginning at the outset of World War II, William Goldfarb (1943 et seq.), working along independent lines, conducted a number of careful studies, in which he compared children raised initially in an institution and subsequently transferred into a foster home with children raised in a foster home from earliest childhood. He concluded that early institutional care has a prolonged unfavourable effect on intellectual and character development.

The growth of studies of distressed children during and immediately after World War II was undoubtedly stimulated by the numbers of deserted children, children without families, evacuated and resettled children, and children in concentration camps (D. Burlingham and A. Freud, 1942; A. Freud and D. Burlingham, 1944*a,b*; S. Isaacs, 1941; C. Burt, 1943; K. M. Wolf, 1945; N. Wolffheim, 1959, and others).

Post-war changes in social and economic structure produced a higher percentage of working mothers, problems of housing and a breakdown in war-time marriages. All these conditions contributed to changes in attitudes towards child care, and affected basic stability in the children themselves. Alarming increases in juvenile delinquency and increased incidence of psychological disorders in children (neurosis, attempted suicide, psychosomatic disorders) provoked widespread interest in the problem of distressed children. Finally, interest began to focus on the question of the millions of deprived children in countries still economically under-developed, children physically and mentally starving, children lacking clothing and shelter, maternal or parental care, wandering children without proper supervision and schooling.

The subject of psychological deprivation, despite its severe consequences, would hardly have aroused such scientific interest had there not existed concurrently a theoretical framework within which these problems could be studied. In the preceding decades, knowledge of normal psychological maturation and developmental processes had progressed rapidly. The social-empirical approach to the problem of deprivation was now replaced by a more promising line of attack, which used as a starting point theories of personality development.

Interest in the problems of children suffering from denial of emotional satisfaction was touched off by speculations from psychoanalytically oriented authors (for example, I. D. Suttie, 1935; H. Edelston, 1943; J. Bowlby of the London Tavistock Clinic, 1940; R. A. Spitz in the U.S.A., 1945 et seq.). Their efforts produced a good deal of interesting material and productive theorizing. In this general area of psychological deprivation, a focal point is Bowlby's monograph *Maternal care and mental health* (1951), in which the results of studies up to that time are collated. Bowlby's conclusions can be summarized as follows. A child in infancy should develop in an atmosphere of emotional warmth, and should be tied to the mother (or a mother surrogate) by an intimate permanent bond of affection, which is, for both child and mother, a source of satisfaction and happiness. Deficiency in such a tie leads to a number of mental health disorders, which are severe, and in some cases irreversible, depending on the degree and permanence of such deprivation.

Spitz and Goldfarb also stressed the severe consequences of long-term total deprivation, its dramatic course, its permanence, and its deep penetration into personality structure, which is significantly retarded and deviates in the direction of the psychopathologically "cold" character with delinquent tendencies, and even towards psychosis. The deprivation model usually employs the medical description of illness, with uniform symptomatology and a certain etiology and prognosis (this usually derives from terms such as "hospitalism", "deprivation syndrome", "anaclitic depression", "institutional character", and so on).

These initial interpretations, which sounded the alarm and roused the interest of the scientific community in a problem which had been ignored up to this point, were soon supplanted by more critical and sober attitudes and opinions.

3. The third period, which we describe as "critical", approximately covers the fifties. Following Bowlby's monograph, a large number of studies were reported which to some extent corrected findings from the previous period. Social practice, mainly

child care in institutions, foster care, and the organization of social services, had already been influenced in the meantime by the studies of the second "alarm" period, so that new investigators in their studies were operating in quite different contexts from those in which Spitz, Goldfarb, and Bowlby had worked. Their conclusions tended to be basically more optimistic. Previously, the experience of the child lacking maternal care was regarded as the main source of deprivation, but it now became clear that deprivation could result from other circumstances. It was noted, for example, that many children who lack maternal care do in fact live with their mothers (J. G. Howells and J. Layng, 1955; B. Wootton, 1962). Recognition of the need to study deprivation under family life conditions (J. Robertson, 1954, 1958; Joyce Robertson, 1962) inevitably followed this observation.

While in the previous period it was assumed that nearly all deprived children suffer mental disorders, it became apparent from these new studies that a number of children survive these conditions practically untouched. Bowlby, Spitz, and Goldfarb had been struck by the severity and the uniformity of the syndrome. By contrast, however, some new investigations (D. Beres and S. J. Obers, 1950; H. Lewis, 1954; G. Klackenberg, 1956; R. M. du Pan and S. Roth, 1955) reported that only a minority of such children developed severe disorders, and that, generally speaking, the syndrome is unstable.

Judging both from the results of experiments on sensory deprivation and from new learning theories, it is clear that a single factor operates only in exceptional cases, that in almost all depriving situations the deprivation involves the refusal of more than one important need, which differ from child to child, and that the denial of such satisfactions has a different effect, depending on the child's developmental level. To workers in the previous period, deprivational disorders appeared to be irreversible, and the prognosis nearly hopeless. But the more recent studies pointed up a certain success of preventive and therapeutic measures (M. David and G. Appell, 1951; B. M. Flint, 1966), where the children's institutions were adequately equipped and staffed, and where the directing principle was to respect the personality of every individual child as much as possible. As appreciation of the underlying causes of deprivation and its functional mechanisms increased, the prognosis for directed individual psychotherapy correspondingly improved.

Bowlby himself, in his 1956 study, modified his earlier view in line with these new findings; however, he stressed that, from a practical point of view, there are no grounds for satisfaction and apathy, since the percentage of disturbed children is still high and the possibility of severe disturbance cannot be ignored.

The climax of this critical period seems to us to be reached in the World Health Organization publication *Deprivation of maternal care* (1962). It considered the results of deprivation studies from different theoretical viewpoints, and the validity of the classical conceptions, and dealt primarily with methodological problems involved in current and subsequent investigations.

If we acknowledge that deprivation can occur not only in baby institutes and children's homes but also in familial and other social milieus, the question acquires much broader social implications. We must even consider the possibility of masked deprivation — deprivation of future generations under the aegis of an accelerating technological civilization. There are increasing signs of a social malaise (increasing juvenile delinquency, social passivity, increased suicides, and so on) as a result of limited emotional resources and basic feelings of inadequacy which children appear to experience from an early age. This seems more prevalent in our present cultural conditions than in previous periods.

The question arises — if there is no one clear-cut syndrome of deprivation, what determines the individual etiological features? How do they relate to the internal and external environment of the organism? If remission of symptoms is possible, when, and why, and under what conditions does this occur? In our view, the main task of the next period is to search for the answers to these questions.

4. The fourth period, covering the 1960s, which we describe as "experimental-theoretical", is characterized by depth studies of the interaction between the organism and the environment under deprivational conditions. If not every child is affected by the deprivational situation, and if children are affected differently by the same conditions, we must discard large-scale studies of heterogeneous groups in favour of intensive studies of smaller groups under strictly controlled conditions. We must also change from cross-sectional to longitudinal studies, so that we can measure with a greater degree of accuracy the effects of deprivational influences on the development of the child's personality. Here we are concerned with the product of the interaction between the individually created child's personality and the individually formed life environment — a deprived life environment, one that is impoverished in some important ways. Already progress has been made in this direction by R. A. Spitz in his important work, *La première année de la vie de l'enfant* (1958). Intelligent planning of experiments and efficient methodological techniques characterize a large number of studies (H.F. Harlow, H. L. Rheingold, J. L. Gewirtz, J. A. Ambrose, R. A. Hinde, H. R.

Schaffer, and others) published in four volumes, *Determinants of infant behaviour,* edited by B. M. Foss (1961, 1963, 1965, 1969).

There is, of course, a sound basis for an experimental approach to the problem of deprivation. After 1950, there were notable advances in the neurophysiological area of experimental psychology, based particularly on the studies of Gray Walter, W. Penfield, H. W. Magoun, J. W. Papez, and J. D. French, with ethological bias deriving mainly from the studies of K. Lorenz, W. H. Thorpe, F. A. Beach, H. Moltz, and J. A. King. Added impetus came from experimental studies of psychological deprivation induced by radical limitation of sensory stimuli and by social isolation. These experiments were first conducted by D. O. Hebb and co-workers (1955) at McGill University, and from there interest spread to other psychological and psychiatric laboratories. Theoretically these studies were extremely important in clarifying the mechanisms underlying psychological deprivation, even though the relationship of these findings to the clinical problem of distressed children is still not fully understood. Special mention should also be made of studies developing out of classical Pavlovian and operant conditioning theory in which animals (H. S. Liddell, 1956; R. A. Butler, 1957) and children (J. L. Gewirtz, 1961 et seq.) were employed as subjects. It is obvious from these developments that the fourth period has already rejected the simple unsatisfactory model of illness, and has advanced to a more valid psychological concept based on the findings of modern psychology, the physiology of the central nervous system, and on new psychoanalytic ideas.

A useful way of approaching the problem of deprivation seems to lie in the cooperation of investigators from different countries. A number of cross-cultural studies of deprived children were reported in this period. Different economic and cultural backgrounds, different traditions of child care with very young children, different social conditions, laws, organization of social and medical services, and many other factors undoubtedly affect forms of deprivation in children. Comparison of these different conditions might possibly bring us a step closer to an understanding of what are the basic underlying features of deprivation, and what is contributed specifically by different regional conditions.

As yet, we lack complete understanding of psychological deprivation and its ramifications. Nevertheless, study of this problem has already contributed to a fuller understanding of the psychological development of man. If we can observe what effect the denial of certain needs in the child's early life environment has on his subsequent psychological development, and if we can experimentally manipulate some of these factors, we should finally arrive at a better understanding of their importance in normal developmental processes. Basically, the importance of the psychological deprivation concept lies in its contribution to the perennial problem in child psychology, that of the relative influence of environment and inherited or innate potential in development. In this sense, it is both a working hypothesis and a new method which can significantly enrich the future.

The concept of psychological deprivation undoubtedly has important practical application. It has changed our views about the care of very young children and has influenced child care in all fields — in institutions, in hospitals, in maternity wards, it has affected the organization and planning of further developments in child care, and has modified the attitudes of doctors, psychologists, and social workers in their normal everyday practice.

2 Terminology and rationale

There is considerable inconformity amongst authors when defining psychological deprivation. Frequently they advance highly idiosyncratic ideas, and engage an assortment of descriptive terms. The most commonly used term is deprivation, which implies a loss of something, or suffering through denial of some important need. Here we refer specifically to the denial of some basic psychological need (psychological deprivation), for which analogous terms are nurturance deficit, psychological starvation, psychological carence (*carence mentale*).

M. Tramer (1963) distinguished two levels of deprivation: mental malnutrition (inanitas mentis) and a much more severe kind, a sort of psychical cachexy (inanitio mentis). M. Pfaundler (1899) described the same content when he used the term "psychical inanition".

Some writers limit their definitions to the psychological need they consider most important, and hence to the particular deficit they consider critical in the etiology of the mental disorder. It is usually assumed by these authors that for normal development a child has a basic need for emotional warmth and love. If sufficient understanding and emotional support are provided, lack of other components − sensory stimuli, toys, adequate care and schooling, for example − can be compensated for. Lack of satisfaction of emotional needs, however − i.e. emotional (H. Bakwin, 1942) or affective (L. G. Lowrey, 1940) deprivation (emotional starvation, *carence emotionelle, Gefühlsmangel* are synonymous terms) − is considered to be a primary pathogenic factor producing developmental and character disorders.

Still more circumscribed terms are used by those workers who see the origins of deprivation primarily in inadequate specific emotional ties between the child and the mother, i.e. in deprivation of maternal care (maternal deprivation, *carence des soins maternels,*

privation maternelle, alejamento de la madre, Muttere~
Ainsworth (1962), for example, defines deprivation as ins~
of mutual interaction between the child and the maternal
(maternal deprivation). She correctly emphasizes the dynamic nat~
of the child's relationship to the environment, but limits this
relationship to the mother or the surrogate figure. She suggests that
we should differentiate between (*a*) insufficiency of interaction, (*b*)
distortion in the character of the interaction, irrespective of the
number of stimuli, and (*c*) discontinuity of the relationship brought
about through separation.

A number of other authors, however, favour more embracing
definitions. For example, the term "pedagogical deficit", which is
used mainly by Soviet workers and which describes a lack of care,
the latter being defined in the widest possible sense, has too wide a
connotation. This applies equally to the Clarkes' (1960) definition of
psychological deprivation as "any external event or constellation of
events which significantly interferes with the child's normal
developmental processes and which thus affects adversely his mental
and physical status". However, although the smothering love of
parents, their inconsistency in attitudes and moods, and their
different ways of masking hostility can be included in the Clarkes'
definition, they can hardly be described as depriving. To describe
every damaging environmental influence as deprivational would render
the term meaningless. On the other hand, a term such as "play
deficit" (*"Spieldefizit"*, after F. Schneersohn, 1950) is unduly
restrictive, since it suggests both that the critical developmental need
during childhood is play, and that the denial of the opportunity to
play often leads to developmental disorders.

Some investigators attempt to distinguish the case in which the
child from birth is not exposed to certain stimuli, so that certain
specific needs are not aroused, from that where the need is aroused,
but subsequently the stimuli by which the need can be satisfied are
not available in the child's environment. The first situation is
described (by Gewirtz, 1961) as "privation", the second as
"deprivation", which is considered by some authors to be identical
with separation.

Bowlby speaks of partial deprivation in instances where the
separation between the mother and the child is not absolute, but
where their relationship is impoverished and insufficient for some
reason. D. G. Prugh and R. G. Harlow (1962) describe a similar
situation as "hidden" or "masked" deprivation. They also
differentiate between a damaged and an impoverished relationship
between mother and child.

The specific circumstances which produce psychological hardship are described in a number of ways, for example "children without families", neglect, the Russian *bezprizornost*, the Polish term *chorora sieboča* (orphan's disease), but most commonly the standard phrase is the older term "hospitalism", because it was in hospitalized or institutionalized children that disorders of this kind were originally and most systematically studied. Even here, however, a careful distinction must be made between psychological hospitalism, infectious hospitalism, and hospitalism with symptoms of physical damage. Although hospitalism originally described damage caused only by institutional or collective care (M. Pfaundler's [1924] description of *"Massenpflegschaftsschaden"*), in subsequent studies the term included any environmentally produced damage to both the physical and the mental development of the child (J. Ströder and E. Geisler, 1957).

Finally, some terms describe the typical results of certain psychological hardship: one speaks of developmental retardation through external causes (environmental retardation, A. Gesell and C. S. Amatruda, 1947), sometimes of loneliness of the child (H. Bakwin, 1942), of withering (*"Verkümmerung"*, U. Köttgen, 1964), of homesickness (*"Heimweh,"* A. Nitschke, 1955), of separation anxiety, and of neglect, dread, and so on.

The lack of clarity of the descriptive terms clearly reflects the confusion in this area of psychology and psychiatry. Unfortunately, many authors confuse terms and definitions so that the original meaning of the concept sometimes broadens, sometimes narrows, sometimes overlaps into other areas of meaning. Very often the terms are described inadequately. For example, the word hospitalism, which a number of authors equate with psychological deprivation, only partly embraces this latter concept. Such a definition limits deprivation to the institutional environment (in fact to the hospital environment), and in addition neglects the fact that the institutional situation harbours influences which, although not depriving, are nonetheless dangerous (higher probability of infection, change of regime, lack of sleep, increased opportunity for conflict during participation in the group situation, and so on). It also fails to consider that under optimal conditions deprivation need not occur in institutions. This same consideration applies to the concept of separation of mother and child, where it is impossible to equate deprivation and separation.

It is obvious that terms which are relevant only to certain specific situations or circumstances are unsuitable for psychological theory, and that we should choose broader, more comprehensive terms which better describe the psychological basis of the resulting handicap.

DEFINITION

Definitions of psychological deprivation which proceed from the analogy between psychological and biological carence seem closer to the nub of the problem, although such an analogy has been questioned in the literature. In the same way that serious disorders can be due to an overall nutritional deficit, to carence of protein, of vitamins, of oxygen, and so on, so serious psychological disorders can arise from psychological deficit — from denial of love, stimulation, social contact, child care, and training. In both cases, the product is a state of general or partial starvation, and the consequences — irrespective of the actual mechanisms involved — are shown by decay, withering, and general impoverishment of the organism. This type of definition also distinguishes implicitly, from both the biological and the psychological points of view, between toxic disorders, other developmental disorders, and the carence-type disorders.

D. O. Hebb (1958) offers the closest approximation to this concept when he defines deprivation as the result of a "biologically adequate but psychologically restricted environment". The expression "restricted" here obviously refers to quantitative impoverishment, which would be understood as a deficit of certain elements in the environment — stimuli as such, or stimuli of a specific kind, or certain structuring of stimuli which is necessary for normal development and for the maintenance of psychological functioning. Of course, we must define precisely which elements in the environment are psychologically so important that their unavailability is the prime determinant of subsequent disorders. From the dynamic point of view, it would be preferable to speak about the sum total of the inadequately met needs of the organism.

After consideration of these points we think the concept is best defined in a preliminary way as follows: "psychological deprivation is the psychological condition produced by life situations in which the subject is not given the opportunity to satisfy some of his basic (vital) psychological needs sufficiently and for a long enough period, so that their appropriate actualization and development are obstructed or distorted".

As we understand it, psychological deprivation is thus a characteristic inner end product of the prolonged impact of an impoverished environment which the child reaches through the deprivating situations — in other words, it is a psychological state resulting from continuing restricted interaction of the child with his physical and/or social environment.

The psychological condition of deprivation is reflected on the behavioural level in characteristic ways, so that we can detect its effects in the actual pattern of the child's developing personality, and in present structure. Here we speak of the "consequences of deprivation" or "deprivation damage". We are avoiding the use of the phrase "deprivational syndrome", because it leads to the erroneous view that we are dealing with a clearly defined group of pathological symptoms, from which deprivation can be diagnosed in the same way as other entities of somatic or mental illnesses.

Sometimes reference is made to "deprivational experiences". This means simply that the child has already experienced a deprivation situation, and that if he later experiences similar situations he will approach them with an already changed, more sensitive, or more "hardened" psychological structure.

In dealing with the link between the depriving situations and their consequences in personality development, we shall speak subsequently about the "mechanisms of deprivation". These are conceptualized simply as a sequence of events brought about by inadequate satisfaction of basic psychological needs in the child, which, in a characteristic way, leads to changes in the structure of the developing child's personality. Thus "deprivating" describes the events which lead to deprivation.

BASIC PSYCHOLOGICAL NEEDS

The complex and controversial issue of basic psychological needs will be dealt with fully in chapter 10, where we shall attempt to explain the theoretical assumptions underlying the concept of deprivation. At this preliminary stage, it is necessary only to postulate the following four main categories of basic psychological needs.

1. The need for a certain level of external stimulation, i.e. for a certain amount and complexity — or variability — of stimuli in general, or of stimuli in certain modalities. This is obviously necessary for the development and maintenance of adequate levels of attentiveness and activity, which is a necessary condition for the child's active relation to the surrounding world.
2. The need for sensory-cognitive structuring, i.e. for meaningful

sequences or order of stimuli, as a necessary condition for the child's effective learning.

3. The need for objects permitting specific affectional attachment, i.e. for stable classes of stimuli which concentrate the child's individual activities. This is a prerequisite for the development of feelings of security.

4. The need for primary personal values, for stimuli (objects and goals) which are critical for the growth of personal identity and self-fulfilment; the child needs appreciation, recognition of his worth, confirmation of his autonomous conduct and approval of his assumed, distinct social roles. This again is clearly a precondition for effective personality integration.

Of course, we can only evaluate the significance of these needs in relation to the individual child and to the society in which he lives. It is probable that basic needs will be much the same in all human cultures, but the further we ascend the hierarchy of needs we have described above, and the more detailed and specific we become, the greater the degree of differentiation occurring. In different cultures, particular needs are experienced with varying degrees of urgency. For example, in some cultures, withdrawal and passivity are valued, while in others social activity and enterprise are preferred. In some cases, a continuing emphasis is placed on the establishment of certain habits, which subsequently enter into complex ceremonials, while in others the child is permitted to lead as free a life as possible. Alternatively, in some societies a strong degree of dependence on parents is encouraged in children, while in others they are encouraged to be independent as early as possible. We can only assess the effect of psychological deprivation, therefore, in terms of generally accepted values in a given culture or social class or individual family. In this sense, these effects will be reflected in the extent to which an individual suffering the effects of long-term non-satisfaction of needs is unable to adapt himself to situations which are normal and desirable in a given society.

Our definition of psychological deprivation is sufficiently robust to allow us to detect a common basis for psychological disorders produced in different deprivational contexts (in an institution, in the family, whether we are dealing with a healthy or defective child, and so on) produced by different mechanisms and reflected in different symptoms. The definition per se, however, does not specify either the psychological needs which are particularly strong in particular developmental stages or those which cause specific damage when they are not adequately satisfied. The fact that we cannot yet reliably identify and classify all of the child's needs at different developmental levels, however, may have a positive aspect. We hope that this concept of deprivation will act as a stimulus for the study of needs of the child and for the recognition of their relative significance in the development of the child's psychological structure.

This definition, of course, refers only to psychological needs and ignores material, biological needs which may, but need not be, at the same time adequately satisfied. Hebb's definition, mentioned above, is therefore narrower, as is the rather more clinical definition of H. Lewis (1956) who views the deprived child as one whose material needs are sufficiently satisfied but whose need for parental affection is denied.

ISOLATION

Our definition allows us to identify the logical content and limitations of other related concepts in this area. Among those of importance for subsequent analysis are two general, closely connected concepts — "isolation" and "separation". Clearly, as set forth, these are "deprivation situations", and not deprivation per se. We should remember that children respond differently and are affected differently when they encounter the same deprivation situation, since they differ both in psychological resources and in stages of personality development. We shall attempt to show, for example, how different children react to the kind of uniform isolation which can be found in a baby or nursery home, or to the same abrupt separation from the family milieu.

The first of these two concepts — "isolation" — denotes the situation in which the child is cut off (more or less continuously) from contact with his stimulating environment (whether physical or social) and hence prevented from forming meaningful relations with it. Isolation exists at different levels (the extreme case is represented by the so-called wolf children, the more moderate level by young shepherds living alone with the herd for long periods). It can involve impoverishment of the physical environment (when a child is restricted to a bed, for example) or of the social environment (a child isolated from the family or peer group, or a child living with his parents in an isolated rural area). It is possible that these factors may interact with certain other factors, e.g. with separation experiences during repeated placements in children's homes, with physical hardship during an isolated existence in the wilderness, with painful experiences during a stay in hospital, and so on.

If there is complete isolation from human contact over a long period of time, we can expect that basic psychological needs which remained unsatisfied from the beginning will not develop and will remain at a very rudimentary level. Under less extreme isolation, delay and retardation in the development of needs will be less marked; it is reasonable to predict clear relationships, within the range from nearly normal to extremely pathological, between the amount of deprivation and the effects noted above. As we shall indicate later, isolation in this sense is present in all social situations which involve deprivation. In institutes of permanent collective care (if we ignore the extreme cases of isolation from human society — wolf children, children criminally neglected by their parents, and so on) the child is isolated from stimuli which he normally encounters in the family context, and suffers a certain monotony of sensory and social stimuli. During a stay in hospital a similar situation may exist. In partial collective care establishments this danger is substantially reduced but not eliminated.

We should also be concerned about the inner, psychological isolation of a child in a family where he is ignored or where parents are unable to reach him emotionally. A child living under normal family conditions, and indeed, the family as a whole, can be isolated from the larger society (for example, a family living in rural isolation, migrant families). Isolation can also result from extraordinary social circumstances (life in a concentration camp, in prison, and so on).

SEPARATION

A second type of depriving situation is the disruption of an already established relationship between a child and his stimulating environment. This kind of situation is most likely to occur if the child is separated from those persons who were previously the source of satisfaction of his basic needs. It was J. Bowlby (1951) who probably most clearly expressed the opinion that repeated long-term separations of a child from his mother or mother surrogate during the first three to five years of life usually result in permanent disturbance to the mental health of the child and that this significantly affects total personality development. In this way the term "separation" was introduced into psychology to serve as a severe pathogenic agent.

This view was first supported by psychoanalytically oriented authors, since it was in general agreement with the emphasis they placed on the relationship between mother and child. Bowlby himself, in asserting that this relationship played the decisive role in the formation of the child's personality, influenced a number of subsequent theorists to limit this concept of separation to the severance of the specific bond between mother and child. A broadening of this concept, however, at times reached such proportions that the logical distinction between cause and effect disappeared, and the concept of separation merged into the concept of deprivation. Thus it was not surprising that this terminological and conceptual confusion attracted the critical attention of other investigators. However, extensive research into maternal deprivation (L. J. Yarrow, 1961; L. Casler, 1961; R. G. Andry, 1962; S. Lebovici, 1962; J. de Wit, 1964) considerably reduced this terminological confusion, and resulted in a more precise definition of the concept. These studies were undoubtedly a positive contribution to the understanding of maternal deprivation. This work also pointed up the methodological weaknesses of a number of separation studies, and contributed to the more careful planning of subsequent investigations and more cautious interpretation of results. As far as the pathogenic effects of the early social separation of a child are concerned, however, the original hypothesis, stated by Bowlby, remains valid.

Originally M. D. Ainsworth and J. Bowlby (1954) tried to differentiate, from a methodological point of view, the situation in which a child is separated from his mother before a specific relationship is established, from that in which the bond is already established and is subsequently suddenly interrupted or severed for a long period. Both situations were considered within the general context of separation. But in her later work, Ainsworth (1962), responding partly to well-founded criticism, recommends that the term separation be applied only to those situations in which there is interruption of an already established bond. We agree with this suggestion, and define separation as the situation in which a specific relation between the child and his environment is interrupted.

It seems reasonable to hypothesize that the biological dependence of the child on his mother is transformed into emotional dependence during the weaning stage, and that separation would be most detrimental to psychological development after such a specific tie has been established. Until this time it is possible that the so-called social stimuli are not perceived as different from stimuli in the physical environment, and that the child's reaction to severed contact with such stimuli does not differ from his reaction to a change in the physical environment. It is only after the establishment of emotional dependence that the response to separation takes on significant proportions.

We ought also to consider in this context the development of independence in the individual. Separation, broadly conceived, is an aspect of normal development in the child. Gradually the child, through the loosening of strong dependency ties with the mother, behaves more and more independently, is able to tolerate distance from her for longer periods of time, and penetrates more and more into wider social groups. This gradual separation is obviously a critical aspect of the child's social maturation, his assertiveness and finally of his mental health. What makes social separation dangerous and pathogenic, above all, is the time factor, when it occurs too early. If a child of school age is temporarily separated from his family (at summer camp, for example) this could strengthen the development of independence. But it is dangerous if the separation occurs when he is still strongly dependent on his mother or a mother surrogate, and when the separation itself is not actively sought after by the child, but is demanded by environmental conditions which he does not understand. When he is developmentally unprepared, he is "betrayed" by this separation.

Separation, then, is a particular external circumstance which may be, but is not inevitably, a depriving factor. Separation often initiates a cycle of events during which deprivation occurs, but it is not itself this cycle of events nor is it a necessary condition. Doubtless deprivation can exist without the actual separation of the child from his mother or from his familiar social environment (see "Deprivation in the family" in chapter 5), but there are many cases of separation which persist for long periods of time, and clearly do not create deprivation.

A child establishes a bond not only with his mother, but at very early stages with other members of the family and all who interact with him. In addition, a special personal relation is formed between the child and the home environment, the existing emotional atmosphere, and certain objects — toys and so on — so that every separation is a complex, complicated psychological act. Certain other factors are also relevant. Separation can be sudden or gradual, total or partial, short-term or long-term. It can also vary in its traumatic effect and in the extent to which it activates mechanisms of frustration. The child employs these mechanisms to adjust to the situation in which his need for emotional contact with those persons constituting his social environment cannot be met because of obstacles, which in this case are physical (and possibly psychological) separation.

In the severance of contact, it is not only the child who is affected by the separation. The mother also experiences frustration of her needs to be with the child, to help and defend him and so on.

We must assume also some separation anxiety on her part if she is separated from the child (employment, study trip abroad, for example). The child's behaviour during separation affects her attitudes and behaviour and, at the same time, her behaviour has some effect on the way in which this separation is tolerated by the child.

In addition, we should consider the compensating role of other family members, and the public at large. Certainly the total social background in which specific cases of separation occur is important. If we are concerned with a society in which frequent separation is quite normal, for example, one in which there is a high level of female employment, this would influence the attitude of the mother towards the child, and stimulate a search for means by which the unfavourable effects of separation could be avoided or softened (availability of adequate home help and so on).

We mentioned in the previous section that if separation is long-term, it sometimes changes into a state of social isolation. Like isolation, separation exists in practically all social situations in which deprivation can occur. Thus, for example, a child committed to a children's home is necessarily separated from the family. But the child also experiences a specific form of separation when he is transferred from one institution to another, from department to department, or whenever staff changes occur. A similar state exists in every hospital situation and in all cases where changes in care-supervision occur. The child, however, can also experience psychological separation when he remains within the family (for example, the advent of a new baby or when the mother, father, or other member leaves the family). The child, with the family as a whole, may also be separated from the rest of society for economic, socio-cultural, or psychological reasons (families with high social mobility, families which have become "prominent", immigrant families belonging to different religious sects, families discriminated against after sudden political changes). Finally, separation plays an important role in those unusual social situations created by natural disasters (floods, earthquakes), or by social catastrophes (wars, revolutions).

FRUSTRATION

Although our concept of deprivation has much in common with the concept of frustration, it is not identical with it. These terms, therefore, should not be used interchangeably. Frustration is variously defined — as the inability to satisfy an aroused need, because of some impediment or obstacle (H. Symonds, 1955), as the state of tension generated by the blocking of the path to the goal, or as a situation in which "the organism meets with some more or less insurmountable impediment or obstacle in its path to the satisfaction of some vital need" (S. Rosenzweig, 1944). In the widest sense, the term frustration is identical with deprivation only where it is impossible to satisfy a need over a long period of time. This does not apply when only one of a number of possible paths to the goal is blocked.

Most of the studies of frustration are concerned (as indicated in the above definitions) with the satisfaction of the aroused need already directed towards the goal. It is clear that in this narrower sense frustration is less damaging than deprivation. As a concrete example: frustration occurs when a child is deprived of a favourite toy and is given a chance to play with something else which is less attractive, while at the same time he observes something which attracts him more. Deprivation occurs if the child is not given the opportunity to play at all (for a sufficient period of time) or if he cannot satisfy his natural drive towards activity and play. We think that this distinction between frustration and deprivation is important, even though at times it may be difficult to distinguish clearly between them.

It is likely that long-term frustration merges into deprivation, and that probably the initial stage of the deprivation situation is simply the frustrating situation. Thus if a two-year-old child is separated from his parents and placed in a hospital, his immediate reaction to this can be viewed as a frustration response. But if he stays in hospital for a year, and is confined chiefly to the same room without visits from his parents, without walks, and where the monotony of the environment is disturbed only by the occasional routine duties performed by nursing staff, a distinct condition of psychological deprivation will develop.

CONFLICT

Similarly we can differentiate psychological deprivation from conflict, even though in ordinary life situations the two sometimes overlap, and initially deprivational situations can produce effects which are characteristic of recognized conflict stages. By conflict we mean a particular type of frustration in which the obstacle which prevents satisfaction of an aroused need is another aroused need which has a competing valence. The organism in conflict is drawn by forces directed to different but equally attractive goals, or is at one and the same time attracted and repelled by the one goal object. Thus approach-approach, approach-avoidance, eventually avoidance-avoidance conflict ensues. M. Tramer (1963) explains how a conflict state, based on deprivation (emotional insufficiency) can be aroused in the child. If the child is starved for love which he vainly tries to win, he will develop initially a certain feeling of emptiness, dissatisfaction — a lack of something essential — and possibly later will direct a feeling of anger and hatred towards the mother or father who deny him this satisfaction. A conflict exists between the motive to injure, punish, or even destroy the parents, and the original motive to love, find security with, or please them, all of which stem from the original vigorous need for love.

NEGLECT

Finally the term "neglect" is differentiated from the concept of deprivation. By neglect we mean simply insufficient care. Neglect profoundly affects the child's overt behaviour, even though it need not directly disturb his mental health. The neglected child usually lives under primitive conditions, with poor hygiene and care supervision, he lacks good models of responsible social behaviour and has poor schooling opportunities; despite this, he can show a well-balanced mental and, more importantly, emotional development. With such a child there are often no grounds for anticipating emotional "withering", or neurotic or other personality disorders.

Psychologically deprived children, however, often develop under excellent hygienic conditions and conditions of correct supervision and care, but their mental, and particularly their emotional, development is seriously disturbed. We face the paradox that the neglected child may be removed from the family and placed in an institute where neglect is eliminated, but where, at the same time, he is exposed to the danger of deprivation, which is, prognostically, far worse. Of course, in this respect, deprivation and neglect are usually not distinguished clearly enough, and in fact the majority of neglected children are, at the same time, deprived. This will be dealt with later on.

In this discussion we have dealt only with the psychogenic conditions, but there also exists a wide range of organic damage, disorders, and deviations which directly or indirectly influence and depreciate the behaviour of the child. An adequate explanation of the interaction of all these factors would require a far more extensive treatment than has been attempted up to this point. In the following chapters we shall at least attempt to identify some of these factors.

3 Methodological approach

The great volume of studies in psychological deprivation makes an overall review almost impossible. Even if we limit ourselves only to the most important studies, we are forced to the conclusion that the reported data and the interpretations of these are often contradictory. An analysis of the different methodological approaches adopted by individual researchers, however, can account for some of these contradictions.

In clinical studies of deprivation any method suitable for studying the effect of any environmental variable on the development and behaviour of the organism can be used. Thus, a number of methodological criteria can be used to categorize studies of this sort.

The first of these is the procedures, techniques and the actual measuring instruments used in the studies.

A second criterion is the method of selection and size of sample. While some studies report individual cases, others are concerned with small, highly selected samples of children, while still others use a large N and few variables.

A final criterion is the time dimension, i.e. the elapsed time between the child's deprivational experiences and the actual observations of their presumed consequences.

Using these three criteria, we shall discuss the advantages and limitations of various approaches in studies dealing with the main question of how depriving situations affect the child's behaviour and development. We do not intend to present a complete critical evaluation; rather we shall limit ourselves to the questions most often raised by clinical workers involved in individual and group work with deprived children.

PROCEDURES USED IN ASSESSMENT OF CRITICAL VARIABLES

A wealth of various developmental scales, psychometric tests, projective techniques, rating scales, questionnaires, behaviour sampling methods, and so on have been used in clinical studies of deprived children. Clearly, the relevance of the conclusions reached in these studies is at least partly dependent on the validity of the applied instruments and on the conditions of administration and interpretation. Hence, the possibility of generalizing the results is often extremely doubtful and it is very difficult to make valid comparisons of data obtained in such different ways. In addition, the depriving life situations are usually so complicated and poorly defined that any demonstration of cause-effect relationships is highly questionable.

It is most difficult to disentangle all the interrelated biological and social variables usually encountered in clinical studies of deprived children. For example, it would be hardly possible to find cases in which the child's separation from the mother is the only factor producing an emotional response from the child. A child in these circumstances is usually isolated from the family environment, he may be ill, subjected to medical treatment and to changes in his daily routine, and he may be placed in an unfamiliar group of children and adults. M. D. Ainsworth and J. Bowlby (1954) observed that this problem can be partly avoided if we study groups of children for whom separation is the common factor, so that the common effect can be attributed to separation.

In addition, however, we encounter other confounding factors — hereditary, social, cultural, and economic — which combine in different ways, and which can produce unpredictable effects in the child's behaviour. We can criticize a number of well-known studies — the Spitz studies, for example (see S. R. Pinneau, 1955b) — for not taking these factors into account. In a number of studies an initial error is made in selecting for comparison groups which differ in a number of important respects. In other studies, control groups are not used, and conclusions are based on assumed norms. Obviously, in carefully planned research these difficulties can be partly overcome (for example the Mersham experiment of Hilda Lewis, 1954).

Difficulties of this sort in clinical studies have stimulated experimental psychologists and physiologists to undertake a number of studies in which they have attempted to control for certain variables. This can be most easily achieved, of course, with animal subjects. The results of these studies are obviously important, and in some cases contribute to our understanding of the factors underlying deprivation. We must be cautious in generalizing these conclusions to clinical practice, however, since the responses of the child are far more complex and variable than those of animals. Similarly, sensory deprivation experiments with adult subjects are only marginally relevant to real psychological deprivation in childhood. For ethical reasons, critical experiments of this sort with children are impossible.

We should note, however, the courageous experiment of W. and M. G. Dennis (1938, 1941) in which they studied the development of grasping, sitting, and standing as a function of maturation or learning. Twin girls of the Dennises, from the end of the first month to the end of the fourteenth month of life, were placed in a special experimental room where their behaviour could be controlled. All hygienic and biological needs were adequately met, but motor behaviour was severely restricted. Social stimulation, according to the authors, was kept to a minimum. For example, when they were fed, the babies' hands were kept under the blankets, and immediately after feeding they were returned to their cots and laid on their backs. All aids which they might use to lift themselves were removed from reach. They were first given toys at eleven months of age. The authors report that there was no noticeable retardation before nine months of age in the observed behaviours, and as soon as the twins were given the opportunity to "learn" (after fourteen months) they quickly recovered the deficit which had become apparent between the ninth and fourteenth months.

M. D. Ainsworth (1962) comments, however, that fortunately for these children, the conditions were not too depriving, since the parents came when the children cried, spent a good deal of time in their company (when making observations), and showed pleasure when they behaved appropriately. In addition, no satisfactory comparison was made between the social and emotional behaviour of the twins and those of other children raised under normal conditions. For these reasons, no definite conclusions can be drawn from this study.

So-called "natural" experiments involving extreme social isolation or criminal neglect approximate more closely the type of clinical deprivation normally encountered. Strictly speaking, these cannot be regarded as valid experiments, since they lack adequate controls. However, as regards specificity and degree of depriving situations they often resemble true experiments, and usually it is possible to define very precisely the stimuli excluded for a specified period of time.

Certain organizational measures taken in child care in some countries provide another example of "natural experiment", since they involve substantial changes in the stimulating environment for large segments of the child population. Evidence of this sort is available from studies of the personality development of children living under relatively strict uniform conditions of permanent collective care in Czechoslovakia after 1950.

SAMPLE SIZE

While most of the clinical studies employ samples of medium size, there are some often disregarded possibilities offered by study of individual cases, on the one hand, and of very large samples — in fact the entire child population — on the other.

a. Detailed studies of individual cases, particularly if continued over a long period of time, are probably the best way of identifying both those mechanisms underlying the development of deprivational disorders, and the close relationship between deprivational symptoms and various internal and external factors. Mechanisms underlying the re-adaptive process can also best be identified using this method. The history of Monica, cited by M. David and G. Appell, is such a case. Case histories of psychiatric patients with extreme separation anxiety (D. L. Burnham, 1965) can be quite revealing in discussions of late severe consequences of early deprivation. Normally, such studies can use the method of naturalistic observation, and can be extremely detailed. Some workers, in pointing out the inadequacy of large sample research, have suggested that future research will probably concentrate on individual cases over longer periods of time. Of course, in such studies one should always guard against over-subjectivity and premature judgment.

In this context, one should also note the sociologically oriented studies of individual families. These throw light on the relationship between the child's behaviour and responses from his family environment under normal everyday conditions (P. Wolf and M. Lewis, 1961).

b. Despite all the advantages accruing from intensive study of individual cases, or small, carefully selected groups, there is a major disadvantage of this technique — it is not always clear whether and in what sections of the population the situations under consideration are typical or representative enough to allow us to generalize, or atypical enough to be classed as deprivating rather than normal. Broad sociological or psychological population surveys are therefore very important, because they show the frequency of occurrence of certain situations which have particular effects under usual conditions.

These data are essential before we can understand the incidence, the forms, and the significance of deprivation in certain societies.

An example of this type of survey is the interesting study by J. Newson and E. Newson (1965) of infant-rearing practices in families in Nottingham, England. Other authors have compared child-rearing practices in advanced Western societies and African and Asian societies (M. D. Ainsworth, 1963). Such comparisons, however, raise a number of methodological problems, since identical events can have entirely different significance in different cultural settings.

THE TIME FACTOR

Immediate reactions to deprivation

Many studies report observations of the immediate reactions of children exposed to deprivating conditions during a prescribed, limited time period.

From a methodological point of view, the simplest examples are the many studies of the child's response to separation from the family and his response to a stay in an institution. A group of English and French workers (J. Robertson and J. Bowlby, 1952; J. Roudinesco, M. David, and J. Nicolas, 1952) have conducted the best-known studies of this type. They report the immediate reactions of children between the ages of twelve and twenty-four months to separation from their mothers. Similar observations have been made in the United States by D. G. Prugh et al. (1953), in Germany by G. A. Harnack and M. Oberschelp (1957), and in Czechoslovakia by M. Damborská (1959), M. Tautermannová (1961), L. Srp (1953), and J. Langmeier (1959) (mainly with children admitted to hospital).

Some of these studies report individual, usually precise and detailed case histories, while others involve larger samples, and the results are evaluated statistically. The behaviour of children of a certain age is recorded in the deprivating situation, and compared with the behaviour of control groups. Most frequently, a developmental and behavioural comparison is made between children from institutions and children raised in their own or foster families (R. A. Spitz and K. M. Wolf, 1946; L. G. Lowrey, 1940; I. Gindl, H. Hetzer, and M. Sturm, 1937; D. Burlingham and A. Freud, 1942; K. M. Simonsen, 1947; J. Roudinesco and G. Appell, 1950) or in different types of nurseries – daily, weekly, or permanent (O. Meszárošová and M. Jurčová, 1956). If the sample is sufficiently large, these comparisons can provide valuable information. This method can also be used for detailed, well-controlled study of certain developmental features amongst children of a particular age (for example, the studies by J. L. Gewirtz, 1961, 1965; H. L. Rheingold, 1961; and others).

A difficulty in using this method is that one can neither judge the persistence of the behavioural deviations recorded, nor make predictions about their further development. In this case, it is particularly important, because we are concerned with modifying the future life environment of the child, so that development can progress as favourably as possible. This method, therefore, should be supplemented by other methods.

Retrospective (anamnestic) approach

This involves the selection of children or adults with certain behaviour disorders, and an attempt to detect possible deprivational factors in their life histories. Implicit in this approach is that clinicians know in detail the final outcome, and therefore look for causes in the life histories of the subjects.

For example, J. Bowlby (1946) sought evidence of early deprivation in the case histories of psychopaths who had records of stealing; L. Bender (1946), C. J. Carey-Trefzer (1949), and H. C. Archibald (1962) looked for evidence of institutional or partial family care in the case histories of patients in psychiatric clinics and counselling centres (J. Langmeier, V. Konias, and M. Dolejší, 1957, did similar work in Czechoslovakia).

Because of easy access to the more or less homogeneous samples of psychiatric patients, retrospective studies are often preferred. Thus they have been used in searching for deprivational situations in histories of psychopathic (sociopathic, delinquent) persons — mostly with positive results (I. Gregory, 1958; S. Glueck and E. T. Glueck, 1950; P. O'Neal et al., 1962; S. Greer, 1964); of schizophrenics (H. Barry, Jr., 1939, 1949; M. Berg and B. B. Cohen, 1959; J. R. Hilgard and M. F. Newman, 1963a, b; J. Langmeier, 1965; J. E. Oltman and S. Friedman, 1965 — with essentially contradictory results); of depressed patients (A. D. Forrest, R. H. Fraser, and F. G. Priest, 1965; A. T. Beck, B. B. Sethi, and R. W. Tuthill, 1963; B. B. Sethi, 1964; S. Greer, 1966 — with positive results; F. N. Pitts, Jr., J. Meyer, and M. Brooks, 1965; I. Gregory, 1966 — with generally negative results); and of neurotics (H. Barry, Jr. and E. Lindemann, 1960, 1965).

Critical features of the retrospective approach are a careful selection of well-defined and complete samples from patient populations, adequate control groups, special inquiry into the life histories of both patients and controls, careful differentiation between types of deprivation situations, and consideration of demographic and cultural changes.

Conclusions based on retrospective data fulfil a number of functions. They usually suggest the initial hypotheses (as in the case of the early Bowlby studies), point to relationships between present states and previous environmental conditions, and steer subsequent studies in more appropriate directions. The basic flaw in this method, however, is that those cases which escape psychiatric detection, and those which develop normally, despite adverse circumstances, are excluded from the sample. This cannot be rectified by using a correction term based on the frequency of similar deprivating backgrounds in the "normal" child population, since these figures are unknown. There are also a number of other facts which tend to bias sample selection (for example, in Czechoslovakia, psychiatric care, for obvious reasons, is more readily available to institutionalized children than to children from families, even if the disorders are of equal severity).

Finally and most important, as there is no necessary connection between the present state of the individual and previous circumstances, extreme caution should be exercised in suggesting cause-effect relationships. For example, the generalization cannot be made from Bowlby's findings that all children who grow up without their mothers necessarily develop into affectionless psychopaths.

Prospective (catamnestic) approach

Here, the sample is selected at an earlier point in the life histories of the children on the basis of specific deprivation criteria. Subsequently the developmental status of the children thus selected is assessed and evaluated. Clearly, this approach avoids to some extent the difficulties inherent in the retrospective methods.

Subjects may be exposed to different living conditions between the two selected points in time; in one type of investigation conditions are obviously deprivational, while in the other type the deprivation experience is interrupted and replaced with another set of living conditions. This second type of investigation is typified by a number of W. Goldfarb's (1943 et seq.) classical studies: a group of children who had been institutionalized between the ages of six months and three and a half years approximately and placed subsequently in foster families were observed and compared at ten to fourteen years of age (the control group lived in foster care from the earliest age). Similarly, J. Bowlby et al. (1956) observed a group of school children aged from six to fourteen years who had been hospitalized in a TB sanitorium for a period prior to four years of age. A more recent example is Gregory's (1965*a*) study of all pupils leaving the ninth grade of Minnesota schools (11,329 children). After three years he found delinquency more often in boys who lost their fathers and in girls who lost their mothers, compared with a sub-group of children living continuously in complete families.

In one of our studies, we assessed school readiness in children who had spent different periods of time in pre-school children's homes. In another study, we compared the behaviour and school achievement of all children who had lived together in one children's home from one to three years of age, and were then transferred to adoptive families, to their own families, or remained under institutional care.

If the number of observations are increased, i.e. if we use an extended catamnestic method, it approximates the longitudinal method. Although this extended form is possibly more useful, it still retains a number of drawbacks, most importantly that we are trying to determine, at a particular point in time, the effects of past events, which may not be well enough documented, and which, especially from the psychological point of view, cannot be given precise etiological meaning and significance, if not accompanied by the direct observation of reactions to the prior critical event. In addition, the impact of the conditions existing between the two respective time points is usually not controlled, so that the course of development of subsequent disorders cannot be precisely evaluated.

Longitudinal approach

This method, which is both the most promising and the most demanding one, affords us — relatively speaking — the most accurate description of the developmental dynamics of the child's personality under deprivational conditions.

Roughly two variants of this method can be identified:
1. The child is observed over the whole period during which deprivation occurs
2. The child is initially observed in the depriving environment, and subsequently in the non-depriving environment.

The starting point for longitudinal studies is the observation of the immediate response of the child to a given situation, followed by systematic observation of further psychological development over a certain period of time. What is the exact time period needed for a classification of "longitudinal"? Opinions differ. It seems to be determined by the aims of the study. R. A. Spitz (1955), for example, described any study as longitudinal if it was sufficiently long-term to allow observation of marked changes in the subject's behaviour, e.g. he considers a span of two or three months in the first year of life as adequate. S. R. Pinneau (1955b), on the other hand, rightly comments that if we are concerned with the child's development during the first year of life, a two—three months' period is not long enough.

To evaluate the effects of deprivation on the development of character and personality, and to determine their reversibility, we must systematically study the child threatened with deprivation from the earliest age to adolescence and possibly adulthood. To date, however, no such studies have been reported, although valuable data might be lying in the records of paediatricians and psychologists who have systematically observed threatened children over a long period of time.

A multitude of difficulties beset longitudinal studies. Children move from place to place, records are incomplete, children die, parents refuse to cooperate, for example. It is rather difficult, in these circumstances, to maintain an intact sample and to ensure systematic examination. There is also the danger that in the data analysis individual differences in the behaviour of subjects might be statistically depreciated so that the final indices are often only rough, almost meaningless averages of individual developmental curves.

Selection of an adequate methodology, which is important for further progress in this field, is always dictated by the particular hypotheses tested and to some extent by the theoretical viewpoint of the individual workers. Psychoanalytically or dynamically oriented workers, for example, prefer to consider personality as an entity, and attempt intensive study of individual cases. Learning theorists, on the other hand, generally prefer observation of single behaviour patterns with small groups of children under well-controlled conditions; most psychiatric workers (psychiatrists and psychologists in medical services) base their assessment, prevention, and therapeutic measures on directed anamnestic and catamnestic studies with larger groups of patients under "normal" life conditions.

To a certain extent, of course, these methods overlap. For example, a number of questions may be raised by individual case studies which must be tested on a larger sample to establish the generality of the original conclusions. The relationship between present symptoms and pre-existing conditions which has been indicated through the anamnestic method suggests a hypothesis which, in turn, must be tested using the catamnestic and longitudinal methods. This again raises problems which can be approached only through detailed, direct observational studies.

From this, it seems obvious that future work in this field must involve greater cooperation between the experimentalist and the clinical worker. The experimental hypothesis should normally be suggested by clinical observations, which are themselves redirected by the experimental results.

We hesitate to make categorical judgments about any of the methods discussed. We doubt that any of them has been fully exploited, and think that it would be advantageous to increase their utility by complementing one with another. Our views on methodology are basically eclectic. We think that this is theoretically sound, as we shall try to demonstrate in our discussion of the multi-level approach to the analysis of child deprivation.

4 Extreme isolation and separation

EXTREME SOCIAL ISOLATION

The only genuine cases of complete deprivation of specific human needs involve children who develop either totally or almost totally without human society and intercourse. Older children and adolescents — like Robinson Crusoe — can sustain a bare existence for a period of time, relying solely on their own resources. The young child, however, is dependent on external sources for satisfaction of his biological needs, which in these special cases may be provided at a minimal level either by people or, as claimed in some cases, by animals.

Interest in cases of deserted, lost, wild, or "wolf" children has persisted throughout recorded history. There are stories and reports by chroniclers in the Dark and Middle Ages (Herodotus, Livy, Salimbeni), and a good deal of philosophical and pedagogical discussion of this topic during the Renaissance and again in the eighteenth century (J. J. Rousseau, J. G. Herder, and others).

In order to illustrate the point that "a man can become a man only when he is raised in human society", John Amos Comenius (in chapter 6 of *The great didactic,* 1657) cites, from the reports of observers who witnessed these events, two examples of "wolf children". He writes: "Cases are recorded of people who were captured in childhood by wild animals and raised amongst them, whose behaviour was that of wild animals, and who were incapable of behaving differently from animals with their tongues, hands, and legs, unless they lived again for some time amongst people. The first, from about 1540, concerns a three-year-old boy who was lost from a Hessian village situated in the middle of a forest through the carelessness of his parents. Several years later, the peasants saw a strange animal with a man's-face running with wolves. It was four-legged, but did not have a wolf's body. Rumours of this apparition spread throughout the district and the governor asked the peasants to try and catch the animal and bring it to him alive. It was caught and taken to the Landgrave at Kassel. But as the creature was led into the castle it tore itself free, fled and hid under a bench, from where it glared fiercely at its pursuers and howled horribly.

The creature was kept continually in the company of men, and gradually his savage habits extinguished. He began to erect himself on his hind legs and walk like a biped, and at last began to speak intelligently and behave like a man. He related, as well as he could, how he had been seized and raised by the wolves and had learned to hunt with them.

The second example is from Geulartius (in *Marvels of our age*) who recounts a similar case from France in 1563. Some locals went hunting and after they had killed twelve wolves they caught in their net something that resembled a naked boy, about seven years old, with yellow skin and curly hair. His nails were talons, and he could only utter wild shrieks. When he was brought into the castle he struggled so fiercely that it was extremely difficult to restrain him; after a few days' starvation, however, he quietened down. Within seven months he had begun to speak. He was exhibited in various towns, and his masters made a good deal of money from this. Eventually a certain poor woman acknowledged him as her son."

This is all that Comenius narrates. Even though it is doubtful that the boy in the first example cited could have recalled after so many years what had happened when he was three years old, and even though the mother's "recognition" in the second case could have been motivated by the profit which exhibiting the boy might bring to his owner, the recorded details tally on many counts with more accurate and better documented reports in later periods.

C. Linneus, in volume 1 of *Systems of nature* (1767), cites ten cases which show the three typical characteristics — mutus, tetrapus, hirsutus (mute, four-legged, covered with hair) of "wild men" *(Homo sapiens ferus)*. This question has been examined subsequently by anthropologists J. F. Blumenbach (1814) and A. A. Rauber (1885) and more recently by R. M. Zingg, a professor of anthropology from Denver. In his study, Zingg (1940) cites thirty-one relatively well authenticated cases, which can be classified in three ways according to the conditions under which the child was raised: (*a*) wild children who ran away or were chased into the wilderness and survived through their own resources; (*b*) "wolf children" who were kidnapped and survived with the help of domestic or wild animals;

(c) children whose basic needs are met by people, but who are otherwise completely isolated from human society (because of criminal or mentally defective parents).

Wild children

The first scientific account of wild children is a report on the wild boy of Aveyron, a child about twelve years of age, who was discovered by hunters near Aveyron, southern France, in 1799. It is assumed that he wandered or ran away into the wilderness and lived like a wild creature. He climbed trees, fed on wild berries and roots, did not speak, and generally behaved like an animal. J. M. G. Itard (1775–1838), a physician and teacher of the deaf and dumb, undertook the boy's retraining. The results, however, were poor; although the boy lost his feral appearance and behaviour and became a pleasant person, he acquired only a very limited vocabulary and remained at a very primitive intellectual level (see J. M. G. Itard, 1807). He survived only to the age of forty. The prominent French psychiatrist of this time, P. Pinel, who examined the boy, proclaimed him an idiot. One can seriously question this judgment, however, since the boy was intelligent enough to sustain life in the wilderness without outside help. (Fig. 1.)

A similar case is reported from the territory of Czechoslovakia by Michael Wagner in volume 1 of *Philosophical anthropology* (1794).

In the Spiš district, he discovered a half wild man, "Tomek", aged thirty. Up to this time, Tomek had lived in the woods on roots and raw meat. He accepted food from people but otherwise tried to avoid them. His only speech was the word· "ham", which was accompanied by a gesture of catching. In winter, he slept in sheds and stables.

Wagner took him home and tried to retrain him. Tomek soon began to understand the gestures and speech of other people, and finally learned to speak Slovak and even to understand German. His speech, however, was idiosyncratic — e.g. he labelled everyone wearing a pigtail a soldier, and although he was often able to give amazingly precise answers, he never learned to count or to memorize a prayer. He performed minor jobs around the house eagerly and reliably. An interesting fact (which recurs in descriptions of other wild people) is that he appeared to show no sexual drive. His progress led the author to conclude that "here we are not dealing with feeble-mindedness or madness, but rather wildness due to neglect".

A more recent case of a wild boy (Tarzanito) is cited by R. M. Zingg (1940). The boy, aged about five years, was found in the tropical jungles of Central America, where it was claimed he had lived on wild fruits and raw fish, and slept in caves and trees. He could not speak, produced only piercing screams, climbed trees with ease, skilfully avoided capture, and repeatedly escaped. But he was eventually socialized, and learned to speak and progressed in school. The case history, however, lacks details of the circumstances under which he came to live in the jungle, and it is doubtful whether he could have survived there from such an early age.

There are many similar, though probably less dramatic, reports of older children living alone without human society in periods following major wars such as the Napoleonic wars or the civil wars in Russia, Spain, and China. Occasionally reports appear of "wild" adults who have been lost in the jungle or wrecked on an island, who on meeting people display panic reactions and demented behaviour.

Thus contact with human society seems to be necessary not only for the development but also for the stability and balanced structuring of personality.

"Wolf" children

It has been fairly well established that a child can be suckled by a domestic animal. A number of reports describe how a child can learn to suckle from a goat's udder, and how an animal can learn to respond to the cry of the hungry child. H. Brüning (1908) reports a number of studies in which goats were observed to nurse children at the Leipzig children's clinic. It is not difficult, therefore, to believe that a baby or a toddler can survive in the wilderness with the sole help of an animal. Most frequently she-wolves, but sometimes she-bears, leopards, and wild sows, are described as wet nurses who raise such children. This theme is repeated in folk lore from the Dark Ages (Romulus and Remus, Zarathustra, Wolf Dietrich, for example) to modern times (e.g. Kipling's Mowgli). In recent history, however, a few reports have appeared which claim to be authentic and warrant scientific investigation.

The best known and documented report is that from the Indian missionary J. A. Singh. This case was carefully investigated by A. Gesell (1940) and by R. M. Zingg (1940).

While visiting Godamury village not far from Midnapore, Singh heard reports of a strange "human spirit" running with a pack of wolves that was terrorizing the countryside. On investigation he observed in front of the wolf's den two creatures in company with three large wolves and two cubs. When an attempt was made to capture these creatures, two adult wolves escaped, and the she-wolf who was defending the cubs was killed. The two "wolf children" and two cubs in the den were captured.

The younger child was a girl (Amala) about eighteen months old, the older a girl (Kamala) about eight years old. From an examination of their physical condition, which indicated thorough adaptation to life in the wolf's den, Gesell judged that the children had lived in the company of the wolves from about six months of age. Kamala used her arms and hands solely for locomotion and gripped and caught only with her mouth. Her huge shoulders and strong legs were striking – she had large callouses on her knees, the soles of her feet, elbows, and palms. She ran so quickly, on all fours, that it was almost impossible to catch her in an open space. Although her skin was surprisingly clean, her hair was matted into a large ball.

In November 1920, the Reverend Singh transferred both children to his orphanage at Midnapore, and began systematic retraining. Details were carefully noted in his diary. Only hunger forced the children to accept food in the new surroundings and they drank from a bowl in the animal way. They were frightened by people and Kamala promptly bit any child who approached her. During the day they slept curled up in a corner but during the night they roused, prowled, and periodically "howled" three times, in the manner of wolves. Their voices were neither "human nor animal-like" and at first this frightened the workers in the orphanage. The only other sounds they made were during feeding. When approached by another child, Kamala would growl and bare her teeth threateningly. (Fig. 2.)

Before her death, within a year, the younger girl, Amala, made reasonably rapid progress, but the retraining of Kamala progressed slowly and with difficulty. After two years her vocabulary consisted of one word, after four years of six words and after eight years she could speak only short simple sentences. After three years she reached an erect posture, but the first independent steps were recorded only after six years of retraining. During this time, she participated with reasonable ease in group activities and could be trusted with small jobs and duties, and her emotional life was relatively rich. She died from uremia when she was about seventeen, after nine years in the institute. Gesell considers that the most significant aspect of this case is the "slow but systematic and lawful progress in the readjustment of Kamala's retarded mental development". In his opinion she would have reached her full·developmental level at thirty-five years of age, when her mental age would have been about ten or twelve years. Amala, developing more quickly, could have reached this level at about seventeen years of age.

In addition to this important case, a number of similar examples have been cited by different authors. Numberg describes the case of a boy living amongst pigs (Klement from Overdyk). Professor J. H. Hutton cites the case of a boy living from the age of two to five years amongst leopards, and Alfred Greil (1953) the case of a Polish girl kidnapped by wolves in early childhood. As recently as 1957, a report appeared in Indian newspapers about two new wolf children who had lived in the wilderness for six years. Like so many cases, however, this report is based on the evidence of the parents who claim to recognize the children as their sons who were carried off by wolves.

If the accounts about "wolf" children had been always adequately documented, they would have considerable scientific importance because such cases would be a convincing natural experiment in the rearing of a child in non-human society. They should indicate with considerable accuracy which mental attributes of men are genetically and which are environmentally determined. The majority of reports reveal that such children are not only severely developmentally retarded but also that they acquire a number of animal habits. Retraining is very difficult, and the potential for human development appears to be irreversibly curtailed.

Some investigators have accepted and used these observations to support their theories (psychologists such as W. N. and L. A. Kellogg [1933] and A. Gesell [1940]; biologists such as A. Portmann [1951, 1964]); others however (the zoologist O. Koehler [1952], the paediatrician A. Peiper [1958]), have strenuously repudiated the veracity and accuracy of these reports. To ascertain the validity of the accounts, an examination of the children is obviously critical; however, the case histories, which should be the starting point, are in nearly all instances incomplete and suspect. Details such as the events leading up to the child's exile in the wilderness, how long and under what conditions he lived, are usually unknown; the circumstances surrounding their discovery are also not reported in sufficient detail. In only two accounts, from Singh and one of the Indian children in 1957, are we told that the children were actually seen in the company of animals. In other cases this is only assumed, witnesses' reports are inexact, and often quite clearly influenced by widely accepted superstitions and beliefs.

It is not implausible that a she-wolf who loses her cubs during the nursing period would care for a child and accept him as her own.

What is doubtful, however, is whether a child after a short period of suckling by a she-wolf (say four months) could adapt rapidly to such food as raw meat and carrion. A less cogent argument is that the child can hardly acquire such extensive animal habits when the opposite case, i.e. of animals raised with humans (e.g. the Kellogg experiment studied a chimpanzee raised with a same-aged boy under a similar regime), shows such poor results. Equally unconvincing is the argument based on the categorical assumption that a child is dependent exclusively on its human mother.

A. Peiper (1958) resolutely rejects the evidence for "wolf children" and tends to support the view stated by Dr. Wishaw of the Indian Psychiatric Institute in 1873 that these were feebleminded children who were possibly deserted by their parents. On the basis of Singh's detailed and impressive case history, however, it is difficult to accept such an explanation.

Since many of the details about these children are equivocal or in dispute, it is impossible to arrive at a final judgment.

Kaspar Hauser and children isolated from society

Of greater significance for clinical practice are cases of children who live for a certain period of time in almost social isolation to which they have been condemned by cruel, psychopathic, or psychotic parents. Although such cases are rare, they occur from time to time, and are usually well documented. The classic case, that of Kaspar Hauser, has excited a good deal of speculation and has been the subject of a novel (J. Wassermann).

Hauser appeared mysteriously in Nuremberg in 1828, aged about seventeen years. According to his later statements he was isolated from early childhood in a dark cellar in which he hardly saw a human face; bread and water were placed at his side while he was asleep. He knew only one uninterpretable sentence, which he repeated over and over. He was so weak that he could hardly walk, but he could write Kaspar Hauser, the name by which he was known throughout Europe from that time on. Obviously some degree of social contact had been maintained during his period in the cellar.

He was entrusted to the care of the well-known teacher G. F. Daumer, who in a period of five years changed a boy with a mental age of three into a young man who could both speak and write fluently and even use some Latin. In 1833 the boy was found dead, and it was unclear whether this was a case of murder or suicide. Much has been written about Hauser, there has been a good deal of speculation about his genuineness (was he the legitimate Prince of

Baden, or was he a swindler), but few valid conclusions have been reached (a summary of the case is given by H. Pies, *Kaspar Hauser*, 1926).

In more recent times a number of similar cases have been described. K. Davis (1940) in the U.S.A. reported two cases of children locked in a cellar for a number of years. Their mental development at the time of discovery was severely retarded. One of the children progressed very slowly in his retraining, but the second child (who was less isolated from people) made considerable developmental progress. In Germany, K. Mierke (1955) reported the case of an illegitimate child who was hidden and severely neglected for nearly nine years. This child also was unable to overcome his developmental retardation and remained at the debile level. B. E. Willis described a similar case in England (reported by the Clarkes) where progress during psychotherapy was interrupted by the premature placement of the child in a children's home.

We have encountered two children who suffered this type of isolation for a number of years.

F. J. was the illegitimate child of a psychopathic mother and an unknown father. During pregnancy the mother attempted to procure an abortion by eating raw poppy heads. There is no information about the delivery other than that it was premature and "difficult". The mother's life was very undisciplined, she was unstable, and constantly changed jobs. Soon after the birth, the mother left her parents and worked initially as a hat-check girl in a hotel; then she worked as a nurse-aid in a district hospital and concealed the fact that she had a child. Up to almost two years of age the boy was left alone for days at a time, locked in her room, in complete isolation, hungry, without any care, and obviously without any form of training.

When the case was brought to official notice the child was taken from the mother and entrusted to the foster care of very good and intelligent parents. At this stage (after two years of age) the child still could not walk properly, cried all the time, and was fearful of everything (a car, a dog, a cat, wind, even people and toys — it was a long time before he dared to take a toy into his hands). He did not speak at all, and made only one meaningless sound — "takn".

With great devotion and patience the adoptive mother — a former teacher — attempted retraining. The boy veered from being very frightened of people to embracing and kissing everybody on first encounter. He began to speak only at about three and a half years of age, but his subsequent speech development was rapid, and soon he could speak quite intelligibly in whole sentences. Training in personal hygiene, however, was slow — he soiled himself until he was four years old.

Both in the kindergarten and at home he was very inattentive and restless; he attacked other children and was a disciplinary problem. In school he was a relatively good scholar and showed progress, although he lacked persistence and concentration. Soon, however, unending complaints began about the child; he contradicted, lied, was cheeky, urinated on other children, touched their genitals, tickled them, and rolled naked over another boy in the playground. He wanted only to cuddle and kiss his parents all the time. He could not be disciplined in any way, or delay gratification, and was impatient and insubordinate; and at the age of eight he still had to be fed like a small child. His resistance to infection was markedly reduced.

His intelligence, on repeated examination, was quite normal (Stanford-Binet IQ at eight years was 107), his speech was developed, and his comparative wealth of knowledge attested to the excellent training he had received at home. During observed play with a group he attempted to attract the psychologist's attention by constant questioning, by showing off, and by frequent cuddling which he employed when he wanted to get something. If his desires were not met he became cheeky and restless. When the opportunity arose he took off his pants and touched his genitals. Sometimes he masked sexual tendencies by aggressiveness, crying, by being naughty, and by attempting to make others envious of him.

These abnormal character features were still evident at fifteen years. He was still stubborn, playful, and restless; the school complained constantly that he disturbed other pupils, that he was exhibitionistic and always attempted to attract attention. He participated in sport to the point of complete exhaustion. He learned very quickly and easily, but forgot equally quickly because he was unstable and his attention wandered. He lacked any clear goals.

At eighteen, he became a skilled mechanic, but left his job and entered military school; he terminated his studies just before graduation and started work as an unskilled labourer. For two years, he attended an evening course at technical college, but again did not complete his course. At twenty-five, he again changed his job. He has no qualifications and only very superficial interests — for the most part he sits around in pubs doing crossword puzzles and reads paperbacks. He has no real friends, no girl friend, no stable affectional ties of any sort.

M. S. came to the children's home from his family at the age of three and a half years. The father had maintained that the child was not his, and so the child was left alone in a stable. He was brought food, but no one spoke to him. It was obvious that the parents wanted to be rid of him. At the time of admission to the children's home he was in very poor condition; he was hardly as tall as the average twenty-month-old child, he showed signs of rickets, and his muscles were weak. His physical condition improved quickly and internal examination showed nothing abnormal. But the boy did not speak at all; he produced only some indistinguishable noises, and could not understand spoken language. He soiled himself, he could not eat with a spoon. He was apathetic, indifferent to human contact, had slow reactions and showed no emotional reactions (he did not cry even when he was being hurt). At the same time, however, he displayed a certain inventiveness in his play with the test objects — on the level of a two and a half to three-year-old child.

After two and a half years in the special institution, his development in several areas had improved considerably. Although physical growth was still below average, otherwise the child was healthy. He established contact more easily, he cooperated willingly, he could feed and dress himself and be responsible for personal hygiene. His speech had developed, he understood and constructed sentences and asked questions — but pronunciation was still very unclear. His overall intellectual development was mildly retarded, but there was considerable imbalance — practical and motor abilities were clearly better developed than verbal abilities. Finally, the child was diagnosed as debile, and admitted to the special children's home for mentally retarded children.

A similar case of criminal social isolation of two boys (identical twins) for a prolonged period was reported recently by L. Pelikán et al. (1969). P. M. and J. M., whose mother died after their delivery, were raised until they were eleven months of age in an infant home. The father's sister then took the boys into her care, but after two months she returned them to a toddler home. At about eighteen months of age, the boys were returned to their father, who had remarried. The family had quite a good reputation in the locality and were comfortably off. However, the stepmother — an educated woman who adequately cared for her own two older children — refused to look after the boys. The father's care regressed quickly to cruel beatings and complete neglect. Both boys were confined to a small unheated cell, where they spent almost all their time in complete isolation. Their existence was concealed from even the nearest neighbours. When the twins were called to the paediatric centre for preventive examination and compulsory inoculation, the parents found some excuse, so that they were never examined by a physician. It was only when the children were due to enter school (after almost six years of isolation) that the situation was disclosed. At seven years, the twins were hardly able to walk, so that initially some form of myopathy was suspected. Detailed clinical examination revealed grossly subnormal growth (3.2 and 2.9 SDs below average for their age), delayed ossification, and symptoms of severe rickets. They spoke only a few words, with a tendency to echolalia, and were unable to name objects presented pictorially. They knew no toys but simple cubes, and play was limited to primitive, stereotyped, manipulative activity. Their further development was relatively good as reported by J. Koluchová (1972).

Although reports on children who are partially or completely socially isolated are usually less accurate than we might wish, they afford a number of tentative conclusions. Social isolation is clearly the most severe deprivational situation. Its results are very marked. The mental development of the child is grossly retarded, speech is not developed at all, and useful social habits are not established. The child appears to be severely feebleminded, and is often regarded as such. There are, however, a number of factors which differentiate these children from cases of congenital feeblemindedness. Children of the wilderness are able to survive dangers, and perform in some tasks at a near normal level. A. A. Rauber (1885) speaks of *"dementia ex separatione"* A. F. Tredgold (1929) of "isolation amentia", the Clarkes (1958 et seq.) of the "feeblemindedness" of deprived children as being diagnostically different from the feeblemindedness of children living in a normal environment.

The prognosis also is clearly different. For children suffering the most severe isolation, developmental improvement is very slow and is always incomplete, while children less affected by isolation, although they progress initially very slowly, subsequently overtake their retardation very quickly. Other factors, of course, must be considered. Neglecting hereditary factors and the possibility of organic CNS (central nervous system) damage, these might include malnutrition, accidents, illness, and with children locked in cellars, the obvious sensory deprivation.

Even in cases where improvement occurs in intellectual development, however, serious personality disorders remain. These children are at first fearful of people; later relationships are unstable, undifferentiated, and strikingly obsequious, and reflect their insatiable demand for love and attention. Sexual behaviour is either autoerotic or uncontrolled and undiscriminating. Emotional behaviour also is very immature; it is characterized by a hunger for intense stimulation (creating uproar by tantrums, by participating in sport until complete exhaustion), and by a very low frustration tolerance. Higher emotions are almost completely absent and human moral values are established only partially and superficially. Clearly the most characteristic human qualities cannot be developed without the influence of early human care.

The cases of extreme social isolation we have described are rare. They serve rather as a particular model of deprivation, against which we can judge and evaluate the consequences of isolation which is less total in nature, and which may exist in combination with other factors to greater or lesser degree. Less severe cases are more important from the point of view of clinical practice; they occur more frequently and are more complicated because they are determined by a greater variety of life circumstances. We will consider such cases in greater detail in more appropriate sections — in the chapters on institutionalized care, on deprivation in families, on culture deprivation, and in the chapter on the experimental approach to the problem of stimulus impoverishment.

SEPARATION

Retrospective studies of clinical cases of separation

The effect of separation from the parents and home on children was first noted by clinical workers amongst cases of psychologically disturbed children. H. Edelston (1943) from the London Child Guidance Clinic described forty-two case histories in which he could detect neurotic symptoms resulting from hospitalization. He maintained that separation of the child from his parents threatens denial of a basic need for security and dependency. Because the child cannot logically cope with the situation he interprets it as "rejection" or "punishment". This generates emotional insecurity and separation anxiety, fear of loss of mother, which cause a number of neurotic disorders. The most severe reactions occur in those cases where vulnerable backgrounds of sensitive, fearful, or aggressive personalities already exist, so that the newly aroused anxiety re-evokes old conflicts.

The most important of these early separation studies was reported by J. Bowlby (1946), who compared a group of forty-four adolescent delinquents (stealing) with a control group. There was no difference between the groups in hereditary background. They differed in one respect only — viz. in long-term lack of maternal care (separation from the mother or surrogate figure for more than six months in the first five years) (table 1). The difference is more

Table 1. Incidence of early separation in the two groups

Group	Early Separation	No Separation
Delinquent	17	27
Control	2	42

significant if those children whom Bowlby classified as "emotionally cold personalities" are treated separately (table 2).

On the basis of these findings, Bowlby concluded that children who in the first five years of life lack maternal care have suffered permanent damage to their capacity for establishing emotional relationships with others. Stealing is an attempt to satisfy their need for love and stolen things become symbols of affection. The "affectionless" psychopaths are extremely superficial in their social relationships and their behaviour is highly irresponsible. They reject help when it is offered, they cannot learn from experience, and have not developed abstract ways of thinking.

In this study, Bowlby developed and popularized a concept which had already been proposed by Edelston (1943) and the older workers of the London school (I. D. Suttie, 1935; H. V. Dicks, 1939; J. A. Hadfield, 1962), a concept which suggested that separation primarily disturbs the normal process of coping with feelings of anxiety. According to this view, every child not only has instincts of love and dependency, but also of hate and defiance. Because of this the child feels guilty and fears that he might lose his parents as a punishment for his wicked thoughts. Under normal conditions, the presence of the parents helps to overcome and channel these feelings. When the child is deprived of this steering and soothing influence, however, anxiety is roused, and this disorganizes the whole of the child's behaviour and interferes with development. Personal possession can become a means of gaining control over aroused separation

Table 2. Incidence of early separation in delinquent and control groups

Delinquent Group	Early Separation	No Separation
"Emotionally cold personalities"	12	2
Other delinquent types	5	25
Control Group		
"Emotionally cold personalities"	0	0
Control Ss of other types	2	42

anxiety (I. D. Suttie, 1935).

More recently, a number of studies have indicated that separation (especially if it is early, long-term, and repeated) can have a number of adverse effects. Ian Oswald (1958) reported significantly more frequent histories of separation – particularly early separation – in a group of soldiers presenting a variety of neurotic symptoms, compared with a group of patients with occasional epileptic paroxysms. In their well-known study, S. Glueck and E. T. Glueck (1950) found separation from parents for various reasons in 60 per cent of delinquent boys and in 34 per cent of matched controls. Significant differences of this sort have also been demonstrated in studies of delinquents and sociopaths reported by other authors (P. O'Neal et al., 1962; S. Greer, 1964; I. Gregory, 1965a). J. W. B. Douglas and J. M. Blomfield (1958), in a large study of 5,386 randomly selected children, reported significant differences in the occurrence of emotional difficulties and "bad habits" (nightmares, nail biting, thumb sucking, enuresis, withdrawal) between children with a history of long-term (at least four weeks) separation in pre-school age, and children without separation experience (47 per cent and 21 per cent). This applied only to children who were completely separated from the parents and the home. If the child was separated from only one of the parents and remained at home, the difference was not significant. This finding, if replicated, would be of considerable importance. The authors employed only a very rough criterion of emotional difficulties and more detailed analysis might have revealed additional differences.

Different findings, however, were reported by B.H. Sklarew (1959) who analyzed case histories of adolescents who were being treated in a special institute and who were experiencing difficulties in social adjustment. When he assessed social adjustment using a number of criteria (number of offences, active participation in working and social activities, abscondings, and so on) he found that boys with a history of early separation from parents showed poorest adjustment, while girls with similar histories conformed to standards at a somewhat better level than the non-separated girls. The fact that girls, if separated from their parents, interact better than if left in their bad families, while with the boys the opposite is the case, is considered by Sklarew to be due to particular attributes of the male and female psyche.

This finding conflicts partly with the original view advanced about the effect of separation. J. G. Howells and J. Layng (1955), however, completely denied its validity. They maintained that the effects of separation are overstated, and that they are unimportant in the etiology of mental disorders, compared with the emotional deprivation the child would suffer in his own bad family. This conclusion, however, is based on a comparison between a relatively small sample (thirty-seven) of emotionally disturbed children (neurotics and delinquents) treated in a child psychiatric clinic and a matched control group. Separation was about equally frequent in both groups, but long-term separation (longer than three months) before five years of age was far more frequent amongst neurotics (six to one). In explanation of this, the authors suggest that the cause of the separation (maladjustment of parents, sickness of the mother, family breakdown) had a direct bearing on the emotional disturbance of the child. They emphasize that the majority of the separations (61 per cent), according to the parents, were welcomed by the child, and maintain that where the child did suffer through the separation, the effect was only temporary. The Howells and Layng study, however, can be criticized (small N, questionnaire method), and H. Edelston (1955) rightly comments that both the extreme opinions stated — that separation inevitably produces disorder, or that separation is quite innocuous — are only partly true.

Some more recent studies also question the decisive influence of early separation on subsequent delinquent behaviour. R. G. Andry (1960) reports no difference in the frequency of separation in the case histories of eighty delinquents and eighty matched non-delinquents. In a subsequent study (1962) he emphasized the role of the father in the child's social development, and pointed out that separation from the father is still little considered compared with maternal separation. He found no indication that separation from mother, father, or from both parents caused deprivation, but he reported a significantly higher incidence of disturbed father-son relationships among the delinquent boys. He related this to internal "psychological separation" irrespective of whether it was instigated by father or son. S. Naess (1959) reported more frequent early separation in the case histories of forty-two non-delinquent boys compared with an equal number of their delinquent brothers.

These findings contradict those of Bowlby and his colleagues. The studies have a number of methodoligical shortcomings, however, which M. D. Ainsworth (1962) has rightly criticized — the use of the questionnaire method in Andry's study, too narrow classification, which does not include, for instance, separation through death or divorce — and therefore cannot be regarded as conclusive. Despite this, they do offer some support for the inference, independently reached by other investigators, that the disturbance of a certain groups of juvenile delinquents can be attributed to early separation only when this occurs in combination with other stressful conditions.

Even if we assume that separation produces traumatic effects in only a small percentage of cases, however, this is an indication that something is wrong. We should, of course, distinguish between cases of especially sensitive children, for whom separation can have serious consequences, and resistant cases which are unaffected by temporary separation, or in some cases may benefit from it.

To illustrate the point, we cite one of our cases which indicates how important it is to look for separation experiences in the case histories of disturbed children and to evaluate them psychologically.

Boy M. R. is in third grade, where he is probably going to fail, although he is obviously gifted. He is very restless and unstable, wants to play all the time, is not interested in schooling — the school and the school minding centre frequently complain about his disruptiveness; at the same time he is very apprehensive, does not want to be alone, up till the age of eight refused to sleep unless put in his mother's bed, he is still anxiously over-dependent on his mother, infantile, naive, and retarded by comparison with other children. His heredity is suspect, and we should therefore consider the possibility of increased sensitivity. Physical and psychological examinations reveal no serious abnormalities, and his intellectual ability is average. When directly supervised, the boy cooperates well, and he orients himself well in problem-solving tasks. The case history records repeated separation, followed by a strong reaction from the boy, which can be related to his present difficulties. When he was seven months old, his mother became ill (severe heart condition) and the boy was placed in a baby institute, where he appeared to be passive and apathetic. At twelve months he returned home, where he adapted well in two months. When transferred to the toddler home he became more deeply inhibited. When visited by the mother, he would not utter a sound, but would sit apathetically on her lap. After another three months, he was again taken home, where he again became a lively child, but he clung to his mother. In the nursery to which he was sent daily he held her frantically, cried and screamed and every afternoon waited for her by the door, refusing to do anything else. He was again sent to a children's home, and was then hospitalized for a month (otitis media). When he was visited by his mother he was withdrawn, but when she took him from the hospital to the institute he objected and angrily struggled against her. At two and a half years of age he finally returned to the family, was again sent to a day care centre, then to a kindergarten, before he entered school. He still showed restlessness, playfulness, autistic behaviour, and poor level of contact with other children, accompanied by an anxious dependency on his mother.

Sometimes we meet children who lose their neurotic symptoms after temporary separation, and obviously achieve greater emotional and social maturity. The temporary separation of a child who shows neurotic symptoms (anorexia, enuresis, for example) from parents (who are also usually neurotic) has long been employed as a therapeutic technique, and even though it has been criticized, it certainly can be effective. A temporary stay in a hospital or sanitorium is often the first step towards re-adaptation of apparently neglected children, which can then be advanced more efficiently by other means. These children, by their indifference towards their home, or by conscious or barely conscious refusals to return home, differ from other patients, who during their stay in hospital anticipate their return home and eagerly count the days. In hospital the former rapidly lose their symptoms, which reappear, however, when they learn they are to return home. Usually, though not inevitably in these cases, we are dealing with children with poor socio-economic backgrounds who are physically neglected, undernourished or overworked by their parents, who otherwise care little for them. Although the majority of these are older children, we have met some cases of pre-school age.

A number of recent studies have attacked the problem of early separation through analysis of the case histories of children who have failed in foster care. G. Trasler (1960) compared two groups of children in foster care, an unsuccessful group (where a change of foster family was required) and a successful group (no changes or complaints). There was some relationship between failure and early separation from parents in 56 per cent of the first group. The child felt rejected. This created anxious attention in the foster parents, who then offered the child a lower level of positive reinforcement. Generally speaking, in these cases the disorder resulting from separation can be superficial and temporary if the child is given opportunity to make contact with the surrogate mother figure, but deepens if the opportunity is lacking.

J. M. Williams (1961) has also studied failures in foster care. She compared a group of failures (aged five to eleven years) with children who were separated from their parents for only a short period of time in an assessment centre. Eighty per cent of separations in the failure group occurred before two years of age (this study has been criticized by S. Z. Gross [1963] on grounds of questionable interpretation of test results and inadequate sampling).

Another problem is whether early separation contributes to the development of more serious disorders such as schizophrenia. M. Berg and B. B. Cohen (1959) report early permanent separation (usually suddenly after the mother's death) significantly more often in the case histories of forty female schizophrenics. They maintain that sudden and severe long-term deprivation of basic emotional needs can be one of the important factors (in addition to constitutional and other factors) in the etiology of schizophrenia.

Similarly, J. R. Hilgard and M. F. Newman (1963a,b) in their study of 1,561 schizophrenics, 929 alcoholics, and 1,096 controls, report a significantly greater frequency of parental death before nineteen years of age in schizophrenics (25.6 per cent) compared with controls (21.3 per cent). This difference, however, was significant only in the group of young patients (twenty–thirty-nine years of age). Schizophrenics who lost their parents did so at an earlier age than did controls.

In our own retrospective studies (J. Langmeier, 1965; J. Langmeier and D. Langmeierová, 1967) we also found a significantly higher frequency of parental death in the child's early life in 328 schizophrenic patients when compared with a matched control group (20.1 per cent against 14.6 per cent). The difference is even more significant when other types of separation are taken into account (table 3).

On the other hand, J. E. Oltman and S. Friedman (1965) dispute the existence of any causal relationship between parental deprivation and schizophrenia. Indeed, some investigators, who regard the pathologically close tie of a child to his family and the ensuing social isolation from the wider community as a fundamental dimension in the etiology of schizophrenia, have attempted to demonstrate that the child's separation from such a family has positive value. Thus, G. F. Nameche and D. F. Ricks (1966) found a lower incidence of separation of any kind in chronic schizophrenics: half of the sample experienced no separation from parents, while only one-fifth of discharged schizophrenics and one-seventh of controls had no separation experience of any sort.

To what extent does separation through parental death or from other causes contribute to depressive illness in later life? Higher incidence of parental loss in patients with depressive illness has been demonstrated by A. D. Forrest, R. H. Fraser, and F. G. Priest (1965), F. Brown (1961), A. T. Beck, B. B. Sethi, and R. W. Tuthill (1963),

Table 3. Percentage incidence of various forms of deprivation in schizophrenic and control groups

	Schizophrenic	Control	$P_{diff.}$
Family never established	4.9	0.9	0.01
Broken family	25.6	15.5	0.005
Incompatibility in family	22.3	1.8	0.0001
Child removed from family	11.3	3.7	0.0005

and B. B. Sethi (1964). In A. M. and B. V. Earle's (1961) study of a heterogeneous psychiatric sample, depression was significantly more frequent in patients where separation was due to the death of the mother rather than to other causes. S. Greer (1966) also reported a higher frequency of parental death in early childhood in suicidal neurotics compared with other neurotics. However, essentially negative results were reported by F. N. Pitts, Jr., J. Meyer, and M. Brooks (1965) and I. Gregory (1966).

More recently, the significance of parental death in the etiology of depressive illness in later life has been demonstrated by D. L. Alkon (1971), in an extensive study of the case histories of 1,100 psychiatric inpatients (Payne Whitney Clinic, New York) and 1,432 controls (who had been employed as control group in the previous Midtown Manhattan study). On the whole, the inpatients showed a much higher frequency of parental deprivation in early childhood compared with controls. However, separation through maternal death in childhood occurred much more often in manic depressives than in all other psychiatric categories, while, for example, alcoholics showed significantly higher frequency of separation due to parental divorce. The incidence of parental loss and early parental deprivation was significantly more frequent in female than in male patients.

In summarizing the evidence from a large number of retrospective studies of psychiatric patients — both children and adults — one can say that separation from parents and home in childhood is clearly a significant event which can have many adverse consequences. However, the precise effect of separation is unclear, and depends apparently on many factors, particularly on the kind of separation experience (whether resulting from death, illness, divorce, family breakdown, and at what age and for how long it persists). If different forms of separation are not treated as independent categories, contradictory results are almost inevitable. Another confounding factor is the use of heterogeneous psychiatric samples and poorly defined control groups. Clearly, the use of more refined methods and direct observation of separation reactions are critical in future research in this important area.

Direct observation of separation reactions

Clinical and survey-type studies using the retrospective method often do not give clear-cut results. We should also keep in mind that in the majority of cases the situation we are dealing with is one of isolation rather than separation, isolation so protracted that we have gone far beyond the initial traumatizing stage. At the same time, the child is in an environment where the input of emotional and sensory stimuli is obviously severely restricted. It is necessary, therefore, to obtain further data through study of the immediate reactions of the child to separation, and through continuing follow-up studies.

The most usual circumstances in which the child is separated from the mother in early life are these. The mother nurses the child for a short time and then leaves the baby home; the child is sent from the family to a hospital, sanatorium, children's home, or possibly a weekly nursery; the child is transferred from one institute to another; the child is returned from the institute, to which he has become adapted, to his family; the mother or father leaves the family (through illness, divorce, military service, evacuation, death of one of the parents). We shall discuss the first four situations, which are concerned with institutional care, and leave consideration of the other points to the chapters dealing with deprivation in the family and deprivation during war-time.

The child's reaction to the mother leaving the baby institute

The very strong reaction of the child to being left by the mother who has nursed him in the institute was described by R. A. Spitz and K. M. Wolf (1946) as anaclitic depression. The child, who up to this point was smiling, happy, spontaneously active, who maintained a friendly, free contact with the environment, becomes very fretful, sad, or anxious. If an attempt is made to interact with him, he anxiously clings to the adult, demands attention and stops active play. In the next period, moroseness and irritability increase. He screams when anybody approaches — he no longer reacts to the departure of the adult. Gradually the fretfulness disappears, and the child increasingly withdraws from the environment. He lies in bed with his face turned away, or is pathologically passive, lying on his belly. Apathy and autisms increase, the child develops a frozen or melancholic expression, sits or lies without moving, his eyes staring, for long periods, lethargic, as if completely ignoring his environment. Sometimes there is also autoerotic activity. Contact with the child becomes increasingly difficult and eventually impossible. If some appropriate remedial measure is not taken his condition deteriorates, and may become irreversible — it becomes the classical hospitalism syndrome, and in some cases approximates stupor catatonia or agitated idiocy. DQ (developmental quotient) decreases further and further, the child loses weight, cannot sleep, and has little resistance to respiratory infections and eczema.

The syndrome usually appears during the period six to eleven months of age, and is contingent on the sudden disappearance of the mother, who up to this point has lovingly cared for the child. It usually onsets four to six weeks after separation. Spitz did not record one case of this syndrome when the mother remained with the child, although it did not occur in all cases when the mother left. The syndrome was severe in 19 cases and mild in 26 cases from a sample of 123 children. The probability of the syndrome occurring after the mother leaves, according to Spitz, is a function of availability of a suitable mother surrogate and of the relationship existing between the child and the mother before separation (the child with too intense a relationship is less able to tolerate separation than a child with a superficial relationship). The syndrome differs from the normal anxiety which children of eight months show when faced with a stranger, an anxiety which can be readily dissipated, given the right approach. In many respects it is similar to adult depression, and because it is caused by severance of the child's social bonds — the anaclitic bonds of support and dependency on the mother — Spitz described it as anaclitic depression.[1]

Although this syndrome rapidly disappears if the mother returns within a certain period (there is sometimes a dramatic increase in DQ), some effects may persist. J. B. Richmond and L. Hersher (1958), who observed one child with typical anaclitic depression which disappeared after the child's placement in a foster home, report some emotional disorders at five and a half years despite good intellectual development.

Only a few systematic studies dealing with this syndrome have been reported. It is a moot point, however, whether this is because

1. The term is taken from psychoanalytic theory and evidently derives from the Greek *ana-klino,* "I lean on somebody". Libidinal cathexis to a person who up to this point has satisfied the life-sustaining needs of the child, i.e. offered him food, care, and protection, is described in this way. These bonds, according to psychoanalytic theory, are subsequently replaced by more permanent social bonds based on sexual impulses and desires.

the syndrome is usually not diagnosed, or whether it is rare, or whether in some studies, for theoretical reasons, its existence is ignored. The first possibility is hardly likely. It also seems clear enough that in the Spitz studies conditions were extremely conducive to the development of anaclitic depression. In the institute where the interned mothers were deprived of all other social satisfactions, they developed unusually strong relationships with their children who were thus exposed to an unhealthy surfeit of emotional stimuli. They reacted more strongly, therefore, to subsequent separation than they would have under different circumstances. G. Klackenberg (1956) who observed, for at least three months, fourteen infants who were admitted to a baby institute after six months of age (they had been cared for to this point by their own mothers), recorded only one case with symptoms resembling anaclitic depression. He noted, however, that the emotional instability which is reflected in a variety of symptoms amongst institutionalized children can be the initial stage of the disorder which when fully developed shows the tragic features of anaclitic depression. One should remember, of course, that the institute in which Klackenberg worked was far better staffed and the emotional atmosphere considerably better than in the institutes in which Spitz was working.

In Czechoslovakia, M. Damborská (1957a, 1957b, 1961) observed over a six-year period the reactions of 150 infants to separation from their mothers who previously had been fully responsible for their care. With babies younger than two months no reaction was recorded, but 90 per cent of older infants responded in some way (two-thirds of them very strongly), by loss of weight (or at least a retardation on the weight curve) and/or by changes of mood or activity (fretful restlessness or apathy, lack of interest in toys, lack of appetite, decreased vocalization and spontaneous movement). These reactions varied in persistence and intensity as a function of the personalities of the mother and child, although usually they did not approach the severe level recorded by Spitz. M. Damborská and E. Blažková (1959), however, have described the case of a particularly strong reaction of a child to separation from the mother, which to a certain extent resembled anaclitic depression (although the authors do not use this term). Subsequently the child also showed clear "neuropathic" behaviour patterns, especially to every separation from the mother. Z. Brunecký (1959) aptly comments that here we are dealing with the child who perceives everything strange as dangerous and the mother as the only source of security. It is a matter of speculation, however, whether this is a result of previous severe traumatization in the home environment, as he suggests; one might also accept the alternative view that the intense relationship between child and mother was appropriate to the child's age and that the child, if not separated, might develop normally. It appears that under certain circumstances children of both types (the child with a normal close relationship with the mother and the child with the pathologically close and conflicted relationship) react strongly to separation.

The child's reaction to placement in an institution during toddler age

Reactions to separation from the family in the second year of life were recorded by a team of French and English scientists working under the auspices of Centre Internationale de l'Enfance (CIE) in the early fifties. J. Roudinesco, M. David, and J. Nicolas (1952) reported a detailed study of twenty children between twelve and seventeen months separated from their parents and placed in a diagnostic ward, where they remained for about fifteen days. Some of the children, from the outset, cried persistently or adopted a wary attitude with a sad, tense expression. Others appeared to be initially unaffected (they were cheerful and playful). This reaction was only temporary, however, as all the children eventually broke down and showed unequivocal symptoms of despair. A fully developed disorder was indicated by a range of symptoms (loss of appetite, apathy towards toys, unfriendly attitude to other children, moodiness, and at times somatic disorders). The critical symptom, however, appeared to be distortion of the child's relationship with the nursing staff. The children either ignored adults or actively rejected their attempts to establish contact, or frantically clung to anybody and persistently demanded attention. At this point in the child's life, when he experiences the greatest dependence on the mother, the type of reaction appears to be determined by two factors − the need for the presence of an adult who represents a source of security and support, and fear of strangers. Children who have achieved a certain level of independence, who, for example, can accept nursing from someone other than the mother, adapt relatively more easily. Where the child's reaction evokes a negative reaction from adults − impatience, rejection − this again creates further disorders in the child.

In a later study, J. Aubry (1955b) recorded children's reactions immediately following separation, and noted still more striking reactions of uneasiness which were combined with either crying or apathy. She concluded that every normal child of one to two years of age, when separated for the first time from parents, shows symptoms of uneasiness. The severity of these, however, depends on a number of factors, primarily on the degree of previous dependence of the child on his parents, and on the quality of the surrogate care. Irrespective of how severe this uneasiness is, it is always accompanied by difficulties in establishing contact with people, and therefore also by psycho-motor regression and behaviour disorders. Return home does not produce immediate remission of these symptoms — anxiety and over-sensitivity to any even minor change in the life environment often persist for a long period of time. If there is long-term lack of maternal care these disorders increase and reach serious proportions (behaviour disorders, severe developmental retardation, anxiety neurosis, or even psychotic states of the autistic type). Thus the acute shock of separation is transformed into real deprivation which permanently affects the child's ability to establish interpersonal relationships.

The English team of J. Robertson and J. Bowlby (1952) extended the work of the French scientists in their studies of the reactions of children of eighteen to twenty-four months of age to separation. They noted three typical phases in the behaviour of children separated at this age for the first time from their mothers and placed in an impersonal institute (children's home, sanatorium, hospital): (1) a protest period when the child cries and struggles, calls for mother, and on the basis of previous experience expects that she will respond to his crying; (2) the despair period, when the child gradually loses hope that he can recall mother; he cries less, rejects the environment, and withdraws into a state of deep uneasiness; (3) the period of detachment, when the child suppresses his desire for mother, and either attaches himself to somebody else on the staff, or, if no one is available, relates to objects rather than to people.

There are individual differences in the length (a few hours, days, or weeks) and in the sequence of these stages. The third and possibly the second stages are regarded by some as simple forgetting. Robertson and Bowlby, however, reject this view since they consider that here we are dealing with a defensive reaction, which can adversely affect the child's further development. In their view, these reactions are quite natural responses to the situation — if they do not occur, this suggests that the child has not yet experienced a close bond with the mother, and is "immune" to separation.

At the same time, however, we should note additional complicating factors. G. Heuyer (1958), when assessing mental disorders in institutionalized children, repeatedly states that we still do not consider fully enough the possible influence of organic brain damage. C. Launay (1956) reports that regressive reactions to separation amongst children placed in institutes are very pronounced in physically weak children, irrespective of whether this weakness is due to congenital defect or to previous sickness and inadequate nursing. Psychological improvement usually follows physical recovery. In Czechoslovakia there have been repeated references to the high incidence of MBD (minimal brain dysfunctioning) children in permanent collective establishments, and to the relationship between deprivation and organic damage (J. Jirásek, in O. Kučera et al., 1961; J. Langmeier and J. Lhoták, 1960; Z. Matějček, 1963b).

Our own observations indicate that the separation reactions of toddlers admitted to institutes are frequent and pronounced, but are less sequential and predictable than those described above. In fact, individual children react very differently to placement in an institution; their responses vary in intensity, persist for different periods of time, and the final outcome may be very different. These reactions are obviously determined by the innate constitution of the child, by the quality of his relationship with his mother and his home, by his previous separation experiences, and by his degree of resistance to stressful conditions.

With our sample, we were unable to record reactions immediately following admission to the children's home. The course of the adaptive process during the first three months, however, clearly attests to great individual differences amongst children in initial types of reaction and in the forms of adaptive behaviour following the first traumatic experience of separation.

The active protest reaction, typified by emotional outbursts, aggression towards other children, wickedness, and provocation, is probably less frequent, but is very noticeable and difficult to handle from a custodial point of view. The inhibitory reaction, which is characterized by apathy, autistic tendencies, and melancholia, which could probably be regarded as a precursor of anaclitic depression, is more frequent, but may be more easily ignored, for such a child is not as disturbing in a group as the actively protesting child. It is not uncommon to find the child who for a couple of months seems to the nurses to be quite dull and unable to benefit from the child-care programmes but who then in a short time blossoms and surprises by his abilities. What is sometimes attributed to successful care by the institute is in fact only the remission of prolonged separation symptoms.

We recorded the case of one child, who for the first three months in an institutional setting would speak only a few words, and whose vocabulary, in typical "institutional" fashion, was developing very slowly. One day, as if he remembered, he began to speak quite normally, in sentences, and used words which are quite unusual for the institutional population. We also noted the development of one boy who after being separated from his family did not smile or show any sign of pleasure for eight months. He was mildly aggressive, although he behaved quite actively and maturely in the group. By the end of his stay in the institution, he actively demanded the attention of the staff, but did not identify with the peer group. When he was alone he sucked his fingers, and the wall around his bed was chewed.

Another boy, admitted to the institute at three years of age, had developed normally in all respects and was outstanding in the peer group. But subsequently his level of activity dropped, his verbal behaviour deteriorated, he began to wet himself and after two months became encopretic. This boy also actively sought the presence of adults, snuggled up to them and was considered more lively during such contacts. The staff reported that, despite all efforts, he had begun to deteriorate, and recommended return to the mother as the only possible recourse.

Yet another boy showed quite different but no less striking behaviour. He strongly rejected all adults, except the nurses, by withdrawing in a tantrum. He behaved in the same way and was dreadful to his mother when she frequently came to visit him. He expended tremendous effort in indiscriminately demanding the nurses' attention, but was obedient and cuddly. Psychological examination (six times in two years) was very difficult because of his utter rejection of strangers, and could be conducted only with great effort and help from the staff. In the peer group, the boy was initially "jealous" and aggressive towards other children — he liked to boss children about — then he participated normally.

Even though such protracted separation reactions sometimes disappear in institutes or after return to the family, we cannot assume that such children will restart their development at the exact point where development was arrested a few months previously. The intervening period, with its pathological overtones, not only suspends development, but also causes the child to forget what he could not utilize under the new conditions. In addition, it is most likely that separation also changes the basic ways in which he organizes experiences, and that this has some effect on his motivation and thus on his overt way of responding; this again produces a reaction from adults in that they attempt to change or punish his new behaviour. A vicious circle of cause and effect can begin here.

From the examples cited, it is obvious that the range of reaction to separation and environmental change is surprisingly large, and that any attempt at classification is inevitably an over-simplification. With this proviso, in table 4 we have attempted a classification of the characteristic behaviour of forty-four children admitted after one year of age to an institution from their families (generally very bad families) and of eighty-five children admitted from a baby institute. The classification is based on the results of psychological examination in the first three months after admission, on nurses' reports and on neuro-psychological data from the institute.

From table 4 it is clear that very adverse, or at least striking, reactions to transfer to the new environment are shown more frequently by children from families than by children from baby homes. We ought to remember, however, that family backgrounds in these cases usually offer the children neither the necessary amount of developmental stimulation nor full emotional satisfaction, and that these children are more or less deprived. This may account for the relatively high percentage of children who show no obvious difficulties when transferred to an institute.

An inhibitory reaction is recorded significantly more often in children from families than from baby institutes. On the other hand, children from baby homes more frequently attempt to attract the attention of adults, or to directly own new people in the environment (though the difference between the groups is not

Table 4. Comparison of typical behavioural features of children admitted to children's homes at one year

	Children Admitted from Families	Children Admitted from Baby Institutes
Pronounced passivity, apathy, minimal contact with environment, autism, anxiety attacks, behavioural regression	14	9
Striking irritability, temper tantrums, aggressiveness	3	6
Exaggerated social activity and interest — child frantically demands attention from adults	3	10
No particular abnormality or difficulty — child appears to be relatively well-adjusted	17	52
No reliable data	7	8
Totals	44	85

significant). We shall discuss this type of behaviour, which is very characteristic of institutionalized children, in a later section.

Response to transfer from one institute to another

The fact that the significant variable in the separation reaction is not always interruption of contact with the loving maternal figure, but withdrawal from the whole complex of life circumstances, is well illustrated in the reaction of the institutionalized child who is transferred from the baby home to the toddler home and subsequently to the pre-school children's home. We cannot assume that these children have any particularly intense emotional relationships with mother surrogates, yet their reactions to the transfer to a new institution are often very pronounced and dramatic, and in some cases very protracted. The symptomatology is in many respects identical with that described above. Table 4, in which we compared reactions of children from families and from baby homes when transferred to toddler homes, shows that in 61 per cent of institutionalized children adaptation proceeds without any severe disorders or abnormalities (the figure for children from families is 38 per cent). The remaining 39 per cent, who show obvious adaptive disorders, merit our special attention. In terms of our classification, these disorders should be viewed as serious. As we mentioned previously, the inhibitory reaction is significantly less frequent amongst institutionalized children than amongst children from families; on the other hand, one encounters in the former more frequent social hyperactivity and attempts to attract attention from adult strangers.

It is quite a normal occurrence for children entering a toddler home to "forget" certain skills and ways of behaving. For this reason, baby institutes are often accused of over-evaluating the child's behaviour. The toddler home, however, is in precisely the same position after another two years, when the children are transferred into pre-school children's homes. This applies again when the children are transferred to school-age children's homes after another three years. Personnel in child psychiatric services who observe the child's development in all types of institutes of course can rectify this, since they record not only disorders of a regressive character, but also a number of other disorders which accompany transfer from institute to institute. Possibly only the fact that the child in Czechoslovakian institutes was denied the opportunity to establish deeper emotional relationships protected him from more severe traumatizing during frequent environmental changes, which characterized this system of child care.

A study by M. Mikešová (1957, unpublished) provides indirect support for this assumption. She observed the reactions, a few days after admission to a toddler home, of sixty-eight children raised from the age of three weeks in a baby institute, where the emotional relationships between the nurses and babies were very strongly emphasized, and where the organizational structure was tailored to this requirement (every nurse cared for two—three babies from the group). Sixty-six per cent of the children showed a noticeable loss of weight and increased temperature (37.5 to 39 degrees) without any other symptoms of illness, half of the children developed bad habits not previously observed (especially excessive sucking), 76 per cent were moody (morose, fearful, lacked contact with the environment) and in nearly 40 per cent of the cases there was obvious behavioural regression. Only ten children (15 per cent) showed no pronounced reaction. These were mainly children who in the baby institute appeared to be slow, quiet, and unexcitable.

The lower percentage of adaptive difficulties in our study, compared with Mikešová's figures, may be due to two factors. In our study we did not record immediate reactions, but only those remaining after a certain time lapse, and thus we observed only the most marked and serious disorders. Secondly, it is probable that in the institution from which we drew our sample care was not directed specifically towards the establishment of an emotional bond. These children, therefore, would be less sensitive to the development of separation reactions.

Let us present one case of strong and protracted reaction to two changes of institutional environment.

Illegitimate boy S. M. was admitted from the delivery ward of a hospital to a baby institute. When transferred to the toddler home (at twelve months of age) he seemed to be severely developmentally retarded, apathetic, fretful, he had minimal contact with nurses and other children. He started to walk and crudely vocalize only at two years of age. There was a strong suspicion that he was feebleminded. He did not play with the other children, nor sit up at the table. If a stranger approached he cried fearfully, screamed, rolled on the floor, and hid his head. He only passively held a toy when it was offered. If the examining psychologist took it away and offered a new one, the boy immediately started to cry. During the next year he showed improved adaptation, development speeded up and in the next ten months — at age three and a half years —

he was approximately normal (by peer group standards), he spoke in short sentences, recited poems and sayings, and was interested in all activities in the institute. All behavioural abnormalities disappeared. He was re-examined at four years of age, one month after transfer into a pre-school children's home. Again there was developmental stagnation with behavioural difficulties; he was defiant, lay on the floor, screamed, and held his breath. Although he knew the psychologist well from previous contacts, in this new environment there was an almost exact repetition of the behaviour he showed during the first examination in the toddler home. He only held the toy, and when the psychologist tried to offer him a new one he again cried fearfully and showed negativistic behaviour. Establishing contact was nearly as difficult as it had been three years before. During his stay in the pre-school home, however, he gradually adapted, emotional outbursts and other difficulties again disappeared, and development speeded up, so that mentally he was only slightly below average when he entered school.

There still remains the question of whether we should be complacent about the fact that 61 per cent of institutionalized children failed to show any response at all when transferred from one institute to another. It is quite evident that children who even in young toddler age are oriented primarily towards material objects and who generally regard adults as secondary objects are included in the "well-adapted" category. These are children whose social development and emotional development are probably seriously retarded. Lack of response to change in the institutional environment may indicate absence of any previous emotional bond rather than good adaptive resources. Nurses describe such children as "always the same". Other children, whose orientation, according to psychological tests, is mainly social, in staff neuro-psychological reports are described as passive, dull, and drooping following transfer. After a certain period of time, however, they begin to develop, show interest in social play, go to the nurses for cuddling and petting, and in general seem to be completely changed. Children who show a predominantly material interest have essentially the same environment when transferred to another institute, since the material equipment of institutes is much the same and the human faces are only secondary. On the other hand, children with predominantly social orientation, who are already emotionally bound to some person, lose this environment when transferred to another institute. They are obviously shocked, and need time and suitable care before any improvement can be expected.

Another aspect of this problem involves toddlers who for some reason are transferred from one day-care centre to another after they reach twelve months of age. Reaction to the new environment is usually minimal. One obvious reason is that the physical differences between nursery environments are very small (standard buildings and equipment), but secondly, and more importantly, the child's emotional bond remains intact at home, in the family. Change of nurseries, therefore, has far less social impact than a change of institute for children without families.

The child's reaction to return home

Since the child's separation from his mother and family environment does in fact produce certain psychological effects, one might expect that his return to the family would also produce a number of striking behavioural changes. The more the behaviour of such a child deviates from normal adaptation to environmental changes and the more rigid the pattern of such behaviour, the greater the justification for assuming that previous separation has left an abnormal psychological condition. Present clinical experience and the data from certain studies appear to support this assumption.

Reaction to returning home — according to J. Robertson, who observed children in their families after return from hospital — depends on the separation phase the child is experiencing (see page 28). Children who have not yet reached the detachment period, and particularly those who are still at the stage of active protest, show separation anxiety. They cling to their mothers more fiercely than before, continually follow them around, and become extremely fearful when separated for even short periods of time. This pattern of behaviour typifies cases where a good relationship between the mother and the child existed before the short-term separation. Some children respond in this way immediately after return, others only after a period of time, during which they seem to be alienated or directly reject the mothers. Where the separation is short-term, the fearful behaviour persists for only a few weeks; it reappears, however, whenever the danger of another separation threatens. If the separation lasts more than six months, and the child lacks a surrogate mother in hospital, so that he enters the detachment period, anxiety is not shown after his return home, and the child is unable to re-establish a normal attachment to his mother.

M. D. Ainsworth (1962) cites a number of studies which basically support Robertson's conclusions. For example, L. Jessner, G. E. Blom, and S. Waldfogel (1952) and K. Jackson et al. (1952) reported persistence of similar abnormalities (infantile behaviour, clinging to mother, sleep disorders) in a number of children a few months after return from the hospital (tonsillectomy). D. G. Prugh et al. (1953) reported that fearful behaviour and increased dependency on mother after return from hospital were greatest in children in the age range two to four years. With hospitalized children, of course, we should remember that the behavioural outcome can also be affected by other traumatizing experiences − by narcosis, operations, pain, feelings of helplessness and so on − independently of separation from the family.

It appears likely that Robertson's observations are valid for short-term separation only. From the point of view of long-term separation, we are particularly interested in the reactions of pre-school children to return to their families or to adoption after a long stay in a children's home.

We studied (Z. Matějček, 1969b) the reaction to transfer into families of 114 children who spent a period of time between one and three years of age in the same children's home. Forty-nine showed no abnormalities, 15 an inhibitory reaction, 10 (9 per cent) a fearful response (in Robertson's sense), 7 psycho-motor restlessness, while in 10 cases the most marked reaction was mental stagnation (regressive forms); 7 children showed other reactions, and in 19 cases the behaviour was too difficult to classify. Time spent in the institute was of no significance. Of 10 fearfully reacting children, 6 had been institutionalized since baby age; of 15 inhibitory types, 11, and of 6 hyperactive types, 4.

We selected all those children (seventy-one cases) now of school age who had lived together in the institution from baby age up to three years of age; twenty-six had returned after three years to their own families, twenty-two had remained in institutes, and twenty-three had been adopted. Rather interestingly, these groups showed no significant differences in reaction to the new environment. The most frequent classification was "without abnormalities", the second "inhibitory"; fearful clinging to the supervisors was reported in the first group in two cases, in the second group in one case, in the third in two cases. A more important finding was that girls were relatively more adaptable (they predominated in the group "without abnormality", and boys in the "inhibitory" category).

Obviously, therefore, it is difficult to compare the situation of a child returning home after a long stay in an institute with that of a child returning from hospital. The variety of constitutional factors in the child's make-up, the diversity of conditions during the institutional stay, and great differences in individual families after return home are confounding factors.

M. D. Ainsworth (1962) aptly remarks that the interaction between the original separation and deprivation experiences of the child and other factors present on return home throws up a number of variables which are difficult to control. Unexpected events can occur in the family, for example, the death of one of the parents, divorce, conflict between parents, and so on. Failures of some of the children we studied after transfer from children's homes to their own families at three years of age were often more attributable to these external factors than to the limited adaptability of the child. The fact that some children, even after three years' stay in an institution, adapt to the new environment rather rapidly and acceptably, without special pre-adaptive training, suggests that the child's experiences in our institutes cannot be regarded as completely depriving.

On the other hand, a certain percentage of adaptive difficulties indicates that the capacity of the child to adapt should not be over-estimated, and that it would be wise to follow the example of certain workers (for example, I. Bielicka in Poland, 1963; B. M. Flint in Canada, 1966) who suggest techniques for the gradual preparation of a child to be adapted for transfer into the richer and differently structured stimulus environment.

Fig. 1. The wild boy of Aveyron (contemporary portrait).

Fig. 2. Kamala eats in a wolf-like fashion.

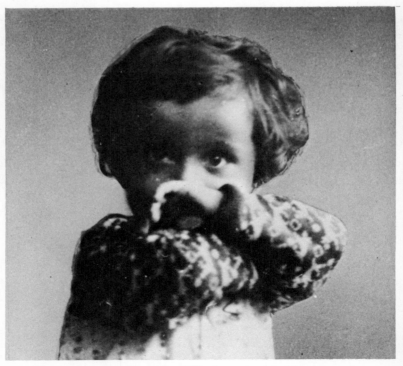

Fig. 3. Typical reactions of a child when approached by a stranger.

Fig. 4. Drawing by a six-year-old child in a pre-school children's home which provides a low level of stimulation.

Fig. 5. Drawing by the same boy after five months in a more stimulating school children's home.

5 Environmental factors underlying deprivation

The conditions which produce psychological deprivation in childhood can be extremely varied and complex. Lack of opportunity for satisfying basic needs, certain types of physical, nutritional, social, and cultural neglect, adult attitudes likely to produce trauma, conflict situations, for example, can have some influence. We should take cognizance of this diversity — which has been repeatedly emphasized by experimental psychologists — if we intend to use the deprivation concept in everyday clinical practice. Despite this, however, we think that the term can be applied to certain typical situations in a child's life, and that this is defensible on both practical and theoretical grounds.

It is difficult to categorize all types of environmental situations which we would regard as significant sources of deprivation. In fact, in our present state of knowledge, it is difficult even to suggest a viable psychological classification — for example, according to the kinds of needs which remain unsatisfied over a long period of time. From the point of view of clinical practice, the most useful classification is still the empirical one, based on the types of social conditions in which the child most frequently experiences psychological starvation. Although there are obvious weaknesses in such a system — there is overlap between categories, and there is the fact that a child can experience, cumulatively or concurrently, a number of different types of deprivation, and that the severity and type of deprivation can vary even within categories — it has utility, and is not intended to be final or definitive. We think it is an advance on preceding systems which often have postulated that deprivation occurs only under conditions of institutional care.

TOTAL COLLECTIVE CARE

The institutional care of children was recorded in harrowing terms many centuries ago.

The fact that the legal codes in the Dark Ages specifically forbade the killing of children suggests that it is not unlikely that "unwanted" children were severely neglected. The early church councils were the first to regard child neglect as murder, and appealed for a more humane attitude.

Probably the first institution for neglected children was established in Constantinople in the year 335, and the first foundling home in 787 in Milan through the initiative of Bishop Datteus. Similar institutions were established subsequently in Siena, Padua, Montpellier, and other cities. Pope Innocent III established the foundling home attached to the Hospital of the Holy Spirit in Rome in 1198. This home was equipped with the famous revolving box, the "torno". Niched in the wall of the monastery, the box fitted infants up to a certain size and allowed mothers to desert their children under cover of darkness. The abandoned child was then under the protection of the patron saint of the church. The torno became so widely used that in the year 1811 the Emperor Napoleon ordered its installation in all foundling homes in the French provinces.

Even in the Middle Ages, however, this method of protecting children was abused. Not only sick and dead children, but also children of well-to-do parents, were abandoned in this way. The torno might have actually encouraged child neglect. In the city of Mainz, for example, during the period 1799 to 1811, when the torno was unused, only thirty cases of neglected children were recorded. This number increased to 516 in the next three years when the torno was introduced in accordance with the Napoleonic edict. The torno was then dismantled. Only seven children were deserted in the following nine years. However, since there are no reports available about the number of unwanted children who were deserted in other ways, or murdered, during this time, one cannot attach too great significance to these figures.

By the end of the last century the use of the torno had declined, but even in the year 1906 464 tornos were still operating in Italy. There is some disagreement about the date of the last used torno. M. Lautererová (1964) cites the year 1913 in Toledo, whereas A. Peiper (1955) states the year 1939 in an orphanage in Warsaw. In 1952, however, one torno was still functioning in Cuba, in its original form, fulfilling the traditional community function of preserving the anonymity of the person who deserted the child.

The charitable institutions established by the monasteries in the Middle Ages admitted not only neglected and foundling children, but all indigent persons – the sick, the impoverished, the old. Only gradually were separate foundling homes, orphanages, and child institutes set up, mainly in the post-Reformation period. The founders of such establishments were usually motivated by a sincere desire to save children who otherwise would certainly have perished, or been bartered or abused. Thus, St. Vincent de Paul, the founder of the well-known Paris foundling home (1638), could state with satisfaction that in ten years he had saved 600 deserted children.

However, the paradoxical results of such noble efforts were becoming apparent. It was evident that more children perished than survived, and that the future for the survivors was bleak. Dotti, in 1678 (see M. Červinková-Riegrová, 1894) reported that of the 2,000 children admitted to Venetian foundling homes, only 7 survived after a period of ten years. Child mortality rates in a foundling home in Florence at the beginning of the seventeenth century ranged from 66 to 97 per cent. In the London foundling home only every sixth child could be expected to reach school age. At this time, transport of children from the country to city foundling homes was a recognized occupation. It is reported from England that only one-eighth of the children survived this journey, and they did so only because the mother walked behind the wagon feeding and caring for the child. One can appreciate the recommendation of a French doctor, Villermé, that children's institutions should bear the inscription "ici on fait mourir les enfants aux frais publics".

Conditions were unchanged at the middle of the last century, and the institutional environment was probably similar to that described by Charles Dickens in his novels (e.g. *Oliver Twist*). This is clearly indicated in table 5, cited by A. Peiper (1955) from the older work by L. Pfeifer (1882).

Table 5. Mortality rates in foundling homes

		%			%
Paris	1780	60	Dublin	1701–97	98
Vienna	1811	72	St.Petersburg	1772–84	85
Paris	1817	67	St.Petersburg	1785–97	76
Brussels	1811	79	St.Petersburg	1830–33	50.5
Brussels	1817	56	Moscow	1822–31	66
Ghent	1823–33	62	Dijon	1838–45	61
Bordeaux	1850–61	18	Prague	1865	19.6

The figures in table 5 are the more striking when we remember that at this time the number of abandoned children in some cities had reached gigantic proportions. According to C. F. Meissner (quoted by A. Peiper, 1955), 18,713 children were baptised in Paris in 1772, of whom 7,676 were foundling children. Some comparative figures, taken from A. Peiper (1955), are shown in table 6. (Fig. 6.)

Table 6. Admission rates to foundling homes (percentage of live births)

		%			%
Lisbon	1815–19	26.3	Madrid		25.6
Rome	1801–21	27.9	Paris	1815–21	20.9
Brussels	1816–21	14.7	Vienna	1815–21	23.4
St.Petersburg	1820	45.0	Moscow		27.9

In the Vienna foundling home, established in 1784, the mortality rate ranged from 70 per cent under the most favourable conditions to more than 90 per cent under unfavourable conditions. The Prague foundling home was established in 1789 to care for illegitimate children from the city hospital. It was to provide a temporary shelter for children who were subsequently placed in foster care. Only weak and sick children were treated here for longer periods of time. In addition, illegitimate children born in other hospitals and in prisons, foundling children, and children picked up by police were accepted. Every year about 3,000 children were admitted, and the infant mortality rate ranged between 50 and 70 per cent.

Improved conditions, which were introduced shortly after 1858,[1] significantly reduced the mortality rate. In 1864, it decreased to 31 per cent, and in 1881 still further to 10.5 per cent. Three facts contributed to this — children were institutionalized for shorter periods of time, they were committed to foster homes sooner, or they were more frequently returned to their own mothers, who received a limited amount of government support.

This emphasis on foster care and support of the families themselves was not only a response to the very poor hygienic-epidemiological conditions in the institution, which were commented on by physicians at that time, but also to new philosophical trends in education initiated mainly by J. J. Rousseau (1712–78).

1. In the records of A. Epstein (1882) who was director of the hospital from 1880, there is an amazing mortality figure (103 per cent) for the year 1858. This figure, however, represents all children younger than twelve months of age who died during the year in the institute or in foster care outside the institute, as a percentage of the number of children under one year of age who were admitted to the institute in that year.
    During the year in question the overall mortality rate of the institute was 36 per cent.

In this connection, we might mention *On orphans* by J. A. Comenius, a hundred years earlier (1634), in which the author, influenced by conditions after the Thirty Years' War, had suggested that the solution to the problem of orphans lay in different types of family care.

From the end of the eighteenth century the unnatural state of the institutional environment was increasingly criticized, and the advantage of family care stressed; for example the Hamburg Arts and Crafts Guild in 1770 arranged an open concourse on the topic "Is it preferable to raise orphans in institutions or in supported foster families?"[2]

At this time some philanthropically oriented philosophers and theologians attempted to implement more progressive ideas. Among these was the great Swiss educator J. H. Pestalozzi (1746–1827) whose theories and ideas guided P. E. Fellenberg to establish in 1799 a quite novel type of institute; this was reorganized by his successor, Wehrli, who introduced the so-called family system, in which children were cared for in small groups.

The future of children who survived the foundling homes or foster care which followed and were then returned to their birth place[3] was extremely grim. By comparison, certain orphanages were progressive and successful establishments. Some of them resembled the family type of small children's homes which are common today, and which a number of workers, from practical experience, consider to be the optimal environment.

These innovations are quite recent, historically, and from this point on efforts to help neglected children were to some extent guided by scientific research. This research history can be conveniently divided into four periods, which are distinguished by the different methodological approaches adopted, along the general lines suggested in the survey of deprivation studies (chapter 1).

1. The empirical period (the second half of the last century up to the twenties of this century)

This research was still overshadowed by the high mortality rate among institutionalized children. Outstanding paediatricians of this

---

2. The modern equivalent of a concourse would be a public examination or competition.
3. It was common practice at this time for children to be returned at the age of thirteen or fourteen from foundling homes to their birth place, where they became community charges.

time (A. Czerny, J. Parrot, M. Pfaundler, J. Ibrahim, J. Brennemann, A. Schlossmann, and others) were concerned about the causes of this and inclined to the view that it was due to conditions of treatment, of stimulation, and of child care. However, nutritional deficit was still considered the major contributor, and the majority of child mortality cases were diagnosed as atrophia infantum, debilitas vitae, or marasmus. The emphasis subsequently shifted to infection, and institutional deaths, for which the diagnosis was unclear, were attributed to rhinopharyngitis and its complications.

The renovation of institutional environments, based on new concepts of hygiene (quarantine, individual cubicles, asepsis during treatment, vaccination, and planned diet), decreased mortality rates so markedly that A. Schlossmann (1920), for example, reported that in the course of eight years (1912–20) the mortality rate of infants below one year of age was reduced from 71.5 per cent to 17.3 per cent, and in another institution to as low as 10.6 per cent. This latter figure was no higher than the then mortality rate in Germany. According to O. Tezner (1956), the infant mortality rate in the Wizoheim Institute in 1949 was still 6 per cent, but in the following year reduced to 0.78 per cent. E. Schmidt-Kolmer (1959b) reports that between 1943 and 1956 the infant mortality rate in the largest institute in Berlin (Königsheim) was 1.12 per cent and in the largest institute in East Germany (in Güstrow) 1.2 per cent, which was a lower figure than the infant mortality rate in East Germany.

The type of illness that these children suffered also changed; the dreaded childish infections were less frequent, and if they did occur, their progress was usually uncomplicated. The decreased resistance to benign illnesses in these children, however, was very marked. The average duration of illness was twice that of children from daily nurseries (E. Schmidt-Kolmer, 1963). Some retardation in physical development was also noticeable. E. Schmidt-Kolmer (1963) reported data on 8,000 institutionalized children in Berlin; on the average they were 8 to 10 centimetres shorter, and 1.5 kilograms lighter than children from daily nurseries, although there were no differences in physical measurements at birth. Similar conclusions were reached when the typical development of three- and six-year-old institutionalized children in Czechoslovakia was investigated by Z. Matějček (1960) and Z. Matějček and S. Reithar (1963). Although the weight gain is noticeable, the overall growth pattern of institutionalized children has not changed much in the last thirty years.

As the mortality rate and disorders of physical development amongst institutionalized children decreased, emphasis shifted to a new problem, that of psychological damage. This approach precipitated a fierce controversy in the early twenties of this century between two outstanding German paediatricians, M. Pfaundler and A. Schlossmann, who had jointly authored a textbook of paediatrics (1910) which was for a long time authoritative in this field. Pfaundler (1924, 1925) was highly suspicious of the baby institutes. He felt that the child, instead of experiencing personal, individual, maternal care, was pushed into "nursery factories" or "baby barracks", where he suffered, in Pfaundler's description, *"widernatürliche Massenpflege"*.[4] Schlossmann, however, thought of baby institutes as places where the severely neglected child could be helped towards normal development. He maintained that if it was possible to radically decrease infant mortality in foundling homes through improvement in hygienic conditions, and if a modern baby institute introduced up-to-date medical practices, the "inferiority stigma" which children from poor institutes in the past had carried with them into later life should be eradicated. Hospitalism, according to Schlossmann (1926), is produced by three factors – the indifference of doctors, lack of care, and poor diet. Because all three can be eliminated, it is possible to eliminate hospitalism as such. Schlossmann was successful in implementing his ideas. He established (from a medical point of view) an "exemplary" baby institute. Soon afterwards (1926) however, his daughter and close colleague, E. Eckstein, reported that, despite the great amount of care, the institutional children did not develop as well as children growing up in their own or foster families.

The controversy, therefore, was unresolved, and the basic problem of whether "to eliminate institutions or improve them" has continued to reappear in different guises. Nevertheless, the dispute showed quite emphatically that the problem of deprivation in institutionalized children cannot be resolved if approached solely from the medical point of view. This has been an important factor in promoting further study of the life of children in institutions, in which psychologists and psychiatrists played a prominent role.

2. The alarm period, which spanned the thirties and forties of this century

The psychologists who first attempted to analyze the factors underlying psychological hospitalism belonged to the Vienna school of C. Bühler. A leading figure was H. Hetzer, with her concept of

4. Unnatural collective care (ed.).

"Milieuforschung" (1929, 1932). These workers introduced the second period which, in its final phase, became alarming, and overlapped into the early fifties.

In one of the earliest studies of this type, H. Durfee and K. Wolf (1934) used "baby tests" to compare the developmental level of ninety-four babies of different ages in eight baby institutes. These institutes differed in level of hygienic care, in the amount of stimulation offered by the environment (toys, opportunity for activity, and so on), and in the type of social environment (some children were cared for by their unmarried mothers, others by nurses and some by baby sitters, for example by mothers of other institutionalized children).

The results of this study were: (1) that the social environment had the greatest stimulation value, and (2) that maternal care was undoubtedly more important than care by trained staff. These findings established the importance of the mother in a more clear-cut fashion than a simple comparison of children from institutes with children from families, which has a large number of uncontrolled variables. The true value of maternal care was illustrated even when it was offered by unmarried, neglected, and poorly educated mothers, for whom the child was probably a burden.

The authors attribute this to three factors — economic (the nurse has to care for more children), physiological (nursing), and most importantly, psychological (the interest and motivation of the mother to play with the child). They noted, however, that if contact was very close between a psychopathic mother and a child this frequently caused more profound disturbances to the child's development than an impersonal relationship with a nurse, and that the combination of both types of care — maternal love and professional nursing — promises the most satisfactory results.

They also reported a negative correlation between hygiene level and the mental development of the children, i.e. development was poorest in the institutes with the best standard of hygienic care. Over-strict observance of hygiene requirements often produced extreme monotony (bare walls, isolated cubicles, no toys, care for specific purposes only, and so on). It seems that a sterile environment, which is hygienically ideal, is also sterile insofar as mental stimulation is concerned.

This study led to further work by members of the same school (I. Gindl, H. Hetzer, and M. Sturm, 1937). I. Gindl, using similar techniques, plus a special verbal test, compared children between twelve and twenty-four months of age raised in institutes, in foster families, and in their own families (N = 20 in each case; similar socio-economic backgrounds). She was concerned with children from the poorest families, neglected children, and children from broken homes. These children if left in families, showed, overall, better development than children transferred to institutes — but the best development was recorded from children placed in good foster homes.

Retardation of institutionalized children was uneven; social behaviour, mainly speech development, was most severely retarded, but there was also much greater disturbance in their attitudes to persons and to material objects. They were passive, lacked initiative, and reacted fearfully or with excessive irritability to every change in daily routine. The primary disadvantage of institutes, according to Gindl, is that the child has no opportunity for normal personal interaction. In a family the child participates in the communal life of the whole family, has his place and status, and sees the outcomes of all his behaviour. The institutional child, however, is socially isolated, his environment is artificial — like living in a glass house, everything is done for him and therefore he relinquishes his social responsibility. Over-zealous treatment and child care stifles the spontaneity and normality in human relations which the child obtains in the family.

M. Sturm extended Gindl's findings with a careful twenty-four-hour observation of the daily routine of children raised in an institution up to six years of age with children raised in devoted homes (twelve children in each group). She reported significant reduction in opportunities for creativity and independence amongst the institutionalized children, which was due to the limited life space, lack of personal participation, and excessive life monotony. While the child in the family spent about eight hours a day in free activity (play) and two hours in directed activity (hygiene, domestic duties, directed play, walks with the parents, and so on), time allocation is the reverse for the institutionalized child. He spends quite a lot of time "waiting his turn", is given the opportunity to handle only one-seventh of the toys and other objects which the family child experiences, and, particularly during the first two years, is left alone to a much greater extent (in the family an adult directs his attention to a child 97 times a day during the first year, 141 times a day in the second year; in institutes only 19 and 50 times a day respectively). In addition, the institutional child has far less opportunity to actively seek adult attention (in the second year only 12 times a day, compared with 121 times a day for the child in the family, and in the sixth year, 35 times a day, compared with 132 times a day for the family child). Most importantly, the child entirely lacks the experience of normal human social interaction. This artificiality of the institutionalized environment is then the main disadvantage. No planning can substitute for normal life conditions.

It is noteworthy that, even at this time, the Vienna psychologists could envisage only one effective solution — the establishment of small homes, "nests", in which groups of approximately ten children, ranging in age from three to ten years, would be given the necessary individual care, sufficient freedom, and where their lives could be relatively normal — i.e. where they are given all that they most require.

The studies of the Vienna school and other workers in the thirties contributed a great deal to our understanding of the basis of deprivation in institutionalized children. These studies were interrupted by World War II, and were subsequently "rediscovered", only to be relegated to the background by later and often methodologically less sophisticated studies.

The well-known work of R. A. Spitz, especially his study of hospitalism (1945—46), is indebted to this earlier work. Spitz, with his colleague K. Wolf, studied 91 children in one foundling home, and 122 children in a prison nursery, over an extended period. Each institution represented an extreme type of institutional environment. The foundling home admitted children, with normal hereditary backgrounds, for social reasons from the unselected city population. They usually spent the first three months of life in the care of their mothers, and were then separated and- entrusted to a nurse, who looked after eight to ten children.

The prison nursery admitted children born in prison of delinquent mothers; they were cared for by the mother (under the supervision of the medical staff) for twelve months. Spitz considers this to be most important. Heredity was obviously poorer in the prison nursery than in the foundling home. In the foundling home, however, children experienced far greater lack of stimulation. They had fewer toys, they lay in glass cubicles up to fifteen to eighteen months of age, and unless they were able to stand up, saw nothing except the ceiling. Their mobility was limited not only by the bed but also by the depression in the mattress. The fact that every child was given only about 10 per cent of effective maternal care is considered by Spitz to constitute total emotional deprivation.

Spitz subsequently extended the research to include two additional groups of children raised in families but under different social conditions — children from a city environment and children from an isolated fishing village.

Study of the mental development of the children in the first year led to the following conclusions.

Children raised in the foundling home began nearly as well as the best group, but their further development was considerably arrested. The decrement was already noticeable in the third month, and by the fourth to fifth month their development lagged behind that of children in the prison nursery. At the end of their first year, instead of the normal reaction to strangers, they either constantly screamed or were extremely friendly to everyone. At the same time they showed great fear and avoidance of objects. (Fig. 7.)

After two years, their DQ had decreased to 45. The children became passive; they lay on their beds with empty expressions, did not roll over, and their bizarre twisting finger movements resembled the movements of catatonics or decerebrates (spasmus nutans). Despite good hygienic conditions, their lowered resistance to infection led to marasmus and mortality. This weakness was evident in measles epidemics (during two years of observation, 37 per cent of the ninety-one children in the home died, while in the prison group there were no deaths, although medical supervision was casual). The children in the prison developed satisfactorily. At the end of their first year, they had no difficulty in walking or speaking, but they found it difficult to contain their curiosity and ingenuity. Prison conditions, however, were not normal for the mothers. Because they were deprived of other means of satisfying their needs, they tended to emotionally smother their children. The severe effect of this was shown in the occurrence of so-called anaclitic depression which followed sudden separations of the mother from the child.

Spitz systematically observed the development of the children from the foundling home at four-monthly intervals for a further period of two years. He concluded that improved conditions and increased stimulation after fifteen months (arranging of children in groups, active stimulation, constant presence of three to five nurses) do not compensate for the damage already caused. This seems to be an irreversible process. Some of the prison nursery children were also observed after a lapse of a year; their development was good, they

Table 7. Changes in DQ (developmental quotient) in the first twelve months

	Mean DQ in First 3 Months	Mean DQ in Last 3 Months
Foundling home children	124	72
Children from urban families	133	131
Children from prison nursery	101	105
Children from fishing village families	107	108

could speak, run, play, and were very active.

The importance of Spitz's studies is that they show clearly that complete emotional deprivation may have very serious consequences. His studies alarmed, in the very real sense of the word, all workers involved in institutional child care, and they were a very strong impetus towards various remedial and preventive measures.

Even such extensive studies, however, have left a number of questions unanswered. For example, one can hardly accept without additional evidence Spitz's statement that the absence of the mother, or the surrogate, is the sole or principal cause of general retardation and of all the severe disorders recorded, when other factors were obviously involved (e.g. extreme sensory and motor deprivation). Generally speaking, in Spitz's writings one should carefully distinguish between valid data and psychoanalytic interpretations of such data. S. R. Pinneau (1955*a*) has made a detailed criticism of the Spitz studies; his objections are mainly methodological, but he comments on the inadequate documentation and statistical analysis.

Other authors quite rightly point out that Spitz's conclusions do not mean that the developmental prognosis for institutionalized children, under improved conditions, must always be extremely poor. L. Casler (1961) concludes a critique of this fact with the statement by C. W. Eriksen (1957). Eriksen maintains that Spitz was unable to answer the questions posed. He writes (pp. 194—95): "While most of us will continue to believe in the importance of mothering during infancy, we must recognize that this belief has more the character of a faith and less the basis of demonstrated facts." We would like to add the rider "at present", for doubtless Spitz's contribution was that although he may have been unable to solve the problem, he did accord it dramatic expression. Criticism of his work did a good deal to clarify the basic problem and to stimulate new, better planned, and more intensive investigations.

A different theoretical point of view, coupled with practical experience, provided the basis for the extensive and well-controlled studies by W. Goldfarb (1943—49), who followed the pioneer work by L. G. Lowrey (1940). Goldfarb compared matched groups of children who differed basically in only one respect; the children in the first group lived from the earliest age in foster families, while children from the second group were admitted to an institute before six months of age, and stayed there for an average of two and a half years, after which they were also placed in foster families. Hereditary factors would be rather more favourable in the second group, since the first group were children of mothers who were unable to provide any sort of care from the beginning The institution provided adequate physical care, but was very impersonal (children initially lived in individual cubicles, later in groups of fifteen to twenty, the nurses were poorly trained and uninterested). He used IQ tests, the Rorschach test, special tests, rating scales, and so on, both during the time of their institutional stay, and when they were about four, six, eight and twelve years of age. Results were very clear-cut. For example, the two groups of fifteen children at thirty-four and forty-three months of age showed differences as in table 8. Comparison of these two groups between the ages of ten and fourteen years gave the results as in table 9.

L. Casler (1961), in his review of the maternal deprivation literature, makes no major methodological criticisms of the Goldfarb studies. He simply comments on the small sample size and the lack of clear selection criteria. Other criticisms noted are Goldfarb's

Table 8. Comparison of children living in institutions and foster families

	Institutionalized Group		Foster Family Group	
	Tested at 34 months	Tested at 43 months	Tested at 34 months	Tested at 43 months
Verbal IQ (Terman)	68.1	75.8	96.4	101.5
Non-verbal IQ (Merrill-Palmer)	78.9	77.8	90.5	89.7
Social maturity (Vineland Scale)	100.5	88.0	103.3	109.3

Table 9. Comparison of groups at ten to fourteen years of age

	Institutionalized Group	Foster Family Group
IQ (Wechsler)	72.4	95.4
Concept formation:		
Weigl score	2.4	6.8
Vigotski score	0.5	4.7
Social maturity (Vineland Scale)	79.0	98.8
Ability to establish normal social relationships (N = 15 in each group)	2	15
Submits to authority	3	12
At least average speech development	3	14
Inability to concentrate	10	1
Intensive need for love	9	2
Bad school record	15	1

interpretation of Rorschach protocols, and the fact that S. Z. Orgel (1941) and Lowrey (1940) report more favourable results than those obtained by Goldfarb with children from the same institute. The last objection is hardly valid, however, since the Orgel and Lowrey studies involved different children, different time periods, and different methodologies, so that it is impossible to make simple comparisons.

The Goldfarb studies, of course, did not provide answers to all the important questions in this area, and had certain deficiencies, primarily that they did not determine the relative importance of the factors underlying deprivation. Generally speaking, however, they did suggest that institutional deprivation produces severe disorders in emotional and intellectual development. During adolescence, deprived children still behave in many ways like pre-school children — in an immature, undiscriminating, primitive fashion. Retardation seems to be irreversible and is not fully recovered. Development is not accelerated in the later, more stimulating environment of foster families, under careful social supervision, or through special psychotherapy. The retardation results finally in "quasi-constitutional fixation on the most primitive level of conceptual and emotional behaviour". While it is true that children raised from birth in foster homes can and do exhibit behaviour disorders, these are of a different type, and originate in disturbed family relationships.

The most comprehensive review of the investigations completed during this second period was reported by J. Bowlby in the monograph *Maternal care and mental health* (1951). Bowlby concludes his review of the effects of early deprivation on the child's development in this way: "The evidence is now such that it leaves no room for doubt about the general proposition — that prolonged deprivation of the young child of maternal care may have grave and far-reaching effects on his character and so on the whole of his future life" (p. 46). Bowlby considered that group care, particularly with children younger than six years of age, was one of the main sources of early deprivation, since it "cannot be too strongly emphasized that, with the best will in the world, a residential nursery cannot provide a satisfactory emotional environment for infants and young children" (p. 132); "the reason why the group care of infants and young children must *always* be unsatisfactory is not only the impossibility of providing mothering of an adequate and continuous kind, but also the great difficulty of giving a number of toddlers the opportunity for active participation in the daily life of the group . . . " (p. 133 — our italics).

In contrast to the first period, during which the philanthropic conception of social care for the deprived child was widely acknowledged, Bowlby stresses at the conclusion of his monograph that "the proper care of children deprived of normal home life can now be seen to be not merely an act of common humanity, but to be essential for the mental and social welfare of the community. For, these children, whose care is neglected, as happens in every country of the western world today, grow up to reproduce themselves ... Yet, so far, no country has tackled this problem seriously. Even so-called advanced countries tolerate conditions of bad mental hygiene in nurseries, institutions and hospitals to a degree which, if paralleled in the field of physical hygiene, would long since have raised a public outcry" (p. 157).

Bowlby completed his severe condemnation of modern society with the alarming comment: "Let it be hoped, then, that all over the world men and women in public life will recognize the relation of mental health to maternal care, and will seize their opportunities for promoting courageous and far-reaching reforms" (p. 158).

3. The period during the fifties and sixties of "critical investigation of the effects of institutional care on child development"

Bowlby's monograph is a milestone in our approach to the problem of institutionalized children. He took a relatively strong and apparently justifiable stand against collective care for small children, and made a vigorous demand for radical changes in the care of children outside their own families. His studies produced positive responses from a number of workers who accepted his conclusions and applied them in various fields of child care. Other workers, however, were critical, and, in some cases, antagonistic. But it was Bowlby who helped subsequent workers in this field to formulate ideas with more care and precision.

The period following the publication of Bowlby's monograph is marked by three main types of studies:

a. Those aimed at verifying and extending the results of previous investigations ("supplementary" studies)

b. Studies in which the findings of previous investigators were questioned, and the concepts modified through the investigator's own research ("correcting" studies)

c. Those in which the arguments for and against institutional care were discussed, and the present-day concept of deprivation advanced ("evaluative" studies).

"Supplementary" studies

In France, J. Roudinesco and co-workers (1950) reported a number of extensive investigations. She presented film documentation of a number of cases of extremely severe deprivation disorders which produced developmental regression to the level of idiot. At the same time, however, she showed that, with more effective maternal care, even these children could improve.

In Belgium, E. A. Sand (1957) compared children raised in families with children living from birth in institutions (three very well-equipped Belgian institutes were selected); he reported statistically significant differences at all age levels.

In Switzerland, M. Meierhofer (1961) completed an extensive investigation of the development of children between three months and six years in institutes in Zurich Canton. She described in film documentaries the unfavourable outcome of lack of maternal care. On the basis of her research, she concluded that the majority of the children in the district baby institutions and pre-school children's homes showed signs of marked hospitalism, retarded motor and psychological functioning with pronounced behavioural apathy.

In West Germany, J. Weidemann (1959) compared 121 children in the age range one month to six years in six institutions, with 62 children in the same age range raised in families; using four different rating scales, he found retardation of institutionalized children at about 20 per cent below the norm and below the level of children raised in families. Retardation, however, which was most pronounced between the ages of three and five years, was shown mainly in learning, social behaviour, and speech development. The author assumes that greater concern with the care of institutionalized children caused an age-shift in developmental retardation but could not fully prevent it. He also reported that the differences in development of children from different institutes favours those children from small homes with "a family atmosphere".

A. Dührssen (1958) noted, in her monograph, that only 25 per cent of institutionalized children were mature enough to begin school, as against 85 per cent of children from families, and 60 per cent of children in foster care.

E. Schmidt-Kolmer (1957, 1959a) in East Germany compared the retardation of institutionalized children with that of children from daily nurseries. By the end of the third year, institutionalized children were at DQ 75 in motor behaviour while development in other areas remained below DQ 70 (see fig. 8).

Of some relevance also was the "experiment" conducted by the Nazis during World War II. Although we lack detailed information which would allow us to evaluate the children's development more precisely, this horrible programme ("Lebensborn" — see O. Kraus and E. Kulka, 1958) answered the question of whether disorders of institutionalized children can be caused primarily by poor hereditary endowment. After a thorough psychiatric examination, men and women were selected according to racial criteria; they were required to be physically and mentally sound and strong, and untainted by hereditary mental deficiency. The couples lived together in special secret camps until the woman became pregnant. Shortly after the birth, the child was removed from the mother and raised in a special children's home in which the aim was to produce racially pure "supermen". According to a report from one of the institutes in Neubiberg, the twenty children raised in this environment became severely developmentally retarded. Only one child was "normal"; in others speech development was delayed. Many of the children were more than five years old before they learned bodily hygiene, and some of them were idiots. The reasons for this were reported as follows: "They lacked the most important factor — love, real maternal care. The babies lay like dead fish. Nobody approached them with a kind word."

G. Trasler (1960) compared a group of children who were regarded as successful cases of foster care with a group of children regarded as unsuccessful cases who had to be transferred to other foster families. He reported that length of institutional stay after separation from the child's own family and before placement in the foster family is the most significant predictor of success or failure. For a child younger than three years who is given the opportunity to interact with a surrogate maternal figure, the damage can be mild and temporary. It becomes deeper and more permanent, however, where such opportunities are lacking.

The unfavourable influence of early institutional care on speech development was reported by M. L. Kellmer-Pringle and V. Bossio (1958, 1960) who compared eighteen pairs of four-year-old children from daily and permanent nurseries. Careful assessment showed that, in all cases, speech development of children from daily nurseries (although they lived in poor families) was significantly better than that of children from permanent institutes. The authors also observed similar retardation in subsequent studies with older children — at eight, eleven, and fourteen years of age. Institutionalized children were more frequently not ready for school, they were

educationally retarded (there were twice as many poor readers
as in the normal population), they showed more serious
symptoms of emotional disorder, either regressive or
exhibitionistic behaviour. At the same time, however, the fact
that more than 30 per cent of the children were reasonably
well adjusted reinforces the view that institutional stay does not
inevitably cause serious damage — it depends solely on the
quality of the human interactions available to the child. By
comparing well-adjusted with poorly adjusted children,
Kellmer-Pringle and Bossio reached the important conclusion
that the badly adjusted children were, in fact, "psychologically
deprived", i.e. unwanted, ostracized from the youngest age, and
lacking deep emotional attachment with somebody outside the
institute (parents, relatives, friends).

"Correcting" studies

In our review of these studies, to some extent we have to
revert to the past. A number of authors in this third period
referred back to certain conclusions from the Iowa
investigations of the thirties and forties (M. Skodak and H. M.
Skeels, 1949, and others), which cast some doubt on the
alarming conclusions of that period. A group of children from a
pre-school children's home was given formal training (following
kindergarten methods); when this group was compared with a
similar untrained group, it was noted that the first group
improved in "intelligence", motor and social development, and
general behaviour. Although these studies were not concerned
with disorders of institutionalized children, it is obvious from
the authors' description that they were concerned with deprived
children, a group similar to the children in the Goldfarb and
Bowlby studies. And although these studies can be criticized on
statistical grounds, their principal findings — that deprivation
disorders can be compensated for, at least to some extent — are
indisputable.

A relatively favourable prognosis of the development of
deprived children was also given by D. Beres and S. J. Obers
(1950). They studied thirty-eight adolescents and adults who
had spent varying periods of time before four years of age in
the same institute from which Goldfarb had selected his
experimental subjects, and who subsequently also lived in foster
homes, adoptive homes, or in family care. Notwithstanding the
fact that their selection was biased (in that well-adjusted
subjects escaped the follow-up), they still found that 18 per
cent (seven persons) of the sample were quite satisfactorily
adjusted. Of course they did not exclude the possibility that
even with these subjects careful examination might expose

traces of their deprivation experiences.

With twenty-eight cases retesting was possible after the lapse of a number of years; they found in sixteen cases an increase in IQ from 10 to 45 points, and in one case an extreme improvement from IQ 59 to IQ 105. On this basis, the researchers assumed that deprivational consequences can be partly compensated for in late adolescence and adulthood. This might be the reason why their conclusions differ from those of Goldfarb, who studied children only up to the stage of puberty.

A similar conclusion was reached by H. Lewis (1954) who studied 500 children admitted to correction homes; about 50 per cent of these children were separated from their families at pre-school age and in the majority of cases experienced institutional care. These institutional children were obviously more disturbed than the other children, who, in most cases, had extremely bad social backgrounds. Nevertheless, about 16 per cent of these institutionalized children were relatively well adjusted, a figure which corresponds roughly with the percentage reported by Beres and Obers (18 per cent).

J. Bowlby himself, in a later study (1965), tested his hypothesis about the effects of prolonged separation on the child's character development. His experiment was a better planned follow-up study of sixty children placed in a TB sanatorium for different periods of time (usually less than eighteen months) before the age of four years. He compared this group with a control group, three times as large, selected from their fellow pupils, and approximately matched for sex and age. The conditions in the sanatorium, as far as one could judge, were less likely to be deprivational than, for example, in the Goldfarb institute, but even here an adequate mother surrogate was not available.

The sanatorium children differed at a later age from the control group primarily in their stronger inclination to daydream, in lack of concentration, initiative, and self-reliance, and secondly, in a greater tendency towards roughness, aggressiveness, and fits of rage. The groups were identical in intelligence; more significantly, however, 14 per cent of these children were very well adapted indeed (according to very strict criteria) although the percentage of maladjusted children (64 per cent) seems to be high. Juvenile delinquency was surprisingly quite rare. Bowlby therefore changed his original view that children raised in institutes for a certain period of time during early age display overall severe personality disorders (psychopathic, affectionless character) and that they develop as a relatively homogeneous group of institutional children. In fact, the individual differences between children who experienced similar institutional deprivation were quite great –

some children were relatively untouched — and were often related to the mother-child relationship before separation.

In recent years a number of additional studies have been reported which clearly indicate that far-reaching improvement in psychological care in institutes is possible. For example, R. M. du Pan and S. Roth (1955) observed fourteen children placed from birth in a baby training institute in Geneva. The staff and material environment were very good (one trainee nurse per two to three children) and great emphasis was placed on the need "to create a life for the children as similar as possible to family life". The average DQ, using Gesell's norms, was 95 (lower in speech and social behaviour, higher in motor behaviour) and the children's behaviour appeared to be quite normal. H. Wissler et al. (1954) studied the development of twenty-seven children who were hospitalized for an average of five months before the age of three years for TB and general respiratory ailments. The children had adequate motor freedom, and during the day each child was looked after by a nurse, who supervised four to six other children. Seventy-five per cent of the children showed no significant decrease in DQ.

In Sweden, G. Klackenberg (1956) compared the development of children from a baby institute with two groups of children, one raised for at least six months by mothers, and then for at least three months in the institute, the other raised for the entire first year in foster care. He reports results as in table 10. Although developmentally the children in the third group were significantly more advanced than the children in the first two groups, the development of the institutionalized children was very good; emotional disorders still occurred, but they were not as severe as in Spitz's samples. The institute was careful to provide a certain amount of surrogate care and stable treatment with good individual care — one nurse to two or three children.

P. Bertoye (1957) studied 1,219 hypotrophic babies in a sanatorium in Lyon; he reported that decrement in psycho-motor development is not inevitable if certain measures are enforced — by

Table 10. Development of three groups of children at one year

	Mean DQ (Bühler)	N
Children in baby homes	105	46
Children in care of mother for 6 months, then admitted to baby homes	108	44
Children in foster families from birth	120	21

which he understands, for example, one nurse for every two children, minimal staff changes, and the selection of staff on the basis of personal qualities.

In the U.S.S.R., a number of workers have emphasized the problem of hospitalism and of "pedagogical deficit", primarily in speech and emotional development (E. I. Tichajeva, 1948; N. M. Ščelovanov and N. M. Aksarina [1949]). Recently, however, there has been more frequent reference to institutes in which such problems have been almost eliminated. Unfortunately, however, we lack accurate documentation of this.

H. Bakwin in the U.S.A. (1949) refers to a large foundling home in which he failed to find, amongst 250 children, a single clear-cut case of emotional deprivation, and where children showed what even a few years ago was quite a rarity — normal development.

O. Tezner (1956) reports a range of IQs from 75 to 100 amongst four-year-olds in a children's home; he detected retardation in some children, but also points to significant improvement in some children coming from very bad families.

B. M. Flint (1966) has described an experimental programme which was planned to eliminate deprivation amongst babies and toddlers in a normal children's home in Toronto. Far-reaching organizational changes were effected, and the care of the children was planned so as to maximally stimulate their spontaneous activity, and to emphasize their individual personalities (including their specific needs); they were also encouraged to establish relatively deep emotional ties with adults, which is the basis of the feeling of "life security". The results, which are backed up by individual case studies, were very favourable. This was also supported by a follow-up of the children when they were placed in foster care and in adoptive families. We should remember, however, that the ratio of children to staff was nearly 1:1, and that even under such favourable conditions the author does not claim that the danger of deprivation was completely eliminated.

The Polish psychologist H. Spionek (1963) also maintains that great opportunity for improvement of institutional care lies in the way in which individual children's needs are satisfied.

In this connection we must mention the frequently quoted studies of W. Dennis (1941), and W. Dennis and P. Najarian (1957) which were conducted in children's homes in Teheran and Beirut, where, in contrast to the previous cases cited, the number of staff was so small that conditions would have to be equated with those in institutes described by Spitz in his very early work. One might assume, therefore, that the result would be the same as that reported by Spitz. This, however, only occurred in the case of institutionalized children of less than one year of age (average DQ 68) when compared with the control group. In the pre-school period, these differences almost disappeared, although there were no great changes in the living conditions for the institutionalized children. In this case, therefore, there was spontaneous adjustment of the developmental process. Dennis maintains that the retardation was caused by the lack of opportunity for learning, and that his findings contradict the notion of permanent deprivational damage. His studies, however, have a number of methodological weaknesses (M. D. Ainsworth, 1962) and it is difficult to consider them as definitive in any sense.

"Evaluative" studies

At the beginning of the sixties a number of studies appeared which reviewed and evaluated the evidence up to that point (for example, L. J. Yarrow, 1961; L. Casler, 1961; proceedings of WHO *Deprivation of maternal care, 1962*). M. D. Ainsworth (1962) made an important contribution in critically examining the overview presented so far. The Dutchman J. de Wit (1964), in turn, critically examined Ainsworth's new conception.

There is a consensus from these different authors, which can be summarized in the following manner. While it is not denied that a number of children raised for a long period of time in an institutional environment show retardation and damage in physical, mental and emotional development, the so-called lack of maternal love is significant only when the child reaches a certain level of emotional reactivity; namely, at about seven months of age. The symptoms observed earlier are most likely produced by other factors; probably the most important of these is sensory deprivation.

The institutional environment can be considerably improved, and it should be possible to ensure conditions promoting the development of personality. These conditions approximate closely those found in families. Severe deprivational disorders nowadays are rare — the mild disorders predominate. Their characteristics are varied. Prognosis is basically more optimistic. Recovery can occur spontaneously (A.D.B. and A. M. Clarke, 1959), or as the result of certain educational and psychotherapeutic programmes (B. M. Flint, 1966).

The practical conclusion derived from this overview is a recommendation to improve institutions rather than to eliminate them.

4. The "experimental-theoretical" period

The conclusions of the alarm period, which seemed to Bowlby and other workers to be convincing, were neither confirmed nor denied by subsequent studies. It became evident that comparisons of groups of institutionalized children gave quite different results depending on the situational and other factors involved, and that the applied techniques were not powerful enough to clearly establish what aspects of institutional care should be considered the critical deprivational factors, whether and at what age additional deprivation caused irreversible damage, and what mechanisms were responsible for changes in the child's personality and intelligence. In the late fifties and sixties more sophisticated methods of analyzing the child's reactions to his environment under deprivating conditions were applied to the problem. New theoretical models were also sought which might suggest a more thorough and parsimonious interpretation of the deprivation symptoms. This takes us to the present, to the beginnings of a new period. While it is too early to make judgments, we can at least identify a number of trends in recent studies.

Firstly, we note attempts by some learning theorists to apply conditioning principles to problems of institutionalized children. The advantages of this approach lie not only in the logical coherence and parsimony of the theoretical constructs (which were developed primarily by J. L. Gewirtz [1961, 1969a], S. W. Bijou and D. M. Baer [1961, 1965], for example) but also in their utility in experimentally handling specific problems (as shown by H. L. Rheingold, 1960, for example). According to this model, typical changes in the behaviour of institutionalized children are due to single, recurring contingencies between the eliciting stimuli and the child's reaction, rather than to a globally impoverished environment (lacking love, warmth, stimulation value, and acceptance). The "retarded" behaviour of these children may be caused by the severe limitation in the quantity and quality of the available controlling stimuli, or by inadequate or intermittent reinforcement of instrumental acts (valued social reactions). The depriving effect of a dull, monotonous, limited, and rigid institutional environment can be viewed as a specific lack of some controlling stimuli, which those involved in child care should provide. Certain supplementary stimuli can counteract these depriving effects and improve the development of retarded infants and institutionalized children (Y. Sayegh and W. Dennis, 1965).

Although the advantages of such an approach — its objectivity, economy, and precision — are obvious, some workers objected on the grounds that this type of behaviour analysis ignores a whole class of phenomena which we must consider if we are to fully understand the problem of the deprived child. They advocated a "phenomenological" approach, through which we might better "understand" the subjective experience of separation and deprivation, and its significance for human psychological development. Studies in line with this orientation not only have a general philosophical importance, but can also contribute to a better understanding of clinical problems, to developments in psychotherapy, and to the rehabilitation of deprived children. Although most of these studies, generally speaking, were addressed to broader issues (for example the development of the emotional bond between the mother and the child, the development of trust, security, love, loneliness, bereavement) and were only peripherally concerned with the problems of the institutionalized child, they have some relevance. Up till now, however, they have offered no systematic theoretical formulation or reliable methodology, although this has been attempted in recent years (M. J. Langeveld, 1967; C. Moustakas, 1961; E. H. Erikson, 1966; E. Fromm, 1956; C. Bühler, 1959, 1962; J. F. T. Bugental, 1967).

A number of workers, rather than totally committing themselves to a wholly behaviouristic or phenomenological approach, consider that both have made valuable substantive and methodological contributions which have advanced psychological theory. As yet, however, no rapprochement between these views has been achieved, and the two bodies of information remain irreconcilable.

The approach to the problems of the institutionalized child, however, has been enriched from other sources. For example, E. Goffman (1961), using his concept of "total institution", generated a sociological model of the typical institute, incorporating characteristics common to all institutions, although to different degrees. The behaviour of the child raised in an institution from earliest age should be moulded by the characteristics of that institution. Using this conceptualization, J. Tizard (1967) and N. V. Raynes and R. D. King (1968) attempted to develop a methodology to measure those sociological characteristics of the institutional environment they considered more important (particularly role structure, type of management practice — whether institution-oriented or child-oriented — as against aspects such as staff numbers and qualifications, for example).

*   *   *

When we consider the development of institutional care, we note how closely related it is to the development of society as a whole. Generally speaking, it is obvious that the value accorded collective care is inversely related to the value placed on family care. From the time of Plato on, philosophers and social reformers who have attempted to establish a more "just" society and more "desirable" qualities in the new generations have advocated the separation of children from families, and collective care from the earliest age. Thus, during times of "great ideologies", the institutional concept tends to be supported, while during periods in which the intimate aspects of human co-existence are emphasized aid to deserted children through foster care is recommended. From the eighteenth century on, we note two contrasting trends — to eliminate institutions, and to improve them. Both views have been advanced by eminent workers, and supported by scientific evidence which at the time appeared to be adequate (Villermé vs. Pestalozzi; Pfaundler vs. Schlossmann; Spitz and Bowlby vs. Schmidt-Kolmer and Aksarina). In each of the four periods these opposing tendencies are evident — the difference lies in how and where the emphasis is placed.

Up to the middle of the last century collective care was guided largely by humanitarian principles. Attention gradually focused on principles of planned social care, which developed psychological, medical, and pedagogical overtones. It was only after World War I, however, that the social care concept predominated, although the humanitarian aspect remained and was a stimulus to practical measures.

The nature of the institutionalized population also changed, as did sources of deprivation, and thus at different periods different therapeutic approaches were advocated. In the last century the institutional population was overwhelmingly orphans and deserted children. Gradually the children of employed, unmarried mothers and neglected children from slums formed the majority. Today the pendulum has swung to children from broken homes and children threatened by cultural deprivation, who are sought out by social agencies, and for whom the only possible means of "re-education" seems to be acculturation outside the family.

Institutional care methods have changed in line with advances in scientific knowledge and changes in social structure. When there was a high mortality and illness rate among institutionalized children, medical care was emphasized. When this problem was resolved — in our first period — problems of developmental retardation became apparent. The third and fourth periods were dominated by disorders in character formation and social participation. In the baby institutes, medical concerns, which earlier had predominated, were relegated to the background, and psychological and pedagogical problems were emphasized. Thus while in the first period the concern was simply to keep the child alive, in the second it was to prevent developmental retardation, in the third to ensure emotional stimulation, and in the fourth period to guarantee complete care on all levels so that the threatened child can fully participate in society.

PARTIAL COLLECTIVE CARE

From a psychological point of view, institutions which only supplement family child care in various ways have a quite different character. This implies that the danger of deprivation will vary as a function of the type of institution.

In judging an institution, the initial criterion is the extent to which it substitutes for the role of the family. We can place institutions on a continuum ranging from those which substitute almost totally (weekly nurseries and weekly kindergartens, schools offering whole-day supervision) to those which only minimally supplement family care (for example a few hours daily stay by the child in a day nursery).

A second criterion is age classification (nursery departments for young babies, for younger and older toddlers, age-structured kindergartens, school minding centres [after-school care] which are organized by grade, and so on). We should note that the effect of collective care will depend on whether we are dealing with very young children or toddlers who are still not mature enough for this type of experience, or with the older child who already actively seeks social interactions with peers.

The role of the child-care institution, its relation to the child's family, and its internal organization form a third criterion. The institution can fulfil several different purposes, and satisfy different expectations. Its organization, therefore, can vary from the impersonal approach to children when they are organized in large groups to the sometimes very intimate contact between a supervisor and a small group of children in the so-called micro-nurseries. Other important factors which should be given consideration are the personalities of the parents as well as of the supervisors, their experience and training, their numbers, stability, and permanence, the traditions and material resources of the institute, the richness of the environment, and the possibility of contact with nature.

Substitution for family care

In dealing with partial child-care institutions from the point of view of the amount of time the child actually spends in them, we can make an initial distinction between daily and weekly institutions. Each of these presents its own particular problem. The weekly-care institutions are closer to the permanent institutions, while the daily institutions only partly substitute for family care. The mechanisms leading to deprivation can be triggered in both cases, of course, but the extent of this danger, and the interaction between these mechanisms, are vastly different. A child in a weekly establishment is in greater danger of being denied adequate emotional and social stimuli and therefore of living in an impoverished environment. While this danger is reduced for the child in the daily institute, the problem of frequent separation from mothers is greater, and the problem of adaptive behaviour in this situation is increased. In both cases the internal structure of the family — specifically, its capacity to compensate for possible deficits in collective care — is important. This concerns the extent to which parents are aware of the child's needs and their attitudes towards him. Thus, dependence on the compensatory role of the family will be more important for children in weekly than in daily establishments.

In fact often parents are not absolutely forced to place their children in weekly nurseries or kindergartens or in schools with whole-day care for economic or employment reasons. Sometimes they are not interested enough to arrange their lives so that they can live with the child. Life without the child can be quite attractive, even if the parents do not consciously admit to this. In such cases we cannot assume that the family can compensate the child either for his impoverished life or for the extreme stress which he may have suffered during the week. The task of the therapeutic worker therefore must be to change the attitudes of individual members of the family, and to improve internal relations in the family as a whole.

The period of separation from the family has a different significance for children of different ages. For very young babies and younger toddlers, a five- or six-day separation represents a "long time". At school age, this time "shortens", so that such a period is not dangerous, and in some cases it can even have a positive value. During the middle and older school age periods, qualitative changes in reactions to separation occur. The child is able to understand the situation, and can direct his fantasy into the future and past. Now a week's separation from the home for him represents only short-term deprivation; during this time the intensity of unsatisfied needs increases, the child is homesick, he directs his thoughts towards the home, looks forward to the weekend, the home has greater value for him, he intensively experiences all that has happened at home. His relationships with the home are therefore strengthened and deepened rather than weakened. At the same time, the child of this age is capable of benefiting from experiences in the peer group. This is one of the real values of summer camps, nature schools, and boarding schools.

The age of the child

The age of the child is the basic criterion determining classification of particular types of partial collective child-care establishments. It is erroneous to consider collective child care in general terms, or to assume that positive results obtained, for example, in kindergartens can be expected in nurseries, or vice versa. During the weaning period the child is still strongly dependent on the personality of the caring adult. At about three years of age, when, under normal conditions, this dependence perceptibly reduces, and when the child independently seeks the company of other children, the danger of deprivation of basic psychological needs substantially decreases. At this age, therefore, daily kindergarten attendance for the majority of children has some positive value, since in addition to the benefit gained from working under skilled supervision, they can cultivate social relationships with their peers.

The school as a daily establishment can hardly be regarded as a source of psychological deprivation as we understand the term. Through its obvious insistence on employment of mental skills and on a certain degree of both cooperation with authority and competition with other children, however, the school is usually the place where the results of previous deprivation are clearly shown. We shall return to this question in chapter 6.

If the child's age is considered to be a critical factor, therefore, we should be particularly concerned with those daily establishments which cater for children under the age of three years.

The role of the child-care establishment

While parents are usually only minimally and indirectly involved in permanent collective care, the family plays a particularly important role in partial collective care. Depending on the parents' attitudes to the child and to the establishment, the nursery can either become thoroughly "institution-like", maintaining only formal contact with the family, or it can be a useful partner in child care and a source of effective developmental stimulation. We constantly encounter tragic cases of parents who "forget" or even "desert" the child in the nursery, although today such cases are much less frequent than previously. Generally most families are concerned not to be separated from the child for a longer period than is absolutely necessary.

At the same time, however, we must not ignore complicating factors in the personalities of the parents themselves. These may be shown, for example, in their immediate reactions to separation from the child — in extreme anxiety or in feelings of guilt, and after the child returns home, in an effort to compensate for separation by extreme permissiveness, by an unconscious effort to be constantly reassured of his love. Many children have difficulty adapting to life in daily establishments, not so much because of their own insecurity, but because of the insecurity of their mothers who are unable to tolerate separation from the child. The greater the number of such factors present (e.g. children left for the whole week, children not mature enough for the institution, parents with uncertain relations with the child), the greater the danger to the child.

On the other hand, daily collective care can have a positive value in cases where family care is neglecting, casual, or emotionally unstable. Collective care in such cases can withdraw the child from an unfavourable environment and compensate for the care-deficit which will otherwise be created by the family. The handling of the child in an expert, efficient way, from both the hygienic and child-care point of view, is an example to parents, and their daily contact with nursery or kindergarten workers is undoubtedly salutary. Ignoring the situation in which the mother's employment and the child's placement in the nursery are matters of economic necessity, the fact that nurseries allow employment of mothers who wish to utilize their training and abilities or to extend their social environment undoubtedly has some value. If this gives the mother some inner satisfaction it improves the family atmosphere and thus strengthens rather than weakens emotional relationships.

NURSERIES

In the 1960 Centre Internationale de l'Enfance (CIE) seminar in Paris a nursery was described as "a medical child-care establishment for healthy children of working mothers", a definition which was internationally approved.

The purposes, legal standing, material resources, and methods of operation of nurseries, however, differ greatly from country to country. Nurseries in socialist countries, and in France, Belgium, and Italy, meet the requirements implicit in the definition given above; children are admitted immediately after maternity leave, and stay there until three years of age. In Holland, the Scandinavian countries, England, and the U.S.A., nurseries have been established by private organizations, and function more as social agencies. In addition to children of working mothers, illegitimate children, children from disturbed families, neglected children, or children disadvantaged in other ways are admitted to nurseries, children who in Czechoslovakia would normally be admitted to baby or children's homes. Only in cases where a child is completely neglected is he committed to a permanent children's home, which is usually only a way station to adoption or to foster care.

Besides classical nurseries, there are the so-called family nurseries, mainly in Scandinavian countries, either in the form of a small shelter for five to seven children in a selected family, or the type providing specialist supervision in the family for the child who will not adjust to normal nurseries. A variant of this is the so-called daily foster care which is popular in Anglo-Saxon countries, and which subsequently is continued in kindergartens and in schools for non-adapting children (J. G. Howells and J. Layng, 1955). The extension of nursery care rather than institutional care is preferred in some countries (Holland and Scandinavia, especially Sweden), where special nurseries have been established for physically and mentally retarded children, for spastics, for deaf and blind children, and so on. Adequate treatment and educational care is encouraged in this way from an early age with the minimum of deprivation through long-term separation from the family.

In addition, from the psychological point of view, certain parents would probably prefer nurseries to institutions. In this respect, the experiences gained in the newly established daily nurseries in Prague which provide an intensive rehabilitation programme for spastic children are most encouraging. Parents of defective children often suffer feelings of guilt which are sometimes increased by separation from the child; even mentally defective children progress much better when the intimate emotional relationships with parents are preserved rather than destroyed. There is the further consideration, of course, that the cost of providing daily rather than permanent care would be lower.

Nurseries, like other collective-care facilities, were established to meet social and medical rather than psychological and child-care needs. Initially nurseries were largely protective in character. In other words, a child was placed in a nursery to protect him from the dangers of serious health and care neglect. The main concern was for children of working mothers and for children with very poor socio-economic backgrounds. Because of improvement in living standards, nurseries in Czechoslovakia now very rarely perform this function. However, this is still true in a number of developing countries where (according to the report of WHO experts in 1962) children are admitted to nurseries for the sole purpose of feeding them and keeping them clean and warm. In this connection it is interesting to note that this protective function has to some extent directed certain new types of nurseries established in highly developed countries (e.g. in the U.S.A.) to aid children from social groups in which attitudes of indolence, anti-social behaviour, negative attitudes towards education, and so on persist through a number of generations because of the very low cultural level of the parents.

At the present time, when female employment is very widespread, nurseries have mainly a supportive role. They permit society to utilize the working potential of women, and additionally, allow women to obtain the advantages which employment brings. From the social point of view, nurseries are obviously very useful institutions. We must be sure, however, that they do not severely disadvantage children, an outcome which would negate their social value. We shall deal with this problem later.

Some experts consider that in addition to the supportive role of supplementing family care, nurseries offer children certain special developmental advantages which in themselves justify their existence, even if they did not directly meet any economic need. Before we can accept this view, however, we must establish firstly that the nurseries give a child experience of a sort which some families, because of their very nature, cannot offer, or which, where it is offered, has a negative rather than positive effect. We shall try to critically review all the pros and cons.

1. Supporters of the developmental role of nurseries maintain that nursery care can rectify certain negative child-rearing attitudes of parents.

Differences in child-rearing attitudes between parents and nursery supervisors have been reported in a number of studies. Thus for example, M. Nováková (1966) using the PARI method, compared forty-two housewives who did not have children in nurseries, forty-two working mothers whose children attended nurseries, and forty nursery supervisors. The three groups agreed that the child needs developmental stimuli appropriate to his age. The two groups of mothers, however, were more anxious (in their attitudes) and in addition were more authoritarian and less patient that the nursery supervisors (although the differences were not highly significant).

On the other hand it is very likely that changes in parental child-rearing attitudes can be produced outside nurseries by suitable instruction, expert advice, or even by planned psychotherapy. It is possible that under these conditions such changes would be more effective and permanent. There is the added consideration that the anxiety of some parents would be increased by separation from the child and that the authoritarian attitudes of other parents would be hardly changed by such separation.

2. Because of the present trend towards only children there is a possibility that a child today will grow up alone at home. Children's groups in nurseries, therefore, can offer substitute siblings.

Of course one might object that siblings play a different role in the family from children in nurseries, and that the family creates richer, more complex, and more differentiated social relationships than nurseries. The characteristic feature of the sibling relationships is permanence, which cannot be achieved in nurseries. In the family, the baby or young toddler usually has an older sibling, while in the nurseries all children are of the same age. It is obvious enough that an adult or even an older child understands the needs of a baby better than does another baby. For this reason there is a move towards experimenting with mixed age groups in nurseries, particularly in institutions in which nurseries are integrated with kindergartens (this is now a major development, particularly in the Soviet Union).

With pre-school or school age children, placement in a peer group can compensate for lack of siblings more efficiently.

3. Some workers (e.g. N. M. Aksarina, 1966), suggest that young children have a very important stimulus value for each other. One can observe a significant increase in alertness even in a baby of six to twelve months of age in the presence of another child of the same age, e.g. in a play pen.

While one would not quarrel with this statement, it is important to establish that this increase in stimulation of itself has certain specific (and positive) effects on the development of the child's personality. One can argue, of course, that adequate stimulation and alertness can be achieved in the family as well.

With older children it is clear that contact with peers has some specific value. We assume that loss or permanent denial of such contact is one element in psychological deprivation.

4. It is also argued that nursery care is more readily influenced

by new scientific findings, and because of this, is more professional and systematic.

One can accept that the results of pedagogical and psychological studies can be more readily implemented in nurseries than in families, so that in nurseries a child can learn certain skills which would not be available in the family, or at least not at the appropriate time. On the other hand, one cannot deny that this might be achieved by suitable instruction of parents and by improvement in social services. In any event, at baby and toddler age we are not yet concerned so much with the development of particular skills, but rather with establishing the basis for such development. From this point of view this argument would be valid only for older children.

We doubt that the pros are fully convincing. Arguments which are valid at upper age levels may not be valid when applied to younger children, where the psychological conditions are quite different.

However, while we would consider placement of a child under three years of age in a permanent care institution as dangerous, we would view his placement in a nursery as, at worst, demanding. Criticisms which have been recently levelled at nurseries, often as simple variations of criticisms of permanent institutions, are generally quite unwarranted. For the child in a nursery, the emotional bond with the mother and with the home is preserved, although of course it is strained to a degree, and is possibly impaired by the establishment of new relationships with the surrogate figures. Strictly speaking we are not concerned here with the danger of lack of maternal care or impoverishment in the input of critical stimuli. The situation most likely approximates that of intermittent or multiple mothering.

Because the relationships of a child in the nursery are richer and more varied than those of a child in a permanent institution, and because other environmental factors are also more complex and difficult to control, it is difficult to plan a research project which would adequately evaluate the results of nursery care. On the basis of investigations to this point in time, however, it is apparent that the development of children in daily nurseries does not differ basically from that of children growing up in families. We base this on nearly fifty years' experience of Soviet workers which shows that under optimal material, staffing, and organizational condition, very favourable outcomes can be achieved in children's development. N. M. Ščelovanov and N. M. Aksarina (1949) in deriving their developmental norms, have reported that in certain respects nursery children show developmental acceleration. More detailed comparative studies are not yet available.

The WHO report on nurseries (1965) describes the work of Professor B. Górnicki of Warsaw, who compared 500 children from families with 400 children from daily nurseries. Developmental differences were not significant, but a significantly higher incidence of infectious illness in nursery children was noticed.

In Czechoslovakia I. Pavlásková (1966) found no evidence of differences of physical and motor development between nursery children and children from families, except for a significant change in the weight curve as an immediate reaction to admission to a nursery. O. Meszárošová and M. Jurčová (1956) report that the mental development of their group of 186 children from daily nurseries approximates the Koch as well as the Ščelovanov norms, while children from weekly nurseries and toddler homes remain below these norms.

However, B. R. Arlt (1966) from the German Democratic Republic reports somewhat different findings. She compared physical and motor development of 726 babies from families, 208 babies from daily nurseries, and 100 babies from weekly nurseries and permanent institutions. In development of the ability to maintain an erect posture, using the Schmidt-Kolmer criteria, boys and girls from the nurseries occupied a position mid-way between the children from families, who developed more quickly, and those from permanent institutions who showed the most retarded development.

Nowadays children in nurseries are observed mainly by doctors and supervisors, less frequently by psychologists. This might explain why relatively so few studies have been concerned with development of play, speech, emotional expression, and social relationships, criteria which could possibly give some indication of the extent to which the mental development of a child being cared for in daily institutions is influenced by deprivational factors.

There is evidence from existing data concerning children in nurseries, mainly in socialist countries, that attention should be focused on two types of problem: (a) difficulties associated with adaptation to the new surroundings (basically separation difficulties), and (b) greater incidence of illness (morbidity).

Adaptation

The first problem has been carefully studied by Soviet paediatricians and psychologists (V. I. Dobrejcerova, A. A. Loginov, and others). They concluded that adjustment difficulties (loss of appetite, poor sleep, disruption of the weight curve, disturbed behaviour, emotional instability) in children after admission to nurseries are more severe in older babies, in spoiled, over-dependent children, and in those with poor physical health and unbalanced nervous processes. A. B. Nikolskaya (1960) studied children who showed particular emotional sensitivity to separation from the family. Some adapted after a few hours or days, some took weeks. Others — usually those who had been brought up solely amongst adults, and who had seldom left the family — had to be returned home. In addition, difficulties arose when children were transferred from nursery to kindergarten or from one department to another, in cases where the child had become attached to a particular nurse as he would to his mother, and where he had difficulty adapting to the different regime. Nikolskaya, therefore, stressed the importance of a planned transfer from situation to situation and of integration of all levels into one system of child care. Each transfer should be adequately prepared for; the child should be gradually introduced — initially only for a short period — into the new social and physical environment. She particularly emphasized the integration of nurseries and kindergartens. In this way a system of gradual separation can be established, similar to the system certain workers (e.g. D. Burlingham and A. Freud, 1942) attempted to establish in England during the war, though using somewhat different methods.

In Czechoslovakia, M. Mečíř (1959) studied adjustment difficulties in children immediately following admission to daily nurseries. He found that of thirty-two children admitted, fifteen adjusted in fewer than four days, eleven in fewer than ten days, while six children required several weeks to adjust. Even after a year, however, one child remained unadjusted. Clearly great individual differences are shown by children in their adaptability to such situations. Children younger than six months adapted more quickly. Adaptive disorders were shown in loss of appetite, sleep disturbances, distortion of the weight curve, emotional and behavioural disturbances. Mečíř also recommends some form of gradual separation; the child should be admitted some time before the mother begins employment, so that he can come to the nursery on the first few days for a short period of time.

M. Nováková (1959), who studied the behaviour of 1,030 children in forty-three day nurseries in the Middle Czech county, reports that 5.72 per cent of the children showed long-term, severe behavioural disorders often connected with adaptive difficulties (fear, passivity, inhibition, or psycho-motor restlessness, defiance, negativism). She cites cases of children who up to the time of admission had shown no behavioural abnormalities, but afterwards cried for hours at a time, refused to eat, and even after a year's stay in the nursery still showed difficulty.

I. Pavlásková (1966) investigated eighty-two children with normal pre-natal history admitted as babies into one daily nursery in Prague which had a very high standard of total care. Adaptive reactions to environmental change or separation from families were evident in all children, although not of the same severity. In some cases there were mood changes, frequent crying, marked restlessness, and in others, apathy and lack of interest. For some time it was impossible to elicit the smiling or cooing response. With some children there were obvious, gross sleep disorders, loss of appetite, vomiting. At the same time somatic symptoms − loss of weight or at least plateaus in weight-increase curves − were recorded. The author suggests that the first illness, which did not appear to be related to time of year or to the epidemic situation in the nurseries, was due to a certain extent to the child's adaptive reaction to the new conditions. The best adjustment was shown by children between three and six months of age on admission and poorest adjustment by those admitted between nine and twelve months of age. Sixty per cent of the latter were ill during the first week. Variation in the weight curve, however, took longer to adjust with children from the youngest group. Nevertheless, after their adjustment, weight appeared to be above average for the child population of Prague.

It is obvious that adaptive difficulties are greater in weekly institutions which create a more severe disturbance to the relationship between the child and the mother.

Bowlby's co-worker C. M. Heinicke (1956), in comparing groups of children from daily and weekly nurseries after three weeks' stay, noted a number of important differences. The efforts of children in weekly nurseries to gain contact with their parents were frantic and direct, similar to those they make to achieve positive relations with the nursing personnel. At the same time they showed stronger rejection of their parents when they were visited in the nursery and were negativistic towards the demands of the supervisors. More frequent aggression, autoerotic activities, and neglect of bodily cleanliness were also observed in these children. They often were more subject to common infections.[5]

---

5. A subsequent interesting study on "brief separation" has been reported by C. M. Heinicke and I. I. Westheimer (1965).

E. Schmidt-Kolmer (1966) describes loss of weight, behaviour disorders, and developmental regression as characteristic symptoms, which are particularly obvious between six months and eighteen months of age. The author recommends that children not be admitted to weekly nurseries at all during this period. From her earlier work it is obvious that children in weekly nurseries show greater developmental retardation, and that their environment resembles more a permanent institution than a daily nursery.

In Czechoslovakia, O. Meszárošová and M. Jurčová (1956), who studied children from daily and weekly nurseries and from toddler homes, report no significant developmental differences during the first year (judged by the Koch and Ščelovanov norms). Nevertheless in the second year differences in speech development between children from daily and weekly nurseries begin to be statistically significant.

Morbidity

L. Šamánková (1968) studied susceptibility to illness in a group of 100 children in three daily nurseries in Prague over a period of three years. The children averaged five illnesses per year, each of which lasted approximately ten days. Seventy per cent of the children were ill during the first three weeks and 94 per cent in the first three months. The illnesses were usually respiratory. The presence of adenovirus antibodies was shown in 6 per cent of the children admitted; during their stay the figure rose to 93 per cent. K. Kubát and A. Syrovátka (1966) reported two or three times the frequency of illness in a group of 609 children in daily nurseries compared with a control group of children from families. Hospitalization was also three times higher with nursery children. Nevertheless, physical development was not seriously disturbed, so that on the average nursery children did as well as children from families. The authors suggest that this is due to increased care in nurseries, but they direct our attention to common respiratory illnesses, and particularly to spastic bronchitis, which has a much higher incidence in children from nurseries than in children from families.

I. Pavlásková (1966) investigated the illnesses of 126 children admitted to nurseries as babies or toddlers. The most frequent illness occurred in children admitted between nine and eighteen months of age. These children also showed the most unfavourable reaction to the nursery environment. The youngest group of children admitted — between three and nine months — recorded the lowest incidence of illness. This group, however, when compared with family children, had a strikingly higher incidence of illness.

E. Pomerska (1966) studied 200 children from families of approximately the same socio-economic background, half of whom remained at home and the other half attended nurseries in Warsaw during the years 1960 to 1962. The incidence of infectious illness was 68.2 per cent in the nursery group as against 19.3 per cent in children in families. But when digestive illnesses were compared, nursery children held a slight advantage — 20.3 per cent against 24.5 per cent in the children from families.

In this general context, we should also consider the additional problem of the psychological meaning of the child's illness for the parent and for family life, particularly in cases where the mother, because of her employment, has not enough time for the children.

KINDERGARTENS

Kindergartens even today can have the same protective function as nurseries in the case of children from problem families (e.g. gipsy children) who must be safeguarded from the unfavourable effects of their social environment.

Like nurseries, kindergartens play a supportive role for children of working mothers. As distinct from nurseries, however, in kindergartens the educational role supersedes the supportive role, so that kindergartens have developmental significance. Contact with peers for a certain period of the day allows a child to satisfy his needs for social contact which are developing at this age. The kindergarten is the natural environment in which new social roles are developed, and where a child develops certain skills and is prepared for school. The arguments advanced for the developmental importance of nurseries (see page 97) are generally valid for kindergartens, but only for kindergartens.

Therefore, the usual type of kindergarten cannot be viewed as dangerous from a deprivational point of view — even the term "demanding" is applicable to only a small number of children, who on admission to kindergartens are developmentally immature, neglected or "sensitized" by previous experience in a permanent care institution.

During the pre-school period, of course, the amount of time spent outside the family is still a very important factor. If, for example, daily care is replaced by weekly care, all the advantages noted are overshadowed by the demands created by long-term separation from the family and by the long-term stress of institutional life. Repeated contact for certain periods of time with critical stimuli, which is very important for learning, is replaced under weekly care by monotonous stimulation which will limit developmental and learning progress. Weekly kindergartens, like weekly nurseries, in many respects resemble permanent institutions.

E. Vančurová (1962) in a careful study of children in a weekly kindergarten reports a significantly higher frequency of negative emotional responses, particularly at the beginning of the week (after the children return from home) and again at the end of the week when the children are waiting to go home. Aggressive and autoerotic behaviour, psycho-motor restlessness, and tearfulness are significantly more frequent. Negative responses during the week appear to be inhibited; in addition, the emotional behaviour of these children, when compared with the average, is generally very flat. In a subsequent study (1966) Vančurová compared paintings of groups of children from daily and weekly kindergartens. Differences were particularly marked when children were instructed to draw "how the home looks when we are all together". Children from daily kindergarten generally drew themselves surrounded by the family, or at least in the company of one family member. The children from weekly kindergartens, however, tended to draw only themselves without the family, the family without them, or both the family and themselves, but separated, possibly with a puppy. In this way they expressed their alienation from the family. Detailed analysis of the drawings showed that they reflected the real situation, since family relations in these cases were clearly not harmonious, and even during the rare visits of the children to the home on Sundays — which they valued highly — they did not spend much time with their parents.

SCHOOLS AND BOARDING SCHOOLS

Schools, as educational agencies, do not usually threaten deprivation. On the contrary, it would be severely depriving if a normally gifted child did not attend school, since he would be denied the opportunity to meet his peers, and participate in activity which is an integral part of school life. From a developmental point of view, we do not even regard boarding schools for older children as dangerous. The threat of persisting deprivation develops, of course, in cases where the child has already suffered deprivation at previous developmental stages, either through family neglect or through experience of permanent institutions. Behavioural disorders most frequently occur in school age children and in adolescents where the home either cannot offer, or where it ceases to be a source of, emotional security for the child. In such cases, belonging to a group is viewed by the child as compensating for unrealized intimate emotional relationships, and tends to produce extravagant, demonstrative, violent responses.

Nevertheless, under certain circumstances the school environment itself can be a source of deprivation. This is usually due to the personality of the teacher, especially when he ignores the emotional and social needs of the children and fails to provide adequate opportunity for successful achievement. In addition, the educational system as such can place obstacles in the path of healthy child development by its rigid adherence to teaching methods and to a particular disciplinary system.

The situation in schools offering whole-day care, where the child often spends a number of hours in the same room with the same children under the control of the one teacher, and subsequently under the control of a supervisor, is somewhat different. Here we are concerned mainly with stimulus monotony and total stimulus overload; it is impossible to fully satisfy the special interests of individual children or their individual needs for motor activity, for intimacy, quiet, or rest. It is generally agreed that here not only problems in the children's behaviour are accumulating, but also problems in the relationships of the child with the parents and of parents with the child.

In this area, however, no more detailed information is yet available.

HOSPITALIZATION

The data reported by Spitz, Bowlby, Aubry, and others have been widely published and accepted. The conference of paediatricians, psychologists, child psychiatrists, and social workers held in Stockholm in 1954, under the auspices of WHO, reached the almost unanimous conclusion that hospitalization of a child, which is the most frequent situation in which long-term separation of a child from the family occurs, can pose a threat to mental health (A. Wallgren, 1955; H. Harbauer, 1955). Based on available evidence, certain preventive measures were recommended: the avoidance of hospitalization if possible, the admission of the mother with the small child, daily visiting, and a radical modification and humanization of the overall regime and environment of hospitals.

During the following period, although these recommendations were generally accepted, the dramatic emphasis placed on the reported findings was viewed more soberly. Previous attitudes and opinions, and practice based on these, were modified in a number of ways. Thus M. Schmaderer (1956), for example, noted that nearly all children admitted to a clinic initially showed a period of protest or primary despair (in J. Robertson's sense), but that most of the children adapted to the new environment after a certain time. She maintained that this adaptation is positive, not merely a denial of the child's longing for mother, or suppression of his feelings of distress (as suggested by Robertson), since young children are incapable of deception. There is no evidence of permanent damage. On the contrary, separation may sometimes have a positive developmental value. Schmaderer also noted the second protest reaction which occurs after release from hospital. According to her, both forms of protest are reactions against any change from the known environment rather than reactions to separation from the loved person. Unfortunately, however, her conclusions lack more detailed description and support from actual case material.

Schmaderer's criticism of the concept of "denial", although certainly justified, is based partly on a misunderstanding. The mechanisms involved in the presumed reactions are obviously more primitive than conscious deception, and nobody equates them with simulation. Of greater importance, however, is that she takes the extreme and unrealistic opposite view, in that she denies the possibility of permanent damage through hospitalization. On this point we would comment that although her work (and our own at times) suggests that separation can have therapeutic value for a disturbed child, this does not mean that healthy children will not suffer damage through hospitalization. The same applies to the findings of Ylppö et al. (1956) who found in fifty children under the age of seven years quick adaptation to new surroundings after the initial transitory reactions of irritability and tension (symptoms of tachycardia and hypertension).

Other more critical studies employing more systematic observation and evaluation of reactions and their results, however, to a certain extent support the original assumption, but do not justify the view that such reactions are always very intense, nor that these reactions develop with predictable regularity.

G. A. Harnack and M. Oberschelp (1957), in a study of 140 children admitted to hospital, report strong protest or rejecting behaviour in 74 per cent of toddlers, in 59 per cent of pre-school age children, and in 25 per cent of school age children. Only 10 per cent of the children, however, completely failed to adapt during the whole period of hospital stay. These were primarily children with an unfavourable child-rearing background (spoiled children, children from broken homes, and so on). Nearly 50 per cent of babies and toddlers and nearly 33 per cent of pre-school children experienced difficulty in adapting after returning home; many of them showed extreme anxiety about the possibility of another separation and desperately clung to their mothers, whom they refused to leave for a moment. They also exhibited sleep disorders, loss of appetite, lack of personal hygiene, and certain behaviour disorders. About 55 per cent of toddlers deteriorated in their behaviour and only 7.5 per cent improved (the rest were unchanged).

J. Ströder and E. Geisler (1957) also report frequent occurrence of initial protest reaction (screaming, crying, motor restlessness) and less frequently negativism and the more severe depressive states, which may continue after discharge from hospital. They maintain, however, that a child has a natural capacity to adapt to social life, particularly when this is facilitated by the environment. A blanket refusal to hospitalize children where there is an adequate medical reason (or where investigation is required) is wrong. P. Bertoye (1957) comes to essentially the same conclusions in his study of the behaviour of 1,219 hypotrophic babies and toddlers hospitalized in a Red Cross sanatorium near Lyon.

Adaptation, of course, is most difficult for small children. Bowlby maintains that the most sensitive period is from one and a half to two years of age, and Ylppö that it is from two and a half to three and a half years of age. L. Hausam and H. Spiess (1958), from their study of 140 children, consider the critical period to be between one and two years. The time taken to adapt or get used to the children's ward, therefore, will depend primarily on the age of the child. The small child is emotionally and intellectually unprepared for the traumatizing experience of hospitalization (E. B. Nordlund, *"fehlende Krankenhausreife"*, lack of hospital "readiness"). (Fig. 9.)

In this connection the question of the traumatizing effects of hospitalization on the smallest children arises — that is, on babies up to six months of age. There is no unanimity on this matter in the literature. While Bowlby regards the child of less than six months of age as still relatively insensitive to separation, others have recorded significant separation and deprivation reactions. For example, the

Bakwins (1960) describe in detail several cases of children of only a few weeks of age who developed severe disorders during hospitalization which quickly disappeared after they had returned home. They describe the main symptoms of separation reaction in young babies as apathy, loss of weight, paleness, lack of motion, lack of cooing, poor sleep, lack of appetite, diarrhea, and a tendency to febrile episodes which apparently have no organic basis.

Similarly, A. Nitschke (1955) describes as "hopelessness" a separation reaction following loss of the family, which represents for a child of this age the basis of security. In such circumstances, babies from two to six months of age are fearful, enfeebled, talking fails to calm them, they are pale, with sunken eyes as if exhausted, they often refuse food or vomit, they have diarrhea, and show a rapid, inexplicable rise in temperature. Nitschke observed this type of reaction not only after admission to hospital, but also after return home, particularly where the children have become attached to some devoted sister who for them, together with the hospital environment, represented "home". (M. Damborská [1957a, 1961] also reports separation reactions in babies of two to six months of age.) With older babies and toddlers, separation disorders approximate the known types of violent, nostalgic reaction, combined with crying, screaming for mother, and possibly aggression and refusal of any attempt to make contact. After the initial violent reaction has ceased, the child either adapts (if there are favourable conditions, primarily if a mother surrogate is available) or gradually sinks into apathy and helplessness (*"Leben ohne Hoffnung"*). In the latter case there is very pronounced dejection and lack of movement from the child, who no longer plays or participates in any activity. Subsequently he does not even cry, becomes dystrophic, is subject to infection — "life is fading through sheer emptiness". A similar but more dramatic picture is presented by children from institutions who lack a home with a loving figure from the very beginning ("homelessness").

Very careful and systematic observations of the reactions of hospitalized babies are reported by H. R. Schaffer and W. M. Callender (1959), who studied the reactions of seventy-six children aged from one to twelve months during a period of hospitalization (average a fortnight) and after their return home. They report that in children over seven months of age the classic picture of separation emerged, with the initial protest, negativism towards staff, with periods of submission to and rejection of the environment, and a period of gradual re-adaptation after return home, when the child showed uncertainty and extreme dependence on the mother. On the other hand, separation does not cause any protest in babies younger than seven months of age; a stranger is accepted readily as a mother surrogate, the level of reaction is not significantly altered, and the child adapts very well even to a radical change in routine. The only behavioural change is reduced cooing (they failed to observe the other symptoms noted by the Bakwins). When the children returned home there was a clear, dramatic, very short-term reaction (twenty minutes to four days); the children carefully observed their surroundings, did not concentrate on anything in particular, and seemed to be so deeply involved in this activity that it was impossible to interest them in toys or in social contact. This global response is described by the authors as a reaction to the perceptual monotony of the hospital environment.

On the basis of his observations, Schaffer considers that the separation reaction develops initially after seven months of age, that it occurs relatively quickly and at full strength, and persists at the same level of intensity during the following months. He considers this to be in line with the perceptual and cognitive development of the child, who around seven months of age begins to establish real relationships with certain persons (mother). He maintains that the severe symptoms described by Spitz and the Bakwins are probably not typical under present-day hospital conditions. Where it is possible to select the age of hospitalization (e.g. for surgery or for treatment of some congenital anomaly), it is recommended that this be done before seven months of age. (Figs. 10 and 11.)

In Czechoslovakia, M. Tautermannová (1961) studied the behaviour of forty-four children in the age range three to six years who were admitted to the inpatient ward of the children's hospital. She observed initial protest reactions in some children which developed into an inhibition phase; 43 per cent of children adapted quickly (they played, and within three days established contact), while a similar number of children adapted slowly (over a period of weeks or longer). Our data from 232 children observed continuously over a period of three days (J. Langmeier, 1959) showed disturbances in different autonomic functions and sleep disorders due to hospitalization. The most severe disorders of this type were noted with babies and toddlers. Concerning effects persisting after the return home, A. Mores and J. Vyhnálek (1957) observed negative reactions mainly with toddlers, while with older children they report more positive reactions (improvement in development and behaviour).

Separation reactions in a "humanized" hospital system

The fact that the original studies reported more severe reactions than later studies did indicates that changes in hospital regimes can lead to very marked improvements. Those conditions which encourage easier and quicker adaptation of a child are of course extremely varied (L. Srp, 1961), but in this context we are concerned primarily with those variables which involve the child's relationships with parents or with surrogate figures.

From a practical point of view the question of visits is very important, since we think that these help to maintain a close bond between the child and the mother. It is obvious, however, that children are usually more disturbed after such visits. R. S. Illingworth and K. S. Holt (1955) report that 86 per cent of children aged from one to two years, 70.5 per cent of children aged from five to six years, and 39.3 per cent of children in the age range seven to nine years are disturbed by a visit. Older children soon adapt to visits, but with younger children the disturbance persists for a much longer time. M. Schmaderer (1956) cites this in support of her argument against increasing visits; on the other hand, Illingworth and Holt maintain that it is justifiable to do everything possible to maintain the mother-child bond even if this results in disturbances. This is preferable to a child's suffering all the time, and coming to the conclusion that his parents have deserted him.

A careful study of the effects of a "humanized" hospital environment is reported by D. G. Prugh et al. (1953). They compared fifty children in an experimental group (the parents helped the child during the initial difficulties in adapting to the hospital, they cared for him, played with him) with a control group of fifty children subjected to normal hospital routine with a visit once a week. The authors concluded that in the experimental group the frequency of reactions is roughly what might be expected on the basis of the child's previous adaptation, while in the control group the frequency of reactions is significantly higher (see table 11).

The psychological value of more humanized treatment is quite obvious. We must remember, of course, that the disorders observed during the period of hospitalization can be influenced to an unknown degree by a number of other factors — being confined to bed, the type of illness and treatment, the unfamiliar routine, and the completely new environment, for example. In addition, we should also consider the resources of the individual child (we observed, for example, the quick adaptation of a child whose mother worked as a

Table 11. Reactions to hospitalization in two groups of children

Control Group			Experimental Group		
Adaptation before Hospital- ization %	Direct Reaction to Hospital- ization %	Reaction after 3 Months %	Adaptation before Hospital- ization %	Direct Reaction to Hospital- ization %	Reaction after 3 Months %
Excellent 56	Minimal 8		Excellent 34	Minimal 32	
Moderate 42	Moderate 56	} 58	Moderate 54	Moderate 57	} 44
Poor 2	Marked 36		Poor 12	Marked 14	

sister in the hospital, and who was with him frequently). It would be interesting to compare the reactions of children who are transferred to a strange environment with the mother with those of children who remain in the known environment from which the mother is withdrawn. Systematic studies of this type, however, are still rare (M. Damborská).

RAISING OF CHILDREN IN THE KIBBUTZ

A special case of partial collective care is child-rearing practices in the kibbutz. This is an important ideological influence in Israel, although the number of kibbutz members does not exceed 4 per cent of the total population. The kibbutz is a self-supporting, productive, ideological community based partly on Jewish religious tradition, and founded partly as a protest against the traditional patriarchal nature of the Jewish family. For these reasons the kibbutz movement created a special type of collective care extending from birth to eighteen years of age; the most clearly comparable system is that of weekly nurseries, weekly kindergartens, boarding schools, and trainee institutes. From a psychological point of view, kibbutz child rearing resembles closely the model of intermittent mothering. Children live in homes separate from their parents. The main child-care responsibility is carried by the educator — the metapelet — who has sole charge of a group of children. During the weaning period the group usually numbers four to eight, but as the child grows up, he progressively enters newer, larger groups of children, always with a new metapelet. Thus the surrogate mother changes periodically, and the child is forced to adapt a number of times during childhood to the personality of the new metapelet and to the new peer groups. The relations of a child to his peers are reinforced and developmentally utilized. In adolescence the groups sometimes do not live in the parental kibbutz.

Since this system of child care has been employed for more than forty years, and since, as we will show later, results can be regarded as favourable, the attention of psychologists and educationists has increasingly focused on this type of care (for example, Caplan, Glaser, Woolf, Golan, Rabin, Rapaport, Kaffman, Kraft). Bowlby's critics often cite the kibbutz as evidence that frequent separation of a child from his family does not necessarily have harmful effects. Advocates of collective care use evidence from the kibbutz to support their case for the expansion of child-care agencies from early childhood, outside the family and in other social contexts. For this reason, we shall mention a number of factors which might more clearly explain the position of a child in a kibbutz.

The whole kibbutz movement is essentially child centred. This means that the child's well-being, the satisfaction of his needs, and his proper development are matters of the utmost concern to the whole community. This objective of a happy childhood ranks equal in importance with other goals of the kibbutz movement, goals such as love of country, respect for work, and cooperation with neighbours. Personal relations in the kibbutz are very open and the community as a whole has a special, intimate character. The metapalet is very carefully selected; at the same time, however, she is given considerable supervisory freedom. Her activity is controlled by the group and not by individual parents. The metapelets are trained for their jobs through special courses after which they complete a year's practicum under the guidance of an experienced metapelet. The relationship of the metapelet to parents and her cooperation with them is a very important aspect of this training.

Until the child is one year old, the mother is responsible for his feeding and most of his care. At that point an increasing amount of the responsibility for the child is transferred to the metapelet. The child usually spends Saturdays, holidays, and evening hours with his own family. In addition to this, the parents visit the child whenever working hours permit, and since the parents work and the children live in the same locale, there are few serious obstacles to daily contact. Fathers in the kibbutz, for example, spend on the average more time with their children than most fathers in Western industrial society. The emotional bond with the family is as strong as that in families outside the kibbutz, and this bond possibly is the consolidating and integrating factor which helps a child to adjust to the changing surrogate figures. The metapelet willingly undertakes the unpleasant tasks of encouraging the child to develop hygienic and social habits, and she disciplines and teaches him. To the child, the parents remain loving, patient, and kindly persons.

This situation of course is very different from that usually found in institutions, resembling rather a large family with somewhat special role differentiation.

During the toddler period, however, when a child has very strong emotional needs, it is noticeable that kibbutz children show a certain developmental retardation when compared with children from families (A. I. Rabin, 1958). This lag is fully retrieved later on, and from nine to eleven years of age children from the kibbutz outstrip children from farm families living outside the kibbutz. K. Glaser (see K. Glaser and L. Eisenberg, 1956) also reports retardation in the toddler period and some characteristics resembling those of the institutionalized child in children of five to seven years of age, but subsequently full recovery and healthy adaptation in adolescence and adulthood.

A. I. Rabin (1965) studied the development of kibbutz children in a cross-sectional study comparing 177 kibbutz children with 121 control children from families living outside the kibbutz; the children were compared during the toddler period, at ten years of age, at late adolescence, and in early adulthood. He again reports that the temporary retardation is compensated for by school age. There were no significant differences between the groups in developmental level nor in the incidence of psychopathological symptoms. The same findings were also reported by M. Kaffman (1963), using data from the Institute of Mental Hygiene in Oranim, which provides psychiatric services for nearly all members of kibbutzim. Thumb sucking is more frequent and more prolonged in kibbutz children, due to the permissive attitudes of the metapelets; enuresis is about as frequent as in the Israeli child population; school phobias are practically non-existent and truancy occurs only rarely — in children with minimal brain dysfunction or as an initial symptom of psychotic onset. The majority of emotional difficulties occur where a conflict between the metapelet and the parent exists, where parents are unable to adjust to the necessity of sharing the care of the child with some other person.

G. Caplan (1953) reported that the young people in the kibbutz are stable, well-adjusted, cooperative, without envy and aggression, delinquency, or sexual deviation. The number of neurotic individuals is very small. M. E. Spiro (1965) describes young men from the kibbutz as shy with strangers and withdrawn in the presence of adults. Some workers have described young people in the kibbutz as arrogant, and others again emphasize that in some cases there is excessive individualism. From most reports, however, it seems that the child-care system in the kibbutz generates attitudes and character traits which facilitate group life in young people. Thus, for example, a significantly larger number of children from the kibbutz, compared with the population at large, assert themselves in the army during compulsory military service. Nevertheless, a number of authors consider that during a time of greater uncertainty and individual responsibility outside the protection of the group, their stability may turn out to be illusory.

Early socialization of a child obviously encourages the establishment of strong group solidarity and group control of individual behaviour. This has been shown in a study by H. Faigin (1958). Children very early use such expressions as "we" and "ours", and competition occurs more between than within groups. A. I. Rabin (1965) reports that in the kibbutz sibling rivalry is less frequent. A. W. Moran (1965) reports a surprising degree of mutual help and cooperation amongst these children. Older children accept greater responsibility for younger children in the group than children in urban society.

Kibbutzim, of course, are not uniform in their organization; they differ markedly in their ideological bases, type of work, in the amount of contact with the surrounding environment, and of course in child-rearing practices. From our point of view a particularly interesting development is the tendency described as "familializing". This occurs in some kibbutzim when parents take children home for the night and attempt to have greater, more direct influence on their upbringing. Kibbutz ideologists oppose this, since in it they see an erosion of the mothers' emancipation and a return to the traditional source of inner maternal satisfaction which is encouraged by the care of their own children. The stability of the kibbutz movement, however, is reflected in the fact that 90 per cent of children raised in kibbutzim decide at maturity to stay in the community, and are not enticed by the better opportunities for education, income, and status in the wider society.

In summary it can be said that the most important finding from recent studies is that the differences between children raised under the special conditions of the kibbutz and children raised outside these conditions are ultimately very small and in most cases almost undetectable. We quote the opinion of Ivor Kraft (1966) which we generally support: "If a child is brought up in a human and stable environment, infused with love, tenderness and respect for work and enlightened moral standards, then the basic product will be unspectacular but sound, irrespective of even major differences in child-rearing methods".

DEPRIVATION IN THE FAMILY

Following the early studies in institutional deprivation, the attention of investigators focused more and more on those environments in which deprivation is less obvious, and where it often merges with other negative factors. This is, of course, no less real and dangerous, although from a methodological point of view, more difficult to investigate. The most important situation of this kind is the family.

Evidence that institutionalized care and separation from the family frequently produced serious damage to the child's development led to some extravagant conclusions. Institutional care suddenly became the model of deprivating situations, while family care was considered to be the only reliable defence against such deprivation. This was expressed in the statement "better the worst family than the best institute". Some data comparing early development in institutes and in families, which we discussed earlier, seemed to support this conclusion. In studies of this kind, however, one is concerned with average values, and a great amount of individual variance is ignored, as well as a number of other factors which can influence results (for example, sample selection, since children who are most threatened in the family environment — children with doubtful heredity or congenital defects, feebleminded children, and so on — are more likely to be admitted to baby homes).

Clinical experience suggests that some children who grow up in very poor family environments face a threat not only to their development, but to their very lives. The practical approach to this problem in some countries where studies of psychological deprivation have made some impact has been to leave children in their bad family conditions, and to direct all social effort towards reforming the family, which was to be kept intact at all costs. Because family guidance was rarely adequate, children remained for a number of years in unsatisfactory environments. All clinical workers, however, can cite a number of cases where children from such environments, who were retarded in their physical and mental development, showed a surprising improvement after transfer to an institute. The question arises therefore of whether, and under what conditions, the child suffers in the family through lack of satisfaction of his basic psychological needs.

This problem is familiar to nearly all investigators who have critically evaluated Bowlby's original concept of maternal deprivation (see page 17). They have shown that conditions little different from those found in the institutional environment can exist in the family (for example, a large, fatherless family where the mother, who is employed outside the family, is overworked and exhausted), and that the child can experience maternal separation even though physically not separated from her (for example, because of her depressive illness or psychopathy).

Some workers — for example W. Goldfarb (1949) — maintain that the institutionalized child is threatened more by deprivation than by emotional conflicts, while for a child in a bad family the reverse is true. This opinion is probably shared by R. A. Spitz (1951), who, in dealing with the psychopathology of early childhood, differentiates between carence (deprivation) disorders caused by the actual absence of the mother and psychotoxic disorders created by unhealthy child-mother relationships — for example, where the child is overwhelmed by over-solicitude, by hostility masked by fear, by sudden or prolonged variations in mood, and so on. Bowlby does not express himself very clearly on this matter, since in his monograph he deals primarily with total deprivation, i.e. where the child is completely separated from his parents and placed in an institute. Other authors (Congress of Child Psychiatry, Toronto, 1955), however, correctly point out that the physical presence of the mother is of little consequence if the child is left alone, faced with four bare walls. This, in fact, is real isolation. Again, other workers — for example, R. V. Coleman (1957) — stress the essential similarity, clinically speaking, between some children from neglected families and those in hospitals, and refer to family hospitalism. H. Lewis (1954), the Clarkes (1960), G. Bollea (1958), J. Robertson (1962), D. G. Prugh (1953), H. F. Harlow (1962), and others have broadened the concept of deprivation to include the family situation. They maintain that some family conditions can be more harmful for child development than permanent institutional care. These authors, however, often do not differentiate between real deprivation, as we understand it, and other harmful environmental influences.

M. D. Ainsworth (1962) suggests that in order to avoid further confusion we should distinguish between real deprivation, caused by the inadequacy of the child-mother interaction, and disorders caused either by distortion or termination of this relationship.

From our observations we would suggest that such distinctions are usually rather difficult to make, and that in certain families we can find at one and the same time inadequate stimulus input, distorted relationships, and frequent separation. It is not easy, therefore, to determine which are primary and which secondary causes, which factor is critical and which produces only side effects.

In addition, we should not forget that deprivation in the family often precedes or follows deprivation in institutes. Further, the emotional situation for the child in the family is usually more complicated than that for a child in an institution: parental attitudes, even under unfavourable conditions, are usually more intense, more firmly based, and more discriminating than those of supervisors in institutions. Nevertheless we feel justified in attempting to identify those situations which most likely underlie lack of satisfaction of basic needs, i.e. deprivation of the child in the family context. We can make a twofold classification.

There is, firstly, the simple lack of social-emotional stimuli needed for the healthy development of the child, which may be due to external factors. Examples of this would be incomplete families (mother or father is absent), families where parents spend most of the day away from the home, or families in which the economic or cultural level is so low that the child is denied developmental stimulation.

The second category involves those cases where the necessary stimuli do in fact exist in the family, but are not available to the child because of an internal psychological barrier which has been created in the parents' relationship with the child. This prevents satisfaction of needs even though such satisfactions are physically attainable. This occurs in intact families which are often socially and culturally advanced, but where the mother, the father, or others involved in child care do not emotionally participate or develop relationships with the child, but ignore and rarely nurse the child and handle him only mechanically.

As we stated earlier these categories frequently overlap, e.g. the mother, because of the nature of her employment, may have no time to establish a relationship with the child. She devotes all her interest to her job, and fails to use the limited time available to become involved with him. Another case is that of the illegitimate child who not only lacks a father but often suffers from the rejecting attitude of the mother, who projects onto the child her feelings of disappointment and bitterness arising from her socially difficult situation.

There is some utility, however, in maintaining a distinction between these classifications. The effects of the first type of situation are usually superficial, and re-adaptation is easier than in those situations in which deprivation is due to a serious psychological disturbance in the personalities of those involved in child care. We consider that a differentiation of this sort is psychologically more meaningful than that suggested by the Clarkes (1960) who take a more legalistic approach of differentiating criminal neglect or cruelty and unfavourable child-rearing practices within the limits of social acceptance. What is lawful and socially acceptable, however, can be psychologically disastrous. The amount of psychological damage is not always dictated by social norms. In some clearly criminal cases the damage can be surprisingly small when compared with the poor prognosis in severe cases of emotionally deprived children with socially excellent backgrounds.

Deprivation in the family from external causes

Family structure

In present-day society the family is of critical importance in the psychological development of the child. Every member of the family naturally and spontaneously plays a particular role, and in so doing fully satisfies the vital physical, emotional, intellectual, and moral needs of the child. In normal circumstances the critical person is initially the mother, who not only nurses the child, but also first supplies him with strong emotional stimuli when she cuddles him, plays with him, pets him, laughs at him, speaks to him. The role of the father as a behaviour model and as a source of security and authority increases as the child grows older, but even in the pre-school period his influence is quite marked. The role of siblings, of course, should not be overlooked. The overall family atmosphere, which strongly influences the developing child's personality, is obviously determined by the permanent, intimate interaction between all family members. Thus, there is a danger of deprivation if one of the critical figures is absent from a very early age, for it is not always possible to substitute a figure who would play the same role towards the child and towards the whole family. The time and duration (from birth or later on and whether temporary or permanent) and the cause of such absences (because the child is illegitimate, through death, military service, or divorce) determine the effects of these deprivating conditions and the accompanying conflicts, and help to create the final clinical picture.

Results from a number of retrospective studies, which disclose a high incidence of children from incomplete families in groups examined and treated for different psychiatric disorders, highlight the importance of family breakdown in the occurrence of deprivation disorders. I. Gregory (1958) critically analyzed data from a number of representative studies in the preceding twenty-five years of the relationship between psychiatric disorders and early parental deprivation. He concluded that a high percentage of people showing delinquent, anti-social, or psychopathic behaviour experienced parental deprivation or early separation from their parents for a variety of reasons. A number of studies show a higher percentage of loss or separation from one or both parents (especially in pre-school age) in groups of neurotics. A high percentage of cases where the mother was absent has also been noted in large groups of young psychotic patients (J. R. Hilgard and M. F. Newman, 1963*a, b*; J. Langmeier and D. Langmeierová, 1967).

We recorded the family backgrounds shown in table 12 in 309 children hospitalized in a child psychiatric ward (J. Langmeier, V. Konias, and M. Dolejší, 1957). Only 41 per cent of the children were raised by both parents from birth to the time of admission (ignoring temporary separation due to hospitalization). In our opinion, a particularly significant fact is that behaviour disorders and enuresis were more closely associated with disturbed family environment than other psychiatric disorders (neurosis, specific defects such as dyslexia): only 27 per cent of children with behaviour disorders (difficult children showing anti-social, undisciplined behaviour) and 31 per cent of enuretics lived in a complete family up to the time of admission, as against 51 per cent of children presenting other neurotic symptoms and 63 per cent of children with specific defects. These figures, as with all retrospective data, should be viewed with caution, as it is difficult to gauge the effect of selection factors (for example, non-parental authorities would demand examination for undisciplined behaviour, while the child's parents would likely be more aware of neurotic symptoms; enuretics treated in a paediatric department are a quite different sample from those treated in a child psychiatric department).

Nevertheless these data are important enough to arouse our

Table 12. Family backgrounds of 309 children in a child psychiatric ward

	%
Illegitimate children	4
Parents divorced or separated	11
One parent deceased	14
Both parents deceased	4
Children legally removed from family	10
Intact family	57

interest, especially since they are supported by observations from a number of independent sources. For example, G. Destunis (1957) has emphasized the role of partial family in the development of behaviour disorders, particularly the "without attachment" type of disorder (*Bindungslosigkeit*) with its typical triad of symptoms (wandering, lying, stealing), which basically is a product of the inadequate relationship between the child and parents and the child and society. G. Hesse (1957) reports in his sample that only 7 per cent of children with behaviour disorders of this type lived in a complete family. The type of incomplete family in this case was frequently the fatherless family (64 per cent of children). In our own data from residential schools for boys showing pre-delinquent or delinquent behaviour we recorded a somewhat higher percentage of children from complete families, but the figure (22 per cent) was still disturbingly low. At the same time, however, only 9 per cent of the families of these young delinquents could be regarded as "normal" judged on criteria of the mental development and health of the parents.

The absence of *the mother* poses the most serious threat to child development, especially in early age. On her depends not only physical care, but also the satisfaction of most psychological needs. She is the primary source of the child's relationship with other humans and of his security in the external environment, the person who creates the home for the child. In most cases where the mother is absent, a surrogate can be somehow provided. Many stepmothers are loving and attentive guardians, even though traditionally they have been unjustly condemned by public opinion. Many grandmothers, by their devotion, perform an important function, and many adoptive mothers are ideal mother surrogates. The motherless child today usually has adequate and sometimes a little too much care and love. Obviously in these contexts deprivating conditions are seldom encountered. In such families, however, it appears that conflicts arise more frequently than in natural complete families, since the interrelationships here are more complicated and tense. Actual deprivating conditions are most likely found in cases where the father copes without any outside help after the mother's death, but even here we found instances of completely adequate care.

Paternal deprivation is far more frequent though superficially less tragic. This involves a number of children living with their unmarried mothers or with mothers who are alone for a variety of reasons. Where the helping and stabilizing influence of the father is absent, the mother's personality obviously becomes more critical than it would be under normal conditions. Because in these situations there are many reasons for suspecting a higher percentage of less well-adjusted personalities, we should be aware of the increased threat from the multiplicity of negative factors.

A number of additional factors are also important. As everyday experience and sociological studies (e.g. by J. and E. Newson, 1965) have suggested, the father's role in the family is changing markedly and relatively quickly. The amount of cooperation in families between husband and wife would far surpass that of earlier times. In modern society — obviously not to a similar extent in all social classes — fathers are much more involved in caring for babies (changing, bathing, feeding, taking for walks). In the context of this type of social development, therefore, the absence of the father will produce much greater stress than previously, when all child-rearing responsibilities devolved on the mother. The physical effort and time involved (which is reduced by modern appliances) is less important than the psychological stress that the lone mother suffers when her role and status are compared with those of other females. The help offered these mothers in the communal houses is still not adequate. The male influence in child rearing is lacking, and the fact that mothers help one another in domestic duties and child rearing produces a type of intermittent mothering with all its difficulties and uncertainties.

More importantly, however, the child growing up without a father lacks the model of masculinity which is important in regulating behaviour, especially for an older boy. The child usually does not experience the authority, discipline, and order which the father normally represents, and is therefore usually more frequently undisciplined, anti-social, and aggressive towards adults and children (L. Michaux and H. Flavigny, 1958). Observation of 163 inmates of the residential schools for pre-delinquent and delinquent boys in the Middle Czech county in 1960—61 revealed that 41 per cent of these boys had been raised without fathers.

Of even greater importance can be lack of security and stable social status, for the father's employment is usually the real and symbolic basis of the economic status of the family. In addition the father's physical presence has overtones of security and protection. While the mother offers the child the experience of intimate human love, the father establishes the pathways to and the attitudes towards society. Mothering encourages receiving, and fathering, giving. Both are critical for the development of personality, both are indispensable ingredients if we are to approximate our human potential (A. Grans, 1970). Finally, for the child the father is also the most natural source of information about the world, and about the development of skills, the person who can help him in his orientation to his future job and in the development of socially desirable goals and ideals.

The absence of the father has a further inherent deprivating effect. If a mother is left alone to shoulder all the economic and family burdens she is usually so busy that there is little time left for the child, and her interest is weakened by economic stress. In these circumstances the child is left alone for most of the day unless some supervision is provided, he often begins very early to wander and to indulge in petty crimes and is easily led astray.

R. G. Andry (1962) reports no difference in the percentage of fatherless and motherless families in case histories when he compared groups of eighty delinquent and eighty non-delinquent boys. Amongst the delinquent boys, however, there was obviously a greater amount of tension in father-son relationships. Delinquent boys showed a greater fear of their fathers, but were less obedient and less prepared to accept the father's dominant role in the family. Fathers were usually aware of this problem but were unable to do anything about it.

As in other cases it is obvious that in addition to physical absence, the inadequate role of the father in the family can be an important factor in the anti-social behaviour of the child. Where the father's role is assumed by a surrogate father or possibly by a grandfather, the deprivation threat is again somewhat reduced. On the other hand, however, there is a greater probability of conflict of a different sort, and in such circumstances neurotic disorders very frequently develop.

The fatherless family today is aided in its child-rearing task by a number of child-care establishments; unfortunately however these are neither numerous enough nor do they always provide as appropriate care as we might expect. Sometimes, however, they are not fully utilized, for even if they cannot fully substitute for a father during the child's development, they can compensate for the lack of care and prevent the development of behavioural disorders which lack of guidance and supervision encourages. In addition they can help the mother so that she has more time for the child and thus derives more satisfaction from his development. In some cases it is even possible for the mother to raise her child rather than commit him to permanent institutional care.

Siblings are also part of the normal family structure. Their influence on the development of the child is not as profound as that of parents, but is still recognizable in some of the difficulties shown by children who lack the stimulation of sibling interactions (for example, an only child).

The older sibling from the very beginning participates in the social environment of the baby, he is a very lively element and provides a variety of stimuli which usually are very intense. Initially he strongly stimulates the sensory field and subsequently the affective and social environment. The younger child is of equal importance to the older sibling though presenting a somewhat different type of stimulation. He needs protection and help and this evokes a protective attitude in the older sibling. The opportunity of playing together, of sharing toys, sweets, and parental attention, of resolving petty daily quarrels, the competition and jealousy, amongst other things, encourage healthy child development and facilitate entry into society.

From this point of view, the trend towards only children which is evident in some countries with low birth rates is an important factor. Czechoslovakia is a good case in point. The birth rate, particularly in the older groups of parents, has significantly decreased by comparison with figures from the previous decade. This in fact means a reduction in the number of second and subsequent children (M. Kučera, 1969).

In 1950, 16.3 per cent of children were third and 16.1 per cent were fourth or later in the birth order; in 1967, however, both these categories together accounted for only 16.6 per cent. At the same time the percentage of first children in the child population increased from 36.9 per cent in 1950 to 49.8 per cent in 1967. Family planning surveys indicate that more and more people prior to marriage plan only one or at most two children. The problem remains urgent even if the trend has been evidently changed in the last few years.

In this context separation disorders (which subsequently can be deprivational) can occur in two completely opposite ways: (a) when the child gains a sibling, and (b) when he loses a sibling.

The first case seems to be somewhat paradoxical but can be properly included in the concept of separation. It can occur if the new child commands so much attention from the mother and other family members that suddenly the older child feels completely isolated, compared with his previous situation in which he was given the exclusive attention of his parents. M. Greenbaum (1962) describes

Table 13. Number of live births per 1,000 females in different age categories

Age	Means		
	1950–54	1960–64	1967
15–19	49.0	45.3	47.4
20–29	337.7	315.5	272.6
30–39	137.8	72.9	58.1
40–49	16.3	5.3	3.4

the syndrome of the displaced child, which most frequently occurs following the birth of another child, as one form of chronic separation anxiety.

A long-term separation reaction following the loss of a sibling is illustrated by the following clinical case.

Boy J.S. was five years old when his mother died. He was left in the care of the grandmother with his younger brother because the father deserted the family soon after the mother's death. After two years the grandmother started work, the younger brother was sent to a pre-school children's home and he himself to a school age children's home. During one home visit — as the boy himself describes it — he was told that "it has happened". The younger brother had been adopted by a family living a long way away. Immediately afterwards the boy began to run away from the home to his grandmother. He was transferred to a more distant children's home to prevent his absconding. The behaviour persisted, and he was sent to a more closely supervised institute from which he continued to escape. Eventually, however, he adapted to the home. His most vivid memory is of "his brother" whom he "loves more than anyone else" although the two of them are practically strangers.

The role of siblings is considerably enhanced by the loss of father or mother. The older sibling represents social support for the younger child and sometimes he assumes a parental role. Where both parents are absent the siblings represent some sort of life security for one another. It ought to be quite normal practice, therefore, that when siblings are institutionalized, they are placed in the same home.

In some cases gaps in the incomplete family can be successfully filled by increased care and attention from the remaining family members. This is probably why in a number of fatherless or motherless families, children develop quite normally, and why a number of only children also show healthy development. To a certain extent both the compensating forces and the conflict sources are determined by family circumstances; the situation is different for illegitimate children, for orphans, for children from divorced parents, and for children from families disrupted for other reasons.

The present position of both *illegitimate children* and *unmarried mothers* in the majority of countries has improved considerably, both legally and in terms of more accepting public attitudes. Nevertheless for an illegitimate child there is a higher risk of inadequate nursing and rearing. The reported data (for example by A. Braestrup, 1956) suggest that illegitimate children are more often premature, still-born, show a higher mortality rate and susceptibility to illness, have poorer school records, and show greater difficulty in social adaptation.

This finding, however, needs further investigation and support before it can be fully accepted. Nevertheless, even in socialist countries when there is no legal difference between illegitimate and other children, the former comprise a large percentage of admissions to baby institutes, so that they are more threatened by all the dangers which are encountered in such circumstances.

Following the abortion law in Czechoslovakia in 1958 there was a marked decrease in illegitimate births and subsequently a decrease in the number of illegitimate children in children's homes. In the toddler home in which we have been working since 1954, the percentage of illegitimate children is now below 30 per cent, whereas up to 1961 the figure was about 50 per cent.

Although the position of the unmarried mother has been greatly improved, there still remain a number of unresolved social, economic, employment, and accommodation problems. It appears that the homes for lone mothers with children provide suitable — even though only partial — help; here, in addition to kindergartens and nurseries, communal self-help amongst the mothers may be possible, and the professional advice of a social worker who is employed in this type of home is available. Such establishments are particularly effective for young mothers who have a history of anti-social behaviour or prostitution and whose personalities show the effects of psychological deprivation in early childhood.

Children of such mothers usually are most threatened by deprivation. Concentrated, individualized, directed help of a social, educational, and possibly also psychotherapeutic nature given in such homes may provide the opportunity to break the circle of deprivating and conflict situations without separating mother and child. Indeed, such treatment sometimes allows the mother to be socialized through the child.

Previously many unmarried mothers were forced by economic and social circumstances to give up their children immediately after birth. Today this occurs less frequently. Threat develops, however, from gradual loss of interest in the child. Motherhood without a husband creates a number of constraints and difficulties for a young woman; if she cannot cope with these she gradually turns away from the child who is the prime source of the difficulty.

S. Marzo-Weyl (1965b) studied in 1952 a group of fifty randomly selected unmarried mothers in a large baby institute close to Paris. She reports that thirty-nine of these mothers showed emotionally immature personalities, were infantile, unstable, and unbalanced, with a special need for protection, which forced them to form new unsatisfactory partnerships. Generally speaking they had been raised without families. From childhood they were "selfish" and "incapable" of real love. Ten years later (1962–63) Marzo-Weyl completed her study of the present circumstances of these women and their children. The results were not entirely encouraging. Only 18 per cent of the mothers actively devoted themselves to their children, mainly with the help of daily or weekly collective-care establishments. Ten per cent of the children were cared for by relatives, 16 per cent were in other families. The situation was still unstable for 30 per cent of the children (16 per cent of the children could not be traced and complete data were not available on a further 10 per cent). Women who ten years ago seemed to be good mothers either entrusted the child immediately to a social agency or soon resolved their problem either by taking the child with them or very quickly putting him up for adoption. Women who ten years ago were classified as bad mothers were neither able to reach a definite decision nor make any clear-cut efforts to help the child. They could not establish a stable life situation. Their children were exposed to all the disadvantages which accompany gradual loss of maternal interest: the child loses his chance to be adopted, he experiences frequent traumatizing separation from the mother, he loses the ability to adapt, and his relationship with an infantile mother offers him more traumatic than positive experiences.

The largest sub-group in our survey sample from the psychiatric department consisted of *one-parent orphans* (14 per cent, see page 120). The sudden death of the mother or father produces in the child emotional hunger, mourning, a bitter feeling of injustice at being dispossessed, and in addition, a loss of security resulting from lack of support and guidance. We would describe this as affective deprivation. Such a situation usually creates conflict, since feelings of hostility towards the dead parent are aroused and reinforced, and this engenders feelings of guilt; in addition this loss touches off anxiety states in the child, not only because of the uncertainty of his new position in society, but because he is confronted with death which he cannot understand.

A typical case is that of child H.C., who was first examined at the age of twelve years seven months. Up to about ten years of age the girl's development and her behaviour at school and in the home were perfectly normal. Following the mother's illness and sudden death (from TB) the child developed fits of rage which ended in uncontrollable laughing, crying, or threats to commit suicide by poisoning (exhibitionistically she ate paints and crayons). In the children's home where she was placed after the mother's death she constantly sulked, was withdrawn and still had feelings of injustice. She was cheeky, sometimes stubborn and sulky, and always dissatisfied, as though she wanted to avenge her emotional loss. She fiercely quarralled with her brother who was a year older. She was either fearful or boastful, she was bullying and quarrelsome towards other children and picked fights for no apparent reason. She did not establish any close contact with adults, nor did she develop any close relationships with any of the people concerned with her care, but was devoted to her father and always cried after his visits. Fits of anger or crying occurred sometimes a number of times a day, and lasted at times for an hour; otherwise she was generally quiet. Sometimes she behaved as a model pupil, at other times she was quite apathetic and showed no interest in her appearance. Her weight did not increase during her stay in the children's home. Physically, she was of normal height, was undernourished, had flabby muscles, poor bodily posture, and showed no signs of pubescence. During psychological examination she established contact with great difficulty; she was shy, spoke in whispers, with head bent, was tearful, chewed her fingers, and said she liked "all her supervisors the same". She herself did not know if they liked her. When asked what she wanted she cried and after a while whispered that she would like to have a mother. She spent a trial period after the death of her mother with her aunt but was returned to the institute because of her persistent rejecting attitudes. An attempt was made in the institute to recruit one of the nurses as an emotional substitute for the mother. After a year a certain degree of external calmness was noticeable, but the emotional uncertainty still persisted.

The child in a family disrupted by *divorce* is in a somewhat different situation. Divorce is usually not unexpected; the internal unity and the interpersonal relationships between family members are usually disturbed much earlier. Often the child has only a weak relationship with the parent from whom he will be separated, but sometimes it can be so close that the child experiences nearly as severe a disturbance as that following the death of one of the parents. The internal relationships in a broken family, however, can be very close, and insofar as the child is concerned, can even be over compensated for. In such circumstances the child need not basically suffer deprivation, even if substitution for the missing parent is very difficult. In a number of divorced families, therefore, children mentally develop in a satisfactory way, and are socially well adapted.

Generally speaking, however, children from broken homes are less well adapted, as shown by V. Trnka (1962) in his study of 118 children from divorced families. When assessed by sociometric techniques these children, compared with a control group of children from normal families, were significantly more often described as less popular, more withdrawn, more fearful, more undisciplined, disorderly, and quarrelsome. They obviously lacked emotional-moral security, and this lack promoted distrust and fear of the environment. As a result they became more withdrawn, which in turn produced day-dreaming, so that they were "mentally absent" in class. According to Trnka, indiscipline is due to loss of authority, and quarrelsomeness is a compensatory aspect of their inferiority complex. This condition can of course exist in a family apparently united but exhibiting real "affective divorce". In such cases legal divorce may even produce some stability and calmness.

According to G. Bollea (1958a), internal disunity in a family is psychologically more important than legal unity or disruption. The same conclusion was also reached by W. McCord, J. McCord, and I. K. Zola (1959) in their extensive study of the conditions underlying juvenile delinquency. We note that here we are already approaching the second group of deprivational factors in family life.

To complete this section we should add that divorce is not the only cause of external family breakdown. Breakdown may happen if the mother or father is hospitalized for a long time (particularly in a psychiatric ward), although probably it has somewhat different effects on the relationships between the remaining family members. The effects would be different if one family member is imprisoned because of his anti-social behaviour, different again if he is sent to a concentration camp or interned for political or other reasons, different again if absence is due to emigration or a long stay abroad. Future research in these areas may determine just how serious such situations are, and specify their characteristic features.

The socio-economic and cultural level of the family

At the opposite pole to problems of partial families are those of very large families. The child in such a family often can be given only a small amount of the attention and loving care he needs for normal development. Experimental studies with animals suggest that litter sizes can be a deprivational factor (P. F. D. Seitz, 1954). In early age a child in a large family usually suffers from lack of maternal care, but subsequently deprivation is due rather to the shortcomings of the father's influence and to the lack of guidance and discipline. This usually results in social-behavioural disorders of different types — wandering, truancy, anti-social behaviour (L. A. Hersov, 1960; P. Vodák and A. Šulc, 1960). Our data from the residential schools for boys showing delinquent and pre-delinquent behaviour for the years 1960—61 disclose the interesting fact that more than 30 per cent of the inmates came from families in which there were four or more children. The percentage of such families in the population in the same period was 8.4 per cent.

Factors which still affect such families in many countries are economic poverty, housing problems, bad hygienic conditions, and to some extent low cultural standards. J. Bowlby (1951) maintains that bad social conditions alone do not necessarily cause emotional deprivation. Children from bad families can have such a deep relationship with their parents that when they are separated from them they suffer more than if they were left in the family environment, since it is very difficult to find someone who would care for them permanently. According to Bowlby even bad parents have a sense of duty which staff of institutes lack. This opinion is of course quite biased.

We agree that poor hygienic conditions should not justify removing the child from the home — in this respect we are somewhat more cautious than in the past — and that we should always consider the basic child-care potential and ability of parents, their interest in the child, and their relation to him, as well as the child's relationship with the parents. On the other hand, a child can often suffer so severely from physical neglect that his psychological development is impeded and his bond with the home is only superficial and ambivalent. There are still areas of cities inhabited only by prostitutes, alcoholics, and delinquents. This type of social environment, in addition to permanent economic stress, unemployment, or frequent imprisonment of parents, prevents the establishment of a strong emotional bond between the child and his parents. Parental care in such families is more or less equivalent to having no family at all (M. Törnudd, 1956). To leave a child in a situation in which he is severely neglected, beaten, undernourished, and lives in filth simply because he needs "maternal care" and because we fear the results of separation is quite unrealistic. A number of children "flourished in front of our eyes" when they were removed from this type of family environment and placed in the better conditions of institutes. We find support for this in our data — such children after being transferred quickly start to speak, walk, increase in weight, to show mood changes, initiative, and spontaneity.

The Clarkes and S. Reiman (1958) have reported in a number of studies how young mentally retarded persons with very bad family backgrounds show a rapid and immediate improvement in their intellectual development after removal from their families. In cases where the background is less depriving, improvement is slower and more gradual. These authors maintain that the important factor here is separation from the bad family rather than the special care and training they receive in institutes. (Table 14. See also fig. 15.)

Similar conclusions were reached by H. Lewis (1954) who observed 100 children with very bad backgrounds who were admitted to assessment centres and then transferred to good foster homes over a two-year period. She reports considerable improvement in these children. At the time of admission 60 per cent were in a poor psychological state; after two years, however, only 25 per cent had failed to improve.

More serious effects are also noted in children when neglect due to bad family environment is combined with some physical or sensory defect. Surprising progress in mental development has often been noted, particularly in children with more serious sensory defects (partial vision or hearing) after they are transferred to a special institute.

This is supported by a number of older studies which report a gradual deterioration in the psychological state of children (measured by decrease in IQ) living permanently under bad socio-economic conditions. H. Gordon (1923) has recorded this in children of English gipsies and canal boat workers, E. J. Asher (1935) and subsequently A. S. Edwards and L. Jones (1938) in children from isolated mountain regions, and A. L. Chapanis and W. C. Williams (1945) in Tennessee farm children. Some of these data are presented in table 15. The same trend is evident in some more recent studies dealing with the intelligence of Negroes in the United States (W. Kennedy, V. Van de Riet, and J. White (1963).

Table 14. IQ changes in young adults after removal from poor family backgrounds

	Average IQ (Wechsler-Bellevue)	
	Children with Poor Backgrounds	Children with Less Unfavourable Backgrounds
At beginning of study	59.6	62.3
After 3 years	70.7	66.8
After 6 years	75.8	72.5

Note: Reprinted, by permission, from A.D.B. Clarke, A.M. Clarke, and S. Reiman, 1958.

Table 15. IQ decrease in children living permanently under poor family conditions (comparative data from L. Carmichael [1954])

	Beginning of Study		End of Study	
	Age	IQ	Age	IQ
A.M. Jordan (1933)	6	100	13	85
E. J. Asher (1935)	7	84	15	60
H. M. Skeels and E.A. Fillmore (1937)	4	93	14	80
A. S. Edwards and L. Jones (1938)	7–9	100	14	76
A. L. Chapanis and W.C. Williams (1945)	6	94	15	76

Although interpretation of these data is difficult, since the results could be confounded by the choice of IQ tests (tests for older children require knowledge and thus favour children with good educational backgrounds) and by selective migration (the drift of the more progressive and intelligent persons to the towns), the amount of agreement between the IQ data cited in table 15 and data from the longitudinal studies previously discussed supports the general conclusion that bad family background has a cumulatively unfavourable effect on the child's intellectual development.

Regular schooling partially compensates for unfavourable family background, for amongst other things schooling involves partial separation. This is supported by the findings of H. Hetzer, who in her book *Kindheit und Armut* (1929), reports retardation of one to two years in children from bad families when compared with children from good families, but a gradual bridging of this gap as schooling progresses. The children from very poor families in Hetzer's study obviously had very unstable emotional bonds with parents and siblings and in addition were physically weak. Hetzer suggests that the material hardship leads to psychological neglect and the physical weakness to a poorer psychological state. The entry of such children into society, their selection of jobs, and work adjustment are more difficult, their adult sexual lives less satisfying, and their emotional development more disturbed. (Fig. 16.)

Severe economic hardship is practically unknown in Czechoslovakia but a number of families still function under sub-standard economic and hygienic conditions. Matters of special concern are the problems of gipsy children and of the alcoholic parent. In our study of children admitted to a children's psychiatric clinic in 1952–55 we recorded alcoholism in the parent and possibly also in a sibling in 20 per cent of cases, and in a relative in 54 per cent of cases. We noted roughly similar figures in the sample of boys committed to residential schools for boys with pre-delinquent and delinquent behaviour for petty crimes and problems of maladjustment

— 18.5 per cent of the fathers of these boys were alcoholics.

The naive assumption that removal of all these sources of deprivation is a simple process which is an inevitable outcome of the socioeconomic changes in socialist countries was rejected a long time ago when it was shown that there is a complex interaction between economic, social, educational, and cultural factors. In socialist countries, of course, these factors are different from those in other countries and demand special study.

It seems paradoxical that an extremely favourable socio-economic family situation can be threatening from the deprivational point of view. On further consideration, however, it is obvious that certain dangers exist in such a situation, and it is rather surprising that this problem has been almost ignored.

High social status, which can be hereditarily or economically based, usually carries a number of social responsibilities. It is quite normal for both father and mother to be fully occupied with social life, which distracts them from the child. This problem is usually solved by employing nurses, servants, and aides so that the child lives under conditions of multiple mothering. Whether or not the child suffers from lack of emotional stimuli depends on the quality of the interpersonal relationships between the child, the parent, and caring adults. Sensory and intellectual stimuli are usually plentiful and formal education begins very early. From the point of view of personality development, however, prognosis is often not very favourable. We are probably not exaggerating in suggesting that the unusual character features of some important historical figures can be traced to their early upbringing rather than to their schooling and life experiences.

Today this problem in prominent families is more common in less developed countries. In economically advanced countries the problem shifts to families deeply involved in public life and to families in which members have particularly demanding jobs requiring total commitment, that is, employment of a scientific or artistic nature or possibly public political activities. The threat to the child, however, which is due to "not having enough time for the child", rather than to lack of sensory or intellectual stimuli, is the same. Nannies of the old school are rare today, and household help is very expensive; in addition the number of people prepared to do this sort of work is decreasing. Help is usually sought from relatives or nurseries. In any case we note an increasing tendency towards intermittent care, and the family is unable to compensate for possible lack of emotional and social stimuli which the child may suffer through stay in daily nurseries. The situation is further complicated by the fact that parents feel a deep devotion to the child and may themselves suffer lack of satisfaction of their emotional needs. They are often faced with a fundamental, irresolvable problem — whether they prefer the child or the creative activity. In addition to intermittent care, there is also a certain imbalance in the input of emotional stimuli. Occasional over-attentiveness to the child may be followed by a period of real or apparent lack of interest. Here, therefore, we are dealing with repeated psychological separation with all the problems this brings to both parties.

Although this danger threatens only a small segment of the population, it should not be ignored. It seems probable that the number of children involved will increase in the future with increase in the number of families of higher socio-economic status. In economically developed countries material poverty has almost disappeared. High socio-economic status is very desirable, and the social prestige derived from creative activity (scientific or artistic) is increasing. Under these conditions, an urgent problem facing society is how to balance the needs of the parents, especially of mothers, to advance socio-economically, with the child's need for stimuli which can most adequately be provided by the mother, father, or other close surrogate figures. The pursuit of economic well-being certainly cannot be the goal of social development if this means that the child loses his value, since this threatens the very basis of such development.

Employment of mothers

Mothers have always been involved in other than child-rearing duties, and it would be wrong to assume that their work load has substantially increased. Modern technology and organization have significantly decreased physical demand, so that now we should not encounter the really work-worn mother.

Surveys of planned parenthood in Czechoslovakia (M. Kučera, 1969) reveal that married women who intend to be permanently employed plan roughly the same number of children as those who intend to stay at home at least for a certain period of time after the birth of the child. However, employed women in all categories have fewer children than originally planned, and fewer than the housewife who has roughly the number of intended children. With second, third, and fourth children this difference is at times twofold. There are two possible explanations for this. In the first place the effort to remain in employment may force women to limit the number of children; secondly, if women have more children they are more likely to be forced to stay at home, although originally this was not planned. The surveys also show that this depends to a great extent on the conditions surrounding the birth of the first child (housing and economic circumstances, whether the mother had some home help). If there is economic hardship there is a tendency for the family to be limited to one child even if conditions subsequently improve.

A significant factor is undoubtedly class of employment. In previous times, when the family was both a social and industrial unit, the child was involved from an early age in the productive activity of the family, which represented a large part of communal life. The mother took the child to the fields, the father took him to the workshop — all of them were busy, but they were still close by. Today, when work activity is concentrated in big production units, the mother must leave the child for certain periods of time. If we accept Bowlby's original concept we would view even such short-term separation as dangerous to some extent. Before adopting such a view, however, we would need to thoroughly investigate this threat in carefully planned studies.

Although the problem of employed mothers is a subject of widespread interest and discussion, many views are on the level of well-intended comment and studies directly dealing with this problem are surprisingly rare. E. Herzog (1960) failed to find a single study concerned with the young children of employed mothers in the psychological literature in the United States. L. M. Stolz (1960) also comments on the unsophisticated nature of studies in this field. The situation is no better in Europe, although the percentage of employed mothers in some parts of European socialist states is very high. This may be partly due to the fact that it is methodologically very difficult to plan programmes of study which would isolate the relationships between the mother's employment and the child's development from the large complex of variables involved. Therefore, investigators prefer direct observation of children's reactions to separation or retrospective evaluation of the effects of such separation.

The majority of studies show that on the average children of employed mothers have more difficulties than children of mothers who stay at home. From a very extensive study involving 117,752 children from Prague schools, L. Kubička (1956) reports that children of employed mothers show significantly poorer school performance (specially children in higher grades) and behavioural deterioration (children in lower grades). According to this author, there are two reasons for this, that the mother has too little time for the child, or because she is generally overburdened. In addition, however, he notes shortcomings in the daily-care establishments. Kubička also reports that a relatively higher percentage of children of employed mothers require psychiatric treatment. His figures, however, differ from those of N.N. Dracoulides (1956) who reports that children of employed mothers are psychologically healthier than those in the full-time care of mothers who are confined to the home (this observation concerns only older children).

E. Herzog (1960) also suggests that psychologists and social workers are increasingly of the opinion that some women are better mothers if they do not care for the child during the whole day, and that if they were not employed the children would suffer other, possibly more unfavourable, effects. Generally speaking the majority of workers (L. Kubička, 1956; R. Adam, 1960; E. Herzog, 1960) incline to the opinion that employment of mothers does not necessarily lead to child neglect, which depends more on the quality of the established bond and of the person who substitutes for the mother during her absence. If the mother is employed solely to avoid conflict with her husband, mother, or mother-in-law, or if she needs to be employed to satisfy her emotional hunger, when she returns home she probably will ignore the child, for whom she "never has any time". This begins the disruption of her bond with the child. C. Bennholdt-Thomsen (1956b) rightly points out that it is not so much the time the parents are actually present in the home as the quality of the interaction that is important. A short period spent playing with the child can be more important than a whole afternoon during which the child is given little attention. From studies reviewed by E. Herzog, it is clear that the mother's employment is a secondary rather than a primary factor in the child's development. Critical factors are obviously the personalities of the parents and the quality of the child rearing, irrespective of whether the mother is employed or not.

There is no compelling evidence that certain disorders are typical in children of employed mothers. On the contrary, there are sufficient data to suggest that surrogate care is not necessarily dangerous if it is tailored to the child's needs. The problem is usually solved with the help of nurseries and other partial-care establishments, or by direct help from the family. It is not absolutely necessary for surrogate care to be the responsibility of only one person, but who handles the child and how this is done is important. Traditionally children have been entrusted during the mother's employment to grandmothers, aunts, or friends; thus in previous times multiple mothering was by no means rare in our culture.

From a psychological point of view the employment of mother is still a complex problem. At present it is safe to assume, however, that employment of the mother outside the family is not pathogenic as such, but that it makes certain other factors more critical, particularly the mother's personality and the quality of the surrogate care. If inadequacies in these create deprivation for the child, then obviously the mother's lack of time for the child, because of her employment, can have an aggravating effect. Because this is the most conspicuous in the whole complex of variables it is usually considered to be the primary cause. However, as is evident from our previous discussion, and as we shall subsequently discuss more fully, we must search more diligently for the real causes in other areas.

Deprivation in the family due to psychological factors

Unsatisfying relationships between parent and child can of course be due to internal psychological reasons. Those deprivating conditions within the child himself will be dealt with in the next chapter. In the present discussion we shall concentrate on the parents and those closely involved in child care. The psychological difficulties here are usually deeper, more complicated, and more difficult to deal with than the external social factors which we have just dicussed. Very frequently, however, both sets of conditions — the external and the internal — are combined in various ways and are so intricately interwoven that in practice it is difficult to make clear distinctions between them.

The psychological reasons for unsatisfactory emotional attachment with the child are many and varied. These may be lack of knowledge or incorrect interpretation of child-care manuals, sometimes excessive vocational or social ambitions which distract parents from the child, or in other cases a somewhat different direction of interest. There may be more serious problems, however, such as psychosis, psychopathic personality structure, or severe intellectual subnormality in the mother. Our basic concern here is how deeply these abnormalities are embedded in the personality of the mother or the surrogate figure, and how significantly and at what age these effect the child.

1. Inability to establish emotional bonds with the child often is caused by the immature, unstable personality of the mother or other surrogate person. For example this may apply to parents who themselves were deprived during childhood or who were unable to successfully resolve their childhood and adolescent problems. They

are usually infantile, concerned only with their own problems, have feelings of injustice and denial of love. Sometimes we can detect over-dependency on the mother or the father, from whom they attempted to escape by premature marriage. The case histories of some deprived girls reveal an indiscriminate craving for new emotional experiences leading to sexual relationships which, because of their immature personalities, cannot be permanent or give full emotional satisfaction. Such mothers lack warmth and tenderness in dealing with their children, and often a real understanding of their basic needs. Personality defects of this sort usually also denigrate the relationships between the parents themselves, so that the family is not emotionally close, it lacks a warm home atmosphere and the intimacy of family life.

The case of boy M.M. is a good example. The mother's pregnancy was free from complications apart from hypertension. The delivery was normal and early development progressed normally. The boy was never seriously ill. However, a state of permanent tension existed between the child's parents and the maternal grandparents, who lived in the same house. The parents were over-strict, the grandmother too protective. The mother was married at eighteen, and complained that she "didn't have any fun"; we were told that the boy "hated his parents, who cruelly punished him from the earliest age, and gave him no guidance". He was usually left alone. He was sent home from school after two months because he was not ready, although psychological testing showed his IQ to be about normal. He was unable to adapt to school even after a year's stay at home; he did not progress and was a thorough nuisance in the classroom. The school reported that "it is quite obvious that the parents do not devote enough time to him" — "he has a small vocabulary and a limited range of interests". He attracted attention by constantly showing off, and was uninterested in school work. At home "he doesn't know how to play", he ran about, screamed, and had temper tantrums. He obeyed only his father. There were no somatic symptoms — but psychological investigation showed symptoms of deprivation similar to those in institutionalized children. In his second year at school somatic troubles began — loss of appetite, stomach aches, vomiting, all of which quickly disappeared, however, when he began to eat with his grandmother and was placed in her care. His school performance also improved greatly. In the third grade, when he was again returned to his mother, he was regarded as "mentally sick"; he showed off, created disturbances, rolled under the desk, and was aggressive. When alone with the teacher he was quite normal; but in class he sometimes had tantrums. When he was praised he did not know how to show his pleasure other than by fighting or pushing one of his fellows over. Although all those involved in this case were intelligent and educated people the basic family conflict was unresolved. When interviewed the boy said that he loved his grandmother best "because she is nice to me". His emotional state was reflected in his drawings (fig. 19). The boy himself, his younger brother, and two uncles are on the right, and the grandparents on the left. He did not draw his parents. One might surmise that the gap in the drawing symbolizes their psychological absence in the boy's life.

2. A serious obstacle to contact with the child is mental disorder of a neurotic or psychotic character in the mother. From the deprivational point of view the most serious are the depressive states, where the mother completely turns away from the child and fails to respond to him. There is also a threat, however, from pathologically unbalanced parents whose behaviour oscillates between indifference and displays of hostility, in which their rejection of the child borders on cruelty. All these result in lack of meaningful contact and communication and exchange of positive emotional and sensory stimuli — i.e. in deprivation of one form or another. H. Lewis (1954) maintains that the amount of deprivation depends mainly on the emotional indifference or rejection by the mother, on her emotional instability and posssibly also on her intellectual level. J. R. Wittenborn (1956) also reports a significant (although relatively small) correlation between the emotional disorders of children living in foster care, and the indifferent or clearly rejecting attitudes of the foster parent.

Some very descriptive case histories are available in the literature (R. V. Coleman and S. Provence, 1957; W. S. Langford, 1955; A. Nitschke, 1955). This problem has also been experimentally investigated by Joyce Robertson (1962). She carefully observed the behaviour of twenty-five children and their mothers from the first month of life. Five of the children, when compared with the remaining twenty, showed significantly poor muscle tonus, weak muscles, decreased ability to contact the environment, poor response to mother, and generally inhibited emotional behaviour. These five children were developmentally retarded at one year of age. At the same time it was observed that the relationships of the mothers to these children were poor and lacked any direct emotional interaction. In normal social situations the mothers seemed quite normal, and the inadequacies in their relationships with their children became apparent only after detailed observation of mother-child interactions. The personalities of some of the remaining twenty mothers, when assessed by usual criteria, were "unsatisfactory", but all of them were able to respond relatively well to the emotional needs of the children. None of these children was retarded at one year of age. The author noted neurotic personality features in the mothers of the five retarded children, which produced a subconscious defence against the child, and did not permit the mother to enjoy the child's spontaneous behaviour, or to respond to his needs naturally and without constraint.

Although really severe cases of this type are very rare, clinical workers should always be alert, since early diagnosis can be important in adjusting the child's development. We shall present one case from our own clinical files which indicates how difficult it is at times to adequately assess the deprivation situation without knowledge of family background.

This concerns twins born four weeks prematurely, with a small gap to two older children. The father was an accountant and the family lived in a new flat. Economic and social conditions were quite satisfactory. The birth of twins was an unpleasant surprise for the parents, and they had difficulty in adjusting to the situation. They hostilely refused to be "slaves to the children" and decided "to raise them in a spartan and modern style". Both children were left alone in a room for the whole day without toys, they were not taken for walks because the parents had no time, and feeding and nursing were completed as quickly as possible. They were under the permanent care of a child advisory centre. Their weight increase was normal, but they were still weak, anaemic, and frequently ill with respiratory infections. When they were forty weeks old the family was visited by a paediatrician, a psychologist, and a children's nurse. The boy was developmentally retarded, at the twenty-week level of gross motor behaviour. The girl was somewhat more developed, but in her case also there was pronounced weakness which was particularly noticeable when the child was lying on her stomach. Both children were apathetic, indifferent to nursing, did not demand attention, and were uninterested in toys. Repeated interviews with the parents were needed to change their attitudes and methods of child care. Subsequently both children improved, especially when they started to walk and obtain stimuli independently. At seven years of age development was quite normal; they were lively and school performance was good.

Some mothers who lack a natural close feeling for their children do at least stimulate their children intellectually, possibly motivated by a sense of social achievement. For such mothers contact with the child is only a means of achieving certain personal goals and social approval. They cannot spontaneously enjoy the child. The child thus lives in an emotionally cold atmosphere and remains in nearly total isolation, although still living amongst people. What the mother lacks in spontaneity she supplies logically and from books; she reads paediatric and psychological literature, is strict in observing hygienic rules and daily routines, strictly follows child-care precepts, and attempts to establish desirable habits too early. In such cases developmental retardation is specific rather than general. Such children often have very good, even too well-developed memories, they know a number of poems and songs and are socially precocious. At the same time they are emotionally withdrawn from people, whom they contact only when they want something. Otherwise they tend to turn away as if they are being annoyingly distracted from their loneliness. Their autism in early life sometimes reaches such a pitch that they seem to be deaf because they ignore the human environment. Even where their IQ is good they encounter a number of difficulties when entering school, as they find it difficult to tolerate children, and efforts by teachers to make more intimate contact produce strong rejection. They adapt best to the relatively strict impersonal regimes imposed by certain teachers.

During adolescence these children stand out through their lack of adaptability to juvenile groups — they are lone wolves and show an extravagant interest in reading or some eccentric hobby. Notwithstanding their strangeness and emotional coldness however, these "autistic" children can play a positive role in society because they are intelligent and often possess surprising knowledge.

In the literature the term "autistic child" is sometimes limited to the extreme case of early psychotic disorder, which is characterized by obsessive clinging to the present, and is often accompanied by serious retardation in speech development. Disorders of this sort were described as early infantile autism by L. Kanner (1943) who suggested that here we might be dealing with an early form of schizophrenia which to a certain extent is a product of the emotionally cold, obsessive, and regimented attitudes of parents who have largely intellectual interests. A number of doubts and arguments, however, have been raised against this interpretation of early autism as early child psychosis caused by emotional deprivation in the family, and the whole question remains open (K. Goldstein, 1959; D. A. van Krevelen, 1963; R. Nesnídalová and V. Fiala, 1961; B. Rimland, 1964; G. Bosch, 1962; J. K. Wing, 1966).

Where parents not only ignore the child through indifference, ignorance, or emotional coldness but show strong emotional rejection which may have overtones of cruelty, obviously the child is not only emotionally and socially isolated, but also severely traumatized and forced into unresolvable conflicts. Doctors, social workers, and magistrates must consider the possibility of criminal neglect and of intentional physical and psychological abuse of children by cruel, psychopathic, or psychotic parents. In Czechoslovakia there are annually about forty cases of child murder by parents. Every year a number of children injured by the cruelty and neglect of parents through beating, intentional hardship (sometimes resulting in death), and sexual abuse are admitted to children's clinics. Although the number of cases is small, one should not ignore the fact that they do occur, which seems quite unpalatable to many physicians (C. H Kempe and H. K. Silver, 1959; E. Elmer, 1960; H. Bakwin, 1960). It is surprising how often a child is left in such cruel circumstances without legal intervention. The deprivation picture in such cases often contains some extraordinary features.

This was shown in the case of a six-year-old girl, L.V., who was referred for examination because of apparently inexplicable behaviour. In the previous month she had cut to pieces on a number of occasions her mother's linen, tablecloths, curtains, and dresses. The mother was obviously a very irritable, dissatisfied, tearful, and quarrelsome but normally intelligent person. The natural father was in prison, the stepfather was mentally retarded, infantile, and dependent on the mother. The child was physically well developed and normally nourished. During the examination it was discovered that the whole of her body was covered with bruises, sometimes as large as the palm of the hand. She was intellectually quick, her mental abilities were rather above average. At first she was uncertain and hesitant; later she relaxed but was still defensive and showed obsessive behaviour. Her free drawings were very unusual; she drew her mother with a baby in the pram in the cemetery. During the interview reasons for her strange behaviour were soon evident: "I do it because I am angry . . . . because mother always chases me away . . . she does not like me at all. I like her but she doesn't like me . . . father doesn't like me either but he likes mother". At times she would like to go somewhere else "but I had better not, as then I would again be homesick for my mother". She was unwilling to admit that she was often whipped by her mother and did not want to show her bruises. During the interview the mother rejected the suggestion that the child was an obstacle, but she said that she was too busy to wait on the child, she just couldn't do it. She admitted beating the child but "she [the girl] doesn't care, she is stoical, it does not hurt her ... I was in a much worse situation, I grew up with strange people ... I was beaten far more; all parents beat their children ... she [the daughter] must be beaten – it's the only way". The mother blamed everything on the husband; he did not like the child around, he was jealous, could not bear to watch the mother caring for the child in his presence and always complained that she preferred the child to him. The mother rejected out of hand any suggestion that the child be placed in a foster family. "She could meet some lady that she might like and this is not right. She must go amongst strangers to realize that she has a mother." The mother agreed to temporary placement in a home to punish the child. After transfer to the children's home the girl improved, she was pleasant and liked by others, her school performance improved, and her neurotic behaviour soon disappeared. (Fig. 20.)

3. The opposite extreme is represented by the mother who has good emotional relationships with the child, but is unable to supply the necessary intellectual stimulation. Here we are dealing with feebleminded and in some cases also with deaf and dumb mothers. One could say – and this is suggested by some authors (K. Glaser and L. Eisenberg, 1956) – that a child in such circumstances would probably not suffer emotionally to any marked degree, since the intellectual level of even such a mother is adequate to fully satisfy the child's basic psychological needs, as long as the mother offers the child her full emotional commitment and spontaneous interest. That this is relevant only at a very early age, and only to a limited degree, is indicated by the generally neglected appearance of such children when they are admitted to children's wards. Such mothers, despite their positive attitudes towards the child, cannot understand his behaviour and do not react appropriately to it. In addition, she cannot devise a reasonable programme of child care. Her ability to understand is only superficial and indiscriminating. She reacts to every cry from the child by suckling; when handling the child, she is dominated by her primitive emotional feelings. The fact that older children in these families suffer intellectual deprivation and deprivation from inadequate supervision is well documented in studies of the intellectual level of children of feebleminded mothers.

It is clear that although intellectual retardation is usually not evident in the first years it subsequently becomes quite marked. G.S. Speer (1940) reports the figures in table 16.

IQ decrement, according to Speer, is greater than that shown by children of intellectually normal mothers who have very bad social and economic backgrounds. There is indirect support for this finding. H. M. Skeels (1940) reports that 87 per cent of children of mentally

Table 16. Average IQs of children of feebleminded mothers

Number of Years under Mother's Care	Average IQ	N
0–2	101	12
3–5	84	19
6–8	75	12
9–11	72	9
12–15	53	16

retarded mothers reached a relatively normal level of intellectual functioning in adoptive care.

Follow-up studies of adopted children in Czechoslovakia also showed similar results. Adopted children reach higher intellectual levels and show better school performance than one would predict from the social background of their parents. This trend towards improvement, however, decreases as a function of the age at which the child was adopted.

In one of our studies (Z. Matějček, 1969b) we observed all 160 children of normal intelligence who were raised in one toddler home throughout the period 1954 to 1966. Of this group 101 children had spent almost the entire period from birth to three years in the institutional environment (they were raised in baby homes before transfer to toddler homes). By the end of 1966, 72 of these were in higher school grades, and of these, 25 were in adoptive families, 24 had returned to their own families, and 23 had remained in school children's homes. When they left the toddler home at the age of three years there were no significant differences in physical or mental development between the children in these three sub-groups (according to Gesell's developmental norms).

As most of the available and suitable children are adopted from baby homes, those adopted from toddler homes show far less desirable characteristics — uncertain heredity, developmental lags and irregularities, signs of psychological deprivation due to a long institutional stay. Ten per cent of mothers of this group of children were diagnosed by the psychiatric and social services as psychotic and 60 per cent as feebleminded. The decreasing ability of the older children to adapt themselves to the new family milieu must also be taken into consideration.

We noted the very quick progress of adopted children during pre-school age. This progress slowed down a little during school age, however, and when they were in higher grades sometimes bad marks appeared in their school reports (though not one of the adopted children has failed in school so far). Our findings are in agreement with those of H. M. Skeels and I. Harms (1948) who reported that the favourable development of adopted children tends to slow down in later school age so that on the average they do not reach the intellectual level of their adoptive parents, although they may considerably surpass that of their natural parents.

The effect of higher level of stimulation and better care in adoptive families can be best seen through a comparison of the achievements of these children with those of children who returned to their own parents or remained in children's homes (table 17).

Another study (J. Melicharová in P. Vodák et al., 1967) involved 170 children (82 girls and 88 boys) placed in adoptive families during the years 1943 to 1950 and followed up until 1963, that is, over a period of thirteen to twenty years. The children finished their compulsory school attendance and many of them became of age. The children were adopted at different ages from birth to fifteen years. Evaluation of the success and failure of adoption was based first of all on the statements of the adoptive parents themselves. Four separate categories of statement were derived (table 18). The proportion of unsatisfied adoptive parents increases as a function of the age of the child when adopted. There are only 2 per cent of fully unsatisfied parents where children were adopted before the end of the first year, and 14 per cent where children were adopted after six years of age. In school achievement, results were relatively favourable (table 19). The same general tendency is obvious here. While a large majority of adopted children reach a far higher social and economic level than that achieved by their natural parents, the fact that 23 per cent of them have poor

Table 17. School achievement of seventy-two children who lived in the same institution until three years of age, and were then adopted (A), returned to their families of low socio-economic level (F) or remained in children's homes (ChH)

School Achievement	A	F	ChH
Superior	11	3	3
Average	10	9	2
Below average	4	3	4
Failure (repeated at least one grade or in a special school for slow learning children)	0	9	14
Totals	25	24	23

Table 18. Success or failure of adoption in relation to the age at which the child was adopted

Age of Child When Adopted	Fully Satisfactory	Satisfactory	Partly Satisfactory	Unsatisfactory
Up to 1 year	36	20	0	1 (2%)
From 1 to 3 years	14	11	5	3 (9%)
From 3 to 6 years	17	10	2	4 (12%)
From 6 to 15 years	29	7	3	8 (17%)
Totals	96	48	10	16

Table 19. School achievement of adopted children ("A" level and Polytechnic examinations after twelve–thirteen years' schooling, "0" level examinations after nine years' schooling). (School data on three children not available.)

	N	%
Passed "A" level or Polytechnic examinations	51	30
Passed "O" level examinations with average or superior results	77	47
Below-average performance on "O" level examinations	39	23

school records prevents us from being as optimistic as we might be judging from their performance during pre-school and school age.

We can conclude therefore that deprivation in the family can take different forms and is far more complex and difficult to analyze than institutional deprivation. It is no less real and threatening to the child's development, however. In fact, it usually marks the beginning of the child's deprivational history.

DEPRIVATION IN THE WIDER SOCIAL ENVIRONMENT

The problem we intend to raise here is that of the child who lives in a family but is completely or partly isolated from the broader social environment, and for this reason is denied both the stimuli and the values which the environment normally offers. He has not suffered from lack of sensory stimuli in early childhood, nor from lack of critical social stimulation. He has been able to establish satisfactory emotional relationships within his own family. What he does lack is social stimulation at higher levels − from peer groups, from the experience of school, from meeting the opposite sex.

Since psychological deprivation would normally not be the only factor affecting the development of the child who lives in this sort of social isolation, but is merely one in a complex of negative influences, it is difficult to establish the precise role it plays in such a child's abnormalities and difficulties.

There are a number of situations in which this type of deprivation can occur.

1. The child cannot fully participate in extra-familial society because of some severe sensory, motor, or psychological defect. We shall deal with these cases in the chapter on the internal organismic factors underlying deprivation.

2. The family itself isolates the child from his environment. This is usually attributable to certain attitudes and beliefs of parents arising from a particular philosophy (a religious sect, for example) or more frequently from their neurotic, psychopathic, or psychotic personalities. These parents either prefer to have the child entirely dependent on them, or fear that the child is in physical or moral danger when outside the family.

3. The family as a whole is socially isolated for internal psychological reasons, or because of external circumstances.

These are usually families living in isolated areas or in small hamlets which are denied access to normal social and cultural life. We also include in this category families which voluntarily embrace a certain system of socio-economic, political, or religious values which completely isolates them from other sections of the community, families which do not actively reject assimilation into the social environment but maintain their old value structures in their new environment (immigrant families which have not yet integrated), or families which are rejected by society (e.g. families with very low cultural standards).

Although it seems unlikely that the personality development of a child isolated in these ways will be seriously affected, we should not under-estimate the extent to which this impoverishment, and the subsequent difficulties and distortions, limit the child's opportunity to learn social roles, and thus social participation and achievement.

A child in any of the circumstances we have described is severely restricted in his contact with the peer group even in pre-school age. His needs for both social play and motor activity are not fully satisfied. He is usually at home meeting only familiar objects and people. His emotional dependence on the parents is grossly prolonged. He lacks sufficient opportunities to develop relationships with other children, to compete, to make social judgments, to test his own strength and ability, to experience friendship. His behaviour is not submitted to the social control of the broader society, and thus he lacks one of the important elements steering behaviour. The behaviour models and systems of values in the nuclear family in which he is isolated persist for a long period.

The great importance of the broader social environment is suggested in J. H. S. Bossard's (1951) study. He was concerned with the development of independence and social maturity in children through visits to relatives, friends, and peers. Short visits by the child outside the family are the most important means of "psychological weaning" — they are the first real "short flights of the fledgling". Some children find these visits difficult to tolerate, for others they are joyous occasions. In any event, they are new experiences and a stimulus to independence. A number of difficulties which we see on school entry in children from isolated areas and in children otherwise socially isolated are due to some extent to deprivation of play, group life, and social experiences.

Although under normal circumstances school itself is an important anti-deprivational influence, deprivation of this sort can continue through school life. Lack of satisfaction of the need for free social contact with peer groups in games, competitions, sports, and adventures, which is very typical of the middle school age group, would now be more difficult to tolerate than previously. This is indicated in the increased efforts by these children to enter the peer group against the wishes of the restrictive family and the rejecting attitude of the peer group itself.

One result of previous deprivation of social relationships is that the child does not know the appropriate form of social approach to his peers. He is unaware, so to speak, of the social strategy. Thus he is often rejected by the group, not because of some personal trait or external circumstance (which is often the explanation of parents) but because of the inappropriate, unskilled, immature way in which he attempts to make contact. The child experiences repeated frustration and conflict, until he learns to adapt to the demands of the peer group, or gives up and withdraws and seeks other means of satisfaction, which widens the gap between him and society.

H. H. Commoss (1962) reports that children who have an adequate number of friends in the class and are accepted (as measured by sociometric analysis) are more confident in their interpersonal relationships, in their ability to communicate, and even in their motor coordination than socially more isolated children.

When the child reaches sexual maturity and there is a greatly increased need to communicate with the opposite sex, social isolation affects another important aspect of personality structure. Isolation from the surrounding world, restrictions due to membership of certain social groups which are discriminated against, or because of the attitudes in the family, can be so strong that they can seriously restrict the development and extension of erotic relationships which are important for a fully developed life in the maturing adolescent. Deprivation obviously plays a part in the etiology of a number of psycho-sexual disturbances.

Job satisfaction can be unattainable under conditions of social isolation and this contributes to the picture of the deprived personality. Chronic unemployment in certain areas, races, and social classes has both its psychological causes and consequences, which have obvious deprivational overtones.

Failures to satisfy these needs at the particular levels we have discussed clearly interact and are summative in their effects. It is probable also that the help we offer to a child at any one of these stages can have a positive value at the next stage, and that the re-adaptive effects will summate if the measures employed are thorough and systematic enough.

EXTRAORDINARY LIFE SITUATIONS

Deprivation can occur in some situations which are difficult to classify on the basis of preceding criteria. Characteristic features of such situations are the unusualness of the event itself, its sudden onset, its broad social significance, its dramatic course and limited time duration. In addition to deprivational factors such as temporary isolation or separation of a child from the family, here we must also weigh the effects of frustration, conflict, traumatic experiences, and so on, which are very difficult to control. Since all these factors contribute, to an unknown degree, to the dramatic features and abnormalities in the psychological development of the child exposed to these situations, it is extremely difficult to isolate the specific effect of the deprivational factors from this complex interaction.

The uniqueness of the event prevents the planning of psychological experiments in this problem area, and during the course of the event, those involved usually have neither time nor incentive for systematic psychological observations. We must base our studies therefore only on subsequent reconstruction of the events, after a certain period of time, during which the primary traumatizing experiences have faded.

We can distinguish two categories of such unusual events: (a) those due to natural catastrophe, and (b) those due to social changes.

Situations created by natural catastrophe — by large-scale flooding, fires, typhoons, catastrophic drought, and so on — occur quite frequently throughout the world. These are usually followed by evacuations or by the voluntary movement of population, by the temporary disruption of family relations, by hunger, exhaustion, and other physical suffering. It is easy to imagine that in such circumstances a child can temporarily suffer from lack of satisfaction of basic psychological needs. In cases where this stress persists for a long time, where it involves a child with reduced tolerance for deprivation (possibly because he has previously suffered similar experiences), and where the child is at a vulnerable age, it is probable that the danger of deprivation is no less real than in the situations we have previously described.

Fortunately emergency measures are usually short-term, and with return to normal life the reduced input of important developmental stimuli can be corrected. Nevertheless in diagnosing subsequent behavioural disorders in the child we must not ignore the possibility of deprivation. Relief measures should also take this into account, and should be concerned with both the child's physical and psychological health and security. There should be particular concern about the extent to which children have to be separated from families and kept in isolation. At present we lack observational data on the psychological reactions of children in natural catastrophes and their social consequences.

Far greater attention has been directed to the second category — to social catastrophes such as wars and revolutions. From this point of view World War II was a cruel natural experiment of vast magnitude. We shall therefore concern ourselves mainly with this event.

Children in World War II

Millions of children lost one or both parents, and were torn from their homes and their usual surroundings, which to this point had offered security and warmth. It is estimated that about 30 million families were disrupted by the war, and that many millions of children found themselves homeless (approximately 8 million in Germany, 6.5 million in the U.S.S.R., 2 million in Yugoslavia, for example). Children were opposed to the horrors of bombing, they saw murder and death, suffered hunger and cold, cruel and degrading treatment, they did not go to school, and some of them even suffered the hell of the concentration camps.

During the war and particularly in the aftermath, workers in the field of child care were faced with new problems of unusual severity. We are still feeling the effects of these. In studies dealing with these problems, however, differences in experimental samples and in methodological approaches led to different interpretations of results which make comparisons extremely difficult. However, the time lapse permits a more evaluative stance.

Special studies were made of two groups of children suffering from the effects of the war: (*a*) children evacuated from threatened to safer areas and who were in most cases separated from their families, and (*b*) refugee children and children from concentration camps.

Evacuated children

The evacuation of children from areas under threat of bombing was quite common, particularly in England, where nearly three-quarters of a million children were separated from their parents. They were usually placed in foster families, less frequently in a special institution in a safe area. Comparison of these children with children who were left with their parents and who experienced the horrors of bombing shows quite conclusively that evacuation (i.e. separation) had a more severe effect on the child's mental health than the bombing.

W. M. Burbury (1941), for example, reported neurotic symptoms in 52 per cent of evacuated children compared with only 20 per cent in children who lived through the bombing. C. J. Carey-Trefzer (1949) also reported more severe disorders (which were resistant to psychotherapy) amongst evacuated children than amongst those who lived through the bombing. This has added significance, in that the sample consisted of children of less than five years of age. M. Meierhofer (1949) in Switzerland concluded that the severe acute trauma due to war experiences does not produce such deep lasting effects as chronic psychological deprivation and isolation. The security which the child obtains from the presence of his parents compensates to a great extent for shocking war experiences. J. M. Sutter, in 1952, reported increased emotional fragility in children who had been evacuated from French cities in age groups, compared with children evacuated in family units (mother with all the children, or at least all the siblings together).

These effects, of course, depend not only on the bonds between the child and his parents, but also on the overall social situation of the child and the family. Children who lived in camps, cut off from normal society, showed symptoms of psychological deprivation, irrespective of whether they were with their parents or separated from them (e.g. children in Terezin concentration camp), since the parents themselves also suffered from this isolation. Nic Waal (1955) reports that children who escaped during the war from Norway to Sweden, where they lived a normal life, fully integrated into the community, showed no symptoms of deprivation, irrespective of whether they lived with or without their parents.

The incidence of neurotic disorders in evacuated children is estimated by most workers to lie between 25 and 50 per cent. It is obvious of course that some of these disorders would have occurred even if the children had not been evacuated — only one-third of the disorders were thought to be directly caused or exacerbated by evacuation. The most common neurotic symptom was enuresis (S. Isaacs, 1941; C. Burt, 1943) which, compared with pre-war figures, showed about a 50 per cent increase. In addition, anxiety states, restlessness, inability to concentrate, and occasionally anti-social behaviour and delinquency occurred. These behavioural disorders sometimes interfered with the integration of the child into the foster family. In other cases, however, even severely disturbed children adapted remarkably well. Usually it depended on the quality of the foster home (fearful children, for example, integrated well in quiet conventional homes; aggressive and quarrelsome children adapted better in free unconventional families). Although the response of the majority of children to evacuation was behavioural deterioration and sometimes neurotic symptoms, the behaviour of some children improved — they became more independent, disciplined, and quiet (similar to the effects noted following hospitalization). This applies mainly to spoiled children whose parents previously had given them whatever they wanted, and who were fixated at an infantile level.

Generally, children who had healthy positive relationships with their parents tolerated evacuation with relative ease. It is clear that this relationship with their parents provided the basis for security, which helped them to adapt to the new situation (as for most children placed for a time outside the family). These children did not often try to recall their homes, and when they did, the description was vague and in conventional or formal terms (K. M. Wolf, 1945). But children who had conflicted relationships with their parents were incapable of adjustment, and their conflict usually increased and was overtly expressed. Adolescent children (thirteen–sixteen years) experienced particular difficulty in integrating into the new foster homes; they had difficulty in developing relationships in the new family. Not unexpectedly the evidence shows that children of pre-school age were more disturbed; in this matter, however, different studies failed to agree.

Although undoubtedly evacuation, with all its demands and consequences, produced a considerable amount of stress and certain behavioural problems in the majority of children, the incidence of disorder and maladaptation, relatively speaking, was considerably lower than we might expect. Increased incidence of neurosis, as mentioned previously, varied around 33 per cent. The number of children who did not integrate into the foster families was reported by S. Isaacs (1941) to be only about 6 to 7 per cent. Many children, therefore, must have survived such experiences relatively untouched. This does not mean, of course, that evacuation did not disturb them, nor that it did not produce a greater vulnerability in the child, which would become obvious if he was subsequently confronted with other difficult or conflict situations.

Refugee children and children from concentration camps

These children were obviously exposed to more severe conditions and their disturbance was far greater. Those subjected to racial discrimination were most affected. Yet even with these there was often surprisingly high potential for re-adaptation and relatively quick recovery in a healthy environment.

In Czechoslovakia, fifteen thousand Jewish children passed through Terezin concentration camp alone. Although some of them lived with their mothers, most were separated. Many of them experienced indescribable hardship and horrors during transport to the camp. Camp conditions prevented any planned child care — there was no time for play with small children, and for the older children no permanent schooling was available. Hunger, dirt, cold, forced hard labour, and degrading treatment by guards was as much the daily lot of children as of adults. In an atmosphere heavy with the fear of death, all efforts were directed towards self-preservation at any cost.

Very valuable data on the psychological conditions existing in the ghetto of Terezin were reported by some outstanding psychologists who themselves were interned there as adults (for example, Professor E. Utitz, 1947), and by those who spent part of their childhood there, and subsequently became psychologists (J. Diamant and M. Kosová), sociologists (O. Klein), or artists (H. Hošková-Weissová). (See figs. 21, 22, 23, 24.) From their reports, it is clear that a very complicated psychological environment existed, in which there was a never-ending conflict between lack of satisfaction of basic self-preservation needs and satiation of other needs. The town which previously numbered ten thousand now housed three times as many. In today's post-war world Terezin is an "empty town", "a lifeless backdrop" to the person who lived there during the concentration camp period. People were literally pressed one on the other, there was no privacy. Family relationships remained basically unchanged, even where the older children were separated from their parents. There was a curious mixture of biological and social deprivation (need for food, peace and quiet, free movement, rest, and sleep) rather than sensory or emotional deprivation. Needs for security, support, privacy, life goals, permanent lasting values, job satisfaction, and stable interpersonal relations were denied to a tragic degree. A state of chronic frustration was shown mostly by the older generation, and through them the children were also psychologically influenced.

In this environment the behaviour of all children — even those from well-adjusted families — quickly deteriorated; they stole, cheated, paid little attention to adults, and established gangs in which amoral and anti-social attitudes flourished. However, mental disorders and even childish neurotic symptoms were not frequent in concentration camps — on the contrary, neurotic difficulties, which a child may have shown previously, disappeared. But powerful effects were accumulating in the child's psyche — anger, vengeance, anxiety, degradation — which were to characterize and sometimes dominate his later development.

After liberation some of these children were repatriated, some were sent to Israel or other countries. However, the majority of them (as were the children of deported or executed parents) were collected in special homes, and from there — after a certain adaptation period — were placed in adoptive families or in permanent children's homes. In these homes a considerable amount of data was accumulated; we must remember, of course, that these data must be viewed in the context of the conditions in the institute, and of the methodological approach of the particular worker involved. We shall try to select some generally accepted conclusions from reports of research workers from different institutes, partly from the review publication by Nelly Wolffheim (1958–59).

Although the majority of children were physically damaged to a considerable extent, their recovery was surprisingly quick. After two to three months' hospital care in a displaced persons' camp in Czechoslovakia, their nourishment and general physical health had improved to such an extent that when they arrived at the transit homes they appeared to be quite healthy children (except for a susceptibility to infection and relatively frequent skin eruptions, which occurred shortly after admission). Psychological damage, however, showed itself very quickly in nearly all children, and, as E. Hejlová (1947) noted, was obviously deeper.

Young children coming to institutions seemed to be extremely restless "little animals". They were indescribably irritable, and most of the time they seemed to be aimlessly running up and down, screaming, tearing and destroying everything. Obviously, they were developmentally retarded in all areas, but most severely in their social behaviour. They did not know how to eat, they had no idea of personal hygiene, they did not know how to play. C. François (1948) reports that nearly all the four- and five-year-old children, who were separated from their parents before the age of three years and were admitted to the home "Le Renouveau" near Paris, showed severe physical, psycho-motor, social, and mental retardation — they were usually of small stature, generally did not speak, and were mentally debile.

Socialization of children from concentration camps progressed very slowly. A. Freud and S. Dann (1951) describe the development of six of these children who lived in Terezin concentration camp for the first three years of life. When admitted to a children's home with individual care of the family type, the children initially rejected the social and physical environment. They slowly learned to tolerate the new conditions, primarily through living together. These interrelationships were revealed in the way they imitated and helped one another, in some cases to establish relationships with adults. Emotional disturbances — panic responses to animals, constant fear that somebody would take something from them (toys, food), separation anxiety, and generally a striking distrust of people and of the environment — persisted for a long time. Nevertheless, all these children managed a substantial and surprising degree of adjustment, which was reflected in their behaviour and development.

A similar account is given of twenty-five children who were forcibly removed from their mothers (who were interned in labour camps) and raised secretly in a home in Austria, where they lived in a small hut in the middle of a wood. They were not allowed to go out, to play with toys, or to see any person other than three indifferent nurses. After liberation these children also initially screamed for days and nights, did not know how to play, did not smile, and had difficulty in learning bodily hygiene, which had been previously conditioned by brute force. After two to three months they developed some semblance of normality. Their re-adaptation was clearly facilitated by their group feeling.

Disorders in school age children and adolescents were at first sight less obvious; some of the children adapted very quickly under the improved conditions, and their behaviour normalized. But in nearly all cases character structure was deeply affected. The most marked symptom of disturbance in these children was their distrust of people. They suspected everybody, they did not believe in promises; they doubted sincerity, expected always to be betrayed, and because of this, were constantly hypercritical, envious, incapable of gratitude. Most of them had better relations with other children, mainly with siblings, who had shared the same fate. It was sometimes possible (as we have already seen with younger children) to start re-education at this point, rather than through direct relationships with adults.

Despite a profound distrust of their new supervisors, and a complete lack of willingness to accept gestures of friendship, these children had a strong need for love which was often shown on particular occasions and in rather indirect ways. For example, a common tactic was exaggeration of physical complaints, by which the children obtained increased individual attention. For many of them a period in the isolation ward with a nurse in attendance was highly valued.

The pronounced disturbances in interpersonal relationships clearly indicated that these children suffered more acutely from loss of family and home than from physical hardship. This is suggested in the children's spontaneous productions — in their stories, poems, and drawings. Margaret Loosli-Usteri (1948) in 1944 asked 97 children living in four homes for Jewish refugees in Switzerland to freely express themselves on the topic of "What I think, what I wish, and what I hope". She used essays of 173 Swiss children from a number of schools on the same topic as a control. Feelings of a sort of emptiness, of lack of satisfaction, permeated nearly all the work of refugee children. Separation from parents seemed to be the most tragic event in their lives. While home and parents were the main themes in their description, for Swiss children these were so much taken for granted that they were not even mentioned. The refugee children compensated for this painful feeling of emptiness by recalling the happy past, and in longing for a better future. While the Swiss children had a happy full life in the present, for the refugee children the present time was only a sort of empty and unsatisfying hiatus between the past and the future.

Similar motives can also be detected in the children's poems written during their Terezin internment, and are projected in a very touching way, into their drawings, which were analyzed by a Czech psychologist, O. Vaňouček (1959, unpublished). Motives of home, travel, open spaces, and escape are frequently expressed. We can recognize here the burning desire to escape from the unsatisfactory present and to return to the secure past, or to escape into the fantasy of a more hopeful future.

The essays and drawings, however, not only were vehicles for expression of fantasies during the time of great hardship, but also obviously met additional needs in some children. Adults who suffered the ordeal of concentration camps say that artistic creativity was encouraged by these experiences. This supports our view that psychological deprivation under certain conditions (where personality development has advanced beyond a certain point) can make artistic creativity and inspiration more profound.

Although during the actual experience children found comfort in a happier past, after liberation most of them either consciously or unconsciously avoided past memories. It was as if they avoided irritating open wounds. Where this wound was only superficially healed, there still remained a high sensitivity to frustration, to any changes in their situation, to re-allocation and repeated separation which, because of international agreements, was quite frequent in the post-war era. It is interesting to note that most of these children, despite their intense conscious longing for a real home, found it hard to leave the displaced persons' camps and enter new families into which they integrated only slowly and with difficulty. This is supported by observations of children sent to Israel; those placed in the kibbutzim adapted best while the greatest conflict occurred in foster homes (only in Switzerland, where psychological advice was available to meet difficulties, has successful placement in families been claimed).

The loss of security and support which these children suffered through the destruction of their homes is regarded by C. François as underlying all the behavioural disorders observed in adolescence. In girls, symptoms were passivity, dull behaviour, possibly an emotional desire to wallow in self-pity, to tearfully remember parents and the happier past. In boys the same feelings were expressed in more active forms as anger, desire for revenge, and destructive tendencies.

Other authors have often referred to the destructiveness of these children which, though often senseless, obviously provides compensatory satisfaction. The boys destroy and tear things apart for the sheer pleasure of it, some of them show sadistic tendencies or at least sadistic fantasies, and others are strikingly hungry for excitement. Motor restlessness, which is such a florid symptom in severely deprived young children in this age group, is accompanied by psychological instability and inability to concentrate on any form of activity where positive feedback is not available.

The tendency to compensate for loss of parental love and the security of the home through over-sentimentality or aggressiveness can be directed into useful social channels. Re-education should offer sufficient opportunity for directed social learning. Thus, in the home established by C. François, special emphasis was placed on intensive school work in group situations, and the results were outstandingly successful. Nearly all the children who had lost two to three years of schooling fully made up this leeway, although many of them would have preferred immediate job placement.

Other authors have also emphasized this motivation to make up lost ground. They have noted in such children a special effort to quickly learn the language of the new home, to acquire new forms of behaviour, and to establish a new status both in the home and in work.

Of particular interest is the finding of a relatively low incidence of delinquency after liberation amongst children who spent even longer periods in concentration camps. In displaced persons' camps some children stole food, which they collected and concealed in their beds, as they had previously done. They were also inclined to take advantage of others, to cheat and bribe. These symptoms, however, usually soon disappeared and did not develop into really delinquent forms. Quite the contrary, overall improvement in moral values paralleled improvement in social behaviour.

Generally it can be said for children who were deprived of family life in concentration camps or in refugee centres that the damage was more severe and deepseated than in evacuated children, who retained some contact with their family, and usually lived under relatively good life conditions. Children who lived from the youngest age under camp conditions usually suffered physical and particularly neuro-psychological effects on a global scale, which influenced their development. Older children tended to show character disorders, primarily a disturbance in interpersonal relations and self-perception (in other words lack of trust in people and in themselves). It is surprising that the majority of severely deprived children adapted reasonably well in a relatively short time, and that about 60 per cent of them showed no frank symptoms of mental disorder. Almost all of them, however, were scarred in certain ways by their great suffering; this was reflected mainly in their increased vulnerability and mental instability and in the fact that minor changes in their life situations tended to produce breakdowns.

Individual differences, of course, are clearly of considerable importance. Children from stable families who had happy early lives and who were mentally very healthy withstood these conditions relatively well. Character traits developed in early childhood (notwithstanding a superficial appearance of maladjustment) resisted even the most severe stress to a certain extent. Children who had developed independence also showed higher tolerance of these difficulties. While it is probable that certain long-term anxiety states in all afflicted children could lead to the development of neurosis in later life, actual neurosis during the stay in concentration camps was relatively rare. In more emotionally unstable individuals, however, severe neuroses often developed after liberation and following transfer to better conditions (D. Müller-Hegemann [1964] describes a similar condition with adult patients as *"Entlastungsreaktion"* — relief response). Where the children are given good care conditions, the prognosis for such deprived children is generally good, if we can accept reports from a number of institutions. At present, however, evidence about later character development is still too meagre to allow more definite conclusions. (See also P. Matussek [1971].)

Fig. 6. Bedroom in a Paris foundling home, 1846. (Reprinted, by permission, from R. Dirx,

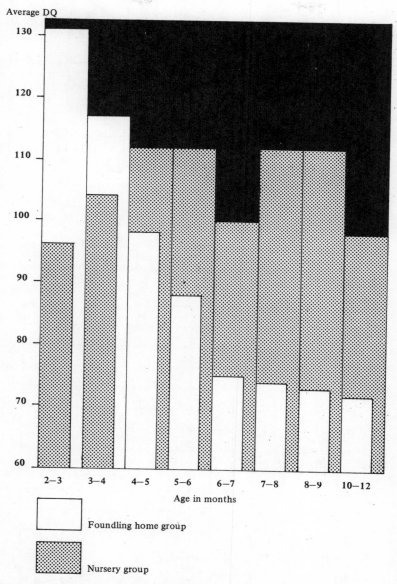

Fig. 7. DQ changes in foundling home and prison nursery groups. (Reprinted, by permission, from R.A. Spitz, 1945.)

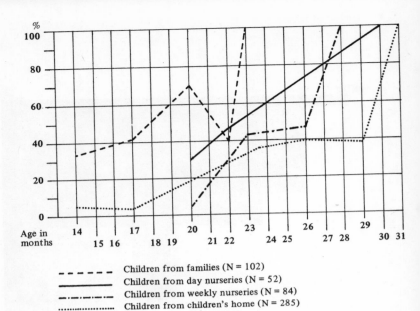

Fig. 8. Speech development in children from families and institutions, showing the age at which children with different backgrounds first use meaningful language. (After E. Schmidt-Kolmer, 1959a.)

Children from families (N = 102)
Children from day nurseries (N = 52)
Children from weekly nurseries (N = 84)
Children from children's home (N = 285)

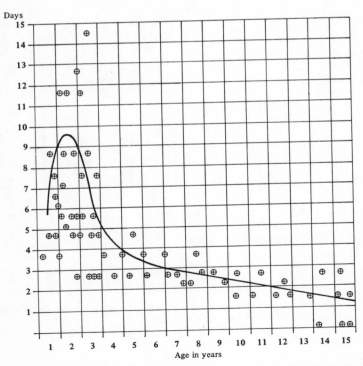

Fig. 9. Time taken to adapt to the hospital environment in relation to age. (Reprinted, by permission from L. Hausam and H. Spiess, 1958.)

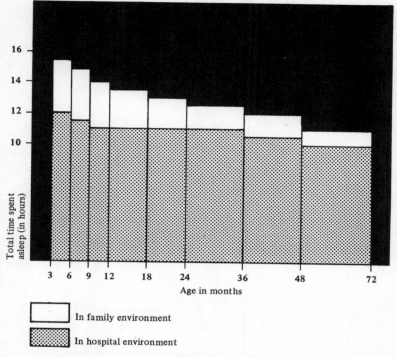

Fig. 10. Average sleeping time of children of different ages in a twenty-four hour period at home and in hospital. (After J. Langmeier.)

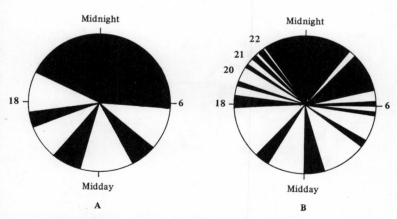

Fig. 11. Sleep periodicity in an eight-month-old baby at home (*A*) and in hospital (*B*). Total time asleep in four periods at home was fourteen hours thirty-five minutes, in thirteen periods in hospital ten hours forty-five minutes. (After J. Langmeier.)

Fig. 12. Drawing of "Our family" by an eleven-year-old boy of normal IQ showing deprivation symptoms relating to emotional security in the family, which is the boy's ideal, but which is non-existent. This is also suggested by the question mark after the title.

Fig. 13. Drawing of "Our family" by fourteen-year-old boy F.Z. of normal intelligence who was first institutionalized in school age children's homes and ended up with his younger brother in a residential school for boys with delinquent or pre-delinquent behaviour. The boys have only peripheral contact with parents and siblings. In the drawing the two boys constitute the family. This is an example of the type of sibling relationship which develops between children who stay for long periods in children's homes.

Fig. 14. Drawing of "Our family" by a fifteen-year-old feebleminded boy who lived from early childhood in institutes, who at four years of age spent a short time in a foster family and was then sent to a special home for retarded children. The boy drew himself as a small baby sitting in a pram while the father builds a house for the family. This typifies escape into an imagined happy childhood.

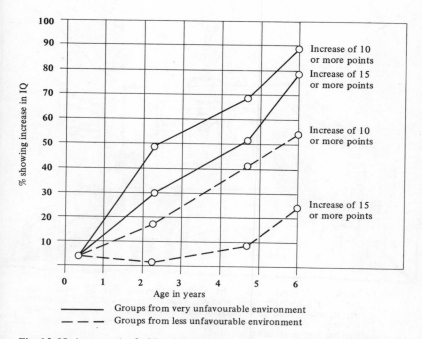

Fig. 15. IQ increase in feebleminded children after removal from unfavourable home environment and placement in an institution. (Reprinted, by permission, from A. D. B. Clarke and A. M. Clarke, 1960.)

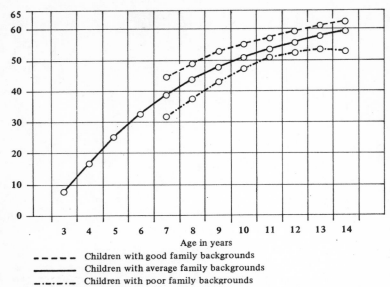

Fig. 16. IQ data from children with different social backgrounds. (After H. Hetzer, 1937.)

Fig. 17. Drawing of "Our family" by a twelve-year-old boy of slightly above average IQ, an only child who was raised from an early age by parents, grandparents, and in collective care establishments. The father was a scientist, the mother an artist. The boy's longing for a home and mother has never been satisfied.

NAŠE.RODINA

povídají.

Mišo a sestřička si

Fig. 18. Drawing of "Our family" by an eight-year-old boy of below average IQ showing symptoms of deprivation and who has no emotional ties with his parents. He finds compensation in his relationship with his younger sister. The drawing shows his sister talking to her teddy bear. No other members of the family are present.

Fig. 19. Drawing by boy M.M.

Fig. 20. Drawing by girl L.V.

Fig. 21A

Fig. 21. Five drawings by H. Hošková-Weissová, who as a girl of twelve to fifteen lived in Terezin and in Auschwitz concentration camps. *A*, Life space for one family in Terezin; *B*, Arrival of a transport at Terezin; *C*, Arrival of Polish children at Terezin; *D*, Night count of the children's legs; *E*, Deprivating conditions in Auschwitz camp.

Fig. 21B

Fig. 21C

Fig. 21D

Fig. 21*E*

Fig. 22. Painting by unknown child in Terezin: a house full of flowers.

Fig. 23. The world outside the fence: the tree and the sky full of stars symbolize the beauty of the outside world which the child is denied by the high wall. Painting by unknown child in Terezin.

Fig. 24. Fantasy drawing with overtones of sadness. Painting by unknown child in Terezin.

6 Culture and deprivation

In previous chapters we attempted to identify those conditions which most frequently threaten children with psychological deprivation. However, these apply only in the present European-American cultural context, to certain sections of the population, and at the present time. We must take cognizance of these facts, since some of the findings about causes and effects of deprivation from the classical studies of the "alarm" period are valid only within these constraints.

Conclusions from these studies, however, were loosely generalized. This provoked a strong wave of criticism, which was followed by such rejection of the corrective measures recommended that it could still be claimed twenty years later that "hospitalism still flourishes" (A. Mehringer, 1966). Obviously the problem of psychological deprivation cannot be resolved without taking into account a number of broader cultural factors which up till now have not been systematically studied.

Although in the fifties and sixties a number of studies presented trans-cultural data, the main purpose was to support the general conclusions previously advanced. For example, R. A. Spitz (1958a) reported that in highly advanced cultures, the chance of emotional (maternal) deprivation is much higher than in so-called primitive societies, where the child is nursed on demand schedule for a long period of time, where physical contact between mother and child is close and long-term, where hygiene training is not forced, and where adaptation to cultural norms is slow and relatively simple. The child can express his instinctive tendencies more freely, and there is less suppression. All these conditions contribute to an ideal in child rearing – a highly permissive upbringing with minimal interference (M. Mead, 1955, 1962a; J. Bostock, 1958).

This view is based on the psychoanalytic assumption that the basic needs of the child are biologically determined, that they are identical across cultures,[1] particularly at an early age, that in the main the limits of these need satisfactions are culturally determined, and that denial of satisfaction of the child's basic instinctive needs in the early critical period will produce certain undesirable personality traits and possibly disturbances in general mental health.

For example, correlations have been reported between deprivation of normal child needs (limited period of suckling) and lack of self-confidence or optimism in adulthood (A. H. Maslow and I. Szilagyi-Kessler, 1946; F. Goldman-Eisler, 1950, 1951), between suppression of aggressive tendencies and later shyness in the presence of others (J. W. M. Whiting and I. L. Child, 1953), between restriction of free movement (swaddling) and passivity (G. Gorer and J. Rickman, 1949), and between punitive parental attitudes and general neuroticism (K. Horney, 1937).

A number of studies, however, have questioned the one-to-one relationship between early deprivation of specific instinctive needs and later personality structure (for example, W. H. Sewell, 1952; J. R. Thurston and P. H. Mussen, 1951; H. Thomae et al., 1962). Although undoubtedly the culture provides the milieu in which certain needs of the child can be satisfied, and has a far-reaching effect on the individual's development, the relationship between the child's needs and cultural provisions for their satisfaction is far from simple. In the first place, the basic needs of the child are not always fixed at birth. They tend to change in intensity and direction in response to environmental, particularly cultural, influences. Secondly, the cultural effect cannot be viewed simply as restriction of instinctive needs. The culture, which stimulates the development and shaping of needs, by its very nature never insists on a particular course of action to which the individual must submit but always provides a number of alternatives; within these constraints, the child has a certain degree of freedom and opportunity for creativity and self-direction in his spontaneous activity and development. This has been very well described by R. Bierstedt (1963): "culture is not a uniform pattern that impresses itself alike on all who are exposed to it, nor is it a uniform that all must wear".

Cultural anthropologists (J. M. Roberts, B. Sutton-Smith, A. Kendon, 1963, quoted in B. N. Colby, 1966) have shown that every culture offers a number of models describing ways of behaving and coping with life's difficulties. Such models are presented in ballads,

1. In this context we interpret culture in a somewhat narrower than usual sense, as the value structure shared by the majority of the members of the society, also the attitudes, motivations, habits, and mores which are more or less binding on all members.

fairy tales, plays, toys, in art, and so on; they are handed down from generation to generation verbally or in written form, they are preserved in sayings, in the advice of older people, and in the exemplary behaviour of certain people to serve as guide lines for training. People always subconsciously search for clearly expressed behaviour patterns in these models which, when perceived, are organized into mental structures ("templates" — Colby), as concepts or correct (acceptable) ways of behaving. These templates direct the behaviour of members of the society, and at the same time are the material for the continued recreation and expansion of the cultural process. Thus we see a cyclical process of behavioural patterns being objectified in models from which the members of the society individually abstract certain behavioural norms (templates). An individual, of course, is selective and accepts a model only from a certain region; at the same time, he himself contributes to its transformation and further development. In some cultures models are fixed and stable, they change very little, and have relatively great authority. In other more open cultures, models change quickly and constantly.

In all societies there are certain children whose needs are not developed and satisfied in accordance with these valid cultural models, even though they are subject to the same social demands, and their behaviour is judged according to these norms. In such a case we might refer to individual deprivation, that is, deprivation of individual children who live under conditions different from those imposed on the majority of children as they are codified in the models. For example, in a culture where unrestricted emotional contact is approved, "rationed" contact with an adult would be regarded as deprivating. The opposite is true in cultures where control and discipline are emphasized. The child's normal striving for emotional contact would be regarded as extravagant and tyrannical. Thus children who in one culture would be regarded as deprived in another would be considered quite normal. In the same way, it is quite likely that the concept of the deprived child changes historically within a culture; children who today would be regarded as deprived were previously considered a quite normal section of the child population. Only in cases of very severe deprivation (for example, extreme social isolation) can one assume that a child is considered to be deprived in every culture. These cases, however, are rather exceptional.

If we confine ourselves to one culture (fixed in space and time) we can speak only about the deprivation of individual children. If we transcend this cultural milieu, however, and base our judgments of children raised in this particular culture on criteria derived from models in another culture, we can describe whole populations of children as deprived. In contrast to the individual deprivation previously described, we can use the term cultural deprivation in a somewhat idiosyncratic, but we think quite justifiable, sense. For example, in the present middle-class culture, the need for verbal learning is encouraged and satisfied from an early age (language construction, symbolic expression, objective descriptions, motivation to learn through reading and later on to academic achievement), while in other classes and ethnic groups there is a much greater emphasis on the need for motor activity, physical fitness and skill, and ability to look after oneself. Children in these groups are considered to be deprived by middle-class social workers and teachers, although this deprivation would have gone unnoticed except for the close contact and overlap between the two cultural groups. In those periods when there was relatively autonomous development of different cultures, and interaction was limited, cultural deprivation was not as great a problem as it is today, when it describes not only certain population groups in the Western cultural sphere (gipsies in central Europe) but whole populations in developing countries, in which traditional cultural models are being replaced by new models of child rearing. In times of rapid cultural change, cultural deprivation of children can be seen when the extant models are not relevant to new values and ideals, and are forced to retreat in the face of new, more adequate, models.

SOCIAL DEVELOPMENT AND DEPRIVATION

It is often assumed that deprivation is a modern scourge which was not experienced in the golden idyllic past. Any realistic historical approach indicates, however, that this view is quite wrong. Only the causes and types of deprivation are different.

It is not easy to attempt a socio-cultural history of deprived children. Our present essay is tentative, incomplete and inexact, but we hope at least that it will provoke better documented studies. It is based on a content analysis of books[2] on child rearing published in the Czech language (original and translated) from 1850 to 1962, and directed towards parents. We have used only those data relevant to general changes in models along the main dimensions of affection and discipline, data documenting important shifts in value orientation

2. Seventy-eight books from the Library of Charles University, Prague.

shown in these models, and those describing changes in the concept of the child who is difficult to rear or actually deprived. We have also briefly described changes in family structure. We must emphasize that changes in cultural models described in popular literature probably reflect changes only in certain classes of the population, and therefore do not represent all directional changes in models in the overall adult population. We have attempted to integrate this information into the framework of the general development of European society in the preceding period, and to deduce unrecorded trends.

The social and cultural development of European countries progressed somewhat differently in response to a number of economic, social, and political factors. For present purposes, it is only necessary to identify basic trends which were probably identical in all countries, although they occurred at different points in time and with different intensities.

1. European society experienced a long and complicated development up to the beginning of the period under discussion. Cultural historians (particularly P. Ariès [1960, 1962] whose interpretation we shall adopt here) note that the concept of childhood from the Middle Ages to the sixteenth century was different from the present one. The child spent the first few years of his life probably in close contact with his mother or other females who satisfied all his needs and allowed him an unimaginable amount of freedom. As suggested in the old ballads, his survival depended on this kind of close maternal care. As soon as the child was weaned and ceased to be physically dependent on the mother, governess, or wetnurse (at about five to seven years of age) he became a "small adult" and no longer belonged to the parents. He moved from the family into the larger social group, accepted certain tasks, dressed and enjoyed himself in the same way as adults, and shared their company. He mixed with them on all occasions in the village square, in pubs, in military camps, at work. From this time the family was not so much an important source of emotional relationships (the child often served as a trainee page or servant in other families). Although the child's life was very hard he had numerous and intense emotional relationships with people outside his own family, with members of the group to which he belonged and with whom he fully identified, whose values and norms he absolutely accepted. Often he was more devoted to his master than to his parents and was bound to him in an absolute way.[3] The family was rather a means of ownership of

3. Translation reads: With life and death solidarity.

things and people, a natural place of production, and included the whole group of kinsmen and servants. In the same way the state — organized society — was viewed as a unity, a hierarchy of patrimonial institutionalized families.

Under such conditions the deprived child was the child who lacked the protection and the physical and emotional care necessary for survival from an early age — he was the totally deserted child, the neglected, rejected child, or the child who, because of his behaviour, illness, or disability, was excluded from his whole group. The outcome for a person in such deprivating circumstances was bare survival and often death, unless he was given special protection. It was in this context that the first institutions for social protection were established by the monasteries in the Middle Ages. Age was not an important criterion; these institutions accepted old, ill, and neglected persons as well as neglected children.

2. Between the sixteenth and seventeenth centuries and the first half of the nineteenth century, family organization, and thus the child's place in society, underwent a significant change in Europe. The family gradually lost its importance as a productive centre and as an institution conferring name (honour) and property. There is evidence of increasing concern for the child and acceptance of responsibility for his care and education. As P. Ariès notes, it was only at this time that the real concept of childhood developed, both inside the family and in society, as indicated in the writings of the great moralists and educationists. Within the family, emphasis was mainly on emotional factors. The parents perceived the child as a nice unsophisticated person, interesting, playful, gay; they played and talked to him, they kissed and cuddled him to a greater extent than previously, told him stories, and so on.

There was also an increased awareness that the child not only needs cuddling but moral care and training, for which discipline is necessary. Children must be raised from their imperfection and ignorance to moral perfection and wisdom. The school began to take on this function and ceased to be a place where only mental skill was developed and children mixed with adults. It became more and more oriented towards the rearing of the child, who was subjected to a strict disciplinary regime. The rough way of life of the medieval student, for whom begging, wandering, and stealing were normal activities, was gradually replaced by the strict discipline of barrack-like boarding schools. The new concept of loving care in the family and strict discipline in the school, to which children were sent rather than being apprenticed, created a new educational ideal of the moral and well-behaved child. This ideal predominated first in the middle classes; amongst the lower classes the old ideal persisted for a longer time, although the greatest educational authority of the time, J. A. Comenius (1592–1670) advocated universal education, for both sexes, for rich and poor, and he himself devised an educational system, very modern in conception, from pre-school age to the university.

In these circumstances it was the child who lacked loving care in the family and, more importantly, discipline (which was the medium for moral and spiritual reconstruction), who maintained the old standards of coarseness, immodesty, and immorality. The deprived child was thus the child who was morally deserted, without discipline and without moral supervision by society. The vagabond type who begged, thieved, sang in the streets and taverns, bickered and quarrelled, rioted at festivals – behaviour which earlier was not only tolerated but approved by the general public – came to be regarded more and more as unacceptable and as socially deviant. The institution which society at this time developed to combat moral desertion of children was the new type of school whose influence became wider and more specialized through government support and because of its value in parents' eyes.

Initially education was aimed at no particular age group, but subsequently schooling became oriented towards children of a certain age, was extended (from one or two years to five or more years), and gradually differentiated into the *lycée* and other types of secondary schools offering classical education, and primary schools offering basic practical education. This differed from the medieval school in its emphasis on effective discipline. In addition, social medicine, which was developing at this time and which was concerned with childhood and the prolongation of life (macrobiotics), laid great emphasis on discipline and the moral way of life. School was the medium through which knowledge of a moral, logical, and useful life could be disseminated. Children who lacked any or adequate schooling were therefore seriously threatened. This applied particularly to the vast majority of children of the lower classes who previously had mixed freely with other children, but who now were isolated and disadvantaged, particularly in the first half of the nineteenth century, when the industrial revolution created a demand for child labour which delayed the development of full-time universal education.

3. These two concepts of childhood, the first emphasizing the need for love (particularly in the family) and the second the need for moral discipline (particularly at school) were incorporated into one model of child rearing in the second part of the nineteenth century

(which is the first period of our above-mentioned study). Warm emotional feelings towards the child and strict discipline now became conditions of adequate care in the family (fig. 26); the mother usually supplied the love and the father the discipline. A new bourgeois patriarchal family in which both children and adults participated in the satisfaction of emotional needs through intimate interrelationships, while relations with people outside the family were emotionally more neutral, replaced the old institutional patrimonial family. In such a family the child from his earliest years developed a sense of moral discipline. Moral education in the family was broadly based on a hierarchy of authority which included kinship groups. The parents increasingly accepted responsibility for the child's upbringing, his behaviour and professional training; for these reasons the size of upper-class families began to reduce. Both the emotional significance of the child for his parents and of the mother for the child considerably increased. At this point we see the development of the concept of maternal love which is irreplaceable.

Under such conditions the main threat to the child was lack of love and authority in the family; the orphan child, the illegitimate, the posthumous child, growing up without maternal love and parental authority, was now the most deprived child (the mother's death was as great a tragedy for the child as the child's death was for the mother; previously neither was considered of any particular significance, being a normal part of life). Parental deprivation was a special kind of moral desertion which could lead to moral delinquency, which in terms of this child-care model, was now considered the greatest evil, a denial of the ideal itself (fig. 29). Orphanages — special institutes caring for such children, who otherwise would have been committed to community care — had been established earlier than this, but at this time their role was extended, broadened, and deepened to cater for the needs of older children of school age. Institutes were founded for unmarried mothers, (state) supported foster care was introduced; the beginnings of organized social care were established, and activities of charitable women's clubs were extended. In 1874 the Society for the Prevention of Cruelty to Children was established in Philadelphia.

4. At the beginning of the present century (the second period of our study, from 1900 to 1920), the earlier child-rearing model persisted, but emphasis on the positive emotional relationships of the family with the child was replaced by a more rational approach to child care. Discipline based on authority gradually declined (fig. 26). Rational rather than blind obedience was demanded of the child. "Monkey love" or "training of despots" was repudiated. While moral

values were still considered important (fig. 27) now, instead of the old ideals of "private" morality (trustworthiness, modesty, application to work, generosity, lack of envy, and so on), ideals of "public " morality were emphasized (humanity, progressiveness, learning, tolerance of others, a critical attitude, and interest in science). At this time the family freed itself from the bonds of the patriarchal hierarchy and was liberalized and democratized. Equality and education of women were emphasized, and there was a greater respect for the personality and the uniqueness of the child. "Respect for the child, and the understanding of his soul" was demanded.

Thus while the family was still the greatest source of deprivation, it was not only a matter of a child being orphaned, but also of being denied moral care by the parents, who themselves were not sufficiently educated, moral, and humanistic. Attention was focused more on the morally degenerating than the fully neglected child — the child from marginal families, from families which did not fulfil their social or child-care obligations, i.e. the child from families forced by modern civilization onto the periphery of society, families from city slums whose anti-social way of life was a product of social disorganization and pathology. The moral shortcomings of children were still attributed to the sins of parents (alcoholism, prostitution, living off the state). Society's attack on problems of child deprivation was waged through education of the public, parents, and teachers. War was declared on poverty. Social medicine was established as a discipline (the first conference on social medicine was convened in 1899) and a systematic attack was made on the problem of high mortality of children with bad social backgrounds.

At this time there was a great increase in the number of sophisticated studies by medical and other workers of deserted, neglected, and maladjusted children. These no longer had a charitable, philosophical, or religious orientation but reported findings on which practical recommendations for helping these children could be based (the empirical period in the development of the concept of psychological deprivation — see page 3). These first scientific attempts to solve the problem of deprivation also disclosed deficiencies in hygienic care and in the rational approach to child care which influenced the general approach of the public to this problem in the following period.

5. Emphasis on strict discipline, which had been the outstanding feature of European child-rearing models since the seventeenth century, and which had reached its peak in the second half of the last century, began to decline after 1900 and particuarly after World War 1 (fig. 26) (the third part of our analysis, covering the

period 1920 to 1950). The authority of the teacher, the father, parents, adults, and the establishment generally decreased, and the child was not expected to submit unconditionally and blindly to all authority. Punishment, either physical or psychological, was not regarded any more as a necessary or always effective recourse, and was replaced in the new child model by order and strict routine, based on medical rather than moral grounds. Moral care (which was now considered to be only the establishment of regular habits or conditioned responses) was referred to far less frequently. More emphasis was placed on ability, efficiency, and achievement (fig. 27) in line with the demands of a modern industrial civilization.

The rational principles which proved successful in organizing industry were now employed as guiding principles in child care. The purely emotional and superstitious notions from the past must be disregarded and we must defer to the only correct and effective authority, that of science and reason. In their outbursts against spoiling and sentimentality, some of the experts echoed certain humanists of the sixteenth and seventeenth centuries (e.g. M. D. Montaigne 1533—92). From this rational, impersonal point of view, those involved in child care should avoid too much cuddling, over-protection, meeting the child's irrational demands, giving way if the child demands something by crying. All these things are damaging and produce a child who is tyrannical, spoiled, dependent, and fundamentally an unhappy person. These results can be viewed as behaviour disorders caused by unreasonable or inconsistent treatment rather than by moral decay (fig. 29). The small child needs satisfaction of his biological needs (food, sleep, and rest) in a measure considered adequate by the supervisor. Over-stimulation is obviously damaging. If the supervisor consistently follows these rules and adopts a rational approach from the cradle or even from the first hour of life, punishment is unnecessary. The establishment of and strict adherence to an effective child-rearing programme is a task for both parents, for they are the most important rearing influences in the child's life. School becomes more and more academic in nature. The family is more and more the centre of the child's environment and rearing. Interpersonal relations within the family become more straightforward and friendly, and offer to all participants greater and greater personal satisfaction. Relationships outside the family are increasingly directed towards material advancement, productivity, and effective cooperation in the working environment.

Under these conditions the most threatened child lacks order and firm, effective — i.e. rational — supervision. This can be the child who is neglected and undernourished, who lives in disorder and dirt, and who has a bad school and work record because the parent is uneducated and/or uninterested in him. Or it can be the child who lacks order and control of his life by rational principles for different reasons — because of over-zealous, unreasonable, and for the child unhelpful, love, i.e. over-protection. If the parents cannot follow the experts' advice (especially medical advice) and if they allow themselves to be swayed by emotional rather than rational considerations, it is better for the child to be placed in an appropriate institution — in a nursery, a kindergarten, a hospital, a sanatorium, a boarding school, or a rehabilitation institute.

At this time, there was rapid development of such institutes, which were more specialized and scientifically based than previously. Greater success in the medical treatment of the child — decrease in mortality, illness, nutritive disorders, and the most serious epidemics — lent support to those advocating this concept of child care. This development was paralleled by the growth of case work with individual families.

Successful development of medical, social, and educational institutions based on this child-care model brought sharp criticism from a number of quarters, mainly from psychologists and child psychiatrists. They argued strongly against impersonal institutionalized care and the emotionally cold attitude of those concerned with child care. In this "alarm" period they were already suggesting new concepts of emotional or maternal deprivation, which was the crux of the deprivational problem in the next period.

6. This period dates from immediately after World War II. In dealing with Czechoslovakian conditions, we have limited this period to the years 1950 to 1962, but it is obvious that trends shown in this period developed in different countries at different times — for example, somewhat earlier in the U.S.A.

The pendulum has swung from the totally permissive medieval child-rearing model to a model of strict authority and discipline in the sixteenth century, reaching its zenith in the second half of the nineteenth century, then back to the ideal of permissive care. In the period under discussion the pendulum had swung to its extreme position (fig. 26). Over-strict discipline (moral or routine) and authority were thought to frustrate the child's needs for spontaneous expression, and could quite easily lead to neuroticism. The rational approach had also led to child-care practices which seemed to resemble the "stable-like" upbringing of animals, rather than the development of a sensitive human personality. The child, because of advances in medical science, could survive without the mother, but his personal development was impossible without a stable satisfying relationship with some maternal figure. The child primarily needs love, and this can be provided only in the family — in the small nuclear family which gradually became the centre of the emotional satisfactions which were previously spread diffusely through the whole of the familial in-group.

The family was now an enclave, which offered both the child and adults emotional satisfaction and protection which were unobtainable elsewhere in a complicated and competitive world. Without the mother or the family, the child lacks a background of love, security, and assurance. This was now recognized as the worst possible misfortune a human being could suffer during his development. The prototype of the deprived child was the child without maternal love, the child separated from the mother, possibly the child from a broken home which cannot provide this emotional background. In this general context, the danger of hospitalism in institutionalized children was seen to be due mainly to lack of maternal care, which even the best scientifically directed child-care programme cannot replace.

This view was the stimulus for a radical change in social child care which occurred in the fifties in Western Europe and in the U.S.A., and which also appeared in different guises in European socialist countries. Removal of huge impersonal institutions, which had previously developed as social care institutions in Europe, or their radical reorganization into small family units, the use of the surrogate family environment, greater emphasis on prevention, and increase in effective and more sophisticated social help for the family have been outstanding features of recent progress in this field.

7. Since we lack the perspective of the uninvolved observer, the most difficult task of all is to describe the present state of affairs. We attempt this reluctantly, and are fully aware of the speculative nature of our assumptions.

The year 1962 (the point at which our analysis finished), in which the WHO monograph *Deprivation of maternal care* was published, probably is the beginning of the next important period in the developing history of the concept of the deprived child. A number of studies emphasized anew the need for discipline and order — even if only to a minor extent — after the period of extreme permissiveness. Again the spectre of the "omnipotent child", the product of too permissive care, appears. At the same time, however, the importance of the emotional needs of the child is fully recognized. In the last hundred years we have gone full circle in our emphasis on the relative importance of both discipline and the emotional needs of the child (fig. 26).

The path we have traversed, however, has been valuable. It has led to a decrease in moralistic attitudes to child care, and to an increased emphasis on an understanding of and sensitivity towards human interactions (fig. 27) — on the need to consider individual needs and individual approaches to every child. Since every child should be treated differently, the single cultural model of child rearing becomes inadequate. This far-reaching individual approach to child-care practices and ideals has, however, created uncertainty in supervisors, children, and adolescents, which is exacerbated by the rapid change in models which had remained relatively unchanged for centuries. Advances in industrial technology have significantly reduced the danger of non-satisfaction of the child's basic material needs, but have increased the emotional deprivation of a child living under conditions of material and educational well-being but lacking emotional interaction and understanding. The emotionally alienated child seeking secondary sources of emotional satisfaction becomes the new model of deprivation. This may begin at an early age, but crystallizes in adolescence when the young person leaves the relatively satisfying and protective family environment and enters the external environment, which, governed by different laws, is alienating and anonymous.

How far have we moved from the small child who could mix freely with the group, and identify with it? The need for group membership still exists in modern man; he seeks to restore his lost capacity to interact which would bridge the gap between the protected nucleus of the small intimate family and the hostile world. Resurgence of interest in the psychological basis of love (H. F. Harlow, 1958; E. Fromm, 1956; P. A. Sorokin, 1967), which we have been too reluctant to discuss, is an expression of such seeking.

TRANS-CULTURAL APPROACH TO PSYCHOLOGICAL DEPRIVATION

It is impossible to find an idyllic period in the past, or a culture in the present complicated and insensitive world, where people do not suffer materially or psychologically, and where the psychological needs of all children are fully satisfied. In every culture we can find conditions which from certain points of view are more favourable than those in our own society, so that personality development in that culture seems more natural and less subject to dangers. Thus we tend to view a culture traditionally offering the child rich sensory stimulation and unlimited opportunity for satisfaction of all his instinctive needs as ideal; we approve the permissive attitude of some cultures (e.g. Oceanic) towards the sexual behaviour of adolescents. Adults and children in some relatively segregated communities (for example the Hutterite communities in North America) may seem to live under ideal conditions of mutual understanding and support. When we take a closer and more objective look, however, we realize that the seeds of danger and difficulty are only differently sown and that "at the present time no cultural group offers optimal conditions for all aspects of child rearing" (W. W. Lambert, 1966). The resources of every society for the determination of the form of the cultural model of child rearing are limited, and therefore its influence on the upbringing of individual children is also restricted. Since the distribution of these resources is different in every culture the distribution of sources of deprivation also varies.

It is beyond our present scope to attempt a detailed discussion of the most important sources of child deprivation in different cultures. We lack adequate and relevant comparative data. Studies by cultural anthropologists are only peripherally concerned with this problem, so that we can draw support for our contentions only from superficial observations or deductions from material which is addressed to different problems (e.g. most frequently to the effect of cultural factors on the development of personality). The methodological problems involved in trans-cultural studies have been frequently discussed and a number of solutions suggested. No one approach, however, can offer the necessary frame of reference.

Despite this, we can compare a few typical cases of deprivation in certain cultural regions, which we think may suggest some general conclusions. There are some analogies with the development of conditions of psychological deprivation in European society, which were previously discussed, but these analogies are very weak. Differences between societies which developed independently are far greater than differences within a society, even though such a society has become complex and differentiated during its historical development.

1. Let us first consider conditions in some traditional so-called "primitive" cultures (which of course are not primitive in their complex diversified structure nor in the richness of their cultural inheritance), for example in some native tribes in Africa, Australia, Polynesia, South America, and Asia. In these cultures child-rearing practices typically permit extensive, and for Europeans, exaggerated permissiveness and emotional warmth by the mother towards the child from the earliest age. Childhood, however, is quite short and

Table 20. Cultural models of child rearing

Historical Period		Sources of Psychological Deprivation	Model of Deprived Child	Development of Social Care	Development of Concepts of Psychological Deprivation
Middle Ages	High emotional level (unstable) and extreme permissiveness / Short childhood / Extended patrimonial family / Early separation from family, strong extra-familial ties, dependency on in-group / Mixed age groups / Concept of child as a small adult	Non-acceptance or rejection by group	Deserted (cast-off, rejected) child	Establishment of founding homes and hospitals in monasteries	(Pre-scientific period)
Seventeenth to nineteenth centuries	Extended childhood / More restricted patriarchal family / Increased extra-family discipline (school), high emotional level in family / Idea of well-bred child	Lack of discipline (in society)	Lone child (vagabond)	Establishment of age-grade schools (boarding schools)	
Second half of nineteenth century (1850–1900)	Strong discipline and high emotional level in family, nuclear patricentric family / Emphasis on moral values / Idea of moral childhood	Lack of authority (father) and emotional ties (mother)	Child without family (orphan) or illegitimate child	Child-care institutes / Charitable social care	
Beginning of twentieth century (1900–20)	More moderate discipline, growing rationality in the family / Emphasis on social-moral values / Liberalization and democratization of family / Idea of a well-educated child	Lack of supervision in family (through lack of social support)	Morally "decaying" child (from marginal families)	Social care, public enlightenment / Universal education	"Empirical" period

				Public health services	
Second quarter of twentieth century (1920–50)	Reduced discipline, increased rationality (routine, persistent) Continued democratization of family Idea of productive (successful) child	Educationally neglected child	Lack of rational upbringing	Orthopaedagogic care	Schlossmann, 1920 "Alarm" period
Post-war period (1950–62)	Return to increased emotional and permissive level in family Nuclear (isolated) family, egalitarian Emotional dependence on family Emphasis on interpersonal relationships Idea of adjusted child	Child emotionally deprived (without maternal love)	Inadequate emotional relationships in small family	Mental health services, surrogate family care	Bowlby, 1951 "Critical" period
Present trends	Greater emotionality – slightly increased discipline Openness and planning (programming) in society Expansion of emotional ties from small family to extra-familial environment Idea of sensitive child	Alienated child	Lack of meaningful relationship to the environment and to himself	Socially oriented psychological services	Ainsworth, 1962 "Experimental-theoretical" period

Table 21. Trans-cultural approach to the problems of psychological
deprivation: some types of society and corresponding
models of the deprived child.

Type of Existing Society	Model of Deprived Child
1. Traditional tribal society (Nigeria, Uganda)	Child physically deserted (in infancy), rejected, excluded from the tribal group
2. Traditional minority groups during re-acculturation as response to external pressure (gipsies in Czechoslovakia)	Morally deserted child, unsupervised, undisciplined (vagabond), social parasites
3. Lower socio-economic groups in developing agricultural-industrial societies (e.g. *barrios* in Puerto Rico)	Child deserted by the family, orphan, child entrusted to care of another family, child with low social status
4. Marginal groups barely existing on borders of developed industrial societies: children from slums and so on (e.g. *scugnizzi* of Neapolitan streets)	Child morally decaying, severe physical neglect, anti-social behaviour
5. Rapidly developing but previously extremely backward groups (e.g. Northeast Slovakia)	Child lacking adequate care, culturally retarded, lacking hygienic habits and schooling
6. Socialist countries in the fifties (e.g. Czechoslovakia after 1948)	Emotionally deprived child, "collectivized" child
7. European and North American cultural regions (excluding disadvantaged children)	The alienated child

the change sometimes occurs quickly, sometimes more gradually,
sometimes earlier, sometimes later. Usually, after weaning or around
five or six years of age, there is a conscious effort to discipline and
socialize the child, who is thus subjected to a rigid, closed system of
social norms and values. Another general feature of child rearing in
such societies is the extensive participation of female − and later
male − members of the extended family and neighbours (adults and
older children) in the nursing and supervision of the child. Under
such circumstances the child quickly develops emotional dependence
on the group to which he belongs, he accepts its norms and values as
his own, and identifies himself with the society. In those societies in
which social status is a function of age, this dependence of the child
on the society is mediated by his close dependence on the peer
group, and the acquisition of full status is accompanied by initiation
rites. In other g oups the mixing of children and adults is much freer

and the adoption of adult roles is a more continuous process (R. Benedict, 1954).

For example, T. A. Lambo (1969) describes child-rearing practices in polygamous, consanguinal, patrilocal, patriarchal, and authoritarian families in major African cultures as being completely permissive during the very early years. The newborn infant, whose every need is anticipated and met by a confident mother before he is aware of needing anything, experiences an unbroken state of satisfaction, without effort, such as doubtless exists in intra-uterine life. He is born into a warm, affectionate, and welcoming culture. In the early months he is inseparable from his mother, who feeds him at the slightest whimper, and he enjoys all the emotional security of the extended family, including grandmothers, who are notorious coddlers of children. The amount of loving stimulation far exceeds that deemed adequate in our culture. For most of the day the child is cuddled, carried, rocked, petted, tickled, is sung and talked to. In the extended family, which includes the father, mother, other wives, grandparents, uncles, aunts, siblings, and cousins, the child very quickly learns to accept frequent mother substitution, and subsequently father substitution. The group as a whole, and particularly the peer group, especially after five years of age, has much greater influence. Group socializing pressures are very strong and the child is forced to adopt certain behaviours to avoid sanctions and possible isolation, which is intolerable. Strong group loyalty is developed very early. Permissive and strong emotional relationships between mother and child in these conditions are limited by two factors — primarily by the mother's new pregnancy, and thus the necessity to care for the other child, and secondly by the mother's household duties and food gathering. Different societies differ quite markedly in their solutions to these problems.

There has been thorough documentation of the almost unbelievable change which occurs in these traditional societies in the relationship between mother and child after the mother becomes pregnant or when the child is weaned. R. C. Albino and V. J. Thompson (1956) report the change in the mother's attitude after the sudden weaning of the child between eighteen and twenty-four months of age. The group studied was a South African Zulu tribe. On a day nominated by the mother (or grandmother) the child is prevented from sucking and the permissive regime is changed into one of harshness and cruelty. The child's usual reaction to the mother's behaviour is apathy and fretfulness, or possibly irritation and aggression (which may extend to the whole family). His attempts to regain his lost position can continue for a few weeks until he adapts to the changed situation and begins to develop his social behaviour. Nutritional disorders are quite frequent.

M. D. Ainsworth (1963) and M. Gebber (1964) describe a similar case of sudden change of maternal behaviour in tribal groups in Uganda. Some time between the twelfth and fifteenth months of the child's life, the oldest female in the family determines the weaning day, and from that time the child's whole life is radically changed. The suckling suddenly stops, and the child must immediately feed himself from the common bowl. He is often entrusted to the care of a distant grandmother and the mother adopts an indifferent, even negative, attitude to him. She no longer carries the child nor spends her time with him. She does not react to his crying and even teases him. In the presence of adults he must sit quietly without moving. Even if he remains in the care of his parents, his relationship with his mother is terminated. When the child returns from his grandmother, in his place he finds a younger child who has now usurped his former, now definitely lost, status.

Under such conditions the development of the child in the first few months of life is unbelievably rapid. At three months he can sit for a few moments without support, at six months can stand up with support, can grasp objects between thumb and forefinger, at nine months starts to walk and mumble, and is very active and full of curiosity. His DQ is 120–140, according to European norms. At about eighteen months, however, the child appears to lose his developmental advantage, his activity level decreases, he often cries and is restless, and if this trend continues, at about three years he becomes apathetic, and at about four to five years his DQ decreases to 70–90. A trusting attitude towards strangers is replaced by a suspicious, alert awareness. Malnutrition, e.g. rickets, or kwashiorkor, often occurs.

S. Biesheuvel (1959), however, gives a quite different account of the marked effects of changes in maternal attitude on weaning; he states: "There is no feeling of rejection following on a period of apparent indulgence, because by now the child has learned to accept substitutes early. Indeed, overt rejection is minimized by the voluntary attentions of the maternal grandmother or aunt" (quoted by T. A. Lambo, 1969).

The second problem — the mother's dual responsibility towards household duties and looking after the child — is also solved in different ways in different cultures. In some instances the mother carries the child while she is working — for example, in the fields (in some parts of India) or on the river (fig. 34), in other cases the child is left alone at home (Alora tribe), deserted and hungry. In other groups an old female from the extended family cares for the child. M. Mead suggests that in those societies in which the child from the beginning is usually separated from parents, he becomes dependent on the group, and the specific relationship to the mother depends on subsequent personal independent decision making. M. D. Ainsworth has a different concept. She maintains that usually under these conditions the child initially develops the specific relationship to the mother and that this attachment quickly generalizes to other people.

From this very short and over-simplified account we consider that there is some danger of deprivation even under these developmental conditions. Insofar as input of sensory and emotional stimulation and the close mother-child relationships are concerned, conditions seem to be generally very favourable up to the time of weaning. It is also clear that the child subsequently is given adequate substitutes which prevent suffering as we know it in the European context. When T. A. Lambo (1969) discusses emotional deprivation, he can claim, with some reservations, that "in clinical work in Africa, this condition is not encountered under normal circumstances", and can also say (referring to J. Kenyatta's [1961] description of the development of Kikuyu children) that illegitimacy appears to be "almost an unknown social condition in Africa — children who are born out of wedlock still have social recognition". Because of the extended system of relationships they belong "to some male, either the natural father, or the maternal grandfather". The death of parents in such societies is not a deprivational crisis: the child does not lose his home, and still retains membership of his primary group of adults and peers. The child who has lost one of his parents by death or divorce, which sometimes occurs in these societies, always remains in the natal household. Even in such circumstances, however, a child can still be threatened by deprivation.

This can occur through sudden separation from the mother — which may be real or emotional (e.g. psychological rejection by the mother), particularly if the attitude of all other persons is rejecting. A change in attitude by the whole primary group is seen by the child as rejecting, and can be experienced as an unbearable reality to which he cannot adapt. The result is increased irritability and social hyperactivity and subsequent depression and apathy, which is followed by marked retardation in mental development, poor physical progress, malnutrition, sickness, and eventually death.

The above, however, is an extreme case of rejection by the group or of actual isolation. Any hint of group rejection, for example teasing, is very effective and can have an unfavourable effect on the child's development. Total rejection by the group is a matter of life and death, for group belongingness is the source of all life security and values; it is fundamental to the whole of mental life and the balance of the natural and social environments. So-called voodoo death amongst Australian Aborigines, after ritual exclusion from the group, is an extreme example of this form of deprivation.

2. As we have suggested, certain child-rearing practices and conditions which threaten deprivation in traditional tribal communities are similar to conditions which existed in the early period of the development of European society. Even today, however, we can still see these conditions in certain groups of people in Europe and North America. An example is the gipsies, who immigrated from northwest India in the Middle Ages and who live in relatively large numbers in Europe. Some features of their life-style and child-rearing practices still resemble those of the Middle Ages, while others approximate more closely child-rearing practices in Europe in the sixteenth and seventeenth centuries.

The 250,000 gipsies who today are scattered through Czechoslovakia are not a homogenous group. Some of the families have been fully assimilated, while others still maintain their traditional ways of life. They have their own language, habits, traditions, behavioural norms, songs, fairy tales and ballads, handed down, usually in verbal form, from generation to generation. They also have their typical child-rearing practices. Their nomadic way of life has changed markedly, but frequent moving about and change of job is still typical. The gipsy family is very extended, and consists of closely related members from different generations (clan). A census is often quite impossible. Marital relations are free, unstable, quarrelsome, but always very affectionate. The mother carries the infant most of the time and satisfies his needs fully on demand. Her relationship with the child is very intense but unstable. The dramatic scenes when a gipsy child is hospitalized, and the participation of the whole extended family with the appropriate displays of affection during the first visit, often surprisingly change to complete indifference towards the child when he is due to return home after two or three weeks. Often the parents do not even collect the child after repeated notification, and he has to be taken home or cared for. He is emotionally deserted and is regarded as a stranger after he has been absent from home for a short period of time.

Gipsies obviously enjoy group life, and they have extensive emotional involvements outside the family. Identification with the in-group is very strong. For a gipsy, rejection by the group is the most severe punishment, and can be a great tragedy. Attempts to assimilate the gipsy population and to house them in permanent, dispersed settlements (for example, in Czechoslovakia under the 1958 law) have been generally unsuccessful, since this severs generation and kinship bonds without which gipsies lose their life security and emotional stability.

Since the eighteenth century, considerable pressure has been applied to gipsies, particularly about the disciplining of children and adolescents. For example, in the region that is now Czechoslovakia, a law was promulgated in 1761, enacting, amongst other things, compulsory schooling for gipsies and the placement of older boys in proper employment. This attempt to ensure schooling, however, failed because of poor motivation, neglect at home, speech difficulties, and so on. Even today only 10—12 per cent of gipsy children complete all grades of primary school. Efforts to socialize gipsy children to the level of other children in the population at large have also been unsuccessful. Gipsy adolescents generally have unstable work records, they wander about from job to job, and their economic and cultural level is still considerably below average.

Under such conditions, typical features of the gipsy child's behaviour are wandering, pilfering, truancy, poor scholastic achievement, and subsequently a poor job record; he is unstable and quarrelsome in his emotional relationships. These children and adolescents resemble, to a certain extent, the type of student-vagabond dating from the Middle Ages, although the latter was a product of different social conditions.

The IQ of these children, when conventionally tested, is usually below average to dull-normal, although practical ability and social "cleverness" suggest good inherited potential. Judged by the standards of society generally, we can regard this state as a specific example of cultural deprivation. From the point of view of traditional gipsy culture, which regards the type of behaviour described as relatively normal, a deprived child is one who lives in the family but is rejected emotionally, and whose behaviour is apathetic. Our experience suggests that the child who is rejected in this way is usually the child with some marked and obvious handicap (malformation, illness, or sensory defect), the child who is lethargic because of mental retardation or defect, or the child separated earlier for various reasons. Toddler institutes, children's homes, and asylums are overcrowded with gipsy children of this type who have been deserted by their families.

3. Let us now briefly consider the sources of child deprivation in one type of agricultural-industrial society which, with regard to child-rearing models, to some extent resembles European society of

the last century. This is the socio-economically depressed group living in *barrios* (villages) of Puerto Rico.[4] A typical community in this Spanish Catholic sub-culture consists of two generation families with numerous children who live in close proximity with grandparents, kinsfolk and *compadres* (ritual co-fathers). The characteristic feature of these families is the strong patriarchal authoritative structure. In the family, obedience to the father is absolute and natural, male superiority is asserted in self-reliance, aggressiveness, freedom of action, knowledge of the world, freedom of movement, and positive attitude to sexuality (the *machismo* — masculinity complex), which contrasts with the submissiveness, sexual inhibition, and attachment to the home (the "cloister pattern") in females. A child born into such a culture is faced from the beginning with two realities — in nearly every case he is exposed to many maternal figures and his status in the family depends on sex and birth order. The child's well-being or the form and severity of his deprivation depend on these factors, as well as on the basic economic level of the family.

The multiple-mothering pattern in this society, however, is very different from that found in traditional tribal societies, for example in Africa. The significant feature here is the instability of the mother figure; every time another child is born, or the mother is sick, or another crisis develops, many female relatives and ritual co-mothers are available as substitutes and assume the mother's role. Under these conditions the quality of the mother-child relationship seems to be less intense and certainly less stable; often the child may become temporarily more attached to an aunt or grandmother, and such attachments are accepted by the mother without any apparent sign of resentment. One might expect that future relationships based on such initial unstable ties would be diffuse rather than being concentrated on one or two love-objects. Under unfavourable conditions the child may become emotionally lost in this network of relationships and his capacity to form any sort of relationship might be impaired.

Cultural expectations about the nature of the sexes and the generally different social statuses ascribed to them lead to extremely different developmental opportunities for boys and girls (in the sense of freedom of movement, environmental exploration, free expression of aggressive and sexual impulses, acceptance of work tasks and responsibilities). The desire to have a male heir is usually very strong and may encourage higher fertility when female offspring occur

---

4. This discussion is based primarily on a study reported by L. Mendez in a seminar organized by one of the authors at the University of Alberta, Edmonton, Alberta, Canada, in 1968, and on the published works of J. M. Stycos (1955), K. M. Wolf (1952), and D. Landy (1959).

earlier in the birth order (J. M. Stycos, 1955). Girls who are the eldest, therefore, find themselves in a very difficult position. They are set aside as soon as another child is born, and are trained early to assume household responsibilities and the care of smaller children. At about eight or nine years of age many of them act as substitute mothers in all household duties. At the same time they must be strictly obedient, devoted, self-denying, are "under-valued" but "over-chaperoned", carefully watched (particularly after their first menstruation) to avoid any kind of dating and even talking to strangers. Under these circumstances many of them actively seek the only possible way of escaping from home — elopement with a lover.

The child most threatened with deprivation is probably the one who, for some reason or other, cannot establish a satisfying relationship with the significant maternal figure in the family and who is literally passed "from hand to hand" during the early years, and lives for long periods with families other than his own. This applies particularly to the so-called *hijos de crianza* (children of rearing), whose parents, either through poverty or because they expect that later on this will be advantageous to the child, lend them for a fixed or indefinite period to a relative or friend. Very frequently, however, these children feel rejected and are given away under some pretext. In the close community of the island towns, where members accept definite responsibilities towards one another, this arrangement might not be too harmful. In the impersonal and bigger communities of some metropolises (Puerto Rican children in New York city), however, this practice can be detrimental. In either case, the child's life becomes difficult, and he experiences a feeling of rejection and confusion when he is faced with different family environments, to each of which he is expected to be loyal and obedient.

Other groups of afflicted children are stepchildren, the children of legal and illegal alliances (the so-called *hijastros*), and children committed to foster care by a public welfare agency. Usually these children have low social status and are often exploited in different ways. Although they very often express positive feelings towards the person who raises them (K. M. Wolf, 1952), they must have a deep feeling of rejection. Sometimes their inability to establish any relationship whatever with either their real parent or with their new (substitute) parent leads to severe personality disorders and anti-social behaviour.

This type of sub-culture, with its specific familial and community structure, creates a predictable pattern of social behaviour and conditions which can lead to certain forms of deprivation. Since the placement of children in institutions is highly disapproved of, the problem of hospitalism as such is non-existent. Different types of family deprivation constitute the greatest problem. This concerns children who at the time of birth, or as a result of a subsequent social catastrophe, lose their social status — orphans, illegitimate children, rejected children, children transferred to another family for an indefinite period of time, children from very large poverty-stricken or alcoholic families. Their destiny and the form of deprivation are rather similar to those of children in analogous circumstances in Europe in the past century.

4. In some areas of Europe and America we can still find groups living in extreme poverty on the periphery of developed or fast-developing industrial societies, in slums, *bidonvilles,* or whatever name is given to those rotting areas which often exist side by side with high class areas in the city. In the worst cases they have nowhere to live and they look for shelter every night, building shanties which hardly protect them from cold or rain. In a society in which public agencies are increasingly adopting supervisory roles, and which is directed by a complicated set of rules, sanctions, ways of interacting and permissible ways of need satisfaction, this sub-proletariat group is subjected to constant environmental stress with only infrequent and usually unsuccessful attempts at help. These people form a special sub-culture which has its own social norms, values, sanctions, ways of behaving, language, and model of child rearing which reflect in a particular way the culture of the country, and which aim to equip the child for survival under primitive social conditions. It is quite obvious of course that all groups of this sort do not operate at the same level. We treat them as one category, however, since the risk of deprivation in all these cases is extremely high and to some extent the results are similar.

In the majority of cases, children born under these conditions lack planned early maternal care. From an early age they usually spend most of their time outside the family, surviving as best they can. There is almost a total lack of love and discipline both inside and outside the family. Very often the only guarantee of some protection, authority, and supervision is the gang, with which the children very quickly show solidarity and identification. They have little schooling, and continuous care is practically non-existent. There is no actual discrimination between legitimate and illegitimate children, between orphans and children who have an existing family, between a neglected child and a child rejected for psychological reasons — all these children are to some degree exposed to the same dangers. In extreme cases they live under conditions of nearly total social deprivation — starved, dirty, concerned only with survival. Their mental development is severely retarded and is completely primitive in structure (A. Schlosser, 1969). In the majority of cases such an environment produces a child who is extremely socially undisciplined, morally delinquent, a child who from the point of view of the surrounding "normal" society is habitually anti-social. For the child, however, such habit patterns are necessary for the maintenance of a bare level of subsistence.

There are many reports about such sub-cultural groups, such as W. F. Whyte's (1943) classic study of the Italian slums in the U.S.A., and some more recent studies of so-called cultural deprivation. These suggest, among other things, that we cannot find an effective solution to this problem unless we understand its cultural and social etiology.

Let us briefly consider the special group of deprived children from the streets of Naples through the eyes of the person who made contact with them and offered effective help. Father M. Borrelli (1969, personal communication; M. Borrelli and A. Thorne, 1963; M. West, 1957) every night dressed in rags, joined the gang and suffered cold, dirt, hunger, pests — and his own anxiety that he might fail to understand the children and gain their trust. Only by these means could he persuade them to accept a different way of life in the "Casa dello Scugnizzo" which the children, after an initial period of scepticism, could accept as their own and in which they were able to forget the past and begin a new life.

In Naples three to four thousand children lived on the streets, slept in gutters covered by papers, ate out of garbage bins, stole, and lived in close contact with the most brutal facts of life. Their ages ranged from seven to over twenty; in the gang all of them gained at least a little security and love which were denied them in their homes. As we described before, they have different family backgrounds, but they have one attribute in common, that they have been denied any form of family care. Their homes, *bassi,* are one-room dwellings facing directly onto the street, so that the street becomes the only real home. Amongst these children are both the strong and self-reliant professionals and those who only partly support themselves by petty crime. The range of family background is matched by the spread of personality and behaviour. All of them, however, because of their lives without love, basic physical care, discipline, or schooling, learn to fight, to beat others, to cheat, to steal, and to distrust. They even distrust the members of their own gang. They are sexually experienced from an early age and frequently consort with prostitutes. "Innocence has been denied them and they have never been taught morals." The "proper" society of the city chooses to ignore them, but they exist — uncontrollable, unreachable. This group is one of the many examples of the most shocking type of deprivation which is still being produced in our advanced society.

5. In countries which today are accelerating their economic and cultural development, the most serious form of deprivation is usually lack of development of cultural needs which are normal in European-American civilization. Children have not yet learned to live the kind of life which the new conditions demand; they have a low level of verbal expression, have not acquired hygienic habits, their achievement motivation, their motivations for acquiring new knowledge, academic education, and higher social status are minimal. This type of deprivation typifies a group living in a mountainous region in the most eastern part of Czechoslovakia.[5] Up to the end of World War II this community was practically isolated from the surrounding areas by bad communications. The people spoke a different dialect, lived on a primitive agricultural level, and their living standard was considerably lower than that of other parts of the region. Families (two generation) were very large, with ten or more children, but there was a high infant mortality rate. Medical care' was almost unobtainable, or was distrusted and rarely sought. People lived with the farm animals in sub-standard houses, often consisting of only one room. The diet of pregnant women was inadequate, as was the care given to the mother and child during and after delivery. Children were suckled for two years, and then began to eat adult food, which lacked the necessary calorific value and variety (especially protein). The incidence of TB was extremely high and lack of control over domestic water supply, contaminated food, and insects caused frequent epidemics. A tooth-brush caused curiosity and surprise amongst all the villagers.

Mothers in this community had strong emotional ties with their children but quickly accepted their loss, which was frequent. Often they could not remember how many children had been born, and how many had died. A typical answer to the question of cause of death was "got ill, died". Most families in the village were related, and lived in a close group relationship, so that there were many substitutes available if the child lost his parents. There were very few divorces, but alcoholism was almost the norm. The mother's involvement with the child was seriously impeded both by the birth of other children and by the onerous task of supporting the family. Schooling was spasmodic and in some remote places almost non-existent. The illiteracy rate was high, although in the western

5. This report is based on a social survey conducted by a group of students in 1946 (D. Langmeierová, unpublished).

part of Czechoslovakia this had been almost unknown since the nineteenth century. Feelings of nationalism were very weak, and many could not name the country in which they lived. The social environment, however, was relatively stable, and the child-rearing models were handed down from generation to generation in the same way as folklore, songs, stories, folk weaving and so on.

Soon after the war an extensive and systematic effort was made to improve the economic, medical, and educational state of the region. Industrialization quickly developed, communication was improved, free medical and community hygiene services were extended, and child-care institutes such as kindergartens, nurseries, and schools were established. Under such rapidly changing conditions the greatest problem was the training of children and adolescents in hygienic habits, and persuading the community about the value of using medical and educational services and the newly available social and working opportunities. From this point cultural deprivation (in the sense of the relative deprivation of the population as a whole) changed more and more to individual deprivation. While rapid improvement was recorded in some individual families and villages, and with individual children, in other places change was slow or almost non-existent. Infant mortality decreased but it was still very much higher than the national average.

6. Let us now attempt to describe deprivating conditions in Western society of today and in the immediate future. There is, of course, the same range of differences amongst Western societies as, for example, amongst traditional African societies. Here also we shall concentrate on basic features which to some extent typify present-day society in Western Europe and North America, and are to some degree also present in the social structures of Eastern European countries.

Possibly we could describe the state of the modern child – or modern man as such – as being characterized both by increasing freedom and by increased planning (which is reflected in the two marked features of child care – striking permissiveness on the one hand and rationality on the other). By saying that Western society is becoming freer we mean that greater opportunities are available to the vast majority of the population for higher education, the acquisition of new knowledge and skills, the understanding of different (sometimes conflicting) points of view, philosophical and religious concepts, new artistic trends, opportunities for meeting people from different countries and different cultures, better job opportunities, different ways of relaxation, and so on. Through educational facilities, mass media, and rapid communication, modern man is offered access to the whole world and beyond to a far greater degree than ever before. The open society permits an individual to see life as a kaleidoscope of choices, alternatives, and preferences, in which his personal decision making is governed mainly by his individuality. Parents and educators, when faced with this, can do little more than allow the child greater freedom in his decision making than at any previous time, primarily because parents themselves cannot envisage the larger number of alternatives and in many situations lack knowledge and certainty, and because the value structures adopted by different authorities which the child encounters are often vastly different and sometimes contradictory. Thus to a far greater degree the child of today, from the very beginning, can become aware of his own individuality and can insist on the actualization and fulfilment of this individuality. The child can strive for the satisfaction of his most basic needs, ignoring the strict limits of absolute ethics.

Life outside the broad kinship and neighbourhood environment without the emotional satisfaction of group participation results in withdrawal into the privacy and the intimate circle of the small nuclear family, which like the individual carries individual values and behavioural norms. At the same time, however, decision making by the child and parents causes uncertainty about what is right and wrong, valid and binding, the consequences of different acts of choice. The child or adult can develop different defences against the resulting anxiety. The situation can be perceived as threatening and dangerous, demanding submissive conformity to a strong ideal — a powerful individual, an influential idea, or a protective group. On the other hand, it can be viewed as desirable and exciting, one promising great opportunities in pursuing the goal of development of an autonomous individuality.

Societies can also differ in the degree to which they maintain old values, inherited forms and traditional beliefs which offer security and protection, and in the extent to which they permit freedom to change values and ideologies. In order to survive, however, society must adapt to the new norms and values. This must be a rational process — that is, one based on the widest possible range of information. Programming or planning, which is shown in increasing technocratization and bureaucratization of life, is the inevitable price we pay for greater freedom in modern society. Acceptance of technical or organizational roles, which is necessary for productivity and effectiveness, is the essential condition for mass production in a society which is becoming more and more a consumer society, and increasingly oriented to improving the material standard of living. An unfortunate side effect of this, however, is the increasing feeling amongst individuals that they are being manipulated by society — by its economic, ideological, and political forces against which they have no defence. The human being is lost in this monstrous complex net, which he does not understand and where the real puppeteers are as anonymous as were the sources of natural energy in the past.

Under such conditions the "I" becomes more and more the programmed self, part of the programme written by the society; the role is played for an audience and the self is the facade displayed to the environment. This programmed self smothers the real self, which is based on how the individual really evaluates himself, his experiences and emotional relationships. This feeling of loneliness, alienation, and helplessness is probably the most characteristic feeling of modern man. This was aptly described in the beginning of this century by an employee of a Prague insurance company, Franz Kafka, who wrote a visionary description of the desperate and hopeless efforts of a nameless individual in a nameless society to conquer the manipulating and hidden forces, to penetrate the facades distorting human life and to reach true reality, the true self, and to establish worthwhile relationships with human beings.

Such is the grotesque world of the alienated modern man which is better described by novelists (A. Camus for example) and dramatists (E. Ionesco, Albee) than by psychologists. But what creates this type of personality? Does the alienated child or adolescent with feelings of loneliness and alienation really exist? If the answer is yes, then what sort of a world is it that nurtures such a child or adolescent?

Even his birth is unique. He is delivered under excellent medical conditions, he is placed immediately in a special bed in a special room separated from his mother, and is given only a carefully regulated amount of handling, movement, attention, and tenderness. All that he needs is provided from a bottle, according to the rules of proper nourishment. All his basic needs are automatically satisfied without his cooperation or consent, and in fact without any consideration at all of his wishes and feelings. He does not experience the strong pangs of hunger, the relief and pleasure derived from satiation, he does not experience cold or the pleasure of radiating warmth. He has many toys and other developmental stimuli, but he gains little joy from them, he does not experience the fear of separation from his mother and the joy of reunion. He is surrounded by many incomprehensible objects which miraculously meet his material needs — sometimes simply by pressing a switch. His many complicated toys, for example, his electric engine, car, aeroplane, demand little active participation — he simply observes or switches them on and off. He spends many hours in front of the TV, observing pictures passively and without effort. Not only objects, events, and words, but also the people surrounding him come and go without obvious reasons, for unknown destinations, they have their own interests, they have little time for him, they do things he cannot understand. All they demand from him is compliance with a materially oriented, impersonal set of rules. Otherwise the child can do as he likes. Under such conditions, he must learn conventional ways of exchanging objects and symbols. Rational principles govern not only the world outside the family but increasingly the behaviour of individuals within the family.

In such a world, the child is supplied with all he needs, judged by rational principles — all his material needs are satisfied as well as his need for education. But his self is more and more determined by expectations created by the environment. The child conforms, lives more and more in the future, in terms of what is expected, what should happen. He does not realize that he can bring to other people joy or sadness and share their experiences.

We can see examples of this type of child even at kindergarten level; he accepts supervision as normal, usually is not troublesome, as if the environment has no significance for him. Behaviourally he seems to be very mature and intellectually precocious; he uses adult language. He seems to be urbane and "good", until he surprisingly shows an insensitivity to his own pain or that of other people, by his cold experimental attitude and indifference. He accepts presents with the same coldness as he accepts the coming and going of people. Some of these children obviously seek compensatory satisfaction of their emotional needs — they eat too much, are TV addicts, play until exhausted, listen to exciting music, voraciously read adventure stories. At a later age, some seek satisfaction from psychedelic drugs. Others run away from home and seek satisfaction in life outside society, in an unconventional life without money, routine, and responsibility, a life of "love". During adolescence some of these children become keenly aware of their internal conflicts and tend to respond by protest or aggression. Some passively realize the emptiness and senselessness of life and seek vainly for satisfying fulfilment. They feel disgusted by the senseless rat race, by their lives, they feel distaste towards their parents and all those people who previously had some credibility. Others simply experience unending loneliness and live through severe depressive stages in isolation. Of course, only a fraction of the child population is affected in this way, but the danger is nonetheless real.

How can one help these children suffering this paradoxical form of deprivation in the midst of plenty and increasing knowledge? It is not enough to simply offer additional food, housing, better medical care, schooling, child-care supervision, even controlled emotional stimulation (tender, loving care) and planned social control (which, in any event, is never adequate of itself, irrespective of the type of deprivation the child is suffering). Here one should be concerned with more extensive help — in developed societies we are only now beginning to realize the nature of this — to eliminate inhuman and crippling conditions in developed industrial societies, to increase active participation in all social activities, to release the child and the adult from the enslaving bonds of manipulating bureaucracy, and further, to make a positive effort to increase the sensitivity of man so that he might understand human values, be willing to listen to others and to himself, to understand rather than to morally judge or impersonally manipulate. Psychology can make some contribution by experimenting with certain techniques which may potentiate human sensitivity (group techniques, T-groups, encounter groups, family therapy, and so on) and encourage its development at an early age (for example, different programmes for development of sensitivity from pre-school age, as for example in H. Bessel's [1968] Human Development Programme). These techniques, of course, can be successful only to the extent that they are integrated into a total programme involving both the reformulation of the values of modern man and the total transformation of society "through the power of love", for "love is the experience that annuls individual loneliness; fills the emptiness of our isolation ...; breaks and transcends the narrow walls of our little egos; makes us co-participants in the highest life of humanity ...; expands our true individuality to the immeasurable boundaries of the universe" (P. A. Sorokin, 1954). Nevertheless any increase in mutual harmony in social groups "produces perhaps unspectacular but general altruization of the masses on a vast scale". If so, even a small effort to improve conditions by psychological means can help to solve the emotional and moral crisis of the human race today.

*   *   *   *

Our attempt to consider the development of European society and to adopt a comparative approach to different present-day societies — we trust in a valid, though obviously sketchy and over-simplified, way — points to two general conclusions.

1. The more highly developed the society or the more

complex its cultural basis, the higher is the status consciously conferred on the child, the more deliberate are all aspects of child care and education, the more stable and directed is the child-adult relationship, the more concentrated and significant are family influences on his development, and thus the more fully satisfied are his basic life needs.

Since Roman times, when exposure of new babies was quite normal, when the father could sell the child (even when adult) into slavery (*patria potestas*), and condemn him to torture or death, European society has progressed through a long period of evolution. Relatively indifferent attitudes to small children were quite normal throughout the Middle Ages. The concept of a child needing love and rearing (discipline) developed only slowly. Gradually, increased value was placed on the child and his rights were respected — initially the most basic rights, that is, those concerned with satisfaction of his material needs, but eventually the right to satisfy his psychological needs. The family became more and more child-centred, parent-child relationships became more intense, and more importantly, more stable. It is interesting to note that this development occurred earlier than changes in the material condition of life; interest in child rearing and the enhanced value of the child considerably preceded the marked decrease in infant mortality and the development of contraceptive practices to limit the number of children in families.

Mother-child relationships were better understood and became more responsible. The concept of blind "mother-love" was replaced by a rational, real interest directed by a progressively developing concept of a child's needs, which produced the concept of mother (parent) care responsible for their satisfaction. The child's behaviour — his special speech, ways of thinking — which were previously ignored as being unimportant, achieved a special importance and were observed, recorded, and studied. As described at the beginning of this century by one Czech philosopher and educator, "the more the culture progresses, the greater the increase in regard for and understanding of the child" (F. Drtina, 1912).

Child-rearing practices which were previously (and still are in certain areas) regarded as normal were increasingly rejected and recognized as deprivational and pathological. This was accompanied by more humanitarian attitudes towards the child and his care.

2. Counteracting this tendency to ascribe special value to the child's life, and to emphasize his health, development, and education, is a contrasting but closely related tendency, one of depersonalization and alienation.

While a child must be given that amount of satisfaction of his basic needs necessary for his full development and social participation, child care must to some extent be logically planned, must be related to changes in social structure, to the functions of different institutions, and to the overall complex of social activity. Consequently the life of the child depends to an increasing degree on intermediate relationships, while the original close primary relationships with humans and with the world are weakened. The child learns to use other humans as instruments in reaching his goals, learns to rely on his skill, knowledge, productivity, and social direction. As described by M. Buber (1923), "the child perceives all surrounding human beings as machines, able to perform different tasks, machines whose strength ought to be assessed and used for his own purposes. But he views himself also in a similar way ... the child appreciates himself also as an object".

Today this trend is most clearly expressed in the most highly developed societies. But it is not a sickness only of our age — "it is a malaise of all ages" (M. Buber). Statesmen, philosophers, and social thinkers have repeatedly attempted to create conditions producing the most radical and quickest approach to the social ideal (Utopian society), and in so doing have been willing, in the name of "the new age", "the new society", or "the new man", to sacrifice the personality of the individual, even of whole generations. They have tended to blame the family — to some extent justifiably — as the enemy of social change, since it is the vehicle of traditional attitudes and behavioural norms which pass from generation to generation relatively unchanged, and have attempted to weaken or destroy its influence. Thus Plato, in his *Republic*, suggested that children (because they should learn to accept the perfect class structure of society) should be cared for from birth by special teachers in state institutions. This has also been suggested by humanist Utopians (for example, T. Campanella, "Sun State", 1623), and by modern Utopians, who with understandable impatience seek to establish a new, better human race using an accelerated developmental process.

In the history of European society expression of the idea of moral childhood in the seventeenth century was followed by a strong tendency to separate the child early from the family, to enclose him in a monastic environment of boarding school, and to give him there the fullest possible formal education and strict disciplinary supervision, neither of which the family could offer. The child who was previously only of necessity separated from his parents was now willingly sent away from home for reasons of upbringing and education. In the middle-class family of the last century, which disapproved of this type of separation, child care became more dependent on other intermediate relationships which were a product of the social conditions of bourgeois society. This is suggested in protests against "false moral" or "inhuman" care. The twentieth century, which is the exciting stage of strenuous efforts to establish real humanity, has also witnessed the most monstrous expression of human bestiality, which had its side-effect on the concept of motherhood and parenthood.

Doubtless the family under normal conditions is, in fact, the retarding and limiting factor in the social and intellectual development of the human race. The family itself must change if it is to satisfy new concepts and new needs. The conversion of the old extended patriarchal family into a small family which is the focus of the sensitivity and emotionality of modern man is obviously the first requirement, although this has not yet been realized. The same changes have occurred in education, although not so obviously. The school, like the family, in the words of the outstanding humanist J. A. Comenius, should be "the workshop of humanity", the centre where the conflict between the two developmental tendencies is resolved.

The history of psychological deprivation in children is closely related to the central conflict in the development of human society, the conflict between developing humanity and repeated exposure to new forms of alienation. A solution to this problem of modern man, modern parent and modern child, the search for ways to strengthen the development of humanity, to counter the dangers of new alienation, underlies every large-scale approach to the problem of deprived children, and at the same time is affected by any attempt to solve this problem. At present we know that this can be achieved only by the cooperation of people all over the world.

25. Jesus entering Jerusalem, from the Bible of Henry II, dated 1002—14; the concept of the child as a "small adult" is clearly represented.

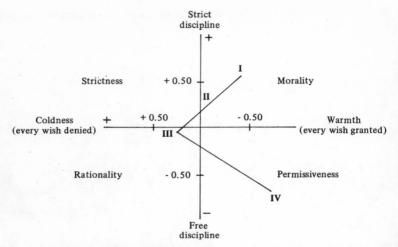

Fig. 26. Emphasis placed on different concepts in child-rearing models in the four periods from 1850 to 1950.

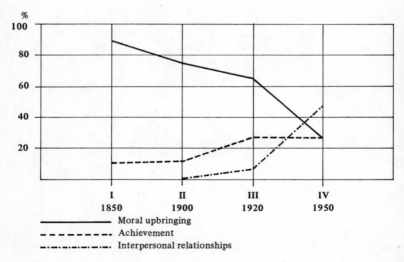

Fig. 27. Changes in value orientation in child-rearing models in the four periods from 1850 to 1950.

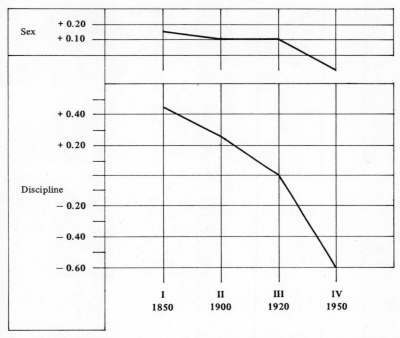

Fig. 28. Attitudes of parents to sexual curiosity and discipline in the four periods from 1850 to 1950.

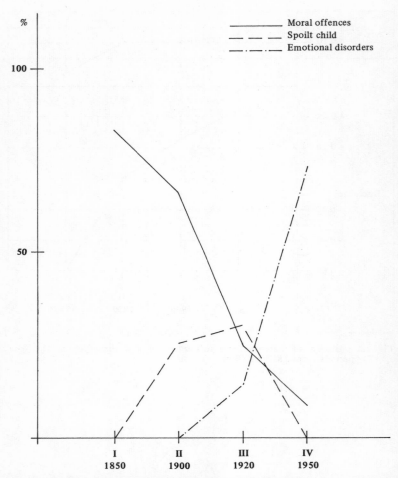

Fig. 29. Critical factors underlying different child-care models and concepts of deprivation from 1850 to 1950.

Fig. 30. By Chodowiecki, 1770: the patriarchical family, in which the father was the authority figure. (Reprinted, by permission, from R. Dirx, 1964.)

Fig. 31. Children working in a paper mill, Aschaffenburg, 1858. (Reprinted, by permission, from R. Dirx, 1964.)

Fig. 32. Kindergarten conditions in England about 1830 following the Wilderspins' methods. Encouraged by an industrialist and guided by teachers from the Owen's Institute, the Wilderspins established a number of kindergartens which were designed to "protect children from evil, and society from neglected children". (Reprinted, by permission, from R. Dirx, 1964.)

Fig. 33. Permanent contact between mother and child can still be found in certain groups such as the Munde tribe of Western Brazil. (Courtesy of Professor C. Lévi Strauss, College de France, Paris.)

Fig. 34. Close contact between mother and child continues after weaning. (Courtesy of Mlle. Dominique Darbois, UNESCO.)

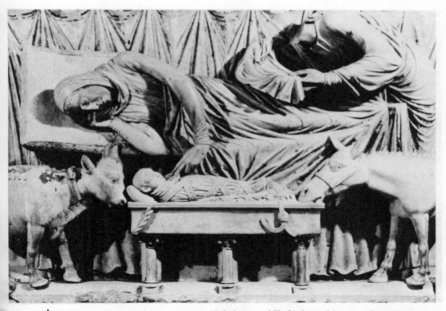

Fig. 35. In earlier times, babies were so tightly swaddled that this constituted motoric deprivation. The large input of sensory and emotional stimuli, however, is clearly shown in the fresco (Holy Family, Chartres Cathedral, France).

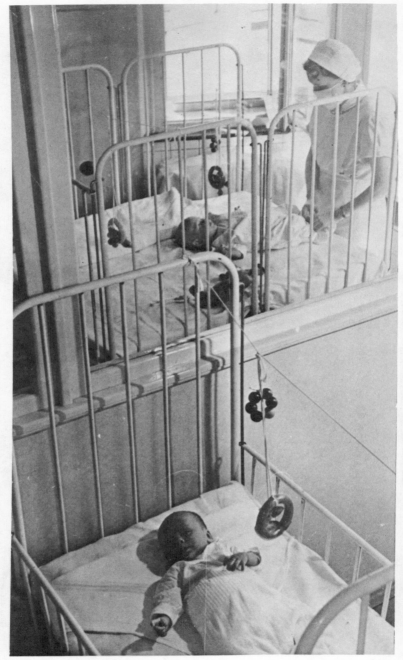

Fig. 36. Conditions in a modern baby home. (Photograph by L. Sitensky.)

7   Institutional care in Czechoslovakia

In Europe, when the second ("alarm") period had reached its climax (marked by J. Bowlby's 1951 monograph), and the dissolution of the large impersonal institutions in favour of adoptive or foster families was being mooted, an opposite trend was developing in Czechoslovakia. Up to this time, in that country, the care of deserted children had largely paralleled that of Western Europe. Now planned, scientific, and to some extent economically sounder, child-rearing programmes in larger groups were favoured, both because of the ideological emphasis on child care as a method of creating a collective feeling, and in an effort to overcome shortcomings of individual family care. Small institutes were replaced by large institutes, which were organized in same-age groups and completely controlled by the state; programmes, working methods, and training of personnel were standardized. Previous types of substitute care, which had been to some extent justifiably criticized, were discontinued and no consideration was given to some undeniable advantages, or to possibilities for their improvement within the new social system. Adoption was neither officially encouraged nor discouraged.

From the early fifties to the middle sixties institutional care was the most approved method of dealing with deserted children. This was widely publicized and strongly supported by the mass media and was therefore accepted by the public as the only possible way of dealing with the problem. The campaign was carried to such extremes and the placement of children in collective care establishments (especially in baby institutes) was made so attractive to parents that it encouraged "child desertion". Workers inside and outside institutes were concerned primarily with developing methods of child care in large homogeneous groups and with the organization of institutional regimes and improvement of the qualifications of personnel. Although some lasting improvement did occur, it was very slow, and the system remained practically unchanged for nearly fifteen years.

The development of Czechoslovakian institutes in this period, therefore, differed from that in Western countries. These different orientations, however, are beginning to re-converge on both theoretical and practical levels. While in the U.S.A. and certain other countries foster care is being increasingly criticized and institutional care is again being approved for certain selected groups, e.g. for children threatened with cultural deprivation, in Czechoslovakia there is a move towards greater variety of substitute care, adoption is being encouraged, SOS villages and children's family homes are being built (see chapter 13).

One contributory factor is the increasing convergence of scientific-social goals throughout the world. Today geographical and other barriers can be more easily penetrated by certain trends in scientific thinking and social action. Secondly, the traditional Czech sense of realism and criticism produced a number of "alarming" studies, which suggested that institutional rearing was not as beneficial as was believed. A number of studies followed, which, judging by generally acceptable criteria, we would describe as "critical". These not only demonstrated the developmental retardation of institutionalized children, but also focused on the total personality of the deprived child. They noted that a number of children survived institutional treatment undamaged, and suggested that the solution to this problem should be sought in understanding the specific dyadic relationships between the developing child and his environment. These studies clearly ushered in the fourth (the experimental-theoretical) period in Czechoslovakia, during which an attempt was made to conceptualize this relationship.

This general development, although specific to the Czech conditions, may have much wider implications. It can be viewed as a unique natural experiment which was systematically observed and studied (since the public health system is generally oriented towards prevention). For this reason, we shall discuss the findings of this period at some length.

CHILDREN IN BABY INSTITUTES

Over a number of years, M. Damborská systematically studied babies in the institute of which she is the director. In her original (1957) study, in which she compared institutionalized and family children (twenty-four matched pairs of six-month-olds, and twelve matched pairs of nine-month-olds) she reported the following results (using Gesell's norms). Up to three months of age, institutionalized children, compared with family children, do not appear to be retarded. In the three to six month period, there is noticeable developmental retardation, particularly in motor development, but also in the preparatory stage of speech. After six months of age, institutionalized children are retarded in sitting posture, but crawl earlier, which may be due to special programmes of motor training. The most marked retardation is in speech. In most cases physical condition is quite favourable, but weight gain, particularly in the second and third quarters, is less than in family children. Institutionalized children have more respiratory infections, especially persistent colds. Damborská recorded good development in visual perception in the third month; the first symptoms of visual retardation were evident when the child was observing the visual field while sitting up. In the following years (Damborská, 1961) she was successful through an extensive programme of child care in offsetting developmental retardation to some extent, except in speech development (particularly expressive speech). The most pronounced remaining symptom of institutionalization was certain emotional disorders.

When she compared children from institutes and families (forty pairs aged twenty-four to forty weeks) in unfamiliar situations and when they were presented with unfamiliar toys, Damborská reported very much poorer adaptation in children from baby institutes. Pronounced tension symptoms (poorer vocalization and concentration, disappearance of smiles, increased respiration, crying) were recorded three times more frequently in institutionalized children in unfamiliar test situations; strong fear responses when faced with an unknown object were seven times more frequent than in family children. The author suggests that the main reason for this is that children from families experience a more varied environment and get used to changes while the mother figure is constantly present. This does not apply to institutionalized children. If they do have intense emotional relationships with one person, however, they can overcome their tension and fear much more easily when that person is present.

M. Damborská (1967) carefully studied the development of emotional responses of babies in the institute as a function of their age and various social and material conditions. She reported that the most important source of positive and negative emotions is the presence and behaviour of adults. The babies suffered most from lack of satisfaction of their need for social relationships. The presence of other babies caused uneasiness. They derived the greatest pleasure from direct contact with adults, and showed greatest sadness when this contact ceased. The older baby takes notice of other children but establishes contact with them only after he has satisfied — at least to some degree — his natural desire for contact with adults. The fact that satisfaction of the baby's physiological needs eliminates negative emotions but in itself does not elicit marked positive emotions we consider to be a most important finding. Positive emotions develop only through contact with the human environment.

J. Koch (1961) compared the development of babies in families and babies in nine baby institutes. He reported that at five months of age, developmental norms were reached by 90 per cent of children in families and 70 per cent of institutionalized children. At ten months, however, only 35 per cent of the institutionalized children mastered the relevant tasks. Figures 37—40 show the ages at which certain basic functions develop in both groups of children. The greatest differences are shown in speech development and social contact; at ten months of age, only 12 per cent of institutionalized children reach criterion level, compared with 90 per cent of family children.

A detailed study of children over a period of time showed that 75 per cent of time awake for babies in families is spent in direct contact with adults and active play, and the rest of the time in observation and non-reacting states. With institutionalized babies, however, direct contact occupies the smallest amount of time, and passive observation of adults is much more extensive. Significant differences were also noted between these indices in different institutes, although all the institutes were organized, materially equipped, staffed, and directed in largely the same way. For example, in the "best" institute, the children had twice as much contact with adults as in the "poorest" institute. This applied also to "observation of adults"; insofar as inhibitory states were concerned, the ratio was 1:4. The author maintains that the extent of inhibitory states in children is a direct index of the rearing standard of the institute.

It is obvious that some children, even when in the same room and under the care of the same nurse, receive different stimulation. For example, the most attractive child of the group has three times more contact with adults than the least attractive, who spends six times as long in an inhibitory state. Today, the best institutes can offer nearly as much as the average family in some aspects of child care. In nearly all institutes the popular children develop almost as well as children in families. As Koch points out, this offers great possibilities of improvement in institutional care.

INSTITUTIONALIZED CHILDREN FROM ONE TO THREE YEARS OF AGE

Children's homes for one- to three-year-olds have been investigated in a number of careful, long-term studies, because it is recognized that children of this age are still seriously threatened by deprivation. In one study (Z. Matějček, 1960), we observed all children (eighty-two) in one toddler home over a period of five years. They were periodically tested by one psychologist using the same test (Gesell). The survey explored the relationships between specific developmental factors over time and their dependence on a number of established and well-controlled environmental variables. The results indicated that children of this age, under the given conditions, are more retarded in body weight than height, but that their motor retardation is not severe; intellectual retardation is pronounced, and social behaviour and speech have deteriorated to the level of borderline debility (IQ 50). While retardation in all functions is pronounced in the second year, in the third year there is some improvement. The most marked retardation therefore is shown in those functions which require emotional contact between child and adults for their development, and at the time when, under normal conditions, this need is most urgently felt. (Figs. 41 – 42.)

This group of children was subdivided into a group raised from birth in the institute, and a second group of children who entered the institute after spending the first year with their families (in almost all cases very bad families). The developmental curves for both groups were surprisingly similar, as was the temporal sequence of retardation in different functions. The figures for children from families, on admission to the institute, however, were on the average significantly higher and were maintained at a higher level throughout the course of the observations. At three years of age, these children are more likely to attain the developmental norms than the first group of children.

Finally, a comparison was made of development over two time periods. The results obtained in the first three years (period 1), where no special effort was made to improve conditions in the institute, were treated independently of those in the next two years (period 2) when full attention was paid to improvement (staff was increased, staff qualifications and material conditions were improved, special training for staff was introduced, child development was closely followed up). The results of these innovations were clearly reflected in the development of adaptive and motor behaviour, but less so in social behaviour. There was practically no improvement in speech development. Generally speaking, the gap between the most and least developed functions was even greater. (Fig. 47.)

These results show clearly that very impressive advances in child development can be achieved through material, technical, and organizational improvements in institutes. For these reasons, such measures should be more thoroughly investigated and developed. Complete success, however, demands adjustment and improvement of the emotional relationships between the child and the institutional personnel.

It is probable that the wide range of intra-individual differences in psychological functioning in our institutional children of toddler age (motor and adaptive behaviour is slightly below average, while speech is severely retarded) creates a certain amount of internal tension which leads to increased irritability, restlessness, aggression, and anxiety episodes. Under these conditions social and work habits tend to develop in unpredictable ways, so that the child cannot fully utilize his intellectual capacities even if they are essentially normal.

SCHOOL READINESS

Study of the development of children in pre-school children's homes (three—six years) was attempted in two ways — either by systematic observation over a period of time, or by very intensive investigation just before the child entered school.

In an intensive study (J. Langmeier, 1961, unpublished) of twenty-six children (oligophrenics were excluded) from one institute who were due to enter school in a few months' time, we tested the hypothesis that children from these homes were not ready for school at six years of age (the age at which children normally enter school in Czechoslovakia). Nine of these children (group 1) were admitted to the institute before their third year, while seventeen (group 2) spent their earliest years in their own families, often under very bad conditions, and were placed in the institute only after three years of age, usually after legal intervention. There are highly significant differences between these groups on a number of variables (see table 22). Kern's school readiness test and a number of other tests indicated that children of the first group on the whole were not ready for school (only three could be classified on certain criteria as having reached the middle level and none the late level), while group 2 children on the average achieved the middle level. There were no clear differences in basic EEG rhythms, which were used as an index of cerebral functioning; in this respect most children of both groups showed a relatively mature record (quite different from oligophrenics) irrespective of time of entry into the institute.

Table 22. IQ results for two groups of six-year-old children with different
backgrounds

	Terman-Merrill Average IQ	Seguin Average Time	Seguin Average Number Errors
First group	78.2	50.7	7.3
Second group	93.3	35.4	2.2

From 1960 to 1962 we completed a detailed analysis of the results of social, physical, and psychological examination of 145 children (average age six years two months ± four and a half months) who entered school from pre-school children's homes in the Middle Czech county (Z. Matějček and S. Reithar, 1963). The final examination was conducted in May or June of the appropriate year.

Experienced social workers from the Child Psychiatric Centre completed social and developmental analyses of every child, using case material from the children's homes or direct interview with the parents in the Centre. Physical examination, which was conducted by the paediatrician, covered general evaluation of the child's physical condition, his state of health, sensory and motor functioning and laterality, and a special neurological investigation aimed primarily at detection of possible CNS damage (minimal brain dysfunction).

Psychological examination included measurement of the child's development using the Terman and Merrill test; the relationship between verbal-abstract and non-verbal-practical abilities was determined for each child by comparing verbal sub-tests 5-III and 6-I with performance sub-tests 5-I,II and 6-III,VI. All children completed a drawing test, speech development was tested (articulation, vocabulary, structure, and social use), and work attitudes and behaviour in specific test situations were recorded. The children were also observed in groups; in addition, our data were supplemented by questionnaire information obtained from the chief supervisor in the institute.

Only nine children (6 per cent) had normal family backgrounds (adequately functioning families); their institutional placement was usually temporary, due to long-term illness of the mother or both parents. Excluding these children, most children in the group had suspect heredity. From this point of view there is no significant difference between children entering earlier or later. The hereditary background of all sub-groups, therefore, can be assumed to be relatively the same.

The group was significantly shorter (χ^2 = 23.3, df = 4, p < 0.001) and lighter (χ^2 = 17.3, df = 4, p < 0.01) than normal, judging from the child population norms (fig. 48). Insofar as height-weight ratio is concerned, although the short-fat category is slightly more frequent than the tall-thin category, normal proportional development predominates. We are not dealing here with a particular somatotype, therefore, but with a segment of the normal child population which is less well developed physically.

Head circumference in 42.5 per cent of the group was more than one SD below the normal for six-year-olds (i.e. less than 49.53 centimetres in boys and 48.76 centimetres in girls). This difference is also highly significant (χ^2 = 29.6, df = 3, p < 0.001). Only seven cases (4.7 per cent) showed a deviation of more than +1 sigma.

The mean Terman-Merrill IQ was 86 (± 10.1). A similar performance deficit was shown also on the Goodenough Draw-A-Man test, on our own Geometric Figures test, and in speech development. In a more detailed comparison of verbal and performance scores, we noted that 38 per cent of children failed in verbal tasks, while only 9 per cent failed in performance tasks.

We divided the children into four sub-groups on the basis of time spent in the institute:

1. Twenty-four children (17 per cent) who were raised in the institute since babyhood (their mental development could not have been affected by adverse family environment)
2. Twenty-three children who were institutionalized during toddler age (one – three years)
3. Forty-four children admitted between the ages of three and five
4. Fifty-four children (37 per cent) admitted after five years of age, who stayed in the institute for one year at most (their mental development could have been most severely affected by an unfavourable family background).

Generally speaking, the longer the child has spent in the institute, the better his physical development. The difference between

Table 23. Mental and physical development of children differing in length of institutional stay

Under Institutional Care since	Mean Deviation		Percentage of Smaller Heads	Average IQ
	Height	Weight		
Baby age	−2.3 months	+0.4 months	26	80.4
1−3 years	−6.6 months	−7.4 months	30	84.1
3−5 years	−6.6 months	−8.5 months	57	87.1
5 years	−7.4 months	−5.1 months	41	88.5

groups 1 and 4 approaches significance for height (t = 1.85) and weight (t = 1.68). This relatively favourable physical outcome might be due to good medical care which is available from babyhood. The lowest percentage of small heads found in the first group might also suggest that it is not the worst constitutional background which makes for the lowest performance of these children on intelligence tests.

The development of intellectual abilities, however, sharply contrasts with physical development. The earlier the child enters the institution, the greater the intellectual retardation. Although the only highly significant difference is that between groups 1 and 4 (t = 2.84, p < 0.01), the other differences are consistently in the same direction. If we assume that hereditary background is relatively the same in all groups, we cannot account for the mental retardation of children institutionalized since babyhood in terms of sample selection or basic care neglect, since the medical and material conditions of children in baby institutes are very good. The most probable causes are deprivational factors, i.e. lack of sensory and particularly emotional-social stimulation in the artificial institutional environment.

Children who grow up in bad families suffer lack of hygiene and care, and usually emotional stimuli, and their basic psychological needs certainly are not fully and continuously met, so that in this case we are also dealing with deprivation. But this is obviously less severe and qualitatively somewhat different, so that the effects, which involve other developmental factors, are not as detrimental to a child with this background entering school as for children permanently cared for in institutions since an early age.

CHILDREN FROM PRE-SCHOOL CHILDREN'S HOMES DURING SCHOOL AGE

At this point we posed the question of how institutionalized children develop in school age and in particular how they handled the first serious life encounter, i.e. schooling (Z. Matějček, 1969c). The group studied consisted of all children who left the pre-school children's homes in the middle Czech county in the period 1960—62 (see above).

We added 6 to our previous sample, so that N was now 151 children (83 boys and 68 girls). Sixty-two children recorded average Stanford-Binet IQ, 49 fell in the 90—80 range, 31 in the 80—70 range, and 9 below 70. By the end of the 1966—67 school year the age range was ten—fourteen years. The oldest child had seven years and the youngest five years of schooling – sufficient time to allow us to evaluate their school records.

Seventy-six children (44 boys and 32 girls) returned to their families from the pre-school children's homes; 24 of these spent some time in school children's homes, and 2 children were adopted. Although adoption at such a late age is regarded as very difficult and generally is not recommended, these two adopted children are "coping". Seventy-five children (39 boys and 36 girls) remained under institutional care. Two of them returned to the children's homes after a short stay with their families. Forty-six are in normal children's homes, 24 are in homes for retarded children (special boarding schools), and 5 are in corrective boarding schools. The children who were admitted to institutional care in babyhood more frequently remained permanently in children's homes than children who were admitted at a later age. For example, 68 per cent of children in group 4 but only 28 per cent in group 1 returned to their families after six years of age. This difference is significant ($\chi^2 = 11.41$, df = 5, p $<$ 0.005).

School record

If we view our sample as a whole, the outlook is rather bleak. Eighty-five children (57 per cent) can be classed as unsuccessful pupils – twenty-six have failed or are failing, but are still in the primary school, and fifty-nine are in special schools. Because the intellectual level of the group was slightly below average on school entry, one might expect that school records would not be exceptional; only rarely should these children fail, however, and only those of lowest intelligence. Here, however, twenty-three (nearly 40 per cent) of sixty-one children of average or above average intelligence are failing or are in special schools.

As expected, results indicated that children who have lived in institutes from earliest age and children who have remained in institutes during school age have the poorest school records. There are, however, certain circumstances which seem to us to be particularly important. With children of average or above average IQ (90 and above), the number of unsuccessful children is around 40 per cent, irrespective of whether they are in their own homes or in an institute. There is no significant difference between those who have long or short stays in institutions. In the lower intellectual ranges, however – IQ 70–80 – all those who remained in institutes (nineteen) failed hopelessly, while five of the twelve children who were returned to their families could be judged successful. This difference is significant at the 2 per cent level. The psychological deprivation which a child suffers in an institution, therefore, seems to be more threatening to children of lower ability than to children of average intelligence, although even the latter react unfavourably.

The school age child in a bad family, of course, also experiences unfavourable conditions, the most important being psychological deprivation. We were interested, therefore, in establishing the extent to which the child's school record reflected the general level of child care in the family. We divided the families (on the basis of available data from school records) into four groups:
1. Families showing generally favourable signs
2. Unfavourable, but not too serious, symptoms are evident
3. The unfavourable symptoms predominate
4. The family is regarded as very unfavourable, and it is recommended that the child be placed in an institute.

The ratio of successful to unsuccessful pupils in school are as follows: group 1, 3:1, group 2, 1:1.2, group 3, 1:1.7, and group 4, 1:6. This refutes the claim that "a bad family is better than the best institute", not so much because our institutes produce such good results, but because there are families which are still very bad, with such low economic standards and levels of stimulation that the child has no chance of normal school achievement.

Children's work habits

We were able to obtain some idea of the children's working tempo, concentration, interest in school work, and attitudes towards physical work from school records.

Children who have been institutionalized from early childhood are usually described as over-active, with a limited span of attention; at the same time, however, they show greater involvement in work than children who were admitted to institutes later on. The latter are more frequently described as indifferent, athough the differences are generally not significant. Children who show a low level of activity are usually below average intellectually, but in this group span of attention and work involvement do not seem to be related to intellectual level. Children of average and below average intelligence are equally likely to be described as *Flinks* (wasters) showing a low level of work involvement. This of course applies more to boys than to girls who are more frequently placed in the zealous category. Here again, however, the differences are not significant.

From the point of view of work attitudes, children who returned to their families after six years of age seem to be a more balanced group. There are fewer extreme cases. On the other hand, when compared with these "family" children, four times as many institutional children are described as "zealous" and "keen" and three times as many as "extremely lazy". Here we are dealing with a phenomenon which has often been referred to in other studies in this field; long-term institutional care from early life (in a uniform, stimulus-impoverished environment) produces polarization rather than developmental regression to the mean.

Social behaviour

From school records, we could also satisfactorily assess the total social activity of the child, his relationship to his teacher, his participation in the group, and his relationships to other children.

There were no significant differences in total social activity, irrespective of how we construct our sub-groups (according to sex, intelligence, time spent in the institution in the pre-school period, and so on). Striking differences emerged, however, in children's relationships to the teacher. The children who were admitted to institutions later — i.e. after three years of age — were more frequently described as defiant, cheeky, provocative; they more often actively opposed the teacher's authority. Children who have lived in institutes from an early age do not behave in this way.

We can note, retrospectively, similar trends in relationships with other children. The children entering the institution after three years of age more often attempt to attract the attention of others by showing off, or are aggressive — they start fights with other children and beat them up. The number of such children in our sample is eighteen, compared with only three children who were placed in institutional care before three years of age. This latter group, however, predominates in other types of social behaviour — they are often described as "tittle tattles" (eleven against six in the group of later admissions). Both differences are statistically significant, the first at the 2.5 per cent level and the second at the 5 per cent level.

In the group of children who have been in institutes from pre-school age to the present, there are more abnormalities and negative assessments (52 per cent) than in the group of children who returned to their families. The number of tittle-tattles is also higher (fifteen against two children from families) and the amount of overt aggression lower (five as against eleven children from families) ($\chi^2 = 12.4$, df = 2, p < 0.01). Predictably, boys more often show more overt aggression (fourteen boys compared with two girls), but tittle-tattling is equally frequent. These children, however are more often described as unsuccessful than successful (fourteen to three), although intelligence is not a significant variable. The tittle-tattler in our sample is thus the child who entered the institute before three years of age and who is unsuccessful at school irrespective of his intelligence (and sometimes despite it).

It is difficult to find a reliable and plausible explanation for this kind of behaviour. It is probable that here however we are dealing with a deeper disturbance in social relationships than in the case of the overtly aggressive child. Tittle-tattling is the hidden form of aggression. Because the child is unable to participate directly in his group, he seeks other means of participation, hiding his aggression behind the authority of the powerful outsider — in this case the teacher. While children from families (in our sample mostly from bad families) are often cheeky and defy the teacher, children from institutes either merge into the background or tend to be submissive. We view this as a symptom of their deeper social uncertainty which arises from their early experience in the deprived institutional environment, and which was not effectively dealt with at a later stage. The specific emotional attachment to the maternal figure was not established at the right time, or was inadequately developed. Thus in their development they lack the organizer which allows them to establish meaningful social relationships at a later developmental stage.

TYPES OF DEPRIVED PERSONALITY AMONGST INSTITUTIONALIZED CHILDREN

Classification of institutional children into inhibited (passive) and aggressive types at infancy and pre-school age had already been suggested by L. K. Fischer (1952), M. Damborská (1957b), and M. Nováková (1957). We should pay particular attention to this difference when considering the subsequent development of certain types of deprived personality.

In Czechoslovakia, school age children of relatively good intelligence can be found in so-called normal institutes, in residential schools for retarded children, and in institutes for children with serious behaviour problems. Unsatisfactory development in these cases cannot be due to bad family conditions or social neglect, since these children have had practically no experience of family life. Personality development, however, has obviously progressed in quite different ways, as the children ended up in different types of institutes. Since the environment of the institute in which they were raised in pre-school age is fairly uniform, this cannot entirely account for developmental differences. These are due rather to the interaction between this environment and certain aspects of the basic psychological equipment of the individual child (the influence of heredity, which is unfavourable in the majority of these cases but is very difficult to assess, is an open question).

Most of our institutionalized children continue to live in normal children's homes, and we can therefore classify them as more or less reasonably adapted. We shall discuss these cases later on; for the moment we shall turn our attention to different types of children in the other two types of institutes.

Socially hyperactive types

In 1960 we examined all children in residential schools for retarded children in our survey region and all children admitted to these institutes in the following three years (1961–63) (Z. Matějček and J. Langmeier, 1970). The sample consisted of 666 children in the age range seven–fifteen years, divided into four sub-groups:

1. Retarded children from normal families who were placed in these schools because it was impossible for them to attend school daily for geographical reasons (197 children)
2. Children who were removed from poor, primitive anti-social families (315 children)
3. Children from bad families who were placed in institutions in the pre-school period, i.e. after three years of age (73 children)
4. Children entering institutions before the age of three years (81 children).

All these children were given a battery of 10 tests – Terman-Merrill, Goodenough, Raven, Kohs, Visuo-motor and drawing tests, a test of social information (DOI), and standard tests of reading, writing, and arithmetic. Family and developmental case histories were carefully analyzed and anthropometric, paediatric, neurological, and, in certain cases, psychiatric examinations were conducted.

It is generally assumed that a child's school failure is due basically to low intelligence. This is clearly supported in the first group of children from good families, less so in children from bad families, and still less in children with a previous institutional history. Institutionalized children admitted to the special school have higher average IQs than children from families (irrespective of whether they are good or bad families). This suggests that they cannot capitalize on their intellectual ability in school work, and despite good IQ fail more often than children from bad families.

Table 24. IQs of children with different family backgrounds in residential schools for retarded children

	Average IQ (T–M)	SD	t	p
1. Children from good families	61	10.6	5.9	0.001*
2. Children from poor families	67.2	13.0		
3. Children in institutes from 3 years of age	70.5	9.4	2.4	0.02
4. Children in institutes before 3 years of age	72.3	9.4	1.0	NS

*   't diff. between groups 2 and 4 = 4.0 (p < 0.001)

Under institutional conditions, children are not given the kind of developmental stimulation which encourages the development of good working habits and personality maturation to the level necessary for coping with school demands. What sort of children are affected in this way? Certainly we encounter a number of institutionalized children and some children from bad families who do not fail at school, and for whom a good IQ is a guarantee of school success.

From our sample we selected a group with IQs above 80 who showed a gross discrepancy between IQ level and school achievement. This consisted of fifty-one children from families and twenty-three from pre-school institutions. A combination of external and internal factors, ranging from neglect to mild brain damage, accounted for school failure in this group. As far as social behaviour is concerned, two extreme forms could be detected — marked inhibition and passivity to the point of apathy in making contact with the social environment, and exaggerated social interest, a form of social hyperactivity or restlessness.

We are particularly interested in that type of socially hyperactive child who is found significantly more often amongst children admitted to special boarding schools (residential schools for retarded children) from pre-school children's homes than amongst children admitted from families ($\chi^2 = 11.63$, df = 2, p < 0.01). These children develop contact freely and unhesitatingly, and are

Table 25. Social behaviour of children from families and from institutions

	Children from Families	Children from Institutes
Inhibitory type	12	1
Socially hyperactive type	14	16
Other types of social behaviour (variable)	25	6

dramatically exhibitionistic, but the contact is superficial and temporary; they are extremely interested in ongoing events in the environment, but they themselves participate only superficially. They are interested viewers of the kaleidoscope of life. For them, schooling and psychological examinations are more social than working encounters. Social interests completely predominate over material, play, and work interests. (Fig. 49.)

A characteristic of institutionalized children who are admitted to residential schools for retarded children is that they are not aggressive or socially provocative. They are often quite liked by the staff. They are somewhat disappointing to the teachers since they obviously under-achieve academically.

We observed the majority of these institutionalized children from an early age and were able to record their typical behavioural features at baby-toddler age. They could establish contact with a strange psychologist "quite spontaneously, without hesitation or difficulty". Constructive play was difficult to introduce but they found a simple social game extremely interesting. They clung to every stranger, cuddled up to him, showed off, but they did not establish deeper relationships, and were superficially affectionate to everybody. They acquired new habits and new knowledge with difficulty. Because of their diffuse social interest they ignored the material environment and had poor school records.

Socially provocative type

From 1960 we paid particular attention in our survey area to children in residential schools for children with serious behaviour problems. These institutes have large, specially qualified staffs, and the school is located inside the institute. Generally children (boys in our sample) are admitted after coming into conflict with the law because of petty crimes or disciplinary offences (Z. Matějček, 1964). The sample consisted of a total of 268 boys in the age range eleven—fifteen years (mean fourteen years). IQs were average to below average (only one inmate was classified as feebleminded). School performance, however, was not consistent with IQ classification, as 32 per cent of the boys repeated one class, and more than 30 per cent two or more classes. Grounds for committal were firstly stealing, then wandering, very undisciplined behaviour, truancy from school, absconding from home or institute, aggression, fighting, and sexual deviancy.

The present behaviour of these boys is ranked by supervisors in the institutes in the following order: (1) lazy, indolent, uninterested in school and work; (2) disobedient, cheeky, negativistic, rebellious; (3) work interests and behaviour highly unpredictable; (4) restless, inattentive, unstable; (5) extremely moody; (6) impulsive, uninhibited; (7) infantile, playful.

Although boys in these institutes are a very heterogeneous group, we can easily identify a group of 25 (about 10 per cent) who were institutionalized from pre-school age. Their IQ is average, their school records slightly better (fewer than 15 per cent repeated), and their average age lower (12.7 years) than the other inmates. An interesting fact is that three of these boys have been placed in two other institutes, and nineteen of them in four or more institutes before admission to the present one. The grounds for admission are ranked in an order different from that applying to other inmates: (1) aggression, fighting, attacking smaller children; (2) highly undisciplined, provocative, breaking institutional rules. Stealing is ranked only fourth. Equally interesting is the description of their present behaviour: (1) unstable, restless; (2) moody; (3) playful, infantile behaviour. Uncontrollable aggression, the initial reason for admission, is now ranked only seventh, and is seldom displayed.

If we compare the behaviour of these children from early childhood with that of the groups of children who continue in the normal children's homes or in residential schools for retarded children, it is obvious that they show another type of reaction to permanent institutional care, which we would describe as socially provocative. Even at twelve months of age these children demand attention from known adults by being provocative. They exact toys by angry outbursts and refuse to give them up, demand preferential treatment, and are aggressive and jealous with other children. They want to have the nurses to themselves. It is very difficult to introduce social or constructive play. Nurses usually react to their persistent conflict with other children by punishment and prohibitions, and by refusing to show them any favours. The nurses think such children are dreadful – but surprisingly they find that when alone with the child he can be completely changed and unrecognizably pleasant. In the institutional system, however, this child cannot "own" the nurse, and punishment and restriction produce further provocation and aggressive behaviour. At school age the aggression of these boys increases further. They disturb the group until they finally end up in residential schools for children with serious behaviour problems, and are diagnosed as uncontrollable by normal custodial methods. There they quickly lose their aggressiveness in the group of older and stronger boys, but they retain certain basic personality characteristics, which can best be described as "infantilism".

From psychological test data (drawings on the topic of "my home", "our family", case histories, questionnaires, sociograms) it is clear that these children have special personal problems with strong anxiety overtones. The peer group usually judges them as uninteresting "cowards". (Figs. 50—54.)

Inhibitory type

In addition to the two types described above, we find other behavioural types amongst institutional children. Most conspicuous is the inhibitory type, which had been described earlier under various labels by R. A. Spitz (1946a), L. K. Fischer (1952), and M. Nováková (1957). This child is extremely passive, sometimes apathetic, and in some cases there are very pronounced regressive tendencies. It is not unusual, therefore, for such a child to be classified as feebleminded on the basis of superficial psychiatric or paediatric examination. We noted in our group of institutionalized children of this type that developmental retardation was most marked from eighteen to twenty-four months (see page 199), and that DQ in the speech area remained at the debile level throughout the second and third years. This implies that the opportunities these children have for verbal contact and social interaction are severely restricted.

During a long-term study of 160 children who lived together between the ages of one and three years in one toddler home (Z. Matějček, 1969b), we noted, amongst other things, characteristic behaviours from time of admission until they were released from the institute. There were individual differences in ease of adaptability to the new environment, but with 33 children (20 per cent) adaptive problems persisted for more than a month, and developmental retardation was so severe in 9 cases (6 per cent) that it was very difficult to record any sort of reaction when the child was transferred from one institute to another. Inhibition was the outstanding feature in most of these 33 cases. The inhibitory reaction was shown mainly by children coming to the institute 'from their families during the second year, but was also recorded in some children coming from baby institutes, i.e. children who had adapted to a certain extent to the particular stimulus structure of institutions.

One hundred and one children came from baby institutes to this toddler home. In twenty of these cases (20 per cent) the inhibitory reaction predominated during the period twelve to twenty-one months. During the time the children spent at the toddler home this percentage decreased to 14 in the first half of the third year, and by the end of the third year to less than 9. This is a reaction characteristic of boys rather than girls, who generally show better social adaptability and more active searching for contact at every age level. On entering a new environment when older than three years, irrespective of whether this is a family or institutional environment, four times as many boys as girls show inhibitory reactions. Overall, 11 per cent of children living in institutes from babyhood showed a predominantly inhibitory reaction during the initial period after transfer to a new environment after three years of age. Roughly the same percentage was recorded by children of school age in our sample. Three (13 per cent) from twenty-three children who were under institutional care from babyhood were classified as inhibitory types. These are in special boarding schools for retarded children. Of twenty-four children who spent the first three years in the same institute but at school age were returned to their families, three (12 per cent) are classified as inhibitory type. None of the children who were adopted during the pre-school period are classified in this way.

In a similar type of study with children from residential schools for retarded children (see page 208) (Z. Matějček and J. Langmeier, 1970), we also noted that of twenty-three children who came from pre-school children's homes and who had IQs higher than 80 only one is classified as an inhibitory type while twelve of seventy-four children (17 per cent) who came from families fall into this category.

Finally, in a third study (Z. Matějček, 1969c) we observed children who at six years of age had been transferred from pre-school homes either to homes for school age children or were returned to their families (see page 203). Of 32 children only 2 (6 per cent) who had been under institutional care since babyhood were classified as inhibitory types, compared with 14 (12 per cent) of 119 later admissions.

It is obvious, therefore, that inhibition is a quite frequent response of a child to separation during the whole of the pre-school period, and that this is the typical behaviour of about 20 per cent of institutional children for whom separation from the family has created a deprivational situation. Gradually this inhibition decreases, however, so that during school age it is rarely encountered in a severe form. Frequency stabilizes at about 12 per cent. It is shown more frequently by boys than by girls and is particularly marked in developmentally retarded children. Here a particularly unfavourable situation is created by the combination of negative factors. Where this produces very severe developmental retardation, the child cannot be cared for even in special schools and is admitted to an asylum type of institution. Retarded children as well as the child of average intelligence can suffer psychological deprivation, but the former can hardly summon adequate defensive resources or create sufficient opportunities to compensate, even partly, for lack of appropriate stimulation and interaction.

We can describe the characteristic personality traits of a child of this type as follows. The relationship of the child to his group, to his nurse, and to the examining psychologist is extremely passive. If offered a toy, the child hesitates for a long time and then plays repetitively and primitively, though quite persistently. Since material interests usually predominate over social interests, it is easier to introduce tectonic rather than social play. Because the child shows almost no response to the nurse's approach, he does not attract her attention or interest, and exchange of reinforcing stimuli occurs at only the most elementary level — in routine medical examinations, during feeding, and in group games, when the nurse tries to involve all the children at the same time. The inevitable outcome of this is increased danger of developmental retardation. (Fig. 55.)

In our institutional setup, even this type of child receives some input of social and emotional stimuli which helps him to adapt gradually. From our observations, most of the children of the inhibitory type, when they reach school age, can be described as balanced. Where this adaptation occurs very slowly (in some cases there may be relapses, particularly when the environment is changed) or not at all (so that we would still describe the child as inhibitory) this is probably due both to the effects of the institutional environment and of the basic psychological structure of the child.

To illustrate, we shall describe one inhibitory case from our sample who was studied from babyhood to adolescence.

Girl J.D. was placed in a baby institute following legal intervention because of family neglect. The family lived in one room, the parents were not permanently employed, and the children were roughly handled. We have no information about the child's delivery, but a thorough physical examination showed no evidence of early brain damage.

When the child was examined at fourteen months, she was mentally retarded at about the ten-month level. Physical development was good; her weight was above average throughout the course of development. She was keenly interested in toys but established social contact only when forced to do so.

Examination in the third year showed the girl to be slow and clumsy; she lacked any lively social response and was passively led around. She followed instructions as far as she could understand them, but lacked spontaneity and initiative. She was helpless, inhibited, a simpleton in the work· situation. Examination at four years seven months disclosed that the child played alone, and that there were long periods of inactivity when she was working. Her social response, however, had increased, and she recorded a Terman IQ score of 78. At six years, her IQ was 88. Working with her was protracted, but there was some willing effort. She was examined again at seven years seven months, after being transferred to a school children's home. Again there was marked inhibition. Her mental age had only slightly progressed so that her Terman IQ score was now 74. At school she was passive and quiet, and lagged far behind the other children. She took small things from the teacher's desk. She was transferred to a residential school for retarded children; no other outcome was possible, as her mother had previously died and her alcoholic father could not look after her. The retardation continued in this new environment; at ten years six months her Terman IQ was 68. She showed no interest in mental activity but still participated relatively well in practical tasks. There was again evidence of an upward trend at thirteen years seven months; she was praised at school and her school achievement was at a socially acceptable level. On leaving the residential school, her IQ, on Raven's test, was 96, her reading achievement quotient 108, and her mathematical quotient 82.

She was sent to a special school to be trained as a gardener. After six months (when our observations temporarily ceased) her adaptation was again poor. She was apathetic, disobeyed her supervisor, but was well integrated in the peer group. She was indifferent when reprimanded. She swallowed a coin and different pills to gain attention. The school authorities thought her untrainable and recommended transfer to another institute, where she should work "under supervision" (these words were underlined twice in the report, suggesting that in their opinion she had to be forced to work). This is a repetition of the sort of thing we saw at the start of schooling and following all changes of institutional environment.

The relatively well-adapted type

In our children's homes there are always a number of children who show no deviations or behavioural abnormalities, judged by strict criteria, which we could relate to institutionalization. It was obvious to us from the beginning that these are children who, in their own particular ways, are constitutionally more resistant to adverse life conditions, or children who by their adaptive, pleasant behaviour can obtain an adequate supply or developmental stimuli even in a stimulus-impoverished environment.

In a long-term study of 151 children who spent long periods during pre-school age in institutes (Z. Matějček, 1969c), 32 (21 per cent) were considered to be fully adapted during older school age (from fifth class upwards). A higher frequency is reported amongst children who returned to their families from pre-school institutes (22 from a total of 76 [30 per cent]) compared with those who continue in institutes (10 of 75 cases [13 per cent]). Twenty-seven per cent of girls and 17 per cent of boys from the total sample were of this type. The number of well-adapted children tended to decrease as a function of time spent in institutes during pre-school age (see table 26).

Finally, in a following study of 160 children institutionalized since infancy (Z. Matějček, 1969b), we obtained the following results. In the period from twelve to twenty-one months 31 per cent of children were considered to be well adapted; in the period twenty-one to thirty months the percentage was 32 and in the second half of the third year this had increased to 44. This percentage decreased only slightly in the pre-school period (41 per cent) and was subsequently maintained in school age (42 per cent). Again there were many more well-adapted types amongst children who were adopted (48 per cent) or returned to their own families (36 per cent) than amongst those who continued in the school children's homes (22 per cent).

The percentage of well-adapted institutionalized children during the school age period is surprisingly similar in different studies and represents approximately one-fifth of the institutionalized population. This child, as early as the end of the first year, can "find his own place", and "his own people", in the institutional environment. Even if the staff constantly changes, he can attach himself to a nurse or

Table 26. Number of well-adapted children of older school age who were either returned to their families at six years of age or remained in institutions, as a function of age of admission to the institution

Age of Admission to Institution	Returned at Six Years of Age to Families (N = 76)	Remained under Institutional Care (N = 75)	Total	%
Baby age (N = 32)	3	3	6	19
1−3 years (N = 27)	2	3	5	18
3−5 years (N = 44)	7	4	11	25
5−6 years (N = 48)	10		10	21

caretaker and gain her favour. He is often the so-called "loved one" who attracts the attention of most people who come into contact with the group, not only those concerned directly with child care. This child does not provoke visitors, he does not flirt or show off in front of strangers (as do the children of the socially hyperactive type) but calmly and methodically establishes contact with them. He eventually accepts an invitation to come closer, then puts his head on the visitor's lap and smiles nicely at him. He receives in response quiet, tender petting. He also evokes in adults calm and emotionally warm behaviour. The danger for this child lies in change of environment which severs the existing emotional bonds. But because his efforts to satisfy his emotional and social needs in the new environment are usually directed into acceptable channels there is a good chance that he will again settle down. It is obvious therefore that here again we are dealing with an interaction between the specific institutional conditions and the basic psychological structure which children bring with them into the situation.

We must not forget, however, that their good adaptation is valid only for the environment in which it was created, and that this environment, generally speaking, is basically more impoverished in level of stimulation in that the structure is simpler and less demanding than the family situation. The fact that these children can play well, that their learning capacity is adequate at pre-school age, and that they can progress through school and the institute without serious difficulties is no guarantee that they will adapt adequately to conditions outside the institute. Although there is no clear evidence that these children fail in later life when they leave the protected environment of the institute and participate in so-called normal life, we have encountered some cases which tend to support this assumption.

Type characterized by compensatory satisfaction of emotional and social needs

From our experience with institutional children we can identify at least one more type which has certain characteristic features. These features, however, have different patterns in different children, so that they do not always co-exist in the one developmental period as was the case with previous types, but tend to follow one another according to the child's progress through specific developmental stages, and occur with different intensity. The common element is a certain degree of compensation for unsatisfied emotional and social needs.

For example, children raised from an early age in institutions eat better and are heavier than children who are admitted later from families (see page 202). Some of these children are greedy — they "stuff themselves". They are aptly described by nurses — "the child compensates for his sadness because he hasn't a mother". For others it is the only relaxed activity, when they have no need to compete with other children or to demand their rights.

We also noted that children who have spent a long time in institutes are very often described as tittle-tattles in school age, while the children who enter institutes later and leave earlier show more overt aggression (see page 206). We interpret tittle-tattling as a type of compensatory satisfaction for children who cannot obtain social satisfaction from direct participation in the group or who cannot secure their own status by their own efforts.

It is significant that the compensatory activities are usually at a fairly basic level, that they are closer to biological needs — eating, masturbation, sexual activity, manipulation of objects rather than contact with other children, tittle-tattling rather than an active effort to cooperate and/or compete in the group, narcissism, and a wicked delight in the sufferings of other people rather than positive feelings of friendliness and participation.

Since statistical analysis of these data is hardly possible, we cannot determine the frequency of this type in the institutional population. They are not concentrated in certain types of children's homes as are the other types, but are distributed through different institutes depending on the type of compensatory activities. We find them in residential schools for children with behaviour problems, in residential schools for retarded children, in normal children's homes, but also in child psychiatric clinics to which they are usually sent for assessment since their behaviour is often strange and abnormal. In these children, the most common features are autistic self-orientation at an early age, precocious and exaggerated sexual curiosity which is difficult to deal with under institutional conditions, sadistic behaviour, and later homosexual tendencies.

Compensatory satisfaction of needs is sought most frequently by children who were admitted to institutional care during the third year, the previous years having been spent in the family environment, where they were denied basic care and attention. However, other factors, which were beyond our control, are probably involved. At present, therefore, we are still on uncertain ground in classifying this type although we can detect the presence of the compensatory mechanisms through study of individual cases.

For illustrative purposes we shall cite a few cases on a simple descriptive level, without attempting interpretation.

Boy J.S. has been under institutional care since babyhood. He was legally committed because of neglect by the family. Through the whole of the toddler period he was slightly developmentally retarded but he ate heartily. He showed specific automatisms — when he bent over he rubbed his head on the ground so that he removed the hair above his forehead. He cuddled the nurse eagerly, he refused contact with strangers, he did not communicate with other children, who were indifferent to him. When the nurse passed by, he brightly smiled at her. Otherwise he was interested solely in simple manipulation of toys. When going for a walk he was happy, running about playfully. He persistently over-ate, and was the fattest child.

Girl A.S. entered the children's home after the second year. Both parents were alcoholics and six siblings had also been placed in institutes. According to Gesell's norms there was slight developmental retardation, but there were no indications of more serious defects. She had a lively interest in the social environment, was happy and full of activity. She cooperated well — even too zealously. She ate well and was always above average in weight. This state was maintained throughout her stay in the pre-school children's home and later in the school age children's home. IQ on repeated examination was between 93 and 100. Gradually, however, enuresis developed and behaviour deteriorated. When she was nine years old she was described as follows: "She wets herself daily — works willingly only if rewarded — is friendly to children who can give her something — she fights with weaker children, sneaks on the older ones — she uses her sexual knowledge — she seduces boys — she swears — it pleases her if she can hurt somebody — she beats small children — she tortured and tried to drown a small kitten in a puddle."

Boy Z.T. was admitted to a children's home when two years six months of age. He was very neglected, the mother was dead and the father was unable to raise the boy. He avoided children, and was apathetic and uninterested. He wet and soiled himself. Later he was hostile to other children and was wicked and selfish. During the pre-school period this state persisted. Although his IQ was only slightly subnormal this institute demanded his transfer to an institute for severely retarded children because he was uncontrollable in the group. He still soiled himself. Masturbation began at six years of age; he liked to wander and "confiscated" the property of others. In the school age children's home he was described as selfish. He liked to tittle-tattle, and toadied when dealing with adults. He showed excessive interest in girls and hurt small children. When examined by a psychologist he demanded a reward for every visit. He was sent to a training school for retarded children. He seemed to be a loner, but could not work independently — he could not learn to be a tractor driver. He was again psychologically examined at eighteen years, when he sexually assaulted small boys. He felt no self-guilt or remorse. His explanation was a mixture of infantilism and vain attempts to achieve satisfaction, for which he could find no socially acceptable forms.

Boy L.Z. entered the institute during his third year. The father was an alcoholic and the mother could not cope with the household duties and the rearing of five children. The pre-school home reported that he did not like to cooperate with others, he teased children, he lied and stole. He was transferred to an institute for children with behaviour disorders and subsequently to a school for retarded children, although the results of verbal and performance IQ tests were average. At fourteen years of age he was described as follows: he is very conceited, unselfcritical — he does daily body-building exercises — he is possibly the only boy who does not secretly smoke — he buys cheese and fish oil to increase his strength — he is extremely narcissistic — he is scrupulously clean — he is cowardly but at the same time he manages to use two small boys as servants. In the sociogram he is described by the other boys as a "show-off", "slimy" — he can be vandalistic — he was suspected of homosexual tendencies but it is obvious that this is extreme narcissism. He writes letters to girls and boasts about his experiences with women.

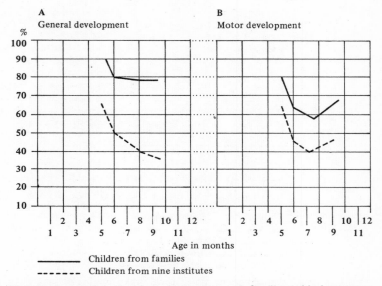

Fig. 37. Percentages of babies from institutions and families achieving neuro-psychological norms for general (A) and motor (B) development. (After J. Koch, 1961.)

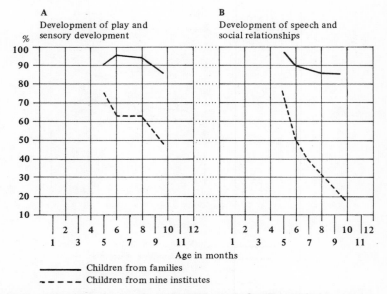

Fig. 38. Percentages of babies from institutes and families achieving neuro-psychological norms for play and sensory development (A) and for speech and social development (B). (After J. Koch, 1961.)

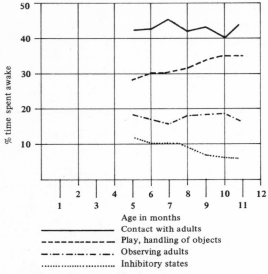

Fig. 39. Utilization of time spent awake by babies in families. (After J. Koch, 1961.)

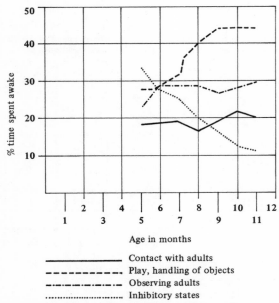

Fig. 40. Utilization of time spent awake by babies in institutions. (After J. Koch, 1961.)

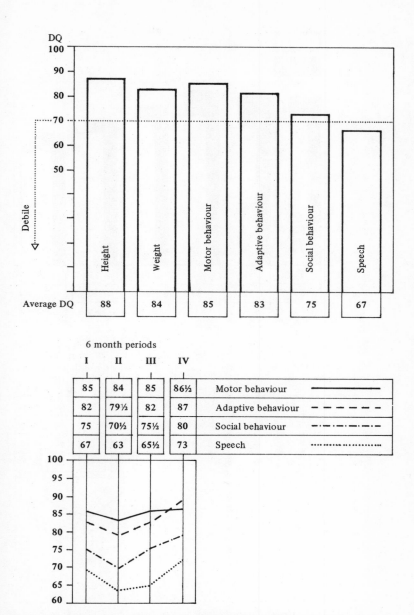

Fig. 41. Development of eighty-two institutionalized children through the two-year toddler period. (After Z. Matějček, 1960.)

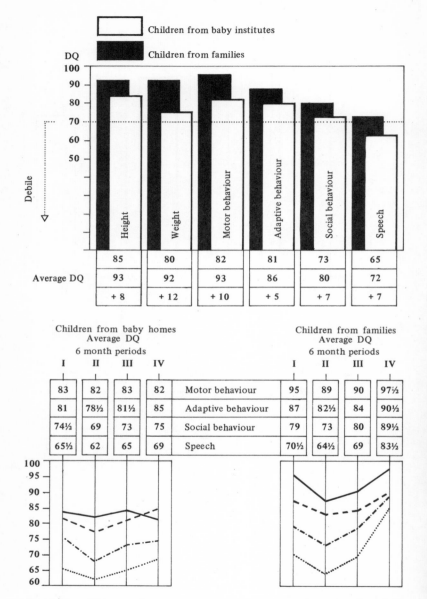

Fig. 42. DQ differences between children admitted to toddler homes from baby homes and from families. (After Z. Matějček, 1960.)

Fig. 43

Fig. 44

gs. 43, 44. "Collective life" in a toddler home, where the children, rather than creating a collective feeling, are simply a collection. (From film *Children without Love*.)

Fig. 45. Speech training in a group. (From film *Children without Love*.)

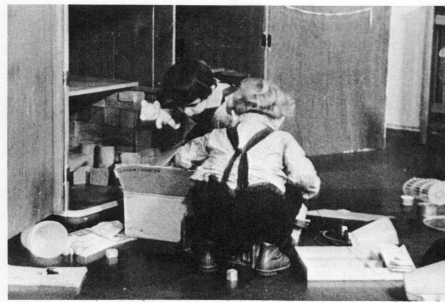

Fig. 46. A method of testing the feeling of collective ownership. The nurse leaves the door the toy cupboard slightly ajar and leaves the playroom. Within a few minutes children take out all the toys, throw them around, squat down, and aimlessly through them. They do not engage in individual or collective play. (From film *Chil without Love*.)

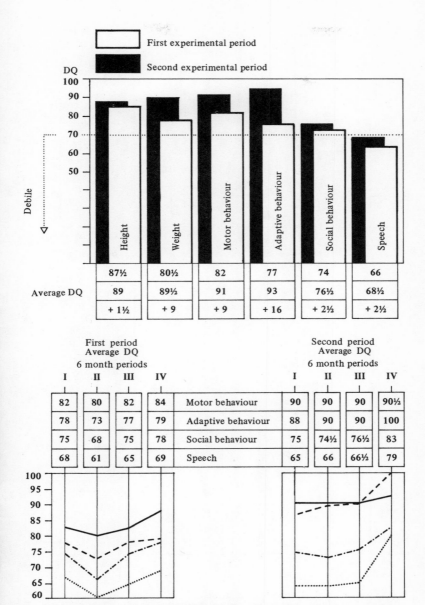

Fig. 47. Comparison of average DQs in the first and second experimental periods. (After Z. Matějček, 1960.)

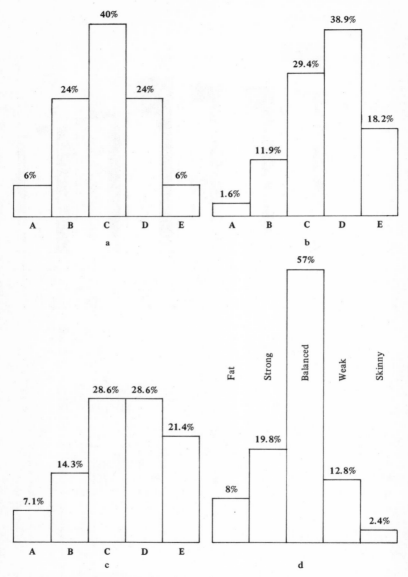

Fig. 48. (a) Normal distribution; distributions of height (b), weight (c), and height-weight ratios (d) among institutionalized children. (After Z. Matějček and S. Reithar, 1963.)

Fig. 49. The socially hyperactive type.

Fig. 50. A child with a predominantly material orientation.

Fig. 51. Drawing by a boy without any feeling for his family. He depicts an empty room, without people.

Fig. 52. Family scene full of aggressive activity.

Fig. 53. The family viewed as a working unit.

54. The family viewed as an ideal emotional interaction. This boy lived in six children's homes, and had little actual experience of family life.

Fig. 55. Negative image of the father, who severely neglected the boy and sent him to the children's home at the age of six, soon after the mother died. The father had died six months before the boy drew this picture.

8 Deprivation conditioned by organismic factors

DEVELOPMENTAL CONDITIONS

Identical deprivation conditions have a different effect on children of different ages and developmental levels, while the needs of the child and his sensitivity to inadequate satisfaction of these needs also change with increasing age.

In line with general theorizing about early mental development, present evidence suggests that the child in the first six months of life reacts strongly to a lack of various stimuli. The monotony of the institutional environment produces indiscriminating global psychosomatic reactions which have been frequently described in the literature (the child is passive and apathetic, shows poor physical and mental development — see page 74). R. A. Spitz and K. M. Woᴎ (1946) first described this state as "mild depression"; subsequently, however, it became apparent that this condition is neither mild, nor is it depression, and that there is a qualitative difference between the reactions of these very young children and those of older children ("anaclitic reactions" or variants of these). This latter syndrome, according to H. R. Schaffer and P. E. Emerson (1964), usually onsets quite suddenly and at full strength shortly after seven months of age.

Schaffer studied the responses of sixty healthy unweaned babies from working-class Glasgow families in seven different separation situations which occur quite normally in the life of every child (the child is left alone in a room; he is left with strangers; an adult passes him without noticing; adults cuddle him for a while and then put him down; he is placed in his pram outside the house; he is left in his pram outside a shop; he is put to bed and left alone).

Schaffer recorded the first occasion on which the child in any of these situations showed a protest directed towards a particular situation. Table 27 suggests that this particular kind of attachment first occurs in the seventh month, and that from six to nine months

Table 27. Age of development of reactions to persons

Age in Weeks	Specific Attachment	Specific Attachment to Mother	Fear of Strangers
	N	N	N
21–24	4	3	0
25–28	15	13	10
29–32	17	18	15
33–36	7	8	19
37–40	7	8	7
41–44	4	4	4
45–48	3	3	2
49–52	1	1	0
53–78	2	2	3
Totals	60	60	60

of age is the critical period, during which, under normal conditions, this reaction develops. Up to this point the child reacts positively but indiscriminately to social stimuli. Subsequently, he begins to show a preference for certain persons, and characteristically attempts to renew the contact by protest.

Table 27 records the number of children in particular age groups who develop this first attachment to some person (specific attachment), when this attachment is directed to the mother, and the time at which the first anxiety responses occur when the child is with strangers. There are no significant sex differences.

From the data it is clear that the attachment need not be initially directed towards the mother, and that the anxiety responses to strangers occur about a month after development of the specific attachment. Obviously here we are dealing with two behaviour patterns which, although having a common basis and developing concurrently, are independent (J. D. Benjamin, 1961; K. H. Tennes and E. E. Lampl, 1964). Some children are strongly attached to their parents and show no fear of strangers, while others panic when faced by strangers, although they have no very strong attachment to the parents.

What conditions predispose children to develop specific attachments at the appropriate age? Schaffer looked for an explanation in his empirical findings. He compared two groups of children, separated from their families at approximately eighteen weeks of age and returned at thirty weeks, the age at which, under normal conditions, they ought to be ready for the specific attachment. The first group of children (N = 11) were in a children's hospital, where the environment offered limited opportunity for social and other types of stimulation. Nurses were constantly changed and during the day they stayed in the ward only for short periods of time. However, the children were periodically visited by their mothers, at least once a week. Children in the second group (N = 9) were admitted to a children's home because of TB in their families. Although there were many more staff and the children had more frequent contact with adults during their stay, they were never visited by their parents.

Schaffer noted the first signs of specific attachment after the children returned home. Neglecting certain individual differences, the results clearly indicate a quicker development of attachment by the second group (from the children's home). They developed a specific attachment in nineteen days, while children from the hospital required fifty-five days (the difference between means is highly significant). All the children from the hospital, barring one, needed more than four weeks to establish a specific attachment, which the majority of the children from the second group developed in fewer than five days.

It is clear that during this time the sum total of social stimuli experienced is relatively more important than continuing contact and more extensive experience with the person with whom the specific relationship should be established. It seems that the hospitalized children had to re-experience the whole period of nondiscriminating relationship after their return home before they could establish the specific attachment. Social development was in a way "kept in cold storage" at the level existing before their introduction to the impoverished stimulus environment of the hospital.

Schaffer's results suggest not only that the child needs a particular type of social stimulation from the seventh month, but also that in the preceding period he needs simple social stimulation of a certain amount and variety. Schaffer postulated a further period which is characterized by the need for stimulation — "the infant who at ten months cries for his mother and who at five months cried for the attention of any person, will have cried at three months for almost any form of environmental change". Thus the simple need for stimulation changes in the second quarter of the first year to a general need for social stimulation, which develops after a further two to three months into a need for specific social stimulation.

The dependence of the child specifically on the maternal figure (which is not necessarily the mother and could be more than one person) is probably critical for the development of feelings of security and ways of coping with anxiety, and provides the original mould for the child's personality. A child who fails to develop such a relationship seems to be damaged in his capacity for later normal interpersonal and social relationships. A child who is suddenly deprived of an already established relationship reacts with strong protest behaviour. If this separation continues, his personality development may be retarded. The sensitivity of a child to such conditions persists, with little variation, probably up to three or five years of age. Even short separations can produce disorders during this period, if only because the child cannot yet estimate time and does not appreciate the reassurance that the separation is only for "a day or a week". Sensitivity to maternal deprivation during this period is so high that it dominates sensitivity to other environmental changes. Where change in the known sensory environment (e.g. following admission to hospital) is the only disturbing feature, the child can be reassured in the presence of the mother or mother surrogate, can adapt sooner, and will eagerly explore new possibilities and play freely (even during examinations). On the other hand, the child can more easily tolerate separation from mother if the physical environment at least remains constant (for example, when he remains at home).

Already in the second year of life, the social relations of the child begin to extend to other members of the nuclear family group and to the small group of family friends and relatives. Until this time, the relationship with the mother (or the mother surrogate) determines the relationship of the child to all other figures, in the sense that they are more or less replicas of this relationship. Now, however, the child begins to specify his relationship to individual members of the family and to other people according to their age (strength and influence) and sex. In normal daily interaction, and especially in play, in which the child now displays a greater degree of autonomy, initiative, and creativity, he learns his first simple orientation to society which at this point is primarily the family structure. The family is the principal source of the emotional stimulation which underlies feelings of security, and is the critical environment for the child. Now it is the true "organizer" of all his needs and activities; it is the point of both departure and return for shorter or longer essays into the wider environment.

This relationship between the child and the family also directs the way in which he participates in kindergarten or other extra-familial activities. By the end of this period, the child identifies himself to a marked degree with the same-sex parent in his sexual and family role. Maternal deprivation now tends to be replaced by familial deprivation. The absence of the father or siblings from the family profoundly affects future development, particularly if in both cases substitutes are unavailable (see page 122). At this time, lack of opportunities for play (*"Spieldefizit"* [F. Schneersohn, 1939] — see page 11) has particularly important deprivational consequences for problem solving and socio-emotional development.

At about six years of age, the normally developed child is capable of partial independence, of tolerating a short separation from the family, and can establish new relationships with teachers, school friends, a peer group — he is ready for school. Even at this stage, however, a strong striving for affection in all aspects of family, school, and social life (G. Bollea, 1958a) is evident, so that continued denial of emotional stimuli as, for example, in a broken family, produces behavioural disorders and unbalanced personality development. At this time, the child is extremely sensitive to new emotional events, for example, to judgments and evaluations, and he finds it difficult to tolerate irony or failure in a game. Thus, a continuing poor scholastic record of a less gifted child can be an unfavourable developmental factor. The child's facility in finding support and security within the peer group in this period (six — ten years) allows him to tolerate transfer into an institution more easily, particularly when he can find emotional support and the opportunity to express himself within such an institution.

Children raised in institutions from an early age begin to adjust to some degree at this age, their development is more balanced, and their school record improves. This is most likely related not only to the extension of social relations, but to a change from "global" thinking (sensorimotor syncretism) to operational categorical thinking (J. Piaget, H. Wallon, A. Gesell). Knowledge dramatically broadens, and is of a qualitatively higher level — the child begins to master abstract concepts of time and space and to differentiate more clearly between events of natural and of social origin. At this stage therefore he is less sensitive and adapts better to temporary separation, even in the less personal environment of child-care establishments. For this reason the absence of the father is more critical than the absence of the mother. Around ten to eleven years the child becomes relatively independent, and because at the same time his high plasticity or adaptability reduces in other developmental areas, he loses the capacity to establish deep intimate bonds with parental surrogates. The child of this age therefore often responds better to placement in an impersonal institute than to temporary placement in a foster family.

With the onset of puberty, the child gradually begins to extend his relationships to society as a whole. He learns to perceive its structure, even if initially in a very simple form. He begins to make self-judgments from the viewpoint of society. He seeks his place in society and his identity in complicated and complex social organizations. He tries finally to find his place in the cosmos, his place in space and time dimensions, the meaning of life. This search is very difficult and painful, and the child seeks new models of identification which can offer precedents and security. This model, which is thus a new organizing influence, can be a real person from whom the child abstracts certain idealized notions, or an abstract fantasy figure from literature or the movies — a pop singer, an actor, a sportsman, an artist, or a scientist. At this time, the adolescent needs access to new sources of social interaction. His search should be supported by the environment, for example through willingness to discuss and debate issues which to adults may seem quite pointless. Lack of such opportunities can produce "identity confusions" (E. Erikson, 1966). Need for such contact and communication has been well documented by E. Horáčková and A. Čulík (1967), in their study of emotional deprivation in adolescents, as it is reflected in their desire to make contact with famous pop singers.

Thus the danger of maternal deprivation is subsequently replaced at a later age by the danger of family deprivation, then of peer group deprivation, and finally of social-cultural deprivation. Studies of psychological deprivation have focused primarily on the first of these, and today we are poorly informed about forms of deprivation at other developmental periods. We know even less about forms of deprivation in later adulthood, although the odd study, some casual clinical observations and theoretical assumptions about developmental periods ("Eight ages of man", E. H. Erikson, 1966) suggest that deprivation in early and late adulthood and particularly in old age, is no less real and important, although it is possibly expressed in different ways and produces different effects. Such considerations, however, are beyond the scope of this book.

SEX DIFFERENCES

In the majority of studies we have surveyed, the question of sex differences is either completely ignored and children are simply lumped together in a group, or in the introduction the number of boys and girls is noted, without further comment. The reason for this is the naive assumption that at a very early age there are no differences between the sexes in reactivity and developmental progress, although there are numerous references to such differences, which could encourage further investigation. For example, the child psychiatrist treats three times as many boys as girls. The difference between the number of boys and girls admitted to correctional institutes with more serious behaviour disorders is even more marked. Data on mortality and illness suggest increased biological vulnerability in boys, so that the original predominance of boys conceived changes in adulthood to a predominance of females. This higher vulnerability probably dates from the pre-natal period, and produces a higher incidence of minimal brain damage in boys which — as we shall show — predisposes them, in a certain way, to be more sensitive to deprivation. Boys are also slower in speech development, and their social maturation in the pre-school period is usually slower and more uneven. They are often admitted to school "unready".

Workers concerned with this problem, however, are not unanimous in their interpretation of data. On the one hand some claim that inherited differences in basic reactivity of boys and girls underlie subsequent differences in early learning. However, there is no sound support for this in the literature. H. Papoušek (1967a) failed to find any sex differences in rate of conditioning or response latency in any of the groups of infants he studied from birth to six months. On the other hand one can agree with the suggestion that the early upbringing of boys and girls progresses differently from the earliest age. Different parental attitudes towards boys and girls are already established before the birth of the child. From the beginning, each sex is given a different social role and is exposed to different demands insofar as discipline and independence are concerned.

A number of older and more recent studies, although not concerned with the origins of such differences, report clear sex differences in the incidence of behaviour disorders even in the first years. E. K. Beller and P. B. Neubauer (1963) report a greater tendency towards aggression and affective outbursts in boys, i.e. increasing impulsivity, which is often associated with a tendency towards negativism and an apparent lack of separation anxiety. When we consider the case histories of these boys, however, we note that the aggression and impulsivity, according to the authors, are rooted in pre-existing intense anxiety. With girls, on the other hand, there is clear evidence of over-emphasis on self-control and projection of emotional feelings. The authors suggest that these differences arise through different development of separation anxiety, and consequently of aggression and the expression of defiance in the two sexes.

Some tentative findings from our own studies suggest that we should consider sex differences in deprivation situations, and that these differences have significance for clinical practice. We cannot claim that some types of deprived personality identified in our sample of institutionalized children were primarily male and others primarily female. Both sexes were represented in every type. Nevertheless the socially provocative type, which is characterized by aggressive behaviour, is largely male, while the relatively adjusted category numbers more girls.

We attempted (Z. Matějček, 1969b) to obtain more precise data in a longitudinal study of 160 children (84 boys and 76 girls) from a toddler institute (see page 212). In our experiment, as in Schaffer's study, in which he investigated sex differences in the development of social attachment and desire for cuddling, sex differences were recorded, but were not significant. Some tendencies, however, were so persistent throughout the whole period of observation that they are worth mentioning.

In the age range twelve to twenty-one months, for example, there were no differences in adaptive behaviour (assessed by Gesell's method) although in motor development girls are somewhat superior to boys, and in social behaviour were more frequently described as well adapted and less frequently as angry. For this reason the nurses viewed them as more lovable, and this, in turn, had an effect on the children's attitudes. Girls show a higher frequency of adjusted behaviour throughout the whole of the toddler age. In our comparison of orientation to the social or to the material environment, girls were much more stable, more frequently being placed in the balanced category. On the other hand, boys up to twenty-one months of age generally were more strongly oriented to the material environment; in the period twenty-one to thirty months, the focus shifted to the social environment, and it was only in the thirty to thirty-six month period that a balanced orientation was shown. We attribute this to the slower social development of boys, a delay which is exacerbated in the institutional environment (see table 28). Boys also seem to be more vulnerable to a change in environment, which suggests that their previous adaptation was probably superficial. We recorded the responses of 114 children on leaving the toddler home to return home, to the adoptive home, or to the pre-school institutes. Of the 63 boys, only 20 (32 per cent) adapted quickly and easily, as against 28 (55 per cent) of the 51 girls. This difference is significant at the 0.02 level. The boys were usually either inhibited or became restless and more irritable.

In the school age range (between the second and the fifth classes) there were no significant sex differences in tested intelligence or school performance, although there were significant differences in

Table 28. Dominant orientation

	Age 12–21 Months % of Total		Age 21–30 Months % of Total		Age 30–36 Months % of Total	
	Boys N=84	Girls N=76	Boys N=84	Girls N=76	Boys N=84	Girls N=76
To material environment	39	20	36	22	29	21
To social environment	30	27	37	32	29	33
Balanced orientation	30	45	25	39	42	46
Other abnormalities	1	8	2	7	0	0

Table 29. Response to new life environment after three years of age

	Boys (N=63) % of Total	Girls (N=51) % of Total
Without abnormalities or difficulties	32	55
Inhibition dominant – passive, apathetic	19	6
Fearful behaviour (clinging to new mother or surrogate)	10	8
Striking restlessness, tension	6	4
Other abnormalities	19	10
Unclassifiable (no reliable data)	14	17

Table 30. Social behaviour of children in second and fifth grade

	Boys (N=46) % of Total	Girls (N=38) % of Total
Well-adapted, without abnormalities	24	71
Aggressive, wilful, dominating	37	5
Restless, hyperactive	22	13
Hypoactive, inhibited, passive	3	3
Strikingly infantile	7	0
Other abnormalities	7	8

behaviour assessed by teachers. At this point adjustment, which we first assessed between twelve and twenty-one months, showed new trends. Twenty-seven (71 per cent) of the thirty-eight girls, but only eleven of the forty-six (24 per cent) boys were judged to be well adjusted. This difference is highly significant ($p < 0.001$).

It is obvious that we are very poorly informed about sex differences in sensitivity to deprivational experiences and about their effects. This is clearly a new field of study.

CONSTITUTIONAL DIFFERENCES

Undoubtedly certain constitutional factors underlie the differential effects produced by identical deprivation conditions. As we previously mentioned, R. A. Spitz, W. Goldfarb, and J. Bowlby, in their classic studies, attempted to describe deprivational effects occurring in certain environments and at a certain age, and, consonant with the psychological and psychiatric theories of that time, looked for a "deprivational syndrome". From the early 1920s on, these theories (Watson's behaviourism, Pavlov's reflexology, different learning theories, Freud's psychoanalysis) focused largely on the effects of environment on child-rearing practices rather than emphasizing the inheritance of certain characteristics, which the older school (Kraepelin) had favoured. For this reason, they looked for an invariant relationship between different environmental conditions and the average organism (the "child" as such), which, in practice, meant a search for the etiology of the disorder in environmental factors — in child rearing, in parental shortcomings, or in institutional conditions. They demanded in principle equal care and education for all children whom they assumed to be endowed, though in different degrees, with similar characteristics and abilities. In dealing with the child's development, they described types which were related to developmental periods — they referred to the personality of the "pre-school child", of the "school child", of the "adolescent".

Periodically, the inevitable question arises of why all children who are raised in identical environments do not develop identically, and why only some of them suffer from certain disorders. It has been repeatedly demonstrated that the "average" child does not exist, only individuals who differ from one another, who are differently equipped, and who respond differently to certain external conditions. The stability of these individual characteristics has been examined in a number of studies, particularly in the early longitudinal studies of A. Gesell (1928, 1939) and the long-term study of P. M. Symonds (1961). The latter showed, for example, that the "adolescent personality" which has been so carefully described in a number of studies, is fictitious — it is simply the average of a number of individual cases. Every adolescent is an individual with unique features which can be observed to adulthood. The myth of the average child, however, persists, and real individuality is overlooked or deliberately excluded by the statistical techniques employed. Individual differences are viewed as unwelcome intrusions which obstruct efforts to find general laws. If we refuse to recognize individual constitutional differences amongst children, however, we cannot appreciate the different effects of a number of deprivational conditions, or predict the outcome of certain therapeutic approaches in particular cases.

The problem of individual constitutional differences is, of course, an extremely complex one. In the first place, it is difficult to establish the extent to which the observed differences are due to genetic or other factors. Even in neonates simple responsiveness can be affected by a number of factors, and it is not always easy to establish precisely what these effects are. H. Papoušek (1967a), in his studies of conditioned head-turning responses with food reinforcement in neonates and infants in the first few months of life, demonstrated large differences between fast and slow conditioners. Based on analysis of the factors which we might assume to underlie individual differences in performance — sex, age, birth weight, weight increase, hunger drive, satiation, and so on — he concluded that his results generally supported the hypothesis that the conditioning procedures were tapping differences in innate, genetically determined, higher nervous functioning.

A second very difficult problem in this area is the development of indices of individual differences in infants and their stability during the life history of the individual under a variety of conditions.

O. Jánoš and H. Papoušek of the Institute for Mother and Child, Prague, have pursued this problem over a number of years through their careful studies of eye-blinking and head-turning responses in babies. They report marked individual differences in CR acquisition and latency — differences which are highly correlated ($r = 0.68$, $p < 0.01$) — in neonates and in babies up to six months of age. The range of differences in head-turning response is clearly shown in the acquisition curves for neonates and three-month-old infants (H. Papoušek, 1967a).

While experimental data to date do not warrant highly general conclusions, it seems reasonable to postulate at least one element in the newly born child's behaviour which is relatively stable, and which has a very profound influence on further development — viz., level of activation.

For example, B. Birns (1965) reported clear individual differences in the responses of five-day-old babies to arousing stimuli (soft and loud sounds, a cold metal ring placed on the thigh). Some babies responded with strong movements and were generally aroused to all stimuli, others reacted moderately or rather weakly. In another experiment from the same laboratory the child was initially exposed by a painful stimulus (striking the foot) and then calmed by a continuous deep tone, by rocking, by warmth, or by a rattle (W. H. Bridger, 1966). In this experiment large individual differences were also shown in speed of relaxation. E. Haar, J. Welkowitz, and A. Blau (1964) have shown that difference in activation level is the basic dimension on which the behaviour of newly born babies differs and on which the ability to attract the attention of the staff is based. W. Kessen (1967) reported that in his experimental group of three- to four-day-old children strong suckers were more active initially than weak suckers. A number of other studies (B. T. Brazelton, 1962b; S.K. Escalona, 1962; U. Pulver, 1959; R. Meili 1961; S. C. Hess, 1966) support the view that inherited differences in activity most likely persist almost throughout life. We note also that psychoanalytically oriented workers today acknowledge inherited differences, and refer to strong or weak "oral instincts" in the newborn baby, which are closely related to the mother's behaviour and the extent to which she can satisfy the basic oral needs of the child (M. Békei de Mezei, 1963).

In this general context of level of activity or stimulation of the central nervous system, a number of experiments reported by J. Lát (1958 and later studies) and others with rats observed from birth to late adulthood are of considerable importance. Lát emphasized the vast inter-individual variability (400–600 per cent) in general activity, indexed by searching and grooming behaviour, speed of CR acquisition and frequency of spontaneous inter-signal reactions. Animals with high CR activity also showed a high level of CNS excitation (strength of excitation in Pavlovian terminology). Level of excitability (or arousal), which is probably mediated by the brain stem reticular formation, is a type of general factor influencing different types of performance. Lát also reported an inverted U relationship between excitation and both discrimination learning and tendency to neurosis. This implies that there are certain optimal (moderate) bands of excitation within which discriminability is greatest and inclination to neurosis least. At higher or lower levels of arousal, however, discriminability decreases and neurotic predisposition increases, although in individual cases the reasons for this differ. Lát also reported similar relationships between excitability and bodily growth, and size of the adrenals. Since excitation level is apparently genetically based, special strains of fast or slow learning rats (with high or low excitation levels) can be selectively bred. Excitation level, however, can be changed in two other ways — either directly, by increased tactile (through "handling", see Levine) or visual and acoustic (Lát) stimulation, or indirectly by altering the internal environment of the organism, for example, through diet (see page 130).

Some children are obviously more sensitive to tactile, kinaesthetic, or thermal stimuli, others to auditory or visual stimuli. Differences of this sort are sometimes surprisingly large. These are probably the factors underlying differences between "cuddling" and "non-cuddling" babies reported by H. R. Schaffer and P. E. Emerson (1964). They reported a careful observational study of a group of thirty-seven babies from early weeks to eighteen months. Nineteen were classified as "cuddling", nine as "intermediate", and nine as "non-cuddling" babies. The latter did not reject all bodily contact (during feeding, nursing, and so on) but strongly resisted all moves towards intimate contact, i.e. through cuddling. This refusal was maintained even when they were tired, ill, in pain, or frightened. The total number of physical contacts was much smaller than with the cuddling type, and, in addition, the specific attachment to the maternal figure was established somewhat later, and was weaker. There were no significant differences between the groups in sex, position in the family, and kind of nursing. However, mothers obviously vary in their need for close physical contact with the child, so that either a positive or a negative interaction, which has a profound influence on the development of basic relationships, can exist between mother and child.[1]

From the very beginning there are also individual differences in the tendency to smile, to cry, to be fearful. We can find, side by side, in the same environment, serious and happy-go-lucky children, tearful and quiet children.

H. R. Schaffer (1963) reported large individual differences in the reactions of children older than seven months to short separations from the maternal figure, and to the presence of a stranger. It is obvious enough that in some children strength of relationship to the parent is relatively independent of the parent's own behaviour, and that this applies also to fear of strangers. However, we can very well imagine a withdrawn child in the hands of a mother who strongly needs intimate contact and who forces the child to demonstrate love and devotion. On the other hand we sometimes encounter a child with a strong specific bond (towards the maternal figure) which in the case of the withdrawn mother appears to be too demanding and restrictive. In both cases deprivation conditions are created which are masked by the parent's misperception of her behaviour towards the child.

---

1. A positive interaction can occur when the mother and the child both reject or both desire physical contact, a negative interaction when one of the two demands physical contact which the other resists.

According to Schaffer, differences in the intensity of social attachment or in the generalization of this attachment (the number of persons included) and in behaviour towards strangers have a common basis in social sensitivity, which is largely genetic in origin, and which develops out of the more basic factor of general reactivity, which we have already discussed.

Less clear are the hereditary factors involved in certain complex structured behavioural patterns (of emotional, imaginal, and logical nature) described by M. Tramer (1960) in his concept of *"formae innatae vitae infantilis"*. (He gives as an example inability to free oneself from the protective mantle of the mother and enter a strange environment, greater and prolonged need of play, and so on.) This applies also to the observations of the Japanese investigators S. Naka, K. Abe, and H. Suzuki (1965) who report that some families exhibit certain character features (for example, dependence on mother, stubbornness, shyness, tongue-tied in a strange environment, and so on). However it is impossible to judge the extent to which hereditary or child-rearing factors are determinative in these cases.

Despite the fragmentary nature and paucity of our present knowledge about individual constitutional differences in children, it is clear that children's reactions to deprivation situations differ from the very outset. We mentioned some cases at an earlier point, and we shall meet this problem again in the following chapters. A tremendous variety of such reactions is produced, for example, by experimentally induced sensory deprivation. The great range of individual reactions to short-term deprivation (a child left alone with a stranger) has also been experimentally demonstrated (for example by D. B. Gardner, D. Pease, and G. R. Hawkes, 1961).

Our own studies, in which we originally attempted to describe an institutionalized type, forced us to conclude, after years of work with children from a number of institutions, that institutionalized children are not a homogeneous below-average group, but show significant individual differences in total activity, intelligence, temperament, character, and social behaviour. Though many of them were raised from earliest age in an identical environment, their development progressed in such different ways that they were subsequently transferred to different types of institutes – to institutes for "normal" children, for the mentally retarded, or for children with behaviour disorders. They do show similarities in habits and lack of knowledge; their social behaviour, work interests, learning ability, general activity level, and level of concentration, however, all varied significantly. Thus, although when discussing such differences we refer to "types" (see pages 207, 318), this is only the first step towards better understanding of individual personalities of afflicted children.

In 1954 we observed at four-monthly intervals all children in one toddler home in the Middle Czech county (children from one to three years of age). Staffing was relatively stable and the rearing environment on the whole could be described as above average. The institute was small (twenty-five beds) and the atmosphere rather familial. Every child, therefore, could be adequately observed. The nurses knew all the children very well, so that we were able to supplement our own observations with their reports, and at the same time to cross-validate their reports with our own observations. Our examination included physical development and health, individual mental development using the Gesell method, development of child-nurse and child-child relationships, difficulties and abnormalities in behaviour, and a number of other measures. At three years of age the children were separated into three groups — some went to adoptive families, some were returned to their own families, and the rest were transferred to pre-school children's homes. During pre-school age, examinations were less frequent, but from school age on we could obtain additional information from school records.

One hundred and sixty children — eighty-four boys and seventy-six girls — were studied in this way. (See table 31.)

Let us first consider the 101 children who were admitted to the toddler institute from baby institutes, i.e. children who up to the age of three years had practically identical developmental environments. Their individual case histories show highly varied patterns, and obviously we cannot class these children under a single syndrome. Nevertheless, even here there are certain clear behavioural trends.

1. Our prime concern was the activity level of the child. It is obvious that the uniform institutional environment, which we assumed lacked adequate stimulation, does not function as a moderating influence. On the contrary, two extremes were evident — children were either strikingly inhibited or strikingly restless. Closer examination, however, led to more precise differentiation. One group of eight children showed a gross decrease in reactivity level — they remained passive not only to people but also to toys. This behaviour

Table 31. Age of admission to institute in the sample tested

	N
Admitted to institutional care at birth or during first year	101
Admitted between 12 and 17 months	28
Admitted at later age	31
Total	160

was shown mainly by children who were already retarded before admission to the toddler home. Not all the children who were classified by the nurses as passive and inhibited, however, are in fact non-active. They only appear to be so by comparison with other rather hyperactive children. They show little interest in the social environment and tend to be more materially oriented. They spend a good deal of time playing, although at quite a primitive level. Here we are dealing with a particular direction of activity or with its transfer from the social to the material environment rather than with an overall reduction.

At the other extreme we find children who are strikingly restless, irritable and hyperactive. Some of these are obviously classifiable as having minimal brain damage. Nevertheless, we also find this high level of activity — a sort of undirected hunger for stimulation — in children who, on the basis of anamnestic and neurological data, cannot be classified in this way. In addition there is a large group of children whose hyperactivity is socially directed — they show a hunger for social stimulation. Children of this group show very little interest in play and material objects but very great interest in human interaction. Between the two extemes was a group (N = 30) who showed normal levels of activity.

2. We attempted to evaluate the general character of the children's social behaviour in their normal daily activity (relations with other children, with nurses and supervisors, with visitors, and with the visiting psychologist). Here also we failed to detect a uniform picture. In the younger toddler range (between twelve and twenty-one months) we used the behavioural categories as in table 32.

The groups showing predominantly social interests behave in quite different ways. Children displaying diffuse undirected social activity (group 3 in table 32) run after every nurse or visitor and attempt to make as close contact as possible. Their need for contact can be expressed in a socially acceptable way. For example, such a child suddenly runs up and puts his head in the experimenter's lap, has "come to be cuddled". The presence of other children does not seem to inhibit this need for intimacy. During examination, these children show greater interest in the experimenter than in toys or play, but try to cooperate. Because of their indiscriminating attempts to obtain social contact, children of this type deny themselves opportunities for play, for handling material, for work activities. They are retarded, therefore, in the development of working habits, techniques, and strategies. Their level of adaptive behaviour is relatively low. They usually react to termination of contact without

Table 32. Social behaviour of children of young toddler age

Behavioural Characteristics	N
1. Adjusted normal behaviour	30
2. Markedly passive, inhibited, lacking spontaneous activity or any significant response	20
3. Clearly expressed social activity (sometimes hyperactive) but diffuse and undirected (these children were equally friendly to all people, and actively established contact, but did not protest when the contact was terminated; social relationships were superficial; they observed all activity around them with interest)	14
4. Socially provocative behaviour; the children attempted to attract attention by provocative behaviour; they rejected and were aggressive to other children; they established contact with an adult when they were alone, outside the children's group	11
5. Strikingly irritable, angry and spiteful, but displaying little initiative or directed activity	10
6. Normal behaviour in children's groups but very inhibited and uncertain in unfamiliar situations	8
7. Other forms of behaviour	4
8. Unclassifiable	4
Total	101

protest, without making scenes; any resistance can be easily overcome when the nurse returns them to their peer group. These children, however, try to find excuses to return to the examination room — they peep in, they show off and try to attract attention (see page 208).

The group of eleven children (group 4 in table 32) characterized as socially provocative in behaviour is particularly conspicuous. Within their peer group they are extremely irritable, aggressive, and unbearable. They are well described in this typical example. Children are playing freely on the floor. The nurse hands a toy to one child. On the other side of the room another child has a tantrum, throws away his toy car, snatches another child's car and possibly attempts to bite him. In this way the child forces the nurse to give him some personal attention. For one reason or another, he sulks for most of the time. If he is alone with the nurse, however, he seems to be completely "changed", "unbelievably pleasant". Nurses say of such a child that he would like to have the nurse for himself, that the presence of other children profoundly disturbs his need for intimacy (see page 211).

Contact with the examiner is poor — he is "a stranger". Gradually, however, the child relaxes and shows reasonable cooperation, although he strongly inclines to do exactly as he pleases. If he is forced or fails to perform some task, he actively refuses to cooperate any further. He reacts negatively and strongly to the termination of contact, he makes scenes, refuses to be taken away — he sulks.

There is another smaller group of ten children (group 5 in table 32) whom we described as generally hyperactive, but who show little directed activity. They seem to be in a state of constant increased alertness. They scream if approached by another child. If anything slightly upsetting occurs they throw away their toys, so that the nurse either willingly or unwillingly has to devote attention to them. This behaviour prevents constructive activity. When examined they do not establish contact — they are wary — but hold on to toys and refuse to give them back; they are concerned only with having, maintaining, or defending something. When an attempt is made to replace one toy with another they resist, and further contact is usually impossible.

In dealing with the total sample, we can employ an additional secondary index for classificatory purposes — the type of stimulation which generally attracts the child's interest (see table 33).

We have already dealt with the first category in table 33. Children of the third category generally belong to that group described in table 32 as "adjusted social behaviour". Children with a strikingly material orientation (category 2) in general belong to the groups described as "inhibited, passive", and "angry behaviour but lacking initiative". These children are usually quiet and satisfied as long as nobody tries to take away their toys, when they defend themselves. They can also be aggressive towards a child from whom they have had bad experiences. During examination, we noted a relatively high level of play in these children, and that their adaptive behaviour is often close to the norm.   In test situations they display greater interest in toys than in the examiner. Termination of contact is accepted by them without protest, providing it is made clear to them that they are returning to their toys, and that they can take some of the toys back with them to the group. They quite often

Table 33. Orientation to different types of stimulation

Marked orientation to social stimulation	25
Marked orientation to material stimulation	30
Relatively balanced social and material orientation	38
Extremely variable	8
Total	101

attempt to return to the examination room to play a little more. Their relationships with adults are indifferent, and the nurses often describe them as "looking through us".

3. We were further interested in special patterns of child-adult and child-child interaction, determined by constitutional traits, in institutionalized children. Behavioural patterns in the toddler home are an extension of those described by J. Koch (1961) (see page 198) in the baby institutes. Certain behaviour from the child produces certain responses from the environment, in this case from the nurse, and from the group of other children with whom he shares his life space. From the weaning stage, and particularly in toddler age, when the child actively invades both the material environment (he crawls, starts walking) and the social environment (he starts to talk), he encounters strong social reinforcement of his behaviour. This reinforcement is of a rather special character in the insitutional environment.

In the course of social learning, how do children of the particular types described interact with the staff? Children who are hypoactive, socially passive, inhibited, with regressive forms of behaviour, demand extensive physical care, they progress rather slowly, and do not offer adequate satisfaction to the nurses. For this reason, they tend to be further neglected, and experience only a limited amount of important social and emotional stimulation.

Children who are oriented primarily to the material environment remain in the background of the group. They are not sources of disturbance. Nurses view them as pleasant — they amuse themselves. There is the ever-present danger, however, that in the future they will be given less social and more material stimulation, and that their social passivity will thus become more and more pronounced.

Children who are socially hyperactive, who show a diffuse undirected type of social interest, frequently disturb the nurses' routine by their persistent demand for attention, a demand which, however, is impersonal in that it is not directed at any one particular nurse. The child seeks attention in non-aggressive ways — by joking, by peeping, or by pleasant indiscriminate cuddling, which hinders the development of deeper contact. Such a child is widely tolerated but has no special emotional attachment with any one person.

Children showing provocative social behaviour are the greatest trial for nurses. They disturb their work with the group, they forcibly demand personal attention by aggressive or by particularly vengeful or wicked tactics. For these reasons they are sometimes described by nurses as "extremely selfish or jealous". It seems inevitable that such a child in an institute is given only negative reinforcement. In the conditions under discussion it is hardly possible for such a child to obtain the necessary satisfactions and thus he is forced more and more into new displays of provocation.

Children with relatively normal levels of activity and social interaction and a balanced material and social orientation, who can obtain adequate stimulation and develop specific social attachments (even if these are weak) to a number of staff members, are pleasant for nurses to deal with, and offer them greater satisfaction from a child-care point of view. Among these are the so-called "loved ones" (favourites), on whom most of the interest and sympathy of all the staff, or at least one of the nurses, is focused, and who develop satisfactorily in the favourable context of multiple mothering. These are included in the category of relatively well-adjusted children (see page 215), and predominate at the present time in Czechoslovakian institutes.

4. We would point out that on occasions the relationships between behavioural indices change over time, during the course of the child's development. For example, when recording social behaviour, we noted that inhibition and social hyperactivity decrease gradually during the period twelve to twenty-four months, and particularly by the end of the third year, and that the percentages of institutionalized children classified as "relatively well adjusted" and "balanced social and material orientation" also increase. In addition there are some specific changes which are obviously determined by the individual child's experience of the institutional environment. For example, some children, after the initial extravagant demand for emotional contact with nurses through emotional outbursts and persistent sulking, eventually found more socially acceptable ways of attracting adult attention. At two years of age, they were described by nurses as "especially pleasant and cuddly", but with other children they were still aggressive "because of jealousy". This sort of behaviour, of course, is very familiar to nurses. It is interesting that we find this behaviour pattern quite frequently in children who during the third year, or even later, were adopted, and suddenly gained new parents, which brought with it a sudden increased input of emotional stimuli. As table 35 suggests, this behaviour is maintained during the school age period, but in most cases it is expressed in socially acceptable ways.

Other children showed developmental stagnation and quite opposite characteristics. It was not until the age of three years that the initial inhibition changed to an exaggerated social interest; the child was now so strongly oriented towards people that he gained little advantage from the working programme, from handling materials, sensory development, group play, and so on.

Finally, there are those children who up to three years showed a predominantly material orientation, but at the end of this period showed an interesting developmental surge, when they finally found their place in the group, actively participating and thus receiving greater attention from the staff.

5. Our final comment here refers to the tremendous capacity for rehabilitation in individual children even in late pre-school and school age. The children observed were not subjected to any special medical or remedial programme, and improvements, as far as we can establish, were due mainly to normal maturational factors.

By the end of 1966, 72 of the 101 children from our group were enrolled in second grade or above. Of this group, 23 were in school age children's homes, 24 had been returned to their own families, and 25 were in adoptive families. The average age of these sub-groups was practically identical − 12.0 years, 11.9 years, and 11.7 years respectively.

On leaving the toddler home soon after reaching three years, the groups showed no significant differences in physical (height and weight) or mental development (motor, adaptive, social behaviour, speech − according to Gesell norms). It is obvious therefore that the adopted children were no better than the others, they were simply available at the time. Nor were those who remained in the institution necessarily the worst children, they were children whose parents did not desert them but who could not offer them an acceptable rearing environment. More boys remained in institutions − girls were more frequently adopted − but the difference is not significant. The most favourable hereditary background was shown by the group of children returned to their own homes.

School achievement was as expected, with the best progress made by adopted children, the worst by those remaining in institutes (see table 34).

Table 34. School achievement of children with different backgrounds

Grade of Last School Report	Adopted Children	Children Returned to Their Own Families	Children Remaining under Institutional Care
1−2	11	3	3
3−4	14	12	6
Failed, is failing or in special class	0	9 (37%)	14 (61%)
Totals	25	24	23

If we compare the behaviour of these children during the school age period and during the period twelve to twenty-one months (see page 216), there are some interesting changes. Inhibition and diffuse social hyperactivity usually change to adjusted behaviour. On the other hand the type characterized as socially provocative and strikingly irritable but lacking initiative remains the same. Such children are described in school records as not adaptable to groups, aggressive and dominating and unpopular. Behaviour of this sort is relatively most frequent in the adopted group, less so in children returned to their families, and is most infrequent in children remaining in the institution (see table 35).

From our point of view, the group of children who remained permanently under institutional care merits special attention. Relocation of these children at school age to different types of school children's homes, and the extent to which these decisions were subsequently justified, are shown in table 36.

The sample is too small to permit definite conclusions; nevertheless, the final referral can be predicted from the behavioural classifications. Inhibited children and children showing diffuse social hyperactivity, despite good intelligence, progress rather poorly in school and most frequently are admitted to residential schools for mentally retarded children. Children of the socially provocative type most frequently find their way into corrective establishments, as indicated in our previous studies (see page 210).

Table 35. Social behaviour of children with different backgrounds

Social Behaviour	Adopted Children	Children Returned to Their Own Families	Children Remaining under Institutional Care
Adjusted, without abnormalities	12 (48%)	9 (37%)	5 (22%)
Aggressive, unpopular in group, dominating	9 (36%)	8 (33%)	7 (30%)
Hyperactive, restless, unstable	1	2	5
Passive, apathetic, inhibited	0	3	3
Dominant infantile features	1	1	0
Other abnormalities	2	1	3
Totals	25	24	23

Table 36. Behaviour of twenty-three children remaining since baby age in children's homes

| | Residential Schools for | | |
	Retarded Children	Normal Children	Children with Pre-delinquent Behaviour
Normal	2	3	0
Inhibition dominant	3	0	0
Diffuse social hyperactivity	4	1	0
Socially provocative, aggressive	0	1	3
Irritable but inactive, rebellious, stubborn	0	3	0
Other abnormalities (variable)	0	2	1
Totals	9	10	4

INDIVIDUAL DIFFERENCES DUE TO PATHOLOGICAL STATES

Identical deprivation conditions affect normal children and children suffering from some organic or mental defect in different ways. Probably in certain extreme cases organic defect in the child can result in decreased sensitivity to deprivational conditions. With some notable exceptions, this is true of children with serious brain damage which results in mental deficiency (idiots or idio-imbeciles). The more frequent and more important case, however, is that where the child, because of some defect, becomes more sensitive to deprivational conditions. If sensory, motor, or other defect prevents the child from satisfying his basic psychological needs in the usual way in an environment otherwise normal (that is, normal for the healthy child), he is forced either to completely abandon his drive towards satisfaction, to accept partial satisfactions, or to find substitute satisfactions. Deprivational danger is thus embedded in the very core of the defect, and the child himself carries this danger with him into his environment. In addition, one should remember that the environment of a handicapped child is seldom normal; it usually has certain deprivational features itself. We shall again ignore a number of other factors which affect the development of these children — primarily frequent social conflicts — and focus attention on the effect that psychological deprivation has on the development of a defective child's personality. We think that this has not been sufficiently emphasized in deprivational studies or in studies of handicapped children.

Sensory disorders

1. The extreme case of limited sensory stimuli from the normal environment is that of deaf-blind children. Successful examples of the rearing of such children are usually well documented, so that from the point of view of psychological deprivation they are useful case material.

An outstanding example is Helen Keller, who was certainly an exceptionally intelligent child, but whose supervision and care were neglected, so that she lost contact with the external world. Her behaviour was wild and undisciplined, she showed turbulent emotional outbursts, and her behaviour became quite intolerable. For these reasons she was admitted to the Boston Institute for the Blind, where she began her incredible improvement. As soon as she understood the signals from the environment, social contact systematically progressed, the girl became adequately socialized in a surprisingly short time, and conditions were created for the use and development of her mental capacity, which up to that point had been hardly touched. Similar cases of successful re-education under such difficult conditions have been reported from time to time (see O.I. Skorochodova, 1956).

2. Although there have been many studies of the development of blind children, until quite recently the basic question of the specific effect of lack of certain sensory stimuli on mental development has been almost ignored. It was only the discovery of serious mental disturbance during experimentally induced sensory deprivation that generated interest in this problem, and clarified a number of older observations — for example, the cause of frequent temporary behavioural confusion in patients recovering from cataract operations. When improved surgical techniques reduced the period of time the eyes had to be covered to twenty-four hours, the incidence of post-surgery psychosis reduced from 7 to less than 1 per cent (E. Ziskind, 1958). In such cases, in addition to sensory restriction itself, one has also to take into account a kind of fearful anticipation and despair. P. H. Leiderman et al. (1958) report in one older woman who was suddenly blinded visual hallucinations and time and space disorientations, disorders similar to those experimentally induced.

Such dramatic disorders do not occur in children suffering from congenital or partial blindness developed after birth; usually in these cases, however, the whole psychological development is deeply affected. The blind child not only suffers lack of visual stimuli, but also significant impoverishment of all other sensory stimuli to a far greater degree than the adult who has already developed his intellect and personality. If the child is afflicted by blindness while he is still fully dependent on the environment and has not yet developed full mobility, he has great difficulty in contacting and spontaneously selecting sensory stimuli. This does not, of course, produce the type of psychotic disorder experienced by adults or experimental subjects, for the development of such states requires a higher level of psychological organization. The effects are similar to those shown by normally seeing deprived children (institutionalized children, for example) and unless special remedial measures are taken, there is total or partial developmental retardation (especially in motor and speech development), and there are certain motor (automatisms) and other behavioural abnormalities, as well as a more prolonged period of dependency than in the case of normal children. In addition to the actual sensory deprivation, we note also that child-care neglect, and more frequently and importantly, possibly emotional deprivation in the family which may result from rejecting parental attitudes, can promote mental abnormalities (B. Lowenfeld, 1952). The developing personality of the blind child is also influenced by different familial and social conflict situations. Let us briefly consider those factors relevant to deprivation.

Thorough observation of the development of blind children at an early age was reported in Chicago by M. Norris, P. J. Spaulding, and F. H. Brodie (1957). They reported that some abilities develop in blind children at a later stage, but in the same general sequence. Developmental progress was determined very largely by the opportunity to learn and to experience (far more so than by the extent of blindness, intelligence, socio-economic factors, and so on). Development was quite favourable under optimal environmental conditions which compensate for sensory defect. Blind children showed delayed speech development, not only because they are unable to observe and mimic speech movements, but also because it is extremely difficult to match the image to the object when critical sensory stimuli are not available. Their initial speech is somewhat idiosyncratic; often there are meaningless echolalia, they use words in the wrong context, there are grammatical errors, usually involving personal pronouns, and although they are strongly motivated to speak, speech sometimes remains at the level of playing with words. Similar disturbances have been recorded in children left in one place — in bed (for safety reasons or through ignorance) — without adequate stimulation.

The personality of the blind child is also marred by inadequate sensory and emotional stimulation — he is usually egocentric, lacks initiative, is often very suggestible and generally socially withdrawn.

His relationships with others are impoverished by difficulties of contact and communication, such as inability to observe expressions and reactions of other people. The special institutes in which blind children are cared for from pre-school age are educationally very good and offer adequate care for most of the children; even here, however, difficulties arise in establishing intimate emotional relationships, difficulties inherent in the very nature of all institutions. Worst off are those blind children with pronounced mental deficiency; if, in addition, they are neglected, they are quite frequently placed in mental institutions.

Lack of visual contact with the environment is directly responsible for retardation of motor behaviour, for its restricted nature and paucity of expression in nearly all blind children. In addition to the frequent movement stereotypes (similar to those noted in sighted children in institutes offering a low level of stimulation, or in chronically ill children confined to bed), eye-rubbing, which was described in detail in 1947 by the ophthalmologist A. Franceschetti as the "oculodigital phenomenon", is particularly marked. He recorded this behaviour in children with congenital cataract in both eyes, and suggested that the child, by pressing the eyeballs, produces retinal phosphene, and that this stimulation is actively sought after. J. Kurz (1959), however, pointed out that this behaviour is no more common than other stereotyped behaviours amongst small children in institutes for the blind, and that this occurs in children suffering from central blindness[2] and even in sighted children. He rejected both Franceschetti's view and the opinion of those concerned with education of the blind, that here we are dealing with a bad habit resulting from inactivity, and maintained that the oculodigital reflex is related to CNS disorders.

Quite compelling and relevant data have been reported by K. Müller (1959a) who systematically observed 340 blind children and adolescents over a period of a week. He noted very frequent incidence of this type of abnormality (in 34 per cent of all children) mainly amongst pre-school children (in this group approximately 60 per cent). He also reported that the oculodigital reflex occurred most often in combination with other types of stereotyped and autoerotic behaviours, and assumed that this phenomenon is subject to the same laws as other psychomotor and neurotic abnormalities, especially when one is dealing with occurrence as a function of age. He found no relationship between these abnormalities and the underlying

2. As distinct from blindness resulting from some defect in the visual system, e.g. cataracts.

causes of blindness, but did not report a direct relationship with lack of developmental stimulation.

Although A. Peiper (1956) recorded movement stereotypes more frequently amongst dull than amongst bright institutionalized sighted children, K. Müller reported a higher frequency of these behaviours amongst lively, restless, nervous blind children (we suspect that the dullness Peiper observed is more a function of deprivation in the institutional environment than an index of congenital mental defect). We cannot attribute Müller's results to mental defect, since only 5 per cent of his sample were diagnosed as feebleminded.

From the data presented in this chapter and in the chapter on institutionalized children, we suggest that in both cases we are dealing with similar phenomena, which are related to psychological deprivation, in the one case wholly a product of the external conditions of a monotonous environment and in the other of organic defects in the child which also produce a similar monotony of stimulus input. This also accounts for the observation that this type of behaviour probably occurs more frequently with feebleminded children and encephalopaths of good to average intelligence. Lack of control over the after-effects of motor movement in these cases is caused by basic intellectual and/or perceptual disorders. An interesting parallel to the movement stereotypes of the blind is found also in so-called spasmus nutans (shaking and turning of the head) which is usually connected with nystagmus. This was long ago thought to be due to inadequate illumination (R. W. Raudnitz, 1897) or to be a symptom of hospitalism (H. Finkelstein, 1898) which suggests that the cause in any case is psychological deprivation (sensory, emotional).

Some interesting data have been reported by M. Strnadová (1969) in a study concerned directly with plateaus in mental development due to deprivation in children suffering from different degrees of visual defect. All children from the second and fifth classes in a special school for the blind, for children with arrested vision, and for poorly sighted children were examined on a number of standard and specially devised psychological tests. The control group was an equal number of randomly selected normally sighted children from a normal school. From our point of view, the arrested vision group of children is rather interesting. Here we are dealing with children who until recently were considered blind, who usually had spent most of their lives in the company of blind children, and who were educated using methods suitable for blind children. The use of modern optical techniques, however, allowed the majority of them to use what sight they had, so that they could become oriented in the environment, could look up even as far as the sky, which is a particularly exciting experience for them, and learn to write and read using visual methods. A special school for these children, probably the only one of its kind in Europe, was established ten years ago in Prague.

Here we are concerned with children who have been liberated from total visual deprivation by modern technology. The most striking characteristic of this group of children is their extraordinary hunger for light stimulation, which is indicated in their drawings. At school they are taught to read and write both normal script and Braille, but 50 per cent more of school time is devoted to learning the Braille script. However, they often achieve better results through normal (i.e. visual) methods of teaching reading, probably because of the much higher level of intrinsic motivation for visual activity, even if this is more demanding than tactile communication. (Fig. 56.)

3. The development of the deaf child is also affected by a number of factors ranging from parents' attitudes at the one end, to frustration through inability to establish auditory contact at the other. The most critical factor, however, is lack of auditory stimuli. It places the child in comparative sensory isolation, and emotionally and socially impoverishes his world (he has never experienced his mother's "loving talk", her singing, the richness and colour of tones, the sound of crying, laughter, and so on). The emotional development of the deaf child is therefore nearly always retarded and indiscriminating.

J. H. Mendelson, L. Siger, and P. Solomon (1960) studied the effect of sensory deprivation on the development of the fantasy world of deaf people by analyzing the dreams of deaf university students. They recorded the very frequent, strikingly real, colourful, three-dimensional dreams resembling real visual imagery, and the hallucinatory experiences of their subjects during induced sensory deprivation. They consider that the difference between the dreams of deaf people and the blurred dreams of normal people is due to lack of sensory stimulation which normally suppresses dream activity, and quickly erases dreams from memory. The fact that the dream characteristics of deaf people are most striking if the person is deaf from birth, less striking if deafness occurred before five years of age, and least striking in those who subsequently became deaf, is further evidence of the importance of sensory input in early years.

Dramatic reactions, similar to those experimentally induced, are recorded in the majority of children and adolescents following deafness. D. Müller-Hegemann (1964), for example, described the onset of schizophrenia in a person who became deaf at seventeen years of age. Such disorders can be explained either as a direct result of sensory deprivation or of social isolation.

It is well accepted that subsequent mental development is severely affected by deprivation of auditory stimuli, particularly if this occurs in the first years of life, and that this effect is expressed particularly in speech development. R.A. Chase (1969) maintains that the greatest problem for children with hearing disorders is that they have been deprived of early auditory experiences, which are essential for the development of auditory perceptual abilities underlying accurate and efficient speech perception. He also refers to the well-established fact that sometimes we encounter children whose audiograms suggest that they should have much greater speech production capability. He maintains that in many of these cases a careful search reveals early auditory deprivation. This can be as damaging as, and possibly more damaging than, a lesion in the peripheral auditory system. When early amplifications of sounds is necessary and the parents are instructed to speak more closely to the child's ear and to speak more loudly, there are considerable gains in speech acquisition.

The child with congenital deafness also suffers severely from lack of communication with the social environment, and subsequently from lack of satisfaction of his basic social needs. Additional deprivational factors are often the rejecting attitudes or indifference of parents, and the institutional environment which, from an educational point of view, is certainly favourable and essential, but from the emotional point of view is obviously less adequate than the normal family environment. Under such conditions, the only way in which a deaf child can attempt to develop the necessary amount of personal security is a rigid clinging to certain ways of thinking and behaviour, constriction of his modes of social action, and impoverishment and primitivization of needs and motives. E. S. Levine (1952) has reported that these effects are evident in the personalities of deaf children. From Rorschach protocols she noted that the outstanding personality characteristics were a high level of rigidity, constriction, lack of ability to conceptualize, and retarded emotional development.

An important observation is that despite fundamental differences in the life environments of deaf children and normal institutionalized children, there are a number of similarities which we suspect are due to psychological deprivation. In both cases there is marked retardation in development of conceptual thinking (the paucity of abstract thinking which W. Goldfarb recorded in institutionalized children was also noted by E. S. Levine [1952] in deaf children), and in emotional development (primitive and undifferentiated emotional responses); both groups incline towards unreal and socially non-conforming fantasies, lack of rational control, and frequent impulsive and aggressive behaviours.

4. Speech and communication disorders, where other intellectual abilities are preserved at a normal level, produce conflict rather than deprivation as such. More severe disorders of this sort, however, can severely impede the child's interaction with the environment, and can produce a certain degree of isolation. According to our findings, for example, a severe specific speech defect at an early age in a child of above-average non-verbal intelligence (described variously as developmental aphasia or idiopathic speech retardation) is often expressed in later life in an overall below-average personality with a low level of abstract ability, and in retarded emotional and character development.

Motor disorders

It is generally agreed that psychological disorders (hallucinatory) quite frequently accompany poliomyelitis with bulbar involvement, and that these are caused more by motor and sensory deprivation in iron lungs than by other factors (fever, toxicity, drugs, anoxia, metabolic disorders), although these can also be contributory factors. This is suggested by the fact that these symptoms can be induced in healthy people by placing them in a tank respirator (J. H. Mendelson and J. M. Foley, 1956) or in a small cell which restricts movement (P. M. van Wulfften Palthe, 1958; see later discussion). Similar states are also recorded in other patients immobilized for long periods in bed. The interruption of usual motor activity arouses anxiety and feelings of helplessness, and the accompanying painful sensory restriction stimulates substitute fantasy activity. The content of the fantasies is steered by the ambient conditions (for example, the noise of the respirator evokes images of aeroplanes, air raids, and so on) while the rest of the environment stimulates landscape imagery and so on. These fantasies differ from those reported in other disorders (for example, rheumatic psychosis) and are most frequent in patients who are isolated in a single room at twilight. They usually quickly disappear when the patient is transferred to a larger common ward, and acquires increased social and sensory stimulation. They do not respond, however, to usual pharmacological treatment. One of the present authors vividly recalls the depersonalization experiences and the vivid hypnagogic hallucinations he experienced at fourteen years of age when placed for a few days in a grey hospital ward for observation. A number of similar disorders, sometimes with paranoid overtones, are reported in children hospitalized in a children's ward (they refuse medicine, they are certain they hear the voices of their relatives in the corridor, and so on). Here, of course, other factors may be involved.

Children with obvious motor disorders (cerebral palsy) who are retarded in their early overall development, often show surprising development of mental abilities even in late school age. This intellectual growth dates from that point in time when rehabilitation succeeds in putting the child "back on his feet", so that he can independently acquire environmental stimulation, which normally is available at about two years of age. With children whose mobility is restricted for medical rather than organic reasons (cardiac cases, epileptics), repeated psychological investigations have disclosed a frustration syndrome which is very clearly expressed and severe.

Disorders involving integration of psychological functioning

1. A quite special category among children showing increased sensitivity to deprivation is that group with early CNS damage. The presenting symptoms are usually undetected and quite often are incorrectly diagnosed. The result is often a more or less unbalanced development of psychological functions and a great variety of abnormal behaviour. From our point of view we should concentrate primarily on the group showing so-called minimal brain dysfunctioning (A. A. Strauss and L. E. Lehtinen, 1950; A. A. Strauss and N. C. Kephart, 1955; D. H. Stott, 1962, 1966; O. Kučera et al., 1961, and others).

It is obvious that minimal brain damage can underlie a variety of disorders. R. L. Masland (1966) graphically comments that the precise symptoms of these disorders are determined by a number of factors, such as the individual's genetic endowment, interaction of the child with his physical and social environment, his training and upbringing. This means, therefore, that every deprivational situation for such a child is a more critical event than a similar situation for the normal child.

Authors who are concerned with psychological deprivation have quite naturally tended to overestimate the effect of environmental factors and to ignore the obviously important consideration that effects vary in type and degree depending on the organic state of the child. Experience in Czechoslovakian child psychiatric advisory centres, where many children of vastly different backgrounds —

including institutional — are treated, and where careful, systematic psychological and physical examination of the child is undertaken by a group of specialists, indicates quite conclusively the importance of both early CNS damage and early psychological deprivation and the interaction between these two (J. Langmeier and J. Lhoták, 1960).

The cumulative effect of peri-natal complications and deprived environment on the psychological, intellectual, and social development of pre-school children has been reported in a comprehensive study by Emmy Werner et al. (1967). In a later study (1968), these workers reported the same effect in a large sample of school-children in Kauai (Hawaii); both degree of peri-natal stress and presence or absence of environmental stimulation (socio-economic status, level of child rearing and emotional stimulation) contributed significantly to school achievement and to intellectual and emotional problems. Analysis of variance showed that the quality of the environment was relatively more important during school age, and that at an earlier age the effect of "reproductive casualties" was much greater.

Throughout his life, the brain-damaged child may encounter frequent conflicts, which become acute in certain critical periods (at school entry, for example). These striking and often dramatic conflicts sometimes conceal the less obvious but equally important fact that the child, by the very nature of his defect, has experienced long-term psychological starvation, the basic causes of which are specific perceptual and motor disorders due to minimal brain dysfunction. These predispose the child to select some and reject other stimuli from the environment which, judged by external criteria, is normal. His perception of the environment is different from that of a normal person, and this difference is exaggerated under unfavourable conditions. Every child, to a certain extent, creates its own environment, and the MBD child tends to create a more impoverished and limited environment. Thus retarded motor development in MBD babies means that for relatively long periods of time (before he begins to walk) the child cannot independently obtain adequate stimulation. This applies also to older children who are motorically clumsy. Decreased sensitivity to a certain class of stimulation also produces deprivation in certain sensory fields. It is well established, for example, that the auditory apathy of the MBD child is sometimes shown in pseudo hardness-of-hearing, which inevitably results in speech retardation, unless the environment is individualized so that the child can select meaningful signals from the homogeneous background.

In addition the muscle hypotonia of brain-damaged children is often highly exaggerated under conditions of inadequate sensory and emotional stimulation.

We recorded this in the following case. An illegitimate child, A.H., was left unattended by his mother for hours at a time. At three years of age the child could not even walk with support, and was so apathetic and passive (he displayed only a permanent smile) that it was impossible to test him at all. His general muscle hypotonia was very severe, but suspected myatonia congenita was excluded by histological examination of the muscles. Under conditions of individual hospital care the child quickly became a "loved one", his motor and psychological development progressed remarkably — soon he began to walk and speak and became lively, cuddly, and cheerful. His intellectual development, however, did not progress beyond the level of borderline feeblemindedness, even when he was seven years old. At that point, the neurologist diagnosed a mild residual state of the hypotonic form of cerebral palsy.

Inability to concentrate attention, and an obsessive concern with unimportant details, which are very well-known symptoms of MBD, are also exaggerated under conditions of a monotonous institutional environment or inadequate family environment, and can sometimes reach quite bizarre levels.

To illustrate we present the case of a boy, Z.M., who soon after a difficult forceps delivery was admitted to a baby institute and subsequently to a children's home, from which he was returned to the family in very bad condition when he was three years old (he did not walk, speak, or swallow solid foods). At home the child was severely neglected, was locked for long periods in a barn or cellar, and was often severely beaten. At seven years of age, when the boy started school, his behaviour was quite deviant; he was aggressive and destructive, very infantile, sometimes extremely cuddly, at other times very aggressive, he bit, was dirty, and had not acquired basic hygiene. His restlessness and lack of concentration were marked; he noticed details in the environment which escaped adult attention, so that sometimes he appeared to be hallucinating; he used idiosyncratic language with stereotyped expression. When the father left the family the boy improved a little — he calmed down, his ability to concentrate improved, he was more obedient and his mental development progressed slightly — but he remained borderline feebleminded.

In school age children in whom developmental dyslexia is due primarily to perceptual disorders resulting from minimal brain dysfunction, we frequently note lack of interest in reading, although the child selects some other supplementary activity, for example, recitation or manual activity. In these cases, reading retardation at first appears to be the result of educational neglect, until during treatment we find the basic disorder. A similar state of affairs exists with other specific learning disabilities due to organically based defects in perceptual and mental abilities.

The increased tendency towards paroxysms in MBD children may also become more pronounced under deprivating conditions, and this can result in retarded maturation, impairment of active inhibition, persistence of generalized reactions and stereotyped automatisms, so that the development of higher forms of voluntary behaviour is retarded. In such cases rocking and other automatisms, which are produced by deprivation, can become highly resistant to any therapy.

> This is illustrated in the case of a ten-year-old boy adopted at the age of five from a children's home. Nocturnal head banging was associated with EEG with paroxysmal characteristics, and was not amenable to treatment by normal sedatives and tranquillizers, but did respond very well to sodanton.[3] Although the cause of this disorder is primarily organic and perhaps due directly to specific CNS damage, as we have already noted, we should not ignore the fact that this produces increased sensitivity to deprivating influences.

The child suffering from minimal brain dysfunction, like the blind or deaf child, often provokes negative rejecting attitudes in those who care for him and thus creates for himself an emotionally depriving situation simply by virtue of his condition — particularly through his awkward behaviour (restlessness, impulsivity, emotional excitability). H.F.R. Prechtl (1963) has shown that the mother's attitude is already formed at a very early stage in response to certain behaviours of the child which she cannot interpret or which she misinterprets. Prechtl carefully observed the first ten days of life of a thousand children who showed some prenatal or delivery disorders. The mothers of restless or irritable children showing the so-called hyper-excitability syndrome, when compared with a control group, were from the outset less satisfied, and were particularly uncertain about the adequacy of their nursing. In addition, those doctors who undertook neurological examination during the long-term study were "disgusted" by the exaggerated and unpredictable reactions of these

---

3. An anti-epileptic drug of hydantoin origin.

children. Prechtl maintains, amongst other things, that mothers of obviously severely damaged children adapt better to the existing situation than mothers of children with more minor but less obvious disorders. The mothers of the latter group consciously or unconsciously refuse to accept the child's disability and to treat it appropriately.

We obtained similar results when comparing parental attitudes towards children with MBD of prenatal or delivery origin and children in whom the damage occurred at a later stage as a result of para-infectious encephalitis (S. Doutlík and Z. Matějček, 1965). Parents of the first group responded to their child's abnormalities and difficulties in an ignoring, rejecting, or directly punishing manner, while the parents of the latter group generally showed a protective attitude. We noted also a similar difference in attitude amongst teachers. The importance of the social determinants of the MBD child's behaviour is supported also by H. G. Birch (1968) in a number of case studies.

One further comment is relevant here. The MBD child, whose developmental progress is often unbalanced and retarded, whose abnormal behaviour disturbs his entire environment, and whose care requires very great effort and often great self-sacrifice, is often more readily committed to an institution by the family than is a child who progresses normally and offers full satisfaction to his parents. From the toddler period onwards, therefore, we find an increased percentage of MBD children in the institutionalized population (20 per cent in institutions as against 3—5 per cent in the general population). At pre-school age and particularly after the age of school entry the usual social motivations for placing such a child in an institution are reinforced by educational problems — parents do not know how to plan the child's education, or the school demands the withdrawal of such a disturbed child from the class and insists on institutional placement, which obviously is of dubious value. The primary difficulties, for such a child, however, are organic in nature, and the educational difficulties are only secondary; even in the children's home the MBD child continues to be a disturbing element, is still misunderstood and neglected, and even worse, is frequently moved from place to place, and eventually ends up in a residential school for children with serious behaviour disorders.

We present the case of a boy K.V. as a typical example of a combination of deprivational and encephalopathic symptomatology. He was born posthumously, one of twins; his birth weight was 1,850 grams. We have a very sketchy account of his early life; his motor development was normal, but he started to speak only at about thirty months. At eighteen months he was admitted to a children's home where he stayed for four years, until his mother remarried and took him home. His restlessness and unpredictable behaviour, however, caused severe difficulties. The new father could not stand him and punished him severely, so that after a year he was returned to institutional care. When he was examined at six years seven months, he seemed to be a typical institutional inmate; he was not ready for school, he was enuretic and encopretic, uninterested in learning, playful, emotionally unattached. In addition he showed a number of MBD symptoms — staring with strong strabismus, a low startle threshold, striking motor clumsiness, he failed abysmally in performance tests, and drew quite primitively, which was at variance with his good verbal level. The school and the institute regarded him as feebleminded, and there was strong pressure for his transfer to a special school. He repeated his class. Complaints increased, his restlessness was a disturbance in the classroom, he rolled under the desk, lost books, played truant. He was transferred to a detention home, and shortly afterwards to another children's home. MBD diagnosis was verified by additional physical and psychological examinations; at the same time he seemed to be a real "old hand", able to avoid trouble. At ten years he was transferred to yet another institute, where under adequate supervision the enuresis disappeared. Finally he displayed an interest in schooling and social and hygienic habits were established. Some of the worst results of institutional deprivation were also eliminated, but it proved impossible to reduce his troublesome psychomotor restlessness, impulsivity, and typical encephalopathic dependence on stimuli; at the same time his intellectual development was unbalanced. The boy was returned to an intermediate institute and then to another institute — his eighth placement. The improvement continued, however, and with this improvement gradually the most serious brain dysfunction problems disappeared. At school he was sometimes an excellent pupil and left to learn a trade after the seventh grade (after extended school attendance covering ten years).

From our studies we would conclude that some of the MBD children would not be behaviourally abnormal if they had not been exposed to depriving life conditions. We think it also self-evident that a mild degree of deprivation, which a normal child can tolerate quite easily, does represent a severe problem for the encephalopathic child. For example, in our group of 163 boys from a residential school for boys with serious behaviour disorders of delinquent character which we studied during the years 1960 and 1961 (Z. Matějček, 1964), in

30 cases (nearly 20 per cent) a strong possibility of MBD was indicated after careful physical (including neurological) examination. As a group these boys showed behavioural characteristics quite different from those of other groups. They had been transferred more frequently from institute to institute (57 per cent lived in at least two institutes before being admitted to this residential school), half of them repeated classes, they more frequently had good family backgrounds (47 per cent), and their siblings were more often described as free from abnormality (43 per cent as against 24 per cent in the rest of the group). The primary reason for placement in the special residential school was lack of discipline, which covered restlessness and school disturbances, and only secondarily stealing, truancy, running away from home, and other misdemeanours. As far as their present behaviour was concerned, they were frequently described firstly as impetuous, restless, unstable, impulsive, secondly as insolent, and finally as deviant in their attitude to work and in their general behaviour.

It is likely that minimal brain dysfunction is the factor underlying the rearing difficulties and the onset of those behaviours which bring some children with a history of early institutionalization into the corrective institutes. It is difficult to obtain definitive data in this area, however, as the anamnestic records, which are so important for MBD diagnosis, are rather fragmentary in these cases. A combination of MBD and deprivation which, as we have just suggested, is by no means rare, constitutes a serious danger for a child and points up the futility of looking for one cause of the disorder. Detailed analysis of the case is always necessary to establish weak links in the child's psychological equipment which would make him particularly vulnerable to sensory, emotional, and social deprivation, and to uncover these resources which would contribute to a therapeutic and educational programme. Many deprivational studies are remiss in that they overlook or only superficially consider the possibility of multiple causation of the disorders under consideration.

2. Mentally retarded children (with or without encephalopathic complications) are also quite frequently threatened by deprivation, usually again by the attitudes of rejecting parents, who after the initial critical period in which they seek help from all sources, become embittered and begin to neglect the child or unconcernedly place him in a hospital or institution. For a mentally retarded child, a suitable institute can often be a favourable environment, for in such a place he is given specialized training which is otherwise hard to obtain. Even here, however, the child obviously is deprived of deep

emotional ties with the family, and lacks emotional support, supervision, and normal opportunities for gaining social experience.

This has been well demonstrated by A. P. Beley and G. Netchine (1958) in their study of the development of feebleminded children in an overcrowded children's ward attached to a psychiatric clinic near Paris. In this large institution the children had no opportunity whatsoever to find any sort of parent surrogate. Their lives were monotonous and restricted by bureaucratic rules. The authors carefully observed the children daily for three months using direct observation and Zazzo's test "Le Bestiaire". The sample consisted of six boys (IQ 55 to 70) who came from broken homes.

The authors report that the boys' behaviour, which was initially restless, disturbed by family conflict, aggressive, and sometimes anti-social, gradually normalized in the institutional environment. This conformity, which was positively valued by the supervisors, is hardly a favourable outcome for the child, however. In fact, it implies the passive acceptance of rules, conventional obedience, and adjustment to a restricted social environment which has no relationship to the external real world. While boys in the control group (living with their families and visiting the special school daily) freely expressed family conflicts and were aggressive in frustrating situations, the institutional children "forgot" conflicts before they were resolved. They gradually lost all social perspective, the meaning of different social roles, and the hierarchy of social values.

Mild mental retardation is a relatively frequent complication of early CNS disorders, and is usually accompanied by motor clumsiness, sensory and speech defects. In addition, these children frequently come from families with the worst socio-economic backgrounds, where familial and rearing conditions are unstable. This is also suggested in our data from pupils of residential schools for retarded children in the Middle Czech county in the period 1961—62 (see page 208). Twenty-nine per cent of the children had good, 47 per cent poor family backgrounds (as described by social workers), and 24 per cent were from pre-school children's homes (which usually indicates poor family background). Here deprivational factors exist in different combinations, and it is difficult to isolate the specific effect of each of these from the resulting complex of developmental disorders and disturbances. Today, according to our findings, residential schools for retarded children cater for children suffering from psychological deprivation of many different types and expressed at different levels. This area is thus a particularly appropriate one for research; for the same reasons, however, it is very demanding in terms of child care and training. Such institutions, therefore, should be given close attention and effective help.

Children with moderate mental retardation (imbecility) are generally thought to be safe from the dangers of psychological suffering under institutional conditions (H. Bakwin, 1960). It is usually assumed that the child whose slow developmental progress is due to retarded psychological functioning can hardly be further retarded by limitation of his stimulus field. Our own practical experience, however, has led us to question this assumption. As we have seen, normal infants as early as two months of age react strongly to environmental changes (A. Nitschke, 1955; M. Damborská, 1957b), and a range of reactions to socially depriving conditions from the seventh month has been widely recorded (H. R. Schaffer, 1958). It is highly likely, therefore, not only that a child who has progressed developmentally to the level of young or middle toddler age is susceptible to depriving conditions, but also that the effect of these becomes more severe depending on the length of time the child remains fixated at the low developmental level. There is an additional source of psychological suffering here in that such a child is often neglected, and is sometimes rejected by the family which will go to a good deal of trouble to have him placed in an institute.

With the most severe cases it is clearly impossible to assess the contribution of deprivation to the very low level of functioning. Even with less severe cases of idiocy and imbecility, however, we often encounter children who in the neglecting family environment are hopelessly bedridden, but who under devoted institutional care recover surprisingly quickly, stand up, are lively, and start to actively seek stimulation. There are cases, however, where a child from a family which gave him proper care is surprisingly well trained in self-sufficiency and other useful activities, can handle material, has a surprisingly rich vocabulary, and who, on being admitted to a poor institute, within a year has deteriorated to an unrecognizable degree, has forgotten how to speak, and has become socially dependent on the nursing staff. The fact that previous training in hygienic and social habits was successful and that speech had developed suggests that emotional factors are of considerable importance here. In our investigation of so-called ineducable children from a large area before placement in social institutes for the mentally retarded, where their development could be systematically controlled, we noted a quite striking relationship between developmental progress — particularly in socialization — and the stimulating value of the institutional environment. Children of similar mental level in the same institute but in different wards and under different supervision sometimes showed completely contrasting developmental progress.

One could argue, of course, that this finding has little practical significance in view of the seriousness of the defect and the relatively poor prognosis. We maintain, however, that in such circumstances any developmental progress is of considerable value. The more independence such a child achieves, the less custodial care he requires; if he can perform even small tasks, less financial support, less time, and more importantly, less nervous strain for all those involved is expended.

The view that both mildly and severely defective children can suffer acutely from psychological deprivation has recently been advanced by a number of clinical workers. M. J. Farrell (1956) emphasizes the unfavourable outcome of too early placement of these children in institutions. R. H. Deisher (1957) reports that even a mongoloid child has certain potential which is better utilized if his needs are reasonably well satisfied during the first years of life (it is known that a mongoloid child has considerable need for emotional attachment). S.A. and W.R. Centerwall (1960) support this view in a study comparing a group of thirty-two mongoloid children placed in an institute immediately after birth with a control group cared for initially at home and then placed in an institute (after two and a half years of age). Subsequently both groups (otherwise very similar) were cared for in the same institute. Children of the second group were on the average superior to children of the first group, judged on the basis of physical growth, nutrition, motor development, average IQ and SQ (social development quotient). These differences had some practical significance, in that while the first group of children deteriorated to the level of almost ineducable idiots, the second group maintained a level of imbecility and were trainable in certain ways (this study has been criticized by H. G. Birch and L. Belmont [1961] on methodological grounds and because of dubious interpretation of results: nevertheless it merits attention because of its obvious relevance and because some other studies point in the same direction). The combination of the constitutional inertness of the feebleminded child and the inertness of his environment is obviously a catastrophic event, which results in permanent incarceration in an asylum rather than training for a relatively independent or at least helping social role appropriate to his limited intellectual capacity.

Fig. 56. Drawing on the topic "House, garden, and children playing" by a six-year-old boy of
normal IQ who has extremely weak vision. Everything connected with light is
emphasized – the switch, lamp, wires, streetlamp. Exaggerated interest in sensory
stimuli dominates all other interests. This is an example of hunger for light
stimulation, which is severely restricted because of defective vision.

9 The experimental approach

Clinical observations usually depend on a number of factors which are difficult to control and which vary from study to study and from series to series, although the conditions may appear to be identical. The fact that such observations lead to only the most general conclusions stresses the need for a more precise experimental approach to our problems; otherwise it is unlikely that we will answer the central question of the pathogenesis of deprivational disorders in children and adults.

In recent years considerable advances in a number of pertinent areas have clarified (although not finally resolved) some important problems (e.g. the subsequent effects of early experiences, the so-called critical period, the relationship between sensory and social deprivation, and so on). It has also become clear that experimentally induced deprivation is a valuable method for explicating a number of other problems which are important for theory and clinical practice, e.g. explaining the relationship between innate (species-specific) and acquired behaviour, the relationship of certain environmental conditions to biological and histological changes in the brain, resolving current problems in aviation and space psychology, in work and traffic safety, in clinical psychiatry and psychotherapy. Here these problems can only be touched on briefly in connection with our basic theme.

EXPERIMENTS WITH ANIMALS

In deprivation experiments with animals it is possible to vary the degree of sensory deprivation, of motor restraint, of environmental complexity, of social isolation from animals of the same species, and of affective or emotional deprivation. In such experiments any physical duress (biological deprivation – starvation, dehydration, any deficit in physical care) must be minimized. This is much more difficult than it appears, especially if one is dealing with neonates who are still dependent on the mother for sustenance.

Primarily sensory deprivation

S. M. Vyržikovskij and F. P. Majorov (1933) raised puppies in isolation. They were housed in special cages and compared with puppies reared freely under normal life conditions. The isolated animals were fearful and more subject to external inhibition. B. J. Hymovitch (1952) conducted a similar experiment with young rats which he raised in isolation in small cages but which were able to exercise (in an activity wheel). In this experiment the rats were given no experience either in problem solving or in social interaction with other rats; as far as possible any painful experience was avoided. Compared with a control group of rats raised in a free environment, the deprived animals showed significantly poorer ability in problem solving.

D. O. Hebb (1955) and his co-workers (W. R. Thompson, R. Melzack, and T. H. Scott, 1956; W. R. Thompson and W. Heron, 1954; R. Melzack and T. H. Scott, 1957) raised one-month-old Scottish terriers in a similar type of impoverished environment for periods ranging from seven to ten months. The surroundings varied in level of external stimulation (dark box, covered cage). During the experimental period the dogs raised in isolation were quite content, grew and gained weight normally, while dogs who were raised under normal conditions and then subsequently transferred to such an environment were obviously "unhappy" and progressed poorly. (We could perhaps draw an analogy with the behaviour of children reared from an early age in institutions compared with that of children separated from their families.)

The consequences of such early deprivation were most marked and persisted into adulthood: dogs were "stupid", strange, hyperactive and emotionally immature, and unable to learn (mainly from painful experiences). In the monotonous environment of the cage these animals were active and full of interest for days at a time, "as if they didn't have the sense to become bored". A dog raised under normal conditions would take two minutes to inspect the surroundings; he would then become bored, lie down, and pay no further attention. For the experimental animals, the greater the reduction in stimulus input, the greater the amount of exploratory activity. They would repeatedly sniff a burning match and did not learn to avoid an electrically charged grid; in such situations the animal ran round and round aimlessly (J. Kestenberg reports that deprived psychopaths showed a similar inability to learn from failures). Under certain conditions of sensory deprivation even more bizarre behaviours occurred — seizure-like behaviour, fearful howling and snarling, tail gnawing. None of the control animals (from the same litter) showed similar disorders. The authors maintained that the retardation shown in the behavioural development of these deprived dogs is due to their inability to develop a general perceptual frame of reference into which new stimuli can be incorporated.

Lasting deficits resulting from long-term partial deprivation in one sensory modality (tactile-kinaesthetic) in infancy have been demonstrated by H. W. Nissen, K. L. Chow, and J. Semmes (1951). A young chimpanzee was grossly deprived of tactile and manipulative experience between the ages of four and thirty-one weeks by placing paper tubes on his limbs. When the tubes were removed the animal recorded a large aesthesiometric index over the whole body, slowly and inaccurately located sources of irritation with his fingers, and could not cling to the keeper or climb. These effects persisted to some extent after four months. Even sensitivity to pain was markedly reduced; a pinprick evoked the kind of reaction expected from tickling. (Figs. 57 and 58.)

R. K. Davenport, Jr. and E. W. Menzel, Jr. (1963) reported stereotyped movements and other developmental disorders in four groups of chimpanzees raised in isolation and under conditions of stimulus impoverishment. In an enriched environment, as under natural conditions, such disorders do not occur.

The effect of short-term partial deprivation with adult animals has also been reported in a number of studies. R. A. Butler (1957), for example, deprived monkeys *(Macacus rhesus)* of visual experience for 248 hours. He reported that the greater the amount of deprivation the greater the reinforcement value of visual stimuli during conditioning. He maintained that the visual exploratory drive operates in a similar way to primary biological drives. An experiment by K. C. Montgomery (1953) suggests that the exploratory drive can be viewed as a relatively independent primary drive and not simply as one form of general activity. He reported that rats, following deprivation of general activity (exercise in an activity wheel), showed no significant increase in exploratory behaviour in a simple maze.

In apparent contradiction to these experimental findings are data from a number of experiments showing the important part played by maturation in the development of certain forms of behaviour and their relative independence of learning. Pigeons and swallows, denied the opportunity of learning to fly for a certain time, after release performed no differently from control birds of the same age who had had normal experience of flying. E. Thomas and F. Schaller (1954) deprived newly born kittens of visual stimuli for a considerable period. They reported that after the kittens were freed from isolation they jumped and held on to lures in the same way as normally raised kittens. The authors also report, however, that the usual repertoire of instinctive behaviours occurred during the period of stimulus impoverishment, in the form of different compensatory (playful) activities *(Leerlaufreaktionen)* which may have facilitated subsequent learning. A number of older studies with animals (rats and chickens) raised during early life in isolation also report negative or inconclusive results (A. G. Bayroff, 1936, 1940). These findings, of course, do not negate the results of more recent experiments in which conditions were better controlled. At best they suggest that certain behaviours are less affected by deprivation than others and that this is dependent on the degree and type of deprivation.

Earlier works on the neurophysiological — mainly metabolic and histological — effects of sensory deprivation are also largely negative. L. Goodman (1932), for example, who raised rabbits in darkness, concluded that continuous functioning is not a necessary condition for the maturation of the visual system. However, more recent studies using more sophisticated experimental techniques (e.g. histochemical analyses on different animal species) show quite conclusively that in animals deprived of visual experience — either through enucleation (not excluding the possible influence of local degenerative changes) or through stimulus deprivation — different degrees of retardation (up to the stage of atrophy) in the development of ganglion cells and optical nerve fibres occur. S. O. Brattgård (1952), for example, using micro-radiographic techniques, reported that lack of adequate stimulation leads to retarded development and disorders in the metabolism and chemical structure of nerve cells. A. H. Riesen (1960) and his co-workers report from extensive experiments with young chimpanzees who were reared in darkness for different periods (mainly from birth) that long-term stimulus deprivation in early life leads to atrophy of ganglion cells of the retina and the optic nerve. If the deprivation lasted no longer than three months, full recovery usually occurred; with longer deprivation, however, recovery was only partial. If the total or nearly total deprivation lasted sixteen months or more, changes in the neural substrate were irreversible. However, similar periods of deprivation did not produce cell atrophy in cats, and the author suggests that transneural changes (transneural atrophy) develop much faster in primates, where there is very great specificity of cell connections in the visual system.

Workers of this group, using histochemical analysis, reported a significant drop in the concentration of ribonucleic acid in cats, rats, and chimpanzees who were subjected to sensory (visual) deprivation. A. W. Wase and J. Christensen (1960) reported biochemical changes in the brains of adult rats raised for a period (fourteen to thirty-one days) in total isolation under conditions of severe sensory deprivation (visual, auditory), and concluded that the abnormal behaviour (restlessness, neurotic disorders, hostility, particularly when transferred into a group) of animals subjected to such stress was due to the destructive process resulting from biochemical and metabolic changes. They demonstrated a significant reduction of phospholipid metabolism in the brains of isolated animals (by measuring the assimilation of isotope $P^{32}O$-phosphate into the lipids of brain cells). The study by T. C. Barnes (1959) is relevant here; by the use of tranquillizers (mainly chlorpromazine), he abolished the abnormal behaviour of 90 per cent of the group of rats and mice kept isolated for seven to ten days; this is in line with the observation that chlorpromazine in smaller doses stimulated phospholipid metabolism (in larger doses it inhibited such metabolism).

In this context the experiments reported over a number of years by workers from the University of California, D. Krech, M. R. Rosenzweig, E. L. Bennett, and M. C. Diamond (D. Krech, M. R. Rosenzweig, and E. L. Bennett, 1960, 1962, 1964; M. R. Rosenzweig et al., 1966, 1968, 1969) are of considerable interest and importance. Rats (carefully selected for strain, age, sex) were divided into two groups. The first group were raised from the 25th to the 105th day after weaning in an enriched environment; ten to twelve animals lived in a spacious cage equipped with complex stimulus material (ladders, merry-go-rounds, boxes, etc.). From the 55th day approximately these animals were trained to run a number of mazes. Group two animals were raised under impoverished conditions, isolated in cages without any opportunity to see or contact other animals, and with minimal sensory input. A third group of animals lived under standard conditions, i.e. approximately halfway between the two extremes. Although the investigators were primarily concerned with the biochemical effects of different early experiences rather than with specific anatomical changes, significant changes in the weight of the cortex were recorded. The total weight (excluding other brain structures) in animals raised in the enriched environment was approximately 4 per cent greater than in deprived animals; the grey matter was thicker and the diameter of the capillaries was greater. The largest difference was in the visual area (6 per cent), the smallest in the somaesthetic region (2 per cent).

Further experiments showed that it is possible to vary the weight of particular areas of the brain, depending on the particular type of sensory enrichment. From biochemical analysis it appears that the most important effect is the increased total activity of the enzyme acetylcholinesterase (AChE); particularly important is the increase in activity of the less specific enzyme, cholinesterase (ChE), in the cortex of animals from enriched environments. In other parts of the brain the differences are non-significant. The authors suggest that this involves the proliferation of different kinds of glial cells in response to environmental demand. Glial functioning is very likely more significant than was originally thought and is possibly related to metabolic functioning or branching of neurons.

Results of these investigations indicate that the mere handling or locomotor activity of an animal, or a combination of these, does not significantly influence the growth and functioning of the brain. Nor can changes in these be attributed solely to the effects of isolation stress. Animals bred in separate cages were not particularly aggressive and their physical condition was satisfactory. In the original experiments the effects of the enriched environment seemed to be more significant than the effect of isolation. Under conditions of extreme environmental impoverishment, however, the negative effect of stimulus deprivation was heightened. The most important factors in the enriched environment seem to be social interaction (twelve animals in a big cage) followed by the opportunity to play with complex apparatus. Formal training (twice a day in a maze) had relatively little influence, though one cannot ignore the fact that more intensive training might have led to more significant effects. These results also suggest that the increase in weight and the change in biochemical properties of the brain are closely connected with changes in the ability to learn, particularly in more demanding situations.

An interesting experiment on oxygen consumption in isolated fish compared with fish living in shoals has been reported by workers from the Physiological Institute of the Biological Faculty of Lomonosov University, Moscow. Oxygen consumption of fish living in shoals is lower than that of fish living in isolation, even if isolation is only partial (produced by a glass plate which allows them to see other fish).

The mechanisms of biochemical changes in animals as a result of isolation are unknown. Obviously we must investigate other biochemical factors before we can specify the relationships between biochemical changes and observed changes in behaviour. At this point, however, we can state that under certain conditions of sensory and social deprivation, metabolic biochemical and structural changes are undoubtedly produced in the central nervous system, and that maturation is not entirely independent of experience.

Mainly emotional and social deprivation

In the experiments described above sensory deprivation was usually the most critical factor under investigation. In other experiments with animals, however, emotional deprivation is the important variable. P. F. D. Seitz (1954), for example, raised new-born rats in two groups of six and twelve. Because a female has twelve nipples, some of which usually are not functioning, the youngsters in the large group experienced partial deprivation. After weaning, at three weeks, the rats were reared under identical conditions, in identical individual cages, and were tested in adulthood. A number of differences were clearly shown; the rats who were deprived in the early stage were malicious, bit more, resisted handling, reacted more fearfully to new experimenters, showed less exploratory activity, hoarded food to a greater degree, and showed a higher level of pre-mating sexual activity. The control experiment with adult rats reared in similar sized groups for the same period of time did not show these effects.

Seitz interpreted the results of his interesting experiment to mean that emotional deprivation in early age produces behavioural changes in adulthood and leads to neurotic disorders. However, J. Lát, of the Academy of Sciences, Prague, has proposed a possible alternative interpretation based on the results of an experiment which he conducted with E. M. Widdowson and R. A. McCance (1960). Young rats arranged in groups of either three or fifteen to twenty were fed different amounts of food up to the time of weaning (twenty-one days), when all animals had free access to standard food. It was shown that young rats fed ad lib in the first three weeks grew significantly more quickly and were more active and curious. It is possible then that higher activity is a result of quick growth, and that both depend on early nutrition. In Seitz's experiments it was noted that animals raised in small groups not only showed greater exploratory behaviour in novel situations, but that they were heavier as adults. The nutritive factor in early age therefore ought to be carefully considered and controlled when we are investigating the effects of deprivational variables.

L. Bernstein (1952) raised rats for forty days after weaning in individual cages under conditions which were identical insofar as food and general surroundings were concerned. One variable was manipulated; control rats lacked external stimulation, while rats in the experimental group were taken every day from the cages, were played with and petted for ten minutes, then returned to their cages. At the end of the experiment, rats from the experimental (handled) group weighed significantly more, gave evidence of better skeletal growth and utilization of food, performed better in a maze, and had greater mean retention rate during the extinction period. In further experiments, Bernstein and his co-workers (L. Bernstein and H. Elrick, 1957) demonstrated the higher ability of handled animals to withstand stress: significantly more of them survived after being injected with a toxic dose of thiourea. Interestingly enough, when handling was interrupted during the extinction period, the animals made a greater number of errors than animals who continued to be handled and even than animals which had not been handled at all (L. Bernstein, 1957). Thus, there is some evidence that interruption of the relationship of the experimental animal with the experimenter may indeed be traumatic (similar to the "anaclitic depression" of Spitz).

M. Czako (1965) of Comenius University in Bratislava has reported the effects of motor and social deprivation in early age on the behaviour of adult rats. Young rats were constrained daily for from four to eight hours in narrow boxes which allowed practically no movement, for a period of thirty days. Motor (and to a certain extent sensory) deprivation began either twelve, eighteen, or twenty-four days after birth. In addition, one group of animals was subjected to social isolation after weaning (each rat lived in its own separate cage). Czako reported that the level of spontaneous activity in adult rats (from seventy days of age upwards) was radically affected by the motor deprivation if the deprivation began at the twelfth or eighteenth day; there was no significant difference in total activity between rats deprived at twenty-four days and the control group. Similar results were obtained in maze performance, the performance of rats who were deprived from the twelfth or eighteenth day being significantly poorer. Social deprivation also strongly affects emotionality (measured by defecation, freezing, grooming behaviour, and so on).

M. Harminc (1965) from the same institute studied

discrimination learning following similar deprivation in ninety day-old rats. He used a Y maze involving a simple black-white discrimination, where the contrast was reduced through various shades of grey; the positive reinforcement was food and the negative reinforcement electric shock. The results again showed that the performance of rats deprived from the twelfth or eighteenth day is significantly poorer than that of control rats or of those animals deprived from the twenty-fourth day. It was also reported that in "intellectual" tasks the effects of social deprivation are more severe than those of motor deprivation. The socially deprived rats showed on the whole marked aggressiveness, a greater show of fear, and inability to learn from punishment (from painful experiences).

J. S. Rosenblatt, G. Turkewitz, and T. C. Schneirla (1961) studied the relationship between the development of sucking in kittens and degree of isolation, the age at which isolation occurs, and the behaviour of the mother cat. Kittens separated from their mothers and from other kittens were kept in special incubators and fed through nipples placed in appropriate positions. It was reported that isolation for the first seven days and subsequently for various periods up to the twenty-third day after birth had no effect on the kitten's sucking after return to the mother. Isolation from the twenty-third to the forty-fourth day after birth, however, produced a decrease in sucking, and long-term isolation from the mother from the second to the forty-fourth day produced no sucking at all after return to the mother. All kittens in this group showed behaviour disorders involving fear. But kittens experiencing later isolation — between the thirty-fourth and forty-ninth days or between the forty-sixth and the fifty-fourth days — began to suck on the mother immediately they were returned to her.

Of great interest also are the extensive studies by H. S. Liddell (1958) and his co-workers (H. Blauvelt, L. Hersher) with kids and lambs. A conditioned reflex was developed in these animals; reduction in illumination was the CS and an electric current applied to the shin (the animal jumps or lifts the leg) the UCS. A programme of twenty trials a day produced experimental neurosis in all but the young animals of two to three weeks of age, who were still dependent on their mothers. The presence of the mother was sufficient to defend them from the traumatizing effects of this treatment. When very young kids (from twelve hours after birth) were used as subjects and separated daily for a period of an hour from their mothers for experimental purposes they rapidly deteriorated; six from a group of seven died during a period of six months although they were given the greatest care and attention. In a further study it was shown that separation of a kid from its mother directly after birth for a period of one hour a day significantly interfered with the mother-kid relationship to the extent that she refused to feed, defend, and in fact have any normal contact with it. While the kid who was raised uninterruptedly with its mother freely played around after the traumatic conditioning, the deprived kid (a twin sibling) was fearful, crouched in a corner, was "psychologically frozen". (Fig. 59.)

Long-term isolation of animals who in nature live in herds, or at least in permanent company with animals of their own species, raises questions about the effects of deprivation of intra-species contact. The effect of isolation in pacifying wild animals who have just been captured is well known. They accept the presence of tamed members of their own species more willingly, and these play a significant role in the adaptation of the wild animal to the new environment (e.g. the taming of elephants). J. C. Lilly's (1961) experiments with dolphins (which, incidentally, he regards as creatures closest to man in intelligence) have some relevance to the commonly accepted notion that a man socially isolated for a long period of time and enclosed in a restricted, limited environment which inhibits activity regards the presence of other people as extremely rewarding even when he does not understand them and has little in common with them. He can adapt to their demands, language, and attitudes to a very large extent. A dolphin kept for a period of two months in isolation from members of its own species adapted extravagantly to human society, and learned to adapt even its vocalization to human language, compared with a dolphin living with other dolphins. When the first dolphin was allowed contact with members of its own species, it quickly lost touch with the human world, which, however, was re-established when it was again isolated from its own species.

Effects like those noted following sensory and social deprivation can also result from stimulus flooding and overcrowding, due probably to a mechanism similar to that suggested by Seitz's findings. The same effect has also been observed in a number of cases of animals living in unrestricted free space. It is well known, for example, that rodent populations decrease as a result of over-population. Whereas previously this was explained simply in terms of epidemics, it is now clear that such epidemics occur only when certain neurohumoral conditions exist. Lack of need satisfaction, primarily psychological (lack of security, never-ending fight for survival, for food, for sexual partners, and so on), produces such stress and exhaustion of all regulating mechanisms that shock disorders result. This is reflected in increased adrenal weight (J. J. Christian and D. E. Davis, 1955).

In a very careful ethological study (non-experimental), R. F. Dasmann and D. Taber (1956) reported that aggregation of animals in a small area produced behavioural changes — Columbian deer for example displayed increased aggressiveness and escape readiness, smaller satisfaction from play, and significantly poorer care of the young animals.

Experiments with primates are obviously of critical significance for our understanding of the mechanisms of deprivation in humans. H. F. Harlow (1958 et seq.) of the University of Wisconsin with his co-workers has systematically studied the behaviour of rhesus monkeys over a period of years in a variety of depriving situations. Newly born monkeys were initially kept in individual cages with access to two models of the mother, one constructed of wire and the other of cloth. The young monkeys became much more attached to the cloth mother and made greater bodily contact with it, even when the nipple was placed on the wire mother. Thus, Harlow demonstrated the relative unimportance of hunger and the extreme importance of bodily contact for the establishment of the relationship between the neonate and the mother. He has also suggested that this relationship is influenced by other factors, for example, by movement (neonates preferred the swinging or moving cloth mother and the moving bed to the immovable mother and bed), by the experience of clinging to the mother, and possibly also by the availability of certain visual, auditory, and other stimuli. (Figs. 60—63.)

These experiments proved not only that the young monkey is attracted to the mother by the emotionally positive stimuli she offers, but also that it is "instinctively" attracted to her in situations which involve sudden fear. When the young monkeys were faced with a novel object (a toy bear moving and playing a drum), they retreated in panic and crouched somewhere in a corner. But if they were in the vicinity of the surrogate cloth mother, they quickly ran to her and clutched her. Gradually they calmed down and started to turn towards the novel fear-producing object, then approached it, and started to manipulate and investigate it, thus resolving the conflict between two opposing tendencies, to escape from and to investigate the unknown. While the young monkeys without mothers remained frozen somewhere in the corner, those with mothers were able to adventurously investigate the environment. Because the monkeys were partly grown and the cloth mother was lightweight they carried her on such expeditions. They behaved in a similar fashion when the mother was placed in a translucent box made of plastic material.

Harlow's findings of the relationship between "life security" and curiosity drive and learning remind us of experiments with children raised from early childhood in institutions. The results show that even pre-school age children of average intelligence do not play well and those of school age fail dismally in their scholastic work (see page 204). The anxiety responses of children from baby institutes when faced with a large unfamiliar toy (M. Damborská's experiments, see page 197) are similar to the reactions of fear and anxiety shown by young animals deprived of the maternal "harbour of security".

Harlow investigated further the effects of social isolation on behaviour at a later stage of development. If the young animals are raised with fabric mothers for 180 days and then separated from them for 90 days, they demonstrate, during and after the experiments, the same warm feeling towards their mothers that they had previously exhibited. Thus separation at a certain age did not interfere with established emotional relationships when contact was briefly renewed (during experimental procedures, for example). In another experiment, three groups of young monkeys were compared. Group A were raised without mothers for 180 days, then made initial contact with other young animals in a common play-pen to which there was access from two opposite cages. In group B the young animals were raised with fabric mothers for 180 days, then they were allowed social contact with their peers for the first time. In group C, contact was permitted from the beginning. The most striking results were noted in group B, where there was no play or communication amongst the young animals. Under normal conditions, at approximately 90 days of age the emotional tie or relationship between the mother and the young ceases to be protective and becomes ambivalent. The mother punishes and rejects to a greater degree. The fabric mother cannot do this, and the extended intimate relationship hindered socialization of the young with its peers. It was clearly shown that all types of play were affected; even that between the mother and the young is considerably less than in other groups. The highest level of contact and common play was in group C; in group A a fair amount of intra-group contact was observed, although play still remained somewhat primitive.

Comparison of young animals raised by real mothers with those reared by surrogate mothers produced some interesting results. For example, the young animals raised by the real mother rarely entered the play-pen during the first sixty days — they were prevented from doing so by the mother. Young animals with cloth mothers spent more time in the play-pen. After three months this balance was adjusted; the young animals with the real mothers however were freer and more animated in their social contact and showed more initiative in play. Typical play forms such as mock fighting and chasing occurred earlier in these monkeys.

As time progressed the young animals raised without mothers in Harlow's laboratories grew to sexual maturity. Young animals raised in isolation or with fabric mothers without contact experience with other young animals showed severe disorders in sexual behaviour, even when they appeared otherwise to have developed quite normally. Males were described as heterosexually hopeless; the females rejected the males and they had difficulty in becoming pregnant. Their behaviour towards their young was markedly non-maternal; they either ignored them or beat them and pushed them away; the amount of rejecting behaviour was correlated with the effort of the young to achieve contact. Harlow notes that observing these traumatic scenes often tested the emotional limits of even experienced workers. Young animals who had early opportunity for interaction with their peers behaved normally as adults, irrespective of whether they were raised with surrogate mothers or without mothers.

In Yerkes's well-known laboratories of primate biology, in Florida, where numerous colonies of chimpanzees are raised, young animals are reared without mothers and are artifically fed to the age of two or three years in a sort of children's home. The special need of these animals for social contact is largely met by keepers with whom the young chimpanzees establish very strong emotional relationships. The worst possible punishment is to be ignored by the laboratory worker. In this laboratory they have also reached the conclusion that early and frequent contact between young animals is a necessary condition for the development of normal sexual behaviour in adulthood. Males who lack opportunity for such contact in childhood are "sexually naive" and "unmotivated".

In more recent studies, the Harlows (1966) have been concerned with the therapeutic effect of contact with other young animals on development which has been affected by social isolation. The effect of total isolation (when the young animal is alone in a cage) is little different from that of partial isolation (when the young animal, though alone, can see and hear its mother and other animals in the immediate vicinity). If young animals, after three months of total isolation, are placed in a peer group, they show emotional shock and their behaviour is somewhat comparable with autistic behaviour in children. They gradually establish contact, however, and subsequently achieve normal social and sexual development. Their intellectual productivity seems to be untouched. The fact that learning ability in monkeys is largely unaffected by social deprivation has been demonstrated both by Harlow in a number of further experiments and by W. A. Mason (1960, 1961, 1962) in experiments on different species of monkeys and on chimpanzees. If peer contact is restored to a young animal after six months of total isolation, the effects on social behaviour persist for a number of months. Where the total isolation lasts for more than six months, however, the animals appear to be incapable of interaction with other animals. Certain animals, partially isolated in the first six months of age, at adolescence showed surprisingly strange aggressive (also auto-aggressive) behaviour, which is never observed with this species of monkeys when in the company of peers and adult monkeys. On the other hand adolescent animals which have experienced total long-term isolation appeared inhibited, passive, highly anxious in the same situation.

Studies of young animals raised from birth in groups without mothers report some interesting findings. Initially, they developed a strange, very strong tendency to keep close together — this tendency extinguishes very slowly and their play remains severely limited. Observations over a long period of time, however, suggest that in adulthood the behaviour of these animals is not highly deviant.

H. F. Harlow and M. K. Harlow (1966) sum up their studies to date with the comment that the surest way to normal development with the species of monkeys they observed is both the normal maternal influence and interaction with peers.

Individual differences in reactions to deprivational experiences are obvious in monkeys and other animals. R. A. Hinde and Y. Spencer-Booth (1970), in a series of experiments with rhesus monkeys, were concerned with separation of monkey infants from their mothers. Performance of infants on a variety of tests six months after the separation experience suggests that the effects of separation may be long lasting. On the other hand, the differences in the infants' reactions to the uniform experience of separation (six days during the period twenty-one—thirty-two months) are pronounced, and cannot be attributed to sex differences, age at which the separation occurred, or to the amount of contact with companions other than the mother. Dramatic differences in mother-child interaction on the day of reunion depended more on the individual characteristics of mothers than on those of the infants. Those infants showing the highest "distress index" after separation were usually those which had been most often rejected by their mothers and which had attempted strenuously to maintain proximity to their mothers before separation. They also showed the greatest post-separation disturbances.

It is obvious that emotional-social deprivation of children and young animals is basically different in a number of respects, and that the experimental findings described above, together with a number of others, cannot simply be generalized to clinical practice with children. Nevertheless, some of the similarities are striking and provide clues which could direct the study of certain aspects of emotional deprivation in children. There is experimental evidence that the effect of early deprivational experience on later behaviour (in contradiction to deprivation at a later age) is similar in children and animals. Physical effects such as physical deterioration, lowered resistance to toxic agents and infections and more severe illness, and the extent to which very marked behavioural changes respond to tranquillizing agents are equally striking. Further investigation is necessary, of course, before these findings can be fully utilized to advance our understanding of the symptomatology of deprived children.

EXPERIMENTS WITH HUMANS

It is obviously impossible to subject a child, unlike animals, to severe experimentally induced deprivation during development. But we can conduct experiments involving extensive sensory and social deprivation (relatively short-term) with adult volunteers. Experiments of this kind have recently grown in number and complexity and we anticipate from these answers to a large number of questions of both theoretical and clinical importance.

The impetus to these studies derived mainly from reports of non-veridical experiences. For example, it has been reported that pilots during long monotonous flights react very strongly to the loneliness and monotony of the environment, sometimes by depersonalization and loss of reality contact and, in some cases, by illusions and hallucinations. B. Clark and A. Graybiel (1957) report that up to 35 per cent of jet pilots experience these effects of isolation. Similar experiences are described during night driving on monotonous freeways, by radar observers in submarines, by prisoners in solitary confinement, and by workers doing a monotonous task on an assembly line. Of interest also are cases of polar explorers and shipwrecked sailors who live alone for a number of months in a monotonous environment of snow or sea. For example we can quote the well-known description by Admiral Byrd, who spent six months alone in Antarctica, of a severe depression which he experienced after three months, or the experiences of Alain Bombard (1953) who was a subject in an experiment involving survival on a wreck for sixty-five days in the Atlantic, or the impressions of Christina Ritter who experienced depersonalization and pseudohallucinations during the polar night. All of them describe the feeling of oppression which flooded over them as a result of the monotony of the environment from which they escaped only by involving themselves in some form of stereotyped activity and by the strict maintenance of daily routine. C. S. Mullin (1960), who observed the behaviour of eighty-five members of a group isolated in Antarctica for a period of many months, considered the main stress to be the monotony of the environment and the lack of normal means of emotional satisfaction. The major symptoms affecting the men in this situation were decreased intellectual activity, memory disorders, and disorders of alertness and concentration. Nevertheless, the majority of subjects retrospectively viewed this experience as valuable in terms of their personal growth, since everyone was forced to "turn inwards" and re-evaluate his interests, inclinations, and attitudes in the furtherance of discipline, adaptation, toleration, and patience.

Basic methods: mainly sensory deprivation

1. Basing their experiments on the type of experiences discussed above, a number of psychologists from D. O. Hebb's Canadian group (W. H. Bexton, W. Heron, T. H. Scott, and B. K. Doane, 1954, 1956, 1957) reproduced conditions of extreme monotony in the laboratory. In these experiments healthy university volunteer students lay on a comfortable bed in a small soundproofed room, they wore opaque glasses which admitted diffused light but prevented shape recognition, their arms were sheathed from elbow to fingertips with cardboard, their ears were covered by rubber earphones and there was the masking sound of a fan. For days at a time they lay inactive, moving only when they went to eat or to the toilet. They could speak into a microphone placed in front of them, and could hear instructions through the earphones. After a few hours under these conditions, rational processes were interfered with; it was impossible to concentrate attention on anything, and clearly suggestibility was increased. Mood varied from extreme irritation to mild amusement. The boredom was such that the subject craved for any stimulus, any movement, longingly waited for the task, although when this was presented he felt unable or unwilling to make any effort. There was a marked decrease in ability to solve simple mental problems which persisted for twelve to twenty-four hours after the

isolation period. Although subjects were paid hourly rates, the majority could not tolerate isolation for more than seventy-two hours. Those who did usually experienced hallucinations and delusions. Imagery (mainly visual) enormously expanded into live pictures consisting initially of only dots and lines, and later into whole sequences resembling cartoon scenes. These hallucinations (visual, auditory, somaesthetic) usually had a dream-like quality and were similar to the phenomena produced by Mescalin, LSD–25, in some cases by pulsing light or by sleep deprivation. EEG recordings during the experimental period and the following few hours generally showed a slowing down of the normal alpha activity and evidence of delta rhythm. Thus in this experiment, for the first time a model experimental psychosis was successfully demonstrated simply by the manipulation of the external environment without drugs or their side effects.

2. In Hebb's experiments sensory deprivation was produced by radical reduction in the variability and patterning of stimuli. As distinct from this, J. C. Lilly (1956) and J. T. Shurley (1960) attempted to exclude all sensory stimuli, i.e. to reduce stimulation to an absolute level. Those stimuli which could not be excluded, e.g. warmth, were kept at a constant level; subjects were equipped with breathing apparatus and opaque goggles and were submerged in a tank filled with tepid, very slowly moving water in which they floated freely without gravitational pull. They were instructed to move as little as possible. Under these conditions, after approximately one hour, subjects reported initial tension and intense hunger for stimuli. After two or three hours they experienced vivid visual imagery which to some extent persisted after termination of the experiment. Although disturbances occurred during the experiment, the long-term consequences of repeated experimentation were clearly positive; subjects found "a new inner security, a new integration" and achieved some insight into their motives and real inner desires. (Fig. 64.)

3. Similarly, the Harvard workers J. H. Mendelson and J. M. Foley (1956) and others report that their subjects showed a number of severe mental disturbances. In their experiment healthy volunteers (students, doctors) spent up to thirty-six hours in a respirator similar to that used in cases of bulbar poliomyelitis, with a monotonous background noise produced by running taps and the sound of the motor. Subjects could see only a small part of the ceiling from the respirator and tubes prevented tactile and kinaesthetic sensations; motorically they were severely restricted. Under these conditions only five of the seventeen subjects could tolerate the respirator for thirty-six hours. All of them had difficulties in concentrating,

experienced periodic attacks of fear, eight of them admitted to difficulties in reality testing (from pseudosomatic delusions to real visual or auditory hallucinations), and four of them had panic reactions in which they attempted to force their way out of the respirator.

Here also we find very pronounced mental disturbances in experimental subjects produced not by limitation in the quantity, but by the forced, over-simplified patterning of the sensory stimuli.

Similar experiments have also been conducted in the special isolation cubicle at Manitoba University in Canada. The results of these experiments are described in a number of studies by J. P. Zubek (1969) and his co-workers. They have been particularly concerned with the effects of a limited input of certain types of sensory stimuli (e.g. only tactile or only visual), and in this way have established the relative predominance of stimuli supplied through other sensory channels, judged by the intensity and significance of the stimuli responded to.

Overall results of experimental deprivation

In a number of studies the physiological changes produced by sensory and perceptual deprivation have been recorded — biochemical and circulatory changes, changes in muscle tonus, stimulus threshold, and GSR. However, these data do not present a clear and unequivocal picture.

It appears that the greatest EEG change is produced primarily by reduction in stimulus variability (perceptual deprivation) and secondarily by reduction in the amount of sensory stimulation (sensory deprivation). Zubek and other workers attributed these changes to disturbances in ARAS activity, which is decreased mainly by reduction in the variability of stimuli (i.e. through an over-simplified structure in the stimulus field).

Other experiments point to decreased intellectual efficiency and ability to learn following sensory deprivation. But the results are not unanimous or persuasive. They are obviously a function of individual resistance to the deprivational conditions of the motivational factors involved.

R. L. Vosburg, N. G. Fraser, and J. J. Guehl (1960) report fluctuation in level of consciousness, in sleep patterns, vividness of imaging (which was indistinguishable from hallucinations) and a variety of uncoordinated behaviours following the experiment; S. J. Freedman, H.U. Grunebaum, and M. Greenblatt (1961) noted disorders of coherent thinking, of concentration, changes in body image, hallucinations, and paranoid fears; L. Goldberger and R.R. Holt (1958) report regression from secondary to primary thought processes. N. Rosenzweig (1959) also refers to a disturbed balance between abstract and primitive affective systems — similar to that observed in schizophrenia. In Holland, P.M. van Wulfften Palthe (1958) recorded the reactions of volunteers subjected to short-term (two—three hours) isolation in a narrow, sound-proofed, dark cell under reduced atmospheric pressure (which produced a sensation of flying at a very high altitude). He reported inability to consciously control fluctuations in level of consciousness, which interfered with the continuous performance of difficult tasks, in all his experimental subjects. Some of these subjects experienced panic reactions. B. Jones and J. E. Goodson (1959) reported increased suggestibility in their isolated group subjected to monotonous (but not sensorily reduced) stimulation.

Although the extent of the psychological experiences of individual subjects differs considerably under different conditions of sensory deprivation, the sequence of experiences possibly indicates a certain lawfulness (P. H. Leiderman, 1962; R. L. Vosburg, N. G. Fraser, and J. J. Guehl, 1960). Initially, behaviour appears to be quite adaptive. In his thinking the subject utilizes memories of recent sensory impressions, possibly concentrating on one or other of the stimulus objects in the immediate environment. Gradually he turns more and more towards imagery, he adds new elements, and restructures images so that the whole hallucinatory structure becomes more meaningful, and usually has personal, emotional significance for him. Sleep often follows, from which the subject awakes restless; adaptive behaviour breaks down, symptoms of anxiety and of neurotic defences (e.g. obsessive images) appear, and he loses his previous ability to gain support from memories. Finally there is sometimes a panic attack or an effort to escape and end the experiment.

Although there is a certain agreement between experimental findings in the area of sensory deprivation, there are also a number of contradictions. Some authors, for example, report only very small negative effects, or even desirable or positive results. J. Vernon and J. Hoffman (1956), who isolated volunteer subjects (students) for forty-eight hours, reported improved learning ability with no increase in suggestibility or hallucinations, nor any reduction in concentration. In a subsequent study (1959), however, Vernon and others reported certain perceptual and motor disturbances, although these were not as severe as those described by other authors. E. Z. Levy (1959) also reported far less severe disorders in his experiments with subjects exposed to seven days' confinement in a dark, quiet room, furnished with only a chair and a bed. His subjects lost "the desire to think" during the experiment, but they lived happily in isolation, without undue stress, and experienced no perceptual disorders.

Longer-term sensory and social deprivation decreases intellectual effectiveness and produces changes in attitudes and motivation to learn. Following long-term isolation subjects are more susceptible to propaganda, for example, and are even attracted to it. With appropriate manipulation of the degree of deprivation and the sources of satisfaction, these tendencies can be exaggerated.

J. Vernon (1963) cites a very interesting example. This concerns a hypothetical prisoner who was strongly Protestant, but who had no strong rational support for his beliefs. The following technique was suggested to convert him to Islam. Initially he should be sensorily deprived for four days to make him more responsive to any new stimuli. After four days two switches are placed in his cell without any instructions. If he presses switch A he will hear a statement supporting Protestantism, if he presses switch B a statement favouring Islam, each lasting thirty seconds. The critical difference is that the statement about Protestantism is always the same, while the statement from amplifier B always has a different content, and is read by a different voice. The monotonous deprivational situation will thus become associated with the monotony of the repeated speech about Protestantism, and the desire for something novel will be shown in a preference for the statement from amplifier B. At this stage the prisoner is allowed further opportunities to press the switches — and the conflict is practically over. We have forced him to voluntarily listen to propaganda, and if we can make him listen, we can persuade him to believe this propaganda, providing it is subtle enough. Every increment of change in attitude must be rewarded. For example he can be given questions on Islam, and correct answers can be rewarded by switching on the light, then by different kinds of food and later by social contact. Nothing is produced by force or torture, only by positive reinforcement, i.e. by variation in stimuli.

M. Zuckerman (1964) summarizes the typical effects of sensory deprivation as follows:
1. Difficulties in directed thinking and concentration
2. Highly intimate fantasies which tend to increase with the degree of isolation
3. Somatic discomforts

4. Negative emotional reactions — such as anxiety — predominate over positive emotional reactions
5. These reactions may be externalized in the form of paranoid-like delusions
6. Hyper-alertness to ambient auditory stimuli
7. Non-veridical auditory and visual sensations.

Individual reactions to sensory deprivation

Every individual to some degree reacts differently to sensory deprivation, depending on individual differences in personality structure, differences in need and habit systems and in the structure of defensive and adaptive mechanisms. There are suggestions that extroverts are affected more by this situation than introverts. A. J. Silvermann et al. (1961) selected six field dependent and five field independent subjects from a population of university students, and subjected them to two hours of sensory deprivation. He reported that the field dependent Ss showed poorer performance in perceptual tasks, were more restless and irritable, experienced more fantasies, and were more suspicious. Similar results are reported in some interesting experiments by A. Petrie (1960; A. Petrie, W. Collins, and P. Solomon, 1960) who related tolerance of sensory deprivation to the basic personality dimension of satiability (which is similar to the extroversion-introversion dimension). According to Petrie, subjects differ in the amount of stimulation needed to produce satiation. These differences are shown in the tendency to subjectively reduce the effectiveness of subsequent stimulation. Subjects who display an extreme tendency of this sort, therefore, are able to tolerate long-term pain, but these are the subjects who are more severely affected by lack of stimuli during sensory deprivation. In this connection, Petrie also reports a weaker tendency to reduce sensations in women, but a stronger tendency in children (who tolerate sensory deprivation very badly). A certain attractiveness of pain, which in the sensory deprivation situation gives some relief from the stressful effects of stimulus impoverishment, is also mentioned in experiments with animals raised under conditions of isolation (see page 261) which we described above. D. O. Hebb points out that the need for increased stimulation and excitement is common to humans and animals. Sometimes we even experience a need to create mild frustration and fear.

From a practical point of view the question of individual resistance to sensory and perceptual deprivation is very important, for example in the selection of long-distance pilots, and crews of

Antarctic stations and cosmic space stations. M. Zuckerman and M. M. Haber (1965) suggest that individual differences in reaction to deprivation conditions reflect individual differences in the need for stimulation. D. P. Schultz (1965) tested this hypothesis in an experiment in the floating chamber at Princeton University. During the experiment subjects were allowed to create very simple and quite meaningless visual stimuli: by pressing a switch they lit up simple line drawings which they could observe briefly. A subject's endurance was measured by the number of times the switch was pressed. Six subjects, who, on the average, could not tolerate the experimental situation for more than 37 hours, recorded a mean of 183 seconds of viewing time during the first day. The nine subjects who persevered for 72 hours recorded an average of only 13 seconds of viewing time over the same period.

Other experiments, however, indicate that the subject's motivation to participate in the experiment is equally important; at the present time, therefore, the problem has only been partly resolved.

People who are mentally disturbed obviously react to sensory deprivation in a somewhat special way. Neurotics are more anxious and panic-stricken. P. M. van Wulfften Palthe (1958) reports panic and phobic reactions in the test situation only from individuals with frank psychoasthenic symptoms who had earlier shown anxiety during air travel. Neurotics more often interpreted hypnagogic images in a highly emotional way. Passive and dependent subjects tolerated the depriving situation better than active subjects. Subjects with obsessive character features often showed fixated stereotyped behaviour and sometimes psychotic epidodes in these situations.

On the other hand, psychotics generally tolerate sensory deprivation surprisingly well. B. D. Cohen et al. (1959) reported smaller reactions from psychotics than from normals. H. Azima and F. J. Cramer-Azima (1956) noted clinical improvement (and in two cases complete recovery) in depressed patients, and temporary improvement in hebephrenics. Schizophrenics in A. Harris's experiments (1959) tolerated the deprivational situation better than mentally healthy individuals. During his experiments, their hallucinations were somewhat less vivid and persistent, but there was no lasting improvement in mental state. Because there is some effect, a number of investigators have attempted to develop a sensory deprivation technique as a method of psychiatric treatment (Azima's anaclitic therapy). At present, however, its usefulness is limited by the unpredictability of reactions of individual patients. H. B. Adams et al. (1960) concluded that the more disturbed the mental state of the patient, the greater the improvement from experimental deprivation. R. G. Gibby, H. B. Adams, and R. N. Carrera (1960) found that the positive effects were more frequent than the negative effects and that they were more persistent in psychiatric patients. The therapeutic effect is usually interpreted (Azima and Cramer-Azima, 1956) as a two-stage process; in the first stage there is a disorganization of psychological structure, followed always by a certain reorganization, which can be directly manipulated.

Mechanisms of sensory deprivation

The mechanisms by which sensory deprivation experimentally or clinically produces psychological change are still not well known. Certain assumptions are based on the physiological notion of the brain as an impulse counter (contrary to the classical notion of the brain as a switching device). It is postulated that continuous sensory bombardment is necessary for the maintenance of efficient cortical functioning. This applies also to other structures. R. D. Burns (1960) has shown that the respiratory centre ceases activity if it is denied afferent stimuli, and P. R. Bromage (1960) reports a similar type of reaction at the lower spinal level. Thus the need for appropriate sensory feeding is apparent at the brain stem level. The overall balance between afferent and efferent stimuli is critically important in the functioning of the organism.

A number of authors postulate that disorders in psychological functioning arise from a disturbance in the mediation of normal sensory stimulation by the ascending reticular system (ARS) which is critically important in the maintenance of attention, awareness, and consciousness (G. Moruzzi and H. W. Magoun, 1949). Decreased activity in the brain stem, primarily in the ARS, leads to a decreased state of awareness, and, through this, to the disorganization of psychological processes – similar to that produced by long-term sleep deprivation, or by drug intoxication. In this connection we might also mention the older Pavlovian experiments, in which reduction of external and internal stimulation leads to inhibition and sleep. We cannot exclude the possibility that the subjective hallucinatory states resulting from sensory deprivation are organismic reactions to the need for an adequate supply of stimuli, which it must create internally, since it is denied access to external sources.

J. M. Davis, W. F. McCourt, and P. Solomon (1960) have emphasized that the quantity and the variability of stimuli are not as important as continuing meaningful contact with the external world. N. Rosenzweig (1959) similarly speaks about deprivation of relevant stimuli, and affirms that this can be produced artificially in a number of ways. He maintains that in schizophrenia we are dealing with internally produced relevance deprivation. Generally speaking, the schizophrenic syndrome is produced by limitation of useful information about the meaning of the perceptual world, due to reduced communication between the affective and the abstract systems (primary and secondary).

From the psychological point of view, a number of different interpretations of the mechanisms of sensory or relevance deprivation have been suggested. Some learning theorists (J. S. Bruner, 1959) maintain that limitation of the input of stimuli disrupts the ongoing process of hypothesis testing (feedback), by which an organism normally generates models and strategies, on the basis of which it relates to the environment. If deprivation occurs during childhood, the development of efficient models is threatened, while later in life the maintenance of such models is frustrated, since the models and the strategies previously generated are continually being re-constituted and modified in a highly sophisticated way.

Other authors (H. Azima and F. J. Cramer-Azima, 1956) emphasize more the emotional factors operating during deprivation. The isolation situation always involves considerable dependency (dark room, the covering of eyes and arms, food and toilet on request, and with help, and so on). All these reinforce dependency needs (which exist in different strengths in different individuals) and evoke regressive behaviour (regressive fantasies). Defencelessness and dependency encourage the experimental subject to regress to earlier childhood (to his anaclitic relationship with his mother). Positive effects, that is, enhanced functioning following deprivation (usually the deprivation is short-term and involves only one sensory modality), are considered to be due to the activation of the relevant drive following deprivation and the increased effectiveness of reinforcement in strengthening the CR. R. A. Butler (1957), for example, suggests that increased reactivity to visual stimuli after visual deprivation in animals is due to increased activation of the visual exploratory drive. G. Rosenbaum, S. I. Dobie, and B. D. Cohen (1959) report significant improvement in visual discrimination of tachistoscopically exposed lines of numbers after five minutes' visual deprivation, but that discrimination reduced to pre-deprivation levels fifteen—thirty minutes after deprivation had ceased.

A simple model accounting for the mechanisms of sensory deprivation is offered by J. Inglis (1965). He starts from the assumption that every activity (ranging from simple motor to complicated mental activity) is to a certain extent dependent on sensory control and on the maintenance of sensory impressions (i.e. on memory). Initially the sensory images provide the elements necessary for formulation of a tentative solution, which is then checked against the elements of the problem and its adequacy determined. However, certain elements of the problem necessary for its solution are not always immediately available in perception; in this case, certain sensory images must be stored in memory, at least for a short time, during which the solution is attempted. Any disturbance of any part of this normal sequence of events can lead to behavioural disorders. When sensory input is excluded or reduced, difficulties arise in setting up a tentative solution and in testing its adequacy. Initially, of course, recent learning (elements stored in memory) has high utility, but these elements quickly dissipate; it then becomes more and more difficult to find an adequate solution during limited contact with the sensory environment which contains the basic elements of the problem. Searching becomes more and more widespread and random. A poor memory, for example, in an older person, or in an individual with organic CNS damage, presents further difficulties. Reduced contact with the sensory environment (e.g. in darkness, during the night) for these people is not compensated for by an adequate store of memory elements, and this quickly leads to so-called "night delirium" and similar disorders.

Still another source of disorder is inadequate filtering of sensory elements in the first stage of the cycle of events mentioned above; the input of external non-relevant stimuli from the environment into the system is so overwhelming and their exclusion so inefficient that thought processes are blocked. In this case the input level is too high at a time when a solution is being sought: this happens, for example, with schizophrenics. Here temporary reduction in sensory input can bring relief (and this is the reason for the temporary improvement of schizophrenic patients during sensory deprivation). Lessening of this filtering ability is probably the main effect of psychoto-mimetic drugs (hallucinatory drugs).

A rather singular explanation of the effects observed during experimentally induced sensory deprivation is offered by E. Ziskind (1964a). Change in sensory perception (by deprivation, by monotony, and possibly by overloading), in his view, is not the reason for the symptoms reported. From his experiments on visual illusions, immediately after awaking, and during brief visual deprivation (ten minutes when the eyes are covered) in which the change in sensory input is so short-term that it does not seem to be significant, he concludes that the necessary (though not sufficient) condition for the production of the pseudohallucinations and pseudoillusions usually noted is the state of decreased mental awareness. Here, of course, we should note the effect of internal (organic) stimuli and possibly of additional external stimuli, to which the subject directs his attention in response to experimental instructions. The author demonstrates in his experiments, as well as in the other experiments he cites, that the percentage of reported visual hallucinations produced by sensory deprivation varies as a function of instructions (e.g. "describe everything you see, all your visual impressions", or "only give an account of your own experiences"). In everyday life situations where similar events occur (with pilots, while driving on an empty monotonous road, with radar observers), a similar instruction is in fact coded as an essential part of the particular activity. Ziskind therefore maintains that it is impossible to equate the data from human sensory deprivation experiments with those derived from long-term deprivation studies with animals.

Generally speaking, the number of independent variables in sensory deprivation experiments is so great, and their effects so difficult to control, that an explanation of their functional mechanisms is still lacking. In the majority of current experiments only partial explanations are offered.

Mainly social and emotional deprivation

Another aspect of the experimental approach to the problem of deprivation involves impoverishment of the social environment. Experiments are based on the assumption that social deprivation finally produces sensory, or more specifically, perceptual deprivation. An unchanging, impoverished social environment — even where the input of sensory stimuli is not experimentally reduced — produces stimulus monotony. If a man lives permanently in a sparsely furnished room, or if he lives in a limited space and has a limited range of social contact, this represents a significant reduction in the variety of environmental stimulation, even though he can move about and converse freely and is involved in a variety of problem-solving situations.

A number of experiments involving social isolation of individuals have been reported. D. W. Ormiston (1958, 1961), for example, isolated ten pilots for forty-eight hours, each in a separate cabin in which he could move about freely, smoke, and speak to the controller, and where he worked on a variety of tasks at certain times. A control group of ten pilots stayed in these cabins only for those periods of time required to solve these tasks. There was no difference in intellectual performance between these two groups, but in the experimental group there was an increase in irritability, and some undesirable forms of behaviour which, however, were usually under conscious control.

R. H. Walters, J. E. Callagan, and A. F. Newman (1963) studied the effects of individual social isolation for ninety-six hours on a group of twenty volunteer prisoners. Each subject was isolated in a small room with a bed, toilet, and basin. An additional twenty volunteers served as a control group. Mental efficiency was tested and a number of behavioural measures were taken before, during, and after the experiment. The authors reported increased anxiety in the experimental group; there was no evidence of psychomotor or intellectual disturbance, however, nor was there evidence of susceptibility to social influence after the completion of the experiment.

The work of W. W. Haythorn, I. Altman, and I. I. Myers (1965) (quoted by D. P. Schultz, 1965) can be cited as an example of experiments on isolation of small social groups. Using a number of criteria, they selected several pairs of naval volunteers, who then spent ten days together confined in a small room, where they ate, slept, and worked together following instructions given by radio. Part of each day was devoted to room cleaning and free activities. The control group left the room after completion of the daily tasks. Projective testing indicated that the experimental subjects showed increased fear and tension under the isolation conditions. This reaction, however, was determined to a significant degree by the personality structures of the isolated pairs and by the assertiveness and the competitive feelings of the individual subjects.

Similar interesting experiments have been reported with prospective personnel of scientific teams — polar, cosmonaut, submarine crews and so on.

As an example of isolation of larger social groups, D. P. Schultz cites two of J. E. Rasmussen's (1963) experiments in which a hundred seamen volunteers were housed in a specially constructed bunker, where the living space was no more than one-tenth that provided in an atomic submarine. In the first experiment, conditions inside the bunker approximated "winter" conditions, and in the second experiment "hot summer" conditions. Each experiment lasted two weeks. The subjects were not told how long they would be subjected to these conditions, and in order to control for motivational factors they were not rewarded. The majority of subjects in both experiments complained about the lack of water for washing. In the winter experiment there were complaints about the food, and in the summer experiment about heat, humidity, and dirt.

A considerable increase in irritability was considered to be the most unpleasant psychological effect. However, material conditions appeared to be a greater source of discomfort than the presence of other people as such.

S. E. Cleveland et al. (1963) studied the effects of social isolation on a family of four in a small underground shelter for fourteen days. They reported no changes in intellectual efficiency, but there were clear mood changes due to increased irritability and depression. During the first ten days of isolation the moods of family members were positively correlated, i.e. all shared similar feelings. From the eleventh day, family cohesion began to break down; there was either little relationship between mood oscillations of individual family members, or the relationship was negative (depression in one family member, euphoria in another). Nevertheless, two months after the experiment the family reported deeper feelings of unity. Two weeks spent together in isolation from the outside world strengthened emotional ties.

J. M. Davis et al. (1961) studied the relative influence of sensory and social isolation on the development of mental disturbances with patients in respirators (pairs of experimental subjects either complete strangers or related were subjected simultaneously to sensory and motor restriction, during which they could converse). The authors report that social isolation alone does not produce the same effects as sensory deprivation, and that social contact alone cannot fully prevent mental disturbances. Nevertheless, social contact at least decreased the effects of sensory deprivation, and had some effect on the content of perceptual disorders, particularly where two emotionally empathic individuals interacted. Any opportunity the subject had for contact with the environment (even through a microphone) counterbalanced the deprivation effects; even the feeling of being observed had the same effect. It is clear, therefore, that artificially created conditions of experimental deprivation always avoid the trauma of the real life situation.

Judging from D. P. Schultz's (1965) review of social isolation experiments, there are no definite conclusions from the reported findings which would be of value for clinical practice. The author himself maintains that studies in this field are now at a stage approaching that of the sensory deprivation experiments in the first half of the fifties, when the basic data were being collected.

For our present purpose, of particular importance are the studies of J. L. Gewirtz and co-workers, of the effects of social deprivation on the behaviour of pre-school children. In the first study (J. L. Gewirtz, 1954) the author was not concerned with social isolation as such, but only with levels of interaction between child and adult. Children of four to five and a half years of age painted individually; an adult was present, either sitting by the child and devoting all his attention to him, or sitting some distance off, behind a writing desk, involved in his own writing. He said to the child that he would pass anything over that the child wanted. In this latter situation, the child more often directly demanded the adult's attention, or at least kept peeping at him more often than in the first situation. Boys more often demanded attention from an adult female than from an adult male, and girls vice versa (the difference, however was not significant).

In further experiments (J. L. Gewirtz and D. M. Baer, 1958a, 1958b; J. L. Gewirtz, D. M. Baer, and C. H. Roth, 1958) kindergarten children threw marbles into one of two holes. Throwing into the left hole was initially less frequent but was reinforced (by the word "good"). The value of such reinforcement significantly increased after twenty minutes of social isolation (the child waited alone in one room while the experimenter "arranged" the game in an adjoining room). The value of the reinforcement however decreased after a twenty-minute period of frequent praise. The authors concluded that the situation in which the adult is less available to the child, even when present, and the real case of short-term isolation are analogous, since both involve lack of social reinforcement. On the other hand, the situation in which the adult is at the full disposal of the child, and where he praises him, represents a high level of social reinforcement. Social drives following short-term deprivation or satiation function in a similar way to primary appetitive drives (hunger, thirst).

Gewirtz and Baer's studies were subsequently repeated on a number of occasions using a different methodology and with different age groups (for example, by M. Lewis, 1965; H. W. Stevenson and R. D. Odom, 1961, 1962; and others). The results however were not always interpreted in the same way. Thus, for example, W. Hartup and Y. Himeno (1959) observed the behaviour of four- to six-year-old children in experimental play with plasticine dolls which permitted free expression of aggression (pulling, pressing, tearing apart, and so on, and possibly verbal displays of aggression); they report that after ten minutes of prior social isolation (which was not intended as a punishment) the children's behaviour was clearly more aggressive than that following a similar period of verbal interaction with an adult. The authors maintain that social isolation for the pre-school child produces not only deprivation (the lack of socially reinforcing stimuli which would make such stimuli more effective), but also frustration (non-satisfaction of dependency need), and that this frustration leads, via the frustration-aggression hypothesis, to an increase in the child's aggressive behaviour. Nor can one exclude the possibility of increased anxiety and uncertainty as a result of isolation. The motivational consequences of isolation, therefore, are obviously complex. Studies have also shown that boys are more aggressive than girls, and that the child's aggressiveness following isolation is greater if the experimenter is the same sex as the child.

R. H. Walters and others (1960, 1964) interpreted the results of Gewirtz's and their own studies quite differently. They postulated that the child's isolation produces anxiety, which enhances the value of any subsequent positive reinforcement (thus the reinforcement "good" is anxiety-reducing for the child).

For these reasons, in subsequent studies Gewirtz excluded the concept of social isolation of the child when developing his model of experimental deprivation. His definition of depriving and satiating conditions is relative (partial). Deprivation is described in terms of conditions in which a certain class of stimuli (social) is provided at a lower than normal level; this leads to increased effectiveness of such stimuli as reinforcers. Satiation refers to conditions where a type of stimulus is offered in larger quantities than usual, which leads to decreased effectiveness of these stimuli as reinforcers. Gewirtz and his co-workers elaborated this concept of experimental deprivation in a number of experiments. In one of these, five-and-a-half-year-old children were given a ten minute preparation period, during which they named different pictures presented to them; one group was frequently praised by the word "good" either thirty or sixty times in ten minutes, while the second group was seldom praised (four or twelve times in the same period). This was followed by an experimental series in which the child was asked to select one from two pictures (plants or animals). The non-preferred stimulus category was systematically reinforced by the word "good" during this series. As anticipated, it was shown that after experience of social deprivation the effectiveness of the reinforcing stimulus (the word "good") increased. The child quickly learned to name the reinforced category. After satiation, however, learning decelerated.

Similar experiments with children of different ages and under different conditions show clearly that the negative correlation between prior experience with the reinforcing stimuli (deprivation or satiation) and the subsequent strength of reinforcement – a fact which is clearly recognized with appetitive stimuli (food, water) – is valid also for other (e.g. social) stimuli.

The conditions which heighten or lower the momentary efficacy of social stimuli in their reinforcing role are those operating concurrently or in an immediate past (i.e. short-term deprivation or satiation). The psychological conditions of long-term (clinical) deprivation, however, may be entirely different, and related to the question of how the general availability of social reinforcers in the child's environment influences his social learning. From this point of view, H. L. Rheingold, J. L. Gewirtz, and H. W. Ross (1959) studied experimentally the extent to which a change in amount of social reinforcement altered the frequency of vocalization in institutional babies. In two experiments, the second a replication of the first, they were concerned with the amount of vocalization from twenty-one three-month-old infants over a period of six days. For the first two days (baseline days) the experimenter leaned over the child on a number of occasions for three minutes with a vacant and unchanging expression, and an observer recorded the number of vocalizations from the child. During the next two days the experimenter bent over the child and reacted immediately with a smile, by clucking, or by patting the child's belly to every spontaneous vocalization by the child. During the last two days the original experimental (baseline) conditions were repeated. The authors report that social reinforcement increased the number of spontaneous vocalizations during the two days by 86 per cent. During the final two days, when reinforcement was stopped, frequency of vocalizations retreated to a level close to baseline performance. Similar results are reported by Y. Brackbill (1958). Four-month-old babies in her experiment significantly increased the number of smiles when smiling was reinforced by a social response from an adult. It is obvious that the mother who responds warmly to a child's smiling or burbling facilitates the child's social development to a much greater degree than the cold uninterested mother or nurse.

H. L. Rheingold (1956, 1961) also reported the effects of experimental modification of mothering on the behaviour of small children. Eight babies from an institution were cared for devotedly for seven and a half hours daily by the same person during the period from six to eight months of age. Eight other babies of the same age, who lived under normal institutional conditions, were used as a control group. It was shown that the social reactivity of children who were given individual devoted care increased significantly when compared with the control group; this difference, however, was not maintained a year later when the children (aged nineteen months) were retested in their own or in foster families, to which they had been transferred from the institution. The only maintained difference was in speech, which in children seems to be more amenable to environmental influences than other behaviour.

Although the experimental approach to the problem of deprivation has been systematically developed only during the last decade, it appears already to be highly promising. Although conclusions from experimental data on animals or adult humans are not directly applicable to clinical problems of deprived children, and although experiments with children can involve only the mildest forms of short-term deprivation, certain findings are valid and generalizable, and advance our understanding of theoretical questions which we intend to consider in the next chapter.

Fig. 57. The young chimpanzee in a normal sitting posture. (Reprinted, by permission, from H. W. Nissen; by permission of the Yerkes Laboratories, Orange Park, Florida; Director A. J. Riopelle.)

Fig. 58. Different sitting posture of a young chimpanzee raised under conditions of restricted tactile stimulation. (Reprinted, by permission, from H.W. Nissen, K.L. Chow, and J. Semmes, 1951.)

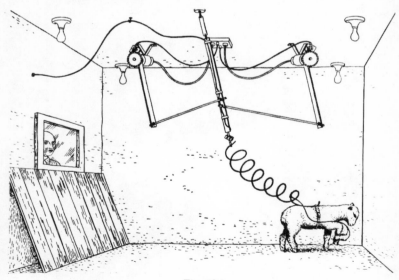

Fig. 59A

Fig. 59. Behaviour of twin lambs in fear-provoking situation without (A) and with (B) the mother present. In C, movements of the lamb without the mother (A) are limited and inhibited; movements of the lamb with the mother present (B) are far freer. (After H. S. Liddell, published by permission of his wife.)

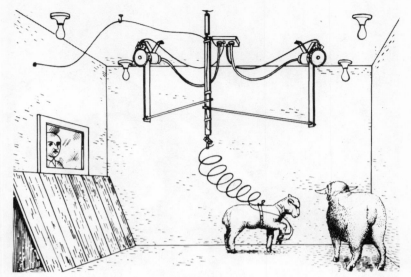

Fig. 59*B*

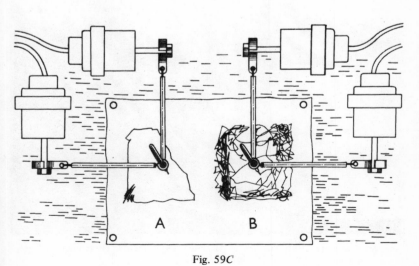

Fig. 59*C*

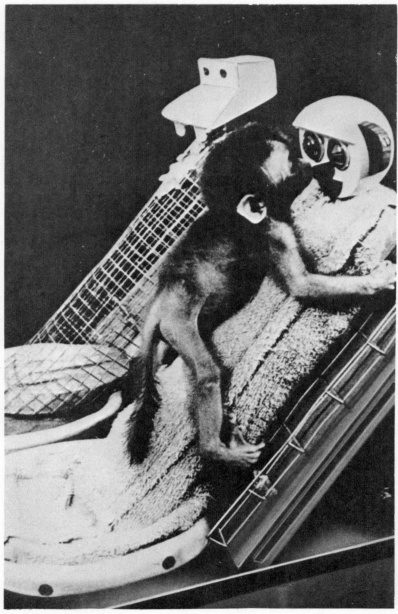

Fig. 60. Surrogate cloth mother in Harlow's experiments. (Reprinted, by permission, from H. F. Harlow, 1959.)

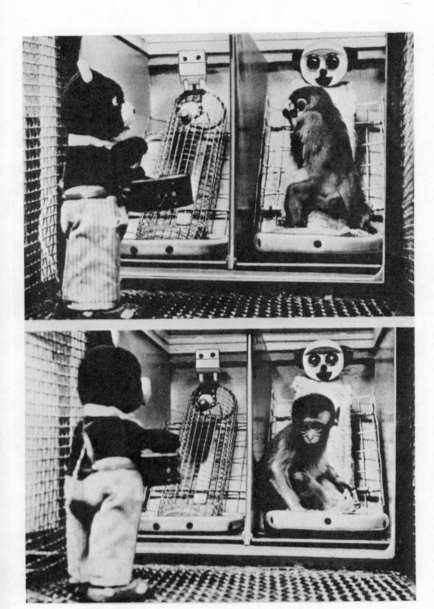

Fig. 61. Fear reaction of a young monkey when faced with an unfamiliar object. He seeks the protection of the surrogate mother, and only after finding security with her does curiosity develop. (Reprinted, by permission, from H. F. Harlow, 1959.)

Fig. 62. Young rhesus monkey immediately after release from isolation which lasted from birth to twelve months. He crouches in the corner with eyes covered. (Reprinted, by permission, from H. F. Harlow and M. K. Harlow, 1966.)

Fig. 63. Behaviour of group of young rhesus monkeys raised without mothers in Harlow's laboratories. (Reprinted, by permission, from H. F. Harlow and M. K. Harlow, 1966.)

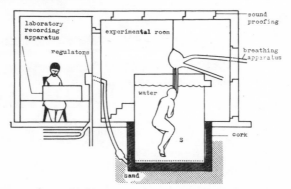

Fig. 64. Apparatus for experiments requiring maximum limitation of external stimulation. S floats in warm water, with air provided through a special helmet. (Reprinted, by permission, from J. T. Shurley, 1960.)

10 A theory of psychological deprivation

One of the prerequisites for a scientific approach to the problem of early deprivation is an adequate methodology for studying the development of small children. This was met at approximately the same time in two systematic approaches, in A. Gesell's developmental scales, and C. Bühler's *"kleinkindertests"* (baby tests). However, Gesell's nativistic theory, which describes and explains psychological development using such concepts as "growth", "maturation", and "pre-determined innate sequence of behaviour patterns", afforded less opportunity for determining the basic influence of the impoverished environment on child development, since this theory postulated that the basic developmental structure is determined by internal factors, and that the environment simply stimulates or retards, modifies and supports this internally directed growth. Bühler, on the other hand, began by recognizing the decisive influence of external factors on the early development of the child; in her theory, the mental growth of the pre-school child reflects environmental features rather than inherited abilities. This led her and her colleagues to systematically investigate the early development of the child under different social and child-rearing conditions. These studies, as we have already noted, initiated the scientific approach to deprivation.

The main trend in initial theorizing about this problem was a reflection of psychoanalytic influences. In recent years, however, exclusive appeal to such concepts has disappeared, and studies taking different theoretical orientations have been reported. This, to some extent, reflects the general confusion and tentativeness of psychological theory in general. Despite this, however, we can recognize a number of trends which we shall describe briefly.

PRESENT THEORIES OF PSYCHOLOGICAL DEPRIVATION

1. As noted above, the pioneering studies were based on, and directed by, psychoanalytic concepts (for example, R. A. Spitz, 1945; D. W. Winnicott, 1948; J. Bowlby, 1946; E. H. Erikson, 1950). Even allowing for the different viewpoints amongst these authors, we can detect a common thread — that deprivation, on the most general level, is conceptualized as lack of gratification of instinctual drives (*Triebe*) in the absence of the drive object. In fact, all behaviour aims to secure gratification of instinctual drives (self-preservation, sexual and death instincts), i.e. to reduce tension whenever it is aroused by these drives. In achieving satisfaction, the organism needs an object (material and personal) which thus becomes a part of the process of gratification, and becomes emotionally charged ("cathected"). Instinctual drives, their objects, and the modes of gratification change from one life stage to another, develop into higher processes, and are better adapted to the surrounding reality. From his analytic treatment of psycho-neurotic patients, S. Freud (1917) came to the conclusion that the various symptoms of neurotic disorders are a compensation for gratifications which the subject was denied in actual life. The patient has to search in his own history until he finds a period in which the satisfaction occurred — even if he has to regress back to his own infancy (S. Freud, 1917, p. 423).

Subsequent differences amongst the various theorists centred on what they understood to be the basic relationship of the child to the prime object of his instinctual drives — his mother — and how they interpreted the mechanisms by which this relationship influences the child's development.

Freud himself gradually changed his views about the "emotional bond to the object". In his early writings (around 1900), he considered that the child's relationship to his mother was based on the direct satisfaction of sexual instinct — we direct our first sexual impulses towards our mothers, just as we direct our first impulses of hate towards our fathers. Subsequently, when discussing narcissism (1914), Freud introduced a new concept, that of an affectional bond, which is more fundamental and primitive, and which is based on the "anaclitic" relationship to the person who offers food, care, and protection to the child, who satisfies his "oral" needs.

This classic psychoanalytic concept was employed by R. A. Spitz (1958*b*) in a detailed study of the development of object relations. He identified three stages during the first year of life: 1, the pre-object period (up to three months approximately) when the child does not distinguish between individual objects, nor does he differentiate himself from the environment – this is the stage of primary narcissism; 2, the preliminary object period (three to six months approximately) when the child reacts with a smile on seeing a face and distinguishes it from the environment. What the child perceives at this time is not an "object" (person or thing), but a signal, a simple image structure (a *Gestalt*) from a simple, particularly significant part of the face (Spitz, 1946); 3, the object period (as such); between six and eight months, the child begins to differentiate the familiar from the strange face, to display fear symptoms when separated from familiar persons. Spitz interprets this reaction as fear of loss of the libidinal object. From this time on, the mother begins to occupy a unique position in the child's psychological life, her image is no longer limited only to the surface quality of the object, but is a fundamental feature which is related to her satisfaction of the child's deepest instinctual needs.

If the child has already established this valid relationship with the object, and if this relationship is shortly afterwards severed, a serious disorder develops, which Spitz called anaclitic depression (see page 53), for here we are concerned with the severance of the anaclitic bond. If lack of maternal care persists, then the deterioration in the process of psychological development merges into the syndrome of hospitalism.

Arguing from the same position, E. H. Erikson (1950) maintains that continuity of maternal care, which satisfies the oral needs of a baby, is the necessary condition for the establishment of a feeling of basic trust which is essential for healthy psychological development. "The first social achievement of the child is thus his willingness to allow mother to move out of his visual field without extreme fear or anger, because the maternal figure has become the internal security as well as the external image." Stability and persistence of external objects and familiar people also constitute the basis for the development of a rudimentary feeling of identity. Inadequacy of basic trust is shown by withdrawal into schizoid or depressive states.

J. Bowlby (1958*a*, 1960, 1961, 1969) in his theoretical investigations of the nature of the child's tie to his mother, of the meaning of separation anxiety and childhood mourning, rejects classic psychoanalytic theory as well as traditional concepts of learning theory, and leans heavily on principles of modern ethology.

The child's attachment to his mother, according to Bowlby, does not originate in the satisfaction of "oral" needs only, nor is it an acquired (secondary) drive. The bond is conceived as determined by a number of innate, instinctual response systems, each of which is built into the organism because of its high survival value — for example crying, smiling, clinging, following. These instinctual systems are activated by certain stimuli in the environment and are terminated by specific situations which tend to focus on a particular individual who is best known and most trusted (i.e. they tend to be "monotropic"). Thus, to form an affectional bond to a person (thing, place) is to regard this person as a terminating object of the instinctual response. Because of the focus on one specific person, the response system develops a very high motivational value. Focusing on one person, therefore, must be viewed in terms of its biological significance: to be in the proximity of a familiar person (or place) is a prerequisite of safety, becoming isolated (distant) from it is extremely dangerous, especially for the young.

As long as the child is close to his mother, the relevant, activated instinctual systems can be terminated; a subjective component of such a situation is a feeling of comfort and safety. If, on the other hand, the child loses mother from his immediate environment, his instinctual systems become activated, but not terminated; the resulting persistent activation is subjectively experienced as tension, distress and anxiety. Such "separation anxiety" is "primary" in the sense that it is elemental, due simply to the rupture of the attachment to the specific person; it cannot be reduced to more primitive components, or explained as a danger signal warning against something worse. A primary anxiety is evoked whenever any instinctual response system is activated, but not terminated — and separation from the trusted person is clearly the most frequent and significant condition of this sort. Hence, separation anxiety is the unavoidable risk in the love relationship with the caring person.

During the course of human life, an individual engages in a whole range of attachments. The most influential among these, however, are the ties formed early in life (mainly during the second and third year of life) when the instinctual response systems mediating the attachments are permanently at the ready for intense activation, and the focus is predominantly on the one person (who has high survival value at that life period). Later on, these systems are less readily activated and become organized around an increasing range of objects. All children in the first three years of life reared under normal conditions react to long-term or repeated separations from the mother with anxiety and distress. If the loss of mother persists, mourning develops, an important aspect of which is aggression, by which the child attempts to restore the lost contact and to achieve reunion with the "mother-figure".

2. An entirely different approach to the problem of deprivation is based on the general principles of learning theory. The original study, using this framework, was that of W. Dennis (1935).

On the basis of his observations of institutionalized children (for example in the Teheran nurseries) Dennis concluded that the mental retardation of children is not caused by maternal deprivation, but that we must seek its causes in the simple lack of opportunity to learn. Especially at an early age, when limited by the confines of the bed, these children have minimal opportunity for movement and exploratory behaviour. Subsequently, even if they remain in the same environment without a mother, they begin to show improvement as soon as they can acquire stimuli for themselves. Dennis maintained that the severity of the disorder is due in large measure to lack of specific experience in the type of situation which is normally used in testing. Subsequently, Dennis experimentally supported this hypothesis, and reported fast improvement in test performance after children had been given special training in the general task area.

Theories based on principles of instrumental (operant) conditioning conceive of deprivation as originating in "an inadequate reinforcement history" of a child living in a dull, routine, unvaried, and restricted environment (S. W. Bijou, 1963; C. B. Ferster, 1958), which results in reduced effectiveness of social reinforcers (E. F. Sigler, 1961, 1963; H. W. Stevenson, 1965). An outstanding example of such an approach is J. L. Gewirtz's (1961 et seq.) theoretical analysis. In line with basic tenets, Gewirtz maintained that deprivation is caused by lack of effective contiguities between responses and reinforcing stimuli. Where such deficits exist from the beginning of the child's development (Gewirtz called this privation), the total of reinforcing stimuli linked to the child's reactions is so small that he does not establish basic habits at the time when such learning would normally occur. A further result of such an impoverished environment is the delayed habituation of fear and other negative emotional reactions which are natural in a small baby. This long-persisting, intense emotional reaction inhibits further successful learning. In the majority of cases of privation, however, not all reinforcers are unavailable, but only a certain class, usually the social reinforcers. Such children eventually "become immune" to fear reactions, they react relatively well to normal stimuli in the material environment, but not to social stimuli, which have a quite specific positive value for other children. Such a child, therefore, does not react readily enough to social stimulation and becomes "autistic".

A different case is that of deprivation, by which Gewirtz means that situation in which social and other environmental stimuli are offered initially to the child in sufficient degree and at the appropriate time so that they become highly significant, but are then subsequently suddenly withdrawn. Immediately following such withdrawal, the behaviour that previously had been effective and normal (for example, calling mother) increases in frequency, as happens in the early stage of CR extinction. Quite abnormal emotional reactions can also occur. Furthermore, Gewirtz maintains that while deprived (institutionalized) children suffer from lack of opportunity for operant conditioning, they may have greater opportunities for classical (Pavlovian) conditioning (as a result of consistent child-rearing practices).

J. S. Bruner (1959), however, maintains that it is the higher type of cognitive thinking that is affected mostly by deprivation. According to Bruner, the deprived child lacks the basic conditions for the development of effective complex problem-solving behaviour, and for effective coping with the environment; these children cannot develop either "models of the environment" or "coping strategies". By "models of the environment" Bruner means the constructs by which the individual preserves the consistent periodicity of the environment (probabilities attached to different occurrences, discrimination between important and unimportant events — signals from noise). "Behavioural strategies" refer to the rules necessary for effective and immediate decision making and for directed behaviour. Under conditions of early deprivation, these rules cannot be derived at the proper time, and thus the basis for selective gating and for differentiation of spheres of activity is lacking. If such a deprived individual meets new tasks, he lacks effective means for non-specific transfer of old experience into new situations.

3. A number of clinical observations, however, indicate that the problem of psychological deprivation cannot be completely accounted for by psychoanalytic theories or by any or all theories of learning. This is suggested by H. R. Schaffer's (1965) study which, although unreplicated, is rather informative. Schaffer compared two groups of children hospitalized before seven months of age, a hospital group and a group in a babies' home. Although both groups of children were separated from their mothers and cared for by a larger than usual number of nurses (due to staff changes), the first group was more deprived in that it received far less social stimulation (the amount of interaction between children and nurses was about 50 per cent less than in the second group). As expected, the children who lacked social stimulation showed noticeably poorer development. There were a number of striking features, however. Developmental retardation immediately following separation was extremely rapid

(average DQs dropped to 84.8 and 97.5 respectively); there was no subsequent drop in DQ (DQs at the end of the separation period were still 84.6 and 95.1); the retardation was adjusted with equal rapidity immediately after return home (DQs recovered to 94.5 and 96.1 respectively, and remained at about the same level three months following discharge — DQ 96.2 and 98.4 respectively). Schaffer maintained, therefore, that the results cannot be explained either by regarding separation from the mother as a major factor (both groups were separated in a similar way and were made up of children who had not yet established the specific relationship to the object) or as due to lack of opportunities for learning (in this case we would have to assume a slow and gradual decrease in DQ as well as a slow and gradual recovery from the deprivational effects).

According to Schaffer, the most likely explanation, at this stage of theoretical development, is offered by motivational theory, which suggests that retardation is a symptom of apathy and inactivity caused by a low level of arousal inherent in the environment. This apathy (reflected, for example, in a low level of vocalizing and spontaneous activity) rapidly onsets when the child is placed in a stimulus-impoverished environment, and it can be changed quickly by increased social interaction. The child's maturation progresses normally under such conditions, but his behaviour (developmentally tested) is well below capacity level.

In this context, Schaffer points to a theory advanced by S. Provence and R. C. Lipton (1952) suggesting that developmental disorders of institutionalized children are due to imperfect adaptation to the environment resulting from "decreased investment".

4. Finally, we should mention some more recent attempts by sociologists to conceptualize child development and its abnormalities within the framework of a total, complex social structure (particularly T. Parsons and R. F. Bales, 1955). According to this view, the social development of the child does not involve only the learning of individual social activities, nor is it restricted only to the child-mother relationship. The child is always a part of an organized social system, and gradually learns the pattern of this system with all its numerous roles (behaviour adequate to certain social positions and statuses). The child learns not only those roles which he himself will gradually assume, but also the roles of other people (as shown, for example, in the play of a three-year-old girl who suddenly copies the mother's role). The child is thus prepared for eventual performance of these roles. The child obtains information about these roles by direct participation in social interactions — initially through his relationship to his mother, later on in the broader context of the

nuclear family and finally through interactions outside the family. In all such interactions, the child meets a number of adults and peers, who perform different functions, and learns to differentiate their roles, on the basis of typical ways of behaving (emotional or emotionally neutral, specific or diffuse, universal or particular, and so on).

If some fundamental element is lacking in the child's social environment, an element basic to some specific social role (relative to certain status) — if, for example, father, mother or siblings are absent from the family, or if the child cannot interact with his peers — it follows "that the aspects of culture learned through interaction with individuals in such statuses are missed by the child and that he remains deficient in learning in this respect, undeveloped in this potential aspect of his personality" (O. G. Brim, Jr., 1960). From this point of view, deprivation can be viewed primarily as inadequate role learning, due to lack of certain fundamental experiences of interactions in childhood. The results of such deprivation are subsequently evident in partial and inadequate socialization; a deprived child is the individual who is badly prepared for appropriate performance in a number of roles which might be expected of him in the course of his normal life in society. His ability to distinguish between different social situations, demands, statuses, and attributes is limited, and his behaviour in social interaction and working performance is immature and deficient.

MOTIVATIONAL BASIS OF CHILD-ENVIRONMENT INTERACTION

Critical evaluation of current theories of deprivation and our own clinical experience convince us that the theoretical approach to these problems must be based on a sound theory of motivation. This is obvious from our definition of psychological deprivation.

Classical motivation theory, to which academic experimental psychology (R. S. Woodworth, 1918) and psychoanalytic theory (S. Freud, 1915) have contributed equally, was based on the assumption that we should look for the real springs of all behaviour in the primary (biological) needs, such as need for food, oxygen, warmth, sexual satisfaction, relief from pain, and so on. Lack of satisfaction of these basic needs is indicated by physiological imbalance and a subjectively unpleasant state of tension which motivates the organism to restore a normal steady state, i.e. to reach homeostasis (W. B. Cannon, 1929). Reduction of the tension produced by an unsatisfied physiological need is thus the source of all activity, the final outcome of which is the achievement of a homeostatic state, a necessary condition for the survival of the individual and of the species. Obviously the drive level which determines whether a man (or animal) is activated or not cannot be directly observed, but it can be inferred from the general energy expenditure of the organism and from the activity directed towards drive reduction.

It is clear, of course, that people (and even animals) have motivations other than simple satisfaction of their basic biological needs, but it has been assumed that these latter needs are somewhat "higher", i.e. derived, secondary, learned by virtue of their association with the primary, basic, inherited needs in the past (C. L. Hull, 1943; J. Dollard and N. E. Miller, 1950).

Over the last two decades a great amount of data suggests that this theory is far from satisfactory. It has been shown (F. A. Beach, 1945) that, for example, children and animal cubs do not remain inactive even when their physical needs are satisfied; on the contrary, rested, well-fed, warm children show quite a degree of spontaneous play activity. Even in the first few weeks of life, we note that the child is concerned with movements of his fingers, curiously observes the environment, is entranced by new sounds. Soon he manipulates objects and his own body with unbelievable persistence, repeats a newly discovered skill hundreds of times. From experiments in which head-turning in babies was reinforced by milk from the bottle (H. Papoušek, 1969) it is clear that CR frequency is unrelated to hunger intensity. Three- to six-month-old babies, though fully satisfied and unable to suck any more milk, still persistently responded to the CS as if they enjoyed making the correct response.

Similarly, well-fed and watered rats thoroughly investigate their new environment, and rather surprisingly, hunger and thirst tend to restrict their exploratory behaviour (D. E. Berlyne, 1950; K. C. Montgomery, 1953). H. F. Harlow, M. K. Harlow, and D. R. Meyer (1950) also report that well-fed and watered monkeys will dismantle and reassemble a mechanical toy for a number of hours without reward, and that they were still interested in this activity (which is quite meaningless from a biological point of view) ten hours later. Of interest here are R. A. Butler's (1954) experiments, in which he reports that a monkey learned to discriminate coloured windows quickly, solely for the reward of looking through them, and that this learning was faster and more lasting if another monkey or a moving engine could be seen in the other compartment, and slower if only fruit or an empty room could be seen.

Obviously these activities cannot be explained solely in terms of biological drive. They do not relate to immediate drive satisfaction;

to some extent, they can have an opposite effect. Thus we should recognize the existence of different kinds of tendencies, whatever we choose to call them (curiosity, exploratory behaviour). Contrary to the view implicit in classical motivational theory, man is not a passive system, who attempts to maintain his homeostasis with minimal energy output, but actively seeks interaction with the external world. This fact is emphasized both by the earlier central European psychologists, and by the Soviet school (L. S. Vygotski [1962] and S. L. Rubinstein). A. Adler (1930), for example, maintained that neither heredity nor environment, although important, is the final determinant of behaviour. The decisive role is played by the emerging creative power of the individual. In a similar manner, E. Spranger (1955) emphasized the contribution of active effort to individual growth.

Striving towards active contact with the world is indicated in man in two ways. In the first place he is spontaneously active (especially in childhood), i.e. he frequently seeks activity even if not "driven" by physiological starvation or by any external stimulus. At the same time, however, this spontaneous activity is continuously extending, constantly growing, directed towards the search for new meaningful stimuli rather than to the achievement of equilibrium.

Man's response to external stimuli is determined by this active attitude — his responses are selective, acquisitive, adaptive, and he is set to cope with emerging problems and to master environmental events. In fact, both spontaneous and selective activity are aspects of the one process. The spontaneous activity aims at promoting a certain level of stimulation through which he can adjust his activity by comparing the expected and real stimulation. It appears that the agreement or disagreement between these two levels plays an important part in the internal motivation for further activity by the child and is related to his emotional life. At the same time it is likely that there are individual differences depending on constitutional and external conditions in this tendency towards active contact with the world.

MULTI-LEVEL APPROACH TO CHILD-ENVIRONMENT INTERACTION

It is perhaps unfortunate that instead of one theory which might account for all forms of psychological deprivation, we must resort to a number of theories. On careful inspection, it is obvious that each of the theoretical approaches discussed describes certain aspects of a very complex phenomenon, which to this point has defied analysis by any one theory. There is no profit in attempting to reduce uncertainty by a priori acceptance of one particular theory, in the hope that eventually it will be robust enough to interpret contradictory results. In our view, a more fruitful approach would be to determine which aspects of deprivation are best explained by particular theories, and to see if we can establish links between them. In this way, it might be possible to erect some sort of conceptual framework which would utilize and possibly temporarily integrate a number of different concepts.

Based on our experience as clinical psychologists, and in line with the views outlined above, we have proposed (1967, 1968) an interpretation of the clinical manifestations of child deprivation on four conceptual levels.

1. On the most basic level, the child-environment relationship is analyzed in terms of the global characteristics of the environment (the quantity, complexity, and variability of stimuli) and in terms of the general level of spontaneous activity and global reactivity in the child. This level of analysis has obvious similarities both with Schaffer's (1965) explanation of the global syndrome in small babies placed in a stimulus-impoverished environment, and with the concept of Provence and Lipton (1962) who viewed retardation in the mental development of institutionalized children in terms of decreased level of investment.

2. On a somewhat higher level of complexity is the analysis of the child-environment interaction in terms of the differential activity of the child in relation to certain specific features of the environment. These are obviously the significant factors underlying the flexible and appropriate adaptive behaviours occurring early in the child's development. From this point of view, the child's development and developmental disorders are analyzed in terms of different learning theories, which are concerned either with different types of contiguity between responses and reinforcing stimuli, or with the processes of transformation of more complex response structures.

3. To maintain or restore the unity of the organism the differentiated specific activities of the child must be concentrated in a certain way. Everything points to the fact that an external object is necessary for such concentration, and that this is so important for the organism that it becomes a centre to which the organism attaches itself and around which all activity concentrates "as peasants around the king". On this level of analysis we are concerned with theories which deal with the development of the child's attachment to the mother figure, the significance of the "relation to the object" which

is the organizer of the varied activities of the child. This owes a good deal to psychoanalytic theories, which emphasize this aspect of the personally important object (rather than significant stimuli) for child development and the role of its absence or loss in the genesis of deprivational disorders.

4. There are grounds for assuming that the "I" of the child emerges out of his relationship to the external "object", and that this "I" represents a new internal organizer, an internally differentiated and organized unity, with a meaningful personal relationship to the environment. We think that the concept of "I" is essential for complete analysis of subject-environment interaction and for a sound interpretation of psychological deprivation. The fact that experimental psychology has for so long avoided this concept has created a wide gulf between experimental and clinical psychology. Through his relationship to "you", the child finds his "I" (W. Dilthey, 1896; M. Buber, 1923), and thus achieves a higher integration and greater independence and flexibility in his striving for a meaningful contact with the world. Irrespective of the way that "I" is established as a new internal "object", a necessary condition for its functioning is obviously the expectation which "you" have about "I". This expectation becomes the expectation of "I". This is the content of the roles which the child adopts in relation to his social environment. Social psychological (or sociological) theories conceive of the child's relationship to the environment in this general way.

The multi-level approach described above can be applied, to some extent speculatively, to both the static and genetic analysis of the child's personality and its deficiencies. The child's personality, at any point in time, can be viewed as a hierarchical structure which can be analyzed on different levels of complexity (P. Lersch, 1951; E. R. Hilgard, 1962; S.H. White, 1965; W.C. Bronson, 1966).

At the same time, it appears that this hierarchy develops in a certain time sequence, and that the particular levels become active or predominate at certain points in time. There are periodic, sometimes overlapping sequences of globality, differentiation, concentration, followed by integration, i.e. by the emergence of a more complex and more autonomous "I". This is analogous to the most general philosophical concept of development, as applied to phylogenesis in the law of complexity-consciousness advanced by P. Teilhard De Chardin (1959).

One should emphasize, of course, that this speculative approach is not fundamentally important to the problem discussed above. The multi-level approach is simply an operational schema which is useful as a working tool and which sooner or later can be replaced by a more useful conceptual framework.

BASIC PSYCHOLOGICAL NEEDS

Since we initially defined psychological deprivation as inadequate satisfaction of basic psychological needs to a marked degree and for a long enough period of time, at this point we should indicate what we mean by "basic psychological needs".

We begin with the assumption that the basic developmental tendency of the organism (in addition to the biological drive for survival) is its need for active contact with the environment, which is realized by a constant widening, differentiation, subsequent concentration and repeated integration of this contact. A living organism is, by its very nature, active, and this activity is, in principle, inevitably oriented towards the world and objects in it: it takes possession of things, learns to recognize their relations and meaning, becomes attached to specific objects and ascribes values to them, and, in the middle of the possessed, grasped and evaluated things and persons, eventually meets its own person and defines its status in the world of things and human beings. This basic activity develops in the process of continuous anticipation and fulfilment, by means of which the organism actively helps to create and realize itself.

If we accept this basic concept, there are some obvious implications. If the trend of the individual towards active contact with the world is to be realized and further developed, the environment itself should possess certain features. In other words, conditions should exist which allow acquisition of objects, the opportunity to influence them and thus to introduce order into the environment. If these conditions are not met, the individual cannot find meaning in objects, and in addition loses the feeling of his own meaningful existence, irrespective of whether or not biological needs are being satisfied.

In line with our previous argument, the external conditions necessary for the satisfaction and further development of the basic drive for active contact with the world can be analyzed on the following four levels.

1. The tendency of the organism to actively contact the world is shown at the most rudimentary level by the effort to establish, maintain, and extend global interaction with the environment, i.e. by the "need" for a certain level of external stimulation.

It is obvious that meaningful interaction with the world cannot exist if the environment does not offer stimuli of a certain quantity and level of complexity and variability. An organism can hardly discover order in a world which lacks basic phenomenological characteristics — i.e. lacks stimulation value.

It is now clearly established that a certain level of stimulation is sought after by the child from the earliest age and that this has a positive emotional and reinforcing value. Most frequently the child reacts to adequate stimulation by positive emotional reactions and optimal attentive and exploratory behaviour. Paucity or surfeit of stimuli (too simple or too complex, too stable or too variable stimuli) are subjectively unpleasant and provoke rejection and indifference, or an attempt to re-establish the optimal level of stimulation.

A considerable number of observations and experiments indicate that a certain degree of environmental stimulation produces searching activity in animals (Bennett, 1958) and that more complex, unpredictable, contradictory, and novel stimuli are attended to for longer periods of time by both adults (D. E. Berlyne, 1966) and small babies (R.L. Fantz, 1961). On the other hand, too complex or too novel stimuli can elicit fear, escape, or "freezing". W. N. Dember and R. M. Earl (1957) maintain that every individual has his own optimal level of amount and complexity of stimuli, which they have labelled the "pacer stimulus". This level determines primarily the extent and type of global active relationship of the individual to his environment, whether we call this activity searching, curiosity, manipulation, or something else. The emotional state of the individual, as an underlying factor in this activity, changes from negative to positive tuning as a function of increasing stimulus complexity. Beyond the optimal level the tuning again becomes negative (S. R. Maddi, 1961a,b; J. McV. Hunt, 1960; P. C. Vitz, 1964, 1966a). The level of stimulus complexity or variability which individuals prefer differs from person to person and is dependent, amongst other things, on age, constitutional features, and previous experience.

We can assume, therefore, that a certain level of stimulation is a basic psychological need in humans at all levels of development. The child, as well as the adult, needs a certain degree of richness of stimulation even if this is not the only important aspect of the environment. In fact, all child-care systems recognize the importance of this type of control, which is incorporated in their child-rearing models; means are prescribed by which kinaesthetic, tactile, or other stimulation is input, especially from the earliest age (by rocking, carrying, cuddling, wheeling in a pram, calming, tickling, singing, the presentation of coloured or bright objects, and so on) or by which over-stimulation is restricted (by swaddling, placing the child in a quiet dark room, and so on). Cultures and societies as well as individuals differ in the degree of stimulation they prefer, permit, or recommend, and judge as appropriate to the emotional and behavioural state of the child.

In the first weeks of life, level of stimulation as such is the most basic feature of "the world" and its representation in the child's environment. At this time, the mother's role is probably quite nonspecific; as the supplier of stimulation she can in fact be replaced by another person, even though this replacement may be hindered by the need for continuous stimulation of the same type and level, and still more by the importance of uninterrupted contact for the mother and thus for the child himself.

In later development also, the basic characteristic of every caring person must be the ability to arouse in the child a positive emotional state — usually based on an emotionally adjusted warm approach — and thus evoke and maintain the child's interest and cooperation. The decisive role here is obviously played by emotionality, the basic variable of maternal behaviour (and of all interpersonal relationships as such). It is obvious, however, that everything — a toy, for example — must have an appropriate degree of stimulation value and variability if it is to play a positive role in the child's development; it must be pleasing, interesting, and attract attention, it must maintain arousal and activity, encourage exploratory behaviour, and permit different types of manipulation.

It seems appropriate to use the explanatory (though somewhat controversial) concept "arousal level" to describe the general psychological and physiological aspects of the organism's drive to ensure relatively global contact with the environment. In the experiments described above, and in a number of other studies, it has often been shown that the amount, complexity, and variability of stimuli not only determine changes in emotional tuning, attention, and readiness for learning, but are also reflected to a significant degree in a number of physiological changes — for example, in changes in basic GSR and in spontaneous GSR fluctuations, in heart rate, in respiration, in EEG changes (primarily desynchronization), in humoral, metabolic, and other changes, which are usually regarded as expressing level of arousal or activation.

Arousal level, of course, constantly changes, depending on the ongoing stimulus flux and on a number of external and internal conditions in the organism. The resulting arousal level is thus some sort of general index of the present relationship of the individual to its environment. The tendency of the individual to maintain balanced contact with the environment can be described, in this sense, as a drive to maintain a certain preferred level of arousal, which, in long-term perspective, profoundly influences both his physiological (his biochemical individuality, metabolism, growth, tempo of neurophysiological maturation) and psychological characteristics (basic emotional tuning, spontaneous activity, reactivity, aspects of learning and attention, tolerance of stress and frustration, for example). It seems probable that this arousal level — although undoubtedly constitutionally determined — can be affected by chronic physical (for example, nutrient) and psychological (richness of stimulation) features of the environment (J. Lát, 1962).

2. The tendency of the organism towards active contact with the world is soon shown behaviourally in another way — in his effort to establish and maintain a significantly differentiated interaction with the surroundings. The environment must be coherently structured for such a differentiated interaction to occur and be meaningful.

The need for external sensory cognitive structure — i.e. for meaningful differentiated sequences or patterns of stimuli — is obviously one of the basic psychological needs from the earliest age.

In deriving meaning from things, global contact — the simple input of any type of stimuli in certain quantities and variability — soon becomes inadequate. The child early strives to find meaning in the hierarchical arrangement of stimuli, attempts to discover their functional value, the direction and meaning of changes, the meaning of previous and present stimulus conformations. Even in the first month of life, and later on to a much greater degree, this motivation to discover the world as a meaningful structure of past and present experiences, of new, expected, and realized experiences, the need to learn, to gain experiences, to seek order, and find solutions through specifically oriented reactions, not simply through global adaptation, can be observed in children at all developmental levels. The effort of a baby to obtain new skills through testing and exercising to the point of obvious fatigue, the endless "why" of the small child, the persistently pursued interests of a school boy, for example, cannot be explained simply in terms of secondary reward.

Lawfulness in the development of differentiated contact between the child and his environment might be described in terms of classical or operant conditioning. Even at an early developmental level, however, it is obvious that the child's learning is far too complex in character to be explained in terms of simple conditioning. H. Papoušek (1969), using modified Pavlovian and operant-conditioning techniques, reports that even at three—six months of age a baby shows effort and well-developed skill in discovering certain simple rules or lawfulness in external stimulation and in using this knowledge to modify his behaviour to reach a certain goal more rapidly and effectively. Babies are obviously pleased if they find meaning in the structure of the stimulus field, and seek solutions even when their learning is reinforced by nothing more than the actual seeking and discovery of the solution. Their behaviour suggests that they attempt to derive a clear concept (model) of the relationship between their behaviour and external stimulation. Obviously the child does not learn simply because the stimulus situation is forced upon him, but rather because the situation, which he actively seeks, encourages learning. The stimulus situation does not fully determine the child's response, but is more a triggering instance which the child responds to or ignores, reacts to positively or negatively, meets with a chosen alternative and with a preferred intensity of response. Learning, by its very nature, is an active process, by which the child tries to check, through his own effort, everything that he has to face. Through learning, the child, rather than passively adjusting, grasps the world and modifies it in terms of his expectations by means of specially devised coping strategies.

If the child's drive towards a significantly differentiated interaction with the world is to be realized and extended, then the environment must offer him relatively varied but distinguishable structures to allow him to discover relationships amongst different parts and different aspects, the relationship between past and present, and between his own acts and environmental changes. For the child the world must not be an uninterpretable — even if fascinating — chaos in which no order can be detected, nor a sequence of events independent of his own efforts, nor should it be a too commonplace and easily perceivable stereotype.

From this point of view, the level of complexity necessary for the stimulation of the child's development is that complexity in the structure of life experiences which the child can master at a particular level of his development. In Papoušek's experiment (1969) mentioned above, it was shown that mastery of simple tasks facilitates subsequent learning of more complex problems. If, however, we attempt to introduce too difficult a level of learning too early, maladaptive behaviour occurs and the time required for learning becomes protracted.

Thus, for instance, a suitable toy must offer the child the opportunity for different types of activity appropriate to his level of ability — it must stimulate discovery of the environment, the concept of the essence of things, it must encourage creativity and richly differentiated activity. Here again we note that child-rearing models, in all times and cultures, include and often directly prescribe different methods by which the child is introduced to the structure of things and events. Each culture prefers certain methods which encourage learning through predetermined control of cognitive templates, which facilitates the growth of knowledge and necessary skills during the whole course of the child's development, and in this way promotes a more effective orientation in and mastery of his surrounding world.

Initially, the child learns only slowly to react in a differentiated way to particular categories of stimuli, but after the second month, such learning progresses rapidly. Under normal circumstances, dependence on complex stimuli of a social character assumes special significance, as is evident from sudden increases in smiling, vocalization, and mimicry, and in the first forms of emotional communication, which lays the foundation for the child's confidence in the trustworthiness of the external world, despite the fact that this is constantly changing. The child rapidly acquires differentiated experience of the external world and readily acquires those skills which permit more efficient contact with the environment. The child who has learned to sit and then crawl, to hold objects, put them down and manipulate them, now has an entirely different, more active relationship with the world than previously. He is not only less restricted by his physical environment, but learns to rely more on the social sources of need satisfaction.

The most interesting "object" for the child, however, becomes the human figure and human behaviour, and the most important experience for him is interaction with humans. The child's experiences with people determine the orientation of his social activity — i.e. his ways of social interaction, cooperation, and conflict resolution. In a similar way, his experiences with the material world determine his activity in the sphere of objects — the mode of his exploratory approaches, his manipulation and adaptive performance.

Substitution of the mother at this level can be only moderately successful, since the child needs a predictable environment. In this very limited sense, even a three- — six-month-old child "recognizes" his mother, because she is a predictable element in the environment, and he may react unfavourably to her withdrawal (M. Damborská, 1967b). At this level, the most significant aspect of maternal behaviour is control of stimuli functional to the child's behaviour. This is clearly a very substantial part of child care and a universal dimension of social interaction, since it determines the framework in which the child develops. The mother in this sense is the first teacher of the child, for she helps to organize his earliest experiences in such a way that he can find his way in a situation, can understand

and govern it, and thus avoid the feelings of anxiety and fear which necessarily occur when the known structure, order, and security are withdrawn and when the child is exposed to the new and unexpected.

3. If the child is to maintain his identity in the world of great flux of stimuli and events, however, his rapidly increasing activity must be somehow concentrated. It is apparent that this concentration can be achieved only through some external object which, for the child, is extremely significant, since it is central to all his strivings and needs. The specific attachment which the child establishes to such an object gives a new meaning to all his different activities.

The principal need of the child, therefore, becomes his need for a specific object to which he relates by a specific close, stable attachment. Initially this object is usually the mother (or mother surrogate). Subsequently, however, other significant objects of social value — the father, the family as a whole, the peer group, the cultural model, and so on — assume this role.

This need of the child is generally recognized, although differently labelled and interpreted (dependency need, attachment need, need for love, affiliative need, for example). For the small child, interaction with the mother soon becomes the most desirable activity, and in certain developmental periods dominates all other activity. The mother at this time represents for the child the "world" as a whole and is a conglomerate of separate "things". A wealth of communication with the mother (verbal and non-verbal, cognitive and emotional) is highly desirable and strongly motivating. The child smiles at the mother, and demands a smiling response from her; he listens to her voice and mumbles back; he reaches for her and cuddles in her arms, he touches her face, holds her, asks for things and hands them back, cries when the mother leaves or fails to come when called, and welcomes her when she returns. As the child's skills develop, his interactions with the mother become more extensive and sophisticated. The extensiveness and creativity, the novelty, the variability and the ingenuity in the child's play with his mother always surprises observers. His contacts with the mother, which obviously in themselves offer satisfaction without further reward, are interminably reiterated; play with the mother in the critical developmental period is preferable to play with an impersonal, even though attractive, toy or to play with another person, no matter how kind and interesting. The mother's presence as such brings pleasure and satisfaction to the child, and at the same time provides him with a sense of confidence, motivates him in all activities, and, in this way, enhances his performance and learning.

If the child's tendency to concentrate his activities around a specific love-object is to be developed, then he must find an object which is not only sufficiently stable and permanent, and offering a warm affectional bond, but also one with unique acceptance of him. The mother must share certain of the child's activities and the child must participate in certain of the mother's activities. Communication must be understandable and meaningful for both of them. The mother's world must become the child's world and vice versa; the mother must understand the child (his needs, his signals, his interests, his activities) and the child (even if only to a limited extent) his mother.

There is some evidence that the child's attachment to the mother occurs quite suddenly at about seven to eight months of age, is rapid and very intense, and remains practically unchanged for a relatively long period of time (H. R. Schaffer, 1963). On the basis of this evidence, some investigators have assumed that the process of attachment cannot be explained as a normal learning process, but that here we are dealing with a different mechanism, possibly similar to imprinting (C. Wolfensberger-Hässig, 1966).

In such a relationship the intimacy of contact is so great that bodily boundaries disappear. The child's world achieves a new dimension and the objects in this world a new meaning. Every culture modifies the child's environment in this sense and controls the ways in which the mother (or other object) relates to the child. Individual societies and cultures, as well as sub-cultures, differ, of course, in the extent and intensity of this bond, and in the closeness and the uniqueness of this specific attachment — amongst other things, in the degree of "monotropism". Nevertheless, a certain degree of involvement by the child in the life space is a necessary condition for the satisfaction of this basic need.

In this relationship, of course, the child is not simply a passive recipient nor is his behaviour dominated entirely by external factors, it is actively oriented towards the establishment and maintenance of contact. Here, as with other needs, there are great individual differences; some children energetically and insistently demand frequent, intimate contact and clearly prefer this contact to all other activities. They can often gain the attention of the nurse even under unfavourable conditions — as typified, for example, by the "loved ones" in institutions. On the other hand, other children are far less active, they prefer the initiative to come from the adult, whom of course they need just as much as does the demanding child.

In the initial period of attachment, the mother cannot be fully substituted, and the child is extremely sensitive to even short periods of interrupted contact. This is very clearly shown in the frequent dramatic examples of separation anxiety. The need for the external object at this time cannot be satisfied by internal activity, or by generally available objects acting as partial substitutes. It can be (successively) displaced onto, or supplemented by, other objects, however, at least partially, although not without difficulty. A toy, a teddy-bear or a doll for example, can be a partial substitute, a central object towards which all the child's activities are oriented, during the period of acute mourning caused by the recent loss of a loved object.

4. Finally the trend towards lively interaction with the world shows itself in the child's effort to establish himself as the central object, the carrier and the source of all his activity in the environment, as well as the recipient of the actions of other objects. This is shown in the need for a strengthening and development of the emerging "I" in its relationship with the environment, especially with the social environment. In other words, the need for personal-social values develops in the child, i.e. the need for objects and goals which support the child's sense of autonomy, his search for identity, for achievement of personal growth and self-fulfilment, and for the establishment of personal integrity.

In the world to which the child turns his attention, amidst the different things which he grasps and masters, and in his relationship to the object (or objects) to which he becomes attached, he soon meets himself — the object of his own body and his mental "I" — as the centre from which all this activity proceeds and to which it returns. The external organizer (the mother as the object around which the total activity of the small child centres) is replaced by the internal organizer, against which the child begins to evaluate all internal and external activity. This internal organizer, which is now always present — inasmuch as it is carried by the child — eventually supplants, at least partially and gradually, those external agents which previously have provided security.

The fact that the child can independently engage in a number of activities which emerge from his "I", and are at variance with environmental demands, presupposes some degree of autonomous functioning. The child who up to that point has been extremely dependent on interaction with the mother now attempts to develop personal relationships with the world, rejects too many intrusions into his personal space, and asserts his own wishes. Thus, the general activity of the child assumes a new meaning, in that now it is the activity of "I" in relation to the environment.

The child is proud of his independent achievements even if initially he is unable to evaluate his performance. In achieving goals which he has established or selected as his own, by gaining new knowledge about things and by acquiring new skills, the child now "realizes" his newly discovered "I" which is satisfying and which motivates further activity. In this respect, individual objects and events are once again re-evaluated, and learning acquires a personal significance.

Through his relation to "you" the child now finds his identity — the basis of his "I". He also recognizes the reciprocity of you-I, appreciates what "you" expect of his "I", and similarly what "I" can expect from "you". Thus the child participates in simple dyadic roles and later also in his roles in more complicated social relationships. He also expects from "you" a verification of his own "I" — he expects praise, acceptance, evaluation of his performance and of his status, acceptance of his assumed or assigned role. Thus the specific relationship between child and mother also acquires a new meaning and value in the polarity of you-I.

The newly created "I" inevitably returns to itself, investigates, understands, and evalutes itself — it seeks and discovers its complexity and meaning. At this point, not only the activity of the "I", its individual characteristics, its attachment to a specific object, but the whole new integration is comprehensively evaluated — meaning is given to its existence, its permanence, its continuity.

At this level, the mother's task (and later on the task of other socializing influences) is particularly onerous and extremely difficult to replace. She still exists, of course, as an object of loving relationship, from whom the child gains personal security; at the same time, however, this relationship becomes the model on which the child's own "I" is based. She is the child's first "you". Thus, it is necessary at this point for the mother to retract somewhat (although superficially) and to help the child to bridge the gap between complete dependency and a growing independence and understanding of his position in the world. She must also help him to discover goals and values which he will internalize and which will reinforce his own "I"; she must help him both to appreciate complex roles, inside and outside the family, and to adopt his own personal role. But in addition she must be primarily the helper in evaluating his tentative but energetically demanding emerging awareness of ego-integrity. "Evaluative acceptance" seems to be the best description of this necessary quality or dimension of maternal behaviour or of interpersonal interaction, out of which emerges satisfaction of the need for personal-social autonomy in human development.

In his relationship to his mother, the child becomes aware of the social implications of his own behaviour. Gradually he introjects the values of the mother and partly internalizes behavioural norms relating to "good" and "bad" behaviour. Thus "I" achieves personal significance. The child begins to adopt very simple social roles, that is, he begins to appreciate what is expected of him, how he can please or offend others, and his behaviour begins to be governed by these criteria. His "I", however, is initially very vulnerable, as was his relationship with his mother: he stubbornly insists on going his own way, and refuses help from other people by making the comment, which he has not previously made, "I'll do it myself".

It is clear that in the later, as well as in the initial stages of development, the child experiences periods of extensive differentiation and of intensive and often difficult concentration of activities, through which the developing "I" becomes more complex, more organized, more independent, and stronger. Thus, in the pre-school period (from two to five or six years), the child learns rapidly and usually more effectively, develops verbal and practical skills, learns new social habits in the family, in the playground and in the nursery school. The centre to which all this activity is related, and where the child finds the necessary security, however, is now the family or the home, rather than solely the maternal figure. The child establishes relationships with all members of the family, he finds his place amongst them, and reappraises his role in the extensive family social interactions. From the conflicts emerging from the child-parent relationships, and out of his drive for independence, there emerges a new and more independent "family I". The child is now able to leave the close family circle for some time and enter a new, wider, more challenging world.

From this time on, in school age, the child's learning again progresses more systematically and directly both inside and outside school. At about eleven years of age, the child usually finds a new model on which social behaviour is concentrated. This is usually a peer group, according to which a child judges his behaviour, his hobbies, his desires, his values. Deviation from this model is as stressful as was the earlier separation from the mother for a small toddler, or absence from home for a boy at about five years of age. Thus from new conflicts and confrontations the "group I" emerges, through which the child achieves new self-assurance and a new image of himself, and finds new ways of participating in human society.

Again, the new "I" is the basis on which new learning rests, learning on an extensive, more general basis, and through more effective methods of abstract thinking. During the adolescent period, the child's activities begin to differentiate, from the point of view of more extensive social, vocational, scientific, ideological, and other interests. In this flux of different ongoing concepts and ideas the adolescent finds a new model in an ideal exemplified by some generally admired figure – a successful adult, a professional authority, a pop singer, famous actor, sportsman, scientist, politician – or possibly only by a figure from the circle of friends from whom he abstracts certain attractive features. In this relationship to society and culture as a whole the adolescent finds his new ego-identity, involving an ideal which he attempts to realize. At this stage the newly developing "I" hesitantly and with difficulty seeks its fulfilment and its role in the social and cultural context of its society and its time.

Obviously, the concept of developmental stages which are always characterized by new differentiations, leading to new integrations, is not the only possible approach to this problem. That this conceptualization recurs in different forms in developmental psychology, however, testifies to a certain degree of utility. For example, the stages described in the establishment of the dyadic, the family, the group, and the social "I" are roughly equivalent to J. Piaget's (1950) stages of the development of intelligence and to the first four "ages of man" in E. H. Erikson's (1950) system.

MULTI-LEVEL APPROACH TO PSYCHOLOGICAL DEPRIVATION

The basis of psychological deprivation is inadequate satisfaction of the basic psychological needs of the child. Since we have described what we consider to be "basic psychological needs" we can now attempt to interpret the concept of psychological deprivation, using the framework of a multi-level conceptual analysis. From this point of view, we can consider psychological deprivation as restriction of those conditions promoting effective interaction between the child and the environment; this restriction can be viewed on four levels: as lack of overall stimulation, as lack of opportunities for cognitive structure, of specific attachment to a particular object, and of personal-social identity.

Deprivation as lack of stimulation

Although the concept of deprivation as simple impoverishment of the stimulus environment has been criticized as an over-simplification and misinterpretation of the real state of affairs (J. L. Gewirtz, 1968), in our opinion this was the first viable approach to the problem which had any firm theoretical basis. In real life, of course, the situation is nearly always more complex, and with the possible exception of the first few weeks of life involves deprivation at other levels. This is true, for example, of deprivation in poorly equipped institutes, of situations of general neglect or indifferent approach to the child, as well as of conditions of undue restriction of the child's mobility and spontaneous activity for various reasons. Under laboratory conditions, we can replicate this situation most closely in the model of sensory or possibly motor deprivation, although, as we have seen, it is difficult to create a simple quantitative impoverishment of stimuli. For this reason, it is difficult to provide compelling evidence of the effects of this type of deprivation. We have grounds for assuming, however, that lack of nonspecific stimulus input results primarily in changes in the intensity of the child's basic drive for interaction with the environment, i.e. in his level of activity and in his readiness to respond. It appears that relatively short-term, partial, or repeated deprivation initially produces increased arousal level, i.e. general hyperactivity in the individual. Long-term or permanent and total deprivation, however, leads to a drop in arousal level, i.e. general hypoactivity. It seems that the organism initially attempts to restore the interrupted environmental contact by increased (diffuse) activity which should ensure a subsequent increase in stimulus input. If this effort fails, i.e. if the child is unable to increase stimulus input through his own efforts, there is increased emotionality sometimes to an extreme level, indicated in crying, screaming, tantrums, and so on. If this situation persists for a longer period of time, some adjustment occurs on a lower level of activity, which is characteristically shown in a decreased level of emotionality.

This view is supported by the results of older and some more recent experiments. It has been reported that following lack of satisfaction of appetitive drives there is an increase, followed by a gradual reduction in drive level, for example with hunger (J. Stavěl, 1937), thirst, and sexual drive. J. L. Gewirtz (1958, 1967) reports that deprivation of social stimuli increases their reinforcement value in a similar way. He maintains, however, that this applies only to short-term, and not to longer (clinical), deprivation. The fact that withdrawal of external stimuli may be associated with heightened arousal has also been reported by a number of recent authors (A. Amsel, 1958; D. H. Lawrence and D. Festinger, 1962; R. H. Walters and R. D. Parke, 1965).

In sensory deprivation experiments, as noted earlier, some authors report that a most striking initial feature is insatiable hunger for stimulation, which after a certain period of time changes to decreased alertness, languorousness, sleepiness, and a sort of "psychological hibernation". Since the complexity of the experimental situations makes it difficult to compare the results of sensory deprivation studies, however, the more recent data do not offer unequivocal answers. M. Zuckerman (1964) maintains that the effects of sensory deprivation depend primarily on the length of the deprivation period. In his experiments, increased arousal was indicated by increased basal skin conductance and by a greater number of spontaneous GSRs (similar results were reported by J. A. Vernon, T. Marton, and E. Peterson, 1961). These signs of heightened arousal, however, were not reported by investigators studying the effects of short-term (two hours or shorter) isolation (A. J. Silvermann et al., 1961; P. H. Leiderman, 1962). Those subjects in Zuckerman's experiment who showed particularly large increases in arousal indices also complained more about the emotional unpleasantness of the sensory isolation, and in other experiments showed a higher level of operant responding to obtain stimulation, i.e. they had a significantly greater need for stimulation.

Based solely on clinical observation of children who were brought up for the most part in the monotonous, uniform environment of an institution, we have identified two basic types (see page 207).

1. The *hyperactive type* is characterized by increase in overall (diffuse) activity, by greater motor behaviour and restlessness, by increased (undiscriminating) liveliness and curiosity, by increased intensity of emotional reaction, by urgent and sometimes even aggressive and provocative demand for valued stimuli, by increased sensitivity to stimuli, by distraction and fluctuating attention, and by performance oscillation.

2. The *hypoactive type* is characterized by decrease in general activity to the point of indolence and torpid reactions, by emotional apathy and indifference, by weakening of the reinforcement value of stimuli, and by a great decrease in performance and learning, even in simple tasks. Growth and maturation is retarded and, in extreme cases, dystrophy occurs. Severe cases of this sort are rather rare amongst institutionalized children, and occur more frequently under conditions of severe family neglect.

3. In addition, one can also find children who appear to have achieved some sort of balance even under conditions of stimulus impoverishment. Children of this *"normo-active" type* show an almost normal level of general activity, which, however, is rather labile, and can rapidly change if a different stimulus environment is imposed. Children of this type are usually older children who have

found their *modus vivendi* in institutes. Transfer of these children to their own families or to foster care is often followed by rapid, striking changes, especially in restlessness, which cannot be explained in terms of a slow, gradual process of learning.

One should note that in this discussion "type" refers to tendencies which are more or less clearly fixed, but which are not necessarily permanent. It can also be objected that such a classification is at least partially based on value judgments, inasmuch as what is considered to be a "normal" level of activity is culturally determined, and even dependent on individual preferences. We feel, however, that this classification has value for clinical practice, and that the standards can be defined in a fairly objective and universal way, at least in the case of the clearly deviant behaviour of deprived children, and in comparison with the baseline activity established in follow-up studies.

Thus R. A. Spitz (1945) reports apathy, rejection of contact, indolence, indifference to stimuli, severe intellectual retardation, and deterioration in physical condition, with decreased resistance to infection in severe cases of hospitalism. L. K. Fischer (1952), who continued Spitz's studies, identifies hyperactive cases, who show strong social responses, and apathetic children lacking such responses in a baby institute. N. M. Aksarina (personal communication), an eminent Soviet expert in this field, reports hyperactivity and greater aggression during frustration amongst children who have lived for a long time in collective care. She maintains that the most important task of the supervisor in a collective is to ensure an optimal state of CNS excitability in the children.

We should remember that a significant factor in determining the final outcome of stimulus impoverishment − whether hyperactivity or hypoactivity − is undoubtedly the basic psychological constitution of the child (in addition to the length and severity of deprivation experiences).

Finally we should note that change in activity level of institutional or otherwise neglected children may be due to factors other than simple lack of external stimulation. One such factor, for example, is diet. A higher basic arousal level has been experimentally induced by a protein-rich diet offered at an early age (J. Lát, E. M. Widdowson, and R. A. McCance, 1960) or by a high fat diet. On the other hand, hypoactivity can be one of the first and most palpable symptoms of malnutrition (J. Cravioto, E. R. de Licardie, and H. G. Birch, 1966). We should recognize the possibility that hypoactivity could be due to dietary deficiencies or to cerebral dysfunctions caused by other pathogenic factors in a number of cases of severely deprived children.

There is another side to this problem. Just as the hyperactive child readily produces a high level of reactivity in his environment (and thus may increase stimulus input, and under favourable conditions normalize his behaviour — an example is the "loved ones" in institutes), the hypoactive child on the other hand, by his behaviour, further increases the danger of stimulus impoverishment. Such a child tends to be unattractive, and thus limits the responsivity of his environment — "the apathy can produce apathy and so contribute to a cumulative pattern of reduced adult-child interaction" (J. Cravioto, E. R. de Licardie, and H. G. Birch, 1966).

Deprivation as lack of cognitive structure

If the child's drive towards effective interaction is to develop, he must be given conditions through which he can learn how to differentially and appropriately respond to the organization and structure of his environment. If the environment does not allow him to discover predictability and order in external events, and relationships between his behaviour and environmental responses to his behaviour, then his interaction with the environment remains on a global, undifferentiated, ineffective level. Under such conditions his psychological needs remain nondiscriminating and undeveloped.

This danger always exists when the external environment (as perceived by the child) has limited structure, i.e. where stimuli (even though numerous and varied) are unintelligible, because they lack meaningful relationships with his spontaneous behaviour and with his intentions. The child is unable to discover meaning in his environmental activities and to direct his activity towards valid goals. This can apply equally to a child living in the monotonous environment of an institute or to a child who is surrounded by toys which are beyond his level of comprehension, or by people who ignore his immediate needs, interests, and wishes. Quite understandably such children have an extremely strong interest in all environmental activity but they themselves are only superficially involved and appear to be "interested viewers of an adventure movie" which however is not meaningful and which does not concern them personally. We frequently noted this amongst our institutionalized children (see page 210).

The lack of meaningful environmental structure which underlies deprivation on this level can be the product of either external, organizational factors (for example, where the environment of children's homes is institution-oriented rather than child-oriented) or of internal factors embedded in the personality of the supervisor (for example, lack of intelligence, sensory defect, or simply lack of attention to the child's needs). Here, in terms of interpersonal relations, we are most likely dealing with a dimension of control of the child's behaviour in the broadest sense (i.e. lack of control of all reinforcing stimuli in general). Thus, deprivation on this level is produced by externally neglecting or indiscriminating care which is only superficially controlling. The child obviously tries to discover a certain structure in his life environment, to find meaning in the environment and to gain access to emotional stimuli. If he cannot manipulate the environment in this way by increased activity, this results in increased emotionality, shown in fear of the unknown (fear of strangers, xenophobia). The effects of such a poorly structured environment, as we might anticipate, are reflected developmentally in a tendency to primitive and indiscriminating, ineffective, unsophisticated interaction with the environment. The needs, the interests, the efforts of the child are undirected, diffuse, and nonspecific.

In extreme cases, the child fails even to discriminate between basic "spheres of activity"; for example, he behaves in an identical way to people and to material objects, to animate and inanimate objects. The higher activity level of the hyperactive child here is quite diffuse and appears to be meaningless and senseless. He welcomes every object — toy or human — with indiscriminating joy, and deserts it without qualms. The indifference of the hypoactive child to humans, objects, or events is equally great. Toys fail to attract him, and the presence of humans neither disturbs nor activates him.

In the majority of cases, of course, there exists at least a crude differentiation between the material and social environments, but more discriminating reactions between known and unknown people, between a doll and a piece of paper, for example, are absent.

In considering social behaviour, we can again identify two categories as we did in previous discussions.

1. The child who is *socially hyperactive* — i.e. who shows extravagant interest in people — clearly attempts to input significant social stimuli through increased participation in social activities. Children of this type who stand out in institutionalized groups show high social dependency. These are the children who run after every nurse or visitor, who go to be cuddled, who stretch out to strangers and try to attract their attention. They are interested in social play and in trying to maintain contact with other people. When left alone with their toys, they rapidly lose interest and their activity decreases to such an extent that they throw them away, lie down on the ground and simply wait for new social opportunities. Because of this

extravagant and indiscriminate striving for social contact, these children develop only limited opportunities for play, for handling material, and for work. Their play, therefore, is very monotonous, lacks creative fantasy, and their working techniques and strategies remain at a primitive level. However, this applies equally to their social behaviour particularly in more demanding or complex situations, and means of communicating with the social environment. In content, their speech is usually poor, although they constantly chatter. With older children of this type, lack of social discrimination is reflected in their failure in tests requiring grasp of social relations, such as the picture-arrangement sub-test of the WISC. Here, poorest performance is usually shown by children raised in institutes from earliest childhood.

2. The *socially hypoactive* child seems to have lost hope that he might satisfy his need for interaction with the environment through participation in social activity. Children of this type limit their social activity and orient themselves more exclusively towards the world of things and impersonal events. They become primarily dependent on material stimuli. Unlike children who grow up in a normal environment, they have been denied the opportunity to evaluate people as a source of stimulation and learning. Their environment offers a greater number of inanimate objects, and the actual manipulation of these is more stimulating than random impersonal contact with the supervisor. Institutionalized children of this type, therefore, are usually quiet and uncomplaining, provided they have their toys. They try to re-enter the examination room not to renew contact but to have another opportunity to play. Their relationships with the nurses and visitors are usually indifferent — they are often described by nurses as "looking through us". We note that in not too severe cases, these children have a relatively high level of spontaneous play. In more severe cases, dependence on the material environment is so extreme that this prevents the child from developing discriminating working strategies and creative activity. Especially where such a child is constantly in a peer group, frequently all of his activity is directed towards keeping and defending his toys and other objects. For this reason, psychological investigation is often almost impossible; as soon as an attempt is made to take away one toy and replace it with another, the child objects, fights, and terminates contact with the psychologist.

We can identify another group of children who show a tendency to substitute satisfaction of biological needs and who become dependent on these substitute activities. These children prefer to eat, to drink, to engage in autoerotic play, movement stereotypes, or other bodily manipulations. We tend to find extreme cases of this sort in families rather than amongst institutionalized children.

It should be emphasized, of course, that the type-categories we have described are not strictly exclusive. We should also recognize that the initial "type" responses may be reinforced or weakened by the consequences of such responding. For example, socially hypoactive children usually give their nurses limited satisfaction, even though their non-demanding quiet play creates little disturbance. Because they can amuse themselves, the nurse tends to "leave them in peace", which, of course, further encourages their social passivity. On the other hand, the socially hyperactive child disturbs the nurse's work through his demands to establish contact with her, but because this demand is very general and undirected, rather than specific and forceful, such a child is tolerated, but "nobody really likes him". This further reinforces the child's undifferentiated striving to achieve social contact.

At a later age, particularly under the stabilizing influence of the school, we note a regression towards more balanced social and material interest. Even here, however, we can observe differences due to the child's individual characteristics, his constitutional features, previous experiences, and his life situation in general. Because of the complexity of the clinical picture, it would be desirable to corroborate this general scheme experimentally, as was possible in the case of sensory deprivation. Unfortunately, the experimental evidence concerning "cognitive" or "relevance deprivation" is at present rather meagre.

Some interesting results relative to this point are reported by H. Papoušek (1969) in his experiments with babies aged three to six months. He concludes that inability to recognize order in situations (predictability) and to create a model or plan on the basis of which information from the environment can be processed and responses stored, initially leads to increased activity in a given sphere, but subsequently to decreased activity and complete apathy. "The incongruity between expected and actual results of activity not only changes the emotional state, but also increases the activity of the baby in those spheres probably most relevant to the achievement of an expected result, in other words, to a more rapid acquisition of information about the situation. But when the baby cannot find the correct solution in time, another behavioural change occurs which can be described as rejection of the problem, escape into another activity, or escape into total passivity." Papoušek presents a number of examples of both types of reaction and maintains that these behavioural changes support K. H. Pribram's (1967) theory about the two types of mechanism of internal control of emotions — those mechanisms involved in the reduction of uncertainty by increased processing of information and those limiting the input of information and decreasing uncertainty by a return to the previous state of integration.

Deprivation as lack of specific attachment

Differentiated and differentiating reactions of the child must always be integrated at a certain point. This occurs in all developmental stages initially through the attachment of the child to some significant social object such as mother, family, peer group. A necessary pre-condition is that such an object must be physically and psychologically present in sufficient degree and for a sufficiently long time. If the child fails to find a permanent object, or if his effort to establish or maintain intimate contact is interrupted at a certain developmental stage, his interaction with the environment remains unconcentrated, non-integrated, and eventually regresses to a less effective stage.

Deprivation of this sort threatens the child whenever an external social object is unavailable. This can occur in early age, if maternal care is offered on a multiple or intermittent basis, as for example in institutes with a large child-nurse ratio, or where the nurses work in shifts. This danger is less obvious in families where the mother is employed. In cultures in which multiple mothering is the traditional model, changes of maternal figures are fewer than in some modern children's homes. As a rule, in such cultures there is also a marked preference for a "primary" emotional object, while others play a supplementary role. In addition, in modern institutes the object may be psychologically as well as physically lacking, e.g. where the approach is impersonal and where there is only routine handling which prevents the child from developing close emotional contact with the object.

Such a situation can occur in families, however, where parental attitudes are rejecting or hostile, or where parents are simply unable to establish intimate relationships with the child, although they are willing and able to supply him with adequate, meaningful sensory stimulation and behavioural control. Such a deficit would most likely be shown in that aspect of the mother-child dyadic interaction which W. Schutz (1958) has termed the "inclusion" dimension. The adult is unable to include the child fully enough in his subjective life space and to share empathically with him his feelings, thoughts, wishes, and decisions (the opposite case is that of the mother who maintains too close a symbiotic, overprotective relationship with the child, which precludes the later severance of the emotional umbilical cord and the development of independence).

The best experimental model of this type of deprivation can be derived from the findings of Harlow and others which we have previously described in some detail. Here we can probably refer to a model of specific emotional-social deprivation rather than a model of sensory or cognitive deprivation.

We might anticipate the outcome of deprivation on this level to be shown in a lack of relatedness to others, in inability to form stable and deep intimate bonds, and possibly in instability and diffuseness of developing relationships with resulting feelings of insecurity. At this level, we can distinguish two extremes in the drive towards attachment.

Attachment-hyperactive children

These children are highly motivated towards establishing the specific attachment. In small children, this is shown in an increased effort to stay in physical contact with the mother or mother surrogate, to cling to her skirts, to have her for himself, to attract her attention at any price and by any possible means. In our institutional sample, the efforts of such children to establish specific contact became frantic, and are expressed in a forced, disturbing, provocative approach to the nurse, often accompanied by aggressive behaviour towards competitors amongst the other children. We described this type as socially provocative (see page 210). Nurses often describe these children as children who "want to have the nurse for themselves alone". The attempt by these children to be cuddled is not as indiscriminate as in socially hyperactive children. It is usually directed towards a particular person, and is therefore very disturbing in the institutional environment.

Within children's groups, and during staff changes, the possibility of establishing a strict one-to-one, face-to-face dyadic relationship is markedly decreased. These children, therefore, are jumpy, aggressive, and extremely jealous. They appear to be extremely wilful, irritable, always prepared for a tantrum, uncontrollable. If such a child is alone with the nurse, he is "changed", is "unrecognizably pleasant", is "cuddly" and "nice". The nurses say that this child does not tolerate the group well. These children do not interact with visitors or examiners as naturally as do children showing diffuse social hyperactivity; for the former, the visitor is a stranger. Once contact is established, however, it is rather difficult to terminate (quite the reverse with children showing diffuse social hyperactivity); after an hour's testing they do not want to leave the examination room, they sulk and make scenes. Because of their difficult behaviour, these children are not usually recommended for adoption; in actual fact however their behaviour in the adoptive family often changes surprisingly, as soon as they understand that the new environment is permanent, and the people involved are willing to accept them fully. In this respect also they differ from children with diffuse social hyperactivity who establish this specific attachment only with difficulty and interact with all alike on the superficial level.

In children of the attachment-hyperactive type who have not established adequate emotional contact, abnormal behaviour persists up to school age and possibly into later developmental stages, as we have indicated previously (see page 211). A number of children who are described by W. Goldfarb as being characterized by a craving for attention are obviously of this type.

Attachment-hypoactive children

The drive to establish specific attachment in these cases is considerably weakened. These children seem to despair of developing specific relationships and have given up. We can assume either that their internal endowment is constitutionally weak or that their deprivation is of such a kind that it has led to the loss of confidence in specific bonds, as such, eventually to the development of defences against them. Their rejection of, or their inability to establish, intimate relationships is apparent sometimes only when they encounter a situation where such relationships are demanded, and where they are the basis for co-existence in a primary group. Such a child, who may be relatively well adapted in an institute, can be a failure in adoptive or foster care. We mentioned previously the case of a boy who, at eight years of age, was adopted by a very good family but after a period returned to the children's home. He himself described the failure: "They only wanted to cuddle me and I did not want it."

To a certain extent, therefore, we can interpret the tendency to hyper- or hypoactivity towards a specific attachment as chronic persistence of the protest and detachment period described by J. Robertson and J. Bowlby (1952; see page 57).

Finally, we should note that even on this level the child can seek compensatory satisfaction, for example, through a relationship with a substituted unreal object, with an inanimate object (for example, a certain toy). We note also that some institutionalized children do not attach themselves to humans but closely identify with some domestic animal. In this category we can include some cases of fetishism in later age.

Deprivation as lack of personal-social identity

Every child is oriented towards achieving personal autonomy, identifying in a social context, and individual integration at a still higher level. To reach this important and difficult stage of individualization, however, the child must find conditions for the development of the "I" in his own social environment.

If the child, for example, does not perceive clearly specified and distinctive values towards which he can effectively orient his behaviour in the immediate environment, or if he is not given the opportunity to realize this goal through his own resources, the establishment of the "I" is delayed or misdirected. Similarly if the child, in his contact with people who are close to him, does not recognize their expectations about his behaviour or about the behaviour of other people, and if this behaviour is not evaluated retrospectively, discriminating, meaningful acceptance of social roles (his own and those of other people) and a satisfying feeling of identity and self-evaluation do not develop.

If the child achieves a certain autonomy and a basic feeling of personal integrity, and then suddenly is deprived of conditions which encourage this development, he experiences existential anxiety — anxiety because the newly established "I" is threatened either physically (fear of body-damage) or on the personal social level (fear of loss of personal integrity, with accompanying feelings of shame and humiliation).

The child is threatened by this type of deprivation whenever the conditions necessary for personal and social participation do not exist to an adequate extent, or where they are unattainable or incomprehensible.

This occurs in the environments which do not reflect the real social relationships in society. For example, in an institution, children do not understand the different roles of father and mother, of younger and older siblings, nor other roles which they would normally experience in the family, and on the basis of which they construct models for their own social behaviour. The child cannot achieve that insight into social structure which incorporates his complementary role and the hierarchy of status which is so important for efficient functioning in society. The inadequate "I" which the child constructs from the available resources is denied the necessary reassurance and support.

In the institutional environment the child is usually not given enough praise, assurance, or advice about achievement or non-achievement of goals through his own efforts. Such a child, therefore, does not learn to value his own success nor does he learn from his failures. His self-image and his perception of other people are distorted; his striving for autonomy dissipates. This is often shown in a dramatic way by apparently well-adapted children when they leave the protective institutional environment at fifteen years of age and enter the more complex social and work environment where they should find their status and create their own independent social existence. Some of these children face a crisis when they are expected to adopt adult roles for which they are unprepared (the role of husband, father, and so on).

Even in the family, however, a child can suffer through deprivation of this sort, for example, in a family of low socio-cultural level, where he does not encounter the roles typical of the broader social environment, or where the values he learns are different from those in society as a whole. Despite this, such culturally deprived children achieve some feeling of ego identity and fulfilment although on a different level of social participation.

The child who lives in a family of normal or high socio-cultural status may face a different problem. Here the family may have created a personally and socially meaningless space for the child. This applies in cases where child care is extremely permissive, where the child is not faced with demands of any sort, nothing is expected of him, his behaviour is not evaluated, nor is he faced with any goals which are difficult to achieve. This contrasts with perfectionist child care which is characterized by absolute norms and expectations which are unrealizable in terms of the child's expectations. The model of such deprivation is thus more likely value deprivation as well as deprivation of social roles.

As on the previous levels, here we can probably distinguish two types of deprived child, depending on the nature of the basic motivational dynamics. We have already noted that the group of socially provocative children (i.e. exhibiting hyperactivity in specific attachment) later subdivides into two groups — the ego-hyperactive children who are aggressive, rebellious, egotistic, and self-demanding, and the ego-hypoactive group who are infantile, playful, with primitive disturbing behaviour, without personal goals and demands (as we mentioned previously, of course, some children oscillate between these extremes). It seems that for some institutionalized children, who only partially achieve their specific object, the search for personal identity, autonomy, and fulfilment at the next developmental level is fraught with considerable difficulty. They either try too hard or give up when their self-realization is obstructed (for example, when stronger and more aggressive individuals are present in the environment).

Ego-hyperactivity

Children of this type seek realization of their "I" — mainly through personal participation in social activities, with particular dedication. Their extreme demand for personal autonomy inevitably leads them into conflict with their supervisors and leaders in the children's groups, they refuse to accept norms in the immediate and broader environment, and in extreme cases they come into conflict with the law. Children of this type are quite common in corrective homes to which they have been committed because of persistent infraction of institutional rules, rebelliousness, opposition, and unwillingness to accept any type of restraint. Their effort to secure personally significant goals leads them to fixate on specific values which are often very primitive, and which are not highly valued by society; for example, they aggressively demand toys and other worthless objects, a better place at the table, a nicer plate, or a better serving of food.

The child's attempt to realize himself in society and to find personal identity is also clearly shown in a strong tendency to assume prominent roles and gain attention or admiration through performance or deviant behaviour. Under normal conditions, of course, individual children perceive their roles in the group differently — either in terms of performance in a particular problem area (because of their strength, skill, knowledge, school record, ability) or in terms of their expressive function (i.e. because of their friendliness, cheerfulness, acceptable social behaviour). The ego-hyperactive child, however, indiscriminately tries to assert himself, takes over any role which promises satisfaction, seeks admiration often through quite inappropriate means; he cannot accurately assess his own strength, or the characteristics and attitudes of others. It is interesting, for example, that amongst children who live in institutes up to school age, by comparison with children who were placed in family care in pre-school age, there are four times as many children who are described by their teachers as "industrious workers" despite lack of success (their school performance is usually very bad). The effort itself is the goal. These children desperately seek admiration and praise from adults (nurses and teachers), but because of their insatiable drive towards self-realization they usually meet only rejection, disapproval, and restriction, which creates further dissatisfaction and only increases their drive. These children show their strong orientation towards personal realization and immediate personal profit by their inability to effectively engage in cooperative tasks and to adopt any but a strictly competitive strategy.

This last fact has been well documented by N. Bauerová and J. Křivohlavý (1974) who compared the performance of twenty boys (aged fourteen—fifteen years) from an institute for correction of behaviour disorders, with that of twenty boys of the same age from families, in an experimental game, "the prisoner's dilemma". The institutionalized boys showed far less willingness to accept a suggestion of cooperation from a partner, and they themselves showed less initiative in leading a partner into cooperation through their own cooperative behaviour. They also expressed less willingness to forgive their partners' non-cooperative behaviour, especially in benevolent strategy. Significantly egotistical behaviour on their part was also shown in other aspects of this study.

We previously referred to a sub-group of children showing tendencies towards aggressive self-realization which emerged from that group of institutionalized children who are characterized as provocative from an early age. If we make a more detailed study during school age of children raised in institutes, we note different types or directions of social hyperactivity. In some children, social hyperactivity is "rather diffuse"; in others it is oriented towards some specific relationship, while in others there is a dominant drive towards self-realization. To a certain extent, all these tendencies are cumulative, they overlap or predominate at different times. As indicated in the sociometric study of Langmeier and Langmeierová (1972) in which social relationships of eleven—fifteen-year-old children in a corrective school home were compared with those of a matched group of children from families, these tendencies characterize the institutionalized population as a whole. Cursory examination of these sociograms shows an extremely wide range of social choices, which clearly indicates the "social hunger" of these children — their simple, diffuse, social hyperactivity. On closer inspection, however, it is obvious that at least some of the children differentiate their positive and negative relationships and attempt to establish specific positive relationships (the average number of positive selections shown by the institutionalized group was significantly higher than that of children from families — 1.28 against 0.65 for boys, and 1.43 against 0.80 for girls). At the same time, the sociograms revealed the intense and diffuse effort of institutionalized children to seek their own roles in the group's social structure, while family children of this age quite clearly differentiate between children whom they select as co-workers in games and competitions (instrumental roles) and those with whom they would like to spend holidays on a deserted island (expressive roles). Children from institutes gave us no sign of such discrimination (cf. sociograms 1—6). By comparison with these two groups, groups of children from children's homes of the family type showed more sophisticated role development than children in corrective institutions, although they did not reach the level of children raised permanently in normally functioning families.

Ego-hypoactive children

These children, either because of insurmountable obstacles or their own limitations, relinquish all effort to achieve their own independence and to find a meaningful status for their "I" in the social environment. They are indifferent to the expectations of others, in social games they play their simple roles in a stereotyped fashion, and accept any role-related status. They willingly remain dependent and show no desire to liberate themselves and act independently. Passive submission to nurses, teachers, and dominating peers seems to give them needed security which they do not want to endanger by risk-taking behaviour. They strive for only the simplest and nearest goals, live for the moment, do not seek and evaluate more distant goals, do not build future goals which they might systematically realize and thus fulfil their "I". Their behaviour reflects a simple ambition and their level of aspiration is low. They are indifferent to success or failure and cannot be motivated either by praise or punishment.

Although this type is less common among institutionalized children than the ego-hyperactive type, nevertheless it is more frequent than amongst family children. As we noted above, amongst children who remain in institutes from baby to school age, there are four times as many children classified by teachers as industrious workers than amongst children transferred into family care. At the same time, however, on the same comparative basis there are three times as many classified as lazy or *flink* (wasters). It seems therefore that if the child remains under institutional care, two extreme forms of behaviour develop — ego-hyperactivity or ego-hypoactivity in searching for social roles and the fulfilment of "I". In this respect children transferred to families are obviously more balanced.

On this level also, we find children who attempt to find

compensatory satisfaction of their drive towards personal integration in immediate sensory experience, in a surfeit of intense sensory stimuli, in complete devotion to work, in the world of fantasy and so on. Some of these individuals, at times, realize the inappropriateness of their goals and the hopelessness of their efforts towards self-fulfilment. Many adolescents experience a bitter feeling of incompatibility between the sought-after goal and the basis of a genuine "I"; they reject unimportant roles which, according to them, people senselessly fulfil, they experience the meaninglessness of all social activity, and an inability to find a personal realization and meaning in life.

The personal-social aspect of deprivation of course has been emphasized mainly by sociologists and social psychologists (see above, O. G. Brim, Jr., 1960). Some authors combine both those aspects which we classified as the third and fourth level in our discussion. Thus L. Bender (1945) considers the basic disorder of the deprived psychopathic child to lie in his primary inability to form an object relationship and in his inability to identify himself in a relationship with other people. Other workers view this type of deprivation as due in large measure to psychopathological defiency in role-playing abilities (H. G. Gough, 1955), i.e. to the inability to anticipate the criticism of others and to share their points of view.

Finally we feel that P. A. Sorokin's (1954) conclusions, which were derived from a quite different type of study, that of large social units, are worth considering. He maintains that reactions to frustration (we would prefer the term deprivation) differ according to circumstances. The possible reactions he describes — egotistic aggression (brutalization, demoralization), dull apathy and patient submissiveness, redoubling of creative powers and other non-aggressive efforts and spiritual and altrustic configuration — resemble the hyperactive and hypoactive solution of self-realization tendencies, eventually adaptation on a more normal level and its substitutional modification.

11   The diagnostic problem

In the classical "alarming" period, a number of workers postulated a syndrome of psychological deprivation. R. A. Spitz referred to hospitalism and anaclitic depression, J. Bowlby to the affectionless psychopath, W. Goldfarb to the institutional child, while others referred simply to the "deprivation syndrome". Research findings to this point, however, do not support such an assumption. Even amongst children raised from an early age under identical institutional conditions, we find different personality development, different symptoms, and differently developed individual characteristics, these differences varying as a function of type, severity, and length of deprivation, and the age at which this occurred.

A number of authors have attempted to apply the Kraepelin-Bleuler diagnostic system in classifying deprivational effects. Where a criterion of developmental rate has been adopted, the effects have been judged in terms of mental retardation; where the criterion of personality disorder has been preferred, categories of psychopathy, neurosis, or psychosis have been employed. Although in recent years this classificatory system, with its specific diagnostic implications and therapeutic perspectives, has been criticized, the fact that it is still used suggests a certain importance and utility.

It is clear that in some cases there is no certainty that psychological starvation is the pathogenic agent. As we noted in previous chapters, symptoms of psychological deprivation can be very different and variable, and can cover a wide range from very mild effects, which can be well within the limits of normal psychological functioning, to severe impairment of intellectual and character development. They can be highly extravagant, resembling a neurotic, psychopathic, even psychotic picture, and sometimes can be converted into somatic symptoms. The fact that all these symptoms can reflect other endogenous and exogenous factors also presents diagnostic difficulties.

DIAGNOSTIC METHODS

In practice diagnosis is based on evidence adduced from anamnestic records and medical and psychological examination, using a number of well-established criteria.

"A deprivation inventory", listing the most common sources of deprivation (M. Dolejši, 1969; J. Šturma, 1970) may be useful, particularly in group studies, but in individual case studies it is usually a very crude instrument.

In the anamnestic records, which should be very detailed, a number of factors appear to be significant — e.g. a history of long-term institutional care, especially when it dates from a very early age, frequent changes in the child-care regime, placement in big "impersonal" institutions, which lack both staff and material resources. Short-term separation tends to produce various neurotic signs rather than marked intellectual retardation, except when conditions are extremely adverse. Deprivations should also be considered likely in those cases where the anamnestic record points to obvious neglect in the family with low social and cultural values, to feebleminded or psychotic parents, to apparently normal families which, to the careful observer, have some "barrier" in the parent-child relationship (sterile, "scientific" care, indifference, demands at variance with a child's capabilities). A thorough check and assessment of the home environment by a social agency should be the starting point of every investigation of developmentally retarded as well as "psychopathic" children. Unfortunately, from this point of view, the anamnestic records of children from one-parent or broken families are usually fragmentary and unreliable, while with institutionalized children we are restricted by lack of information which might throw light on their early life histories. This lack is all the more critical when we remember that deprivation often begins in the family before the child is placed in the institute, and that accurate information from this period is necessary before we can predict the effects of other adverse conditions.

The next diagnostic step is the medical (physical) examination to isolate the physical from other possible etiological factors and to determine their contribution to the psychological disorder. It must also be remembered that deprivation may be a significant factor in some cases showing typical symptoms of physical disorder which are referred to paediatricians — for example, in some babies who show chronic failure to thrive or growth retardation, in dystrophics, particularly when they respond poorly to classical treatment, in children suffering nutritional disorders such as anorexia or hyperorexia, in some children who are markedly hypotonic, have weak postures and unusual motor behaviour, in children with some chronic skin disorders, and in hospitalized and ambulatory patients who require protracted convalescence. The contribution of deprivational and organic factors should be assessed independently. The presence of so-called malformations, degenerative disorders, or less severe CNS dysfunction does not exclude the possibility that deprivation might be involved. In fact, such conditions increase the probability that deprivation, in the long run, will have some effect.

The findings from such examinations, of course, do not always agree. Even if we ignore those cases where the physical and psychological etiological factors are closely related, usually it is difficult to establish whether, for example, disorders of muscle tone and motor disorders are caused by lack of stimulation, or are organically based.

The psychological investigation, which involves a planned programme of testing, and long-term methodical observation of the child in his normal environment, is the most important part of the diagnostic examination. A "test" of deprivation does not exist, nor is it easy to envisage such a test. The judgment of the psychologist about the effects of deprivation, therefore, no matter how uncertain he may be, must be based on his experience and careful evaluation of all available data. The simple numerical statement of mental age or IQ has little value. Such a measure, as a mathematical expression, indicates the average level of psychological functioning at a certain period of time, which does not necessarily reflect the child's true capacity. Changes in IQ in deprived children over a period of time can be surprisingly large — in some cases advancing from debile to normal level. For illustrative purposes, we present one case from our records.

Boy M.O. grew up to the age of fourteen months in the family. The parents were unmarried, they were both retarded, almost illiterate; according to the social worker, the home was "a disaster area". On first examination in the institute, he showed severe developmental retardation (DQ 67). Progress was maintained at this level up to four years of age and the boy adapted to the institutional environment only slowly and with difficulty; he was abnormally irritable and vicious. In his fifth year, however, his mental development progressed to the borderline-normal level, and at the end of the sixth year to the level of low average development (IQ 91). At this stage he was transferred to a special boarding school with a relatively good prognosis.

Today, improved psychometric techniques allow us to make a

detailed, systematic study not only of the child, but also of the parent and supervisor, through projective tests, questionnaires, rating scales, and — perhaps most accurately — through experimental analysis of family group interaction, and so on. In this way, we can assess the relationship of the child to the parents, of the parents to the child, and of the parents to their own parents, so that we can glean some information about the causes of unhealthy tendencies which persist in the family.

The psychiatric examination is also very important. This should differentiate deprivational from other psychiatric disorders, particularly psychosis and organic brain syndromes. Since deprivation is often the underlying cause of frustration and conflict, the child psychiatrist should assess the effect of specific psychopathological factors in the overall clinical picture. Even drug therapy and psychotherapy, which are usually also his function, are, in their own way, diagnostic tests.

DIFFERENTIAL DIAGNOSIS

Clinically, we should make a clear distinction between developmental retardation caused by psychological suffering and mental deficiency, whether hereditarily or organically based, and try to identify the role played by both these types of pathogenic factor. A doctor, if working alone in this diagnostic field, tends to discount the possibility of the psychogenic origin of severe intellectual disorders and is prone also to overlook psychological disorders of a milder sort. R. Dubois and H. Leschanowsky (1957) quote a number of cases of severely deprived children whom the institute's paediatrician diagnosed incorrectly as idiots. His diagnosis was based on assumed encephalitis, heredity, premature birth, innate abnormality, and so on. He proposed committing the children to an asylum which, of course, prognostically, would have been disastrous. The authors comment on the relative frequency of deprivational retardation, which was evident in 72 per cent of the 900 children examined in the medical-psychological centre.

The most frequent difficulty encountered is that of differentiating the mental defective from the regressive, inhibited type of deprived child. As suggested in the reviews of developmental studies of children from Czech institutes (M. Nováková, 1957; A. Smržová, 1957; Z. Matějček, 1960) severest retardation occurs before the end of the second year. In the third year some adaptation is evident, and this increases during the pre-school period and overlaps into the school period. Significant developmental acceleration is one of the outstanding characteristics of deprived children (in the institutional environment) compared with genuinely mentally defective children, whose development continues permanently at about the same level (this also applies to children with MBD who, despite certain speech and motor difficulties, appear bright and curious, especially in the pre-school period, but whose special difficulties mature probably at about school age). Longitudinal observation and developmental assessment at regular intervals, which are sometimes carried out in institutions by child psychiatric and psychological services, are therefore the effective diagnostic, preventive, and therapeutic tools, for they allow us to cope with difficulties which gradually emerge at different stages in the child's development.

Since the child's global developmental quotient is of little value in psychological diagnosis, we must obtain a clearer picture of his developmental level of efficiency by using a number of special tests — of gross and fine motor coordination, adaptability, speech, and so on. With smaller children, Gesell's developmental schedule or the Bühler-Hetzer baby tests, and at times, modifications of these (Brunet-Lézine) have proved satisfactory. The so-called neuro-psychological schedule (J. Koch) which is employed in Czech children's institutes is also useful as a diagnostic tool and for differential assessment of the child's mental development. With older children it is preferable to use a range of selected tests (from drawing and performance tests to tests of knowledge and social information) or intelligence tests allowing differential assessment of verbal functioning and practical aptitude.

Deprivation usually has a different effect at different developmental periods, producing certain characteristic patterns depending on the type and degree of depriving conditions. The classic picture in young children usually includes pronounced speech retardation. In addition to poor pronunciation, which is most marked in institutional children, there is an obvious impoverishment in the structure and content of language. Vocabulary is very poor, and the child gives the impression that he has been "trained" to use certain words, but that he has not "learned to speak". He can name other children, but the use of personal pronouns develops at a very late stage. In addition, words are strung together without any sentence construction; this continues for a long time, often beyond the third year. He is relatively efficient at naming objects in pictures, but it is only later and with difficulty that he can describe the meaning of the events and relations depicted, which presumably would involve an understanding of the underlying relationship between the actual behaviour and its symbolic representation. Lack of early experience in comparing real objects with their graphic representations leads inevitably to a limited understanding of the symbolic nature of the graphical representation. We see in this retardation one of the underlying factors in the characteristic pattern of failure in writing and reading in the first years of schooling. From more detailed analysis, it is evident that here we are not dealing with disorders of perception and orientation in space and time, caused by brain dysfunction, as in the case of developmental dyslexia, but with inability to match perceived symbols with their appropriate content. These disorders, however, are relatively mild, and in many cases there is spontaneous remission at a higher maturational level.

With deprived children, another characteristic speech retardation is in the social use of language. This is usually limited to a commentary on present events, and to statements of present needs. The stage of persistent questioning hardly develops in institutional children, and during the whole of the pre-school period we seldom hear the characteristic "why" of the older toddler. There is also a marked absence of interpretation of ongoing experience and especially the expression of hope, expectations, and wishes for the future. There are few attempts at story telling, or to comment on one's own experiences and expectations. Conversation with adults remains at a very primitive level. The kind of effort made to initiate and maintain such conversation depends on the type of deprivational effect. Children who are socially hyperactive speak a lot, they scream, are exhibitionistic, and at times constantly interrupt. Children who are dominated by material interests tend to speak little, their speech is more defensive than informative.

In addition to retarded speech development, the deprived child has poor social and hygienic habits (bodily cleanliness, dressing, other independent habits). Development of these requires close contact between the child and an adult. Finally with deprived (particularly institutional) children, we note marked retardation in the development of fine motor coordination, which usually contrasts with the relatively good development of gross motor coordination (which appears to be more retarded in cases of family deprivation in the first developmental period) during the pre-school age. Under usual institutional conditions there is evidence that the child has a more limited experience through lying on his belly, a poorer mastery of head movement (he is cuddled less), and some retardation in sitting and walking. As soon as he can move independently, however, gross motor coordination develops relatively quickly. This is aided nowadays by special physical education programmes for infants, which have generally been incorporated into the normal educational programmes of children's institutes. On the other hand, there is less opportunity for development of fine motor coordination, since for reasons of hygiene and protection the child is not given enough small objects to handle before the end of the second year. The effects are usually noticeable throughout the pre-school period, and are shown in clumsy handling of a pencil during the first school years.

The development of adaptive behaviour (perception, object manipulation, play, use of tools, adaptation to a task situation, general expression of practical intelligence) is usually maintained at a slightly under-average or even average level. This is the reason for employing this criterion in assessing the child's real ability. It differentiates the deprived child from the mentally retarded child, and has practical value, particularly in examining children who are offered for adoption.

With older deprived children we find, overall, a lower performance on intelligence tests. There is often a marked difference between the performance and the verbal IQs, the latter being usually well below the former. Under the same examination conditions, which involve a working relationship with the child (which, in itself, has diagnostic significance), we find an unevenness of mental functioning also in the MBD child. Here, however, low level of drawing and low achievement in performance tests, difficulties in spatial orientation and in motor and perceptual tasks are most noticeable. A child with congenital mental retardation presents the picture, overall, of lower performance level, but the profile is fairly even. The deprived child shows marked inability in tests of reasoning, general knowledge, social information, practical judgment and evaluation; on the other hand, the MBD child usually performs relatively well in these tests.

The MBD child typically approaches a given task eagerly, sometimes even hastily, he works impulsively, he adjusts quite well to some tasks but to others surprisingly poorly. The mentally retarded child has difficulty in adjusting and needs direction in every new situation — he is less capable of learning. A deprived child, depending on the type of damage, finds difficulty in working independently, is usually distracted by external stimuli, but may respond relatively quickly to task training, adjusts to the task, works well under directed supervision, and does not experience the characteristic MBD failures. The assessment of institutional children by verbal intelligence tests, therefore, gives a false estimate of their mental capacity.

The majority of six-year-old institutional children show poor school readiness (see page 200). Emotional immaturity, poorly developed work and social habits, in addition to the factors we have already mentioned, ensure that in most cases school progress, usually in the first classes, will be far below the level of capacity.

The quality of the child's reactions to persons and objects provides valuable clues for the diagnosis of deprivational disorder. The typical MBD child immediately establishes contact with the experimenter, unselfconsciously and without any difficulty. A mentally retarded child's behaviour is similar to that of a younger child — he reacts positively to the experimenter's approach if it is appropriate to his mental age. A deprived child, however, has considerable difficulty in establishing effective working relations, although the reasons for this can vary greatly (inhibition, diffuse social hyperactivity, provocation, strong defence mechanisms). We are referring here to the deprivational types (page 318); the type which is most likely to be confused with the classic encephalopathic child is the socially hyperactive type.

Our observations recorded at the time when institutional children were examined in a diagnostic centre rather than in the children's institute itself, which is the present practice, are of some value. While the child was in the larger group in the waiting room, his behaviour was similar to that of other pre-school children waiting in the same room with their mothers. When he was taken from the group and left alone in the examination room with the psychologist, however, after the initial joyous response to the toys his interest quickly waned, he became restless and cried "because the children will go away". Children from families were usually satisfied with the presence of the mother in the waiting room and cooperated fairly confidently with the psychologist. But it was impossible to individually examine most of the institutionalized pre-school children because of their inability to adapt to the new conditions. When they were admitted to the examination room in a group, however, this was possible, since the child received some support from the other children who were playing freely in the room. Here we are obviously concerned with a factor of group dependency, which we consider to be one of the most significant diagnostic indices of the institutional deprived child. As we have already mentioned, this characterized some groups of concentration camp children in a particularly obvious way, and was the basis for later retraining (see page 155).

In some cases a deprived child cooperates better in the presence of a familiar nurse or supervisor; this is an important index of the quality of the surrogate mother care. In a similar way, we might regard the gradual establishment of a positive relationship between child and therapist as a favourable sign, whether it takes a few days, some weeks, or repeated attempts. Usually remission of other pathological symptoms and improved adjustment follows. Success or failure of the therapeutic approach is often a critical symptom of the pathogenic nature of the retardation. We must remember, however, that these approaches can produce similar results in milder cases of organic defect. Another fundamental therapeutic test is the child's reaction to transfer to better conditions.

Strange, even quite bizarre, behaviour, lack of contact with the world, and marked behavioural variability in some retarded children can raise the question of early child psychosis (L. Kanner's [1949] early infantile autism, B. Rank's [1949] atypical development, B. H. Brask's [1959] borderline schizophrenia). Until recently, most of these children were simply classified as feebleminded, and placed in institutions for ineducable children. Today, although many questions are still unanswered, the possibility of early child psychosis is more frequently recognized, and the need for early diagnosis more strongly emphasized. Immediate medical attention is critical for the future development of this type of child, even though the prognosis is always uncertain.

There are three classic symptoms of fully developed early psychosis: (1) early onset, usually beginning in the first year; (2) intolerance of any change; (3) extreme isolation from the human (but not material) environment (H. H. Eveloff, 1960). Lack of anticipatory movements prior to handling (stretching out hands, mumbling, smiling) and expressionless frozen looks are amongst the first symptoms. The older child typically does not recognize his own parents, and gives the impression that he would like to be left alone. Identification of schizophrenic symptoms in a child who up to this point has developed normally presents greater difficulties. We should always consider this possibility when there are sudden marked changes in behaviour or in the general state of the child — refusal of all, or only solid, food, sleep disorders, sudden inexplicable loss of weight, a mournful expression, absence of the normal screaming response when meeting strangers, an obvious shunning of the outside world, a tendency towards stereotyped behaviour of almost obsessive nature.

Parents usually ignore these first symptoms. Initially it is difficult to differentiate between the destructive handling of objects and a certain amount of fearful and impulsive behaviour in these children and the neurotic symptoms of over-sensitive children. If the onset is gradual, diagnosis of child psychosis is more difficult still. It seems clear that today the incidence of early child psychosis is low, although research workers are aware of its existence and are constantly alert.

At times it is hard to differentiate between deprivation disorders of personality and schizophrenia in later childhood. There are some obvious similarities − lack of affective reactivity, low level of interpersonal contact, lack of initiative and interest extending to apathy, paucity of abstract thinking, stereotyped and bizarre motor behaviour. But there are also some fundamental differences. W. Goldfarb (1949) identifies one of these as differences in levels of anxiety. A schizophrenic child reacts to the primary inadequacy of his personality (caused by his psychotic processes) by deep anxiety, which produces a variety of defensive reactions. An institutional child, on the other hand, shows little or no anxiety. He remains generally indifferent to frustrating situations, is not affected by success or failure, does not feel shame or guilt, is not stimulated by competition. A schizophrenic child perseveres, is pedantic and perfectionist, shows dread and bizarre individualized fantasies. Goldfarb supports his claim with consistent findings from Rorschach testing. However, even these differences are valid only in the most clear-cut cases of certain types of institutional deprivation.

Generally speaking, we should consider the possibility of psychological deprivation in cases which present a variety of behaviour and character disorders, and which child psychiatrists usually diagnose as neurotic disorders, conduct disorders, or psychopathy. The symptomatology of these psychiatric disorders is usually very broad; the symptoms of deprivation may cover their whole range. However, in any case, we must distinguish the disorders produced by other factors (overstress, conflict, psychological trauma, illness, for example) from those caused by deprivation. We have already described in some detail the temporary neurotic response of children who are suddenly transferred from the home to an institution or hospital. Some show anxiety, depression, withdrawal, and fear, while others are hostile to adults and other children, are regressive, undisciplined, and suspicious. If the deprivational conditions are severe and long-lasting, more severe symptoms can be anticipated. With pre-school children these are likely to be regressive in character − the child regresses to an earlier period, refuses to eat unaided, wets his bed, is unconcerned about his physical health, and does not speak or play, all he wants is to be cuddled and petted. We strongly suspect deprivation when we encounter atypical indiscriminating − i.e. primitive − relationships with people − the child either refuses to speak to anyone, rejects any attempt to make contact, is shy and indifferent, or is obsequious to strangers, restless, and superficially easily establishes contact with any person at all. In older children this infantile level of behaviour is shown more in efforts to constantly attract attention from an adult — the child repeatedly calls the nurse, issues a variety of complaints, and at times develops severe hysterical attacks. Hostility is sometimes overtly expressed to adults; with other children they are moody, vicious, sly (they will hurt another sneakily, then perhaps "tittle-tattle").

Since simple observation alone is not an adequate diagnostic procedure in these cases, a range of personality tests is particularly useful. Besides the Rorschach test, different behaviour ratings, rating scales, analysis of free and directed play, of artistic productions, and a number of projective methods (Thematic Apperception test, story completion, Wartegg's test, tests of frustration) can be employed. Since the reliability and validity of these tests vary, they cannot be relied on as the sole diagnostic criterion. They are useful, however, in rounding out the total picture and in providing greater insight in individual cases.

In her study of severely deprived children, J. M. Williams (1961) reported striking consistencies in the use of colours in the Rorschach protocols (particularly the use of black and the darker colours), and indications of abnormal family experiences in the responses from the Thematic Apperception Tests devised by L. Jackson and from the Bene-Anthony test. Children often gave accounts of a deserted or neglected child, were convinced of his badness and of the parents' desire to punish him severely. Lack of a feeling of belongingness was very marked. M. L. Kellmer-Pringle and V. Bossio (1958) reported that an idealized picture of the hero's mother was the most prominent feature of deprived institutionalized children's responses on Raven's projective test. Observations from Czech pre-school children's homes also suggest that the content of fantasies produced by some children relate to the idealized mother figure, even when the child is motherless, or doesn't know his mother and has been given no information about her. The mother figure is the subject of discussion and dispute amongst the children (sometimes the child will boast about the mere existence of the mother). Non-deprived children never behave in this way.

The possibility of psychological deprivation should always be considered in cases of delinquency in older children and adolescents. Children who constantly pilfer, wander, play truant from school, who persistently lie, are vicious and aggressive, quite often have suffered emotional stress for long periods during development. Although there is no incontrovertible evidence for the type of deprived delinquent described by J. Bowlby (1946) as the "affectionless" psychopath, the lack of rapport, inability to establish worthwhile contact with other people, emotional flatness, and general lack of social adaptability in these cases support the diagnosis of deprivational disorder. As distinct from other delinquent types, these children are usually lone wolves, do not belong to gangs, are quarrelsome, unreliable, blame other people, and sometimes appear to be devoid of pity of shame.

Lumping all cases together into a general deprivation category of course is not a satisfactory alternative to a thorough analysis of all conditions. In every case of deprivation, it is particularly important to distinguish between emotional and stimulus deprivation, to establish clearly the quality of the maternal or the substitute care, and of the developmental environment, the general family situation, the personalities and attitudes of the parents, and finally institutional conditions and the interpersonal relationships within such institutions. We must remember also that children react somewhat differently to environmental conditions, have different physical and psychological constitutions, abilities, physical endurance, needs and goals, and may have been differently affected by previous early traumatizing experiences. Only a matching of the child's personality to the specific deprivational circumstances will allow us to determine the deprivational mechanisms, and to understand both the short- and long-term effects on behaviour, and to determine when deprivation plays a crucial role, when it operates only as an additional factor, and how it interacts with other conditions to produce the final outcome. While undoubtedly in the past the importance of deprivational consequences was overlooked, today there is a danger that these will be over-emphasized. Professor G. Heuyer (1958) rightly comments that cases of pure hospitalism are exceptional, and that we should study cases of deprivation of the child in the family more closely.

There is a clear case for a team approach involving paediatricians, child psychiatrists, psychologists, social workers, teachers, and possibly neurologists. To a large extent the effectiveness of medical, re-educative, and therapeutic services depends on early diagnosis. Any person who has any contact with deprived children — paediatricians, those involved in child care (particularly in institutions), social workers, and child nurses — should be familiar with the presenting symptoms.

Well-planned diagnostic procedure, which should be careful and detailed, must never disturb the therapeutic prospects, but must be the basis of a remedial programme. Since when dealing with deprived children we are primarily concerned with the extent to which they can establish contact with other people, it is hardly appropriate that such contact should be neutral or coldly objective. It is more appropriate for the investigator to approach the child sympathetically, to interact empathically while observing him, and attempt to establish the most favourable human contact, for this is not only the prerequisite of a reliable diagnosis, but is also the first step towards treatment and rehabilitation.

12 Prognosis and treatment of deprivational disorders

Studies during the "alarming" period led to the very pessimistic conclusion that the effects of long-term psychological deprivation in early childhood are severe and almost irreversible. Placing the child in a healthier environment after the disturbances have developed has no effect. This view was advanced by H. T. Wolley in 1930 from his analysis of selected cases, by W. Goldfarb (1943a) from his catamnestic studies with children aged ten—fourteen, by D. Levy (1937) who states that there is little hope of improvement, and by L. Bender (1945) who insisted that all efforts should be directed towards the prevention of deprivation, since therapy is quite useless.

While opinions vary on the age during which deprivation is critical, and how long-term such deprivation must be before results are irreversible, most authors agree with J. Bowlby's (1951) opinion that therapy can be effective only when deprivation occurs before the sixth or possibly the twelfth month, and that it is always ineffective when this period extends beyond two and a half years. R. A. Spitz (1946a) maintained that the symptoms of anaclitic depression disappear with surprising speed if the mother returns or if a surrogate is found within five months. If the deprivation persists, however, the effects are more or less permanent. According to R. A. Spitz (1946a) a six months' institutional stay, with total separation from mother, almost inevitably has a permanent, adverse effect on the child. Even brief but repeated separations traumatize the child more or less permanently (J. Robertson and J. Bowlby, 1952). All remedial efforts, therefore, must be directed towards prevention.

Later studies, however, were somewhat more optimistic. We have already cited relevant evidence from our own and other studies that successful therapy is still possible at adolescence and early adulthood (D. Beres and S. J. Obers, 1950; the Clarkes, 1959; and others); even in cases of fully developed anaclitic depression, there is normal mental development after placement in a good foster home, although emotional disorders persist (J. B. Richmond and L. Hersher 1958, 1961; S. R. Lewis and S. Van Ferney, 1960). A case in point is the relatively quick adjustment of children who were severely deprived in concentration camps. M. A. Ribble (1945, 1965) also reports dramatic improvement in a number of marasmic babies, "shown in increased appetite and liveliness and greater reactivity", after the babies were committed to the full personal care of selected foster mothers. Similar results were reported when children were introduced to the system of "the beloved". This outcome might be expected, judging from F. B. Talbot's (1913) report of the case of old Anna, who took children in a clinic in Düsseldorf under her maternal care. She was the model for this type of simple emotional treatment, which often produced extraordinary results in cases where medical care had previously been quite ineffective.

In addition to these cases of almost spontaneous remission of deprivational disorders in a more normal life environment, numerous case histories describe the success of planned therapy in severe cases of deprivation. M. C. Gelinier-Ortigues (1955) reports successful therapy of a child with very severe psycho-motor retardation (DQ 38, according to the Gesell norms), functional deafness, and physical debility. R. Dubois and H. Leschanowsky (1957) refer to the case of a child raised in an institute, who, at seventeen months of age, had a DQ of around 10, was diagnosed an idiot, and was recommended to be placed in an asylum. However, following a short hospital stay, and transfer into the tender care of his grandparents, the child progressed so quickly that at the age of thirty-nine months his level of intellectual functioning was normal. In one of our own cases, a child who at first appeared to be an imbecile showed considerable improvement after a few months of intensive hospital care.

We might argue that if improvement is possible in such severe cases, much more should be possible in milder cases. However, we should guard against too great optimism. Although in our opinion the prognosis of deprivational disorders is not hopeless, neither is it highly favourable. Current opinion suggests that severe and long-term deprivation usually produces serious and at least some permanent effects in a child's psychological structure. The younger the child and the longer the deprivation, the smaller the chance that the deprivational effects can be completely abolished. It is also very likely that some effects — mainly emotional — will persist even when the patient shows quite normal levels of social and intellectual development. M. D. Ainsworth (1962) reminds us that even short-term deprivational experiences, which may produce no obvious symptoms, deposit at least one hidden trace — increased vulnerability to repeated encounters with similar situations or other unfavourable life situations.

It is probable that therapeutic outcomes will be improved when we can identify the fundamental mechanisms of deprivation more clearly. The human psyche may have unsuspected adaptive resources. Workers who view deprived children as a homogeneous group with unique symptomatology understandably search for a standard therapeutic approach. If the primary cause of deprivation is considered to be the child's separation from the mother, they attempt to restore contact, or at least to provide an acceptable surrogate. If they see the sole cause as lack of sensory stimulation, the therapeutic treatment involves placement in an enriched environment. When we consider the whole range of clinical patterns of deprivation, however, and the different conditions under which these develop, we should plan individual care and treatment to meet individual needs, basing this on a complete analysis of environmental conditions and a detailed knowledge of the psychological and physical state of the child. The more thoroughly we consider the individual child, the greater the therapeutic effects are likely to be; the earlier we begin, the greater the chance of success.

In a previous chapter we attempted to show that deprivational effects can occur at different levels of mental functioning. From this it follows logically that therapy should involve the four levels we discussed in detail in the theoretical section, or at least those which are most severely affected.

1. Re-activation

If early deprivation produces disorders at the deepest level, as seen in apathy and poor emotional tone, we must withdraw the child from the depriving situaiton, and ensure an adequate input of environmental stimuli. This usually involves very young children, and the effectiveness of these procedures decreases with increase in the child's age. In practice, here we are concerned with adaptive therapy, which includes stimulation of the child's central nervous system by controlled input of sensory stimuli (e.g. by handling and cuddling, "music" therapy, activation therapy, vegeto-therapy, relaxation therapy), by drugs, and through provision of conditions which facilitate motor functioning and normal functioning of the sensory organs (rehabilitation, treatment of sensory disabilities, and so on).

2. Re-learning

Obviously some deprivation effects can be eliminated by direct repetitive learning. A child is given selected, limited, and controlled stimuli, which reinforce the desired behaviour while other stimuli are excluded, so that unwanted behaviours will extinguish. Here, we are basically concerned with substitution of new, more useful habits for old maladaptive habits which are the symptoms of "the deprivational syndrome". The so-called behaviour therapy techniques are included in this category, as are other special training methods — speech therapy, training of motor skills, formal schooling, the development of practical knowledge and skills, training in social adaptation in the peer group, in broader society, and in particularly demanding situations. All means of arousing curiosity and learning drives in the child should be employed so that learning is sought after, and is satisfying, rather than passive — the child is motivated towards discovery.

3. Reattachment

Some disorders can be treated most appropriately by adjustment of the child's relationship to his social and material environment. We must change the child's relationships to humans and other objects and remodel his character. In practical terms, this means that we should employ psychotherapy in its narrower sense of remoulding the personality as an organized entity. We must help the child to discover and acquire the necessary organizational factors in an acceptable way. By this we mean primarily strong feelings of trust, sympathy, security, and love towards those who are concerned with his care.

4. Re-socialization

At the highest level we must re-introduce the child to society and encourage him to achieve true independence and to acquire useful social roles. Within and with the help of society, the child liberates himself from deprivational effects, and establishes new, satisfying relationships with his environment. We could call this process socio-therapy, which would include already recognized family therapy, some forms of group therapy, and less directed and less formally planned child-care approaches in children's groups.

As we noted previously (page 316), if we are dealing with specific forms of deprivation in children growing up in an institutional environment, individual treatment should begin at different levels. With inhibited, passive, regressive children we must increase the general level of awareness and organismic activity. This is the necessary condition for further therapeutic progress. The type characterized by compensatory satisfaction of needs, i.e. by an extravagant interest in the material world, in food, in autoerotic manipulation, and so on, can be trained to extinguish these behaviours, and to establish new, more useful behaviours through conditioning techniques. It is not difficult to engage such a child in play; the difficulty lies in making contact with him. Therapeutic treatment, therefore, should be directed away from the world of objects towards the social environment.

Those types characterized in their social activity by extravagant responsiveness, either aggressive and provocative or superficial and non-involved, need increased input of organizers rather than increased activation to direct their activity and make it more meaningful. The problem here is not one of establishing contact, but of increasing it to the point where the child acquires emotional security, and can quietly engage in normal activity — play, learning, and work. In this case it would be proper to use both psychotherapy and socio-therapy. Therapy should progesss from the therapist towards the objective world.

Finally, we should probably attempt some supportive socio-therapy with those institutionalized children whom we described as relatively well adapted. Children who can develop feelings of security and successful relationships with supervisors even in institutes quite often fail in more demanding situations requiring quick social orientation and independent thinking. We must prepare them specifically for more and more highly developed social roles, and teach them independence and responsibility.

It is quite obvious that in individual cases it is unnecessary and often quite impossible to systematicaly proceed from level one to level four, since these overlap and cannot be clearly differentiated. In practice, our main concern is that therapy will be of widest possible application and suitably adapted to individual children. In the interests of clarity, however, we shall use this schema as a general principle in developing our argument.

RE-ACTIVATION

A considerable amount of evidence attests that the inhibitory regressive deprivational types are usually weak children who show a constitutional tendency towards retardation in motor development. It is obvious that children who are diagnosed as inhibited, passive, and apathetic on transfer from the baby to the toddler home have already shown retardation in motor development from the first months of life. Since the input of stimuli under impoverished environmental conditions is dependent on the child's level of activity, an endless cycle of lack of activity restricting stimulus input develops. It is possible that this cycle can be successfully broken, and that the child can be helped towards more extensive activity through "baby exercises", massage, and special exercises for motor development. On the other hand, children suffering from MBD (even slight), whose behaviour is characterized by a high level of irritability, restlessness, and unbalanced reactivity from the beginning, under institutionalized conditions become strikingly hyperactive through the stress of global input of stimuli (e.g. undifferentiated noise in children's groups). Early diagnosis and drug treatment of these children can damp down the general level of stimulus input, decrease cortical excitability, and lead to a more adaptive, appropriate participation in ongoing environmental activity. The removal of all somatic and sensory defects is also a necessary condition of therapy in all cases where these defects are an inner barrier isolating the child from the surrounding social world (page 243). Often there is spontaneous improvement in the physical condition of some deprived children after transfer to a new, more stimulating environment. This can be either a cause or an effect of improvement in general mental health. One must ensure correct diet, a stable regime, and good hygienic conditions for the child. Involvement of the child's doctor, possibly even a child psychiatrist, is necessary for therapeutic treatment at this level.

Therapeutic progress of a very young deprived child is demonstrated in the following case.

Child R.D. was admitted to the children's department of a hospital at the age of twelve months with symptoms of dystrophy; she was pale, weak, smelly, filthy, and suffered acute rhinopharyngitis. Home conditions were obviously extremely bad. The father, a farm hand, was primitive, selfish, drank too much, and used the mother and children to do his work. The mother was ground down, tearful, exhausted, quite passive, with a pronounced stammer and of low intelligence. Three older children spent most of the day completely unsupervised. At home, the child spent most of the time lying apathetically or rocking, she was sad, very seldom babbled, and was frightened when anybody (even the father) spoke to her. In the first days after admission she continued to lose weight, lay down for the whole day, rocked her arms and head from side to side with her tongue poking out, staring into the far distance. When anyone entered her cubicle, she started to cry fearfully and to suck her thumb strongly; she refused to sit even with help, and threw away toys when they were given to her. After a few days the child began to relax, and could bear the presence of somebody else in the cubicle — at least when the person did not turn directly towards her. The psychologist was able to establish the simplest contact only very gradually — a look from a distance, a smile, soft humming, subsequently even tapping and slight rhythmical movement. Contact at first had to be very carefully managed, and was usually indirect, for any direct approach to the child touched off an anxiety reaction.

Even such minimal contact produced changes in the child's behaviour; with some help she would sit longer, smiled more often, her appetite improved, and the weight curve accelerated (fig. 65).

During this time the child was entrusted to the individual care of one sister, who was devoted to her most of the day, even in her spare time. Three weeks after admission, the child was able to sit and stand up alone, using the bar around the bed, was interested in toys, started to babble; while alone, however, she still maintained her automatisms. During the next month, the child's progress was dramatic. She could tolerate such demanding contact as being lifted and thrown up in the air, and when laid back on the bed stretched out her hands, and by calling, actively demanded further attention. She was cheerful and active, and started walking around the bed. Weight increase was about one kilogram.

At this point she was returned to her mother's care. When she was handed over she began to cry. The mother had previously spent most of the day out of the home, leaving the child completely alone, rarely speaking to her. Although she appeared to love the child, she lacked the time or willpower and interest to become involved. At this point we attempted to change her attitude. As far as possible, she spent the whole day at home, and devoted all her time to the child. The social workers helped to establish more acceptable conditions of hygiene and care through family visits, and contrary to the advice of municipal agencies, it was not necessary to commit the child to permanent institutional care. In the referral examination, when the child was sixteen months old, the wisdom of this decision was obvious; the child was thriving, in three weeks she had gained another kilogram, and her weight was gradually approaching normal. She was active and running about independently, could speak first words in the idiom, and played energetically. Although she was still slightly retarded, the prognosis was favourable, the more so because she was now able to acquire stimuli independently, and because through her new attitudes (acquired in the hospital) she was able to actively demand attention and contact and provoke an emotional response from the mother who had previously been indifferent. The mother admitted that for the first time she derived satisfaction from the child's behaviour and from her surprising development.

RE-LEARNING

The possibility of therapeutic treatment of deprivational disorders through training programmes has already been suggested by a group of Iowa workers. They demonstrated that such programmes can improve intellectual functioning, and adaptation to the social environment and to work demands in deprived children. Therapeutic work, of course, cannot be based solely on planned programmes, but must be directed by the individual needs of the child.

Therapeutic techniques based on modern learning theories have been systematically developed over the past ten years. This approach (usually termed behaviour therapy) involves either classical or operant conditioning procedures — sometimes a combination of both — in the treatment of individual cases.

Although behaviour therapy is not appropriate for all cases, a number of studies affirm its usefulness in suitably selected cases. For example, this has been amply demonstrated in a number of severe cases of infantile autism (discussed more fully on page 141).

G. C. Davison (1964) reports relatively great improvement in the progress of some autistic children. He made the initial assumption that the autistic child does not react normally to social stimuli, and that therapy, therefore, must begin with his primary (mostly physiological) needs as the basis for reinforcement of certain types of behaviour. For example, every time the child paid attention to the therapist or obeyed his instructions, he was rewarded with a sweet. Undesirable behaviours, e.g. fits of rage, were ignored, contrary to the mother's usual response, and gradually extinguished. Type of reinforcement was also varied during therapy. These techniques produced dramatic behavioural changes — e.g. in a nine-year-old boy who from an early age was an isolate, ignored others, refused to be disciplined, had frequent emotional outbursts, did not speak or read, and played only at a very primitive level. After an intensive therapeutic programme directed by a teacher (five hours a day for six months) the boy became more disciplined, reacted to people and surroundings more normally, performed more satisfactorily in a variety of tasks, and began to read and write. Obviously it is necessary to systematically reinforce every positive social response. This is admitted even by those authors who assume that this disorder is biologically based (J. L. Schulman, 1963; B. Rimland, 1964).

Although learning therapy has not been used extensively with very young children, it is clear that best results can be anticipated from this group. B. C. Etzel and J. L. Gewirtz (1966) report successful behaviour modification in two institutionalized children of six and twenty weeks of age, who demanded attention by tyrannical screaming (*"tyranno-tearus infantus"*), through consistent non-reinforcement of the behaviour. Other therapists have used similar methods with pre-school children.

It is clear that a number of disorders in social behaviour and bad habits of deprived children can be treated successfully by the methods described above. Some clinical workers, therefore, have attempted to devise more extensive programmes of treatment of developmental disorders.

One such, though not so firmly anchored in learning theory, has been suggested by B. M. Flint (1966) for toddlers in the usual type of institutional setting. The critical element in the programme is provision of extensive play facilities demanding different degrees of involvement. Staffing, which includes volunteer helping mothers, is so arranged that every child has a companion of his own, so that feelings of individuality are reinforced. These feelings are further reinforced by consistent emphasis on individual behaviours such as dressing, making beds, and so on. The children's attempts to do something independently are approved and reinforced as much as possible. Children are encouraged from the earliest possible age to become independent of the personal care of the staff. Only at this point are small child-care groups formed, for which children are selected according to their behavioural characteristics and, more importantly, according to the personality of the supervisor. This type of programme is important as a preparation for transfer to a foster or adoptive family, where the child is given full opportunity for permanent emotional anchoring for the first time.

REATTACHMENT

With some deprived children, of course, rehabilitation is

possible through psychotherapy in the narrow sense of the word. Although this may be effective only in certain cases (we lack valid data on this point) the psychotherapeutic approach, based on a close emotional relationship between child and therapist, is undoubtedly useful in every case.

Since deprivation is usually due to inadequate satisfaction of the child's emotional needs in his present environment, initially one must provide the opportunity for readjustment of the present level of emotional experience. This means, in effect, that we must provide the child with the significant emotional experiences he lacks. Thus, it is critically important for the child to establish a close emotional relationship with the psychotherapist which can be the bridge he uses to gradually establish the newer, richer, more realistic relationships with the social environment. However, because of the very nature of deprivation, this is particularly difficult to establish. A deprived child creates an environment in which his individual idiosyncratic modes of behaviour are best maintained and further reinforced — he is usually indifferent, or even rejecting, or is totally incapable of establishing interpersonal relationships. The majority of adults, when faced with such an unresponsive child, very quickly give up any attempt to establish contact, and the circle is again closed.

A similar situation develops when the child loses his emotional stability through repeated separation, and for this reason actively rejects contact by aggression and hostile attitudes towards adults. The task of the psychotherapist is to overcome this barrier by patience and skilful treatment, by accepting the child as he is, and by offering him assurance about the validity of the new relationship, an assurance which the child has never before experienced. If the therapist accepts the child's hostility without retaliation, usually the attitudes of the child gradually change and his level of aggression decreases.

Of course, this simple, natural, accepting attitude is in itself not enough — there must also be certain psychotherapeutic knowledge and skill; in addition, the personality of the therapist is very important in determining the outcome of therapeutic work with different children. We must also recognize that work with deprived, usually retarded, children is less satisfying for the therapist than work with neurotic superior children, for example, and that such work is more difficult and prolonged. Dramatic improvement, which provides the therapist with feedback, seldom occurs in this type of work. The theoretical orientation of the therapist, his experience, and his scientific training will decide which psychotherapeutic method will be used in a particular case. At this point in time, adequate criteria on which to base selection of appropriate psychotherapeutic techniques in particular cases are not available.

In the Clinic of Social Paediatrics in Warsaw, I. Bielicka (1963) and co-workers developed so-called pre-verbal psychotherapy, which they used with children of baby and toddler age who were offered for adoption from institutions. This involved establishment of basic contact with the child through tactile, auditory, visual, and kinaesthetic stimulation; an attempt was made to develop an exchange of stimuli similar to that existing between mother and child before they begin to communicate by speech.

Pre-verbal communication of this sort is also the starting point for so-called regressive therapies. These therapies begin with the assumption that the deprived child is locked at a primitive level of emotional and intellectual development, and that before he can achieve a healthy adjustment, he must return to this primitive level and relive his experiences under healthier conditions. For example, C.O. Jonsson in Sweden, B. Bettelheim (1956) and E. Sylvester in the United States, A. Friedemann (1958) in Switzerland, encourage children to behave on a primitive level. Even ten-year-old children can drink from a bottle, are fed, dressed, can speak in childish pattern, and can be totally dependent on their nurses. Since bodily contact is usually the most primitive and the first form of contact, this is the basis on which a relationship between the child and the therapist can be developed. This applies mainly to severely retarded children. The first stage of contact is limited often to petting, placing the head on the lap and cuddling, and only gradually do other types of communication — visual, auditory, and finally speech — develop. Even here, however, we must respect the child's individuality and begin with the situation which evokes the most favourable reaction in the child.

Body contact is also the basis of Nic Waal's (1955) vegeto-therapy, in which contact is initiated by rhythmical cuddling, tender and emotional touching, and by massage of different parts of the body. The child-therapist relationship is initially "activating" in character (clinging and support, feeling of comfort, security of being loved). The integrity of these relationships is the basis for the gradual development of higher-order relationships. Thus the child initially must be allowed to have basic emotional experiences.

One form of regressive therapy, Azima's (1961) anaclitic isolation, uses sensory isolation to induce total dependency of the patient (adult) on the therapist, a relationship similar to that between mother and baby. The patient is fed, cared for, and protected. It is claimed that this method is suitable for patients who have a history of severe deprivation in early childhood, and who are aware of both their need for love and the anxiety which this love brings with it. Bottle feeding in an infant-like state is also an intermediate step (following electrolytic therapy) in H. C. Tien's (1970) "psychosynthesis".

I. W. Charny (1963) describes another form of isolation therapy, in which children were separated in special rooms without toys or other sources of stimulation for two to five months. Social contact was limited to visits by the therapists. Initially these children showed increasing anxiety, followed by a weakening of defence mechanisms, so that their personalities could be rebuilt under the guidance of the psychotherapists.

Progress towards higher levels depends on the resources of the child. In most severe cases we should anticipate progress over a period of years rather than months or weeks. Initially, the therapist must meet the child's basic needs without reservation (possibly the only exception is where the child's health is endangered). He must avoid unnecessary frustrations and must fall in with the child's wishes, since the deprived child gains little from frustrating experiences. We are not advocating cuddling and petting the child indiscriminately all the time; this would soon produce rejection. The therapist must be particularly sensitive to signs of the child's present needs and wishes, which he must meet as they arise. At times, it is enough for him to sit on the bed, to allow the child to approach him, possibly to hold out his hand and wait for the child to approach. Only when the therapeutic relationship is firmly enough established can he proceed to the next stage, which involves independence and control — to the socialization and acculturation of the child.

With the strengthening of his relationship with the therapist, the child leaves his autistic world, and finds his way into the surrounding real world; he gradually becomes more capable of accepting richer stimulation and of more efficient learning. At this point, it is appropriate to supply him with sensory, motor, and verbal stimuli in fuller measure, and to develop his play by all child-care and motivational strategies.

Of course the child-therapist relationship is only an avenue to the development of new relationships with other people, who are his every day caretakers. Gradually, the therapist retreats and entrusts further guidance of the child to them.

The psychotherapeutic programme with children varies also according to the available opportunities. In some cases, daily contact is possible, in other cases contact is limited to one or two short sessions a week. M. C. Gelinier-Ortigues (1955) and J. Aubry (1955b) report marked progress with very young children from regular psychotherapeutic sessions of thirty—forty-five minutes twice or three times a week. The therapist may also use indirect methods, such as a suitably selected nurse, kindergarten teacher, and possibly children's groups. An example of this is the "therapeutic pyramids" suggested by Barbara Henker (quoted by H. E. Dent, 1968) in the training of retarded children by operant .techniques. A small number of professionals train a larger number of retardates, who, in turn, train a still larger group of retardates. We often meet children who, after admission to hospital, do not react to adults but do respond to other children. If the therapist is treating a child in the immediate vicinity, plays with him, and devotes his attention to him, the new child is more likely to accept the direct attention of the therapist. The influence of a well-organized kindergarten in advancing therapeutic aims has been frequently emphasized (A. Alpert, 1954).

RE-SOCIALIZATION

At this point we approach the last stage of remedial treatment, the development of new attitudes and the rebuilding of the present poor and inadequately developed social relationships and attitudes of the deprived child, so that socially he can satisfactorily participate as a relatively autonomous, independent and responsible member, initially in the family, then in the school, in children's groups, in vocational groups, and can develop satisfactory attitudes to the opposite sex, to marriage, to the establishment of his own family. The first step is usually transfer of the child from the depriving situation to the new favourable environment, in which normal social relations exist, so that he can experience and learn normal social roles. He should be encouraged to experience in the social environment what is normally experienced by other children — the intimacy of warm emotional relations, the satisfaction of needs, feelings of security and safety, recognition of his own value, appropriate levels of response. This first step, however, should be thoughtfully considered and carefully implemented.

Returning a disturbed child to his own family, or placing him in another suitable family, often raises a number of problems, since the child relying solely on his own resources cannot adjust to such an environment. L. G. Lowrey (1940) reported that the aggressiveness and negativism of his sample of twenty-eight children who were raised in institutions for the first three years hindered their adjustment in the foster homes. The inability of deprived children to adjust to foster homes has also been reported by others (for example G. Trasler, 1960; J. M. Williams, 1961). In most cases, therefore, the first advisable step is to ensure adequate adaptation of these children by placing them in small groups under the care of an understanding, loving person; only after such experience should they be placed in a new family. It is obvious that the deprived child cannot develop the kind of close relationship which the family demands, and that he can better tolerate the impersonal environment of smaller groups, in which he gradually becomes socialized.

For this reason, pre-adoptive preparation of the child is sometimes advocated (for example, I. Bielicka, 1963; B. M. Flint, 1966) so that he adjusts to the new environment without trauma, and so that the process of natural socialization in the family surroundings can develop normally from the outset. In other cases, mainly with pre-school children, adjustment can be achieved in a specially devised hospital setting. Where organization permits, intensive psychological preparation can lead to highly successful outcomes (for example, A. Nitschke, 1956; R. Dubois and H. Leschanowsky, 1957; P. Bertoye, 1957). Medical treatment itself involves natural concern by adults, and relaxed but frequent and intensive contact with the patient which is a favourable condition for the beginnings of the re-adaptation. Small institutions, or institutions in which children's groups number five to seven, which have an adequate number of specially trained personnel, are also ideal for this purpose. Where possible, re-adaptation should be entrusted to one person (nurse, supervisor, teacher) who, in addition to being sympathetic and giving tender care to the patient, must also have certain psychological knowledge, so that he does not react adversely even to aggressive and sometimes quite provoking behaviour. Selection of the appropriate group for the child is also important. Some children show greater tolerance of younger age groups, others adapt better in peer groups. T. Bergmann and A. Freud (1965) have described such re-adaptive procedures, based on psychoanalytic theory, in a ward for severely and chronically ill children.

M. Hicklin (1945) describes the successful re-socialization of older girls who were engaged as helpers with a group of small children, where each older girl adopted her own child. In the case of severe disorders, however, these children should be admitted to a child psychiatric ward where a coordinated, comprehensive, remedial programme involving a team of workers should be available. Direct placement in the family is the best solution only with very young children. If a child is to become well adjusted to his social environment, it is usually necessary also to influence this environment so that it will accept the child. It is therefore important to work in collaboration with the parents, and when the child is still younger, primarily with the mother.

Intensive therapy with the mother is necessary in all cases where her disturbed mental health is the basic cause of the child's deprivation. Where the causes are obviously social or socio-cultural in nature, the environment, the child-care regime and conditions must be changed, and possibly advisory services provided for the family in the future. On the other hand, favourable results in the child's psychotherapy often produce a favourable change in the mother's attitude.

W. S. Langford (1955) notes that when a child begins to emerge from his lethargy, begins to walk and smile, this provokes interest from the mother who admits that for the first time the child has brought her happiness. Through the effect of the psychotherapeutic treatment the mother herself gains corrective emotional experiences, satisfaction and happiness — which to this point she has been denied — from the maternal bond with the child. She learns to understand the child's needs more fully, to react to them and recognize them more sensitively.

Since behavioural disorders in the deprived child, any improvement or worsening of his state, any retardation or progress in his development, always affect the mental stability of the whole family and the lives of individual members in some way, the study of family interaction processes is of utmost importance in these cases. Therefore, the development of the system of so-called family therapy is a logical growth (J. E. Bell, 1962). This new therapeutic trend is based on the theoretical postulates of modern social psychology and on new findings from clinical work: (1) that treatment of the child in isolation — where the parents and possibly siblings and other members of the family are not involved — is not always successful; (2) that independent treatment of the child and help for the parent tend to be uncoordinated and of minimal effectiveness (the therapist who treats the child is often not even aware of problems of parents, who are treated in the adult department; mutual interaction, which is often the core of the problem, is ignored by both agencies).

For this reason the family therapist always works with all members of the family (even with healthy members) and interviews the family as a whole or in sub-groups. He himself becomes a member of such sub-groups and manipulates the size of such groups as circumstances demand. The therapist attempts to encourage new methods of interaction between group members and to stimulate more effective means of communication, supports the establishment of new personal or social goals and the acquisition of more suitable methods of furthering the goals of the family as a whole, and helps to explain and establish the functions and roles of individual members of the family. Interview methods of course are efficient mainly with children older than nine years; with smaller children other pre-verbal or mixed communication methods based, for example, on play activity accompanied by verbal comments must be employed.

The rehabilitation of deprived juveniles and antisocial persons is particularly difficult. When the personality is already well structured, changes in personality characteristics are difficult, and often attempts are unsuccessful, despite extensive efforts. If we are concerned only with rehabilitating the youngster in his working and social environment, the percentage of success is somewhat higher. In correctional homes we find a number of children with severe deprivational disorders; even here the basic approach of the supervisor should involve consideration of individual emotional needs, while added importance should be given to the influence of the group as a whole, and to the effect of useful work.

In this context A. S. Makarenko's (1951 *a, b*) experiences in rehabilitating deprived adolescents in special collective institutions after the Russian Revolution are particularly valuable. His success is probably due largely to the influence of his own personality as supervisor and on the control of interactions between youngsters both inside and outside the work context. By comparison with Makarenko's success it is interesting to note that in Czech correctional homes it is the deprived children who are adversely affected by collective care (see page 196). Apart from the direct influence of Makarenko's personality, we must attribute a good deal of the success of his training programme to the fact that the type of deprivation experienced by juveniles in his correctional training institutes was different from that experienced by institutionalized children in Czechoslovakia. His children were not stimulus deprived, nor were they isolated from society, even though they lacked the opportunity to establish close permanent emotional relationships with adults. Thus the prognosis for socialization through collective interaction in adolescence was good. However, any form of collective retraining is obviously unsuitable for children who have lived under collective care from earliest age, and whose behavioural disorders and difficulties are a result of such care. One should recommend individual re-socialization of these young delinquents through placement in therapeutic foster families (Swedish reports indicate that this method is more effective and economical than the present form of collective retraining).

Some of Bowlby's critics cite cases of deprived children who spontaneously managed a satisfactory social and vocational adjustment at a later age through normal channels, and conclude that the dangers of deprivation have been overestimated. If we carefully study these cases of spontaneous remission, however, it is obvious that this spontaneity is at best questionable. The very nature of social organization exerts a directing influence on a non-adapting member in certain ways. These forces, however, whether they are parents, relatives, teachers, qualified workers, or other agencies, are difficult to evaluate even though they can be quite effective.

It is possible that during the school and post-school periods there are certain critical points at which we can terminate deprivation and alleviate its worst effects. For example, during the school period intellectual abilities develop. Deprived children are usually poor learners, because they are not strongly enough motivated, although their intellectual ability may be average. Even if we cannot motivate them scholastically, however, it is still possible to utilize their intellectual ability in extra-curricular activities – in solving practical tasks, in games, in competitions, and so on. If we can give the child experience of success, and the social approbation of the group, this may be the first step in developing interest in such satisfying activity, which may generalize to other more complex higher-level activities.

A characteristic feature of middle school age is motivation to display physical strength and skill. The desire for group activity leads children of this age into competitive games. Deprived children are not socially oriented, and thus they are not interested in competitive games, which involve continuing cooperation, self-control, competitiveness, and team spirit (their preference for individual sports is aptly demonstrated in the film *The loneliness of the long-distance runner*). Nevertheless, we can help them to successfully participate in group activity by training in certain bodily skills. They can then be encouraged to participate in group games and sporting competitions, where they will experience the greatest number of useful social contacts. The next step is to involve them in more permanent juvenile sporting groups, where they can be given some systematic training. Sports teachers and coaches sometimes have considerable success in dealing with deprived children.

The next level at which we can influence the deprived child is when he enters employment, when he takes a job consistent with his interests. The small workshop with a stable organization, flexible enough to accommodate a less adaptable member, can play a very positive therapeutic role. The avenue through which the child can enhance his social value and self-esteem is his technical ability. We have noted that some boys with obvious deprivational disorders, who did not adapt to the group situation of the classroom or the children's home, are very quickly "healed" in the workshop situation, even when it is very noisy, but where there is no forced contact with other people and no competition of a verbal-academic nature. We have also noted similar adaptation in some inmates of correctional institutes, whom we have diagnosed as aggressive, socially provocative types of deprived personality.

Maturing sexuality can also be the point of departure for the therapeutic process. Although it is difficult for a deprived individual to fall in love and achieve satisfactory relations with the opposite sex, it is not impossible, providing the partner is able to give emotional support. Happy marriages of former institutionalized children are not unusual. In their effort to idealize their marriages, we can recognize an attempt to gain the highest possible satisfactions, and especially to give to their children what they themselves were denied; in this we can detect a certain degree of compensation for the permanent, deep, dissatisfaction — compensation which in this case, however, is socially acceptable.

This suggests that we can attempt social adaptation or retraining on a still higher level by evoking parental feelings. We have already discussed the retraining of young delinquent mothers through their relationships with their children in the institutional environment (page 126). Usually social workers undertake this type of therapeutic help. Parents' contacts with supervisors in nursery schools, teachers in kindergartens, medical workers in advice centres, in hospitals, in sanatoria, and so on can be classed in this category of therapeutic work.

The essence of deprivation lies in the fact that the afflicted child does not carry with him adequate resources when participating in social life, whether his role is that of a schoolboy, partner in a game, member of a sporting group, a trainee, a member of a work force, a lover, a husband, or a parent. In cases of mild disorder, however, it is possible to treat the disorder in the situations outlined above, providing there is sufficient community goodwill, enough concern about the problem, and sufficient knowledge. Just as a child is sensitized by one deprivational experience to other unfavourable experiences, it is equally true that one positive group experience increases his ability to benefit from another similar experience. Lack of success at any one level of the re-adaptation process therefore does not inevitably mean total failure.

Although today the possibility of rehabilitation in cases of severely deprived children is greater, retraining and treatment of these children is still complicated, long-term, and very demanding, and certain effects seem to persist indefinitely. In these circumstances, a broadly based preventive programme is likely to be more effective and economical. In practice, therefore, our primary effort should be directed towards this goal.

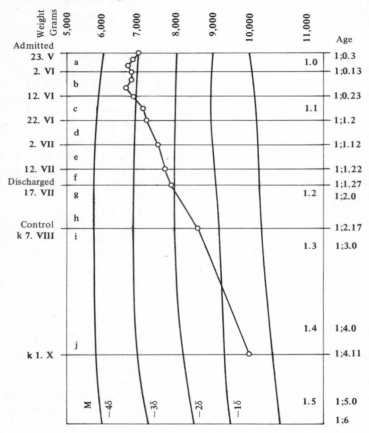

a. Apathetic, crying, stereotyped automatisms

b. Begins to sit, sometimes smiles

c. Starts to mumble, yell, is happily active and cheerful

d. Starts to stand up, walk around bed

e. Tries to attract attention

f. Eats food voraciously

g. Crawls, calls out to adults

h. Walks hand in hand

i. Starts to run

j. Speaks a few words

Fig. 65. Developmental progress of deprived child R.D. after admission to hospital. (After J. Langmeier.)

Fig. 66. Sensory training in a kindergarten. (Photograph by L. Sitensky.)

Fig. 67. Children's activity in a well-run institution. (Photograph by L. Sitensky.)

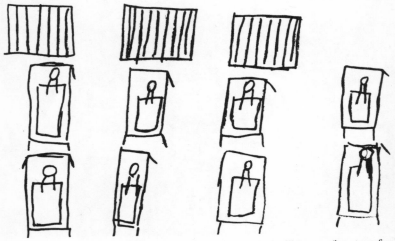

Fig. 68. Drawing by a nine-year-old boy of normal intelligence after transfer from a normal children's home to a family children's home; the drawing calls on memories of his previous environment.

Fig. 69A

Fig. 69B

Fig. 69. Two drawings by a ten-year-old boy of normal intelligence who was transferred to a family home where two "parents" raised ten children of different ages. The drawings show general activities in his previous (A) and present (B) environments.

Fig. 70. First SOS village established in Imst, Tyrol, Austria.

Fig. 71. Goodenough Draw-A-Man test response by an eleven-year-old girl of slightly under average IQ, almost totally blind, who was raised in a special residential school for blind children.

Fig. 72. Goodenough Draw-A-Man test response of a nine-year-old boy of slightly under average IQ who is partially sighted (1.5/50 vision). He is a pupil in the third grade of a residential school for blind children, and uses the Braille method.

Fig. 73. Drawing on the topic of "School" by a nine-year-old girl of slightly under average IQ who is partially sighted (1/50 vision, poorer than the boy in figure 72). She is a pupil in the third grade of a residential school for children with arrested vision, and uses the visual method. Note the lamp by the desk.

13   Prevention

The extent and variety of problems of psychological deprivation have very wide practical implications. Many children are still seriously hampered in their development and the mental health of a considerably greater number is threatened by less severe and less obvious deprivational factors. Today, when infant mortality in most developed countries has decreased markedly and the basic medical problems have been solved, mental hygiene seems to us to be the most important problem in child care.

In some countries the conclusions of the first deprivation studies led to special remedial measures. There was substantial reduction in institutional care, foster care and adoption were encouraged, and the social services were given new tasks and responsibilities. Nevertheless, a certain percentage of children remained in institutes and were given only minimal help, since effort was directed towards abolishing rather than reforming institutes. Examples of bad institutes were cited as evidence against any form of institutional care. Considerable reduction in the length of hospital stay was demanded, outpatient care was recommended, and the view that bad parents were better than good institutes was given some "scientific" support.

It was only in the following more critical period that the reported data were interpreted more objectively. Although conclusions were more sober and restrained, they acted as a stimulus for a large number of preventive measures. The deprivation problem, however, has such wide ramifications, that we must confine ourselves to the most important of these.

A preventive programme can operate at different levels, and if these are not clearly differentiated, implementation of the programme can be difficult and misdirected. Initially, therefore, we propose to describe very general preventive measures, then those measures applied to society as a whole, and finally those concerned directly with threatened individual children.

GENERAL PREVENTIVE MEASURES

A general preventive programme based directly on the concept of psychological deprivation presented in previous chapters should, in our view, meet four criteria, which overlap to a considerable degree.
1. The child should be guaranteed input of stimulation from the external environment adequate in amount and quality, and appropriately structured, i.e. stimulation which will maintain the CNS at an optimal level of awareness and organize the nervous processes at the level which maximally tunes the organism to receive and interpret new stimuli. This should determine the overall activity and reactivity level of the child, which in turn should govern his ability to obtain new stimulation and adjust to life stresses. The child, therefore, should neither be over- nor under-stimulated, nor should stimulation be too monotonous. One should ensure that stimulation is appropriate to the child's developmental level; if it is delayed or offered too early it is less effective and can be damaging. It should also be appropriate to the child's present level of nervous functioning, which changes during the course of the day in relation to sleep, feeding, and a number of other factors (J. Koch, 1957).
2. The child should be provided with conditions necessary for continuous age-appropriate learning, i.e. the stimulation presented should have meaning for the child so that it can be incorporated into the system of his own experiences. In order to guarantee this he needs a certain degree of environmental stability which presupposes the continued presence of adults who are involved in rearing the child. Only those who know the child intimately from day-to-day contact can appreciate his specific needs, capacities, interests, idiosyncrasies, and weak points in his ongoing, everyday learning process. This leads quite logically to the conclusion that within the context of a preventive programme we should pay special attention to those persons on whom feelings of life security should be based.
3. Thirdly, we should create conditions for the development of positive permanent relations between the child and the first person who is concerned with his care, the family environment and later the broader social and material environment. The fundamental aspect of child rearing is not only formal habit training. The emotional bond between the child and the adult is obviously the organizing or consolidating factor which brings meaning and integrity to the habit structure. An impersonal, expert, primarily supervisory or didactic

attitude is ineffective, even with school children; in the rearing of small children it is obviously damaging. Nor can text-book recommendations, no matter how generally accepted, substitute for the motivational value of the positive emotional attitudes of people who love the child.

4. Finally, we should encourage the child to participate in society in such a way that he can subsequently acquire different social roles which allow him to function as an independent member of his community. This means that we should create conditions in which the child experiences not only social roles on the level of the primary social group (family) but also those which lead him to a gradually increasing involvement in the environment. If we equate this with age, then his social activities should extend outwards from the family to the peer group, the school, the job, his own newly created family, and so on.

PREVENTIVE MEASURES CONCERNED WITH SOCIETY AS A WHOLE

The fundamental framework of measures to prevent psychological deprivation in children includes a wide variety of measures applied in society at large or at least on such a wide scale that they influence the basic structure of society.

1. The basic element is the domestic policy of the state. The elimination of poverty and of all forms of material hardship, insecurity, and fear, the realization of an adequate standard of living for the whole of the population, and special aid to families with children are undoubtedly basic anti-deprivating conditions. Further aids are paid holidays for working mothers, and the setting up of institutions, ranging from nurseries to mental institutions, to which severely defective children can be admitted so that the family may devote attention to the normal children. A very important factor is also good medical care, including basic advisory services, which should be free and universal. In these agencies children could be detected who are in need of help and protection, whose family backgrounds are socially inferior — children who in other circumstances would escape detection. Very often the financial burden of a diagnostic or advisory service either makes this type of help beyond reach of such families, or more likely provides them with a plausible excuse for maintaining their present mode of life. Preventive measures based on systematic follow-up of the development of the entire child population, and integrated into a

comprehensive system of paediatric services as implemented in Czechoslovakia in the fifties, seems to be effective. Improved housing and reduced working hours would permit the family to be together for longer periods and the parents to devote more time to the child.

State laws, of course, are concerned only with those external conditions in which psychological hardship can occur. The main problem is whether and to what extent these measures are implemented, whether the public is prepared to make efficient use of existing facilities, and whether the present affluent and rapidly developing society threatens new dangers. The child often loses his valued status in the family in competition with values relevant to material well-being, comfort, and amusement. Laws change slowly, and it is not always possible to respond adequately to new scientific insight. We should be constantly alert, therefore, to ways in which new findings can be integrated into political planning. This can be facilitated by the available propaganda media, which project to the population the views of the state and society about the family, child care, the place of women in society, schooling, and so on.

2. Public enlightenment on problems of psychological deprivation. New data and interpretations of these are fairly quickly available to professional workers, less readily to parents and the general public, and then only after selection and reinterpretation by the mass media.

Usually fifteen or twenty years elapse before new scientific findings are available to workers in applied areas. The lag, however, depends on a number of factors. In some states certain recommendations are relatively quickly implemented — for example, by flexible, partly private institutions, while other institutions within the state may remain highly conservative. In more centralized states implementation is slower, but usually more balanced.

An interesting example of this occurred in Czechoslovakia, where studies from the alarm period in the forties initially excited interest from paediatricians, psychiatrists, and clinical psychologists, but not from those directly involved in institutional care. For a considerable period the only scientific forum for these ideas was the *Paediatric bulletin*. A milestone was the Paediatric Conference of 1961 in which a number of empirical studies and clear statements of the basic theoretical concepts were reported. Only then was the issue publicly debated in avant-garde publications, on radio, and through the medium of a movie. This created a milieu in which institutional reorganization, technical changes, and finally legal measures were possible. The spread of new scientific knowledge to all concerned physicians was achieved through the systematic efforts (courses and internships) of the Postgraduate Medical Institute and related organizations.

In 1964 new family legislation was enacted in Czechoslovakia which rehabilitated the family as the most natural and convenient context in which to rear children. Adoption became more acceptable, and regained its priority amongst possible forms of supplementary care for children without families (compared with the previous emphasis on institutional care).

Public awareness about the problem of deprivation should increase understanding of the basic needs of the child, of the relationship between satisfaction of these needs and family life, of the value of healthy child development for society, and the possibilities and limitations of the existing facilities. We suggest that the most important task in this field is to show how the needs of the developing child can be harmonized with the needs of the developing society. We should, of course, be alive to certain dangers. Popularization of scientific psychological information, particularly about children, is a serious scientific problem. It very often leads to unjustified generalizations and to anxiety and guilt feelings on the part of parents. Whenever we deal with the individual, we cannot state simple generalizations and recommendations about child care. In addition, every implementation of scientific principles is related to the socio-cultural historical conditions from which the psychological empirical data are usually abstracted.

3. A special way of preventing deprivation is the training of young people for parenthood. Sometimes this training is extremely narrow, and involves only informing them about sex; a number of lectures and discussions at school is considered adequate. Training for parenthood, however, is a much broader and intensive task; it takes a number of forms and operates simultaneously on different levels.

Initially one should establish favourable working and housing conditions and eliminate the tension in families caused by economic hardship, lack of public services and transport, by multi-generation families living together, and so on. Surveys in Czechoslovakia and other countries on the problems of young married couples threw up a number of interesting points. For example, many young couples over-emphasize economic problems in an attempt to conceal deeper psychological problems which lead to family limitation or child neglect or the breakdown of the family; for example, they refer to housing problems as the sole cause of the child's institutionalization.

Secondly, there ought to be advisory services for young parents (preferably for expectant parents) to discuss the psychology of married life, developmental psychology, child rearing, and even problems of psychological deprivation. The advice can be offered through books, lectures, discussions, and mass communication media ranging from the press to TV and films. The latter are particularly effective in that all aspects of the problem can be covered in a very concrete way.

We observed the reactions of selected and heterogeneous groups of juveniles in Czechoslovakia and in a number of other countries (including the U.S.A., Australia, and Canada) to K. Goldberger's movie *Children without love*. We were surprised at the extent to which young people could recognize that the film was depicting not only the problem of institutionalized children but of the relationship of society as a whole to children, and the problem of the responsibility of the young to the still younger generation. When asked "What did you think about during the movie?" girls and boys frequently answered "about ourselves and our future children".

Such training should extend beyond simple awareness of responsibility. It should help young people to understand themselves and others. From clinical practice we know that a number of marriages are unsatisfactory and unhappy, because they were not established on a fully responsible basis. Surveys show that a high percentage of children are conceived before marriage (figures vary in different countries) and that the marriage itself is agreed to under duress. Certain obligations, which can stress future family life, are not recognized. A number of marriages are psychologically premature, either because one or both parents seek in marriage the earliest escape from their unsatisfactory present family situation or because they are still emotionally immature. Here again we encounter the problem of deprived children who at adolescence cannot establish satisfying erotic relationships and consequently fail in their parental roles.

We now approach the third level of training for parenthood — the important stage of training in early child care. Long before the child is born young parents have established their attitudes to him, which are based on their own experiences from early childhood — their relationships to their parents, their later erotic experiences and relationships with their partners. Here we are dealing with a structure which is laid down during childhood and develops during life. Child-care measures which should prevent deprivation of the present generation of children help also to prevent psychological deprivation of the next generation.

The fourth aspect of parental training involves the system of social values. All training schemes operate in particular social contexts which in this case is the general moral state of society and the hierarchy of ideals, values, and goals. For example, if in a given society the highest value is placed on material goals, a child in a family with this background would most likely be viewed as "additional expense and work". Judged from the attitudes of the present adult generation, the parents of tomorrow should realize that not only does the child need the parents, but that married people need children to experience a full and meaningful life. Just as a child's personality grows and matures under the care of the parents, the parents emotionally develop, mature, and enrich their lives through their lives with the child. They experience quite specific satisfactions. Lack of experience of this type is deprivation on one of the highest levels — deprivation in adulthood. The value which the child represents is clearly indicated in the attitudes of childless couples who apply for adoption.

4. The establishment of medical and social services to ensure early detection of a child threatened by deprivation. While there has been considerable expansion of medical services in the past two decades social services are usually the weakest aspect of the preventive programme. It is extremely important to establish and organize these services so that every child will be guaranteed the necessary amount and quality of care. Social workers should be equipped to independently recognize and deal with threatening situations. It goes without saying that social workers in such a responsible position should also have certain legal powers. Effective social work in a number of countries is obstructed by division of responsibility between state institutions and partly and fully independent institutions with different ideological orientations (religious, philanthropical, educational).

At the present time the child is usually subjected to a number of ad hoc procedures (often random) in response to external conditions, without regard to his present psychological state and his future care. In institutes for children with behaviour disorders we frequently meet children who were taken from the family, placed in a diagnostic centre, then transferred to a children's home, from which they were returned to their parents, and again sent back to a different children's home. These transfers were possibly interspersed with a number of temporary stays with the family. Although this sort of treatment is now rare, our data on children from institutions for children with behaviour disorders in the Middle Czech county show that 50 per cent of these boys lived in at least two other institutes, some in four or more, in addition to the diagnostic centre.

Child psychiatric or psychological services which observe the mental development of institutionalized children and children from mentally disturbed families should be properly equipped. It is also necessary to generously expand psychological services in the institutions themselves, to involve other communal and state services in this work, and to effectively coordinate all this activity. As far as we could establish, the diagnostic services for emergency cases, that is, aid to children who suddenly for some reason or other have lost their parents, function reasonably well.

We place great importance on refresher courses for graduate workers. We noted the great changes in general orientation of Czechoslovakian medical care when systematic training of paediatricians in psychological aspects of child care was introduced. This should be expanded to cover all categories of workers involved in this problem area.

5. These efforts, however, could not be fully effective unless progress is maintained in the most relevant scientific discipline, child psychology. If we detect threatened children early enough, we must then psychologically analyze the disorders, establish what risk is involved in applying certain remedial measures, what approach we should select, having regard to the child's personality structure, what factors can be utilized in further rearing and as a basis for retraining. This requires broadly based and methodologically sound research conducted on an international scale. We must not only detect deprivation at an early age, in certain geographical and cultural regions, but must also determine what can be attributed to specific geographical factors, and what is valid in a general sense. It is unfortunate, for example, that more longitudinal studies of the child under part-time collective care were not conducted, studies in which similar techniques were employed so that comparable data were available. We feel that such research would be a profitable venture in international cooperation.

PREVENTIVE MEASURES CONCERNED DIRECTLY WITH THREATENED CHILDREN

A preventive programme, in the narrow sense, should include measures directed specifically towards helping threatened children. One way of categorizing these measures is in terms of the social contexts in which the threat occurs.

Help to one-parent families and families threatened with breakdown

J. Bowlby (1951) classified problem families into three categories.
1. The normal type of family was never established (the concern here is mainly with illegitimate children).
2. The normal family is not disrupted but fails to function effectively. This takes into account economic circumstances, for example poverty, housing problems, unemployment, as well as chronic illness or invalidity, psychological instability, psychosis, feeblemindedness and other psychological defects in the caring adults. We could also include in this category families of very low socio-economic and cultural level.
3. The normal family is completely disrupted. In addition to such social catastrophes, as, for example, wars, Bowlby includes the death of one or both parents, their absence from the family through illness, imprisonment, divorce, and possibly also by reason of employment.

Using this classification, we can compare the familial environments of children in toddler homes, homes for pre-school children, and in institutes for school-age children with more serious behaviour disorders in our survey area.

From table 37 it is obvious that the baby and the toddler homes mainly admit children of unmarried mothers. With increase in

Table 37. Family backgrounds of children in different homes

	Children in Normal Children's Homes		Children in Residential Schools for Boys with Behaviour Disorders
	Age		Age
	1–3	6	12–15
Status of the family	N 112	N 145	N 163
Family never established	45	15	5
Family intact, but not functioning adequately	26	28	27
Broken family	20	50	51
Normal family	5	6	17
No reliable data	4	1	—

age the situation changes; the children now come primarily from broken families. A detailed analysis established that the disruption of the family was caused by the death of either the father or the mother in only 6 per cent of cases. The principal causes were divorce, desertion of the family by one of the parents, and imprisonment of one parent where the other could not cope with the children. The percentage of broken families is the same amongst children in residential schools for boys with behaviour disorders. It is interesting to note that the percentage of children coming from families which are well established but which do not provide adequate care conditions is identical in the three types of home. This type of family consistently supplies more than 25 per cent of institutional children.

The fourth group in table 37 consists of families which were well established and functioning properly, and where the placement of the child in the institution is a temporary measure (for example, during the mother's hospitalization). This type of family supplies a higher percentage of children to residential schools for boys with behaviour disorders. Here we are dealing with cases where the general social environment rather than the family has had an unfavourable effect, or with cases of mild brain dysfunction which could not be adequately dealt with in the family.

The unfavourable circumstances mentioned are usually only alerting signals which should attract the attention of social workers. In every case we should thoroughly investigate how and to what extent family conditions can be improved and what kind of support and guidance the family needs. This is of particular importance with families of very low cultural level and in cases where hygienic conditions are clearly unsatisfactory. We are aware that even in such primitive environments children can have such close relationships with parents that the severing of the bond can be extremely threatening to the child, and that the normal children's homes can hardly offer adequate compensation. On the other hand, of course, one should remember that such a child, if undernourished and in poor physical condition, cannot realize his intellectual potential; we have on record many cases of a sudden blossoming of these children after admission to the children's home.

In the light of our present knowledge about psychological deprivation in children the primary concern is the removal of those conditions which lead to a child's transfer to an institute. The initial and simplest way of accomplishing this is to effectively help threatened families. Normally this help should be global, for the threat-producing conditions are usually varied and unpredictable. One can distinguish, however, at least three basic components of this total help — medical, social, and parental guidance.

Medical help is obviously relevant in cases where family functioning is threatened by the illness of the mother or of a family member. One of the first tasks is the prevention of invalidity. A particularly important role is played here by the psychiatric services, since psychopathic, psychotic, or otherwise psychologically afflicted persons are a danger to the child because they fail to provide an adequate or balanced input of sensory and emotional stimuli. Severely depressed mothers are particularly dangerous from this point of view. In these cases close cooperation between child and adult psychiatrists is necessary since we should carefully evaluate the effectiveness of treatment of both the child and the mother, as the latter can be adversely affected by separation from the child (there are, of course, cases where the child's psychological disorder is not the result but the cause of breakdown in the family and of the subsequent difficulties for both parents and other siblings).

Quite frequently children are institutionalized for long periods because of alcoholic parents. Separation of the child from a family in which the father's drinking is the basic problem is the most usual and superficially the easiest solution, but it is also the most questionable. The alternative — treatment and eventually the temporary separation of the alcoholic member of the family (hospitalization in a special medical centre) — although socially more difficult, is usually a more effective measure.

Social and economic help should be directed to families with low cultural and social standards which disadvantage children mainly through lack of medical care and supervision, or overwork. The families of feebleminded parents, who need help both in crisis situations and on a more permanent basis, are a special problem. Preventive measures aimed at so-called culturally deprived families are also included in this category. These aim at interrupting the endless cycle through which the deprivating conditions are transmitted from one generation to the next. We shall return to this problem later on.

Social help for one-parent families, particularly for unmarried mothers, belongs in a different category. Generally speaking, today the baby institutes admit children with mothers for whom the family itself cannot provide adequate conditions. The mothers usually stay in the institutes after the child has been weaned.

Special institutes for young unmarried mothers have a long history in European countries. These operate on the assumption that where the mother has a reasonably balanced personality and where there is some chance of a normal emotional bond developing between mother and child they should be given all possible help and opportunity. Where this is impossible it is better to terminate the relationship than maintain it at a marginal level. In such circumstances we ought to offer the child a balanced developmental environment in a substitute family or in a family children's home. Choice between the two alternatives, and the method of implementing the decision, should of course be based on skilled psychological diagnosis by specialists in this field.

The same can be said for centres for young mothers, who because of prostitution or antisocial behaviour have run foul of the law. They should not be separated from the child during the term of imprisonment. We may be able to capitalize on the increased sensitivity of such women after the birth of the child, and to use their first emotional feelings towards the child in psychotherapeutic treatment and readjustment of their attitudes and values.

Material and social help should not be limited only to the first period of life of mother and child, that is, to the time before the mother enters employment and the child can be sent to the kindergarten. A survey by S. Marzo-Weyl in France (1965b) showed that with a number of unmarried mothers stressful social and economic conditions gradually eroded the mother's interest in the child, a fact which we have verified in our own studies. This is a new task for the social services — to tactfully observe and help to develop the relationship between the mother and the child in these situations of increased danger.

We have suggested on a number of occasions that a source of psychological deprivation in children is the immature or psychopathic personalities of parents who themselves have suffered serious deprivation in childhood. Although we are aware that the personality of an adult can still be modified quite considerably, it is wiser in certain cases to sever such a bond as soon as possible. Abortion laws in some countries have prevented child deprivation by reducing the number of unwelcome children, and to some extent have ensured that those who are born are wanted. We think that such "repressive" measures alone are inadequate, however, and may even be a source of danger. We should not ignore the fact that suppression of maternal feelings and of other parental values impoverishes both children and parents.

Guidance can be provided by a number of organizations which deal with threatened families — divorce courts, psychological-psychiatric marriage guidance services, religious and state institutions, trade unions, and so on. Wherever one deals with this problem (of family breakdown or families with difficult internal states), a special psychological approach is required to the problem of deprivation, and lack of awareness by legal authorities (judges) can have far-reaching and disastrous consequences.

Although guidance is offered by a number of agencies, the key person is usually a social worker who coordinates the diverse efforts of various specialists and institutions and efficiently marshals all the available resources. Traditionally the social worker's approach is either case work with individual family members (the child may or may not be included) or the child's placement outside the home (with or without legal removal). The first method is usually adopted when the parents are willing to change their attitudes and child-rearing practices, the second when there is little hope of this. The latter course, however, can often be "considered a temporary expedient and an attempt is made to engage the parents in ongoing case work so that the return of the child to the home may mark a new and improved relation between the child and his parents" (E. Elmer, 1967).

More recently, new social work methods, such as group work with parents, have been developed to deal with the difficult tasks facing the social worker. A prerequisite is extensive knowledge of all the psychological factors involved and how these can be dealt with.

The problem of children from divorced families has already been fully discussed (see page 128). From the preventive point of view we should concern ourselves not only with separating families but also with families which are being re-established. A person assuming the role of father or mother in a new family is seldom adequately prepared for this task, and rarely appreciates the responsibility involved. Additionally, stereotypes persist about stepmothers and stepfathers, and we still lack an adequate range of services to help maintain and stabilize the newly established family.

Although cases of disturbances and psychiatric disorders which are noted by psychological and psychiatric advisory centres in children from broken or disturbed families are usually due to conflict rather than deprivation, we should not ignore the latter possibility. A child who for one reason or another is unloved always faces the risk that he will be deserted, psychologically rejected, neglected, or denied emotional and sensory stimuli. This applies also to illegitimate children. Although the legal status of unmarried mothers in some countries is equivalent to that of married mothers, and although public attitudes have changed tremendously, the basic psychological problem remains relatively untouched. The child who is the cause of unpleasant experiences for the mother is exposed to a quite different situation from that facing a child who from the beginning of pregnancy was a source of satisfaction to his mother and whose existence is perceived by her as enhancing her own social value. There is the additional fact that illegitimate children, who comprise a significant percentage of children in Czechoslovakian institutions, are usually children of feebleminded, psychopathic, psychotic, delinquent, or otherwise antisocial mothers.

Most child-rearing pamphlets are of limited value unless they are repeated at regular intervals and are aimed concretely at the child's developmental level. Planned sessions for selected groups of parents, as for example in the so-called Universities for Parents in Poland and Les Ecoles des Parents in France, are much more effective. However, we always face the basic problem of how to reach parents who either resist, or are unaware of the need for, instruction, or who have competing interests. In such cases, special psychiatric and psychological centres are of limited value. It seems to us that the preventive advisory services should be expanded to deal with the psychological aspects of the problem on all levels, and should tactfully consider all disturbances in the parent-child relation. In clinics for well babies there is a more obvious emphasis on the training of parents. In Czechoslovakia, we can utilize in the same way the obligatory preventive medical examinations at infancy and at pre-school age and particularly that immediately prior to school entrance. We have already stated that good relations between parents and service personnel have a certain influence on the parents, and in some cases this can be deliberately used to change parental attitudes to children and to improve the internal atmosphere of the family. The same applies to the advisory school services, to medical, marriage guidance and employment centres, and to law courts.

Aid to working mothers

Increasing female employment outside the family is a world-wide problem. The resulting changes in family life and in child-rearing practices have been discussed and scientifically studied a good deal. Remedial and supplementary measures are necessarily dependent on the political and economic conditions in different countries and on their level of social development. In Czechoslovakia improvement of conditions for working mothers has been directed towards the staggering and reduction of working hours, reduced shift work, extended paid holidays after the birth of the child, and improvement in all types of child-rearing services.

In families the supplementary aids are usually grandmothers or available females. Multiple generation families, however, have an effect on the child since the different sets of values, child-rearing practices, and methods employed create a number of obvious difficulties. This method of help, however, is still the most widely utilized, even where nurseries and kindergartens have been systematically established and are perfectly adequate. Because of its importance it is rather surprising that this problem has been and still is largely ignored, so that it is impossible to confirm or deny the advantages of internal self-help in the family. We can note the positive aspects — that the child stays permanently as a family member and that the mother, if she has effective help in the family, is free to play with the child and participate in all his activities after work, factors which are extremely important in the establishment of the mother-child relationship. How far and how effectively the mother exploits these possibilities is of course another matter.

Since grandmothers and other family helpers cannot always provide fully adequate care, however, the establishment of aid services is an important aspect of the overall problem of female employment. In the majority of countries this role is filled by day nurseries which were defined in the CIE Seminar of 1960 as "medical child care establishments for healthy young children of employed mothers".

Generally speaking, experience with nurseries to the present time can be summed up in the statement that in most countries they have become a necessary service for working mothers, and that if psychological, child-care and medical rules are observed, usually they do not adversely affect the child's development. They do, however, create a number of special problems (see page 97), and society should ensure that these problems, which concern all three participating elements, the nursery, the family, and the child himself, do not exceed certain limits.

For the family, provision of adequate nurseries usually means not only the economic contribution from the mother's employment but also the psychological contribution of her personal satisfaction from participation in work and in the accompanying social activity. Another positive contribution is the satisfaction of the whole family that the child is being well cared for when the mother is absent. This of course must be balanced by the other need — of the mother and other members of the family to establish their individual relationships with the child, to get to know him, to reaffirm parental and maternal roles and to gain the social values which these confer.

The main stress for a child placed in a daily nursery is the repeated separation from the family and premature placement in a group. What is required are those measures which can help the child to a quick and successful adaptation. The present development of nursery care in Czechoslovakia is directed towards this goal. For example, very young children are not admitted to nurseries, so that the establishment of the basic bond between mother and child is not interfered with. This has also been a direct outcome of a law which guarantees a full year's paid leave for every mother after the birth of the child (the 1971 act guarantees leave on part-pay until the child is two years old). The maximum period of stay in a nursery is limited to no more than six to eight hours a day with the oldest children. In addition, there is a greater acceptance by employers of the increasing demand by mothers to shorten their hours of work.

In the nurseries themselves, there is a movement away from group planning and the rigid daily routine which was uniform for all children. The individual biological rhythm (J. Koch, 1968) and the specific psychological needs of the individual child (L. Koželuhová, 1966) are being emphasized more and more. The majority of nurseries are increasingly acknowledging the concept of the individualized regime, that is, children are put to bed, dressed, and fed according to their own biological demands, while other children, following their own biological rhythms, play freely. The children are more restful and satisfied, are not dependent on one another, do not need to waste time waiting for other children, and are involved for most of the time in cheerful activity. Groups are smaller, children are encouraged to express themselves more freely and to have more contact with nature. This, of course, places a greater burden on supervisors, but at the same time work becomes really creative and gives greater pleasure and satisfaction. The child is gradually introduced to the group. Initially he comes to the nursery for a short time (the mother usually stays with him), then the time is extended and the mother withdraws. Continuity of child care between the family and the nurseries is emphasized, particularly in child-care methods and attitude to the child; sometimes it is only that a favourite toy is brought by the child from his home. The combined nursery-kindergarten facilities which are rapidly being established in the Soviet Union have the advantage of eliminating the transition from one environment to the other. In addition, if the daily programme is arranged in a certain way, groups of children of different ages can be formed, and we can use the stimulation and developmental values which older children have for younger children and vice versa. Unfortunately, however, for hygienic reasons (fear of cross-infection) this possibility is not fully exploited.

One of the problems in the child-care establishments, from a psychological point of view, is the quality of the supervisors, and careful selection of personnel should be one of the main concerns when setting up these institutions. At present, however, selection is usually inefficient, and there is no consideration of the actual personalities of the applicants. We should consider the implication of this, i.e. that in the majority of countries a great number of children in their most vulnerable years are entrusted to the care of supervisors about whom we know very little.

New trends are also apparent in the organization and equipment in nurseries. Daily nurseries are increasing and weekly nurseries decreasing in number; the latter, which operate twenty-four hours a day except at weekends, at present do not accommodate more than 5 per cent of the total nursery intake in Czechoslovakia. Planners do not envisage that in future nurseries will be the typical child-care establishments for children up to three years of age (in 1970 only 13 per cent of children up to three years of age could be placed in nurseries). The majority will still be cared for in families. Despite all improvements, therefore, nurseries will continue to function as a helping service and eventually only as a social service, more suitable than the permanent institutes, but still having marked disadvantages in caring for very young children.

We should remember, however, that nurseries, and other establishments of a similar sort, can be substantially improved. There are very good and very bad nurseries. In the former, children have much more frequent contact with adults or are involved in individual free play, while in the latter we often find children who are inhibited or who only gaze passively at their surroundings. Nurseries differ widely in availability of equipment, space, staffing, and play materials. According to the official 1966 figures, the staff-child ratio in Czechoslovakia was 1:4.6, and in the U.S.S.R. 1:3.

The greatest problem is staff changes, which depend not only on the age of nurses, but on the nature of the work itself. The work cannot be fully programmed, but demands constant attention, initiative, and readiness, which can be very exhausting. The fact that children come and go means that nurses cannot see the results of their work, and this makes for a low level of personalized care. Since they do not live as closely to the child as the parents, their motivation lacks the important element, as it were, of anticipating the future developmental progress of the child when he goes to school, enters employment, and starts going to parties.

Very good handbooks are available on how to organize a nursery, on child-care programmes, on methods of physical and musical education; there are also information and rating scales for long-term observation of the neuro-psychological development of the child. Whether or not these are used, of course, depends on the attitudes of the personnel.

In addition to these improvements in nurseries along traditional lines, there is also greater use of other methods for encouraging children to develop individually, for example through family type care and by reducing, as far as possible, excessive or over-monotonous stimulation which results from living in a larger institution. Today, new forms of so-called micro-nurseries are being developed, in which three or four children of working mothers stay together in one apartment under the care of another mother. Results to date seem to be favourable. This type of child care is being developed largely for economic reasons, but we think it particularly appropriate for children who adapt poorly to normal nurseries and who for some reason cannot stay at home, and for children from families where care conditions are threatening. In the latter case, this can lead to overall improvement in the family situation.

Supplementary family care

Care in surrogate families involves mainly deserted and orphaned children, and those deprived of care by their own families for a variety of reasons. Where there are sufficient surrogate families and this type of care is encouraged, institutional care is confined to special cases.

Every type of surrogate family care has its own particular features, potential, advantages, and disadvantages. Even where these overlap, we think it worthwhile to have a range of such possibilities available, for only then is it possible to find for every child at least a relatively adequate environment, so that both the child's and the new parents' capacities for adaptation are not unduly taxed.

MEASURES INVOLVING THE EXTENDED FAMILY

Experience suggests that there are still a number of institutionalized children who could have been cared for by their grandparents or by close relatives if the social services had fully investigated the family background or had created such an opportunity.

The child's situation in the family of relatives of course differs from his position in his own family or in the adoptive or foster family, and brings its own particular problems. It is essential, therefore, to tactfully offer help and guidance of the types mentioned above to such families wherever necessary. Although horrifying cases of children living under very bad circumstances on the charity of their benefactors fortunately belong to the past, one should remember that depriving conditions in the family of relatives may be present, but masked, in the personalities of the benefactors and in their negative child-rearing attitudes, of which they themselves are sometimes unaware. Any special service which today or in the future is concerned with problems of adoptive and foster families should also be concerned with problems of children raised by relatives.

ADOPTION

Adoption is one of the oldest forms of child care for children without families. It dates from Roman times and has its own particular psychological problems. For pre-school children who come under public care and who cannot return to their own families, this form of care is undoubtedly the best solution.

Orphans or deserted children were adopted in the past not only for humanistic reasons, but also to maintain family privileges or wealth. Today, in our society, there is one predominant motive for adoption — the desire of married couples for a child who has value in fulfilling their lives. What place the child is given in the hierarchy of values of the childless married couple, however, and the real psychological reasons for adoption, are highly specific, and can be disclosed only by study of the individual case. The dearth of attention devoted to this problem (P. Vodák et al., 1967; M. Bohman, 1970) is highly surprising.

Today, the mortality rate among middle-aged people is low, so that cases of completely orphaned children are quite unusual. The introduction of abortion laws, improvement in the social standard of the illegitimate child, and other social legislation in some countries, including Czechoslovakia, has led to a substantial reduction in the number of children put up for adoption. At the same time, however, there has been a significant decrease — and this will persist in the future — in the number of children suitable for adoption. Today most children who are recommended for adoption come from antisocial, broken families where parents are in some way or another psychologically deviant. The hereditary background of a child in these circumstances is at best doubtful; the situation is usually complicated by the fact that the child has been living for some time in the poor or extremely bad environment of his own family, followed by a period of institutionalization after being legally separated from his family. His development is thus affected by a number of factors, about which we know very little, so that often it is extremely difficult to give a precise estimate of the present developmental level and future prognosis.

From a psychological point of view, adoption is always a very serious, delicate, and complicated problem in which at least three factors are involved in particular ways: (1) the child's own mother or both parents; (2) the child; (3) the adoptive parents.

1. If we ignore the personal problem of the mother who gives up her child, we are left with the problems of the mother's heredity and psychological state and her prognosis. T. Thysell (1952), from an extensive survey of 441 adoptions in Sweden, reports that more than one-third of the adoptive parents wished to know the case histories of the real parents, a figure similar to that recorded in our own survey on adoption in Czechoslovakia (P. Vodák et al., 1967). Such requests can be justified in certain cases on the grounds that if adoptive parents are aware of possible complications they are better prepared and can more easily find a way of handling them, and can refer and seek advice in time. The argument against this is that adoptive parents may consciously or unconsciously look for the image of the parent in the child. There is a danger therefore of misguided upbringing through over-zealous attempts to avoid the consequences of unfortunate hereditary blights. Anonymity in the adoptive process should also eliminate a second risk which could affect the new relationship between the child and his new parents, i.e. any subsequent attempts on the part of natural parents to terminate the adoption and to get the child back. Any of these events can have tragic consequences for the new adoptive bond. J. Bowlby (1951) considers that the mother who is likely to desert the child sooner or later should be persuaded to allow the child to be adopted immediately after birth, and that she should not even nurse him. It is unwise, in Bowlby's view, to assume that if we impose normal maternal responsibilities on an emotionally immature mother this will produce proper maternal attitudes.

2. The second factor in this complex problem is the child himself. Since the majority of adoptive parents want to know his medical and developmental history, physical and psychological examinations should be a matter of course. Early adoption practically eliminates the risk of psychological hardships due to institutionalization, and thus is more desirable than a later adoption. On the other hand, with early adoption there is the risk that we may not be able to recognize hidden defects or mental deficiency in the child, since these cannot yet be validly assessed. In doubtful cases, therefore, it is advisable to foster the child in the family and to delay

legal adoption until toddler or pre-school age.

Other important factors in adoption are the temperament and basic personality of the child. Some children will fit into any family. Experienced nurses in children's homes can quite easily recognize these children. Others, with more rigid personalities, are less adaptable. They require more flexible family environments, which should be carefully selected, to ensure successful development. On the basis of a very searching enquiry, we should inform the adoptive parents about the child's traits, establish him as an independent self-realizing personality, and advise them on how the child should be guided. The adaptation of the child to the family and of the family to the child should begin long before the child enters the family and should be carefully supervised by experienced workers.

On the basis of our own practical experience, we attempted to determine suitability for adoption of different types of institutionalized children, taking into account the possible sources of danger and the type of therapy that might be employed.

The relatively well-adapted type

Here we are dealing with children who develop relatively well in the institutional environment. They show no particular deviations or abnormalities; perhaps it is more correct to say that we cannot detect any disorders.

This type is suitable for adoption, although there are some dangers. One should remember that this child's adaptation was previously to the uncomplicated institutional environment, and it is problematical whether a similar level of adjustment is possible under more demanding conditions. The child is used to institutional "multiple mothering". If he is then faced with a sudden assault of new emotional stimuli in the adoptive family, he is very easily disturbed, becomes frightened, and sometimes defends himself. This creates uncertainty in the adoptive parents. We can assert with some confidence that this type of child has established emotional relationships with adults, but that they have remained relatively weak, shallow, and undifferentiated under institutional conditions.

We suggest that parents be tactful and patient during the initial period of the establishment of the adoptive relationship, even with this type of child.

The hypoactive inhibited regressive type

Here we are dealing with the classic type of deprived

personality described by R. A. Spitz. Characteristic features are mental retardation and overall decreased activity, particularly in the social sphere.

Suitability for adoption is doubtful, and one should be particularly careful in such cases. The child is usually incapable of emotionally responding. A specific emotional relationship to adults has not been established, and if we are dealing with a child of three years or older it is obvious that the optimal conditions for the development of such a relationship have already disappeared. It is unlikely, therefore, that the child can offer to the adoptive family that satisfaction which would reinforce further development of this relationship. The danger is exacerbated by the fact that this type of child is particularly attractive to some adoptive parents. He seems quiet, well behaved and adjusted, is often physically attractive, roly-poly, and smiles happily during simple play.

We maintain that such children should not be adopted without previous therapy, which should be undertaken in a specially selected therapeutic family. To avoid unnecessary transfer from family to family we suggest that in the majority of cases it is more suitable for this type of child to be fostered than to be adopted.

The socially hyperactive type

This type of deprived child would not attempt to establish contact with one particular person and is concerned more with the quantity than the quality of the available social stimuli. He spontaneously establishes contact with the environment and in this sense is hyperactive, but the contact is only superficial and multi-directional; the child is not deeply involved in it.

This child is at risk from the point of view of adoption. His uninhibited spontaneous nature, his social interest and activity make him very attractive. He runs to any embrace. He seems to adapt immediately to new emotional conditions and quite often he himself selects his future adoptive parents. (He runs from the group, grabs the woman who is visiting the institute and ingenuously says "you are my mother?") Quite often, however, within a short time the superficiality of the child's emotional involvement becomes apparent. More than any other child, he lives for the present and cannot completely adjust to intimate family relationships. Both the adoptive parents, who seek in adoption a deep, permanent, full emotional relationship with the child, and those who are concerned with his intellectual development can be disappointed. It is well established that such a child, because of his extravagant social involvement, avoids other forms of activity. His play is unskilled and he has a poor school record, although his IQ may be average or above average.

The adoptive family for such children should be very carefully selected, and the family should be as well prepared for its child-rearing task as if we were dealing with a handicapped child. We would also recommend foster care rather than adoption for extreme cases of this type.

The socially provocative type

Such a child is in a state of constant high tension which is directed towards his unsatisfied attachment needs. He demands attention, is provocative and wicked. In institutions, this child shows abnormal aggression and tantrums, and is regarded by his supervisor as undisciplined. He is generally disliked. When he is alone with the supervisor, however, the picture is quite the reverse. The child is "unrecognizably" quiet, cuddlesome, and tractable.

Because of his abnormal offensive behaviour, this type of child is only rarely offered for adoption. Experience suggests, however, that the results of such adoptions are usually quite fair. If the cause of the increased tension is lack of emotional satisfaction, then there is a reasonable chance that the child will settle down and adapt if the adoptive family offers him the emotional security he seeks. This child needs a stable life environment with permanent caretakers who fully accept him. We have often noted almost miraculous changes in the behaviour of such children after they are transferred into an adoptive family.

In these cases also the adoptive family ought to be carefully selected, thoroughly prepared for the possible reactions of the child and in some cases advised on how to develop this new bond, at least in the early stage of adoption.

The type which seeks substitute satisfaction of emotional needs

These children substitute their primitive, more easily satisfied needs for their unsatisfied social needs — they are sexually precocious, over-eat, are aggressive, tease animals, and so on. Such a child can be considered for adoption only after therapy, that is, following redirection of his emotional strivings into appropriate channels. Since this is a difficult and slow process, we would consider a specially selected therapeutic foster family as a more appropriate life environment for this type of child.

3. The third factor is the adoptive parents. In the majority of cases we are dealing with married couples, since adoption by a single person (usually a single female) is disapproved of by social agencies. An unsatisfied desire for one's own child is obviously a disturbing element in family life and the decision by one or both parties to adopt is often a very difficult, painful, and complicated process. This is a possible reason why psychiatric examination of such people has shown a somewhat higher percentage of instability than in the general population. In any event, specialized psychological and psychiatric examination of future adoptive parents should be as much a matter of course as the psychological and medical examination of the child.

From this point of view it is very important to establish the real motives for adoption. If, from the beginning, adoption of a child is not valued in itself but only viewed as a means to some end (for example, the maintenance of the marriage relationship), adoption has a very doubtful prognosis. We should carefully watch the attitudes of new parents to the child for they tend to overestimate the effectiveness of their loving care, and demand emotional responses and above average developmental progress from the child. At the other extreme we find over-protective and fearful parents. This is often exacerbated by the fact that here we are dealing with older people who have passed the optimal age for parenthood.

Although success of adoption is determined by many factors which are not always under the control and management of professional workers, progressive legislation has always been a very important basis for efficient work in this field. We can cite the Czechoslovakian Family Act of 1963 as an example. The main principle, explicitly stated in this bill, is the welfare of the child. The legal relationship between the adoptive parents and the adopted child is essentially the same as that between natural parents and their children. As the welfare of the child cannot be ensured unless the new parents achieve full satisfaction in having and rearing "their own child", logically full evaluation both of the child and the future adoptive parents becomes an important requirement. This is in compliance with the second tenet of the act, "the right child entering the right family".

The Act recognizes two forms of adoption, reversible and irreversible. In both cases the same family bond which exists between natural parents and their children should develop. The adopted child takes the surname of his new parents and his rights and duties are the same as those of a natural child. He enters into familial relationships with all relatives of his new parents and can, for instance, inherit as if he were a natural child. In the first case however, under certain conditions the adoption can be legally dissolved, while in the second case the adoption is irreversible. The original birth certificate is destroyed and a new one issued in which the adoptive parents are recorded as the natural parents.

The child cannot be adopted before twelve months of age, although he may live in the family of his future adoptive parents before this time (perhaps from birth) under provisional care. In any case, a period of three months' provisional care is obligatory, so that the social agency can establish whether suitable conditions for adoption exist in both the child and the future parents. If not, it is possible to look for another solution.

Adoption can take place: (1) if the natural parents of the child willingly consent to his adoption (a written statement is issued as a court record); (2) without this consent if neither natural parent has shown a real parental interest in the child for at least a period of one year; (3) if the natural parents of the child have been deprived of their parental powers by the court, either because of their lack of interest in the child or because of other circumstances which make their child rearing impossible.

FOSTER CARE

In some countries placement of children in foster families is widely practised. Government or other private organizations financially support one or two children in a carefully selected family. The advantage of this is that the child grows up in a family, and can take advantage of a good deal (usually not all) that the family environment can contribute to child development. The disadvantages are that the child is a stranger and is denied the name of the foster family. The family is not quite his. The financial support offered can become the most important reason for the child's acceptance and can also affect the attitudes of the future foster parents, which are difficult to control. The percentage of failure in foster care is reported to be greater than the percentage in adoptions. We should be cautious in accepting these figures, however, since the child as well as the parents contribute to the failure of both types of child care. Children are carefully selected for adoption and those who remain and are offered for foster care are those who are more demanding and difficult from a child-care point of view. This has been very well demonstrated in an extensive study by J. M. Williams (1961) concerned specifically with children who failed in good foster families.

The reaction against institutional care following the classic deprivation studies led (in some respects uncritically) to overall increase in foster care. Today, when the advantages, disadvantages, and practical limitations of foster care are being critically reviewed, the pendulum appears to be swinging back. In some countries (e.g. the U.S.A.) with the most extensive systems of foster care, there is increasing emphasis on certain advantages of institutional care. In these countries the child often lives in a number of foster families (just as previously in Czechoslovakia children were transferred from institution to institution) and it is difficult for him to find an environment in which to permanently settle.

We recognize that in countries where foster care is the usual form of social care for children without parents, and where it is the alternative to children's homes, we cannot avoid the disadvantages and dangers which accompany every attempt at sweeping, uniform solutions to social problems. Experience suggests that if suitable children are adopted at the right time, if there is a fully developed preventive programme to help threatened families and families of low socio-economic levels, and if family children's homes (which we will discuss later) are established, only a few children are available for foster care. We feel that under these conditions it would be desirable to develop foster care into a direct, specialized type of therapeutic agency from a child-care or medical point of view. We can identify at least three forms of this.

Pre-adoptive foster care

Here we are not dealing with the child placed in his future adoptive family but with the child who is given a special preparation for the changes involved in the transfer from the institute to a family (this system has been well established in Warsaw under the direction of I. Bielicka and others, 1963). The child who has been in a children's home and is about to be adopted is initially placed in a specially selected foster family for some sort of emotional and social therapy, so that he will be better able to accept the emotional impact of the adoptive family. According to quite extensive data, the results are very favourable. One can argue, of course, that if the adoptive parents are well selected and properly advised before adoption, and given intensive advice on child care, at least in the initial period of adaptation, this type of intermediate care is quite unnecessary.

Foster care in special cases

Here we are dealing with children whose heredity is so doubtful that there is a question about the advisability of adoption. We must remember, however, that the kind of family care which will respond sensitively to the special need of this child is a most reliable defence against subsequent serious mental deterioration. If such a child remains in the impersonal environment of a children's home, he is faced with serious danger. Foster care in these cases has a quite specific function.

A similar rationale applies to children with minimal brain dysfunction who also require individual care. Because of their restlessness, impulsiveness, clumsiness, and other abnormalities, they are often an unacceptable risk from the point of view of adoption. In a children's home, however, they suffer tremendously. Children with limited mental abilities who cannot be adopted can derive greater benefit from good foster care than from life in a children's home. Today this type of child, if he lives in a big impersonal institute, usually presents the picture of deprivation.

Finally, we can place in this category those children who because of abnormalities in personality development (including some types of deprived personality) or because of some physical deformity or chronic illness need permanent rehabilitation, treatment, or other measures. These children are also unsuitable for adoption or for collective care in children's homes.

Foster care in the retraining of older children and adolescents with behaviour disorders and of delinquents

This type of care has been established, for example, in Sweden. Reports are generally favourable and emphasize that this is a more effective way of preventing recidivistic juvenile delinquency than care in children's homes.

This of course presupposes that the foster families are able to appreciate their responsibilities. They must have the resources and special training to perform the task, and must be given professional guidance during the fostering period. It is equally important that individual children be carefully selected for individual foster families and matched in such a way that the most effective interaction is assured.

INSTITUTIONAL CARE

Psychological deprivation was most frequently noted and studied amongst institutionalized children. Today we reject the initial radical conclusions that children's homes should be eliminated, since, despite all efforts, some children must remain permanently under institutional care. In any event, it has been demonstrated that improvement of the institutional environment can considerably mitigate the worst effects.

In previous chapters we have described a good deal of what has already been achieved. This account revealed a number of obvious deficiencies. For example, although certain aspects of the institutional environment, which is particularly amenable to direct observation, were examined and the effects on the child noted, little attention was paid to the child who was untouched by this experience. No criteria were established by which we could determine which type of child was best suited to institutional care (or care outside the family). Placement is usually determined by present social needs rather than by the psychological needs of the individual child.

The second serious gap in our present knowledge is our ignorance about exactly what constitutes "maternal behaviour". Nor can it be specified precisely how a nurse (or any other surrogate person) should behave so as to offer the child all that he needs and what he needs most; quite surprisingly our decisions are based on "instinct" or personal experiences. Generally speaking, at present we lack scientific procedures for the proper selection of workers, which is often based on exclusion of negative qualities rather than the contribution of positive attributes.

If the child is to be placed in an institute as a final attempt at a solution when all other methods have failed, we should do this responsibly and with great care. There are obvious cases where institutional care is indicated. J. Bowlby (1951), for example, not only accepts but recommends institutionalization with adolescent or older children (older than six or seven years) who need only temporary placement (through illness of the mother or some similar reason) and for whom the emotionally neutral institutional environment is less damaging than the establishment of emotional bonds in a new family. Institutionalization is also suitable in cases where one has to keep a number of siblings together, in all cases of placement for a temporary period before a final decision is made about the child, or in cases of serious disturbance or behaviour disorders which cause family upheaval. O. Tezner (1956) suggests another category — the physically weak child who is also severely neglected psychologically. For such a child an immediate change of environment is always desirable; sometimes placement in an institute is necessary to save his life.

From our experiences, we would suggest a further category — those children with severely disturbed family backgrounds who become the contentious issue in divorce proceedings, and who are exhausted by continuing tension and the complexity of the situation. We can risk subjecting an older child to mild deprivation if by so doing we protect him from a dangerous, frustrating, and conflicting situation. The emotionally neutral environment of the institute allows him to calm down so that both the child and the family can regain their balance. We have also noted instances of successful emotional adjustment after admission to the children's home of older children who have been traumatized by extreme demands in perfectionist families or by the over-zealous efforts of adoptive parents (in the case of adoption of an older child) to force an emotional response from the child.

Generally speaking, in deciding whether to remove the child from the family and place him in a children's home, we should consider the following factors.

1. The child's age. An institute is far more demanding and dangerous to a small child than to a school-age child. Older school children and adolescents have greater difficulty in adapting to the intimate environment of adoptive families, and are much more suited by boarding schools and bigger institutes with extensive care and training programmes.

2. The child's physical and mental state. Some illnesses and physical defects require institutional care. In some cases of psychological disorder, particularly neurotic difficulties and behaviour disorders, withdrawal from the highly conflicted family environment has therapeutic value. Placement in special boarding schools for educational reasons or in asylums in more severe cases is often necessary for children who are developmentally retarded. In discussing the problem of mentally defective children, M. J. Farrell (1956) reminds us that they also are children and have a right to the same attention and care as other children; in addition they are defective children, and should be given the help which would allow them to live the life of a child, although with some difficulty. Therefore one should assess the condition, the abilities, and the outlook for every defective child and for the whole family, which can be enriched or impoverished by separation from the child. The complexity of this problem is shown in cases where parents do all they can to place their feebleminded children in institutes, then

subsequently take them back home, send them again to an institute, then take them back home. Whether it is better to have an extensive system of small special classes to which the children can be sent daily (and thus remain in the family) or larger and from the educational point of view better special residential schools for retarded children, remains an open question. From our point of view it seems preferable to transport children by bus from the surrounding district to special schools or to institutes for ineducable children. The children can receive special training and still return every day to their families.

3. The situation of the family. In a previous chapter we considered bad, threatened, and indigent families from which the child should be removed. Usually a decision is made to place siblings together, unless there are special reasons for not doing so. Children who for any reason are transferred from one institute to another should also be transferred in larger groups so that feelings of separation are minimized.

From our observations, social agencies show greatest hesitation when faced with the problem of intervening in families where there are a number of children. Quite frequently only one child – the one who disturbs or is otherwise abnormal – is removed from a family environment which is judged by the courts to be extremely unfavourable. Other siblings who remain in the family continue to be threatened by these adverse conditions. Such placement has the character more of punishment of the child and a caution to the family than the protection of the child or the adjustment of the family.

We should also consider how far the child is to be sent from the family. In some cases it is preferable to maintain as intensive a contact as possible with the family, in others separation of the child from his parents is necessary before therapy can begin. We should also consider the fact that every institute has its own specific character so that in a particular institute children of a certain type may progress better, while children of a different type or with a different family background would be better placed in a different institute. With increasing differentiation of institutes (which we shall discuss later on) we should be able to judge accurately the most suitable environment for each child.

An equally serious problem is the child's removal from the institute. Too frequently we still encounter repeated institutional placement (which has an extremely bad effect). This indicates that the first placement of the child was not appropriately handled. Subsequent help, protection, and guidance for such a child are still frequently not available or are inadequate. Contact between the institute and the family should be an important part of the therapeutic process. At present, however, because of distance, but most frequently because of the parents' negative attitude towards the institute, this contact is limited to Sunday visits.

4. Length of institutional stay. It is important that the child who will return to the family in a short time should not establish too strong emotional relationships. On the other hand, the child who is probably going to stay for a long period, or permanently, ought to be provided with all the necessary conditions for successful care. For him, a close emotional contact with the supervisor is a necessary condition. The responsibility for deciding on permanent or temporary separation from the family is very great, and the cooperation of the social agencies with psychological and medical, including psychiatric, services is desirable in making this decision. From the group of permanently placed children we can select those suitable for adoption and those cases of mental defect requiring special care. A long-term plan of care ought to be devised for the rest of the group.

Institutes for children can be classified in a number of ways.

1. Age-group institutes (residential). Here we are dealing with the traditional type of institution which consists of more or less homogeneous age groups (sometimes segregated according to sex). These are staffed by professional workers who tend to be transient. Although some of these institutions are very small, there is a trend towards larger institutions which are more economical, and which from the child-care angle are more stratified. From a psychological point of view this type of institution utilizes the socializing influence of secondary child groups, i.e. of working and recreational groups. In their day-to-day operations they are more institution-oriented than child-oriented, that is, they are concerned more with a stable daily routine, planned work and training programmes. Selection of staff is based more on professional qualifications than on personal qualities. The advantages claimed for such institutions are uniformity, professional care, clear unequivocal goals, planning, organization and stability, and certain economic advantages.

As we noted earlier, however, conditions in these institutes suggest that these advantages are doubtful, and the results of this type of care are often questionable. The concept of psychological deprivation was in fact based on the critical evaluation of this type of institute. There are two reasons for this — the child suffers from the lack of the socializing influence of the mother and the immediate family, and the secondary groups often do not possess the psychological attributes necessary to positively direct the child's development. The personal influence of the staff, despite the best of intentions and effort, is swamped by the mechanical routine and bureaucratic structure of the institute.

In every institutionalized system which is based on the principle of homogeneous age groups, the decisive factor is the number and quality of staff. Any improvement requires increase in staff. Those which achieve the best results have a 1:1 staff-child ratio. An additional problem is the permanence of the staff and of the physical environment, since a child must be able to develop permanent relationships to those who care for him and to his "home".

Notwithstanding these disadvantages it is probable that this type of institution can be changed and reorganized in important ways, and can be useful for certain special purposes.

a. For older children (roughly from eleven years on) who at this age are both independent of the primary intimate family group and beginning to be more and more influenced by the peer group. This type of institution should be reserved for children who are scheduled for long-term institutional care, whose return to their own family is highly unlikely or impossible (for example, after losing both parents). Type of care and training and recreational programmes should be fitted to the needs of children of this age group.

b. The second category is those institutes which cater for a short-term stay in emergency cases where reduced emotional responsivity of the environment is desirable and staff changes are not harmful since we do not anticipate the development of more permanent relationships. These institutions should also have a diagnostic and assessment function, particularly for children who are to be transferred to other homes (homes for children with behaviour problems, homes for older children, homes for children with medical problems, and so on). In most cases, however, the child-family relationships should not be terminated, so that the child can eventually return to the family. The social services should be concerned with improving the internal family situation so that after the child's return the family can provide conditions for healthy development.

2. Family-type institutions. These attempt to replicate the family environment, and use the socializing influence of the primary intimate group, which in normal circumstances is the family. In some countries, this type of institution has a long history. In other countries, development has been more recent and spasmodic. Only in more recent times have such homes been established on a planned professional basis.

The defining characteristic of these homes is that they house a small number of children (usually not more than ten) differing in age and sex, who constitute a sort of large family. The children attend schools in the district and have very good contact with all environmental events and influences.

We can roughly identify three types of family children's homes; these differ in the extent to which they reflect degrees of real family atmosphere, and from the child's point of view, the extent to which they offer opportunities for establishing a permanent intimate relationship with the parental figure.

a. Parental homes. The staff here are husband and wife. The man is usually employed outside the home, and inside the home plays the role of a father, while the woman is concerned solely with the family. These artificially created families either live separately or in small settlements; in some cases they live in family apartments in large city apartment houses or in a large country house. Where more families live together, they can cooperate in economically advantageous domestic and other services. Models of families of this sort are the Albert Schweitzer Children's Village in West Berlin, and the Pestalozzi Hamlet in Trogen in Switzerland, which was established in 1946 by W. R. Corti for post-war orphans. This is an international village which at present houses 220 children of twelve nationalities in nineteen families. The principal staff is a couple *(Hauseltern)* in each family; the nineteen couples are advised by three or four professional staff and aided by one or two helpers. The individual character of the families is created by the personalities of the couple, and is strengthened by the fact that every couple is economically independent. Under such conditions the child's life differs little from life in a very large family. These families are usually composed of children of pre-school and school age, whose prognosis suggests long-term or permanent placement outside their own families, and for whom adoptive or foster care is out of the question (for example a number of siblings of different ages who otherwise would have to be separated and placed in a number of families). Although present experience suggests that such establishments are closest to normal families it is not easy to guarantee their proper functioning, particularly their stability, which is a prerequisite for success. If we can select really suitable couples, the outcome is excellent, but if the couple is for some reason unstable and unable to continue, the results are as severe and in some cases more severe than the breakdown of the normal family. It is clear also that the father figure is the particularly critical factor in selection. When we consider that few couples are interested in such work, it is understandable why in the last few decades the maternal type of institution has been developed on a much wider scale.

b. Maternal homes. Here there is no father in the family. The only person responsible for care is the "mother" who usually has a helper ("auntie"); otherwise the structure of this type of establishment is basically the same as the parental homes. In this case, however, it is essential that the families coalesce into larger groups and use common facilities. The mothers benefit from the communal life, and it is possible to introduce at least some male figures into the child's environment (the landlord, the handyman, and so on). Lack of a male figure is one of the most serious arguments against this type of family. Since we can find a sufficient number of women whose basic personalities are such that, in our opinion, they have a need for motherhood — they have warm attitudes towards children and have considerable emotional resources, although it is unlikely that they will marry and have their own children — the selection of these mothers is much easier than in the previous case. This also creates greater family stability.

The model of maternal institutes is the system of SOS children's villages, founded by Dr. Hermann Gmeiner in Austria soon after World War II, which from very small beginnings developed into a large-scale international movement. In 1970, there were eighty-five villages in forty-five countries, many of them in developing countries. The English National Children's Homes movement, which was founded a hundred years ago (1869) by Reverend Stevenson, has also moved more and more towards the maternal type of institution. (Fig. 70.)

c. Foster or child-care homes. This type of institution is a variant of the two previous types, the main difference being that the supervisors of a group of children are usually two professionally trained workers — sometimes two females (aunties), sometimes a man and a woman, who alternate. Each family lives in individual apartments (in a large city block or in smaller villas) and usually has an individual character depending on the personality of the staff. Here stability is rather doubtful, and the relationship between the child and the staff is usually not as close and permanent as in the previous types of institutions. The communal services and facilities tend to be used more extensively than in previous cases. For example, food is served from a central kitchen, but each family dines separately. The economic independence of the family, however, is limited. Nevertheless this type of establishment is an improvement on the big traditional impersonal institutes. When compared with the latter they are more child-oriented: the child's individuality is always respected, the groups of children are heterogeneous in age and sex, and are usually carefully constructed and followed up. These institutes are also more staff-oriented — the personality of the supervisor is the crucial factor and is more important in the total care programme than professional training and competence.

The well-known Munich "*Waisenhaus,*" which was restructured by its director, Dr. Mehringer, into this type of establishment, serves as a model. Quite independently a large institute in Czechoslovakia directed by J. Kučera, was also remodelled in this way. Very soon this concept began to direct the programme of institutional reform.

Child-care homes are very effective, especially where permanent separation of the child from his family is unnecessary or where a special type of care is required, for example for handicapped and mentally retarded children, or for children with behaviour disorders who do not require psychiatric treatment but who need more than the special educational treatment given milder cases.

3. Medical and corrective institutes. These institutions can follow the pattern of the first or second type of institute already discussed, or in some cases combine features of both. They also have a specific orientation which is dictated by psychological considerations.

a. Homes for children with disciplinary problems and pre-delinquent behaviour. These institutions deal with cases of serious behaviour problems resulting from neglect or unsuitable care. At present the group of children in these institutions is diagnostically heterogeneous, so that possibilities of retraining, using normal procedures, are rather limited. It is important that these institutions perform their true function of corrective retraining centres and not be required to deal mainly with psychopathological problems. One should note that these institutions would benefit from increase in the number and qualifications of the staff. Since most inmates will be returned to their families after successful treatment, the social agencies should again be concerned with improvement of family conditions and should also observe and shield the development of the child. The internal structure of institutions of this sort can be similar to that of the child-care homes.

b. Medically oriented homes. Pre-school and school age children who require a long institutional stay and greater medical and rearing care are admitted to these homes. As far as we can establish, this intermediate link between the child psychiatric clinics and establishments concerned solely with child care is very useful. Many cases where we are not dealing with mental illness or behaviour disorders which can be modified by short-term intensive psychiatric treatment are ill-advisedly admitted to child psychiatric clinics. On the other hand, many children in children's homes show behaviour disorders based on mild brain dysfunction, various neurotic

Table 38. Types of surrogate family care

	Number of Children in Establishment	Number of Children in the Group	Supervisors	Operational since
Family children's homes (individual families), e.g. England, Poland, Czechoslovakia	Average 10	Average 10	Married couple, "father and mother"	World War II
Albert Schweitzer Children's Village, West Berlin	50	8–10	Married couple, "father and mother"	1964
Pestalozzi Hamlet, Trogen, Switzerland	220	Up to 18	*Hauseltern* (married couple) 3–4 supervisors 1–2 assistant supervisors	1946
SOS children's villages, Austria and a number of other countries	50–300	8–10	"Mother" "Auntie"	1949
Villages of National Children's Homes, Great Britain	100–300	7–10	"Sister" and assistant supervisor	World War II (est. 1869)
Mose Pijade Home, Yugoslavia	150	Up to 20	"Auntie" or "uncle"	World War II
Waisenhaus, Munich, West Germany	180	13	"Mother" and "auntie"	1950
Kašperské Hory Children's Home, Czechoslovakia	100	15	Two "aunties"	1967

Note: After J. Dunovský, 1972.

symptoms, and other forms of abnormal behaviour which create insurmountable difficulties from a child-care angle and which cannot be adequately treated in the homes. Some of these children should obviously be transferred to these new establishments, as well as some patients admitted from psychiatric centres for convalescence. In this case also, the child-care programme previously discussed seems suitable.

c. Hospital establishments (see later).

d. Special care institutes for handicapped children (see later).

Since the development of the child does not depend solely on relationships inside the family, but also on his relationship to the wider environment, it is obvious that one cannot guarantee adequate development of children in the protected environment of an institution which is isolated from the external world. Where the children have the fullest possible relationships with children and adults outside the institutions, where they can independently shop and run errands, there is some compensation for lack of stimuli inside the institute. In some cases neighbourhood families take one or more children for a weekend at Christmas or for a trip during vacation. In recent years, a scheme has been devised in some countries (especially in the U.S.A.) in which children from children's homes, hospitals, boarding schools, and other establishments develop relationships with old people. In the broadly based Foster Grandparent Programme, older people (over sixty) provide personal care and attention for underprivileged and/or handicapped children for a few hours a day at reasonable rates of pay. Generally speaking, this programme has proved very effective, both for the children and for the old people, in that it helps them to remain active and feel useful.

In an unpublished preliminary study conducted by A. Berzins (1968) in a seminar organized at the Department of Educational Psychology of the University of Alberta, Edmonton, Canada, the author investigated possible sources of psychological deprivation in elderly people living in homes for the aged. She concluded that both children and old people in institutions are deprived and might benefit from interaction, because their needs are often complementary. Old people could feel needed, sought after, loved, and useful, and could get involved, thus maintaining their feeling of being active, could profit from the humour and recreation which adds to their lives, since children are never dull company. The children, on the other hand, would have much more opportunity to learn language, to listen to stories, to develop their capacities through contact with the talents and hobbies of their foster grandparents. She suggested, therefore, that old people's and children's homes should be placed side by side, so that interaction between the two groups is facilitated. The children could be visited by their foster grandparents and the old people by the children in case of illness.

Much benefit can be gained by institutionalized children from close frequent contact with the natural environment. Summer camps for institutionalized children are extremely stimulating; there are frequent references to surprising improvement in the development of retarded children during a short stay in such camps.

CARE OF CHILDREN WHO REQUIRE SPECIAL MEDICAL TREATMENT

Findings which we previously mentioned also stimulated a move towards humanization and "psychologizing" of medical care. This has been facilitated by an interaction between two different approaches, one based on Pavlovian concepts, the other on psychoanalytic concepts. Pioneer work in this field was the studies and films by J. Robertson (1958, 1962). Today medical care is directed towards both the physical and the psychological well-being of the patient − i.e. from the beginning of treatment it is recognized that the success of the medical treatment must not be at the expense of psychological shock or damage which can be more serious and permanent than the actual physical illness itself.

A number of factors combine to threaten a child during a hospital stay. Some of these are also present in other depriving situations. Compared with a children's home the hospital has the advantage that the child is the focus of greater attention and care from adults. Seldom is contact with the family completely severed and his stay in the strange environment is rarely extended for a longer period than necessary.

Here again we note large individual differences ranging from negative reactions to hospitalization to reactions which are quite favourable from a developmental point of view. We should remember that hospitals and other medical establishments in which the child stays for longer periods of time offer a range of interesting and valuable life experiences, feelings of "verification", particularly to the older child; amongst other advantages, hospitalization dissipates or eliminates neurotic disorders if they are based on family or school conflicts. A. Mores and J. Vyhnálek (1957) report that the effects of short-term hospitalization on toddlers were judged by parents to be twice as often unfavourable as favourable (although favourable effects were observed quite frequently), while older children generally show an improvement in behaviour. From the available evidence it seems probable that the younger the child, the longer the stay, the less well prepared he is for hospitalization, the more demanding the medical treatment to which he is subjected, the greater the psychological danger. Other medical facilities as well as hospitals also have their psychological problems.

We shall attempt to outline the main points of a programme which we think might reduce the danger of deprivational damage in children in medical establishments.

1. All participating personnel at all levels should be informed about the presence of psychological factors during the illness, and ways in which psychological damage to the child can be prevented. How quickly and how successfully the child adapts to the new environment is determined largely by the behaviour of personnel. In addition to desirable personality features, extensive training in psychology and child care is essential. During the training of medical personnel we should aim at a balance between concern for the child's physical well-being (which still predominates) and knowledge about his psychological needs.

2. Stay in hospital should be minimized, especially with toddlers and pre-school children. This means that we should clearly and carefully decide what types of illness should be treated in hospital, or in outpatient clinics, with the decision weighted heavily in favour of outpatient treatment. With some slight variations, the psychological reasons we gave in support of similar practices in children's homes are valid here.

3. The relationship between the hospitalized child and his family or at least with the mother or other family members should be maintained. Hospitalization of the child provides relief for some parents in that somebody else has taken over responsibility for the child. The parent, however, is deprived of an important experience — that of caring for the sick child, of protecting and helping him, of feeling anxiety about his illness and happiness on his recovery. This is one of the greatest opportunities for parents to become aware of their relationships with their children.

Some interesting and encouraging results from the combination of methods of hospital and family care have been reported in England (R. Lightwood, 1957). One aspect of this is a nursing service to families where nurses visit sick children and treat them on medical instructions. An alternative form is the extension of hospital care to families on the recommendation and with the cooperation of the general practitioner. A team from the hospital treats the patient, keeps records, cares for the child, keeps a night-watch and instructs the mother so that she is equipped to handle the situation. The patient remains the responsibility of the general practitioner and contact with the hospital is maintained by telephone or by bedside consultations. This method of treatment is particularly successful with babies and toddlers where family care is highly desirable. The range of illness which can be dealt with in this way is relatively large. Although this method of treatment is aimed primarily at the child's well-being, not only the parents but also nurses, doctors, the G.P., and the hospital derive some benefit from it, primarily through the close contact and cooperation involved.

Physical weakness or helplessness obviously generates a certain amount of anxiety, and increases the importance of sympathetic and loving responses from adults. During a longer stay in hospital the child can suffer from lack of emotional stimulation in the same way as a child in a children's home. The establishment of close relationships with the nurse, which we would encourage in children's homes, is however not desirable here. On the contrary we should try to maintain maximum contact with the family even in these cases, where there is a particular danger not only that the child will get used to life without the family, but also that the family will adapt to life without the child. The best contact with the family environment is maintained where the mother is also admitted to the hospital, a practice which is particularly desirable with children up to three years of age. Reports from hospitals where this practice is employed are generally favourable.

T. F. Main (1958) has given an interesting account of a different practice, that of admitting sick mothers with their healthy children into psychiatric wards for neurotics. It is assumed that the child represents the mother's problems in a live form, and that treatment will be more adequate under these conditions. There are excellent opportunities here for studying the mother's attitudes, and disturbances in these attitudes, and the chance of effective therapy is improved. Mothers are directed into activity, they support one another and in addition they are guided psychotherapeutically. Children who show emotional disorders because of the mother's neurosis adjust quickly following improvement in the mother's state. Similar observations are reported by Y. I. M. Glaser (1962) in the treatment of neurotic, depressive, and schizophrenic mothers.

The second type of contact is through visits. It is clear that demand for free visiting has increased and that the psychological advantages of this are slowly becoming apparent. This places greater demands on the psychological awareness of all those involved in the care of the child, but also creates certain difficulties and conflicts which cannot be ignored (for example, over-excitement of some children). Free visiting requires more careful work by staff, outstanding personality, and tact during contact with parents. There are a number of compromises between open access and fixed visiting hours, of course, and those are being discussed and experimentally studied. Frequently the best solution is to leave regulation of visits in the hands of the medical superintendent who should consider both the medical and psychological state of the child and the attitudes of the parents. This would allow full use of visits both as medical and child-care treatment.

The third form of contact between the child and his family is through letters and other communication media. J. Milotová, V. Kluska, and J. Stejskal (1958), who studied the effects of postal communication with 120 children in an infectious hepatitis ward, have reported that this form of communication can be very effective where personal visits are impossible, and that it can have therapeutic value.

The work of the medical staff is not limited only to the child himself, since his sickness or physical defect intrudes into his whole social environment. Hospitalization of the child should lead to the establishment of contact with the family. The development of mutual trust positively influences treatment. Here we have the opportunity to provide parents with guidance for the future development of the child. If needs be, one should attempt to improve the total family environment. Paediatricians particularly are in a position to detect the first symptoms of psychological suffering in a child and to employ appropriate remedial measures.

4. One should ensure correct handling of a very young patient. This requires psychological preparation before admission to hospital, the planning of individual medical programmes and thoughtful and tactful application. From the child-care point of view such a situation can be used to establish correct attitudes in the child towards physical health and medical treatment and towards medical workers as such. In particularly demanding cases (surgery, narcosis, post-operative anxiety, depression due to hospitalization, and during work with neurotic children and children showing behavioural abnormalities), the help of a psychologist and possibly of a child psychiatrist should be employed.

5. The hospital routine should be effectively organized, and

facilities should be provided for adequate stimulation of the child. As far as possible one should guard against the possibility that hospitalization becomes a period of stagnation or developmental regression. Small children should be provided with the same materials as are available in nurseries or in kindergartens, providing the medical prognosis permits this. For older children the most important factor is schooling and the educational programme. Today, schools exist in the majority of children's hospitals in Czechoslovakia. L. Srp (1961) correctly points to another aspect of hospitalization with older children, viz. that children get used to a comfortable stay in hospital and that this in some cases can be prevented only by a rapid discharge. Greater psychological consideration should be given both to programmes regulating the children's free time and to the whole programme of medical care, to the physical surroundings and equipment of medical centres and to the architectural planning of new institutions. The extent to which relatively simple adjustments can eliminate severe problems (see page 111) has been suggested in the effects of changed attitudes to children's sleep in hospital.

CARE OF CHILDREN THREATENED BY DEPRIVATION DUE TO ORGANIC OR MENTAL DEFECT

In chapter 8 we discussed children who are exposed to deprivation because of specific internal factors, children who, because of some serious sensory defect, disorders in the integration of psychological mechanisms, or limited mental capacities, not only are more neglected, but themselves to some extent create a depriving situation by the very nature of their defect. Protection of these children involves both quick and effective treatment of the actual organic defect so that further psychological difficulties can be avoided, and assessment of the position of the defective child in his life environment and the working out of a suitable care programme. The second task is our proper concern, but not the first, which is essentially a medical problem.

Care of children with visual and auditory defects dates far back into history. As the number of cases of severe defect (blindness and deafness) has decreased, emphasis has shifted to the milder cases (partial vision, bad hearing), and afflicted children are being given considerably more professional care and training.

Today, these groups are subdivided, and treatment is more discriminating. For example, children still retaining minimal vision or hearing are not forced into schools for the blind or deaf. This is in part due to new techniques such as hearing aids as early as toddler age for even severely defective children, and special optical devices for children with reduced vision, which have considerable educational value and in addition allow us to test some psychological assumptions.

M. Strnadová (1969) reports interesting results from her investigation of the social development of children with arrested vision who were sent to a special school in Prague instead of an institute for the blind. She considers that a child's ability to evaluate his own performance and set future goals is the sign of social maturity. She compared levels of aspiration and so-called goal difference (the difference between the child's previous performance and his aspiration about the next task) in a bead-threading test in groups of blind children, children with arrested vision, children with weak vision, and a group of randomly selected normally sighted children. The task occupied thirty seconds, but the time limit was reduced by the experimenter so that the children at a certain stage of the experiment could not reach the pre-set goal. Under such conditions negative and low positive goal difference could be regarded as a sign of good adaptation to reality, and a large positive difference as symptomatic of immature non-adaptive behaviour. Table 39 shows that children with partial vision regress their self-evaluation and adaptation towards the norm, which differentiates them from children with more severe visual defects.

Strnadová reported similar, though less significant, differences, using the revised form of the Rosenzweig Picture-Frustration test. Rosenzweig's "index of socialization", which usually increases with age, was lower for the blind group than for any of the other groups (table 40). (Figs. 71–73.)

Table 39. Goal differences in the four groups

Goal Difference	Blind Children	Partial Vision	Weak Vision	Normal Vision
	% Response			
Negative and low positive	9	45	46	43
High or extremely positive	91	55	54	57

Table 40. Mean indices of socialization (Rosenzweig)

	Blind Children	Partial Vision	Weak Vision	Normal Vision
Young children (first and second grade)	4	7.3	10.4	17.7
Older children (fifth grade)	9	11.5	15.7	17.8

This emphasizes the necessity for a certain maintained level of sensory stimulation so that the child gets used to hearing or seeing from the earliest age, that is, for stimulation appropriate to the developmental period in all sensory modalities. This is clearly supported in the successful results of later care and training. Similar results have been obtained with the acupedic methods devised and developed by the Dutch school in St. Michelsgetel, or the methods for training the deaf (and those with motor handicaps) through the medium of ballet advocated by Virginia Flynn at the Mackay Centre for Deaf and Crippled Children in Montreal, which open up for the deaf child the world of music and dancing, draw him out of his social isolation, permit him to participate more fully in normal social life, and increase his self-assurance. This is well illustrated in a comment by J. Lesák (1961): "When the electro-acoustic ear-phones which the deaf child has used for years are out of order, usually his first reaction is 'now again I am alone'."

Finally, considerable progress has been made in the highly specialized training of the most difficult cases – deaf blind children – since the days of Laura Bridgman and Helen Keller, particularly in the use of the vibrating method.

The basic preventive measure for children with motor disorders, as for children with sensory defects, is to make their lives as nearly normal as possible. Institutional care of these children has a number of obvious advantages. We can supply concentrated training and medical care, personnel is specially trained, special teaching programmes are more skilfully applied, and the children benefit from the technical resources available. In addition the family is relieved of the burden of care and treatment, and the knowledge that the child is adequately cared for is comforting. Often the overall family environment improves in those cases where the presence of the child, as a constant reminder to the parents of a family disaster, has produced unhealthy tensions.

This of course is relevant only to children of school age. Institutional care, which from a medical and educational viewpoint certainly offers a number of advantages, also embodies all those dangers to emotional development which we described earlier. To avoid these we must observe the same precautions which ensure prevention of deprivation with normal children. A logical development of this is the present tendency to establish nurseries and kindergartens for children with various types of defect to which they can go on their own, or possibly can be brought by bus.

We are faced with a somewhat different problem in the case of children with minimal brain dysfunction. The psychological and social problems of these children were discovered only recently, so that special educational and care programmes for these children have not yet been fully developed. However, there are certain preventive measures that we can take.

The first requirement is to inform professional people involved in the care of these children and to make available new information to parents and teachers. This should lead to greater interest in these children and to increasing pressure for the establishment of special facilities. Initial results from the first special classes for MBD children in Prague (classes usually no greater than twelve and the education strongly individualized) are at least encouraging. The special measures produced marked changes in attitudes towards the school and improvement in school achievement.

We would also emphasize the increased need for emotional stimulation of MBD children. Because of their abnormality and behavioural difficulties from early childhood they usually give their caretakers less satisfaction and keep them in a state of permanent high tension. Sleep and waking rhythms in the early period are sometimes disturbed, the children are usually restless, crying, and demand excessive supervision. Motor skills, and particularly speech, develop only with difficulty, and limited contact with the environment leads to irritability and tantrums. O. Kučera et al. (1961) comment: "MBD children are usually so affected by repeated frustration arising out of their abnormality that they require more love than normal children to achieve real emotional satisfaction." Recognition that the feeling of security and protection, based on a close emotional bond between the child and the first caring adult, is a formative element in future character development is even more valid and important for the MBD than for the normal child.

Because sensory disorders in cases of mild brain damage lead to unbalanced input of stimuli from the external environment and because malfunctioning of the integrative mechanisms makes interpretation of input more difficult, the MBD child lives and develops in a somewhat distorted environment. It is probable that some of the later abnormalities and behavioural difficulties are reactions to this distortion of reality. One of the early preventive measures is psychological analysis of mental functioning so that any malfunctioning systems can be detected and appropriate remedial measures planned. This of course assumes further advances in the area of mental testing and in special training methods.

Our data (Z. Matějček, 1961) indicate that the deficits and difficulties of these children are shown to a surprising extent soon after school entry. A wrong response by teachers which may be due to lack of knowledge about the origin of these difficulties produces additional frustration and conflict which further complicates the picture. The ideal solution of course would be for these children to be diagnosed at a very early age — at the latest, at pre-school age, for schooling is the rock on which they perish. Usually special supervision of the child is necessary during the entire course of schooling.

Finally we would advise a very cautious attitude to placement of these children in a children's home. The combination of minimal brain dysfunction and deprivation creates an extremely difficult problem. We noted earlier (see page 255) that these children are most frequently found in baby, toddler, and corrective institutes. While the tendency persists to use institutionalization not only as a care or social measure but as a kind of punishment for the undisciplined child, we shall meet many MBD children in institutes. Just as frequently we encounter teachers who in despair insist that these children be transferred to some special institute. We reiterate that whenever psychological deprivation intrudes into such a sensitive area or is superimposed on an existing organic problem, the outcome is usually far more severe and dangerous than in cases where only one of these factors is present.

Our comments about children with sensory deficiencies and MBD children apply also to some degree to mentally retarded children. We again must emphasize that in every case we must consider the desirability of institutional placement, irrespective of whether we are considering special boarding schools, institutes for severely retarded children, or psychiatric hospitals. We should always be concerned with possibilities for the care, training, and sensory stimulation of the child, and with the level of emotional input.

PREVENTION OF SOCIAL AND CULTURAL DEPRIVATION

In the chapter dealing with psychological suffering due to lack of stimuli from the broader social environment (page 147) we noted three deprivational situations.

a. The child is cut off from broader social contacts because of some physical or sensory defect
b. The child is isolated by his own family
c. The family is cut off from normal social and cultural life.

When we consider problems of re-adaptation and prevention we are faced with a number of possibilities. The easiest remedy involves the use of modern techniques and certain organizational measures. We have discussed how modern techniques allow us to maximize a very small amount of remaining sensory functioning and help people who were previously confined to bed to become mobile. Even if it is still impossible under these conditions to introduce the child to society we can bring society to him — in the last resort by radio and TV.

This applies also to children who are isolated geographically. Distance can be bridged by modern transport, and lack of information remedied by modern means of telecommunication. In Australia, for example, where 75 per cent of the population lives in six large cities, and the remainder mainly in smaller towns, a small percentage is spread over the remainder of the continent. Children are quite adequately schooled by radio. Programming on certain radio stations is directed towards the needs of isolated families. Instructions about child rearing are communicated by radio and even some form of psychotherapy is being introduced through this medium. Throughout the world the introduction of radio and TV has linked small villages and hamlets with the cultural life of the metropolises. Deprivation therefore usually is found in those cases where the family fails to supply the child with an adequate amount of stimulation, so that the general social deprivation is a reflection of family deprivation.

Where a family isolates itself and prevents adequate social participation by the child, help is possible on the level of psychotherapy and sociotherapy. In the case of families which are socially discriminated against, the solution lies in social enlightenment, for the principal task here is to eliminate social prejudice and to allow the families involved to participate fully in the cultural life of the community.

The most difficult case of course is the prevention of so-called cultural deprivation, a problem which we discussed previously (see chapter 6). It is obvious that the usual economic or social aid for such families is inadequate and is often simply a waste of time and effort. Psychological help and guidance is the only method that promises any kind of success, but such help unfortunately is difficult to realize.

Though it appears somewhat paradoxical, it is obvious that the family itself maintains this form of deprivation and that re-education to a certain extent should be directed against the family. The family, however, is surprisingly resistant to external influences and thus is resistant to re-educative efforts. Sociological surveys indicate that primary groups such as the family demand consistent loyalty from their members, and that the family norms have greater significance for the individual than the norms of the secondary social group. Thus this resistance of the family is actually quite understandable.

We must break this endless circle through which different cultural or directly antisocial attitudes are handed down from generation to generation. In the extreme case this would mean removing the child from such a family and giving him "better", "more advanced" care and training than that provided by his parents. An easier way of achieving this is to place the child under permanent or part-time institutional care. But here we face a serious dilemma. We have to balance the danger of individual deprivation in an institute against the danger of cultural deprivation if the child remains in the family and is permanently exposed to its unfavourable influences.

Society would generally regard the continuance of cultural deprivation as more dangerous. The evidence presented in this book, however, suggests that one should be extremely cautious in making such a judgment. There is one further question which we have to answer. As an example we can cite the case of gipsy children who are a large percentage of the institutionalized population in Czechoslovakia. We usually compare the behaviour of these children with that of the non-gipsy child population, and try to raise them in accordance with these norms. What actually constitutes the developing, civilizing, cultural progress of the gipsy population, however, is unclear. Thus we cannot say what developing tendencies should be encouraged to fit with the developing cultural pattern. The present slow progress in the re-adaptation of some groups of gipsies seems to support the view that this problem is a very real one. Opinion is growing that the goal of gipsy re-adaptation should be integration rather than assimilation, that is, participation in the dominant society while retaining the essential features of their own cultural tradition.

At present in the United States there is great interest in new methods of treating cultural deprivation through group care of small children by specially trained and selected persons of the same race, with basically the same social background as the children, who are particularly interested in improving the child's position in society. From this point of view there is increasing interest, particularly in the United States, in observations and findings about child care in nurseries and children's homes in socialist countries. Interest is also being shown in possibilities of simultaneously influencing the child's development and the internal state of the family by placement of children in nurseries and by continuing contact between staff and parents. The necessary condition is the willingness of the family to accept advice of this sort and deal with it effectively.

In a similar way, SOS villages in developing countries can have a specific preventive function. They act as models of a new civilized way of life for the population in areas where the clash between traditional ways of life and new civilizing forces is most violent — for example, on the fringes of large cities (A. Prawoto, personal communication, 1969).

Here we are concerned not only with attitudes and preparedness of the family but also with the attitudes and orientation of the school. As emphasized by M. J. Langeveld (1966) in his article "Educating a whole world", the school in some classes and societies must assume a new role. He maintains that education of culturally deprived children is the most important child-care problem, and that this ought to concern all societies. Only the school can create the conditions which will guarantee every child his natural rights, i.e. encourage the development of native abilities, despite earlier constraints. To be concerned about those whom nobody else cares about is also considered by R. Dellaert (1964) to be an extremely important educational goal. His ideas, like those of many others, originate in the views expressed by J. A. Comenius three hundred years ago.

One of the most important ways of preventing cultural deprivation is to guarantee conditions which will allow successful completion of schooling to children from underprivileged homes, primarily through early and effective preparation for grade one. There are a number of possible avenues, such as the establishment of nursery schools specifically designed for children from large low-income families (H. Wilson's Play Centre for Large Families in Cardiff). Other schemes involve afternoon school, e.g. the experimental programme of the Ontario Institute for Studies in Education (directed by C. Bereiter), in which children attend regular kindergarten in the morning and then a more academically oriented school in the afternoon (dual kindergarten). Still more demanding are comprehensive projects like Head Start in the U.S.A., which attempts to help children in their formative years and their families through all kinds of social, psychological, and educational services. There are also summer programmes for children who will enter school the following autumn and/or full-year programmes available to children aged three to six who live in poverty-stricken areas. Today many more similar programmes are being attempted in different places. The greatest emphasis in most of these is on language education, but some encourage the development of perceptual, motor, and various social skills.

S. Smilansky (1968) studied cultural deprivation in children from families which had immigrated to Israel from the Middle East and Africa. When compared with immigrant children from more culturally advanced countries, these children failed badly in school. Smilansky considers that 'one of the most serious shortcomings is that their activity and verbal behaviour are not sufficiently integrated. These children cannot develop certain concepts, ideas, play, conversation, all of which indicate a discontinuity in the basic structure of conceptual schemata. If we attempted individual or group communication of knowledge and skill, as has been the practice in Israel and other Western countries, we would be unsuccessful. We have to show these children ways in which individual experiences and discoveries are combined into unities, structures, and systems. One possible means, according to the author, is through social play. A survey of thirty-six kindergartens, half of them accommodating immigrant children from the East and the other half children of settlers with middle-class social backgrounds, indicated that in the first group relationships were largely authoritarian and in the second group mainly democratic. Children in the first group laugh at one another, children from the second group laugh together, they have more common satisfactions, are less aggressive, and show stronger role identification in play. Direct observation of the interaction between parents and children indicated clearly that these differences in the children's behaviour are directly related to their different traditions and attitudes and to the general family care atmosphere. The most effective of the re-adaptive techniques tried in the kindergarten was one in which children were taught techniques of social play; only subsequently was an effort made to extend their knowledge through play. The alternative approach, in which the main emphasis was placed on increasing knowledge, was of lesser value. The type of school which rigidly adheres to traditional types of formal education is the final step in the endless cycle for this type of child. Because of his lack of success, the child is excluded from participation in cultural life, in job opportunities, and in the opening up of life prospects.

Here we approach the final problem, that of the attitudes of society to those classes of the population which are on the lowest socio-cultural level, or which are for one reason or another excluded from society, the problems of prejudice and acceptance of social norms and ideology, of moral values and goals acceptable to society. We can cite the Nazi solution to this problem by barbaric liquidation of certain sections of the population. Unfortunately, however, this may not be the last tragic experiment of this sort. These shocking examples stimulate society to seek in itself the resources to solve this problem through its own highly developed culture. Here, however, we go beyond our sphere of discourse, since these values and goals are not the real province of psychology.

Thus our problem of psychological deprivation involves problems of morals and world view, of philosophy and religion. At this point, therefore, we will take leave of our reader with the profound hope that other more qualified workers will continue to study this complex area.

Bibliography

Abello, V. B. 1970. Wolf children: truth or fallacy? *Clin. Pediat.* 9:425–29.

Adam, R. 1960. Die berufstätige Mutter und die Erziehung ihrer Kinder. *Prax. Kinderpsychol. Kinderpsychiat.* 9:220–24.

Adams, H. B.; Carrera, R. N.; Cooper, D. G.; Gibby, R. G.; and Tobey, H. R. 1960. Personality and intellectual changes in psychiatric patients following brief partial sensory deprivation. Paper read at annual meeting of American Psychological Association. Mimeographed.

Adams, H. B.; Carrera, R. N.; and Gibby, R. G. 1960. Behavioral reactions of psychiatric patients to brief sensory deprivation. Paper read at conference of Southeastern Psychological Association, Atlanta, Georgia. Mimeographed.

Ader, R., and Friedman, S. B. 1965. Social factors affecting emotionality and resistance to disease in animals. V. Early separation from the mother and response to transplanted tumor in the rat. *Psychosom. Med.* 27:119–22.

Adler, A. 1930. *Praxis und Theorie der Individualpsychologie.* 4th ed. Munich: J. F. Bergmann.

————. 1931. *Menschenkenntnis.* 4th ed. Leipzig: S. Hirzel.

Aichhorn, A. 1969. *Verwahrloste Jugend.* 6th ed. Bern, Stuttgart, Vienna: Hans Huber.

Ainsworth, M. D. 1962. The effects of maternal deprivation: a review of findings and controversy in the context of research strategy. In *Deprivation of maternal care,* pp. 97–159. Geneva: WHO.

————. 1963. The development of infant-mother interaction among the Ganda. In *Determinants of infant behaviour,* ed. B. M. Foss, vol.2. London: Methuen.

————. 1964. Patterns of attachment behavior.shown by the infant in interaction with his mother. *Merrill-Palmer Q. Behav. Dev.* 10:51–58.

————. 1969. Object relations, dependency and attachment: a theoretical review of the infant-mother relationships. *Child Dev.* 40:969.

Ainsworth, M. D.; Bell, S. M.; and Stayton, D. J. 1971. Individual differences in strange-situation behaviour of one-year-olds. In *The origins of human social relations,* ed. H. R. Shaffer. New York, London: Academic Press.

Ainsworth, M. D., and Boston, M. 1952. Psychodiagnostic assessment of a child after prolonged separation in early childhood. *Br. J. med. Psychol.* 25:169–205.

Ainsworth, M. D., and Bowlby, J. 1954. Research strategy in the study of mother-child separation. *Courr. Cent. int. Enf.* 4:1–47.

Aksarina, N. M. 1956. Some questions of the education of infants. (In Polish). *Pediatria pol.* 31:1081–87.

————. 1957. Physiologische Grundlagen einiger Fragen der Erziehung der Kinder im frühen Kindesalter. *Z. ärztl. Fortbild.* 51:883–87.

————. 1966. Main principles of child care in nurseries. (In Russian). Paper read at First Symposium of Socialist Countries on Nurseries, Prague.

Aksarina, N. M., and Ladygina, N. F. 1954. Language development of infants in nurseries and children's homes. (In Russian). *Pediatriya* no. 3:10–16.

Albino, R. C., and Thompson, V. J. 1956. The effects of sudden weaning on Zulu children. *Br. J. med. Psychol.* 29:177–210.

Alkon, Daniel L. 1971. Parental deprivation. *Acta psychiat. scand.* Suppl. 223.

Allen, F. H. 1955. Mother-child separation – process or event. In *Emotional problems of early childhood,* ed. G. Caplan, pp. 325–31. New York: Basic.

Alpert, A. 1954. Observations on the treatment of emotionally disturbed children in a therapeutic center. *Psychoanal. Study Child* 9:334–43.

Ambrose, A., ed. 1969. *Stimulation in early infancy.* London, New York: Academic Press.

Ambrose, J. A. 1961. The development of the smiling response in early infancy. In *Determinants of infant behaviour,* ed. B. M. Foss, vol. 1. London: Methuen.

Amsel, A. 1958. The role of frustrative non-reward in non-continuous reward situations. *Psychol. Bull.* 55:102–19.

Anastasi, A., and Jesus, C. de. 1953. Language development and non-verbal IQ of Puerto-Rican preschool children in New York City. *J. abnorm. soc. Psychol.* 48:357–66.

Andry, R. G. 1960. *Delinquency and parental pathology.* London: Methuen.

————. 1962. Paternal and maternal roles and delinquency. In *Deprivation of maternal care,* pp. 31–44. Geneva: WHO.

Anthony, E.J., and Benedek, T., eds. 1970. *Parenthood: its psychology and psychopathology.* Boston: Little Brown.

Archibald, H. C.; Bell, D.; Miller, C.; amd Tuddenham, R. D. 1962.

Bereavement in childhood and adult psychiatric disturbances. *Psychosom. Med.* 24:343–51.

Ariès, P. 1960. *L'enfant et la vie familiale sous l'ancien régime.* Paris: Plon.

————. 1962. *Centuries of childhood: a social history of family life.* New York: Knopf.

————. 1969. Le rôle nouveau de la mère et de l'enfant dans la famille moderne. *Carnets de l'enfance* 10:36–46.

Arlt, B. R. 1966. Vergleiche von Wachstum, Statik und Morbidität bei Säuglingen, die im elterlichen Haushalt, in Tageskrippen und in Säuglingsheimen aufgezogen wurden. *Paediat. Grenzgebiete* 5:59–67.

Arnold, J. W.; Thoman, E. B.; and Aileen, D. G. 1971. Effects of early social deprivation on maternal behaviour and male mating behaviour in rats. *Proc. 19th Int. Congr. Psychol.* 115.

Arsenian, J. M. 1943. Young children in an insecure situation. *J. abnorm. soc. Psychol.* 38:225–49.

Arthur, B., and Kemme, M. L. 1964. Bereavement in childhood. *J. Child Psychol. Psychiat.* 5:37–49.

Asher, E. J. 1935. The inadequacy of current intelligence tests for testing Kentucky mountain children. *J. genet. Psychol.* 46:480–86.

Aubry, J. 1955a. The effects of lack of maternal care: methods of studying children aged one to three years, placed in institutions. In *Emotional problems of early childhood,* ed. G. Caplan. New York: Basic.

————. 1955b. La carence de soins maternels. In *Travaux et documents,* vol. 7. Paris: Presses Univ. de France, CIE.

————. 1956. Hospitalisme. In *Cours de pédiatrie sociale,* pp. 321–24. Paris: CIE.

Aubry, J., and Guiton, M. 1960. Les relations du thérapeute et des pédagogues en internat. *Sem. Hôp. Paris* 36:2707.

Ausubel, D. P. 1963. The influence of experience on the development of intelligence. Paper read at a Conference on Productive Thinking in Education, Sponsored by NEA Project on the Academically Talented Student, Washington, D.C. Mimeographed.

————. 1964. How reversible are the cognitive and motivational effects of cultural deprivation? Implications for teaching the culturally deprived child. *Urban Educ.* 1:16–39.

Azima, H., and Cramer-Azima, F. J. 1956. Effects of partial isolation in mentally disturbed individuals. *Dis. nerv. System* 17:117–22.

Azima, H.; Vispo, R.; and Cramer-Azima, F. J. 1961. Observations on anaclitic therapy during sensory deprivation. In *Sensory deprivation,* ed. P. Solomon et al., pp. 143–60. Cambridge, Mass.: Harvard Univ. Press.

Bach, G. R. 1946. Father-fantasies and father-typing in father-separated children. *Child Dev.* 17:63–80.

Bakwin, H. 1942. Loneliness in infants. *Am. J. Dis. Child.* 63:30–33.

————. 1944. Psychogenic fever in infants. *Am. J. Dis. Child.* 67:176–81.

————. 1948. Pure maternal overprotection. *J. Pediat.* 33:788–94.

————. 1949. Emotional deprivation in infants. *J. Pediat.* 35:512–21.

————. 1951. The hospital care of infants and children. *J. Pediat.* 39:383–90.

————. 1960. The infant's love for his mother. *J. Pediat.* 57:643–45.

Bakwin, H., and Bakwin, R. M. 1960. *Clinical management of behavior disorders in children.* Philadelphia: Saunders.

Barnes, T. C. 1959. Isolation stress in rats and mice as a neuropharmacological test. *Fedn Proc. Fedn Am. Socs exp. Biol.* 18:365.

Barnett, S. A. 1955. "Displacement" behaviour and "psychosomatic" disorders. *Lancet* 2:1203–8.

————. 1958a. Experiments on "neophobia" in wild and laboratory rats. *Br. J. Psychol.* 49, pt. 3.

————. 1958b. Exploratory behaviour. *Br. J. Psychol.* 49:290–310.

————. 1961. The behaviour and needs of infant mammals. *Lancet* 1:1067–71.

Barry, H., Jr. 1939. Study of bereavement: an approach to problems in mental disease. *Am. J. Orthopsychiat.* 9:355–59.

————. 1949. Significance of maternal bereavement before age eight in psychiatric patients. *Archs Neurol. Psychiat. Chic.* 62:630–37.

Barry, H., Jr.; Barry, A.; and Lindemann, E. 1965. Dependency in adult patients following early maternal bereavement. *J. nerv. ment. Dis.* 140:196–206.

Barry, H., Jr., and Lindemann, E. 1960. Critical ages for maternal bereavement in psychoneuroses. *Psychosom. Med.* 22:166–79.

Bartemeier, L. H. 1952. Deprivations during infancy and their effects upon personality development. *Am. J. ment. Defic.* 56:708–11.

Barton, R. 1961. The institutional mind and the subnormal mind. *J. ment. Subnormal.* 7:1–8.

Bauerová, N., and Křivohlavý, J. 1974. Co-operative conflict resolution in institutionalized boy dyads. *J. Child Psychol. Psychiat.* 15:13–21.

Baumgartner, L. 1952. The physician and adoptions. In *The child in health and disease,* ed. C. G. Grules and R. C. Elley. Baltimore.

Bayley, N., and Jones, H. E. 1937. Environmental correlates of mental and motor development: a cumulative study from infancy to six years. *Child Dev.* 4:329–41.

Bayroff, A. G. 1936. The experimental social behavior of animals: I.

The effect of early isolation of white rats on their later reactions to other white rats as measured by two periods of free choices. *J. comp. Psychol.* 21:67–81.

————. 1940. The experimental social behavior of animals: II. The effect of early isolation of white rats on their competition in swimming. *J. comp. Psychol.* 29:293–306.

Beach, F. A. 1945. Current concepts of play in animals. *Am. Nat.* 79:523–41.

Beach, F. A., and Jaynes, J. 1954. Effects of early experience upon the behaviour of animals. *Psychol. Bull.* 51:239–63.

Beck, A. T.; Sethi, B. B.; and Tuthill, R. W. 1963. Childhood bereavement and adult depression. *Archs gen. Psychiat.* 9:295–302.

Becker, E. 1962. Socialization, command of performance and mental illness. *Am. J. Sociol.* 67:494–501.

Beley, A. P., and Netchine, G. 1958. Étude psychologique et clinique de quelques jeunes débiles mentaux vivant en situation de carence affective au sein d'une collectivité psychiatrique. *Criança port.* 17:915–16.

————. 1959. Situation de carence socio-affective au sein d'une collective psychiatrique. *Revue Neuropsychiat. infant.* 7:1–15.

Bell, J. E. 1962. Recent advances in family group therapy. *J. Child Psychol.* 3:1–15.

Bell, R. M. 1962. Differential reactions to stress following handling at different ages during infantile development. *Am. Psychol.* 17:307.

Beller, E. K., and Neubauer, P. B. 1963. Sex differences and symptom patterns in early childhood. *J. Am. Acad. Child Psychiat.* 2:417–38.

Bender, L. 1945. Infants reared in institutions, permanently handicapped. *Child Welf.* 24.

————. 1946. There is no substitute for family life. *Child Study* 23:74.

Benedek, T. 1949. The psychosomatic implications of the primary unit: mother-child. *Am. J. Orthopsychiat.* 19:624.

————. 1956. Psychobiological aspects of mothering. *Am. J. Orthopsychiat.* 26:272.

Benedetti, G. 1964. Die Quellen des sozialen Kontaktes. *Acta Paedopsychiat.* 31:145–52.

Benedict, R. 1949. Child rearing in certain European countries. *Am. J. Orthopsychiat.* 19:342–48.

————. 1954. Continuities and discontinuities in cultural conditioning. In *Readings in child development,* ed. W. Martin and C. Stendler, pp. 142–48. New York: Brace.

Benjamin, J. D. 1961. Some developmental observations relating to the theory of anxiety. *J. Am. psychoanal. Ass.* 9:652–68.

Benjamin, L. S. 1961. The effect of frustration on the non-nutritive sucking of the infant rhesus monkey. *J. comp. physiol. Psychol.* 54:700–703.

Bennett, E. L., et al. 1964. Chemical and anatomical plasticity of brain. *Science* 146:610–19.

Bennett, I., and Hellman, I. 1951. Psychoanalytic material related to observations in early development. *Psychoanal. Study Child* 6:307–24.

Bennholdt-Thomsen, C. 1956a. Das gefährdete Kind unserer Zeit. *Öff. GesundhDienst* 18:236–53.

―――. 1956b. Eltern ohne Zeit. *Dt. med. Wschr.* 81:2105–6.

―――. 1957. Die Bedeutung der mütterlichen Fürsorge in der frühen Kindheit. Eine Stellungnahme des Paediaters zu Bowlby. *Revue Neuropsychiat. infant.* 5:434–45.

Beres, D., and Obers, S. J. 1950. The effects of extreme deprivation in infancy on psychic structure in adolescence: a study in ego development. *Psychoanal. Study Child* 5:212–35.

Berg, I. 1966. A note on observations of young children with their mothers in a child psychiatric clinic. *J. Child Psychol. Psychiat.* 7:69–73.

Berg, M., and Cohen, B. B. 1959. Early separation from the mother in schizophrenia. *J. nerv. ment. Dis.* 128:365–69.

Bergmann, T., and Freud, A. 1965. *Children in the hospital.* New York: International Univ. Press.

Berlyne, D. E. 1950. Novelty and curiosity as determinants of exploratory behavior. *Br. J. Psychol.* 41:68–80.

―――. 1957. Uncertainty and conflict: a point of contact between information-theory and behavior-theory concepts. *Psychol. Rev.* 64:329–39.

―――. 1960. *Conflict, arousal and curiosity.* New York: McGraw-Hill.

―――. 1966. Conflict and arousal. *Scient. Am.* 215:82–87.

Bernstein, B. 1960. Language and social class. *Br. J. Sociol.* 11:271–76.

―――. 1961. Aspects of language and learning in the genesis of the social process. *J. Child Psychol. Psychiat.* 1:313–24.

Bernstein, L. 1952. A note on Christie's "Experimental naiveté and experiential naiveté". *Psychol. Bull.* 49:38–40.

―――. 1957. The effects of variations in handling upon learning and retention. *J. comp. physiol. Psychol.* 50:162–67.

―――. 1960. A comparison of the effects of human and machine handling on later behavior in C 57B1/6 mice. *Child Dev.* 31:229.

―――. 1972. The reversibility of learning deficits in early environmentally restricted rats as a function of amount of experience in later life. *J. psychosom. Res.* 16:71–74.

Bernstein, L.; Borda-Bossana, D.; Atkinson, H.; and Elrick, H. 1961. An experimental test of the permanence of learning deficits in the environmentally restricted rat. *J. psychosom. Res.* 5:127–31.

Bernstein, L., and Elrick, H. 1957. The handling of experimental animals as a control factor in animal research: a review. *Metabolism* 6:479–82.

Bertoye, P. 1957. Le comportement psychique des nourrissons placés en pouponnière. *Sem. Hôp. Paris* 33:353–58.

Bessel, H. 1968. The content is the medium: the confidence is the message. *Psychology Today* 1, no. 8:32–35.

Bettelheim, B. 1956. Schizophrenia as a reaction to extreme situations. *Am. J. Orthopsychiat.* 26:507–18.

Bevan, R. T. 1956. The behaviour and education attainments of deprived children. *Publ. Hlth, Lond.* 69:234–37.

Bexton, W. H.; Heron, W.; and Scott, T. H. 1954. Effects of decreased variation in the sensory environment. *Can. J. Psychol.* 8:70–76.

Bibring, G., et al. 1961. A study of the psychological process in pregnancy and of the earliest mother-child relationship. *Psychoanal. Study Child* 16:1–72.

Bielicka, I. 1961. Hospitalism in infant wards. (In Polish). *Szpital Pol.* 5, no.3.

————. 1962. *Reflexions at the cradle.* (In Polish). Warsaw.

————. 1963. Treating children traumatized by hospitalization. *Children* 10, no.5.

Bielicka, I., and Olechnowicz, H. 1962. Attempts at prevention and treatment of hospitalism of infants in conditions of an infant ward. (In Polish). *Szpital. Pol.* 6:203–6.

————. 1966a. Techniques of psychotherapy of very young children. (In Polish). *Pediatria pol.* 41:779–86.

————. 1966b. Theoretical basis of preverbal psychotherapy. (In Polish). *Pediatria pol.* 41:771–78.

Bielicki, I. 1971. *Dein Kind braucht Liebe.* Munich: Kindler.

Biermann, G. 1965. Kind und Krankenhaus. *Prax. Kinderpsychol. Kinderpsychiat.* 14:282–97.

Biermann, G., and Biermann, R. 1967. Kinder in Israel. *Prax. Kinderpsychol. Kinderpsychiat.* 16:97–111.

————. 1973. Die Mutter-Kind Situation in den Kinderkrankenhäusern der Bundesrepublik. In *Jahrbuch der Psychohygiene,* ed. G. Biermann, vol. 1. Munich, Basel: Reinhardt.

Bierstedt, R. 1963. *The social order: an introduction to sociology.* New York: McGraw-Hill.

Biesheuvel, S. 1959. *Race, culture and personality: the Hoernle Memorial Lecture.* Johannesburg: S. Afr. Inst. Race Relat.

Bijou, S. W. 1963. Theory and research in mental (developmental) retardation. *Psychol. Rec.* 13:95–110.

Bijou, S. W., and Baer, D. M. 1961–65. *Child development,* 2 vols. New York: Appleton-Century-Crofts.

Birch, H. G. 1968. Health and the education of socially disadvantaged children. *Devl Med. Child Neurol.* 10:580–99.

Birch, H. G., and Belmont, L. 1961. The problems of comparing home rearing versus foster home rearing in defective children. *Pediatrics* 28:956–61.

Birns, B. 1965. Individual differences in human neonatal responses to stimulation. *Child Dev.* 30:249–56.

Birtchnell, J. 1970*a*. Depression in relation to early and recent parent death. *Br. J. Psychiat.* 116:299–306.

————. 1970*b*. Early parental death and mental illness. *Br. J. Psychiat.* 116:281–88.

————. 1970*c*. Some psychiatric sequelae of childhood bereavement. *Br. J. Psychiat.* 116:346–47.

Blatt, B., and Garfunkel, F. 1965. *A field demonstration of the effects of nonautomated responsive environments on the intellectual and social competence of educable mentally retarded children.* Boston University, Cooperative Research Project no. D-014.

Blauvelt, H.; Herscher, L.; and Richmond, J. 1956. An experimental study of maternal-neonate relationships. *Am. J. Dis. Child.* 92:460–61.

Blumenbach, J. F. 1814. *Handbuch der Naturgeschichte.* 9th ed. Göttingen.

Bodman, F. H. 1941. War conditions and the mental health of the child. *Br. med. J.* 2:486.

Bodman, F. H.; Mackinlay, M.; and Sykes, K. 1950. The social adaptation of institution children. *Lancet* 1:173–76.

Bohman, M. 1970. *Adopted children and their families.* Stockholm: Proprius.

Bollea, G. 1958*a*. Les carences affectives de 6 à 10 ans. *Criança port.* 17, no. 1.

————. 1958*b*. Patologia della crisi evolutiva dei 7–8 anni. *Z. Kinderpsychiat.* 25:29–36.

Bombard, A. 1953. *Naufrage volontaire.* Paris: Editions de Paris.

Bondy, S. C., and Margolis, F. L. 1971. *Sensory deprivation and brain development.* Jena: Fischer.

Borda-Bossana, D.; Elrick, H.; Bernstein, L.; and Atkinson, H. 1961. Effects of handling in the adrenalectomized rat treated with corticosterone. *J. psychosom. Res.* 5:206–10.

Borrelli, M., and Thorne, A. 1963. *A street lamp and the stars: the autobiography of Don Borrelli of Naples.* New York: Coward.

Bosch, G. 1962. *Der frühkindliche Autismus.* Berlin, Göttingen, Heidelberg.

Bossard, J. H. S. 1951. Process in social weaning: a study of childhood visiting. *Child Dev.* 22:211–20.

Bostock, J. 1958. Medicine's need for history. *Med. J. Aust.* 45:557–61.

Bothler, C. 1959. Der Einfluss eines plötzlichen Umweltwechsels auf das Gewicht bei Kindern im Alter bis zu 3 Jahren. *Z. ärztl. Fortbild.* 53:1443–44.

Bowden, D. M., and McKinney, W. T. 1972. Behavioral effects of peer separation and reunion on adolescent male rhesus monkey. *Devl Psychol.* 5:353–62.

Bowlby, J. 1940. The influence of early environment in the development of neurosis and neurotic character. *Int. J. Psycho-Analysis* 21:154—78.

————. 1946. *Fortyfour juvenile thieves.* London: Tyndall and Cox.

————. 1951. *Maternal care and mental health.* Geneva: WHO.

————. 1953. Some pathological processes set in train by early mother-child separation. *J. ment. Sci.* 99:265—72.

————. 1957. An ethological approach to research in child development. *Br. J. med. Psychol.* 30:230—40.

————. 1958*a*. The nature of the child's tie to his mother. *Int. J. Psycho-Analysis* 39:350—73.

————. 1958*b*. A note on mother-child separation as a mental hazard. *Br. J. med. Psychol.* 31:247—48.

————. 1960. Separation anxiety. *Int. J. Psycho-Analysis* 41:1—25.

————. 1961. The Adolf Meyer lecture: Childhood mourning and its implications for psychiatry. *Am. J. Psychiat.* 118:481—98.

————. 1969. *Attachment and loss.* New York: Basic; London: Hogarth.

Bowlby, J.; Ainsworth, M. D.; Boston, M.; and Rosenbluth, D. 1956. The effects of mother-child separation: a follow-up study. *Br. J. med. Psychol.* 29:211—47.

Bowlby, J.; Robertson, J.; and Rosenbluth, D. 1952. A two-year-old goes to hospital. *Psychoanal. Study Child* 7:82—94.

Brackbill, Y. 1958. Extinction of the smiling response in infants as a function of reinforcement schedule. *Child Dev.* 29:115—24.

Braestrup, A. 1956. Children born out of wedlock in Copenhagen: their family milieu at the age of five years. *Acta paediat., Stockh.* 45:352—55.

Brandt, E. M.; Baysinger, C.; and Mitchell, G. 1972. Separation from rearing environment in mother-reared and isolation-reared rhesus monkeys. *Int. J. Psychobiol.* 2:193—204.

Brandt, V. 1964. *Flüchtlingskinder.* Munich.

Brask, B. H. 1959. Borderline schizophrenia in children. *Acta psychiat. scand.* 34:265—82.

Brattgård, S. O. 1952. The importance of adequate stimulation for the chemical composition of retinal ganglion cells during early post-natal development. *Acta radiol.* 96:1—80.

Brazelton, B. T. 1962*a*. Crying in infancy. *Pediatrics* 29:579—88.

————. 1962*b*. Observations of the neonate. *J. Am. Acad. Child Psychiat.* 1:38—58.

Brennemann, J. 1932. The infant ward. *Am. J. Dis. Child.* 43:577.

Brenner, W. 1960. Die psychische Gefährdung des Kindes im Krankenhaus und ihre Bekämpfung. *Kinderärztl. Prax.* 28:479—82.

Bridger, W. H. 1966. Individual differences in behavior and autonomic activity in newborn infants. *Am. J. publ. Hlth* 55:1899—1900.

Brim, O. G., Jr. 1960. Personality development as role-learning. In *Personality development in children,* ed. Ira Iscoe and H. W. Stevenson, pp. 127—59. Austin: Univ. of Texas Press.

Brodberck, A. J., and Irwin, O. C. 1946. The speech behavior of infants without families. *Child Dev.* 17:145—56.

Brody, S. 1956. *Patterns of mothering: maternal influence during infancy.* New York: International Univ. Press.

Bromage, P. R. 1960. Sensory deprivation. *Lancet* 1:226.

Bronfenbrenner, U. 1958. Socialization and social class through time and space. In *Readings in social psychology*, ed. E. E. Maccoby et al. New York: Holt, Rinehart and Winston.

Bronson, W. C. 1966. Central orientation: a study of behavior organization from childhood to adolescence. *Child Dev.* 37:125—55.

Brooks, G. L.; Bain, K.; Burtt, M. M.; Danis, P. G.; Farber, S.; Goldbloom, A.; Grulee, C. G.; McGullough, G. C.; and Seelye, W. B. 1954. The care of children in hospitals. *Pediatrics* 14:401—20.

Brown, F. 1961. Depression and childhood bereavement. *J. ment. Sci.* 107:754.

Bruch, H. 1962. Falsification of bodily needs and body concept in schizophrenia. *Archs gen. Psychiat.* no. 6:18—24.

Brunecký, Z. 1959. Reaction of a ten-month-old girl to separation from her mother. (In Czech). *Cslká. Pediat.* 14:853.

Bruner, J. S. 1959. The cognitive consequences of early sensory deprivation. *Psychosom. Med.* 21:89—95.

Brüning, H. 1908. *Geschichte der Methodik der künstlichen Säuglingsernährung.* Stuttgart.

Buber, M. 1923. *Ich und Du.* Leipzig: Insel-Verlag.

Bugental, J. F. T. 1967. *Challenges of humanistic psychology.* New York: McGraw-Hill.

Bühler, C. 1959. Theoretical observations about life's basic tendencies. *Am. J. Psychother.* 13:561—81.

————. 1962. *Psychologie im Leben unserer Zeit.* Stuttgart, Hamburg: Deutscher Bücherbund.

————. 1967. Human life as a whole as a central subject of humanistic psychology. In *Challenges of humanistic psychology,* ed. J. F. Bugental, pp. 83—91. New York: McGraw-Hill.

Burbury, W. M. 1941. Effects of evacuation and of air raids on city children. *Br. med. J.* 2:660.

Burdina, V. N.; Krasucki, J. V. K.; and Čebykin, D. A. 1960. About the relationship of higher nervous activity of dogs to rearing conditions: ontogenetic view. (In Russian). *Žh. vỹssh. nerv. Deyat. I. P. Pavlova* 10:427—33.

Burlingham, D., and Freud, A. 1942. *Young children in war-time: a year's work in a residential war nursery.* London: Allen and Unwin.

Burlingham, D.; Goldberger, A.; and Lussien, A. 1955. Simultaneous analysis of mother and child. *Psychoanal. Study Child* 10:165—86.

Burnham, D. L. 1965. Separation anxiety. *Archs gen. Psychiat.* no.

13:346—58.

Burns, R. C., and Kaufman, S. H. 1970. *Kinetic family drawings.* New York: Brunner/Mazel.

Burt, C. 1943. War neurosis in British children. *Nerv. Child.* 2:324.

Busemann, A. 1932. *Handbuch der pädagogischen Milieukunde.* Halle.

————. 1951. *Geborgenheit und Entwurzelung des jungen Menschen.* Göttingen: Vandenhoeck u. Ruprecht.

Butler, R. A. 1954. Curiosity in monkeys. *Scient. Am.* 190, no. 2:70—75.

————. 1957. The effect of deprivation of visual incentives on visual exploration motivation in monkeys. *J. comp. physiol. Psychol.* 50:174—79.

Cahn, T. 1962. Un aspect physiologique du problème des collectivités, de la hiérarchie sociale et des individus. *Acta neuroveg.* no. 23:523—33.

Caldwell, B. M. 1962. The usefulness of the critical period hypothesis in the study of filiative behavior. *Merrill-Palmer Q. Behav. Dev.* 8:229—42.

Caldwell, B. M.; Wright, C. M.; Honig, A. S.; and Tannenbaum, J. 1970. Infant day care and attachment. *Am. J. Orthopsychiat.* 40:397.

Cannon, W. B. 1929. *Bodily changes in pain, hunger, fear and rage.* 2nd ed. New York: Appleton.

Cantor, G. N. 1963. Responses of infants and children to complex and novel stimulation. In *Advances in child development and behavior,* ed. L. Lipsitt and C. C. Spiker, vol. 1, pp. 1—30. New York, London: Academic Press.

Čapková, D. 1968. *Preschool education in the work of J. A. Comenius, his precursors and followers.* (In Czech). Prague: S.P.N.

Caplan, G. 1952. The disturbance of mother-child relationship by unsuccessful attempts at abortion. *Courr. Cent. int. Enf.* 2:193—201.

————. 1953. Clinical observations on the emotional life of children in the communal settlements in Israel. In *Problems of infancy and childhood. Transactions of the Seventh Conference,* pp. 91—120. New York: Macey.

Carey-Trefzer, C. J. 1949. The results of a clinical study of war-damaged children who attended the child guidance clinic, the Hospital for Sick Children, Great Ormond Street, London. *J. ment. Sc.* 95:535—59.

Carmichael, L., ed. 1954. *Manual of child psychology.* New York: John Wiley; London: Chapman and Hall.

Casler, L. 1961. Maternal deprivation: a critical review of the literature. *Monogr. Soc. Res. Child Dev.* 26, no. 2.

Centerwall, S. A., and Centerwall, W. R. 1960. A study of children with mongolism reared in the home compared to those reared away from the home. *Pediatrics* 25:678—85.

Červinková-Riegrová, M. 1894. *The protection of poor and abandoned youth.* (In Czech). Prague.

Češmedžieva, S. 1965. Language development of children up to three years in nurseries. (In Bulgarian). *Informacionen Bjul.* no. 2:95—102.

Chambers, J. 1961. Maternal deprivation and the concept of time in children. *Am. J. Orthopsych.* 31:406—19.

Chapanis, A. L., and Williams, W. C. 1945. Results of a mental survey with the Kuhlmann-Anderson intelligence tests in Williamson County, Tennessee. *J. genet. Psychol.* 67:27—55.

Chapin, H. D. 1915a. Are institutions for infants necessary? *JAMA* 64:1—3.

————. 1915b. A plea for accurate statistics in infants' institutions. *Archs Pediat.* 10.

Chapman, A. H. 1960. Early infantile autism. *Am. J. Dis. Child.* 99:783—86.

Chapman, A. H.; Loeb, D. G.; and Gibbons, M. J. 1956. Psychiatric aspects of hospitalizing children. *Archs Pediat.* 73:77—88.

Charlesworth, W. R. 1969. The role of surprise in cognitive development. In *Studies in cognitive development,* ed. D. Elkind and J. H. Flavell, pp. 257—314. Oxford: Oxford Univ. Press.

Charny, I. W. 1963. Regression and reorganization in the "isolation treatment" of children: a clinical contribution to sensory deprivation research. *J. Child Psychol. Psychiat.* 4:47—60.

Chase, R. A. 1969. Biological dimensions of language and language disorders in children. *Bull. Orton Soc.* 19:1—17.

Chess, S. 1963. Interaction of temperament and environment in the production of behavioral disturbance in children. *Am. J. Psychiat.* 120:142—48.

————. 1966. Individuality in children, its importance to the pediatrician. *J. Pediat.* 69:676—84.

Chodoff, P. 1963. Late effects of the concentration camp syndrome. *Archs gen. Psychiat.* 8:323—33.

Chombart de Lauwe, Y. M. J. 1959. *Psychopatologie sociale de l'enfant inadapté.* Paris: Centre National de la Recherche Scientifique.

Christiaens, L. 1962. Les enfants abandonnés. *Sauvegarde de l'enfance* 17:406—17.

Christian, J. J., and Davis, D. E. 1955. Reduction of adrenal weight in rodents by reducing population size. In *Trans. N. Am. Wildl. Conf.,* pp. 177—89.

Claessens, D. 1963. Weltverlust als psychologisches und soziologisches Problem. *Arch. Rechts-und Sozialphilosophie* 49:513—25.

Clark, B., and Graybiel, A. 1957. The break-off phenomenon. *J. Aviat. Med.* 28:121—26.

Clarke, A. D. B. 1972. Consistency and variability in the growth of human characteristics. *Devl Med. Child Neurol.* 14:668—83.

Clarke, A. D. B., and Clarke, A. M. 1959. Recovery from the effects of deprivation. *Acta psychol.* 16:137—44.

————. 1960. Some recent advances in the study of early deprivation. *J. Child Psychol. Psychiat.* 1:26—36.

Clarke, A. D. B.; Clarke, A. M.; and Reiman, S. 1958. Cognitive and social changes in the feebleminded: three further studies. *Br. J. Psychol.* 49:144—57.

Cleveland, S. E.; Boyd, I.; Sheer, D.; and Reitman, E. E. 1963. Effects of fallout shelter confinement on family adjustment. *Archs gen. Psychiat.* 8:38—46.

Cleveland, S. E.; Reitman, E. E.; and Bentinck, C. 1963. Therapeutic effectiveness of sensory deprivation. *Archs gen. Psychiat.* 8:455—60.

Coates, B.; Anerson, E.; and Hartup, W. 1972. Interrelations in the attachment behavior of human infants. *Devl Psychol.* 6:218.

Cohen, B. D.; Rosenbaum, G.; Dobie, S. I.; and Gottlieb, J. S. 1959. Sensory isolation: hallucinogenic effects of brief procedure. *J. nerv. ment. Dis.* 129:489—91.

Colby, B. N. 1966. Cultural patterns in narrative. *Science* 151: 793—98.

Coleman, R. V., and Provence, A. 1957. Environmental retardation (hospitalism) in infants' families. *Pediatrics* 19:285—92.

Comenius, J. A. 1634. *On orphans.* (In Czech). Lešno.

————. 1653. *The school of infancy.* London: T. D. Benham, 1858. (First Czech ed. 1653.)

————. 1657. *The great didactic.* London: T. M. Keating, 1896. (First Czech ed. 1657.)

Commoss, H. H. 1962. Some characteristics related to social isolation of second grade children. *J. educ. Psych.* 53:38—42.

Cooper, G. D.; Adams, H. B.; and Cohen, L. D. 1965. Personality changes after sensory deprivation. *J. nerv. ment. Dis.* 140:103—18.

Corti, E. C. 1937. *Elisabeth, die seltsame Frau.* 19th ed. Salzburg, Leipzig: Pustet.

Couve, P.; Audebert, A.; and Baron, J. 1952. Syndromes de carence affective du jeune enfant en collectivité: essai de traitement. *Pédiatrie* 41:283—97.

Cravioto, J.; Licardie, E. R. de; and Birch, H. G. 1966. Nutrition, growth and neurointegrative development: an experimental and ecologic study. *Pediatrics* 38:319—72.

Crissey, O. L. 1937. Mental development as related to institutional residence and educational achievement. *Univ. Iowa Stud. Child Welf.* 13, no. 1.

Cross, H. A., and Harlow, H. F. 1965. Prolonged and progressive effects of partial isolation on the behavior of macaque monkeys. *J. exp. Res. Personality* 1:39—49.

Cutts, W. G. 1962. Special language problems of the culturally deprived. *Clearing Ho.* 37:80—83.

Czako, M. 1965. Influence of motor and social deprivation upon the spontaneous activity and maze learning in rats. (In Czech).

Psychologica, Bratisl., Fil. fak. Univ. Komenského 14, no. 5:245–62.

Czerny, A. 1908. *Der Arzt als Erzieher des Kindes.* Leipzig, Berlin: F. Deuticke.

Damborská, M. 1957*a.* Actual questions in the upbringing of institutionalized children. (In Czech). *Čslká Pediat.* 12:893–99.

————. 1957*b.* Differences between children brought up at home and in institutions in the first year of life. (In Czech). *Čslká Pediat.* 12:980.

————. 1959. Experience with the training of children in an infants' institute. (In Czech). *Čslká Pediat.* 12:819.

————. 1961. Emotional life of an infant. (In Czech). *Čslká Pediat.* 16:935–38.

————. 1963. Language development of children in an infants' home. (In Czech). *Pedagogika* 13:131–49.

————. 1966. Kinder ohne Liebe. *Monatskurse ärztl. Fortbild.* 16:552–53.

————. 1967*a. Development and education of infants in institutional conditions.* (In Czech). Prague: S.Zd.N.

————. 1967*b.* Investigation of emotional life of infants in an infants' institute. (In Czech). *Rev. Czech. Med.* 13:190–201.

————. 1969. Main positive emotions in infants. (In Czech). *Čslká Pediat.* 24:535–41, 644–50.

————. 1970. Zur Symptomatik des Deprivations-Syndroms bei Heimkindern. In *Das Deprivations-Syndrom in Prognose, Diagnose und Therapie.* Arbeitstagung für Heimärtzte und Heimleiter an Säuglings- und Kinderheimen, 1968. Frankfurt-am-Main: Deutsche Zentrale für Volksgesundheits-Pflege. Schriftenreihe vol. 17.

Damborská, M., and Blažková, E. 1959. The reaction of a ten-month-old girl to separation from her mother. (In Czech). *Čslká Pediat.* 14:658–59.

Danzinger, L. 1961. Social difficulties of children who were deprived of maternal care in early childhood. *Vita hum.* 4:229–41.

Danzinger, L., and Frankl, L. 1934. Zum Problem der Funktionsreifung. *Z. Kinderforsch.* 43:219–54.

Danzinger, L.; Hetzer, H.; and Löw-Beer, H. 1930. *Pflegemutter und Pflegekind.* Leipzig: S. Hirzel.

Dasmann, R. F., and Taber, D. 1956. Behavior of Columbian black-tailed deer with reference to population ecology. *J. Mammal.* 37:143–64.

Davenport, R. K., Jr., and Menzel, E. W., Jr. 1963. Stereotyped behavior of the infant chimpanzee. *Archs gen. Psychiat.* 8:99–104.

David, H. P., ed. 1972. *Child mental health in international perspective.* New York: Harper and Row.

David, M. 1961. Les séparations précoces mère-enfant. *Infs sociales,*

June-July.

David, M., and Appell, G. 1951. Observation et traitement d'un cas d'arriération psychogène. Z. Kinderpsychiat. 18:205–15.

Davis, J. M.; McCourt, W.; Courtney, J.; and Solomon, P. 1961. Sensory deprivation: the role of social isolation. Archs gen. Psychiat. 5:106–12.

Davis, J. M.; McCourt, W. F.; and Solomon, P. 1960. The effect of visual stimulation on hallucinations and other mental experiences during sensory deprivation. Am. J. Psychiat. 116:889–92.

Davis, K. 1940. Extreme social isolation of a child. Am. J. Sociol. 45:554–65.

———. 1947. Final note on a case of extreme isolation. Am. J. Sociol. 57:432–57.

Davison, G. C. 1964. A social learning therapy programme with an autistic child. Behav. Res. Ther. no. 2:149–59.

Décarie, T. G. 1974a. The infant's reaction to strangers. New York: International Univ. Press.

———. 1974b. Intelligence and affectivity in early childhood. New York: International Univ. Press.

Deisher, R. H. 1957. Role of the physician in maintaining continuity of care and guidance. J. Pediat. 50:231.

Delano, J. G. 1964. Separation anxiety as a cause of early emotional problems in children. Proc. Staff Meet. Mayo Clin. 39:743–49.

Dellaert, R. 1964. La corporalité comme vecteur de pédagogie curative. Acta Paedopsychiat. 31:44–52.

Dember, W. N., and Earl, R. M. 1957. Analysis of exploratory, manipulatory and curiosity behaviors. Psychol. Rev. 64:91–96.

De Mezei, M. B. 1963. Manifestaciones espontáneas del recién nacido: despertar de la vida psiquica. Archos argent. Pediat. 59:103–13.

Deniker, F. 1962. Étude sociologique de la population des crèches. Sem. Hôp. Paris 38:281–83.

Dennis, W. 1935. The effect of restricted practice upon the reaching, sitting and standing of two infants. J. genet. Psychol. 47:17–32.

———. 1938. Infant development under conditions of restricted practice and of minimum social stimulation: a preliminary report. J. genet. Psychol. 53:149–58.

———. 1941. Infant development under conditions of restricted practice and of minimum social stimulation. Genet. Psychol. Monogr. 23:143–89.

———. 1951. A further analysis of reports of wild children. Child Dev. 22:153–58.

———. 1960. Causes of retardation among institutional children: Iran. J. genet. Psychol. 96:47–59.

Dennis, W., and Najarian, P. 1957. Infant development under environmental handicap. Psychol. Monogr. 71, no. 436.

Dent, H. E. 1968. Operant conditioning as a tool in the habilitation of the mentally retarded. In *Proceedings of the first congress of the International Association for the Scientific Study of Mental Deficiency, Montpellier, France, 12–20 September 1967*, ed. B. W. Richards, pp. 873–76. Reigate, Surrey: Michael Jackson Publ.

Destunis, G. 1957. Die pathogenetischen Milieueinwirkungen auf die Entwicklung des Kindes. *Medsche Klin.* 52:371–73.

————. 1961. Milieuschädigung und Kinderneurose. In *Das milieugeschädigte Kind*, ed. H. Schwarz, pp. 1–11. Jena.

Deutsch, M. 1963. The disadvantaged child and the learning process. In *Education in depressed areas*, ed. A. H. Passow, pp. 163–79. New York: Bur. Publ., Teachers College, Columbia Univ.

————. 1964. Facilitating development in the pre-school child: social and psychological perspectives. *Merrill-Palmer Q. Behav. Dev.* 10:249–63.

Diamant, J. Notes on the psychology of life in the Terezin ghetto. (In Czech). Manuscript.

Dicks, H. V. 1939. *Clinical studies on psychopathology.*

Dilthey, W. 1924. Über vergleichende Psychologie. Beiträge zum Studium der Individualität. (1895). In *Wilhelm Dilthey's Gesammelte Schriften*, vol. 5, pp. 241–316. Leipzig, Berlin: B. G. Teubner.

Diner-Vlosko, T. B. 1960. Management of educational work in nurseries and children's homes in district of Moscow. (In Russian). *Vop. Okhr. Materin. Detst.* 5:73–77.

Dirx, R. 1964. *Das Kind: das unbekannte Wesen.* Hamburg: Marion von Schröder Verlag.

Dolejší, M. 1969. Some theoretical approaches to the question of mental retardation. (In Czech). (Dissertation thesis, Charles University, Prague.)

Dollard, J., and Miller, N. E. 1950. *Personality and psychotherapy.* New York: McGraw-Hill.

Doniger, C. R. 1962. Children whose mothers are in a mental hospital. *J. Child Psychol. Psychiat.* 3:165–73.

Douglas, J. W. B., and Blomfield, J. M. 1958. *Children under five.* London: Allen and Unwin.

Doutlík, S., and Matějček, Z. 1965. Folgezustände nach parainfektiöser Enzephalitis bei Kindern mit dem Syndrom leichter kindlicher Enzephalopathie. *Paediat. Grenzgebiete* 4, no. 1:1–8.

Dracoulides, N. N. 1956. Le milieu familial et la formation du psychisme de l'enfant. *Revue Méd. préventive* 7:1–2.

Dubois, R., and Leschanowsky, H. 1957. Observations d'hospitalisme. *Acta paediat. belg.* 11:177–88.

Dührssen, A. 1958. *Heimkinder und Pflegekinder in ihrer Entwicklung.* Göttingen: Vandenhoeck u. Ruprecht.

————. 1961. *Psychogene Erkrankungen bei Kindern und Jugendlichen.* 4th ed. Göttingen.

Dunovský, J. 1966. Fürsorge für Kinder ohne Familie in der Tschechoslowakei. *Unsere Jugend* 18:228—30.

————. 1968. Infant institutions in Czechoslovakia. *Devl Med. Child Neurol.* 10:805—11.

————. 1969a. Die soziale Stellung von Kindern, die seit frühester Kindheit in Kinderheimen aufwachsen. *Unsere Jugend* 21:545—57.

————. 1969b. Social status of children brought up since early childhood in children's homes. (In Czech). *Pedagogika* 19:189—205.

————. 1972. Social diagnosis and selection of children for substitute family care. *Rev. Czech. Med.* 18:204—12.

Dunovský, J., and Havlíčková, V. 1968. Some basic data on children in homes for infants and children (1—3 years) from 1960 to 1964. (In Czech). *Bull. SPOK* 3:3—12.

Dunovský, J.; Kučera, M.; and Zelenková, M. 1974. *Children born out of wedlock.* (In Czech). Prague: MPSV ČSR.

Durfee, H., and Wolf, K. 1934. Anstaltspflege und Entwicklung im 1. Lebensjahr. *Z. Kinderforsch.* 42:273—320.

Earle, A. M., and Earle, B. V. 1961. Early maternal deprivation and later psychiatric illness. *Am. J. Orthopsychiat.* 31:181.

Eckstein, E. 1926. Zur Frage des Hospitalismus in Säuglingsanstalten. *Z. Kinderheilk.* 42:31—38.

Edelston, H. 1943. Separation anxiety in young children: a study of hospital cases. *Genet. Psychol. Monogr.* 28:3—95.

————. 1955. Separation experiences and mental health. *Lancet* 2:615—16.

Edwards, A. S., and Jones, L. 1938. An experimental and field study of North Georgia mountaineers. *J. soc. Psychol.* 9:317—33.

Eggers, H., and Wagner, K. D. 1965. Untersuchungen zu körperlichen und psychischen Entwicklung von Kleinkindern in Krippen. *Ärztl. Jugendkd.* 56:157—69.

Ehrlich, A. 1959. Effects of past experiences on exploratory behaviour in rats. *Can. J. Psychol.* 13:248—54.

————. 1961a. The effects of past experiences on the rat's response to novelty. *Can. J. Psychol.* 15:19.

————. 1961b. Note on the effects of differential rearing conditions on weight gain in the hooded rat. *Can. J. Psychol.* 15:244—46.

Eisenberg, L. 1958. Emotional determinants of mental deficiency. *Archs Neurol. Psychiat., Chicago* 79:114—21.

————. 1966. Reading retardation: I. Psychiatric and sociologic aspects. *Pediatrics* 37:352—65.

Eisenberg, L., and Kanner, L. 1956. Early infantile autism. *Am. J. Orthopsychiat.* 26:556—66.

Elliot, O., and Scott, J. P. 1961. The development of emotional distress reactions to separation in puppies. *J. genet. Psychol* 99:3–22.

Elmer, E. 1960. Abused young children seen in hospitals. *Social Wk* 5, no. 4:98–102.

——. 1963. Identification of abused children. *Children*, September-October, pp. 180–84.

——. 1966. Hazards in determining child abuse. *Child Welf.* 45:28–33.

——. 1967. Abused children and community resources. *Int. J. Offender Ther.* 11, no. 1.

Elmer, E., and Gregg, G. S. 1967. Developmental characteristics of abused children. *Pediatrics* 40:596–602.

Elrick, H.; Bernstein, L.; Diamant, E.; Whitehouse, J. M.; and Borda-Bossana, D. 1958. Effects of handling on the adrenalectomized rat. *Proc. Soc. exp. Biol. Med.* 99:696–98.

Elrick, H.; Borda-Bossana, D.; Diamant, E.; Bernstein, L.; and Whitehouse, J.M. 1960. Effects of handling on the thyroid-ectomized rat. *Am. J. Physiol.* 198, no. 1:13–14.

Emery-Hanzeur, C., and Sand, E. A. 1962. Enfants désirés et non désirés. *Enfance* 2:109–25.

Emmerich, W. 1966. Family role concepts of children aged six to ten. In *Role theory: concepts and research*, ed. B. J. Biddle and E. J. Thomas, pp. 361–69. New York, London, Sydney: Wiley.

Epstein, A. 1882. *Studien zur Frage der Findelanstalten unter besonderer Berücksichtigung der Verhältnisse in Böhmen.* Prague.

Eriksen, C. W. 1957. Personality. *A. Rev. Psychol.* 8:185–210.

Erikson, E. H. 1950. *Childhood and society.* 1st ed. New York: W. W. Norton. 2nd ed. 1963.

——. 1966. Eight ages of man. *Int. J. Psychiat.* 2:281–97, 298–307.

Escalona, S. K. 1945. Feeding disturbances in very young children. *Am. J. Orthopsychiat.* 15:76–80.

——. 1962. The study of individual differences and the problem of state. *J. Am. Acad. Child Psychiat.* 1:11–37.

Etzel, B. C., and Gewirtz, J. L. 1966. Experimental modification of caretaker-maintained operant crying in two infants (Tirannotearus Infantus) 6 and 20 weeks old. Mimeographed.

Eveloff, H. H. 1960. The autistic child. *Archs gen. Psychiat.* 3:66–81.

Faigin, H. 1958. Social behavior of young children in the kibbutz. *J. abnorm. soc. Psychol.* 56:117–29.

Falkowska, M.; Kuzańska, M.; and Sieradzki, Z. 1968. *Collective care in children's homes.* (In Polish). Warsaw: Nasza Ksiegarnia.

Fantz, R. L. 1961. The origin of form perception. *Scient. Am.* 204:66–72.

Farrell, M. J. 1956. The adverse effects of early institutionalization of mentally subnormal children. *Am. J. Dis. Child.* 91:278–81.

Fernandez, J. M. 1954. Psychogenic weeping in infancy. *Acta pediat. esp.* 12:707–19.

Ferster, C. B. 1958. Reinforcement and punishment in the control of human behaviour by social agencies. *Psychiat. Res. Rep.* 10:101–18.

Finkelstein, H. 1898. Über Morbidität und Mortalität in Säuglingsspitälern und deren Ursachen. *Z. Hyg. InfektKrankh.* 28:125–58.

Finkelstein, H., and Ballin, A. 1904. *Die Waisensäuglinge Berlins.* Berlin, Vienna.

Fischer, L. K. 1952. Hospitalism in six-month-old infants. *Am. J. Orthopsychiat.* 22:522–34.

Fiske, D. W., and Maddi, S. R. 1961. *Functions of varied experience.* Homewood, Ill.: Dorsey.

Fleck, S.; Lidz, T.; and Cornelison, A. 1963. Comparison of parent-child relationships of male and female schizophrenic patients. *Archs gen. Psychiat.* 8:1–7.

Flescher, J. M. D. 1970. *Childhood and destiny: the triadic principle in genetic education.* New York: International Univ. Press.

Flint, B. M. 1957. Babies who live in institutions. *Bull. Inst. Child Study, Toronto* 19:1–5.

————. 1959. *The security of infants.* Toronto: Univ. of Toronto Press.

————. 1966. *The child and the institution: a study of deprivation and recovery.* Toronto: Univ. of Toronto Press.

Forrest, A. D.; Fraser, R. H.; and Priest, F. G. 1965. Environmental factors in depressive illness. *Br. J. Psychiat.* 111:243–53.

Foss, B. M., ed. 1961–69. *Determinants of infant behaviour,* 4 vols. London: Methuen.

Franceschetti, A. 1947. Rubéole pendant la grossesse et cataracte congénitale chez l'enfant, accompagnée du phénomène digito-oculaire. *Ophthalmologica, Basel* 114:332–39.

Francis, R. D. 1964. The effects of prior instructions and time knowledge on the toleration of sensory isolation. *J. nerv. ment. Dis.* 139:182–85.

François, C. 1948. État psychologique des enfants et leurs réactions à leurs arrivées au "Renouveau". *Z. Kinderpsychiat.* 14:178–85.

Frankl, V. E. 1963. *Man's search for meaning.* Boston: Beacon Press.

Fraňková, S. 1970. Late consequences of early nutritional and sensoric deprivation in rats. (In Czech). *Activitas nerv. sup.* 12:155–56.

Freedman, D. A. 1971. Congenital and perinatal sensory deprivation: some studies in early development. *Am. J. Psychiat.* 127:1539–45.

Freedman, S. J. 1961. Perceptual changes in sensory deprivation: suggestions for a conative theory. *J. nerv. ment. Dis.* 132:17–21.

Freedman, S. J.; Grunebaum, H. U.; and Greenblatt, M. 1961. Perceptual and cognitive changes in sensory deprivation. In *Sensory deprivation,* ed. P. M. Solomon et al., pp. 58–71. Cambridge, Mass.: Harvard Univ. Press.

Freeman, F. N.; Holzinger, K. J.; and Mitchell, C. B. 1928. The influence of environment on the intelligence, school achievement, and conduct of foster children. In *Twenty-seventh yearbook of the National Society for the Study of Education,* ed. G. M. Whipple, Part 1, pp. 103–217. Bloomington, Ill.: Public School Publ.

French, J. D. 1960. Brain physiology and modern medicine. *Postgrad. Med.* 27:559–68.

Freud, A., and Burlingham, D. 1944*a. Infants without families.* New York: International Univ. Press.

————. 1944*b. War and children.* New York: International Univ. Press.

Freud, A., and Dann, S. 1951. An experiment in group upbringing. *Psychoanal. Study Child* 6.

Freud, S. 1917. *Vorlesungen zur Einführung in die Psychoanalyse.* Leipzig, Wien: H. Heller.

————. 1938. Three contributions to the theory of sex. In *The basic writings of Sigmund Freud,* trans. A. A. Brill. New York: Random House. Originally published 1905.

————. 1950. Instincts and their vicissitudes. In *Collected papers,* vol. 4, pp. 60–83. London: Hogarth. Originally published 1915.

————. 1957. On narcissism. In *The standard edition of the complete psychological works of Sigmund Freud,* vol. 14, pp. 73–102. London: Hogarth. Originally published 1914.

Fried, R., and Mayer, M. F. 1948. Socio-emotional factors accounting for growth in children living in institutions. *J. Pediat.* 33:444–56.

Friedemann, A. 1958. Rapport sur la carence affective chez l'enfant de 6 à 10 ans, dans le tableau du développement normal. *Criança port.* 17:103–42.

Fries, M. E., and Woolf, P. G. 1953. Some hypotheses on the role of the congenital activity type in personality development. *Psychoanal. Study Child* 8:48–62.

Frisk, M. 1964. Identity problems and confused conceptions of the genetic ego in adopted children during adolescence. *Acta Paedopsychiat.* 31:6–12.

Fromm, E. 1956. *The art of loving.* New York: Harper and Row.

Gardner, D. B.; Pease, D.; and Hawkes, G. R. 1961. Response of two-year-old children to controlled stress situations. *J. genet. Psychol.* 98:29–35.

Gardner, D. B., and Swiger, M. K. 1958. Developmental status of two groups of infants released for adoption. *Child Dev.* 29:521–30.

Gardner, L. I. 1972. Deprivation dwarfism. *Scient. Am.* 227:76–82.

Gardner, R. W. 1971. Evolution and brain injury: the impact of deprivation on cognitive-affective structures. *Bull. Menninger Clin.* 35:113–24.

Gavrin, J. B., and Sack, L. S. 1963. Growth potential of preschool-aged children in institutional care: a positive approach to a negative condition. *Am. J. Orthopsychiat.* 33:399–408.

Gebber, M. 1964. Le développement psycho-moteur de l'enfant Ganda en relation avec son milieu socio-culturel. *Inf. psychiat.* 40:555–65.

Gedo, J. E. 1966. The psychotherapy of developmental arrest. *Br. J. med. Psychol.* 39:25–33.

Gelinier-Ortigues, M. C. 1955. Maternal deprivation, psychogenic deafness and pseudo-retardation. In *Emotional problems of early childhood,* ed. G. Caplan, pp. 231–47. New York: Basic.

Gesell, A. 1928. *Infancy and human growth.* New York: Macmillan.

————. 1940. *Wolf children and human child.* New York, London: Harper and Brothers.

Gesell, A., and Amatruda, C. S. 1947. *Developmental diagnosis.* New York, London: Hoeber.

Gesell, A.; Castner, B. M.; Thompson, H.; and Amatruda, C. S. 1939. *Biographies of child development: the mental growth careers of eighty-four infants and children.* New York: Hoeber.

Gesell, A., and Ilg, F. L. 1943. *Infant and child in the culture of today.* New York: Harper and Brothers.

Gesell, A., and Thompson, H. 1929. Learning and growth in identical infant twins. *Genet. Psychol. Monogr.* 6:1–124.

Gewirtz, H. B., and Gewirtz, J. L. 1968. Visiting and caretaking patterns for kibbutz infants. *Am. J. Orthopsychiat.* 38:427–43.

————. 1969. Caretaking settings, background events and behavior differences in four Israeli child-rearing environments. In *Determinants of infant behaviour,* ed. B. M. Foss, vol. 4, pp. 229–95. London: Methuen.

Gewirtz, J. L. 1954. Three determinants of attention-seeking in young children. *Monogr. Soc. Res. Child Dev.* 19, no. 2.

————. 1956. Program of research on the dimensions and antecedents of emotional dependence. *Child Dev.* 27:205–21.

————. 1961. A learning analysis of the effects of normal stimulation, privation and deprivation on the acquisition of social motivation and attachment. In *Determinants of infant behaviour,* ed. B. M. Foss, vol. 1, pp. 213–99. London: Methuen.

————. 1965. The course of infant smiling in four child-rearing environments in Israel. In *Determinants of infant behaviour,* ed. B. M. Foss, vol. 3, pp. 205–60. London: Methuen.

————. 1967. Deprivation and satiation of social stimuli as determinants of their reinforcing efficacy. In *Minnesota symposia on child psychology,* ed. J. P. Hill, vol. 1, pp. 3–56. Minneapolis: Univ. of Minnesota Press.

————. 1968. 1. On designing the functional environment of the child to facilitate behavioral development. 2. The role of stimulation in models for child development. In *Early child care: the new perspectives,* ed. L. L. Dittmann. New York: Atherton, pp. 139–68 and 169–213.

————. 1969a. Levels of conceptual analysis in environment-infant interaction research. *Merrill-Palmer Q. Behav. Dev.* 15:7–47.

————. 1969*b*. Mechanisms of social learning: some roles of stimulation and behavior in early human development. In *Handbook of socialization theory and research,* ed. D. Goslin, pp. 57–212. New York: Rand McNally.

————. 1969*c*. Potency of a social reinforcer as a function of satiation and recovery. *Devl Psychol.* 1:2–13.

Gewirtz, J.L., and Baer, D.D. 1958*a*. Deprivation and satiation of social reinforcers as drive conditions. *J. abnorm. soc. Psychol.* 56:165–72.

————. 1958*b*. The effects of brief social deprivation on behaviors for a social reinforcer. *J. abnorm. soc. Psychol.* 56:49–56.

Gewirtz, J.L.; Baer, D.M.; and Roth, C.H. 1958. A note on the similar effects of low social availability of an adult and brief social deprivation on young children's behavior. *Child Dev.* 29:150–52.

Gewirtz, J. L., and Gewirtz, H. B. 1965. Stimulus conditions, infant behaviors, and social learning in four Israeli child-rearing environments. In *Determinants of infant behaviour,* ed. B. M. Foss, vol. 3, pp. 161–84. London: Methuen.

Gewirtz, J. L., and Stingle, K. G. 1968. Learning of generalized imitation as the basis for identification. *Psychol. Rev.* 75:374–97.

Gibby, R. G.; Adams, H. B.; and Carrera, R. N. 1960. Therapeutic changes in psychiatric patients following partial sensory deprivation. *Archs gen. Psychiat.* 3:33–42.

Gindl, I.; Hetzer, H; and Sturm, M. 1937. Unangemessenheit der Anstalt als Lebensraum für das Kleinkind. *Z. angew. Psychol. Charakterkd.* 52:310–58.

Ginsburg, H. 1972. *The myth of the deprived child.* Engelwood Cliffs, New Jersey: Prentice-Hall.

Glanzer, M. 1958. Curiosity, exploratory drive and stimulus satiation. *Psychol. Bull.* 55:302–15.

Glaser, K. 1960. Group discussions with mothers of hospitalized children. *Pediatrics* 26:132–40.

Glaser, K., and Eisenberg, L. 1956. Maternal deprivation. *Pediatrics* 18:626–42.

Glaser, Y. I. M. 1962. A unit for mothers and babies in a psychiatric hospital. *J. Child Psychol.* 3:53–60.

Glueck, S., and Glueck, E. T. 1950. *Unravelling juvenile delinquency.* New York: Commonwealth Fund.

Gmeiner, H. 1960*a*. Das SOS-Kinderdorf als Verwahrlosungs-prophylaxe. *Neue Wege* 2.

————. 1960*b*. *Die SOS-Kinderdörfer.* Vienna.

Goffman, E. 1961. On the characteristics of a total institution. In *Asylums.* New York: Doubleday, Anchor Books.

Gofman, H.; Buckman, W.; and Schade, G. 1957*a*. The child's emotional response to hospitalization. *Am. J. Dis. Child.* 93:157–64.

————. 1957b. Parents' emotional response to child's hospitalization. *Am. J. Dis. Child.* 93:629—37.

Golan, S. 1958. Behavior research in collective settlements in Israel: collective education in kibbutz. *Am. J. Orthopsychiat.* 28:549—56.

Goldberger, K. 1963. *Children without love.* (Film.) Prague: Krátký Film.

Goldberger, L., and Holt, R. R. 1958. Experimental interference with reality contact (perceptual isolation): I. Method and group results. *J. nerv. ment. Dis.* 127:99—112.

Goldfarb, W. 1943a. Effects of early institutional care on adolescent personality. *J. exp. Educ.* 12:106—29.

————. 1943b. Effects of early institutional care on adolescent personality. *Child Dev.* 14:213—23.

————. 1943c. Infant rearing and problem behavior. *Am. J. Orthopsychiat.* 13:249—65.

————. 1944a. Effects of early institutional care on adolescent personality: Rorschach data. *Am. J. Orthopsychiat.* 14:441—47.

————. 1944b. Infants' rearing as a factor in foster home replacement. *Am. J. Orthopsychiat.* 14:162—66.

————. 1945a. Effects of psychological deprivation in infancy and subsequent stimulation. *Am. J. Psychiat.* 102:18—33.

————. 1945b. Psychological privation in infancy and subsequent adjustment. *Am. J. Orthopsychiat.* 15:247—55.

————. 1946. Variations in adolescent adjustment of institutionally-reared children. *Am. J. Orthopsychiat.* 17:449—57.

————. 1949. Rorschach test differences between family-reared and institutionally-reared children. *Am. J. Orthopsychiat.* 19:624—33.

Goldfarb, W., and Klopfer, B. 1944. Rorschach characteristics of institutional children. *Rorschach Res. Exch.* 8:92—100.

Goldman, F. 1950. Breastfeeding and character formation: II. The etiology of the oral character in psychoanalytic theory. *J. Personality* 19: 189—96.

Goldman-Eisler, F. 1951. The problem of "orality" and of its origin in early childhood. *J. ment. Sci.* 97:765—82.

————. 1953. Breast feeding and character formation. In *Personality in nature, society and culture,* ed. C. Kluckhohn and H. A. Murray, pp. 146—84. New York: Knopf.

Goldstein, K. 1959. Abnormal mental conditions in infancy. *J. nerv. ment. Dis.* 128:538—57.

Goodman, J. D.; Silberstein, R. M.; and Mandell, W. 1963. Adopted children brought to child psychiatric clinic. *Archs gen. Psychiat.* 9:451—56.

Goodman, L. 1932. Effects of total absence of function of the optic system of rabbits. *Am. J. Physiol.* 100:46—63.

Gordon, H. (1923). *Mental and scholastic tests among retarded children: an enquiry into the effects of schooling on the various tests.* Board of Education, London, Education Pamphlets, no. 44.

Gorer, G., and Rickman, J. 1949. *The people of Great Russia.* London: Cresset.

Górnicki, B. 1965. Développement des enfants dans le milieu familial et dans les crèches en Pologne. In *Les soins aux enfants dans les crèches.* Geneva: WHO.

Gottschaldt, K. 1954. *Probleme der Jugendverwahrlosung.* Leipzig.

Gough, H. G. 1955. A sociological theory of psychopathy. In *Mental health and mental disorders,* ed. A. M. Rose. New York: Norton.

Graffar, M., and Sand, E. A. 1954. Les dangers de l'hospitalisation des jeunes enfants. *Serv. Social* 1–15.

Graham, P., and George, S. 1972. Children's responses to parental illness: individual differences. *J. psychosom. Res.* 16:251–56.

Grams, A. 1970. Fatherhood and motherhood in a changing world. *Int. Child Welf. Rev.,* September.

Green, C., and Zigler, E. 1962. Social deprivation and the performance of retarded and normal children on a satiation type task. *Child Dev.* 33:499–508.

Green, M., and Beall, P. 1962. Paternal deprivation: a disturbance in fathering. *Pediatrics* 30:91–99.

Greenbaum, M. 1962. The displaced child syndrome. *J. Child Psychol. Psychiat.* 3:93–100.

Greenfield, P. M. 1972. Cross-cultural studies of mother-infant interaction: towards a structural-functional approach. *Hum. Dev.* 15:131–38.

Greer, S. 1964. Study of parental loss in neurotics and sociopaths. *Archs gen. Psychiat.* 11:177–80.

———. 1966. Parental loss and attempted suicide: a further report. *Br. J. Psychiat.* 112:465–70.

Gregory, I. 1958. Studies of parental deprivation in psychiatric patients. *Am. J. Psychiat.* 115:432–42.

———. 1965*a*. Anterospective data following childhood loss of a parent. I. Delinquency and high school dropout. II. Pathology. Performance and potential among college students. *Archs gen. Psychiat.* 13:99–109, 110–20.

———. 1965*b*. Retrospective estimates of orphanhood from generation life tables. *Milbank meml Fund q. Bull.* 43:323–48.

———. 1966. Retrospective data concerning childhood loss of a parent. I. Actuarial estimates vs. recorded frequencies of orphanhood. II. Category of parental loss by decade of birth, diagnosis and MMPI. *Archs gen. Psychiat.* 15:354–61, 362–67.

Greil, A. 1953. *Das Wesen der Menschenwerdung.* Jena: G. Fischer.

Groot, A. D. de. 1948. The effects of war upon the intelligence of youth. *J. abnorm. soc. Psychol.* 43:311–17.

———. 1951. War and the intelligence of youth. *J. abnorm. soc. Psychol.* 46:596–97.

Gross, S. Z. 1963. Critique: Children who break down in foster homes: a psychological study of patterns of personality growth in grossly deprived children. *J. Child Psychol. Psychiat.* 4:61–66.

Grunebaum, H. U.; Freedman, S. J.; and Greenblatt, M. 1960. Sensory deprivation and personality. *Am. J. Psychiat.* 116:878–82.

Guépin, F. 1962. Hospitalisation et immobilisation prolongée chez de jeunes enfants. *Enfance* 2:127–67.

Gunderson, E. K. E. 1963. Emotional symptoms in extremely isolated groups. *Archs gen. Psychiat.* 9:362–68.

Gyomroi, E. L. 1963. The analysis of a young concentration camp victim. *Psychoanal. Study Child* 18:484–510.

Haar, E.; Welkowitz, J.; and Blau, A. 1964. Personality differentiation of neonates: a nurse rating scale method. *J. Am. Acad. Child Psychiat.* 3:330–42.

Hadfield, J. A. 1962. *Childhood and adolescence.* Harmondsworth, Mddx.: Penguin.

Haggerty, A. D. 1959. The effects of long-term hospitalization upon the language development of children. *J. gen. Psychol.* 94:205–9.

Harbauer, H. 1955. Das Kind im Krankenhaus. *Kinderärztl. Prax.* 23: 417–22.

Harineková, M. 1962. Emotional reactions in nursery school children. (In Czech). *Cslká Pediat.* 17:615–20.

Harlow, H. F. 1958. The nature of love. *Am. Psychol.* 13:673–85.

———. 1959. Love in infant monkeys. *Scient. Am.* 200:68–74.

———. 1961. The development of affectional patterns in infant monkeys. In *Determinants of infant behaviour,* ed. B. M. Foss, vol. 1, pp. 75–97. London: Methuen.

———. 1962. The heterosexual affectional system in monkeys. *Am. Psychol.* 17:1–9.

Harlow, H. F., and Harlow, M. K. 1962. Social deprivation in monkeys. *Scient. Am.* 207:137.

———. 1965. The effect of rearing conditions on behavior. *Int. J. Psychiat.* 1:43–51.

———. 1966. Learning to love. *Am. Scient.* 54:244–72.

Harlow, H. F.; Harlow, M. K.; and Meyer, D. R. 1950. Learning motivated by a manipulative drive. *J. exp. Psychol.* 40:228–34.

Harlow, H. F., and Zimmermann, R. F. 1958. The development of affectional responses in infant monkeys. *Proc. Am. phil. Soc.* 102:501–9.

———. 1959. Affectional responses in the infant monkeys. *Science* 130:421–32.

Harminc, M. 1965. Influence of deprivation at an early age upon the discriminative learning in rats. (In Czech). *Psychologica* 16:263–76.

Harnack, G. A., and Oberschelp, M. 1957. Die seelischen Auswirkungen eines Krankenhausaufenthaltes im Kindesalter. *Dt. med. Wschr.* 82.

Harris, A. 1959. Sensory deprivation and schizophrenia. *J. ment. Sci.* 105:235–37.

Harrison, S. J.; Davenport, C. W.; and McDermott, J. F., Jr. 1967. Children's reaction to bereavement: adult confusions and mis-perceptions. *Archs gen. Psychiat.* 17:593–97.

Hartmann, K. 1961. Über die Entbehrung des Vaters und ihre Bedeutung für männliche Jugendverwahrlosung. *Prax. Kinderpsychol. Kinderpsychiat.* 10:249–54.

Hartung, K., and Glattkowski, H. 1965. Erhebungen über Aufenthaltsdauer und Gründe die zur Heimaufnahme von Säuglingen führen. *Prax. Kinderpsychol. Kinderpsychiat.* 14:241–45, 297–303.

Hartup, W., and Himeno, Y. 1959. Social isolation vs. interaction with adults in relation to aggression in preschool children. *J. abnorm. soc. Psychol.* 59:17–22.

Hasselmann-Kahlert, M. 1958. Das entwurzelte Kind. *Medizinische* 36:1365–67.

Hassenstein, B. 1973. *Verhaltensbiologie des Kindes.* Munich, Zürich: Piper.

Hausam, L., and Spiess, H. 1958. Kind und Krankenhaus. *Medizinische* 36:1365–67.

Hauss, K. 1960. Das Kind ohne Familie. *Hippokrates* 31:266–72.

Haworth, M. 1964. Parental loss in children as reflected in projective responses. *J. project. Tech. Personality Assessment* 28:31–45.

Haythorn, W. W.; Altman, I.; and Myers, I. I. 1965. *Emotional symptomatology and stress in isolated groups.* Bethesda, Maryland: Naval Medical Research Institute.

Haywood, H. C. 1961. Relationships among anxiety, seeking of novel stimuli, and level of unassimilated percepts. *J. Personality* 29:105–14.

————. 1962. Novelty-seeking behavior as a function of manifest and physiological arousal. *J. Personality* 30:63–74.

Hebb, D. O. 1955. The mammal and his environment. *Am. J. Psychiat.* 111:826–31.

————. 1958. The motivating effects of exteroceptive stimulation. *Am. Psychol.* 13:109–13.

Heber, R. 1967. The role of environmental variables in the etiology of cultural-familial mental retardation. In *Proceedings of the first congress of the International Association for the Scientific Study of Mental Deficiency, Montpellier, France, 12–20 September 1967,* ed. B. W. Richards, pp. 456–65. Reigate, Surrey: Michael Jackson Publ.

Hege, M., and Bischof, D. 1963. Psychologische Analyse eines Säuglings- und Kleinkinderheimes. *Prax. Kinderpsychol. Kinderpsychiat.* no. 1-2.

Heinicke, C. M. 1956. Some effects of separating two-year-old children from their parents. *Hum. Relat.* 9:105–76.

Heinicke, C. M., and Westheimer, I. I. 1965. *Brief separation*. New York: International Univ. Press.

Hejlová, E. 1947. Psychological state of children after their liberation from concentration camp. (In Czech). *Pediat. Listy* 2:113.

Held, R., and Bossom, J. 1961. Neonatal deprivation and adult rearrangement. *J. comp. physiol. Psychol.* 54:33—37.

Held, R., and White, B. 1959. Sensory deprivation and visual speed. *Science* 130:860—61.

Hellbrügge, T., 1966. Zur Problematik der Säuglings- und Kleinkinderfürsorge in Anstalten: Hospitalismus und Deprivation. In *Handbuch der Kinderheilkunde*, ed. H. Opitz and F. Schmid, vol. 3, pp. 384—404. Berlin, Heidelberg, New York: Springer.

——————. 1970. Zur Prognose des frühkindlichen Deprivations-Syndroms bei Heimkindern. In *Das Deprivations-Syndrom in Prognose, Diagnose und Therapie*. Arbeitstagung für Heimärtzte und Heimleiter an Säuglings- und Kinderheimen, 1968. Frankfurt-am-Main: Deutsche Zentrale für Volksgesundheits-Pflege. Schriftenreihe vol. 17.

Hellbrügge, T.; Becker-Freyseng, I.; Menara, D.; and Schamberger, R. 1973. Deprivations-Syndrom im Säuglingsheim. *Münch. med. Wschr.* 115:1753—60.

Hellbrügge, T., and Pechstein, J. 1967. Pädiatrische Merksätze zur Situation der Säuglingsheime. *Fortschr. Med.* 85:1—2.

Hellman, I. 1962. Hampstead Nursery follow-up studies. I. Sudden separation and its effect followed over twenty years. *Psychoanal. Study Child* 17:159—74.

Heron, W. 1957. The pathology of boredom. *Scient. Am.* 196:52—56.

Heron, W.; Bexton, W. H.; and Hebb, D. O. 1953. Cognitive effects of a decreased variation to the sensory environment. *Am. Psychol.* 8:366.

Heron, W.; Doane, B. K.; and Scott, T. H. 1956. Visual disturbances after prolonged perceptual isolation. *Can. J. Psychol.* 10:13—18.

Hersher, L.; Moore, A. U.; Richmond, J. B.; and Blauvelt, H. 1962. The effects of deprivation during the nursing period on the behavior of young goats. Paper read at seventieth annual conference of American Psychological Association.

Hersov, L. A. 1960. 1. Persistent non-attendance at school. 2. Refusal to go to school. *Child Psychol. Psychiat.* 1:130—36, 137—45.

Hertzig, M. E.; Birch, H. G.; Richardson, S. A.; and Tizard, J. 1972. Intellectual level of school children severely malnourished during the first two years of life. *Pediatrics* 46:814—24.

Herzog, E. 1960. *Children of working mothers*. Washington: U.S. Dept. of Health, Education and Welfare, U.S. Children's Bureau Publ. no. 382.

Hess, R. D., and Shipman, V. C. 1965. Early experience and the socialization of cognitive modes in children. *Child Dev.* 36:869—86.

Hesse, G. 1957. Die familiäre Situation bei der Schwererziehbarkeit des Kindes. *Z. ärztl. Fortbild.* 51:981—82.

Hetzer, H. 1929. *Kindheit und Armut.* 1st ed. Leipzig: S. Hirzel. 2nd ed. 1937.

―――. 1932. Die Entwicklung des Kindes in der Anstalt. In *Handbuch der pädagogischen Milieukunde,* ed. A. Busemann. Halle.

Heuyer, G. 1958. Rapport introductive. Aspects somatiques de la psychiatrie infantile. *Criança port.* 17:295—303.

Heymann, K. 1946. Entwurzelte und disharmonische Kinder. *Psychol. Prax.,* no. 5.

Hicklin, M. 1945. *War-damaged children.* London: Association of Psychiatric Social Workers.

Hilgard, E. R. 1962. Impulsive vs. realistic thinking. *Psychol. Bull.* 59:477—88.

Hilgard, J. R., and Newman, M. F. 1961. Evidence of functional genesis in mental illness. *J. nerv. ment. Dis.* 132:3—16.

―――. 1963a. Early parental deprivation in schizophrenia and alcoholism. *Am. J. Orthopsychiat.* 33:409—20.

―――. 1963b. Parental loss by death in childhood as an etiological factor among schizophrenic and alcoholic patients compared with a non-patient community sample. *J. nerv. ment. Dis.* 137:14—28.

Hill, J. C., and Robinson, B. 1929. A case of retarded mental development associated with restricted movements in infancy. *Br. J. med. Psychol.* 9:268—77.

Hinde, R. A., and Davies, L. 1972. Removing infant rhesus from mother for 13 days compared with removing mother from infant. *J. Child Psychol. Psychiat.* 13:227—37.

Hinde, R. A., and Spencer-Booth, Y. 1970. Individual differences in the responses of rhesus monkeys to a period of separation from their mothers. *J. Child Psychol. Psychiat.* 11:159—76.

Hofer, M. A. 1972. Physiological and behavioural processes in early maternal deprivation. *Ciba Fdn. Symp.* 8:175—86.

Holway, A. R. 1949. Early self-regulation of infants and later behavior in play interviews. *Am. J. Orthopsychiat.* 19:612—22.

Hopkinson, G., and Reed, G. F. 1966. Bereavement in childhood depressive psychosis. *Br. J. Psychiat.* 112:459—63.

Horáčková, E., and Čulik, A. 1967. One-sided relation and a test of projected emotional deprivation. (In Czech). *Activitas nerv. sup.* 9:145—51.

Horn, A. 1966. Zur schädlichen Wirkung des Hospitalismus und Grund von Rorschach-Protokollen. *Schweiz. Z. Psychol.* 25:107—15.

Horney, K. 1937. *The neurotic personality of our times.* New York: Norton.

Howells, J. G. 1972. Monkey therapist. *Am. J. Psychiat.* 129:485—86.

Howells, J. G., and Layng, J. 1955. Separation experiences and mental health. *Lancet* 2:285—88.

Hügel, F. S. 1863. *Die Findelhäuser und das Findelwesen Europas.* Vienna: L. Sommer.

Hull, C. L. 1943. *Principles of behavior.* New York: Appleton-Century.

Humphrey, M., and Ounsted, C. 1964. Adoptive families referred for psychiatric advice. *Br. J. Psychiat.* 110:549–55.

Hunt, J. McV. 1960. Experience and the development of motivation. *Child Dev.* 31:489–504.

————. 1961. *Intelligence and experience.* New York: Ronald.

————. 1964. The psychological basis for using pre-school enrichment as an antidote for cultural deprivation. *Merrill-Palmer Q. Behav. Dev.* 10:209–48.

Hymovitch, B. J. 1952. The effects of experimental variations on problem solving in rats. *J. comp. physiol. Psychol.* 45:313–21.

Illingworth, R. S., and Holt, K. S. 1955. Children in hospital. Some observations on their reactions with special reference to visiting daily. *Lancet* 2:1257–62.

Illingworth, R. S., and Lister, J. 1964. The critical or sensitive period, with special reference to certain feeding problems in infants and children. *J. Pediat.* 65:839–48.

Inglis, J. 1965. Sensory deprivation and cognitive disorder. *Br. J. Psychiat.* 111:309–15.

Irvine, E. 1952. Observations on the aims and methods of child rearing in communal settlements in Israel. *Hum. Relat.* 5:247–75.

Irwin, R. B. 1972. Language of culturally deprived children. *Acta Symbolica* 3:1,29–32.

Isaacs, S. 1941. *Cambridge evacuation survey: a wartime study in social welfare and education.* London: Methuen.

————. 1948*a*. Children in institutions. In *Childhood and after,* pp. 208–38. London: Routledge and Kegan Paul.

————. 1948*b*. Fatherless children. In *Childhood and after,* pp. 186–207. London: Routledge and Kegan Paul.

Itard, J. M. G. 1807. *Rapport fait à son excellence le ministre de l'intérieur sur les nouveaux développements et l'état actuel du sauvage de l'Aveyron.* Paris: L'imprimerie imperiale.

Jackson, K.; Winkley, R.; Faust, O. A.; and Cermak, E. G. 1952. Problems of emotional trauma in hospital treatment of children. *JAMA* 149:1536–38.

Jackson, W. C., Jr., and Pollard, J. C. 1966. Some nondeprivation variables which influence the "effects" of experimental sensory deprivation. *J. abnorm. Psychol.* 71:383–88.

Jensen, G. D., and Bobbitt, R. A. 1968. Monkeying with the mother myth. *Psychology Today,* May.

Jessner, L.; Blom, G. E.; and Waldfogel, S. 1952. Emotional implications of tonsillectomy and adenoidectomy on children. *Psychoanal. Study Child* 7:126.

John, V. P. 1963. The intellectual development of slum children. *Am. J. Orthopsychiat.* 33:813–22.

Jones, B., and Goodson, J. E. 1959. *The effect of boredom on suggestibility.* Research Report, U.S. Naval Aviation Medical Center, Pensacola, Florida.

Jones, D. C., and Carr-Saunders, A. M. 1927. The relation between intelligence and social status among orphan children. *Br. J. Psychol.* 17:343–64.

Joppich, G. 1962. Die kulturelle Vernachlässigung der ersten Kindheit. *Dt. med. Wschr.* 717.

Kaffman, M. 1961. Evaluation of emotional disturbance in 403 Israel kibbutz children. *Am. J. Psychiat.* 117:732–38.

————. 1963. Children of the kibbutz clinical observations. In *Current psychiatric therapies,* ed. J. H. Masserman, vol. 3. New York: Grune.

Kagan, J., and Beach, F. A. 1953. Effects of early experience on mating behavior in male rats. *J. comp. physiol. Psychol.* 46:204–8.

Kanner, L. 1943. Autistic disturbances of affective contact. *Nerv. Child* 2:217–50.

————. 1949. Problems of nosology and psychodynamics of early infantile autism. *Am. J. Orthopsychiat.* 19:416–26.

————. 1958. The specificity of early infantile autism. *Acta Paedopsychiat.* 25:108–12.

Kaplan, J. 1970. The effects of separation and reunion on the behavior of mother and infant squirrel monkeys. *Devl Psychobiol.* 3:43–52.

Kardiner, A. 1954. Social stress and deprivation. In *Beyond the germ theory,* ed. I. Galdston, pp. 147–70. New York: Health Education Council.

Katz, I. 1964. Review of evidence relating to effects of desegregation on the intellectual performance of neuroses. *Am. Psychol.* 19:381–99.

Kearsley, R.; Snyder, M.; Holder, R.; Richie, R.; Ervin, F.; Crawford, J. P.; and Talbot, N. B. 1961. A pediatric procedure for studying relations between psychological environment and the behavior of children. *Am. J. Dis. Child.* 102:748–49.

Keller, S. 1963. The social world of the urban slum child. *Am. J. Orthopsychiat.* 33:823–31.

Kellmer-Pringle, M. L. See Pringle, M. L. K.

Kellogg, W. N. 1931. More about the "wolf children" of India. *Am. J. Psychol.* 43:508–9.

————. 1934. A further note on the "wolf children" in India. *Am. J. Psychol.* 46:149–50.

Kellogg, W. N., and Kellogg, L. A. 1933. *The ape and the child.* New York: McGraw-Hill.

Kempe, C. H., and Silver, H. K. 1959. The problem of parental criminal neglect and severe physical abuse of children. *Am. J. Dis. Child.* 98:528.

Kennedy, W.; Van de Riet, V.; and White, J. 1963. A normative sample of intelligence and achievement of Negro elementary school children in the southeastern United States. *Monogr. Soc. Res. Child Dev.* 28, no.6.

Kennell, J. H., and Bergen, M. S. 1966. Early childhood separations. *Pediatrics* 37:291—98.

Kenyatta, J. 1961. *Facing Mount Kenya.* London: Secker.

Kessen, W. 1967. Sucking and looking: two organized congenital patterns of behavior in the human newborn. In *Early behavior*, ed. H. W. Stevenson et al. New York: Wiley.

Kiehl, W., and Petermann, H. D. 1959. Vergleichende Untersuchungen über die körperliche und geistige Entwicklung von Kindern in Krippen und Heimen der Stadt Halle. *Z. ärztl. Fortbild.* 53:1418—23.

Kiev, A. 1962. Primitive therapy. A cross-cultural study of the relationship between child training and therapeutic practices related to illness. *Psychoanal. Stud. Soc.* 1:185—217.

King, D., and Raynes, N. V. 1968. An operational measure of inmate management in residential institutions. *Soc. Sci. Med.* 2:41—53.

King, J. A. 1958. Parameters relevant to determining the effects of early experience upon the adult behavior of animals. *Psychol. Bull.* 55:44—58.

King, J. A., and Eletheriou, B. E. 1959. Effects of early handling upon adult behavior in two subspecies of deermice, *Peromyscus maniculatus. J. comp. physiol. Psychol.* 52:82—88.

King, J. A., and Gurney, N. L. 1954. Effects of early social experience on adult aggressive behavior in C 57/BL/10 mice. *J. comp. physiol. Psychol.* 47:326—30.

King, K.; McIntyre, J.; and Axelson, L. J. 1968. Adolescent's view of maternal employment as a threat to the marital relationship. *J. Marriage Family* 30:633.

Kirchmann, N. 1972. Anteil und Bedeutung der frühkindlichen Hirnschädigung bei verhaltensauffälligen Heimkindern. Inaugural-Dissertation. Abteilung für Kinder-und Jugendpsychiatrie der Nervenklinik der Universität Tübingen.

Klackenberg, G. 1947. Mental injuries due to hospitalization or custody in children's homes. *Acta paediat., Stockh.* Suppl. 2, 35.

—————. 1956. Studies in mental deprivation in infants' home. *Acta paediat., Stockh.* 45:1—13.

—————. 1971. A prospective longitudinal study of children. *Acta paediat. scand.* Suppl. 224.

Klatsin, E. H. 1952. Shifts in child care practices in three special classes under an infant care program of flexible methodology. *Am. J. Orthopsychiat.* 22:52—61.

Klaus, M.; Jerauld, R.; Kreger, N.; McAlpine, W.; Steffa, M.; and Kennell, J. 1972. Maternal attachment: importance of the first postpartum days. *New Engl. J. Med.* 286:460.

Klein, H.; Zellermayer, J.; and Shanan, J. 1963. Former concentration

camp inmates on a psychiatric ward. *Archs gen. Psychiat.*
8:334–42.

Klein, O. 1947. The psychology of children in concentration camps. (In Czech). (Diploma thesis, Charles University, Prague.)

————. 1969. Crisis of emotionality. *Sociologicky Časopis* 5:129–49.

Klímová, H. 1966. *Allow the little ones to come... or civilization versus children?* (In Czech). Prague: Čs. Spisovatel.

Koch, J. 1957. Change of excitability of the CNS in individual children during periods of wakefulness. (In Czech). *Čas. Lék. česk.* 96:757–65.

————. 1961. An attempt to analyze the influence of infant home conditions on the neuro-psychological development in four- to twelve-months-old children. (In Czech). *Cslká Pediat.* 16:322–30.

————. 1968. The change of conditioned orienting reactions in five months old infants through phase shift of partial biorhythms. *Hum. Dev.* 11:124–37.

————. 1974. *Education of infants in family.* (In Czech). Prague: Avicenum.

Koch, J.; Langmeier, J.; and Matějček, Z. 1965. A proposal for a new system of care of the child educated outside its own family. (In Czech). *Pedagogika* 15:316–26.

Koch, M. D., and Arnold, W. J. 1972. Effects of early social deprivation on emotionality in rats. *J. comp. physiol. Psychol.* 78:391–99.

Koehler, O. 1952. "Wolfskinder", Affen im Haus und vergleichende Verhaltensvorschung. *Folia phoniat.* 4:29.

Kolaříková, O. 1966. Some problems of personality development in the conditions pertaining in children's homes. (In Czech). *Psychol. Patopsychol. dieťaťa* 3:17–25.

Koller, K. M. 1971. Parental deprivation, family background and female delinquency. *Br. J. Psychiat.* 118:319–27.

Koluchová, J. 1972. Severe deprivation in twins. *J. child Psychol. Psychiat.* 13:107.

Komenský, J. A. *See* Comenius, J. A.

Kos, M. 1960. La problematica del rapporto affectivo nella famiglia illustrata da due tests proiettivi. *Rass. Psicol. gen. clin.* 5:1–23.

Kosťukovskaja, M. L. 1957. Experiences with transition of children from children's homes to residential schools. (In Russian). *Vop. Okhr. Materin. Detst.* 2:62–65.

Kotelchuck, M. 1972. The nature of the child's tie to his father. (Doctoral dissertation, Harvard University.)

Köttgen, U. 1964. Die Bedeutung der Reizverarmung, Monotonie, für die frühkindliche geistige Entwicklung. *Z. Kinderheilk.* 91:247–53.

Koželuhová, L. 1966. Organization of the lives of toddlers in collective care. (In Czech). Paper read at First Symposium of Socialist Countries on Nurseries, Prague.

Kraft, I. 1966. Some observations on kibbutz children. *Children* 13:195—97.

Kraus, O., and Kulka, E. 1958. *Night and smog.* (In Czech). Prague: Naše Vojsko.

Krech, D.; Rosenzweig, M. R.; and Bennett, E. L. 1960. Effects of environmental complexity and training on brain chemistry. *J. comp. physiol. Psychol.* 53:509—19.

————. 1962. Relations between brain chemistry and problem-solving among rats raised in enriched and impoverished environments. *J. comp. physiol. Psychol.* 55:801—7.

————. 1966. Environmental impoverishment, social isolation and changes in brain chemistry and anatomy. *Physiol. Behav.* 1:99—104.

Krevelen, D. A. van. 1963. On the relationship between early infantile autism and autistic psychopathy. *Acta Paedopsychiat.* 30:303—23.

Kubát, K., and Syrovátka, A. 1966. Die Entwicklung der Morbidität bei Familien- und bei Krippenkindern während der ersten 3 Lebensjahre. *Ärztl. Jugendkd.* 57:16—23.

Kubička, L. 1956. The influence of mother's employment on the development of psychological maladjustment in children. (In Czech). *Čslká Pediat.* 52:247—56.

Kučera, M. 1969. *Population growth in ČSSR in 1950—68.* (In Czech). Prague: Český Statistický Úřad.

Kučera, O., et al. 1961. *Psychopathological manifestations in children with mild encephalopathy.* (In Czech). Prague: S.Z.N.

Kugel, R. B.; Fedge, A.; Trembath, J.; and Hein, H. 1964. An analysis of reasons for institutionalizing mongoloid children. *J. Pediat.* 64:68—74.

Kunzová, Z., and Havlíčková, V. 1964. Morbidity of children in nurseries in ČSSR in 1961—62. (In Czech). *Čslká Pediat.* 19:912.

Kuromaru, S. 1973. Changes in Japanese mother-child separation anxiety in Japan: 1963—1972. *J. nerv. ment. Dis.* 157:339—45.

Kurz, J. 1959. Oculo-digital reflex. (In Czech). *Čslká Oftal.* 5:193—203.

Ladygina, N. F. 1959. Some problems in the rearing of two- and three-year-old children. (In Russian). *Vop. Okhr. Materin. Detst.* 4:77—81.

Lambert, W., and Levy, L. H. 1972. Sensation seeking and short-term sensory isolation. *J. Personality soc. Psychol.* 24:46—52.

Lambert, W. W. 1966. Le rôle des parents dans la vie de l'enfant. Coup d'oeil sur différentes cultures. In *Le rôle de l'adulte dans la vie de l'enfant.* Paris: OMEP.

Lambo, T. A. 1969. The child and the mother-child relationship in major cultures of Africa. *Carnets de l'enfance* 10:61—74.

Landy, D. 1959. *Tropical childhood: cultural transmission and learning in a rural Puerto Rican village.* Chapel Hill: Univ. of North Carolina Press.

Lane, R. C., and Singer, J. L. 1959. Familial attitudes in paranoid schizophrenics and normals from two socio-economic classes. *J. abnorm. soc. Psychol.* 59:328—39.

Lange, U. 1965. Das alleinstehende Kind und seine Versorgung. *Psychol. Prax.* 38.

Langeveld, M. J. 1964. Zum Problem des Vaters in der Entwicklung des mänlichen Kindes. *Vita hum.* 7:33—48.

————. 1966. Educating a whole world. *Paedagogica Evropaea* 2:1—26.

————. 1967. Intelligence as an educable conglomerate: a synthesis. *Hum. Dev.* 10:22—26.

Langford, W. S. 1955. Disturbances in mother-infant relationship leading to apathy, extra-nutritional sucking and hair ball. In *Emotional problems of childhood,* ed. G. Caplan, pp. 57—76. New York: Basic.

Langmeier, J. 1959. Sleep of young children in families and in hospitals. (In Czech). *Čslká Pediat.* 14:628—39.

————. 1962. The question of psychological deprivation and the development of educational views in Czechoslovakia. (In Czech). *Čslká Pediat.* 17:646—52.

————. 1965. Psychological deprivation in the case histories of schizophrenics. (In Czech). *Prakt. Lék.* 45:890—93.

————. 1968. Psychological deprivation in children. (In Czech). *Pokroky v pediatrii,* ed. J. Houštěk, J. Lhoták, and A. Syrovátka, 1:303—31. Prague: S.Z.N.

————. 1972. Personalities of deprived children. In *Determinants of behavioral development,* ed. F. J. Mönks, W. W. Hartup, and J. de Wit. New York, London: Academic Press.

Langmeier, J.; Konias, V.; and Dolejši, M. 1957. A contribution to the study of children's psychiatric departments. In *Hraniční problémy psychiatrie,* pp. 185—94. Bratislava:SAV.

Langmeier, J., and Langmeierová, D. 1967. The significance of early psychological deprivation for the psychopathological development of personality. (In Czech). In *K problémům psychologie osobnosti,* ed. V. Tardy, pp. 221—29. Prague: Academia.

————. 1972. Formation of peer groups. (In Czech). Prague: KPÚ. Mimeographed.

Langmeier, J., and Lhoták, J. 1960. Psychological deprivation and minimal brain injuries. (In Czech). Paper read at Second Congress of Psychiatry, Prague, October 1960.

Langmeier, J., and Matějček, Z. 1963. *Psychological deprivation in childhood.* Prague: S.Z.N. 2nd ed. 1968. (In Czech).

————. 1966. Problemi psicologici delle instituzioni collettive per l'infanzia prescolastica in Cecoslovacchia. *Atti 1 convegno italo-cecoslovacco sui problemi dell'infanzia prescolastica, Roma, November 1966.*

————. 1970. Mental development of children in families and in infants' homes. *Soc. Sci. Med.* 4:569—77.

————. 1972. Psychological aspects of collective care in Czechoslovakia. In *Child mental health in international perspective,* ed. H. P. David. New York: Harper and Row.

Langová, J., and Šváb, L. 1973. Reduction of stuttering under experimental social isolation. *Folia phoniat.* 25:17–22.

Lát, J. 1958. The mythical average organism and the significance of interindividual (constitutional, biological) variability. (In Czech). *Čslká Fysiol.* 7:97–111.

————. 1962. Über die Möglichkeit der Beeinflussung der Entwicklung der individuellen psychosomatischen Konstitution. *Biol. Lebensälter Tag.* 222–26.

Lát, J.; Widdowson, E. M.; and McCance, R. A. 1960. Some effects of accelerating growth. III. Behaviour and nervous activity. *Proc. R. Soc.* B 153:347–56.

Launay, C. 1956. Réflexions sur l'hospitalisme. *Évolut. psychiat.* 265–71.

Lautererová, M. 1964. The history of social health care of children in Brno. (In Czech). *Čslká Pediat.* 19:936–41.

Lawick-Goodall, J. van. 1971. Some aspects of mother-infant relationships in a group of wild chimpanzees. In *The origins of human social relations,* ed. H. R. Schaffer. New York, London: Academic Press.

————. 1973. The behavior of chimpanzees in their natural habitat. *Am. J. Psychiat.* 130:1–12.

Lebovici, S. 1962. The concept of maternal deprivation: a review of research. In *Deprivation of maternal care,* pp. 75–94. Geneva: WHO.

Lebovici, S., and David, M. 1971. L'influence du milieu sur le développement du jeune enfant. *Assignment Childn* 15:46–57.

Leiderman, P. H. 1962. *Imagery and sensory deprivation: an experimental study.* USAF MRL Tech. Docum. Rep., no. 62-28.

Leiderman, P. H.; Wexler, D.; Mendelson, J. H.; and Solomon, P. 1958. Sensory deprivation: clinical aspects. *Archs intern. Med.* 101:389–96.

Leiderman, P. H., et al. 1961. Contributions of sensory deprivation to the study of human behaviour. In *Neuroses,* ed. O. Janota and E. Wolf, pp. 117–83. Prague.

Lelong, M., and Lebovici, S. 1955. Problèmes psychologiques et psychopathologiques posés par l'enfant à l'hôpital. *Archs fr. Pédiat.* 12:349–67.

Leonard, M. F. 1970. Growth failure from maternal deprivation or undereating. *JAMA* 212:882.

Lersch, P. 1951. *Aufbau der Person.* Munich: J. Ambrosius Barth.

Lesák, J. 1961. The perception of sound by the deaf child. *Otázky Defekt.* 3, no.6.

Levine, E. S. 1952. The deaf. In *Psychological aspects of physical disability,* ed. J. F. Garrett, pp. 125–46. Rehabilitation Service

Series no. 210. Washington, D.C.: Office of Vocational Rehabilitation.

Levine, S. 1956. The effects of shock and handling in infancy on
consummatory response in adulthood. *Am. Psychol.* 11:397.

Lévi-Strauss, C. 1963. *Tristes tropiques.* Paris: Union Générale
d'Editions.

Levy, D. 1937. Primary affect hunger. *Am. J. Psychiat.* 94:643—52.

Levy, E. Z.; Ruff, G.E.; and Thaler, V. H. 1959. Studies in human
isolation. *JAMA* 169:236—39.

Levy, R. J. 1945. Effects of institutional vs. boarding home care on
groups of infants. *J. Personality* 15:233—41.

Lewis, H. 1954. *Deprived children: the Mersham experiment.* New
York: Oxford Univ. Press.

————. 1956. Psychological aspects of the deprived child. *Med.
Wld, Lond.* 84:135—43.

Lewis, M. 1965. Social isolation: a parametric study of its effect on
social reinforcement. *J. exp. Child Psychol.* 2:205—18.

Lewis, S. R., and Van Ferney, S. 1960. Early recognition of infantile
autism. *J. Pediat.* 56:510—12.

Liddell, H. S. 1944. Conditioned reflex method and experimental
neurosis. In *Personality and the behavior disorders,* ed. J. McV.
Hunt, vol.1, pp. 389—412. New York: Ronald.

————. 1954. Conditioning and emotions. *Scient. Am.* 190:48—57.

————. 1956. *Emotional hazards in animals and man.* Springfield,
Ill.: C. C. Thomas.

————. 1958. A biological basis for psychopathology. In *Problems
of addiction and habituation,* ed. P. H. Hoch and J. Zubin. New
York: Grune.

Lightwood, R. 1957. A London trial of home care for sick children.
Lancet 1:313—17.

Lilly, J. C. 1956. Mental effects of reduction of ordinary levels of
physical stimuli on intact healthy persons. In *Research techniques
in schizophrenia.* Psychiatric Research Reports of American
Psychiatric Association, no. 5:1—9.

————. 1961. *Man and dolphin.* New York: Doubleday.

Lilly, J. C., and Shurley, J. T. 1961. Experiments in solitude in
maximum achievable physical isolation with water suspension of
intact healthy persons. In *Psychophysiological aspect of space
flight.* New York: Columbia Univ. Press.

Lipton, E.L.; Steinschneider, A.; and Richmond, J.B. 1965. Swaddling,
a child care practice: historical, cultural and experimental
observations. *Pediatrics* 35:521—67.

Loosli-Usteri, M. 1948. Thoughts, hopes and wishes of refugee children.
New era in home and school 29:1.

Lorenz, K. 1935. Der Kumpan in der Umwelt des Vogels. *J. Orn., Lpz.*
83:137—213, 289—413. English translation in *Instinctive
behavior,* ed. C. H. Schiller. New York: International Univ. Press,
1957.

————. 1965. *Evolution and modification of behavior.* Chicago: Univ. of Chicago Press.

Lowenfeld, B. 1952. The blind. In *Psychological aspects of physical disability,* ed. J. F. Garrett, pp. 179—95. Washington, D.C.: U.S. Govt. Print. Off.

Lowrey, L. G. 1940. Personality distortion and early institutional care. *Am. J. Orthopsychiat.* 10:576—85.

Luria, A. R. 1961. *The role of speech in the regulation of normal and abnormal behavior.* New York: Pergamon.

Lustman, S. L. 1970. Cultural deprivation: a clinical dimension of education. *Psychoanal. Study Child* 25:483—502.

Lutz, J. 1957. Zur Frage der Mütterlichkeit. *Acta Paedopsychiat.* 24:13—18.

Lyle, J. G. 1959. The effect of an institution environment upon the verbal development of imbecile children. I. Verbal intelligence. *J. ment. Defic. Res.* 3:122.

————. 1960. The effect of an institution environment upon the verbal development of imbecile children. III. The Brooklands residential family unit. *J. ment. Defic. Res.* 4:14—23.

Lynn, D. B., and Sawrey, W. L. 1959. The effects of father-absence on Norwegian boys and girls. *J. abnorm. soc. Psychol.* 59:258—62.

MacCarthy, D. 1962. Children in hospitals with mothers. *Lancet* 1:603.

McCord, J.; McCord, W.; and Thurber, E. 1962. Some effects of parental absence on male children. *J. abnorm. soc. Psychol.* 64:361—69.

McCord, W.; McCord, J.; and Zola, I. K. 1959. *The origins of crime: a new evaluation of the Cambridge-Sommerville youth study.* Montclair, N.J.: Patterson Smith.

McKinney, W. T., Jr.; Suomi, S. J.; and Harlow, H. F. 1972. Repetitive peer separations of juvenile-age rhesus monkeys. *Archs gen. Psychiat.* 27:200—203.

Mackler, B., and Giddings, M. G. 1965. Cultural deprivation: a study in mythology. *Teach. Coll. Rec.* 66:608—13.

Maddi, S. R. 1961a. Affective tone during environmental regularity and change. *J. abnorm. soc. Psychol.* 62:338—45.

————. 1961b. Unexpectedness, affective tone, and behaviour. In *Functions of varied experience,* ed. D. W. Fiske and S. R. Maddi. Homewood, Ill.: Dorsey Press.

Magoun, H. W. 1958. *The waking brain.* Springfield, Ill.: C. C. Thomas.

Main, T. F. 1958. Mothers with children in a psychiatric hospital. *Lancet* 2:845—47.

Makarenko, A. S. 1951a. *The road to life.* Moscow: Foreign Languages Publishing House.

————. 1951b. *Works.* (In Russian). Moscow: I.A.P.N.

Malmo, R. B. 1959. Activation: a neuropsychological dimension. *Psychol. Rev.* 66:367—86.

Malrieu, P. 1960a. Evolution et fonction des émotions dans la première année de l'enfant. *Revue suisse Psychol* 19:132—51.

————. 1960*b*. Les conditions de l'évolution des émotions dans la première année de l'enfant. *Revue suisse Psychol* 19:132—51.

Manova-Tomova, V. 1962. Neuro-psychische Entwicklung und Erziehung der Kinder im Alter von O bis 3 Jahren. *Heilberufe* 14:153—55.

————. 1965. Perspectives of research work in children's homes and nurseries. (In Bulgarian). *Informacionen Bjul* no. 2:11—17.

Marzo-Weyl, S. 1965*a*. *Enfants privés de famille*. Paris: CIE.

————. 1965*b*. *La mère seule: le désintéressement*. Paris: CIE.

Masland, R. L. 1966. *Minimal brain dysfunction in children*. Washington, D.C.: U.S. Govt. Print. Off.

Maslow, A. 1955. Deficiency motivation and growth motivation. In *Nebraska Symposium on Motivation*, ed. M. R. Jones, pp. 1—30. Lincoln: Univ. of Nebraska Press.

Maslow, A. H., and Szilagyi-Kessler, I. 1946. Security and breast feeding. *J. abnorm. soc. Psychol.* 41:83—85.

Mason, M. K. 1942. Learning to speak after six and one-half years of silence. *J. Speech Hear. Disorders* 7:295—304.

Mason, W. A. The effects of social restriction on the behavior of rhesus monkeys, I—IV. *J. comp. physiol. Psychol.* 53 (1960):582—89; 54 (1961):287—90; 55 (1962):363—68.

Massé, G. 1971. Croissance et maturation de l'enfant à Dakar. *Assignment Childn* 15:36—45.

Massucco-Costa, A. 1966. Problemi psicologici degli asili nido. *Atti I convegno italo-cecoslovacco sui problemi dell'infanzia prescolastica, Roma, November 1966*.

Matějček, Z. 1960. Investigations of the mental development of children aged one to three years in children's homes. (In Czech). *Čslká Pediat.* 15:234—41.

————. 1961. School failure of some children with normal intelligence. (In Czech). *Čslká Pediat.* 16:877—82.

————. 1962. Investigations of the mental development of institutionalized children by the Children's Psychiatric Service in Central Bohemia. (In Czech). *Čslká Pediat.* 17:621—27.

————. 1963*a*. The question of adoption. (In Czech). *Čslká Pediat.* 18: 842—46.

————. 1963*b*. Über einige Ursachen des Versagens von normalintelligenten Kindern in der Schule. *Paediat. Grenzgebiete* 2:202—9.

————. 1964. Psychological studies in children's homes for children with behavior disorders. (In Czech). *Čslká Pediat.* 19:21—25.

————. 1967. Personality development of institutionalized children. *Psychol. Patopsychol. dieťaťa* 3, no.1.

————. 1969*a*. About foster care in ČSSR. (In Czech). *Čslká Pediat.* 24:654—56.

————. 1969*b*. Mental development of children in our children's homes. (In Czech). (Dissertation thesis, Charles University, Prague.)

————. 1969c. School achievement of children from preschool children's homes. (In Czech). *Čslká Psychol.* 13:8—15.

————. 1969d. Über Persönlichkeitstypen bei Heimkindern und ihre Berücksichtigung im Adoptionsverfahren. *Unsere Jugend* 21:155—60.

————. 1972. New forms of substitutional family care for children. *Psychol. Patopsychol. dietaťa* 7:57—65.

Matějček, Z.; Doutlík, S.; and Janda, V. 1964. The evaluation of neuropsychiatric sequelae in children after parainfectious encephalitis. *Acta Paedopsychiat.* 31:301—9.

Matějček, Z., and Langmeier, J. 1965. New observations on psychological deprivation in institutionalized children in Czechoslovakia. *Slow Learning Child* 12:20—38.

————. 1968. Die zeitweilige Gemeinschaftserziehung im Hinblick auf die psychische Deprivation. *Paedagogica Evropaea* 98—111.

————. 1970. Folgen frühkindlicher psychischer Deprivation bei Anstaltskindern. *Prax. Kinderpsychol. Kinderpsychiat.* 19:85—90.

Matějček, Z., and Reithar, S. 1963. Problems of school readiness in children under institutional care. *Čslká Psychol.* 7:338—45.

Matussek, P. 1971. *Die Konzentrationslagerhaft und ihre Folgen.* Berlin, Heidelberg, New York: Springer.

Mausshardt, M. 1962. Kann Hospitalismus vermieden werden? *Unsere Jugend* 1.

Mead, M. 1962a. A cultural anthropologist's approach to maternal deprivation. In *Deprivation of maternal care,* pp. 45—62. Geneva: WHO.

————. 1962b. *Male and female.* Harmondsworth, Mddx.: Penguin.

Mead, M., and Wolfenstein, M. 1955. *Childhood in contemporary cultures.* Chicago: Univ. of Chicago Press.

Mečíř, M. 1955. The behaviour of infants in nurseries. (In Czech). *Čslká Pediat.* 10:690—94.

————. 1959. Abandonment of home by children and adolescents. (In Czech). *Čslká Psychiat.* 55:157—62.

Mehringer, A. 1966. Geschützte Kleinkindzeit. *Unsere Jugend* 18:5.

Meierhofer, M. 1949. First experience in medical-psychological work at the Pestalozzi children's village at Trogen. Paris: Unesco. Mimeographed.

————. 1955. Fehlentwicklung der Persönlichkeit bei Kindern in Fremdpflege. *Schweiz. med. Wschr.* 85:862—66.

————. 1961. Psychohygiene im frühen Kindesalter. *Acta Paedopsychiat.* 28:1—15.

————. 1971. *Frühe Prägung der Persönlichkeit.* Bern: Hans Huber.

Meierhofer, M., and Keller, W. 1970. *Frustration im frühen Kindesalter.* 2nd ed. Bern: H. Huber.

Meierhofer, M., and Keller, W. 1966. *Frustration im frühen Kindesalter.* 1st ed. Bern: Hans Huber. 2nd ed. 1970.

Meili, R. 1961. Untersuchungen zur Aetiologie frühester persönlichkeitsrelevanter Eigenscheften. *Z. Psychol.* 165:214–40.

Melzack, R. 1969. The role of early experience in emotional arousal. *Ann. N. Y. Acad. Sci.* 159:721–30.

Melzack, R., and Scott, T. H. 1957. The effects of early experience on the response to pain. *J. comp. physiol. Psychol.* 50:155–61.

Mendelson, J. H., and Foley, J. M. 1956. An abnormality of mental function affecting patients with poliomyelitis in a tank-type respirator. *Trans. Am. neurol. Ass.* 81:134–38.

Mendelson, J. H.; Siger, L.; and Solomon, P. 1960. Psychiatric observations on congenital and acquired deafness. *Am. J. Psychiat.* 116:883–88.

Mendez, L. 1968. Psychological implications of child care in Puerto Rico. Paper read in seminar on deprivation at University of Alberta, Edmonton.

Meszárošová, O., and Jurčová, M. 1956. Neuro-psychological development of infants in establishments of collective care. (In Czech). *Čslká Pediat.* 11:832–36.

Meyendorf, R. 1971. Infant depression due to separation from siblings. *Psychiat. clin.* 4:321–35.

Meyer, L. F. 1913. *Über den Hospitalismus der Säuglinge.* Berlin.

Mezei, T. C., and Rosen, J. 1960. Dominance behavior as a function of infantile stimulation in the rat. *Archs gen. Psychiat.* 3:53–56.

Michaux, L., and Flavigny, H. 1958. D'une consequence de l'abus de la notion de frustration affective. *Criança port.* 17:689–700.

Mierke, K. 1955. Quoted by A. Peiper, 1958.

Miller, R. E.; Banks, J. H., Jr.; and Ogawa, N. 1962. Communication of affect in "cooperative conditioning" of rhesus monkeys. *J. abnorm. soc. Psychol.* 64:343–48.

Milotová, J.; Kluska, V.; and Stejskal, J. 1958. Letters to parents as one of the means of combating hospitalism. (In Czech). *Čslká Pediat.* 13:355–59.

Moltz, H. 1960. Imprinting: empirical basis and theoretical significance. *Psychol. Bull.* 57.

Moltz, H.; Rosenblum, L.; and Stettner, L.J. 1960. Some parameters of imprinting effectiveness. *J. comp. physiol. Psychol.* 53:297–301.

Mönks, F.J.; Hartup, W.W.; and Wit, J. de, eds. 1972. *Determinants of behavioral development.* New York, London: Academic Press.

Montagu, A. 1961. Culture and mental illness. *Am. J. Psychiat.* 117:15–23.

Montgomery, K. C. 1953. The effect of activity deprivation upon exploratory behavior. *J. comp. physiol. Psychol.* 46:438–41.

Moore, J. K. 1947. Speech content of selected groups of orphanage and non-orphanage preschool children. *J. exp. Educ.* 16:122–33.

Moore, T. 1964. Children of full-time and part-time mothers. *Int. J.*

soc. Psychiat. (Special Congress Issue) 2:1—10.

————. 1968. Language and intelligence: a longitudinal study of the first eight years. *Hum. Dev.* 11:1—24.

Moragas, J. De. 1958. Conséquences psychiques chez l'enfant repussé. *Z. Kinderpsychiat.* 25:49—51.

————. 1964. L'action nosogène mutuelle entre la mère et l'enfant. *Acta Paedopsychiat.* 31:365—74.

Mores, A. 1959. Reaction of a child on being separated from his mother and his possible feelings. (In Czech). *Čslká Pediat.* 14:946—47.

Mores, A., and Vyhnálek, J. 1957. Hospitalism. (In Czech). *Čslká Pediat.* 12:12—22.

Morsier, G. De. 1965. À propos des enfants-sauvages et les enfants-loups. *Schweiz. Z. Psychol.* 24:148—55.

Moruzzi, G., and Magoun, H. W. 1949. Brain stem reticular formation and activation of the EEG. *Electroenceph. clin. Neurophysiol.* 1:455—73.

Moustakas, C. 1961. *Loneliness.* Englewood Cliffs, N. J.: Prentice-Hall.

————. 1967. Heuristic research. In *Challenges of humanistic psychology,* ed. J. F. T. Bugentat, pp. 101—7. New York: McGraw-Hill.

Mowrer, O. H., and Kluckhohn, C. 1944. Dynamic theory of personality. In *Personality and the behavior disorders,* ed. J. McV. Hunt, vol.1, pp. 69—135. New York: Ronald.

Müller, K. 1959a. Beobachtungen zur Psychometrik blinder Kinder. *Klin. Mbl. Augenheilk.* 134:213—27.

————. 1959b. Bewegungsauffälligkeiten bei blinden Kindern. *Kinderärztl. Prax.* 27:400—402.

Müller-Hegemann, D. 1964. Soziale Isolierung als ätio-pathogenetischer Faktor. I. Die komplete soziale Isolierung. II. Partielle soziale Isolierung. *Fortschr. Med.* 82:478—80, 777—880.

Müller-Küppers, M. 1964. Das Problem der Unterbringung von Kindern und Jugendlichen in Heimen aus der Sicht des Erziehungsberaters. *Prax. Kinderpsychol. Kinderpsychiat.* no. 5:161—68.

Mullin, C. S. 1960. Some psychological aspects of isolated artistic living. *Am. J. Psychiat.* 117:323—25.

Munro, A. 1966. 1. Some familial and social factors in depressive illness. 2. Parental deprivation in depressive patients. *Br. J. Psychiat.* 112:443—57.

————. 1969. The theoretical importance of parental deprivation in the etiology of psychiatric illness. *Appl. soc. Stud.* 1:81.

————. 1970. Some psychiatric sequelae of childhood bereavement. *Br. J. Psychiat.* 116:347—49.

Murphy, G. 1947. *Personality.* New York: Harper.

Mussen, P. H.; Boutourline, Y. H.; Gaddini, R.; and Morante, L. 1963. The influence of father-son relationships on adolescent personality and attitudes. *J. Child Psychol. Psychiat.* 4:3—16.

Myklebust, H. R. 1964. *The psychology of deafness: sensory depriva-*

tion, learning and adjustment. New York: Grune.

Naess, S. 1959. Mother-child separation and delinquency. *Br. J. Delinq.* 10:22.

Naka, S.; Abe, K.; and Suzuki, H. 1965. Childhood behavior characteristics of the parents in certain behavior problems of children. *Acta Paedopsychiat.* 32:11–16.

Nameche, G. F., and Ricks, D. F. 1966. Life patterns of children who became adult schizophrenics. Paper read at annual meeting of American Orthopsychiatric Association, San Francisco.

Nameche, G.; Waring, M.; and Ricks, D. 1964. Early indicators of outcome in schizophrenia. *J. nerv. ment. Dis.* 139:232–40.

Nash, J. 1965. The father in contemporary culture and current psychological literature. *Child Dev.* 36:261–97.

Neale, J. M. 1966. Egocentrism in institutionalized and non-institutionalized children. *Child Dev.* 37:97–101.

Neibsch, G. 1959. Der Einfluss des Milieus auf Länge und Gewicht in den ersten 2 Lebensjahren. *Z. ärztl. Fortbild.* 53:1428–30.

Nesnídalová, R. 1973. *Extreme loneliness: autism.* (In Czech). Prague: Avicenum.

Nesnídalová, R., and Fiala, V. 1961. On the question of Kanner's early autism. (In Czech). *Čslká Psychiat.* 57:76–84.

Neubauer, P. B. 1965. *Children in collectives.* Springfield, Ill.: C. C. Thomas.

Newson, J., and Newson, E. 1965. *Patterns of infant care in an urban community.* Harmondsworth, Mddx.: Penguin.

Nikolskaya, A.B. 1960. *Continuity of education in preschool age.* (In Russian). Moscow: Znanije.

Nissen, H. W.; Chow, K. L.; and Semmes, J. 1951. Effects of restricted opportunity for tactual, kinesthetic, and manipulative experience on the behavior of a chimpanzee. *Am. J. Psychol.* 64:485–507.

Nitschke, A. 1955. Das Bild der Heimweh-Reaktion beim jungen Kind. *Dt. med. Wschr.* 80:1905.

––––––. 1956. Die Bedeutung der Familie für die frühe Kindheit. *Sammlung: Z. Kultur Erziehung* 11:465–77.

––––––. 1962. *Das verwaiste Kind der Natur.* Tübingen: Niemeyer.

Nordlund, E. B. 1952. Erziehungsprobleme in einem Kinderkrankenhaus. *Acta paediat., Stockh.* 41:192–99.

Norris, M.; Spaulding, P. J.; and Brodie, F. H. 1957. *Blindness in children.* Chicago: Univ. of Chicago Press.

Nováková, M. 1957. Disturbances of mental development of preschool children in children's homes. (In Czech). In *Problémy pediatrie v praxi a ve výzkumu,* pp. 138–40. Prague.

––––––. 1959. Special behavior disorders in children in nurseries. (In Czech). Paper read at meeting of Czech. Medical Association, Prague.

––––––. 1961. Développement psycho-moteur de l'enfant et besoins affectifs. *Séminaire sur les crèches.* Paris: CIE.

————. 1966. Attitudes of mothers and nurses to infants. Paper read at First Symposium of Socialist Countries on Nurseries, Prague.

O'Conner, N. 1971. Children in restricted environments. *Psychiat. Neurol. Neurochir.* 74:71—77.

O'Connor, N. 1956. Evidence for the permanently disturbing effects of mother-child separation. *Acta psychol.* 12:174—91.

Oersten, P. A., and Mattson, A. 1955. Hospitalization symptoms in children. *Acta paediat., Stockh.* 44:79—92.

Olechnowicz, H. 1957. Hospitalism in infants reared out of families. (In Polish). *Pediatria pol.* 7.

————. 1965. Schizophrenia-type disturbances in infants as reactions to emotional isolation. (In Polish). *Zdrow. psych.* 6:36—43.

————. 1969. *First steps among people.* (In Polish). Warsaw: Nasza Ksiegarnia.

Olson, W. C., and Hughes, B. O. 1940. Subsequent growth of children with and without nursery school experience. In *Thirty-ninth yearbook of the National Society for the Study of Education*, ed. G. M. Whipple, Part 1, pp. 237—44. Bloomington, Ill.: Public School Publ.

Oltman, J. E., and Friedman, S. 1965. Report on parental deprivation in psychiatric disorders. *Archs gen. Psychiat.* 12:46—56.

O'Neal, P.; Robins, L. N.; King, L. J.; and Schaefer, J. 1962. Parental deviance and the genesis of sociopathic personality. *Am. J. Psychiat.* 118:1114—24.

Oppel, W.; Rider, R.; and Harper, P. 1961. The relationship of maternal deprivation to childhood achievement and adjustment. *Am. J. Dis. Child.* 102:758—59.

Orgel, S. Z. 1941. Personality distortion and early institutional care. *Am. J. Orthopsychiat.* 11:371—74.

Orlansky, H. 1949. Infant care and personality. *Psychol. Bull.* 49:1—48.

Ormiston, D. W. 1958. The effects of sensory deprivation and sensory bombardment on apparent movement thresholds. *Am. Psychol.* 13:389.

————. 1961. *A methodological study of confinement.* WADD Tech. Rep. 61-258, Ohio.

Oswald, I. 1958. Deprivation of parents during childhood. *Br. med. J.* 1:1515—16.

Ourth, L., and Brown, K. B. 1961. Inadequate mothering and disturbance in the neonatal period. *Child Dev.* 32:287—95.

Pan, R. M. du, and Roth, S. 1955. The psychologic development of a group of children brought up in a hospital type residential nursery. *J. Pediat.* 47:124—29.

Papez, J. W. 1937. A proposed mechanism of emotion. *Archs Neurol. Psychiat., Chicago* 38:725—43.

Papoušek, H. 1961a. Conditioned head rotation reflexes in infants in the first months of life. *Acta paediat., Stockh.* 50:565—76.

————. 1961*b*. Über die Beziehungen einiger Formen des Hospitalismus bei Säuglingen zur Ontogenesis der Nahrungsreflexe. In *Das milieugeschädigte Kind*, ed. H. Schwarz, pp. 37—39. Jena.

————. 1967*a*. Conditioning during early postnatal development. In *Behavior in infancy and early childhood*, ed. Y. Brackbill and G. G. Thompson, pp. 259—74. New York: Free.

————. 1967*b*. Genetics and child development. In *Genetic diversity and human behavior*, ed. J. N. Spuhler, pp. 171—86. Chicago: Aldine.

————. 1969. Development of learning ability in children in the first months of life. (In Czech). (Dissertation thesis, Charles University, Prague.)

Papoušek, H., and Bernstein, P. 1969. The functions of conditioning stimulation in human neonates and infants. In *The functions of stimulation in early post-natal development*, ed. J. A. Ambrose. London: Academic Press.

Parkes, C. M. 1955. Bereavement and mental illness. *Br. J. med. Psychol.* 38:1—26.

————. 1964*a*. Effects of bereavement on physical and mental health: a study of the medical records of widows. *Br. med. J.* 2:274—79.

————. 1964*b*. Recent bereavement as a cause of mental illness. *Br. J. Psychiat.* 110:198—204.

Pasamanick, B. 1954. Epidemiology of behavior disorders. *Proc. Ass. Res. nerv. ment.* Dis. 23:397—403.

Patton, R. G., and Gardner, L. I. 1961. Observations on retardation of growth and osseous maturation in association with maternal deprivation. *Am. J. Dis. Child.* 102:761.

————. 1962. Influence of family environment on growth: the syndrome of "maternal deprivation". *Pediatrics* 30:957—62.

————. 1963. *Growth failure in maternal deprivation*. Springfield, Ill.: C. C. Thomas.

Pavenstedt, E. 1962. Introduction to the symposium on Research in Infancy and Early Childhood. *J. Am. Acad. Child Psychiat.* 1:5—10.

Pavlásková, I. 1966. Morbidity and adjustment of infants to the milieu of a nursery. Paper read at First Symposium of Socialist Countries on Nurseries, Prague.

Pease, D., and Gardner, D. B. 1958. Research on the effects of non-continuous mothering. *Child Dev.* 29:141—48.

Pechstein, J. 1967*a*. Hilfe für die Säuglingsheime. *Gesundheitsfürsorge* 17:75—78.

————. 1967*b*. Innere Reform des Säuglingsheimes. *Fortschr. Med.* 85:2—8.

————. 1968*a*. Entwicklungsphysiologische Untersuchungen an Säuglingen und Kleinkindern in Heimen. Beitrag zur Frage der frühkindlichen Deprivation. *Mschr. Kinderheilk.* 116:372—73.

————. 1968*b*. Frühkindliche Deprivation durch Massenpflege. *Fortschr. Med.* 86:409—12.

————. 1969. Die Kinderärztliche Verantwortung in Säuglings-heimen. *Münch. med. Wschr.* 111:1537—42.

————. 1970. Zur Situation der Kinder in den Säuglingsheimen der Bundesrepublik. In *Das Deprivations-Syndrom in Prognose, Diagnose und Therapie.* Arbeitstagung für Heimärtzte und Heimleiter an Säuglings- und Kinderheimen, 1968. Frankfurt-am-Main: Deutsche Zentrale für Volksgesundheits-Pflege. Schriftenreihe vol. 17.

————. 1971. Sind mehr Kinderkrippen wünschenswert? *Fortschr. Med.* 89:756—59.

————. 1972. Das junge Kind im Heim und Krippe. In *Kleinkinder-erziehung*, ed. G. Hundertmarck and H. Ulshoefer, vol. 3. Munich: Kösel.

————. 1973*a*. Das Kind ohne Familie. *Mschr. Kinderheilk.* 121:432—43.

————. 1973*b*. Vermeidung frühkindlicher Deprivation. *Fortschr. Med.* 91:929—30.

Pechstein, J., and Krause-Lang, M. 1966. Das elternlose und elternarme Kind in der Statistik. In *Handbuch der Kinderheilkunde,* ed. H. Opitz and F. Schmith, vol. 3, pp. 156—69. Berlin.

Pechstein, J.; Siebenmorgen, E.; and Weitsch, D. 1972. *Verlorene Kinder? Die Massenpflege in Säuglingsheimen.* Munich: Kösel.

Peiper, A. 1955. *Chronik der Kinderheilkunde.* Leipzig: Georg Thieme.

————. 1956. *Die Eigenart der kindlichen Hirntätigkeit.* Leipzig: G. Thieme.

————. 1958. Kaspar-Hause Kinder, verwildete Kinder (Wolfs-kinder). *Medizinische* 36:1411—16.

Pelikán, L.; Mores, A.; Koluchová, J.; Široký, J.; and Fárková, H. 1969. Serious deprivation in twins due to long-term social isolation. (In Czech). *Čslká Pediat.* 24:980—83.

Penfield, W., and Roberts, L. 1959. *Speech and brain mechanisms.* Princeton: Princeton Univ. Press.

Perret, H. 1962. Einfluss des Milieus auf die Förderung von Gesundheit und körperlicher Entwicklung. *Z. ärztl. Fortbild.* 55:30—36.

Petrie, A. 1960. Some psychological aspects of pain and the relief of suffering. *Ann. N.Y. Acad. Sci.* 86:13—27.

Petrie, A.; Collins, W.; and Solomon, P. 1960. The tolerance for pain and for sensory deprivation. *Am. J. Psychol.* 78:80—90.

Petrov, E.; Kelpazanov, A.; and Angelová, A. 1965. A comparative study of the neuropsychological development of infants in children's home Pleven, in weekly nurseries, daily nurseries, and in the family milieu. (In Bulgarian). *Informacionen Bjul.* 86—95.

Pfaundler, M. 1899. Über Saugen und Verdauen. *Versamml. dt. Naturforscher Ärzte* 71.

————. 1924. Über Antaltsschäden an Kindern. *Mschr. Kinderheilk.* 29:661.

——————. 1925. Klinik und Fürsorge. *GesundhFürs Kindesalter* 1:3.

Pfaundler, M., and Schlossmann, A. 1910. *Handbuch der Kinderheilkunde.* Leipzig: F. C. W. Vogel.

Pfeifer, L. 1882. Die Kindersterblichkeit. In *Handbuch der Kinderkrankheiten,* ed. C. Gebhardt. 2nd ed., vol. 1. Tübingen: H. Laupp.

Piaget, J. 1950. *La psychologie de l'intelligence.* Paris: A. Colin, 1947. English translation: *Psychology of intelligence.* New York: Harcourt-Brace.

——————. 1968. *Le structuralisme.* Paris: Presses Univ. de France.

Pies, H. 1926. *Kaspar Hauser.* Quoted by A. Peiper, 1958.

Pinkerton, P. 1956. Understanding the deprived child. *Lancet* 1:275–76.

Pinneau, S. R. 1950. A critique on the articles by Margaret Ribble. *Child Dev.* 21, no. 4:203–28.

——————. 1955*a*. The infantile disorders of hospitalism and anaclitic depression. *Psychol. Bull.* 52:429–52.

——————. 1955*b*. Reply to Dr. Spitz. *Psychol. Bull.* 52:459–62.

Pitts, F. N., Jr.; Meyer, J.; and Brooks, M. 1965. Adult psychiatric illness assessed for childhood parental loss, and psychiatric illness in family members: a study of 748 patients and 250 controls. *Am. J. Psychiat.* 121, suppl. 9.

Plank, E. N. 1959. *Working with children in hospitals.* London: Tavistock.

Plaut, S. M. 1972. Maternal deprivation in mice and rats. *Lab. Anim. Sci.* 22:594.

Polak, P. R.; Emde, R. N.; and Spitz, R. A. 1964. The smiling response to the human face. I. Methodology, quantification and natural history. *J. nerv. ment. Dis.* 139:103–9.

Pollard, J. C.; Uhr, L.; and Jackson, C. W. 1963. Studies in sensory deprivation. *Archs gen. Psychiat.* 8:435–54.

Pomers, G. F. 1948. Humanizing hospital experiences. *Am. J. Dis. Child.* 76:365–79.

Pomerska, E. 1966. Einige medizinische Probleme in Kinderkrippen. Paper read at First Symposium of Socialist Countries on Nurseries, Prague.

Portmann, A. 1951. *Biologische Fragmente zu einer Lehre vom Menschen.* Basel: B. Schwabe.

——————. 1964. Die Bedeutung des ersten Lebensjahres. *Mschr. Kinderheilk.* 112:483–89.

Pottar, O. 1962. Le drame des enfants-loups. *Sci. Vie* 101.

Prader, A.; Tanner, J. M.; and Harnack, G. A. von. 1963. Accelerated growth following illness or starvation. *J. Pediat.* 62:646–59.

Pražáková, A. 1969. Morbidity of children in daily nurseries. (In Czech). *Čslká Pediat.* 24:466–67.

Prechtl, H. F. R. 1963. The mother-child interaction in babies with minimal brain damage. In *Determinants of infant behaviour,* ed.

B. M. Foss, vol. 2. London: Methuen.
Prescott, E. 1970. The large day care center as a child-rearing environment. *Voice for Childn* 3:12.
Pringle, M. L. K. 1965. *Deprivation and education.* London: Longmans.
Pringle, M. L. K., and Bossio, V. 1958. A study of deprived children. *Vita hum.* 1:65–92, 142–70.
————. 1960. Early prolonged separation and emotional maladjustment. *J. Child Psychol. Psychiat.* 1:37–48.
Provence, S., and Lipton, R. C. 1962. *Infants in institutions: a comparison of their development with family-reared infants during the first year of life.* New York: International Univ. Press.
Prugh, D. G., and Harlow, R. G. 1962. "Masked deprivation" in infants and young children. In *Deprivation of maternal care,* pp. 9–30. Geneva: WHO.
Prugh, D. G.; Staub, E. M.; Sands, H. H.; Kirschbaum, R. M.; and Lenihan, E. A. 1953. A study of the emotional reactions of children and families to hospitalization and illness. *Am. J. Orthopsychiat.* 13:70–106.
Przetacznikowa, M. 1960. Psychological development of infants in three different milieus. (In Polish). *Psychologia Wych.* 1.
Pulver, U. 1959. *Spannungen und Störungen im Verhalten des Säuglings.* Bern.
Putnam, M. C. 1955. Some observations on psychosis in early childhood. In *Emotional problems of early childhood,* ed. G. Caplan, pp. 519–23. New York: Basic.
Quay, H. C. 1965. Psychopathic personality as pathological stimulation-seeking. *Am. J. Psychiat.* 122:180–83.
Rabin, A. I. 1958. Behavior research in collective settlements in Israel. *Am. J. Orthopsychiat.* 28:577–86.
————. 1959. Attitudes of "kibbutz" children to family and parents. *Am. J. Orthopsychiat.* 29:172–79.
————. 1965. *Growing up in the kibbutz.* New York: Springer Pub.
Rank, B. 1949. Adaptation of the psychoanalytic technique for the treatment of young children with atypical development. *Am. J. Orthopsychiat.* 19:130–39.
————. 1955. Intensive study and treatment of preschool children who show marked personality deviations or "atypical" development and their parents. In *Emotional problems of early childhood,* ed. G. Caplan. New York: Basic.
Rapaport, D. 1958. Behavior research in collective settlements in Israel. *Am. J. Orthopsychiat.* 28:587–97.
Rasmussen, J. E. 1963. Psychological discomforts in 1962 navy protective shelter tests. *J. Am. diet. A'ss.* 42:106–16.
Rauber, A. A. 1885. *Homo Sapiens Ferus oder die Zustände der Verwildeten.* Leipzig.
Raudnitz, R. W. 1897. Zur Lehre vom Spasmus nutans. *Jb. Kinderheilk.* 45:145–76, 416–59.

————. 1918. Kritisches zur Lehre vom Spasmus nutans. *Jb. Kinderheilk.* 87:15—46.

Raynes, N. V., and King, R. D. 1968. The measurement of child management in residential institutions for the retarded. In *Proceedings of the first congress of the International Association for the Scientific Study of Mental Deficiency, Montpellier, France, 12—20 September 1967,* ed. B. W. Richards, pp. 637—41. Reigate, Surrey: Michael Jackson Publ.

Reinhart, I., and Elmer, E. 1964. The abused child. *JAMA* 188:358—62.

Rheingold, H. L. 1943. Mental and social development of infants in relation to the number of other infants in the boarding home. *Am. J. Orthopsychiat.* 13:41—44.

————. 1956. The modification of social responsiveness in institutional babies. *Monogr. Soc. Res. Child Dev.* 21.

————. 1960. The measurement of maternal care. *Child Dev.* 31:565—73.

————. 1961. The effect of environmental stimulation upon social and exploratory behaviour in the human infant. In *Determinants of infant behaviour,* ed. B. M. Foss, vol. 1, pp. 143—77. London: Methuen.

————. 1971. Social behaviour in infancy. *Proc. 19th Int. Congr. Psychol.* 88—89.

Rheingold, H. L., and Bayley, N. 1959. The later effects of an experimental modification of mothering. *Child Dev.* 30:363—72.

Rheingold, H. L., and Eckerman, C. O. 1970. The infant separates himself from his mother. *Science* 168:78—83.

Rheingold, H. L.; Gewirtz, J. L.; and Ross, H. W. 1959. Social conditioning of vocalizations in the infant. *J. comp. physiol. Psychol.* 52:58—73.

Ribble, M. A. 1941. Disorganizing factors in infant personality. *Am. J. Psychiat.* 98:459—63.

————. 1944. Infantile experience in relation to personality development. In *Personality and the behavior disorders,* ed. J. McV. Hunt, vol. 2, pp. 621—51. New York: Ronald.

————. 1965. *The rights of infants: early psychological needs and their satisfaction.* 2nd ed. New York: Columbia Univ. Press.

Richmond, J. B., and Hersher, L. 1958. A follow-up study of an infant with anaclitic depression. *Am. J. Dis. Child.* 96:628.

————. 1961. Infantile depression: a seven-year follow-up study of a patient. *Am. J. Dis. Child.* 102:764—65.

Richmond, J.; Hersher, L.; and Ulric Moore, A. 1959. An experimental approach to the study of adoption. *Am. J. Dis. Child.* 98:478—80.

Richmond, J. B.; Hersher, L.; and Stern, G. 1960. A retrospective study of the effects of infant experiences on the development of psychological disorders in childhood. *Am. J. Dis. Child.* 100:775—76.

Riesen, A. H. 1960. Effects of stimulus deprivation on the development and atrophy of the visual sensory system. *Am. J. Orthopsychiat.* 30:23–36.

————. 1961. Studying perceptual development using the technique of sensory deprivation. *J. nerv. ment. Dis.* 132:21–25.

Riessman, F. 1962. *The culturally deprived child.* New York: Harper.

Rimland, B. 1964. *Infantile autism.* New York: Appleton-Century-Crofts, Meredith Pub.

Riskin, J. 1963. Methodology for studying family interaction. *Archs gen. Psychiat.* 8:343–48.

Ritter, C. *Eine Frau erlebt die Polarnacht.* Frankfurt/Main, Berlin: Ullstein Gontt.

Robertson, J. 1953. Some responses of young children to the loss of maternal care. *Nurs. Times* 49:382–86.

————. 1957. Der Verlust mütterlicher Fürsorge in früher Kindheit und einige Auswirkungen auf die Entwicklung der Persönlichkeit. *Z. ärztl. Fortbild.* 51:899–903.

————. 1958. *Young children in hospital.* London: Tavistock.

————. 1962. *Hospitals and children: a parent's eye view.* London: Gollancz.

Robertson, J., and Bowlby, J. 1952. Responses of young children to separation from their mothers: observations of the sequences of responses of children aged 18 to 24 months during the course of separation. *Courr. Cent. int. Enf.* 2:131–40.

Robertson, J., and Martin, R. C. 1961. Sensory deprivation and its relation to projection. *J. consult. Psychol.* 25:274.

Robertson, J., and Robertson, J. Study of young children separated from their mothers and cared for in a family setting. Mimeographed.

————. 1968. *Young children in brief separation.* Films on foster care and residential nursery care. London: Tavistock Child Development Research Unit.

————. 1971. Young children in brief separation. *Psychoanal. Study Child* 26:264–315.

————. 1972. Quality of substitute care as an influence on separation responses. *J. psychosom. Res.* 16:157–60.

Robertson, Joyce. 1962. Mothering as an influence on early development: a study of well-baby clinic records. *Psychoanal. Study Child* 17:245–64.

Robinson, H. B., and Robinson, N. M. 1971. Longitudinal development of very young children in a comprehensive day care program. *Child Dev.* 42:1673.

Robson, K. 1967. The role of eye-to-eye contact in maternal-infant attachment. *J. Child Psychiat.* 8:13.

Rose, J. 1960. The evidence for a syndrome of "mothering disability" consequent to threats to the survival of neonates. *Am. J. Dis. Child.* 100:776.

Rose, J. A., and Sonis, M. 1959. The use of separation as a diagnostic measure in the parent-child emotional crisis. *Am. J. Psychiat.* 116:409–15.

Rosen, J. 1958*a*. Comments on studies of the effects of early gentling experience. *Psychol. Rep.* 4:623–26.

————. 1958*b*. Dominance behaviour as a function of post-weaning gentling in the albino rats. *Can. J. Psychol.* 12:229–34.

————. 1961*a*. Dominance behavior of the adult rat as a function of early social experience. *J. genet. Psychol.* 99:145–51.

————. 1961*b*. Weight gain as a function of early social experience in the albino rat. *J. genet. Psychol.* 98:15–17.

Rosen, J., and Wejtko, J. 1962. Effects of delayed weaning on rat emotionality. *Archs gen. Psychiat.* 7:77–81.

Rosenbaum, G.; Dobie, S.I.; and Cohen, B.D. 1959. Visual recognitive thresholds following sensory deprivation. *Am. J. Psychol.* 72:429–33.

Rosenbaum, M. 1963. Psychological effects on the child raised by an older sibling. *Am. J. Orthopsychiat.* 33.

Rosenblatt, J. S.; Turkewitz, G.; and Schneirla, T. C. 1961. Early socialization in the domestic cat based on feeding and other relationships between female and young. In *Determinants of infant behaviour*, ed. B. M. Foss, vol. 1. London: Methuen.

Rosenzweig, M. R. 1966. Environmental complexity, cerebral change, and behavior. *Am. Psychol.* 21:321–32.

Rosenzweig, M. R.; Bennett, E. L.; Diamond, M. C.; Wu, Su-Yu; Slagle, R. W.; and Saffran, E. 1969. Influences of environmental complexity and visual stimulation on development of the occipital cortex in the rat. *Brain Res.* 14:427–45.

Rosenzweig, M. R.; Krech, D.; Bennett, E. L.; and Zolman, J. F. 1962. Variation in environmental complexity and brain measures. *J. comp. physiol. Psychol.* 55:1092–95.

Rosenzweig, M. R.; Love, W.; and Bennett, E. L. 1968. Effects of a few hours a day of enriched experience on brain chemistry and brain weights. *Physiology Behav.* 3:819–24.

Rosenzweig, N. 1959. Sensory deprivation and schizophrenia: some clinical and theoretical similarities. *Am. J. Psychiat.* 116:326–29.

Rosenzweig, N., and Gardner, L. M. 1966. The role of input relevance in sensory deprivation. *Am. J. Psychiat.* 122:920–28.

Rosenzweig, S. 1944. An outline of frustration theory. In *Personality and the behavior disorders,* ed. J. McV. Hunt, vol. 1, pp. 379–88. New York: Ronald.

Roudinesco, J., and Appell, G. 1950. Les répercussions de la stabulation hospitalière sur le développement psycho-moteur de jeunes enfants. *Sem. Hôp. Paris* 2271–73.

Roudinesco, J., and David, M. 1952. Peut-on atténuer les effets nocifs de la séparation chez des enfants placés en institution? *Courr. Cent. int. Enf.* 2:255–66.

Roudinesco, J.; David, M.; and Nicolas, J. 1952. Responses of young children to separation from their mothers. I. Observation of children aged 12 to 17 months recently separated from their families and living in an institution. *Courr. Cent. int. Enf.* 2:66–78.

Rubin, M. 1972. Auditory deprivation in infants. *J. Communication Disorders* 5:195–204.

Rubinstein, S. L. 1957. *Bytie i soznanie.* Moscow: Izd. Akad. Nauk.

Ruegamer, W. R.; Bernstein, L.; and Benjamin, J. D. 1954. Growth, food utilization, and thyroid activity in the albino rat as a function of extra handling. *Science* 120:184–85.

Rupp, J. C. C. 1966. Disturbing behaviour in adolescent boys. *Paedagogica Evropaea* 2:118–55.

—————. 1969. *Helping the child to cope with the school.* (In Dutch). Groningen: Wolters-Noordhoff.

Rutter, M. 1972. *Maternal deprivation reassessed.* Baltimore: Penguin.

Salfield, D. J. 1956. Reflexions on therapeutic separation of children from home. *Z. Kinderpsychiat.* 23:165–75.

Sälzer, A. 1959. Vergleichende Messungen von Länge und Gewicht bei Kindern aus Familien und Kindereinrichtungen und der Einfluss der sozialen Herkunft auf die körperliche Entwicklung. *Z. ärztl. Fortbild.* 51:1430–33.

Šamánková, L. 1968. Morbidity of children in three Prague nurseries. (In Czech). *Čslká Pediat.* 23:350–56.

Sand, E. A. 1954. L'hospitalisme. *Archs belg. Méd. soc.* 3:77–101.

—————. 1957. Le retentissement des séjours prolongés en institution sur le développement psychologique des enfants. *Acta paediat. belg.* 11:235–47.

Sayegh, Y., and Dennis, W. 1965. The effects of supplementary experience upon the behavioral development of infants in institutions. *Child Dev.* 36:81–90.

Ščelovanov, N. M., and Aksarina, N. M. 1949. *Education of infants in children's institutions.* (In Russian). Moscow: Medgiz.

Schaffer, H. R. 1958. Objective observations of personality development in early infancy. *Br. J. med. Psychol.* 31:174–83.

—————. 1963. Some issues for research in the study of attachment behaviour. In *Determinants of infant behaviour,* ed. B. M. Foss, vol. 2. London: Methuen.

—————. 1965. Changes in developmental quotients under two conditions of maternal separation. *J. soc. clin. Psychol.* 4:39–46.

—————. ed. 1971. *The origins of human social relations.* New York, London: Academic Press.

Schaffer, H. R., and Callender, W. M. 1959. Psychologic effects of hospitalization in infancy. *Pediatrics* 24:528–39.

Schaffer, H. R., and Emerson, P. E. 1964. The development of social attachments in infancy. *Monogr. Soc. Res. Child Dev.* 29.

Schenk-Danzinger, L. 1961. Social difficulties of children who were deprived of maternal care in early childhood. *Vita hum.* 4:229–41.

Schlosser, A. 1969. Paper read at SOS-International Seminar in Hinterbrühl, Austria, October 1969.

Schlossmann, A. 1906. *Über die Fürsorge für kranke Säuglinge unter besonderer Berücksichtigung des neuen Dresdener Säuglingsheimes.* Stuttgart: F. Enke.

―――. 1920. Zur Frage der Säuglingssterblichkeit. *Münch. med. Wschr.* 67.

―――. 1923. Die Entwicklung der Versorgung kranker Säuglinge in Anstalten. *Ergebn. inn. Med. Kinderheilk.* 24:189.

Schlottmann, R. S., and Seay, B. 1972. Mother-infant separation in the Java monkey *(Macaca irus). J. comp. physiol. Psychol.* 79:334–40.

Schmaderer, M. 1956. Entstehen für das Kind bei der Trennung vom Elternhaus seelische Schäden? *Ärztl. Wschr.* 11:419–23.

Schmalohr, E. 1968. *Frühe Mutterentbehrung bei Mensch und Tier.* Munich, Basel: E. Reinhardt.

Schmidt, W. H. O. 1966. Socio-economic status, schooling, intelligence, and scholastic progress in a community in which education is not yet compulsory. *Paedagogica Evropaea* 2:275–89.

Schmidt-Kolmer, E. 1957. Erscheinungen des psychischen Hospitalismus und ihre Verhütung. *Z. ärztl. Fortbild.* 51:895–99.

―――. 1959*a*. Der Einfluss der Lebensbedingungen auf die psychische Entwicklung. *Z. ärztl. Fortbild.* 53:1438–41.

―――. 1959*b*. Erscheinungsformen des psychischen Hospitalismus in den ersten Lebensjahren und ihre Bekämpfung. *Psychiatrie Neurol. med. Psychol.* 11:239–45.

―――. 1960. Der Einfluss des Alters und der Umwelt auf die Grund prozesse der höheren Nerventätigkeit bei Kindern im Vorschulalter. *Z. ges. Hyg.* no. 2.

―――. 1961*a*. Die Rolle der zwischenmenschlichen Beziehungen für die Gesundheit des Kindes. *Psychiatrie Neurol. med. Psychol.* 13:50–55.

―――. 1961*b*. Hospitalismusschäden in Kindereinrichtungen des Vorschulalters. In *Das milieugeschädigte Kind,* ed. H. Schwarz. Jena.

―――. 1963. *Der Einfluss der Lebensbedingungen auf die Entwicklung des Kindes im Vorschulalter.* Berlin: Akademie Verlag.

―――. 1966. Psychologisch-paedagogische Probleme bei Kindern in Kinderkrippen. Paper read at First Symposium of Socialist Countries on Nurseries, Prague.

Schmitz, H. A. 1962. Der Säugling, ein soziales Wesen. *Acta Paedopsychiat.* 29:172–78.

Schneersohn, F. 1939. Einsamkeit und Langweile als psychopathische Faktoren. *Z. Kinderpsychiat.* 5:136–43, 173–78.

―――. 1950. Das Spielalter und seine Bedeutung in der Kinder-

psychopathologie. *Z. Kinderpsychiat.* 17:65–74.
Schneirla, T. C. 1965. Aspects of stimulation and organization in approach/withdrawal processes underlying vertebrate behavioral development. In *Advances in the study of behavior*, ed. D. S. Lehrman, vol. 1, pp. 1–74. New York: Academic Press.
Schulman, J. L. 1963. Management of the child with early infantile autism. *Am. J. Psychiat.* 120:250–54.
Schultz, D. P. 1965. *Sensory restriction: effects on behavior.* New York, London: Academic Press.
Schutz, W. 1958. *Firo: a three-dimensional theory of interpersonal behavior.* New York: Holt, Rinehart, and Winston.
Schwarz, J. C. 1968. Fear and attachment in young children. *Merrill-Palmer Q. Behav. Dev.* 14:313.
Scofield, R. W., and Chin-Wan Sun. 1960. A comparative study of the differential effect upon personality of Chinese and American child training practices. *J. soc. Psychol.* 52:221–24.
Scott, J. A. 1962. Intelligence, physique and family size. *Br. J. prev. soc. Med.* 16:165–73.
Scott, J. P. 1962. Critical periods in behavioral development. *Science* 138:949–58.
Scott, J. P.; Frederickson, E.; and Fuller, J. L. 1951. Experimental exploration of the critical period hypothesis. *Personality* 1:162–83.
Sears, P. S. 1951. Doll-play aggression in normal young children: influence of sex, age, sibling status, father absence. *Psychol. Monogr.* 65, no. 323/6.
Sears, R. S.; Maccoby, E. E.; and Lewin, H. 1957. *Patterns of child rearing.* Evanston, Ill.: Row, Peterson.
Seay, B.; Hasen, E.; and Harlow, H. F. 1962. Mother-infant separation in monkeys. *J. Child Psychol. Psychiat.* 3:123–32.
Seitz, P. F. D. 1954. The effects of infantile experiences upon adult behavior in animal subjects. *Am. J. Psychiat.* 110:916–27.
Selander, P. 1954. Some hospitalization problems from the point of view of the mother. *Svenska Läkartidn.* 51:2361.
Sethi, B. B. 1964. Relationship of separation and depression. *Archs gen. Psychiat.* 10:486–96.
Sewell, W. H. 1952. Infant training and personality of the child. *Am. J. Sociol.* 58:150–59.
————. 1959. Infant training and personality of the child. In *Mental health and mental disorder: a sociological approach*, ed. A. M. Rose, pp. 325–40. New York: Norton.
Sewell, W. H., and Mussen, P. H. 1952. The effects of feeding, weaning, and scheduling procedures on childhood adjustment and the formation of oral symptoms. *Child Dev.* 23:185–91.
Shepher, J. 1969. The child and the parent-child relationship in the kibbutz. *Assignment Childn* 10:47–60.
Shirley, M., and Poyntz, L. 1941. The influence of separation from the

mother on children's emotional responses. *J. Psychol.* 12:251—82.

Short, R. R., and Oskamp, S. 1965. Lack of suggestion effects on perceptual isolation. *J. nerv. ment. Dis.* 141:190—94.

Shurley, J. T. 1960. Profound experimental sensory isolation. *Am. J. Psychiat.* 117:539—45.

Siregman, A. W. 1966. Father absence during early childhood and antisocial behavior. *J. abnorm. soc. Psychol.* 71:71—74.

Silberstein, R., and Irwin, H. 1962. Jean-Marc-Gaspard Itard and the Savage of Aveyron. *J. Am. Acad. Child Psychiat.* 1:314—22.

Silvermann, A. J.; Cohen, S. J.; Shmavonian, B. M.; and Greenberg, G. 1961. Psychophysiological investigations in sensory deprivation. *Psychosom. Med.* 23:48—62.

Simmons, J.; Ottinger, D.; and Haugk, E. 1967. Maternal variables and neonate behavior. *J. Am. Acad. Child Psychiat.* 6:174.

Simonsen, K. M. 1947. *Examination of children from children's homes and day-nurseries by the Bühler-Hetzer developmental tests.* Copenhagen.

Six, M. 1964. Familienpglegekinder. *Prax. Kinderpsychol. Kinderpsychiat.* 51—56.

Skeels, H. M. 1937. A cooperative orphanage research. *J. educ. Res.* 30:437—44.

—————. 1938: Mental development of children in foster homes. *J. consult. Psychol.* 2:33—43.

—————. 1940. Some Iowa studies of the mental growth of children in relation to environmental differentials: a summary. In *Thirty-ninth yearbook of the National Society for the Study of Education,* ed. G. M. Whipple, Part 2, pp. 281—308. Bloomington, Ill.: Public School Publ.

—————. 1966. Adult status of children with contrasting early life experiences. *Monogr. Soc. Res. Child Dev.* 31, no. 3.

Skeels, H. M., and Dye, H. 1939. A study of the effects of differential stimulation on mentally retarded children. *Proc. Am. Ass. ment. Defic.* 44:114—36.

Skeels, H. M., and Fillmore, E. A. 1937. The mental development of children from underprivileged homes. *J. gen. Psychol.* 50:427—39.

Skeels, H. M., and Harms, I. 1948. Children with inferior social histories: their mental development in adoptive homes. *J. gen. Psychol.* 72:238—94.

Skeels, H. M.; Updegraff, R.; Wellman, B. L.; and Williams, H. M. 1938. A study of environmental stimulation. *Univ. Iowa Stud. Child Welf.* no. 4.

Skinner, B. F. 1966. Contingencies of reinforcement in the design of a culture. *Behavl Sci.* 11:159—66.

Sklarew, B. H. 1959. The relationship of early separation from parents to differences in adjustment in adolescent boys and girls. *Psychiatry* 22:399—405.

Skodak, M. 1939. Children in foster homes. *Univ. Iowa Stud. Child Welf.* 16:1.

————. 1968. Adult status of individuals who experienced early intervention. In *Proceedings of the first congress of the International Association for the Scientific Study of Mental Deficiency, Montpellier, France, 12–20 September 1967,* ed. B. W. Richards. Reigate, Surrey: Michael Jackson Publ.

Skodak, M., and Skeels, H. M. 1949. A final follow-up study of one hundred adopted children. *J. genet. Psychol.* 75:85–125.

Skorochodova, O. I. 1956. *How I perceive the surrounding world.* (In Russian). Moscow: Izd. Akad. Pedag. Nauk.

Slater, P. 1973. Cultural deprivation in the mind and heart. *Pediatrics* 51:758.

Sluckin, W. 1966. *Imprinting and early learning.* London: Methuen.

Smilansky, S. 1968. *The effects of sociodramatic play on disadvantaged preschool children.* New York: Wiley.

Smržová, A. 1957. Education of children in children's homes. (In Czech). In *Problémy psychiatrie v praxi a ve výzkumu,* pp. 164–69. Prague: S.Z.N.

Solnit, A. J. 1960. Hospitalization. *Am. J. Dis. Child.* 99:155–63.

Solomon, P.; Leiderman, H.; Mendelson, J.; and Wexler, D. 1957. Sensory deprivation: a review. *Am. J. Psychiat.* 114:357–63.

Solomon, P., et al. 1961. *Sensory deprivation.* Cambridge, Mass.: Harvard Univ. Press.

Sorenson, E. R., and Gajdusek, D. C. 1966. The study of child behavior and development in primitive cultures. *Pediatrics* 37:149–243.

Sorokin, P. A. 1954. *The ways and power of love.* Boston: Beacon. 1967 Chicago: Regnery.

Speck, S. 1956. *Kinder erwerbstätiger Mütter.* Stuttgart.

Speer, G. S. 1940. The mental development of children of feeble-minded and normal mothers. In *Thirty-ninth yearbook of the National Society for the Study of Education,* ed. G. M. Whipple, part 2, pp. 309–14. Bloomington, Ill.: Public School Publ.

Spionek, H. 1963. *Development and education of infants.* (In Polish). Warsaw: Nasza Ksiegarnia.

Spiro, M. E. 1955. Education in a communal village in Israel. *Am. J. Orthopsychiat.* 25:283.

————. 1965. *Children of the kibbutz.* New York: Schocken.

Spitz, R. A. 1945. Hospitalism: an inquiry into the genesis of psychiatric conditions in early childhood. *Psychoanal. Study Child* 1:53–74.

————. 1946a. Hospitalism: a follow-up report. *Psychoanal. Study Child* 2:113–17.

————. 1946b. The smiling response: a contribution to the ontogenesis of social relations. *Genet. Psychol. Monogr.* 34:57–125.

————. 1949. The role of ecological factors in emotional development in infancy. *Child Dev.* 20:145–55.

————. 1951. The psychogenic diseases in infancy: an attempt at their etiological classification. *Psychoanal. Study Child* 6:255–75.

———. 1954*a*. Infantile depression and the general adaptation syndrome. In *Depression,* ed. H. Hoch and J. Zubin, pp. 93–108. New York: Grune.

———. 1954*b*. Unhappy and fatal outcomes of emotional deprivation and stress in infancy. In *Beyond the germ theory,* ed. I. Galdston, pp. 120–31. New York: Health Education Council.

———. 1955. Reply to Dr. Pinneau. *Psychol. Bull.* 52:453–59.

———. 1956. Some observations on psychiatric stress in infancy. In *Fifth annual report on stress,* ed. H. Seley, pp. 193–204. New York: MD Publ.

———. 1958*a*. Experiments in the United States on the consequences of affect deprivation and stimulus deprivation in animal and man. *Criança port.* 17.

———. 1958*b*. *La première année de la vie de l'enfant: genèse des premières relations objectales.* Paris: Presses Univ. de France.

———. 1960. *A genetic field theory of ego formation.* New York: International Univ. Press.

———. 1967. *Vom Säugling zum Kleinkind.* Stuttgart: Klett.

———. 1970. The effect of personality disturbances in the mother on the well-being of her infant. In *Parenthood,* ed. E. J. Anthony and T. Benedek. Boston: Little Brown.

Spitz, R. A. and Wolf, K. M. 1946. Anaclitic depression: an inquiry into the genesis of psychiatric conditions in early childhood, II. *Psychoanal. Study Child* 2:313–42.

———. 1949. Autoerotism: some empirical findings and hypotheses on three of its manifestations in the first year of life. *Psychoanal. Study Child* 5:85–120.

Spranger, E. 1955. *Psychologie des Jugendalters.* 24th ed. Heidelberg: Quelle u. Meyer.

Spurlock, J. 1970. Social deprivation in childhood and character formation. *J. Am. psychoanal. Ass.* 18:622–30.

Srp, L. 1953. Reaction of children to hospital environment. (In Czech). *Pediat. Listy* 8:290–92.

———. 1961. *Psychology of medical treatment of children.* (In Czech). Prague: S.Z.N.

Stavěl, J. 1937. *Hunger: a contribution to drive analysis.* (In Czech). Bratislava.

Stedman, J., and Eichorn, D. H. 1964. A comparison of the growth and development of institutionalized and home-reared mongoloids during infancy and early childhood. *Am. J. ment. Defic.* 69:391–401.

Stein, A. 1959. Resistance to psychological prophylaxis in hospital pediatrics. *J. Pediat.* 55:497–503.

Steinitz, L.; Ryll, G.; and Trettin, I. 1959. Vergleichen der Morbidität in Tages-, Wochenkrippen und Dauerheimen. *Z. ärztl. Fortbild.* 53:1441–43.

Stendler, C. B. 1954. Possible causes of over-dependency in young children. *Child Dev.* 25:125–46.

Stevenson, H. W. 1965. Social reinforcement of children's behavior. In *Advances in child development and behavior,* ed. L. P. Lipsitt and C. C. Spiker, vol. 2, pp. 97–126. New York, London: Academic Press.

Stevenson, H. W., and Fahel, L. S. 1961. The effect of social reinforcement on the performance of institutionalized and noninstitutionalized normal and retarded children. *J. Personality* 29:136–47.

Stevenson, H.W.; Hess, E.H.; and Rheingold, H.L. 1947. *Early behavior: comparative and developmental approaches.* New York: Wiley.

Stevenson, H. W., and Odom, R. D. 1961. Effects of pretraining on the reinforcing value of visual stimuli. *Child Dev.* 32:739–44.

———. 1962. The effectiveness of social reinforcement following two conditions of social deprivation. *J. abnorm. soc. Psychol.* 65:429–31.

Stoddard, G. D. 1940. Intellectual development of the child: an answer to the critics of the Iowa studies. *School Soc.* 51:529–36.

Stolz, L. M. 1960. Effects of maternal employment on children. *Child Dev.* 31:749–82.

Stolz, L. M., et al. 1954. *Father relations of war-born children.* Stanford, Calif.: Stanford Univ. Press.

Stone, F. H. 1955. A critical review of a current program of research into mother-child relationship. In *Emotional problems of early childhood,* ed. G. Caplan. New York: Basic.

Stone, J. 1954. A critique of studies of infant isolation. *Child Dev.* 25:9–20.

Stott, D. H. 1961. An empirical approach to motivation based on the behavior of a young child. *J. Child Psychol. Psychiat.* 2:97–117.

———. 1962. Abnormal mothering as a cause of mental subnormality. I. A critique of some classic studies of maternal deprivation in the light of possible congenital factors. II. Case studies and conclusions. *J. Child Psychol. Psychiat.* 3:133–48.

———. 1966. *Studies of troublesome children.* London: Tavistock.

Straus, P. 1961. L'hospitalisation des enfants: une étude de pédiatrie sociale dans l'agglomeration parisienne. *Monogrs Inst. nat. Hyg.* no. 23.

Strauss, A. A., and Kephart, N. C. 1955. *Psychopathology and education of the brain-injured child,* vol. 2. New York, London: Grune.

Strauss, A. A., and Lehtinen, L. E. 1950. *Psychopathology and education of the brain-injured child,* vol. 1. New York, London: Grune.

Strnadová, M. 1969. Psychological characteristics of children suffering from visual defects. (Dissertation thesis, Charles University, Prague.)

Ströder, J., and Geisler, E. 1957. Das kind im Krankenhaus. *Arch.*
    Kinderheilk. 154:216—38.
Šturma, J. 1970. Psychological deprivation, mild encephalopathy and
    disharmonic development of personality in boys. (Dissertation
    thesis, Charles University, Prague.)
Stutte, H. 1972. Transcultural child psychiatry. *Acta Paedopsychiat.*
    38:229—31.
Stycos, J. M. 1955. *Family and fertility in Puerto Rico: a study of the*
    lower income group. New York: Columbia Univ. Press.
Sun, G. 1959. Morbidität und Gewichtsentwicklung bei Kindern
    berufstätiger und nicht berufstätiger Mütter. *Z. ärztl. Fortbild.*
    53:1415—46.
Suomi, S. J. 1973. Surrogate rehabilitation of monkeys reared in total
    social isolation. *J. Child Psychol. Psychiat.* 14:71—77.
Sutter, J. M. 1952. Conséquences éloignées des émotions de guerre chez
    les enfants. *Pédiatrie* 41:345.
Suttie, I. D. 1935. *The origins of love and hate.* London: Kegan Paul.
————. 1936. Evidence of non-rational factors in "economic"
    behavior. *Br. J. med. Psychol.* 15, part 1:51—62.
Sváb, L.; Grob, J.; and Langová, J. 1972. Stuttering and social isolation.
    J. nerv. ment. Dis. 155:1—5.
Švejcar, J. 1962a. Étude de l'influence de la mère sur le développement
    psychique de l'enfant. *Courr. Cent. int. Enf.* 12:469—73.
Švejcar, J. 1962b. A study of the influence of the mother on the
    emotional development of the child. (In Czech). *Prakt. Lék.*
    42:367—70.
Symonds, H. 1955. The emotional development of children. *Lancet*
    2:814—16.
Symonds, P. M. 1946. *The dynamics of human adjustment.* New York:
    Appleton-Century.
————. 1961. *From adolescent to adult.* New York: Columbia
    Univ. Press.
Szymborska, A. 1969. *Social orphanage.* (In Polish). Warsaw: Wiedza
    Powszechna.
Talbot, F. B. 1941. Transactions of the American Pediatric Society,
    1941: discussion of paper of Bakwin. *Am. J. Dis. Child.* 62:469.
Tamborini, A. 1960. Die Situation des Kindes und Jugendlichen in
    Heimen aus psychologischer und soziologischer Sicht. *Prax.*
    Kinderpsychol. Kinderpsychiat. 9:17—22.
Tatochenko, V. K. 1971. Social action on behalf of the child. A USSR
    experience. *Assignment Childn* 16:72—86.
Tautermannová, M. 1961. Child's hospitalization and resulting disorders
    in mother-child relations. Paper read at meeting of Čslká Pediat.
    Soc.
Teilhard De Chardin, P. 1959. *The phenomenon of man.* London:
    Collins. New York: Harper and Brothers.
Tennes, K. H., and Lampl, E. E. 1964. Stranger and separation anxiety

in infancy. *J. nerv. ment. Dis.* 139:247–54.

Teuber, H. L. 1961. Sensory deprivation, sensory suppression and agnosia. *J. nerv. ment. Dis.* 132:32–39.

Tezner, O. 1956. Zur Frage der Kinderheime. *Annls paediat.* 186:189–209.

Thevenier, D. M. 1956. Troubles psychosomatiques du jeune enfant séparé de sa mère. *Pédiatrie* 11:610–12.

Thomae, H.; Blankenburg, J.; Uhr, R.; and Weinert, F. 1962. "Orale" Frustration und Persönlichkeit. *Z. Psychol.* 167:31–41.

Thomas, A. 1961. Individuality responses in children. *Am. J. Psychiat.* 117:798.

Thomas, A., and Autgaerden, S. 1963. Audibilité spontanée de la voix maternelle, audibilité conditionée de toute autre voix. *Presse méd.* 71:1761–64.

Thomas, A.; Birch, H. G.; Chess, S.; and Robbins, L. 1961. Individuality in responses of children to similar environmental situations. *Am. J. Psychiat.* 127:798–803.

Thomas, E., and Schaller, F. 1954. Das Spiel der optisch isolierten jungen Kaspar-Hauser-Katze. *Naturwissenschaften* 41:557–58.

Thompson, W. R., and Heron, W. 1954. The effects of early restriction on activity in dogs. *J. comp. physiol. Psychol.* 47:77–82.

Thompson, W. R., and McElroy, L. R. 1962. The effects of maternal presence on open-field behavior in young rats. *J. comp. physiol. Psychol.* 55:827–30.

Thompson, W. R.; Melzack, R.; and Scott, T. H. 1956. "Whirling behavior" in dogs as related to early experience. *Science* 123:939.

Thurston, J. R., and Mussen, P. H. 1951. Infant feeding gratification and adult personality. *J. Personality* 19:449–58.

Thysell, T. 1952. About adoption. *Courr. Cent. int. Enf.* 2:377–84.

Tichajeva, E. I. 1948. *Language development of preschool children.* (In Russian). Moscow: Učpedgiz.

Tien, H. C. 1970. Psychosynthesis: the telefusion of modern eclectic psychiatry. *Wld J. Psychosynthesis* 2:49.

Tizard, J. 1960. The residential care of mentally handicapped children. *Br. med. J.* 1:1041–46.

———. 1967. *Survey and experiment in special education.* London: Harrap.

———. 1968. Residential care for the mentally retarded. In *Proceedings of the first congress of the International Association for the Scientific Study of Mental Deficiency, Montpellier, France, 12–20 September 1967,* ed. B. W. Richards, pp. 633–36. Reigate, Surrey: Michael Jackson Publ.

Tizard, J., and Tizard, B. 1971. The social development of two-year-old children in residential nurseries. In *The origins of human social relations,* ed. H. R. Schaffer. New York, London: Academic Press.

Törnudd, M. 1956. *Deprived children in public care.* (In Swedish).

Helsingfors: Työväen Kirjapaino.
Traina Cottone, E. 1966. Critica alla teoria della carenza materna e sui implicazioni. *Atti 1 convegno italo-cecoslovacco sui problemi dell'infanzia prescolastica, Roma, November 1966*, 230–42.
Tramer, M. 1949. *Lehrbuch der allgemeinen Kinderpsychiatrie.* Basel: B. Schwabe.
————. 1960. Das Phänomen der angeborenen Lebensmuster im Kindesalter (formae inatae vitae infantilis). *Acta Paedopsychiat.* 27:129–39.
————. 1961. Eventualadoption. *Acta Paedopsychiat.* 28:81–91.
————. 1963. Säuglings- und Kleinkindernöte. *Acta Paedopsychiat.* 30:167–80.
Trasler, G. 1960. *In place of parents: a study of foster care.* London: Routledge and Kegan Paul.
Tredgold, A. F. 1929. *Mental deficiency (amentia).* 6th ed. rev. New York: Wood.
Trnka, V. 1962. Some personality changes in children from divorced families. (In Czech). *Čslká Pediat.* 17:628–31.
————. 1966. School achievements of children from divorced families. (In Czech). *Čslká Pediat.* 21:351–54.
Tugendreich, G. 1909. *Die Mutter- und Säuglingsfürsorge.* Stuttgart: F. Enke.
Utitz, E. 1947. *The psychology of life in the concentration camp of Terezin.* (In Czech). Prague: Dělnické nakladatelství.
Vančurová, E. 1962. Some questions of emotionality and sociability in drawings of preschool children. (In Czech). *Čslká Pediat.* 17:660–66.
————. 1966. Symptoms of emotional and social carence in drawings of preschool children. (In Czech). *Čslká Psychol.* 10:97–110.
Vaňouček, O. 1956. The problem of play satiation in children's institutions. (In Czech). *Čslká Pediat.* 14:530–40.
————. 1959. Drawings of children in ghetto Terezin.
Vermeil, G. 1974. Le rôle de l'école maternelle dans la prévention des inadaptations. *Méd. infant.* 81:315.
Vernon, D. T. A.; Foley, J. M.; and Schulman, J. L. 1967. Effect of mother-child separation and birth order on young children's responses to two potentially stressful experiences. *J. Personality soc. Psychol.* 5:162–74.
Vernon, D. T. A., et al. 1965. *The psychological responses of children to hospitalization and illness.* Springfield, Ill.: C. C. Thomas.
Vernon, J. 1963. *Inside the black room: studies of sensory deprivation.* Harmondsworth, Mddx.: Penguin.
Vernon, J., and Hoffman, J. 1956. Effects of sensory deprivation on learning rate in human beings. *Science* 123: 1074–75.
Vernon, J. A., and McGill, T. E. 1957. The effects of sensory deprivation on rote learning. *Am. J. Psychol.* 70:637–39.

Vernon, J. A.; McGill, T. E.; Gulick, W. L.; and Candland, D. K. 1959. Effect of sensory deprivation on some perceptual and motor skills. *Percept. Mot. Skills* 9:91–97.

Vernon, J. A.; McGill, T. E.; and Schiffman, H. 1958. Visual hallucination during perceptual isolation. *Can. J. Psychol.* 12:31–34.

Vernon, J. A.; Marton, T.; and Peterson, E. 1961. Sensory deprivation and hallucinations. *Science* 113:1808–12.

Veselkova, K. P. 1957. Physical development of children in nurseries. (In Russian). *Pediatriya* 40:64–69.

Vitz, P. C. 1964. Preferences for rates of information presented by sequences of tones. *J. exp. Psychol.* 68:176–83.

———. 1966a. Affect as a function of stimulus variation. *J. exp. Psychol.* 71:74–79.

———. 1966b. Preferences for different amounts of visual complexity. *Behavl Sci.* 11:105–14.

Vodák, P., and Šulc, A. 1960. School phobia and truancy. (In Czech). *Čslká Psychiat.* 56:109–17.

Vodák, P., et al. 1967. *Problems of adoption of children.* Prague: S.Z.N.

Vosburg, R. L.; Fraser, N. G.; and Guehl, J. J. 1959. Sensory deprivation and image formation. *Psychiat. Commun.* 2:157–70.

———. 1960. Imagery sequence in sensory deprivation. *Archs gen. Psychiat.* 2:356–57.

Vygotski, L. S. 1962. *Thought and language.* Cambridge, Mass.: Massachusetts Institute of Technology.

Vyržikovskij, S. M., and Majorov, F. P. 1933. Study of influence of education on the formation of higher nervous activity in dogs. (In Russian). *Trudÿ fiziol. Lab. I. P. Pavlova* 5:171.

Waal, N. 1955. A special technique of psychotherapy with an autistic child. In *Emotional problems in childhood,* ed. G. Caplan, pp. 431–49. New York: Basic.

Wagner, M. 1794. *Beiträge zur Philosophischen Anthropologie und den damit verwandten Wissenschaften.* Vienna.

Walker, E. L. 1964. Psychological complexity as a basis for a theory of motivation and choice. In *Nebraska Symposium on Motivation,* ed. D. Levine. Lincoln: Univ. of Nebraska Press.

Wall, W. D. 1955. *Éducation et santé mentale.* Problèmes d'éducation, no. 11. Paris: Unesco.

Wallgren, A. 1955. Children in hospital. *J. Pediat.* 46:458–72.

Walter, W. G. 1953. *The living brain.* London: Duckworth.

Walters, R. H.; Callagan, J. E.; and Newman, A. F. 1963. Effects of solitary confinement on prisoners. *Am. J. Psychiat.* 119:771–73.

Walters, R. H., and Parke, R. D. 1964a. Emotional arousal, isolation and discrimination learning in children. *J. exp. Child Psychol.* 1:163–73.

————. 1964*b*. Social motivation, dependency and susceptibility to social influences. In *Advances in experimental social psychology*, ed. L. Berkowitz, vol. 1, pp. 231—76. New York: Academic Press.

————. 1965. The role of the distance receptors in the development of social responsiveness. In *Advances in child development and behavior*, ed. L. P. Lipsitt and C. C. Spiker, vol. 2, pp. 59—96. New York, London: Academic Press.

Walters, R. H., and Ray, E. 1960. Anxiety, social isolation, and reinforcer effectiveness. *J. Personality* 28:358—67.

Wase, A. W., and Christensen, J. 1960. Stimulus deprivation and phospholipid metabolism in cerebral tissue. *Archs gen. Psychiat.* 2:171—73.

Washburn, A. H. 1966. All human beings start life as babies. *Pediatrics* 37:828—32.

Weidemann, J. 1959. Das Kind im Heim. *Z. Kinderpsychiat.* 26:1—10, 77—86.

————. 1960*a*. Das "Sozialbild" des Anstaltskindes. Untersuchungen zur sozialen Entwicklung des heimasylierten Kleinkindes. *Prax. Kinderpsychol. Kinderpsychiat.* 9:137—40.

————. 1960*b*. Soziodynamik auf einer psychiatrischen Krankenstation. *Arch. Psychiat. NervKrankh.* 200:174—81.

————. 1961*a*. Das Kind als "Sozialperson". Ausblick und psychodiagnostischer Hinweis. *Prax. Kinderpsychol. Kinderpsychiat.* 10:226—27.

————. 1961*b*. Soziale Verhaltensweisen des kranken Kindes. *Acta Paedopsychiat.* 28:241—48.

Weininger, O. 1956. The effects of early experience on behavior and growth characteristics. *J. comp. physiol. Psychol.* 49:1—9.

Weisberg, P. 1963. Social and nonsocial conditioning of infant vocalizations. *Child Dev.* 34:377—88.

Wellman, B., and Pegram, E. I. 1944. Binet I.Q. changes of orphanage preschool children: a reanalysis. *J. gen. Psychol.* 65:239—63.

Werner, E.; Bierman, J. M.; French, F. E.; Simonian, K.; Connor, A.; Smith, R. S.; and Campbell, M. 1968. Reproductive and environmental casualties: a report on the 10-year follow-up of the children of the Kanai pregnancy study. *Pediatrics* 42:112—27.

Werner, E.; Simonian, B. S.; Bierman, J. M.; and French, F. E. 1967. Cumulative effects of perinatal complications and deprived environment on physical, intellectual, and social development of preschool children. *Pediatrics* 39:490—505.

West, M. 1957. *Children of the sun.* London: Pan.

Weston, D. L., and Irwin, R. C. 1963. Preschool child's response to death of infant sibling. *Am. J. Dis. Child.* 106:564—67.

Wexler, D.; Mendelson, J.; Leiderman, P. H.; and Solomon, P. 1958. Sensory deprivation. *Archs Neurol. Psychiat., Chicago* 79:225—33.

Wheaton, J. L. 1959. Fact and fancy in sensory deprivation studies.

Aeromed. Rev. 5–59.
Wheeler, W. M. 1956. Psychodiagnostic assessments of a child after prolonged separation in early childhood. *Br. J. med. Psychol.* 29:248–57.
White, S. H. 1965. Evidence for a hierarchical arrangement of learning processes. In *Advances in child development and behavior,* ed. L. P. Lipsitt and C. C. Spiker, vol. 2, pp. 187–220. New York, London: Academic Press.
Whiting, J. W. M., and Child, I. L. 1953. *Child training and personality: a cross-cultural study.* London: Yale Univ. Press.
Whitten, C. F. 1970. Growth failure, deprivation, and under-eating. *JAMA* 211:1379.
Whyte, W. F. 1943. *Street corner society: the social structure of an Italian slum.* Chicago: Univ. of Chicago Press.
Wight, B. W. 1970. Cultural deprivation: operational definition in terms of language development. *Am. J. Orthopsychiat.* 40:77–86.
Williams, D. H. 1951. Management of atopic dermatitis in children: control of maternal rejection factor. *Archs Derm. Syph.* 63:545.
Williams, J. M. 1961. Children who break down in foster homes. *J. Child Psychol.* 1:5–20.
Winch, R. F. 1949. The relation between the loss of a parent and progress in courtship. *J. soc. Psychol.* 29:51–56.
Wing, J. K., ed. 1966. *Early childhood autism.* Oxford: Pergamon.
Winnicott, D. W. 1948. Desarollo emocional primitivo. *Revta Psicoanál.* 5:1003–17.
————. 1958*a*. The capacity to be alone. *Int. J. Psycho-Analysis* 39:1–5.
————. 1958*b*. First year of life: modern views on the emotional development in the first year of life. Parts I and II. *Med. Press* 239:228–31, 289–91.
————. 1960. The theory of the parent-infant relationship. *Int. J. Psycho-Analysis* 41:585–95.
Wissler, H.; Flammer, I.; Pfister, M.; and Zangger, K. 1954. Zur Frage der Hospitalisationsschäden bei Kleinkindern. *Helv. paediat. Acta* 9:317–22.
Wit, J. de. 1962. *Problems of mother-child relation.* (In Dutch). Amsterdam.
————. 1964. Some critical remarks on "maternal deprivation". *Acta Paedopsychiat.* 31:240–53.
Witmer, H. L. 1948. *Pediatrics and the emotional needs of the child.* New York.
Wittenborn, J., and Myers, B. 1957. *The placement of adoptive children.* Springfield, Ill.: C. C. Thomas.
Wittenborn, J. R. 1956. A study of adoptive children. *Psychol. Monogr.* 70:1–3.
Wolf, K. M. 1945. Evacuation of children in wartime. *Psychoanal. Study Child* 1:389–404.

————. 1952. Growing up and its price in three Puerto Rican sub-cultures. *Psychiatry*, November.

Wolfensberger-Hässig, C. 1966. Lächeln und Weinen des Säuglings als sozio-psychische Instinktphänomene. *Helv. paediat. Acta* 21:197–223.

Wolfenstein, M. 1953. Trends in infant care. *Am. J. Orthopsychiat.* 23:120–30.

————. 1969. Loss, rage, and repetition. *Psychoanal. Study Child* 24:432–60.

Wolffheim, N. 1958, 1959. Kinder aus Konzentrationslagern. Mitteilung über die Nachwirkungen des KZ-Aufenthaltes auf Kinder und Jugendliche. *Prax. Kinderpsychol. Kinderpsychiat.* 7(1958):302–12; 8(1959): 20–27, 59–71.

Wolley, H. T. 1930. *A study of the experience of a nursery school in training a child adopted from an institution.* London.

Woodward, M. 1959. The behavior of idiots interpreted by Piaget's theory of sensorimotor development. *Br. J. educ. Psychol.* 29:60–71.

————. 1960. Early experiences and later social responses of severely subnormal children. *Br. J. med. Psychol.* 33:123–32.

Woodworth, R. S. 1918. *Dynamic psychology.* New York: Columbia Univ. Press.

Woolf, M. 1960. Gemeinschaftserziehung und Kindergesellschaft. *Acta Paedopsychiat.* 27:170–74.

Wootton, B. 1959. Chap. 4, "Theories of the effects of maternal separation or deprivation". In *Social science and social pathology*. London: Allen and Unwin.

————. 1962. A social scientist's approach to maternal deprivation. In *Deprivation of maternal care*, pp. 63–74. Geneva: WHO.

World Health Organization. 1962. *Deprivation of maternal care.* Geneva.

Worts, H., and Freedman, A. 1965. The contribution of the social environment to the development of premature children. *Am. J. Orthopsychiat.* 35:57–68.

Wulfften Palthe, P. M. van. 1958. Sensory and motor deprivation as a psychopathological stress. *Aeromed. Acta* 6:155–68.

Yarrow, L. J. 1961. Maternal deprivation: toward an empirical and conceptual re-evaluation. *Psychol. Bull.* 58:459–90.

Ylppö, A.; Landtman, B.; Hallman, N.; and Piipari, R. 1956. Effects of short-time hospitalization on the behavior and on some somatic functions of children. *Annls paediat.* Suppl. 8:3–24.

Yule, W., and Raynes, N. V. 1972. Behavioural characteristics of children in residential care in relation to indices of separation. *J. Child Psychol. Psychiat.* 13:249–58.

Zeman, L., and Bryndová, D. 1969. Morbidity of institutionalized infants. (In Czech). *Čslká Pediat.* 24:448–53.

Ziemska, M. 1969a. *Parental attitudes.* (In Polish). Warsaw: Wiedza Powszechna.

————. 1969b. Personality of adoptive parents. (In Czech). *Psychol. Patopsychol. dietaťa* 4:73–84.

Zigler, E. 1961. Social deprivation and rigidity in the performance of feebleminded children. *J. abnorm. soc. Psychol.* 62:413–21.

Zigler, E., and Williams, J. 1963. Institutionalization and the effectiveness of social reinforcement: a three-year follow-up study. *J. abnorm. soc. Psychol.* 66:197–205.

Zimbardo, P. G., and Montgomery, K. C. 1957. Effects of "free-environment" rearing upon exploratory behavior. *Psychol. Rep.* 4:589–94.

Zimmerman, D. W. 1961. The effects of deprivation and satiation on secondary reinforcement developed by two methods. *J. genet. Psychol.* 99:139–44.

Zingg, R. M. 1940. Feral man and extreme cases of isolation. *Am. J. Psychol.* 53:487–517.

Ziskind, E. 1958. Isolation stress in medical and mental illness. *JAMA* 168:1427–31.

————. 1963. Significance of symptoms of sensory deprivation: experiments due to methodological procedures. In *Recent advances in biological psychiatry,* ed. J. Wortis, pp. 111–18. New York: Plenum.

————. 1964a. An explanation of mental symptoms found in acute sensory deprivation. Paper presented at meeting of American Psychiatric Association. Mimeographed.

————. 1964b. A second look at sensory deprivation. *J. nerv. ment. Dis.* 138:223–32.

Ziv, A. 1965. *La vie des enfants en collectivité.* Paris.

Zubek, J. P., ed. 1969. *Sensory deprivation: fifteen years of research.* New York: Appleton-Century-Crofts.

Zuckerman, M. 1964. Perceptual isolation as a stress situation. *Archs gen. Psychiat.* 11:255–76.

Zuckerman, M., and Haber, M. M. 1965. Need for stimulation as a source of stress response to perceptual isolation. *J. abnorm. Psychol.* 70:371–77.

Zuckerman, M.; Levine, S.; and Biase, D. V. 1964. Stress response in total and partial perceptual isolation. *Psychosom. Med.* 26:250–60.

Zuckerman, M.; Levine, B.; Persky, H.; and Miller, L. 1970. Sensory deprivation versus sensory variation. *J. abnorm. Psychol.* 76:76–82.

Zuckerman, M.; Persky, H.; Hopkins, T. R.; Murtaugh, T.; Basu, G. K.; and Schilling, M. 1966. Comparison of stress effects of perceptual and social isolation. *Archs gen. Psychiat.* 14:356–65.

Author Index

Abe, K., 234
Adam, R., 136
Adams, H. B., 282, 283
Adler, A., 302
Ainsworth, M. D., 11, 18, 25, 26, 28, 48, 64, 65, 88, 117, 178, 179, 347
Aksarina, N. M., 87, 98, 99, 319
Albee, 189
Albino, R. C., 177
Alkon, D. L., 52
Alpert, A., 358
Altman, I., 287
Amatruda., C. S., 12
Ambrose, J. A., 7
Amsel, A., 317
Andry, R. G., 18, 48, 123
Appell, G., 6, 27, 28
Archibald, H. C., 29
Ariès, P., 164, 165
Arlt, B. R., 100
Asher, E. J., 131, 132
Aubry, J., 56, 106, 357. *See also* Roudinesco, J.
Azima, H., 282, 283, 284, 356

Baer, D. M., 89, 289
Bakwin, H., 10, 12, 87, 109, 110, 142, 258
Bakwin, R. M., 109, 110
Bales, R. F., 299
Barnes, T. C., 265
Barry, H., Jr., 29
Bauerová, N., 330
Bayroff, A. G., 264
Beach, F. A., 8, 301
Beck, A. T., 29, 51
Beley, A. P., 258
Bell, J. E., 360
Beller, E. K., 227
Belmont, L., 260
Bender, L., 29, 332, 346
Benedict, R., 177

Benjamin, J. D., 222
Bennett, E. L., 265
Bennett, 306
Bennholdt-Thomsen, C., 136
Beres, D., 6, 84, 85, 346
Berg, M., 29, 51
Bergmann, T., 359
Berlyne, D. E., 301, 306
Bernstein, L., 268
Bertoye, P., 86, 108, 359
Berzins, A., 401
Bessel, H., 191
Bettelheim, B., 356
Bielicka, I., 66, 356, 359, 390
Bierstedt, R., 161
Biesheuvel, S., 178
Bijou, S. W., 89, 297
Birch, H. G., 255, 260, 319, 320
Birns, B., 231
Blau, A., 232
Blauvelt, H., 269
Blažková, E., 55
Blom, G. E., 64
Blomfield, J. M., 47
Blumenbach, J. F., 35
Bohman, M., 383
Bollea, G., 117, 129, 225
Bombard, A., 276
Borrelli, M., 185
Bosch, G., 141
Bossard, J. H. S., 148
Bossio, V., 83, 84, 343
Bostock, J., 160
Bowlby, J., 5, 6, 11, 17, 18, 25, 28, 29, 30, 45, 46, 48, 57, 80, 81, 85, 106, 108, 113, 117, 130, 135, 195, 230, 294, 295, 326, 333, 343, 346, 362, 373, 384, 392
Brackbill, Y., 291
Braestrup, A., 125
Brask, B. H., 341
Brattgård, S. O., 264

General Index